Lecture Notes in Artificial Intelligence   4460

Edited by J. G. Carbonell and J. Siekmann

Subseries of Lecture Notes in Compu T0224426

FoLLI Publications on Logic, Language and Information

Stefano Aguzzoli   Agata Ciabattoni
Brunella Gerla   Corrado Manara
Vincenzo Marra (Eds.)

Algebraic and Proof-Theoretic Aspects of Non-classical Logics

Papers in Honor of Daniele Mundici
on the Occasion of His 60th Birthday

Springer

Series Editors

Jaime G. Carbonell, Carnegie Mellon University, Pittsburgh, PA, USA
Jörg Siekmann, University of Saarland, Saarbrücken, Germany

Volume Editors

Stefano Aguzzoli
Università degli Studi di Milano
Via Comelico 39-41, 20135 Milano, Italy
E-mail: aguzzoli@dsi.unimi.it

Agata Ciabattoni
Technical University Vienna
Wiedner Hauptstrasse 8-10, A-1040 Wien, Austria
E-mail: agata@logic.at

Brunella Gerla
Università degli Studi di Salerno
Via Ponte don Melillo, 84084 Fisciano (SA), Italy
E-mail: bgerla@unisa.it

Corrado Manara
Università degli Studi di Salerno
Via Ponte don Melillo, 84084 Fisciano (SA), Italy
E-mail: cmanara@unisa.it

Vincenzo Marra
Università degli Studi di Milano
Via Comelico 39-41, 20135 Milano, Italy
E-mail: marra@dico.unimi.it

Library of Congress Control Number: 2007937644

CR Subject Classification (1998): I.2, F.4.1

LNCS Sublibrary: SL 7 – Artificial Intelligence

ISSN   0302-9743
ISBN   3-540-75938-7 Springer Berlin Heidelberg New York
ISBN   978-3-540-75938-6 Springer Berlin Heidelberg New York

Springer is a part of Springer Science+Business Media

springer.com

© Springer-Verlag Berlin Heidelberg 2007

Typesetting: Camera-ready by author, data conversion by Scientific Publishing Services, Chennai, India
Printed on acid-free paper   SPIN: 12180226   06/3180   5 4 3 2 1 0

Preface

Daniele Mundici is widely acknowledged as a leading scientist in many-valued logic and ordered algebraic structures. In the last decades, his work has reveiled profound connections between logic and such diverse fields of research as functional analysis, probability and measure theory, the geometry of toric varieties, piecewise linear geometry, and error-correcting codes.

In March 2006, the international conference MANYVAL06 was held in Gargnano, Italy, in honor of Daniele Mundici on the occasion of his 60th birthday. Several prominent logicians, mathematicians, and computer scientists gathered together to celebrate the event. This volume is meant as a follow-up to that conference. It consists of a wide-ranging collection of invited papers by established scholars, whose scientific interests are related to Daniele's work.

The paper by Cignoli offers a historical account of the algebraic investigations of Łukasiewicz logic, leading to a discussion of Daniele's work up to 1986. A turning point in such algebraic studies was Chang's introduction of MV-algebras in 1958. MV-algebras are the focus of a number of papers in this collection. Belluce, Di Nola, and Lettieri introduce the class of symmetric MV-algebras, and investigate their relationship with MV-chains of cardinality $p+1$, for p a prime number. Caicedo studies by algebraic means implicit definitions of connectives in Łukasiewicz infinite-valued logic. Di Nola and Navara continue a line of investigation concerned with generalizations of the Cantor – Bernstein Theorem to classes of MV-algebras. Drossos and Karazeris revisit Di Nola's Representation Theorem through Boolean ultrapowers.

Daniele's most celebrated achievement is perhaps the discovery of a categorical equivalence between MV-algebras and lattice-ordered Abelian groups with strong order unit. The paper by Esteva and Godo addresses the question of generalizing that equivalence to the larger class of IMTL algebras. Jenei and Montagna, on the other hand, give to product and related logics a game-theoretic semantics inspired by Daniele's well-known work on Ulam games.

Glass and Point use piecewise linear geometry to characterize those finitely presented lattice-ordered Abelian groups having decidable first-order theory, and also obtain results on the elementary equivalence of such groups. In another paper with a strong geometric slant, Panti relates the automorphism groups of free MV-algebras and free cancellative hoops, and offers a comparison of the dynamics they induce on the dual space.

A number of papers deal with first-order logic, both classical and non-classical. Hájek investigates the import of adding *tertium non datur* to fuzzy predicate logics with Gödel negation. It is well known that several t-norm-based logics do not enjoy strong completeness with respect to evaluations into the real unit interval $[0, 1]$, already at the propositional level. Montagna shows that the addition of a single infinitary rule remedies the situation for Hájek's Basic Logic and some of its notable extensions, even for the first-order case. Avron and Zamansky provide a general semantics for a large class of first-order paraconsistent logics based on a non-deterministic extension of many-valued logical matrices. Baaz shows how to express constructive provability within classical logic, by means of an appropriate translation. Hetzl and Leitsch introduce the notion of profile of a proof in Gentzen's sequent calculus for classical logic, and show its invariance under a large class of proof transformations.

The volume is completed by a series of papers on a variety of topics. Dalla Chiara, Giuntini, and Leporini characterize the fuzzy extensions of binary Boolean functions implementable by reversible quantum gates, showing that the Łukasiewicz connectives do not have such a representation. Riečan studies probability over IF-events both through the well-established theory of MV-algebraic probability and through an alternative approach based on max-min connectives. Finally, Gedell and Hähnle show how to apply automated first-order deduction to formal software verification of Java programs through an analysis of parallelizable code.

Several organizations made MANYVAL06 possible with their financial support. We take this occasion to thank the University of Milan and its two computer science departments DICO and DSI, the Kurt Gödel Society (KGS Vienna), and the GNSAGA department of the Istituto Nazionale di Alta Matematica.

We would also like to thank all speakers and participants in the conference for making the event a success, all authors for their invaluable contribution to this *Festschrift*, and all referees for their help in reviewing the papers.

This volume is collectively edited by the same group of former PhD students of Daniele who organized MANYVAL06. We are all grateful to Daniele for his generosity in sharing his knowledge, for his constant scientific and personal encouragement, and for the long inspiring talks in his office in Milan.

May 2007

Stefano Aguzzoli
Agata Ciabattoni
Brunella Gerla
Corrado Manara
Vincenzo Marra

Table of Contents

Many-Valued Non-deterministic Semantics for First-Order Logics of Formal (In)consistency

Arnon Avron and Anna Zamansky

School of Computer Science, Tel Aviv University

Abstract. A *paraconsistent logic* is a logic which allows non-trivial inconsistent theories. One of the oldest and best known approaches to the problem of designing useful paraconsistent logics is da Costa's approach, which seeks to allow the use of classical logic whenever it is safe to do so, but behaves completely differently when contradictions are involved. da Costa's approach has led to the family of Logics of Formal (In)consistency (LFIs). In this paper we provide non-deterministic semantics for a very large family of first-order LFIs (which includes da Costa's original system C_1^*, as well as thousands of other logics). We show that our semantics is effective and modular, and we use this effectiveness to derive some important properties of logics in this family.

1 Introduction

The concept of paraconsistency was introduced more than half a century ago, when several philosophers questioned the validity of classical logic with regard to its *ex contradictione quodlibet* (ECQ) principle. According to this counterintuitive principle, any proposition can be inferred from any inconsistent set of assumptions. Now the philosophical objections to this principle have recently been reinforced by practical considerations concerning information systems. Classical logic simply fails to capture the fact that information systems which contain some inconsistent pieces of information may produce useful answers to queries. The obvious conclusion from this state of affairs is that a more appropriate logic is needed for such systems. Thus [15] says:

> *Informally speaking, paraconsistency is the paradigm of reasoning in the presence of inconsistency. Classical logic intolerantly invalidates any useful reasoning if there is any inconsistency, no matter how irrelevant it may be. However, inconsistencies, as unpleasant and dangerous as they can be, are ubiquitous in information systems. For novel technology which often is not sufficiently mature before being launched on the market, the risk of inconsistencies is even higher. Hence, a thoroughly revised inconsistency-tolerant logic is needed for databases and information systems, also because many future applications (e.g., the self-organizing cognitive evolution of networked information systems, involving negotiation, argumentation, diagnosis, learning, etc.) are likely to deal directly with inconsistencies as inherent constituents of real-life situations.*

S. Aguzzoli et al.(Eds.): Algebraic and Proof-theoretic Aspects, LNAI 4460, pp. 1–24, 2007.

A paraconsistent logic is a logic that allows contradictory, yet non-trivial, theories. There are several approaches to the problem of designing useful paraconsistent logics (see, e.g. [6,9,7]). One of the best known is da Costa's approach ([12,10,11]), which has led to the family of *Logics of Formal Inconsistency* (LFIs). This family is based on two main ideas. First of all, propositions are divided into two sorts: the "normal" (or "consistent") and the "abnormal" (or "inconsistent") ones. The second idea is to express the meta-theoretical notions of consistency/inconsistency at the object language level, by including in it a (primitive or defined) connective ∘, with the intended meaning of ∘φ being "φ is consistent". (Sometimes the dual connective •, expressing inconsistency is used, see e.g. [8,11]). Using the consistency operator, one can limit the applicability of the rule $\varphi, \neg\varphi \vdash \psi$ (capturing the ECQ principle) to the case when φ is consistent (i.e., $\varphi, \neg\varphi, \circ\varphi \vdash \psi$).

Although the syntactic formulations of the LFIs are relatively simple, already on the propositional level the problem of finding useful semantic interpretations for them is rather complicated. Thus the vast majority of the propositional LFIs *cannot* be characterized by means of finite multi-valued matrices. What is more, for almost all of them no useful infinite characteristic matrix is known either. Therefore other types of semantics, like bivaluations semantics and possible translations semantics, have been proposed for them ([10,11]). However, it is not clear how to extend these types of semantics to the first-order level.

An alternative framework for providing semantics for propositional paraconsistent logics was introduced in [1] (and used in [2,3,4]). This framework uses a generalization of the standard multi-valued matrices, called *non-deterministic matrices* (*Nmatrices*). Nmatrices are multi-valued structures, in which the value assigned by a valuation to a complex formula can be chosen *non-deterministically* out of a certain nonempty set of options. The framework of Nmatrices has a number of attractive properties. First of all, the semantics provided by Nmatrices is *modular*: the main effect of each of the rules of a proof system is to reduce the degree of non-determinism of operations, by forbidding some options. The semantics of a proof system is obtained by combining in a rather straightforward way the semantic constraints imposed by its rules. Secondly, this semantics is *effective*. By this we mean that any legal *partial* valuation closed under subformulas can be extended to a full valuation. This property is crucial for the usefulness of semantics, in particular for constructing counterexamples.[1]

This paper has two main goals. The first is to combine the results of [2] and [3] (which treat different families of propositional LFIs) into one unified framework. The second (and more important) goal is to extend this semantic framework (and to generalize the corresponding results) to the full first-order level.[2]

It turned out that one encounters severe complications when moving (in the context of LFIs) from the propositional level to the first-order one. They are

---

[1] No general theorem of effectiveness is available for the semantics of bivaluations or for possible translations semantics. As a result, effectiveness has to be proven from scratch for any instance of these types of semantics.

[2] First steps in this direction have been taken in [20].

mostly related to the lack of the IPE principle (intersubstitutability of provable equivalents) in LFIs. This is an important principle of classical logic, according to which $\psi(A) \leftrightarrow \psi(B)$ is provable whenever $A \leftrightarrow B$ is provable. Unfortunately this principle does not hold for the family of LFIs studied in this paper (see [10,11]). For instance, already on the propositional level one usually cannot infer $\neg(A \wedge B) \leftrightarrow \neg(B \wedge A)$ from $A \wedge B \leftrightarrow B \wedge A$. This abnormality becomes really harmful on the first-order level. Even the α-conversion principle (identifying syntactic objects differing only in the names of their bound variables) does not hold in the first-order systems which are obtained from the propositional LFIs considered here by the addition of the usual rules and axioms for $\forall$ and $\exists$. Thus although $\forall x p(x) \leftrightarrow \forall y p(y)$ is provable in these systems, $\neg\forall x p(x) \leftrightarrow \neg\forall y p(y)$ is not. This is of course unacceptable in any reasonable logical system. A similar problem occurs concerning vacuous quantification: although $\forall x \forall y p(x) \leftrightarrow \forall x p(x)$ is provable, $\neg\forall x \forall y p(x) \leftrightarrow \neg\forall x p(x)$ is not.

The straightforward solution to this problem proposed by da Costa ([12,13]) is to add an explicit axiom capturing the principles of α-equivalence and vacuous quantification. However, the non-deterministic semantics for systems with such axioms become more complicated. As a result, their effectiveness becomes less evident. Nevertheless, we shall be able to prove the effectiveness of our semantics for all the first-order LFIs studied in this paper. Then we show how this effectiveness can be used in order to prove important proof-theoretical properties of those LFIs.

2 Preliminaries

Notation: Given a first-order language L, Frm_L is its set of wffs, Frm_L^{cl} - its set of sentences and Trm_L^{cl} - its set of closed terms. $Fv[\psi]$ ($Fv[\mathbf{t}]$) is the set of variables occurring free in a formula ψ (a term $\mathbf{t}$). $\psi\{\mathbf{t}/x\}$ is the formula obtained from ψ by substituting the term $\mathbf{t}$ for every free occurrence of x in ψ. $P^+(\mathcal{V})$ denotes the set of all non-empty subsets of the set $\mathcal{V}$.

The following definition formalizes for first-order languages the notion of a *substitution of subformulas* in a sentence.

Definition 1. (Substitutable subformulas) *Given a sentence ψ of L, the set $SSF(\psi)$ of its substitutable subformulas is inductively defined as follows:*

- $SSF(p(\mathbf{t}_1, ..., \mathbf{t}_n)) = \{p(\mathbf{t}_1, ..., \mathbf{t}_n)\}$
- $SSF(\diamond(\psi_1, ..., \psi_n)) = \{\diamond(\psi_1, ..., \psi_n)\} \cup SSF(\psi_1) \cup ... \cup SSF(\psi_n)$
- *If $x \notin Fv[\psi]$, then $SSF(Qx\psi) = \{Qx\psi\} \cup SSF(\psi)$. Otherwise, $SSF(Qx\psi) = \{Qx\psi\}$.*

Denote by $\varphi(\psi)$ an L-sentence φ, such that $\psi \in SSF(\varphi)$. Let $\varphi(\psi)$ and θ be L-sentences. We denote by $\varphi(\theta)$ the result of substituting θ for ψ in φ.

For capturing the principles of α-conversion and void quantifiers, we need the notion of a *congruence relation*.

Definition 2. (Congruence relation) *Given a first-order language L, a binary relation $\sim$ between L-formulas is a* congruence relation *if (i) $\sim$ is an equivalence relation, (ii) If $\psi_1 \sim \varphi_1, ..., \psi_n \sim \varphi_n$ then $\diamond(\psi_1, ..., \psi_n) \sim \diamond(\varphi_1, ..., \varphi_n)$ for every n-ary connective $\diamond$ of L, and (iii) If $\psi \sim \varphi$ then $Qx\psi \sim Qx\varphi$ for $Q \in \{\forall, \exists\}$.*

2.1   A Taxonomy of First-Order LFIs

Let $\mathcal{L}_{cl}^+$ be a first-order language with the propositional connectives $\{\wedge, \vee, \supset\}$ and the quantifiers $\{\forall, \exists\}$. $\mathcal{L}_{cl}$ is the language obtained from $\mathcal{L}_{cl}^+$ by extending its set of propositional connectives with the unary connective $\neg$. $\mathcal{L}_C$ is the language obtained from $\mathcal{L}_{cl}$ by the addition of the unary connective $\circ$.

Definition 3. *Let $\mathbf{HCL}^+$ be some propositional Hilbert-type system which has Modus Ponens as the sole inference rule, and is sound and strongly complete for the positive fragment of CPL (classical propositional logic). The first-order system $\mathbf{HCL}_{FOL}^+$ over $\mathcal{L}_{cl}^+$ is obtained from it by adding the following axioms and inference rules:*

($\forall_{\mathbf{f}}$) $\forall x\psi \rightarrow \psi\{t/x\}$
($\exists_{\mathbf{t}}$) $\psi\{t/x\} \rightarrow \exists x\psi$

$$\frac{(\varphi \rightarrow \psi)}{(\varphi \rightarrow \forall x\psi)} \ (\forall_{\mathbf{t}}) \qquad \frac{(\psi \rightarrow \varphi)}{(\exists x\psi \rightarrow \varphi)} \ (\exists_{\mathbf{f}})$$

where t is free for x in ψ, and $x \notin Fv[\varphi]$.

Remark: It can be shown that $\mathbf{HCL}_{FOL}^+$ is an axiomatization of the negation-free fragment of classical first-order logic (in fact, a proof of this can be extracted from the proof of theorem 24 below). It is also easy to see that the usual deduction theorem of classical first-order logic (If φ is a sentence then ψ is derivable from $T \cup \{\varphi\}$ iff $\varphi \rightarrow \psi$ is derivable from T) is true for any extension of $\mathbf{HCL}_{FOL}^+$ by axiom schemata.

Definition 4. *The system $\mathbf{QB_0}$ is obtained from $\mathbf{HCL}_{FOL}^+$ by adding the schemata:*

(t) $\neg\varphi \vee \varphi$
(p) $\circ\varphi \supset ((\varphi \wedge \neg\varphi) \supset \psi)$

Remark: It is not difficult to provide semantics for $\mathbf{QB_0}$. However, in this paper we concentrate on da Costa's systems, which include the additional explicit axiom (mentioned in the introduction) for capturing the principles of α-conversion and of vacuous quantifiers. For this purpose we define the following congruence relation between L-formulas:

Definition 5. ($\sim_L^{dc}$) *Given a first-order language L, $\sim_L^{dc}$ is the minimal congruence relation between L-formulas, which satisfies:*

- If $\psi\{z/x\} \sim_L \psi'\{z/y\}$, where z is a fresh variable, then $Qx\psi \sim_L^{dc} Qy\psi'$ for $Q \in \{\forall, \exists\}$.
- If $\psi \sim_L^{dc} \psi'$ and $x \notin Fv[\psi]$, then $Qx\psi \sim_L^{dc} \psi'$ for $Q \in \{\forall, \exists\}$.

In other words, $\psi \sim_L^{dc} \psi'$ if ψ' can be obtained from ψ by renaming of bound variables and deletion/addition of void quantifiers.

Definition 6. *The system* **QB** *is obtained from* **QB$_0$** *by adding the axiom schema* $\psi \supset \psi'$, *where* $\psi \sim_{\mathcal{L}_C}^{dc} \psi'$.

Next we obtain a large family of first-order systems by adding different combinations of the following schemata, studied in the literature of LFIs (see, e.g. [10,11,8]).

Definition 7. *Let Ax be the set consisting of the following schemata:* [3]

(c) $\neg\neg\varphi \supset \varphi$
(e) $\varphi \supset \neg\neg\varphi$
(w) $\circ(\neg\varphi)$
(i$_1$) $\neg\circ\varphi \supset \varphi$
(i$_2$) $\neg\circ\varphi \supset \neg\varphi$
(k$_1$) $\circ\varphi \vee \varphi$
(k$_2$) $\circ\varphi \vee \neg\varphi$
(a$_\neg$) $\circ\varphi \supset \circ(\neg\varphi)$
(a$_\sharp$) $(\circ\varphi \wedge \circ\psi) \supset (\circ(\varphi\sharp\psi))$ *for* $\sharp \in \{\wedge, \vee, \supset\}$
(o$_\sharp$) $(\circ\varphi \vee \circ\psi) \supset (\circ(\varphi\sharp\psi))$ *for* $\sharp \in \{\wedge, \vee, \supset\}$
(v$_\sharp$) $\circ(\varphi\sharp\psi)$ *for* $\sharp \in \{\wedge, \vee, \supset\}$
(a$_Q$) $\forall x\circ\varphi \supset (\circ(Qx\varphi))$ *for* $Q \in \{\forall, \exists\}$
(o$_Q$) $\exists x\circ\varphi \supset (\circ(Qx\varphi))$ *for* $Q \in \{\forall, \exists\}$
(v$_Q$) $\circ(Qx\psi)$ *for* $Q \in \{\forall, \exists\}$

For $\mathbf{X} \subseteq Ax$, **QB[X]** *is the system obtained by adding the schemata in* **X** *to* **QB**.

The set Ax' consists of the following schemata:

(l) $\neg(\varphi \wedge \neg\varphi) \supset \circ\varphi$
(d) $\neg(\neg\varphi \wedge \varphi) \supset \circ\varphi$
(b) $(\neg(\varphi \wedge \neg\varphi) \vee \neg(\neg\varphi \wedge \varphi)) \supset \circ\varphi$

For $y \in \{(l), (d), (b)\}$ *and* $\mathbf{X} \subseteq Ax$, **QBy[X]** *is the system obtained from* **QB[X]** *by adding the schema y.*

---

[3] The schemata **(c)**, **(e)** , **(i$_1$)**, **(i$_2$)**, **(k$_1$)**, **(k$_2$)**, **(a$_\neg$)**, **(a$_\sharp$)** and **(o$_\sharp$)** were treated for the propositional case in [3] (**(k$_1$)** and **(k$_2$)** were called there **(d$_1$)** and **(d$_2$)**). The schemata **(a$_Q$)** and **(o$_Q$)** were treated in [20] (for the three-valued case). The schemata **(w)**, **(v$_\sharp$)** and **(v$_Q$)** are treated in the context of Nmatrices for the first time. It might have been more natural to refer to the schema **(w)** as **(v$_\neg$)**, but we keep the name used in [8].

Notation: We shall usually denote **QB[X]** (**QB***y***[X]**) by **QB***s* (**QB***ys*), where *s* is a string consisting of the names of the axioms in **X**. Thus we'll write **QBic** instead of **QB[{(i), (c)}]** and **QBlic** instead of **QB(l)[{(i), (c)}]**. If both (**x₁**) and (**x₂**) are in **X** for **x** ∈ {**i**, **k**}, we abbreviate it by **x**. Also, if **x***y* is in **X** for every **y** ∈ {⊃, ∧, ∨} and some **x** ∈ {**a**, **o**, **v**}, we shall write **x_p**. Similarly, if **x***y* is in **X** for every **y** ∈ {∀, ∃} and some **x** ∈ {**a**, **o**, **v**}, we shall write **x_Q**. For both **x_p** and **x_Q** we shall write **x**.

Remark: Denote by **QC₁** the system **QBlcia**. If we take ∘ψ to be an *abbreviation* of ¬(ψ ∧ ¬ψ), then **QC₁** becomes da Costa's original system C_1^* from [12,13].[4] Note that C_1^* is over the language of {¬, ∨, ∧, ⊃, ∀, ∃}.

2.2 Non-deterministic Matrices

nmatrices Our main semantic tool in what follows will be the following generalization of the concept of a multi-valued matrix given in [1,2,3,21,20].

Definition 8. (Non-deterministic matrix) *A non-deterministic matrix (Nmatrix) for a language L is a tuple* $\mathcal{M} = \langle \mathcal{V}, \mathcal{D}, \mathcal{O} \rangle$, *where:* $\mathcal{V}$ *is a non-empty set of truth values,* $\mathcal{D}$ *(designated truth values) is a non-empty proper subset of* $\mathcal{V}$ *and* $\mathcal{O}$ *includes the following interpretation functions:*

- $\tilde{\diamond}_\mathcal{M} : \mathcal{V}^n \to P^+(\mathcal{V})$ *for every n-ary connective* ◇.
- $\tilde{Q}_\mathcal{M} : P^+(\mathcal{V}) \to P^+(\mathcal{V})$ *for every quantifier Q.*

Definition 9. (L-structure) *Let* $\mathcal{M}$ *be an Nmatrix. An L-structure for* $\mathcal{M}$ *is a pair* $S = \langle D, I \rangle$ *where D is a (non-empty) domain and I is a function interpreting constants, function symbols, and predicate symbols of L, satisfying the following conditions:* $I[c] \in D$ *if c is a constant,* $I[f] : D^n \to D$ *if f is an n-ary function, and* $I[p] : D^n \to \mathcal{V}$ *if p is an n-ary predicate.*
I is extended to interpret closed terms of L as follows:

$$I[f(t_1, ..., t_n)] = I[f][I[t_1], ..., I[t_n]]$$

Here a note on our treatment of quantification in the framework of Nmatrices is in order. The standard approach to interpreting first-order formulas is by using *objectual* (or referential) semantics, where the variable is thought of as ranging over a set of objects from the domain (see. e.g. [16,17]). An alternative approach is *substitutional* quantification ([18]), where quantifiers are interpreted substitutionally, i.e. a universal (an existential) quantification is true if and only if every one (at least one) of its substitution instances is true (see. e.g. [19,14]). [21] explains the motivation behind choosing the substitutional approach for the framework of Nmatrices, and points out the problems of the objectual approach in this context. The substitutional approach assumes that every element of the domain has a closed term referring to it. Thus given a structure $S = \langle D, I \rangle$, we extend the language L with *individual constants*, one for each element of D.

---

[4] The name C_1^* is used in [10] for another, different, first-order paraconsistent system.

Definition 10. (**L(D)**) *Let $S=\langle D, I\rangle$ be an L-structure for an Nmatrix $\mathcal{M}$. $L(D)$ is the language obtained from L by adding to it the set of individual constants $\{\bar{a} \mid a \in D\}$. $S' = \langle D, I'\rangle$ is the $L(D)$-structure, such that I' is the extension of I satisfying: $I'[\bar{a}] = a$.*

Given an L-structure $S = \langle D, I\rangle$, we shall refer to the extended $L(D)$-structure $\langle D, I'\rangle$ as S and to I' as I when the meaning is clear from the context.

Next we define the congruence relation $\sim^S$, which is the semantic counterpart of the syntactic congruence relation $\sim_L^{dc}$ (see Definition 5).

Definition 11. ($\sim^S$) *Let S be an L-structure for an Nmatrix $\mathcal{M}$. The relation $\sim^S$ between terms of $L(D)$ is defined inductively as follows:*

- *$x \sim^S x$*
- *For closed terms t, t' of $L(D)$: $t \sim^S t'$ when $I[t] = I[t']$.*
- *If $t_1 \sim^S t_1', ..., t_n \sim^S t_n'$, then $f(t_1, ..., t_n) \sim^S f(t_1', ..., t_n')$.*

The relation $\sim^S$ between formulas of $L(D)$ is the minimal congruence relation, satisfying:

- *If $t_1 \sim^S t_1', t_2 \sim^S t_2', ..., t_n \sim^S t_n'$, then $p(t_1, ..., t_n) \sim^S p(t_1', ..., t_n')$.*
- *If $\psi\{z/x\} \sim^S \varphi\{z/y\}$, where x, y are distinct variables and z is a new variable, then $Qx\psi \sim^S Qy\varphi$ for $Q \in \{\forall, \exists\}$.*
- *If $\psi \sim^S \varphi$ and $x \notin Fv[\varphi]$, then $\psi \sim^S Qx\varphi$.*

The proofs of the following two easy lemmas are left for the reader:

Lemma 12. *Let S be an L-structure, and t_1, t_2 closed terms of $L(D)$, such that $t_1 \sim^S t_2$. Let ψ_1, ψ_2 be $L(D)$-formulas, such that $\psi_1 \sim^S \psi_2$. Then $\psi_1\{t/x\} \sim^S \psi_2\{t_2/x\}$.*

Lemma 13. *Let $S = \langle D, I\rangle$ be an L-structure.*

1. *Let A, B be two L-formulas. If $A \sim_L^{dc} B$, then $A \sim^S B$.*
2. *Let A, B be two L-formulas such that $I[t_1] \neq I[t_2]$ for any two closed terms $t_1 \neq t_2$ occurring in A and B respectively. Then $A \sim_L^{dc} B$ iff $A \sim^S B$.*

Remark: The difference between $\sim_L^{dc}$ and $\sim^S$ is as follows:

1. $\sim_L^{dc}$ is a relation between formulas of L, while $\sim^S$ is a relation between formulas of $L(D)$.
2. $\sim^S$ is defined with respect to some structure S, while $\sim_L^{dc}$ is purely syntactic.
3. Unlike $\sim_L^{dc}$, $\sim^S$ identifies two sentences ψ, ψ' such that ψ' is obtained from ψ by substituting any number of closed terms for closed terms with the same denotation in S. For instance, let S be an L-structure, such that $I[d] = I[c]$ for two constants $d \neq c$. Then $p(c) \not\sim_L^{dc} p(d)$, but $p(c) \sim^S p(d)$. The motivation for this is purely technical and is related to extending the language with the set of individual constants $\{\bar{a} \mid a \in D\}$. Suppose we have a closed term $\mathbf{t}$, such that $I[\mathbf{t}] = a \in D$. But a also has an individual constant $\bar{a}$ referring to it. We would like to be able to substitute $\mathbf{t}$ for $\bar{a}$ in every context, as will be shown in the sequel.

Definition 14. *(S-valuation) Let $S = \langle D, I \rangle$ be an L-structure for an Nmatrix $\mathcal{M}$. An S-valuation $v : Frm_L^{cl} \to \mathcal{V}$ is legal in $\mathcal{M}$ if it satisfies the following conditions:*

- *v respects the $\sim^S$ relation, i.e. $v[\psi] = v[\psi']$ for every two L-sentences ψ, ψ', such that $\psi \sim^S \psi'$.*
- *$v[p(t_1, ..., t_n)] = I[p][I[t_1], ..., I[t_n]]$.*
- *$v[\diamond(\psi_1, ..., \psi_n)] \in \tilde{\diamond}_{\mathcal{M}}[v[\psi_1], ..., v[\psi_n]]$.*
- *$v[Qx\psi] \in \tilde{Q}_{\mathcal{M}}[\{v[\psi\{\bar{a}/x\}] \mid a \in D\}]$.*

Definition 15. *Let $S = \langle D, I \rangle$ be an L-structure for an Nmatrix $\mathcal{M}$.*

1. *An $\mathcal{M}$-legal S-valuation v is a model of a formula ψ in $\mathcal{M}$, denoted by $S, v \models_{\mathcal{M}} \psi$, if $v[\psi'] \in \mathcal{D}$ for every closed instance ψ' of ψ in $L(D)$.*
2. *A formula ψ is $\mathcal{M}$-valid in S if for every $\mathcal{M}$-legal S-valuation v, $S, v \models_{\mathcal{M}} \psi$. ψ is $\mathcal{M}$-valid if ψ is $\mathcal{M}$-valid in every L-structure for $\mathcal{M}$.*
3. *The consequence relation $\vdash_{\mathcal{M}}$ between sets of L-formulas and L-formulas is defined as follows: $\Gamma \vdash_{\mathcal{M}} \psi$ if for every L-structure S and every $\mathcal{M}$-legal S-valuation v: $S, v \models_{\mathcal{M}} \Gamma$ implies that $S, v \models_{\mathcal{M}} \psi$.*
4. *An Nmatrix $\mathcal{M}$ is sound for a proof system $\mathbf{S}$ if $\vdash_{\mathbf{S}} \subseteq \vdash_{\mathcal{M}}$. $\mathcal{M}$ is complete for $\mathbf{S}$ if $\vdash_{\mathcal{M}} \subseteq \vdash_{\mathbf{S}}$. $\mathcal{M}$ is a characteristic Nmatrix for $\mathbf{S}$ if it is sound and complete for $\mathbf{S}$.*

The following is an extension of Definition 2.9 and Theorem 2.10 from [3] to first-order languages:

Definition 16. (Reduction, refinement) *Let $\mathcal{M}_1 = \langle \mathcal{V}_1, \mathcal{D}_1, \mathcal{O}_1 \rangle$ and $\mathcal{M}_2 = \langle \mathcal{V}_2, \mathcal{D}_2, \mathcal{O}_2 \rangle$ be Nmatrices for L.*

1. *A reduction of $\mathcal{M}_1$ to $\mathcal{M}_2$ is a function $F : \mathcal{V}_1 \to \mathcal{V}_2$, such that:*
   - *For every $x \in \mathcal{V}_1$, $x \in \mathcal{D}_1$ iff $F(x) \in \mathcal{D}_2$.*
   - *$F(y) \in \tilde{\diamond}_{\mathcal{M}_2}[F(x_1), ..., F(x_n)]$ for every n-ary connective $\diamond$ of L and every $x_1, ..., x_n, y \in \mathcal{V}_1$, such that $y \in \tilde{\diamond}_{\mathcal{M}_1}[x_1, ..., x_n]$.*
   - *$F(y) \in \tilde{Q}_{\mathcal{M}_2}[\{F(z) \mid z \in H\}]$ for $Q \in \{\forall, \exists\}$ and every $y \in \mathcal{V}_1$ and $H \subseteq P^+(\mathcal{V}_1)$, such that $y \in \tilde{Q}_{\mathcal{M}_1}[H]$.*
2. *$\mathcal{M}_1$ is a refinement of $\mathcal{M}_2$ if there exists a reduction of $\mathcal{M}_1$ to $\mathcal{M}_2$.*
3. *$\mathcal{M}_1$ is a simple refinement of $\mathcal{M}_2$ if it is a refinement of $\mathcal{M}_2$, $\mathcal{V}_1 \subseteq \mathcal{V}_2$, $\mathcal{D}_1 = \mathcal{D}_2 \cap \mathcal{V}_1$, $\tilde{\diamond}_{\mathcal{M}_1}[\overrightarrow{x}] \subseteq \tilde{\diamond}_{\mathcal{M}_2}[\overrightarrow{x}]$ for every n-ary connective $\diamond$ of L and every $\overrightarrow{x} \in \mathcal{V}_1^n$, and $\tilde{Q}_{\mathcal{M}_1}[H] \subseteq \tilde{Q}_{\mathcal{M}_2}[H]$ for $Q \in \{\forall, \exists\}$ and every $H \subseteq P^+(\mathcal{V}_1)$.*

Theorem 1. *If $\mathcal{M}_1$ is a refinement of $\mathcal{M}_2$, then $\vdash_{\mathcal{M}_2} \subseteq \vdash_{\mathcal{M}_1}$.*

Proof: a straightforward extension of the proof of theorem 2.10 from [3].

3   Effectiveness of First-Order Nmatrices

One of the most important properties of the semantic framework of Nmatrices is its *effectiveness*, in the sense that for determining whether $\Gamma \vdash_{\mathcal{M}} \varphi$ (where $\mathcal{M}$ is an Nmatrix) it always suffices to check only *partial* valuations, defined only on *subformulas* of $\Gamma \cup \{\varphi\}$.

Definition 17. *Let S be an L-structure. A set of sentences $W_S \subseteq Frm^{cl}_{L(D)}$ is* closed under subformulas *if it satisfies the following conditions:*

- *For every n-ary connective $\diamond$: $\psi_1, ..., \psi_n \in W_S$ whenever $\diamond(\psi_1, ..., \psi_n) \in W_S$.*
- *For $Q \in \{\forall, \exists\}$ and every $a \in D$: $\psi\{\overline{a}/x\} \in W_S$ whenever $Qx\psi \in W_S$.*

Definition 18. *Let S be an L-structure and $\mathcal{M}$ - an Nmatrix for L. Let $W_S \subseteq Frm^{cl}_{L(D)}$ be a set closed under subformulas. A* partial $\mathcal{M}$-legal S-valuation *on W_S is a function $v : W_S \rightarrow \mathcal{V}$, satisfying:*

- *$\psi \sim^S \psi'$ implies $v[\psi] = v[\psi']$ for every $\psi, \psi' \subset W_S$.*
- *$v[p(t_1, ..., t_n)] = I[p][I[t_1], ..., I[t_1]]$ whenever $p(t_1, ..., t_n) \in W_S$.*
- *$v[\diamond(\psi_1, ..., \psi_n)] \in \tilde{\diamond}[v[\psi_1], ..., v[\psi_n]]$ whenever $\diamond(\psi_1, ..., \psi_n) \in W_S$.*
- *$v[Qx\psi] \in \tilde{Q}[\{v[\psi\{\overline{a}/x\}] \mid a \in D\}]$ whenever $Qx\psi \in W_S$.*

Definition 19. *An Nmatrix $\mathcal{M}$ for L is* effective *if for every L-structure S and every set of $L(D)$-sentences W_S which is closed under subformulas: if v_p is a partial $\mathcal{M}$-legal S-valuation on W_S, then it can be extended to a full $\mathcal{M}$-legal S-valuation.*

For the propositional case, the proof of effectiveness of an Nmatrix $\mathcal{M}$ is very simple (see proposition 2 in [2]). However, in the first-order case effectiveness becomes less evident because any $\mathcal{M}$-legal S-valuation has to respect the $\sim^S$ relation. In fact, given an Nmatrix $\mathcal{M}$ for L and a partial $\mathcal{M}$-legal S-valuation v_p on some set $W_S \subseteq Frm^{cl}_{L(D)}$ closed under subformulas, it is not necessarily guaranteed that v_p can be extended to a full S-valuation legal in $\mathcal{M}$. Consider, for instance, a first-order language L with a constant c and a unary predicate p. Let $\mathcal{M} = \langle \{t, f\}, \{t\}, \mathcal{O} \rangle$ be an Nmatrix for L with the following non-standard interpretation of $\forall$: $\tilde{\forall}[H] = \{t\}$ for every $H \subseteq P^+(\{t, f\})$. Let $S = \langle \{a\}, I \rangle$ be the L-structure in which $I[c] = a$ and $I[p][a] = f$. Let $W = \{p(c)\}$ (obviously, W is closed under subformulas). Then no partial valuation on W can be extended to a full $\mathcal{M}$-legal valuation v, respecting both the $\sim^S$ relation and the interpretation of $\forall$, because such v should assign f to $p(c)$ and t to $\forall x p(c)$, while $\forall x p(c) \sim^S p(c)$. Thus in order to be effective, an Nmatrix has to satisfy a certain condition:

Definition 20. *An Nmatrix $\mathcal{M}$ for L is* suitable for $\sim^{dc}_L$ *if for every $a \in \mathcal{V}$ and every quantifier Q of L: $a \in \tilde{Q}[\{a\}]$.*

For instance, an Nmatrix $\mathcal{M}' = \langle \mathcal{V}', \mathcal{D}', \mathcal{O}' \rangle$ with the following natural interpretations of $\forall$ and $\exists$ is suitable for $\sim^{dc}_L$:

$$\tilde{\forall}[H] = \begin{cases} \mathcal{D}' & \text{if } H \subseteq \mathcal{D}' \\ \mathcal{V}' - \mathcal{D}' & \text{otherwise} \end{cases} \qquad \tilde{\exists}[H] = \begin{cases} \mathcal{D}' & \text{if } H \cap \mathcal{D}' \neq \emptyset \\ \mathcal{V}' - \mathcal{D}' & \text{otherwise} \end{cases}$$

Proposition 21. *Any Nmatrix $\mathcal{M} = \langle \mathcal{V}, \mathcal{D}, \mathcal{O} \rangle$ for L which is suitable for $\sim^{dc}_L$, is effective.*

Proof: Let S be an L-structure and let W_S be a set of $L(D)$-sentences, closed under subformulas. Let v_p be some partial S-valuation on W_S which is $\mathcal{M}$-legal. We show that it can be extended to a full S-valuation v which is legal in $\mathcal{M}$.

For every n-ary connective $\diamond$ of L and every $a_1, ..., a_n \in \mathcal{V}$, choose a truth-value $\mathbf{b}^\diamond_{a_1,...,a_n} \in \tilde{\diamond}[a_1, ..., a_n]$. For $Q \in \{\forall, \exists\}$ of L and every $B \subseteq P^+(\mathcal{V})$, choose a truth-value $\mathbf{b}^Q_B \in \tilde{Q}[B]$, so that for every $a \in \mathcal{V}$: $\mathbf{b}^Q_{\{a\}} = a$ (this is possible, since $\mathcal{M}$ is suitable for $\sim^{dc}_L$).

Denote by $H_{\sim^S}$ the set of all equivalence classes of $Frm^{cl}_{L(D)}$ under $\sim^S$. Denote by $[\![\psi]\!]$ the equivalence class of ψ. Define the function $\chi : H_{\sim^S} \to \mathcal{V}$ as follows:

$$\chi[\![p(\mathbf{t}_1, ..., \mathbf{t}_n)]\!] = I[p][I[\mathbf{t}_1], ..., I[\mathbf{t}_n]]$$

$$\chi[\![\diamond(\psi_1, ..., \psi_n)]\!] = \begin{cases} v_p[\varphi] & \varphi \in [\![\diamond(\psi_1, ..., \psi_n)]\!] \cap W_S \\ \mathbf{b}^\diamond_{\chi[\![\psi_1]\!],...,\chi[\![\psi_n]\!]} & [\![\diamond(\psi_1, ..., \psi_n)]\!] \cap W_S = \emptyset \end{cases}$$

$$\chi[\![Qx\psi]\!] = \begin{cases} v_p[\varphi] & \varphi \in [\![Qx\psi]\!] \cap W_S \\ \mathbf{b}^Q_{\{\chi[\![\psi\{\bar{a}/x\}]\!]\} \mid a \in D} & [\![Qx\psi]\!] \cap W_S = \emptyset \end{cases}$$

Note that because v_p is $\mathcal{M}$-legal, the value of $v_p[\varphi]$ in the above definition does not depend on the choice of φ (among those satisfying the relevant condition). Hence χ is well-defined. Next define

$$v[\psi] = \chi[\![\psi]\!]$$

The proof that v is $\mathcal{M}$-legal is not difficult and is left to the reader. Obviously, v is an extension of v_p.   □

4 Non-deterministic Semantics for First-Order LFIs

4.1 Finite Non-deterministic Semantics

In this section we provide five-valued (or less) non-deterministic semantics for first-order LFIs obtained from the basic system **QB** by adding various combinations of schemata from Ax (not including the schemata **(l)**, **(b)** and **(d)**. We deal with systems including these schemata in the next subsection). The semantics presented below is an extension to first-order languages of the semantics from [3].

The system **QB** treats the connectives $\wedge, \vee, \supset$ and the quantifiers $\forall, \exists$ similarly to classical logic. The treatment of $\circ$ and $\neg$ is different: intuitively, the truth/falsity of $\neg\psi$ or $\circ\psi$ is not completely determined by the truth/falsity of ψ. More data is needed for it. The central idea is to include all the relevant data concerning a sentence ψ in the truth-value from $\mathcal{V}$ which is assigned to ψ. In our case the relevant data beyond the truth/falsity of ψ is the truth/falsity of $\neg\psi$ and of $\circ\psi$. This leads to the use of elements from $\{0, 1\}^3$ as truth-values, where the intended meaning of assigning $\langle x, y, z \rangle$ to ψ is as follows:

- $x = 1$ iff ψ is true
- $y = 1$ iff $\neg\psi$ is true
- $z = 1$ iff $\circ\psi$ is true

However, the axioms **(t)** and **(b)** rule out some of the truth-values. By **(t)**, at least one of the sentences $\psi, \neg\psi$ should be true, thus ruling out $\langle 0, 0, 1 \rangle$ and $\langle 0, 0, 0 \rangle$. Similarly, **(b)** rules out $\langle 1, 1, 1 \rangle$. We are left with the following five truth-values:

- $t = \langle 1, 0, 1 \rangle$
- $t_I = \langle 1, 0, 0 \rangle$
- $I = \langle 1, 1, 0 \rangle$
- $f = \langle 0, 1, 1 \rangle$
- $f_I = \langle 0, 1, 0 \rangle$

Note that since the first component of a truth-value assigned to a formula should indicate whether that formula is true, the designated truth-values should be those whose first component is 1. Thus we are led to the following definition (which is an extension to first-order languages of Definition 3.1 from [3]):

Definition 22. *The Nmatrix* $\mathcal{QM}_5 = \langle \mathcal{V}, \mathcal{D}, \mathcal{O} \rangle$ *for* $\mathcal{L}_C$ *is defined as follows:*

- $\mathcal{V} = \{t, t_I, I, f, f_I\}$, $\mathcal{D} = \{t, t_I, I\}$.
- *Let* $\mathcal{F} = \mathcal{V} - \mathcal{D}$. *The operations in* $\mathcal{O}$ *are defined as follows:*

$$a \tilde{\vee} b = \begin{cases} \mathcal{D} & \text{if either } a \in \mathcal{D} \text{ or } b \in \mathcal{D}, \\ \mathcal{F} & \text{if } a, b \in \mathcal{F} \end{cases}$$

$$a \tilde{\supset} b = \begin{cases} \mathcal{D} & \text{if either } a \in \mathcal{F} \text{ or } b \in \mathcal{D} \\ \mathcal{F} & \text{if } a \in \mathcal{D} \text{ and } b \in \mathcal{F} \end{cases}$$

$$a \tilde{\wedge} b = \begin{cases} \mathcal{F} & \text{if either } a \in \mathcal{F} \text{ or } b \in \mathcal{F} \\ \mathcal{D} & \text{if } a, b \in \mathcal{D} \end{cases}$$

$$\tilde{\neg} a = \begin{cases} \mathcal{F} & \text{if } a \in \{t, t_I\} \\ \mathcal{D} & \text{if } a \in \{f, f_I, I\} \end{cases} \qquad \tilde{\circ} a = \begin{cases} \mathcal{D} & \text{if } a \in \{t, f\} \\ \mathcal{F} & \text{if } a \in \{t_I, f_I, I\} \end{cases}$$

$$\tilde{\forall}[H] = \begin{cases} \mathcal{D} & \text{if } H \subseteq \mathcal{D} \\ \mathcal{F} & \text{otherwise} \end{cases} \qquad \tilde{\exists}[H] = \begin{cases} \mathcal{D} & \text{if } H \cap \mathcal{D} \neq \emptyset \\ \mathcal{F} & \text{otherwise} \end{cases}$$

Note that the non-deterministic truth tables in $\mathcal{QM}_5$ corresponding to the operations $\neg$ and $\circ$ are:

$\tilde{\neg}$	f	f_I	I	t	t_I
	$\{I, t, t_I\}$	$\{I, t, t_I\}$	$\{I, t, t_I\}$	$\{f, f_I\}$	$\{f, f_I\}$

$\tilde{\circ}$	f	f_I	I	t	t_I
	$\{t, I, t_I\}$	$\{f, f_I\}$	$\{f, f_I\}$	$\{t, I, t_I\}$	$\{f, f_I\}$

Lemma 23. (Effectiveness of $\mathcal{QM}_5$) $\mathcal{QM}_5$ *is effective.*

Proof: This follows from the suitability of $\mathcal{QM}_5$ for $\sim_L^{dc}$, and proposition 21.

The following theorem is a generalization of theorem 3 of [20].

Theorem 24. (Soundness and completeness) *Let $\Gamma \cup \{\psi_0\}$ be a set of $\mathcal{L}_C$-formulas. $\Gamma \vdash_{\mathbf{QB}} \psi_0$ iff $\Gamma \vdash_{\mathcal{QM}_5} \psi_0$.*

The proof of soundness is not hard and is left to the reader.

For completeness, we first note that by definition of the interpretation of $\forall$ in $\mathcal{QM}_5$, $\forall x \varphi \vdash_{\mathcal{QM}_5} \varphi$ and $\varphi \vdash_{\mathcal{QM}_5} \forall x \varphi$ for every formula φ and every variable x. Obviously the same relations hold between φ and $\forall x \varphi$ in $\mathbf{HCL}^+_{FOL}$, and so in $\vdash_{\mathbf{QB}}$. It follows that we may assume that all formulas in $\Gamma \cup \{\psi_0\}$ are sentences. It is also easy to see that we may restrict ourselves to L_r, the subset of L consisting of all the constants, function, and predicate symbols occurring in $\Gamma \cup \{\psi_0\}$. Now suppose that $\Gamma \nvdash_{\mathbf{QB}} \psi_0$. We will construct an $\mathcal{L}_C$-structure S and an $\mathcal{QM}_5$-legal S-valuation v, such that $S, v \models_{\mathcal{M}_5} \Gamma$, but $S, v \nvDash_{\mathcal{QM}_5} \psi_0$. Let L' be the language obtained from L_r by adding a countably infinite set of new constants. It is a standard matter to show (using a usual Henkin-type construction) that Γ can be extended to a maximal set Γ^* of sentences in L', such that:

- $\Gamma^* \nvdash_{\mathbf{QB}} \psi_0$.
- $\Gamma \subseteq \Gamma^*$.
- For every L'-sentence $\exists x \psi \in \Gamma^*$ there is a constant $\mathbf{c}$ of L', such that $\psi\{\mathbf{c}/x\} \in \Gamma^*$.
- For every L'-sentence $\forall x \psi \notin \Gamma^*$, there is a constant $\mathbf{c}$ of L', such that $\psi\{\mathbf{c}/x\} \notin \Gamma^*$.

(The last property follows from property 3, the deduction theorem for $\mathbf{QB}$, and the fact that for any $x \notin Fv[\varphi]$, $(\forall x \psi \supset \varphi) \supset \exists x(\psi \supset \varphi)$ is provable in the positive fragment of first-order classical logic, and so also in $\mathbf{QB}$). It is now straightforward to show that Γ^* has the following properties for every L'-sentences ψ, φ, and $\forall x \theta$:

1. If $\psi \notin \Gamma^*$, then $\psi \supset \psi_0 \in \Gamma^*$.
2. $\psi \vee \varphi \in \Gamma^*$ iff either $\varphi \in \Gamma^*$ or $\psi \in \Gamma^*$.
3. $\psi \wedge \varphi \in \Gamma^*$ iff both $\varphi \in \Gamma^*$ and $\psi \in \Gamma^*$.
4. $\varphi \supset \psi \in \Gamma^*$ iff either $\varphi \notin \Gamma^*$ or $\psi \in \Gamma^*$.
5. Either $\psi \in \Gamma^*$ or $\neg \psi \in \Gamma^*$.
6. If ψ and $\neg \psi$ are both in Γ^*, then $\circ \psi \notin \Gamma^*$.
7. If $\psi \in \Gamma^*$, then for every L'-sentence ψ' such that $\psi' \sim^{dc}_L \psi$: $\psi' \in \Gamma^*$.
8. If $\forall x \theta \in \Gamma^*$, then for every closed L'-term $\mathbf{t}$: $\theta\{\mathbf{t}/x\} \in \Gamma^*$. If $\forall x \theta \notin \Gamma^*$, then there is some closed term $\mathbf{t}_\theta$ of L', such that $\theta\{\mathbf{t}_\theta/x\} \notin \Gamma^*$.
9. If $\exists x \theta \in \Gamma^*$, then there is some closed term $\mathbf{t}_\theta$ of L, such that $\theta\{\mathbf{t}_\theta/x\} \in \Gamma^*$. If $\exists x \theta \notin \Gamma^*$, then for every closed term $\mathbf{t}$ of L': $\theta\{\mathbf{t}/x\} \notin \Gamma^*$.

The L'-structure $S = \langle D, I \rangle$ is defined as follows:

- D is the set of all the closed terms of L'.
- For every constant c of L': $I[c] = c$.
- For every $\mathbf{t}_1, ..., \mathbf{t}_n \in D$: $I[f][\mathbf{t}_1, ..., \mathbf{t}_n] = f(\mathbf{t}_1, ..., \mathbf{t}_n)$.
- For every $\mathbf{t}_1, ..., \mathbf{t}_n \in D$: $I[p][\mathbf{t}_1, ..., \mathbf{t}_n] = \langle x, y, z \rangle$, where $x, y, z \in \{0, 1\}$ and:

- $x = 1$ iff $p(\mathbf{t}_1, ..., \mathbf{t}_n) \in \Gamma^*$.
- $y = 1$ iff $\neg p(\mathbf{t}_1, ..., \mathbf{t}_n) \in \Gamma^*$.
- $z = 1$ iff $\circ p(\mathbf{t}_1, ..., \mathbf{t}_n) \in \Gamma^*$.

Lemma 25. $I^*[\mathbf{t}] = \mathbf{t}$ *for every* $\mathbf{t} \in D$.

Proof: by induction on the structure of $\mathbf{t}$.

Note that in the extended language $L'(D)$ we now have an individual constant $\bar{\mathbf{t}}$ for every term $\mathbf{t} \in D$. For any L'-term $\mathbf{t}$, define $\tilde{\mathbf{t}}$ as follows:

$$\tilde{\mathbf{t}} = \begin{cases} \mathbf{s} & \text{if } \mathbf{t} = \bar{\mathbf{s}} \text{ for some } \mathbf{s} \in D \\ \mathbf{t} & \text{otherwise} \end{cases}$$

Given an $L'(D)$-sentence ψ, define the sentence $\tilde{\psi}$ inductively as follows:

- $\widetilde{p(\mathbf{t}_1, ..., \mathbf{t}_n)} = p(\tilde{\mathbf{t}}_1, ..., \tilde{\mathbf{t}}_n)$
- $\widetilde{\diamond(\psi_1, ..., \psi_n)} = \diamond(\tilde{\psi}_1, ..., \tilde{\psi}_n)$
- $\widetilde{Qx\psi} = Qx\tilde{\psi}$

In other words, $\tilde{\psi}$ is obtained by replacing all individual constants $\bar{\mathbf{t}}$ occurring in ψ by the respective (closed) term $\mathbf{t}$.

Lemma 26.   *1. For any $L'(D)$-sentence ψ, $\psi \sim^S \tilde{\psi}$.*
2. For any $\psi, \varphi \in Frm^{cl}_{L'(D)}$: if $\psi \sim^S \varphi$, then $\tilde{\psi} \sim^{dc}_L \tilde{\varphi}$.
3. For every $L'(D)$-sentence ψ and every $\mathbf{t} \in D$: $\widetilde{\psi\{\mathbf{t}/x\}} = \tilde{\psi}\{\mathbf{t}/x\}$.

Proof: The proofs of part 1 and 3 are straightforward. Part 2 follows from Lemma 13-2 and Lemma 25.

Next we define the refuting S-valuation $v : Frm^{cl}_{L'(D)} \to \mathcal{V}$ as follows:

$$v[\psi] = \langle x_\psi, y_\psi, z_\psi \rangle$$

where $x_\psi, y_\psi, z_\psi \in \{0, 1\}$ and:

- $x_\psi = 1$ iff $\tilde{\psi} \in \Gamma^*$.
- $y_\psi = 1$ iff $\widetilde{\neg\psi} \in \Gamma^*$.
- $z_\psi = 1$ iff $\widetilde{\circ\psi} \in \Gamma^*$.

Let ψ, ψ' be two $L'(D)$-sentences, such that $\psi \sim^S \psi'$. Then by lemma 26-2, $\tilde{\psi} \sim^{dc}_L \tilde{\psi}'$, and by property 7 of Γ^*, $\tilde{\psi} \in \Gamma^*$ iff $\tilde{\psi}' \in \Gamma^*$. Similarly, since $\neg\psi \sim^S \neg\psi'$ and $\circ\psi \sim^S \circ\psi'$, $(\widetilde{\neg\psi} =)\widetilde{\neg\psi} \sim^{dc}_L \widetilde{\neg\psi}'(= \widetilde{\neg\psi}')$ and $\widetilde{\circ\psi} \sim^{dc}_L \widetilde{\circ\psi}'$. Thus $\widetilde{\neg\psi} \in \Gamma^*$ iff $\widetilde{\neg\psi}' \in \Gamma^*$ and $\widetilde{\circ\psi} \in \Gamma^*$ iff $\widetilde{\circ\psi}' \in \Gamma^*$. Hence $v[\psi] = v[\psi']$ and so v respects the $\sim^S$ relation.

It remains to check that v respects the interpretations of the connectives and quantifiers in $\mathcal{QM}_5$. This is guaranteed by the properties of Γ^*. We prove this for the cases of $\circ$ and $\forall$:

- Let $v[\psi] \in \{t, f\}$. Then $\widetilde{\circ\psi} \in \Gamma^*$ and so $v[\circ\psi] \in \mathcal{D}$. Similarly for the case of $v[\psi] \in \{t_I, f_I, I\}$.
- Let $\forall x\psi$ be an $L'(D)$-sentence, such that $\{v[\psi\{\overline{a}/x\}] \mid a \in D\} \subseteq \mathcal{D}$. Suppose by contradiction that $v[\forall x\psi] \notin \mathcal{D}$. Then $\widetilde{\forall x\psi} = \forall x\widetilde{\psi} \notin \Gamma^*$. By property 8 of Γ^*, there exists some closed L'-term $\mathbf{t}$, such that $\widetilde{\psi}\{\mathbf{t}/x\} \notin \Gamma^*$. Then $v[\widetilde{\psi}\{\mathbf{t}/x\}] \notin \mathcal{D}$. Since $\psi \sim^S \widetilde{\psi}$, $\psi\{\mathbf{t}/x\} \sim^S \widetilde{\psi}\{\mathbf{t}/x\}$ by lemma 12. We have already shown that v respects the $\sim^S$ relation, and so $v[\psi\{\mathbf{t}/x\}] \notin \mathcal{D}$. By lemma 12 again, $\psi\{\mathbf{t}/x\} \sim^S \psi\{\overline{\mathbf{t}}/x\}$, and so $v[\psi\{\overline{\mathbf{t}}/x\}] \notin \mathcal{D}$. A contradiction.
- Let $\forall x\psi$ be an $L'(D)$-sentence, such that $\{v[\psi\{\overline{a}/x\}] \mid a \in D\} \cap \mathcal{F} \neq \emptyset$. Suppose by contradiction that $v[\forall x\psi] \notin \mathcal{F}$. Then $\forall x\widetilde{\psi} \in \Gamma^*$. By property 8 of Γ^*, for every closed L'-term $\mathbf{t}$: $\widetilde{\psi}\{\mathbf{t}/x\} \in \Gamma^*$. Then $v[\widetilde{\psi}\{\mathbf{t}/x\}] \in \mathcal{D}$. Similarly to the previous case, we get that $v[\psi\{\overline{a}/x\}] \in \mathcal{D}$ for every $a \in D$, in contradiction to our assumption.

Now for every L'-sentence ψ: $v[\psi] \in \mathcal{D}$ iff $\psi \in \Gamma^*$. So $S, v \models_{\mathcal{QM}_5} \Gamma$ (recall that $\Gamma \subseteq \Gamma^*$), but $S, v \not\models_{\mathcal{QM}_5} \psi_0$. $\qquad\square$

Next we turn to the semantics of the systems obtained from the basic system **QB** by adding various combinations of the schemata from Ax. As explained in the introduction, the main idea is *modularity*: each schema induces some semantic condition, leading to a certain refinement of the basic Nmatrix $\mathcal{QM}_5$.

Definition 27. *The refining conditions induced by the schemata from Ax are:*

Cond(c) : *if $x \in \{f, f_I\}$ then $\tilde{\neg}x \subseteq \{t, t_I\}$*
Cond(e) : *$\tilde{\neg}I = \{I\}$*
Cond(w) : *$\tilde{\neg}x \subseteq \{t, f\}$*
Cond(i$_1$) : *f_I should be deleted, and $\tilde{\circ}f \subseteq \{t, t_I\}$*
Cond(i$_2$) : *t_I should be deleted, and $\tilde{\circ}t = \{t\}$*
Cond(k$_1$) : *f_I should be deleted.*
Cond(k$_2$) : *t_I should be deleted.*
Cond(a$_\neg$) : *$\tilde{\neg}t = \{f\}$ and $\tilde{\neg}f = \{t\}$*
Cond(a$_\sharp$) : *if $a, b \in \{t, f\}$, then $a\tilde{\sharp}b \subseteq \{t, f\}$*
Cond(o$_\sharp$) : *if $a \in \{t, f\}$ or $b \in \{t, f\}$, then $a\tilde{\sharp}b \subseteq \{t, f\}$*
Cond(v$_\sharp$) : *$x\tilde{\sharp}y \subseteq \{t, f\}$ for every $x, y \in V$.*
Cond(a$_Q$) : *for every $H \subseteq \{t, f\}$, $\tilde{Q}[H] \subseteq \{t, f\}$*
Cond(o$_Q$) : *if $H \cap \{t, f\} \neq \emptyset$ then $\tilde{Q}[H] \subseteq \{t, f\}$*
Cond(v$_Q$) : *$\tilde{Q}[H] \subseteq \{t, f\}$ for every $H \subseteq V$.*

Definition 28. *For $\mathbf{X} \subseteq Ax$, let $\mathcal{QM}_5(\mathbf{X})$ be the weakest simple refinement (see Definition 16) of $\mathcal{QM}_5$, in which the conditions of the schemata from $\mathbf{X}$ are satisfied. In other words, $\mathcal{QM}_5(\mathbf{X}) = \langle V_X, \mathcal{D}_X, \mathcal{O}_X \rangle$, where:*

- *If both (**e**) and (**w**) are in $\mathbf{X}$, then I is deleted.*
- *V_X is the set of values from $\{t, f, t_I, f_I, I\}$ which are not deleted either by a combination of both (**e**) and (**w**), or by any condition of a schema from $\mathbf{X}$.*
- *$\mathcal{D}_X = V_X \cap \{t, t_I, I\}$.*

- For any connective $\diamond$ and any $a_1, ..., a_n \in \mathcal{V}_X$, $\tilde{\diamond}_{\mathcal{QM}_5(\mathbf{X})}$ assigns to $\overrightarrow{a}$ the set of all truth-values in $\tilde{\diamond}_{\mathcal{QM}_5}$ which are not forbidden by any condition of a schema from $\mathbf{X}$.
- For $Q \in \{\forall, \exists\}$ and any $H \subseteq P^+(\mathcal{V}_X)$, $\tilde{Q}_{\mathcal{QM}_5(\mathbf{X})}$ assigns to $\overrightarrow{a}$ the set of all truth-values in $\tilde{Q}_{\mathcal{QM}_5}$ which are not forbidden by any condition of a schema from $\mathbf{X}$.

Notation: We write $\mathcal{QM}_5\mathbf{s}$ instead of $\mathcal{QM}_5(\mathbf{X})$, where $\mathbf{s}$ is the string of all the names of the schemata from $\mathbf{X}$.

Remarks:

1. Assume that $\mathbf{X} \subseteq Ax$, and that either $(\mathbf{w}) \notin \mathbf{X}$ or $(\mathbf{e}) \notin \mathbf{X}$. It is not difficult to see that in this case $\{t, f, I\} \subseteq \mathcal{V}_X$, $\{t, I\} \subseteq \mathcal{D}_X$, and both $\tilde{\diamond}_{\mathcal{QM}_5(X)}[\overrightarrow{a}]$ and $\tilde{Q}_{\mathcal{QM}_5(\mathbf{X})}[H]$ are not empty (where $\diamond$ is an n-ary connective, $\overrightarrow{a} \in \mathcal{V}_X^n$, $Q \in \{\forall, \exists\}$, and $H \subseteq P^+(\mathcal{V}_X)$). The case when both $(\mathbf{w})$ and $(\mathbf{e})$ are in $\mathbf{X}$ is different, since these conditions are not coherent in the presence of I. It is easy to see that in this case $\mathbf{X}$ is equivalent to classical logic (and so it is not paraconsistent). An adequate semantics for it can be obtained simply by deleting I. Alternatively, one may delete all truth values except t and f.
2. Note the following dependencies between the conditions:
   (a) $(\mathbf{k_j})$ follows from $(\mathbf{i_j})$ for $\mathbf{j} \in \{1, 2\}$.
   (b) $(\mathbf{c})$ follows from $(\mathbf{a_\neg})$ and $(\mathbf{k_1})$ (taken together).
   (c) $(\mathbf{a_\neg})$ follows from $(\mathbf{c})$, $(\mathbf{k_1})$ and $(\mathbf{k_2})$ (taken together), and from $(\mathbf{w})$.
   (d) $(\mathbf{a_x})$ follows from $(\mathbf{o_x})$ and $(\mathbf{o_x})$ follows from $(\mathbf{v_x})$ for $\mathbf{x} \in \{\vee, \wedge, \supset, \forall, \exists\}$.

Examples:

1. The non-deterministic truth table for $\neg$ in $\mathcal{QM}_5\mathbf{c}$ is:

$\tilde{\neg}$	f	f_I	I	t	t_I
	$\{t, t_I\}$	$\{t, t_I\}$	$\{I, t, t_I\}$	$\{f, f_I\}$	$\{f, f_I\}$

2. The only truth-values which are retained in $\mathcal{QM}_5\mathbf{ci}$ are t, f, and I. The non-deterministic truth tables in this Nmatrix corresponding to the operations $\neg$, $\circ$, $\forall$, and $\exists$ are :

$\tilde{\circ}$	f	I	t
	$\{t\}$	$\{f\}$	$\{t\}$

$\tilde{\neg}$	f	I	t
	$\{t\}$	$\{I, t\}$	$\{f\}$

H	$\tilde{\forall}[H]$	$\tilde{\exists}[H]$
$\{t\}$	$\{t, I\}$	$\{t, I\}$
$\{f\}$	$\{f\}$	$\{f\}$
$\{I\}$	$\{t, I\}$	$\{t, I\}$
$\{t, f\}$	$\{f\}$	$\{t, I\}$
$\{t, I\}$	$\{t, I\}$	$\{t, I\}$
$\{f, I\}$	$\{f\}$	$\{t, I\}$
$\{t, f, I\}$	$\{f\}$	$\{t, I\}$

3. In $\mathcal{QM}_5\mathbf{cio}$ the tables for $\forall, \exists$ change to:

H	$\widetilde{\forall}[H]$	$\widetilde{\exists}[H]$
$\{t\}$	$\{t\}$	$\{t\}$
$\{f\}$	$\{f\}$	$\{f\}$
$\{I\}$	$\{t,I\}$	$\{t,I\}$
$\{t,f\}$	$\{f\}$	$\{t\}$
$\{t,I\}$	$\{t\}$	$\{t\}$
$\{f,I\}$	$\{f\}$	$\{t\}$
$\{t,f,I\}$	$\{f\}$	$\{t\}$

4. In $\mathcal{QM}_5\mathbf{cia}$ the tables for $\forall, \exists$ change to:

H	$\widetilde{\forall}[H]$	$\widetilde{\exists}[H]$
$\{t\}$	$\{t\}$	$\{t\}$
$\{f\}$	$\{f\}$	$\{f\}$
$\{I\}$	$\{t,I\}$	$\{t,I\}$
$\{t,f\}$	$\{f\}$	$\{t\}$
$\{t,I\}$	$\{t,I\}$	$\{t,I\}$
$\{f,I\}$	$\{f\}$	$\{t,I\}$
$\{t,f,I\}$	$\{f\}$	$\{t,I\}$

5. The truth table for $\wedge$ in $\mathcal{QM}_5\mathbf{v}_\wedge$ becomes fully deterministic:

$\widetilde{\wedge}$	$\mathbf{f}$	$\mathbf{f_I}$	$\mathbf{I}$	$\mathbf{t}$	$\mathbf{t_I}$
$\mathbf{f}$	$\{f\}$	$\{f\}$	$\{f\}$	$\{f\}$	$\{f\}$
$\mathbf{f_I}$	$\{f\}$	$\{f\}$	$\{f\}$	$\{f\}$	$\{f\}$
$\mathbf{I}$	$\{f\}$	$\{f\}$	$\{t\}$	$\{t\}$	$\{t\}$
$\mathbf{t}$	$\{f\}$	$\{f\}$	$\{t\}$	$\{t\}$	$\{t\}$
$\mathbf{t_I}$	$\{f\}$	$\{f\}$	$\{t\}$	$\{t\}$	$\{t\}$

Theorem 29. (Soundness and completeness) *Let* $\mathbf{X} \subseteq Ax$. *Let* $\Gamma \cup \{\psi_0\}$ *be a set of* $\mathcal{L}_C$-*formulas.* $\Gamma \vdash_{\mathbf{B}[\mathbf{X}]} \psi_0$ *iff* $\Gamma \vdash_{\mathcal{QM}_5(\mathbf{X})} \psi_0$.

Proof: a straightforward modification of the proof of theorem 24. We only have to check that the conditions imposed by the schemata in $\mathbf{X}$ are respected by the valuation v defined in the proof. We prove this for $(\mathbf{a}_Q)$ and $(\mathbf{o}_Q)$:

- Suppose that $(\mathbf{a}_Q) \in \mathbf{X}$. Then from the definition of Γ^* it follows that that $\forall x \circ \psi \notin \Gamma^*$ in case $\circ Qx\psi \notin \Gamma^*$. Let $Qx\psi$ be an $L'(D)$-sentence, such that $H_\psi = \{v[\psi\{\bar{a}/x\}] \mid a \in D\} \subseteq \{t,f\}$. Suppose by contradiction that $v[Qx\psi] \notin \{t,f\}$. Then $\widetilde{\circ Qx\psi} = \circ Qx(\widetilde{\psi}) \notin \Gamma^*$ and so $\forall x \circ (\widetilde{\psi}) = \forall x(\widetilde{\circ\psi}) \notin \Gamma^*$. By property 8 of Γ^*, there exists some closed term $\mathbf{t}$ of L', such that $\widetilde{(\circ\psi)}\{\mathbf{t}/x\} \notin \Gamma^*$. By lemma 26-3, $\widetilde{(\circ\psi)}\{\mathbf{t}/x\} = (\circ(\widetilde{\psi\{\mathbf{t}/x\}}))$. By definition of v, $v[\psi\{\mathbf{t}/x\}] \notin \{t,f\}$. By lemma 12, $\psi\{\mathbf{t}/x\} \sim^S \psi\{\overline{\mathbf{t}}/x\}$. Since v respects the $\sim^S$ relation (this is proved like in theorem 24), $v[\psi\{\overline{\mathbf{t}}/x\}] \notin \{t,f\}$, in contradiction to our assumption about H_ψ.

– Suppose that $(\mathbf{o}_Q) \in \mathbf{X}$. Then $\exists x \circ \psi \notin \Gamma^*$ in case $\circ Qx\psi \notin \Gamma^*$. Let $Qx\psi$ be an $L'(D)$-sentence, such that $H_\psi \cap \{t, f\} \neq \emptyset$, where $H_\psi = \{v[\psi\{\overline{a}/x\}] \mid a \in D\}$. Suppose by contradiction that $v[Qx\psi] \notin \{t, f\}$. Then $(\widetilde{\circ Qx\psi}) = \circ Qx(\widetilde{\psi}) \notin \Gamma^*$ and so $\exists x \circ (\widetilde{\psi}) = \exists x(\widetilde{\circ\psi}) \notin \Gamma^*$. By property 9 of Γ^*, for every closed term $\mathbf{t}$ of L', $\widetilde{\circ\psi}\{\mathbf{t}/x\} \notin \Gamma^*$. By lemma 26-3, $(\widetilde{\circ\psi})\{\mathbf{t}/x\} = (\circ(\widetilde{\psi\{\mathbf{t}/x\}}))$. By definition of v, $v[\psi\{\mathbf{t}/x\}] \notin \{t, f\}$. By lemma 12, $\psi\{\mathbf{t}/x\} \sim^S \psi\{\overline{\mathbf{t}}/x\}$. Since again v respects the $\sim^S$ relation, $v[\psi\{\overline{\mathbf{t}}/x\}] \notin \{t, f\}$ for every $\mathbf{t} \in D$, in contradiction to our assumption.

Lemma 30. (Effectiveness of $\mathcal{QM}_5(\mathbf{X})$) *For every* $\mathbf{X} \subseteq Ax$, $\mathcal{QM}_5(\mathbf{X})$ *is effective.*

Proof: This follows from proposition 21.

4.2   Infinite Non-deterministic Semantics

We turn now to the extensions of the systems handled in the previous section by the schemata **(l),(d)** and **(b)** (see Definition 7). It is easy to see that any of these schemata entails in **QB** both $(\mathbf{k}_1)$ and $(\mathbf{k}_2)$. Recall that the semantic effect of the latter two axioms is to delete t_I and f_I from the basic Nmatrix $\mathcal{QM}_5$. Thus the infinite Nmatrices provided in this section are all refinements (see Definition 16) of the *three-valued* Nmatrix $\mathcal{M}_5\mathbf{k}$.

To provide some informal intuition about the infinite semantics, note that what all of the above schemata have in common is a conjunction of a formula with its negation. Consider for instance the schema **(l)** $\neg(\varphi \wedge \neg\varphi) \supset \circ\varphi$. Its validity is guaranteed only if $v[\neg(\varphi \wedge \neg\varphi)] \notin \mathcal{D}$ whenever $v[\circ\varphi] \notin \mathcal{D}$. Informally, to ensure this, we need to be able to isolate a conjunction of an "inconsistent" formula ψ with its own negation from conjunctions of ψ with other formulas. This can be done by enforcing an intimate connection between the truth-value of an "inconsistent" formula and the truth-value of its negation. This, in turn, requires a supply of infinitely many truth-values.

The following definition is a generalization of Definition 8 in [2]:

Definition 31. Let $\mathcal{T} = \{t_i^j \mid i \geq 0, j \geq 0\}$, $\mathcal{I} = \{I_i^j \mid i \geq 0, j \geq 0\}$, $\mathcal{F} = \{f\}$. Define the following Nmatrices for the language $\mathcal{L}_C$:

$\mathcal{QM}_3\mathbf{l}$: This is the Nmatrix $\langle \mathcal{V}, \mathcal{D}, \mathcal{O} \rangle$ where:

1. $\mathcal{V} = \mathcal{T} \cup \mathcal{I} \cup \mathcal{F}$
2. $\mathcal{D} = \mathcal{T} \cup \mathcal{I}$
3. $\mathcal{O}$ is defined by:

$$a \widetilde{\vee} b = \begin{cases} \mathcal{D} & \text{if either } a \in \mathcal{D} \text{ or } b \in \mathcal{D}, \\ \mathcal{F} & \text{if } a, b \in \mathcal{F} \end{cases}$$

$$a \widetilde{\supset} b = \begin{cases} \mathcal{D} & \text{if either } a \in \mathcal{F} \text{ or } b \in \mathcal{D} \\ \mathcal{F} & \text{if } a \in \mathcal{D} \text{ and } b \in \mathcal{F} \end{cases}$$

$$\tilde{\neg} a = \begin{cases} \mathcal{F} & \text{if } a \in \mathcal{T} \\ \mathcal{D} & \text{if } a \in \mathcal{F} \\ \{I_i^{j+1}, t_i^{j+1}\} & \text{if } a = I_i^j \end{cases}$$

$$\tilde{\forall}[H] = \begin{cases} \mathcal{D} & \text{if } H \subseteq \mathcal{D} \\ \mathcal{F} & \text{otherwise} \end{cases}$$

$$\tilde{\exists}[H] = \begin{cases} \mathcal{D} & \text{if } H \cap \mathcal{D} \neq \emptyset \\ \mathcal{F} & \text{otherwise} \end{cases}$$

$$\tilde{o} a = \begin{cases} \mathcal{D} & \text{if } a \in \mathcal{F} \cup \mathcal{T} \\ \mathcal{F} & \text{if } a \in \mathcal{I} \end{cases}$$

$$a \tilde{\wedge} b = \begin{cases} \mathcal{F} & \text{if either } a \in \mathcal{F} \text{ or } b \in \mathcal{F} \\ \mathcal{T} & \text{if } a = I_i^j \text{ and } b \in \{I_i^{j+1}, t_i^{j+1}\} \\ \mathcal{D} & \text{otherwise} \end{cases}$$

$\mathcal{QM}_3\mathbf{d}$: This is defined like $\mathcal{QM}_3\mathbf{l}$, except that $\tilde{\wedge}$ is defined as follows:

$$a \tilde{\wedge} b = \begin{cases} \mathcal{F} & \text{if either } a \in \mathcal{F} \text{ or } b \in \mathcal{F} \\ \mathcal{T} & \text{if } b = I_i^j \text{ and } a \in \{I_i^{j+1}, t_i^{j+1}\} \\ \mathcal{D} & \text{otherwise} \end{cases}$$

$\mathcal{QM}_3\mathbf{b}$: This is defined like $\mathcal{QM}_3\mathbf{l}$, except that $\tilde{\wedge}$ is defined as follows:

$$a \tilde{\wedge} b = \begin{cases} \mathcal{F} & \text{if either } a \in \mathcal{F} \text{ or } b \in \mathcal{F} \\ \mathcal{T} & (\text{if } a = I_i^j \text{ and } b \in \{I_i^{j+1}, t_i^{j+1}\}) \text{ or } (b = I_i^j \text{ and } a \in \{I_i^{j+1}, t_i^{j+1}\}) \\ \mathcal{D} & \text{otherwise} \end{cases}$$

Theorem 32. (Soundness and completeness) *Let $\Gamma \cup \{\psi_0\}$ be a set of $\mathcal{L}_C$-formulas. For $y \in \{\mathbf{l}, \mathbf{d}, \mathbf{b}\}$, $\Gamma \vdash_{\mathbf{QB}y} \psi_0$ iff $\Gamma \vdash_{\mathcal{QM}_3 y} \psi_0$.*

Proof: We do the proof for the case of **QBl**. The proofs in the other two cases are similar.

Soundness: Define the function $F : \mathcal{T} \cup \mathcal{I} \cup \mathcal{F} \to \{t, I, f\}$ as follows:

$$F(x) = \begin{cases} f & x \in \mathcal{F} \\ t & x \in \mathcal{T} \\ I & x \in \mathcal{I} \end{cases}$$

It is easy to see that F is a reduction of $\mathcal{QM}_3\mathbf{l}$ to $\mathcal{QM}_5\mathbf{k}$, and so $\mathcal{QM}_3\mathbf{l}$ is a refinement of $\mathcal{QM}_5\mathbf{k}$. By theorem 1, $\vdash_{\mathcal{QM}_5\mathbf{k}} \subseteq \vdash_{\mathcal{QM}_3\mathbf{l}}$. To prove soundness, it remains to show that (1) is $\mathcal{QM}_3\mathbf{l}$-valid. Let S be an L-structure and v an $\mathcal{QM}_3\mathbf{l}$-legal S-valuation, such that $v[\circ\psi] \in \mathcal{F}$. Then $v[\psi] = I_j^i$ for some i, j. Hence $v[\neg\psi] \in \{I_j^{i+1}, t_j^{i+1}\}$ and so $v[\psi \wedge \neg\psi] \in \mathcal{T}$ and $v[\neg(\psi \wedge \neg\psi)] \in \mathcal{F}$.

Completeness: Assume that $\Gamma \nvdash_{\mathbf{QBl}} \psi_0$. Again we may assume that all elements of $\Gamma \cup \psi_0$ are sentences. Like in the proof of theorem 24, we proceed with a Henkin construction to get a maximal theory Γ^*, such that $\Gamma^* \nvdash_{\mathbf{QBl}} \psi_0$ over the extended language L', and Γ^* satisfies the properties from the proof of theorem 24. Let D be the set of all the closed terms of L', and let Cl be the set of all the equivalence classes of $L'(D)$-sentences under $\sim^S$. For every $\mathcal{E} \in Cl$, choose the *minimal representative* of $\mathcal{E}$, $Min(\mathcal{E})$, to be a sentence with the least number of quantifiers of all the sentences in $\mathcal{E}$. (For instance, the sentences $\forall x p(c)$ and $p(c)$ are in the same equivalence class, but $Min(\mathcal{E}) \neq \forall x p(c)$ since $p(c)$ has less quantifiers). Let $\lambda i.\alpha_i$ be an enumeration of all the equivalence classes of $\mathcal{L}_C(D)$-sentences under $\sim^S$, such that their minimal representatives do not begin with $\neg$ (for instance, the minimal representative of $[\![\forall x \neg p(c)]\!]$ begins with $\neg$). It is easy to see that for any equivalence class $[\![\psi]\!]$, there are unique $n_{[\![\psi]\!]}, k_{[\![\psi]\!]}$ such that for every $A \in [\![\psi]\!]$, $A = \overline{\neg}_{k_\psi} \varphi$ for some $\varphi \in \alpha_{n_{[\![\psi]\!]}}$, where $\overline{\neg}_k \theta$ is a sentence obtained from θ by adding k preceding negation symbols and any number of preceding void quantifiers (Note that for any atomic sentence $p(\mathbf{t}_1, ..., \mathbf{t}_n)$, $k([\![p(\mathbf{t}_1, ..., \mathbf{t}_n)]\!]) = 0$). An L'-structure $S = \langle D, I \rangle$, and an $L'(D)$ valuation v in $\mathcal{QM}_3l$ are now defined as follows (where $\widetilde{\psi}$ is defined as in the proof of Lemma 25):

- For every constant c of L': $I[c] = c$.
- For every $\mathbf{t}_1, ..., \mathbf{t}_n \in D$: $I[f][\mathbf{t}_1, ..., \mathbf{t}_n] = f(\mathbf{t}_1, ..., \mathbf{t}_n)$.
- For every $\mathbf{t}_1, ..., \mathbf{t}_n \in D$:

$$I[p][\mathbf{t}_1, ..., \mathbf{t}_n] = \begin{cases} f & p(\mathbf{t}_1, ..., \mathbf{t}_n) \notin \Gamma^* \\ t^0_{n([\![p(\mathbf{t}_1, ..., \mathbf{t}_n)]\!])} & \neg p(\mathbf{t}_1, ..., \mathbf{t}_n) \notin \Gamma^* \\ I^0_{n([\![p(\mathbf{t}_1, ..., \mathbf{t}_n)]\!])} & p(\mathbf{t}_1, ..., \mathbf{t}_n) \in \Gamma^*, \neg p(\mathbf{t}_1, ..., \mathbf{t}_n) \in \Gamma^* \end{cases}$$

$$v[\psi] = \begin{cases} f & \widetilde{\psi} \notin \Gamma^* \\ t^{k([\![\psi]\!])}_{n([\![\psi]\!])} & (\widetilde{\neg \psi}) \notin \Gamma^* \\ I^{k([\![\psi]\!])}_{n([\![\psi]\!])} & \widetilde{\psi} \in \Gamma^*, (\widetilde{\neg \psi}) \in \Gamma^* \end{cases}$$

It is easy to see that v is well-defined. Obviously, $v[\psi] \in \mathcal{D}$ for every $\psi \in \Gamma^*$, while $v[\psi_0] = f$. It remains to show that v is $\mathcal{QM}_3l$-legal.

Let A, B be $L'(D)$-formulas such that $A \sim^S B$. Then $n_{[\![A]\!]} = n_{[\![B]\!]}$, and $k_{[\![A]\!]} = k_{[\![B]\!]}$. Also, $\neg A \sim^S \neg B$, and by Lemma 26-2 $\widetilde{A} \sim^{dc}_L \widetilde{B}$ and $\widetilde{\neg A} \sim^{dc}_L \widetilde{\neg B}$. By property 7 of Γ^*, $\widetilde{A} \in \Gamma^*$ iff $\widetilde{B} \in \Gamma^*$ and $\widetilde{\neg A} \in \Gamma^*$ iff $\widetilde{\neg B} \in \Gamma^*$. Thus by definition of v, $v[A] = v[B]$ and so v respects the $\sim^S$ relation.

The proof that v respects the operations corresponding to $\vee, \supset, \forall$ and $\exists$ is like in the proof of Theorem 24. We consider next the cases of $\circ$, $\neg$ and $\wedge$:

$\circ$: That $v[\circ\psi] = f$ in case $v[\psi] \in \mathcal{I}$ is shown as in the proof of Theorem 24. Assume next that $v[\psi] \in \mathcal{T} \cup \mathcal{F}$. Then either $\widetilde{\psi} \notin \Gamma^*$, or $\widetilde{\neg \psi} \notin \Gamma^*$. It follows that $\widetilde{\psi \wedge \neg \psi} \notin \Gamma^*$, and so $\neg(\widetilde{\psi \wedge \neg \psi}) \in \Gamma^*$. Hence $\circ\widetilde{\psi} \in \Gamma^*$ by **(1)**, and so $v[\circ\psi] \in \mathcal{D}$.

$\neg$: The proofs that $v[\psi] = f$ implies $v[\neg\psi] \in \mathcal{D}$ and that $v[\psi] \in \mathcal{T}$ implies $v[\neg\psi] = f$ are like in the proof of Theorem 24. Assume next that $v[\psi] = I_n^k$. Then both $\tilde{\psi}$ and $\widetilde{\neg\psi}$ are in Γ^*, and $\psi = \daleth_k\varphi$ where $\varphi \in \alpha_n$. Thus $\neg\psi = \daleth_{k+1}\varphi$ for $\varphi \in \alpha_n$, and so $n_{[\neg\psi]} = n$, $k_{[\neg\psi]} = k + 1$. It follows by definition of v that $v[\neg\psi]$ is either I_n^{k+1} or t_n^{k+1} (depending whether $\neg\neg\psi$ is in Γ^* or not).

$\wedge$: The proofs that if $v[\psi_1] = f$ or $v[\psi_2] = f$ then $v[\psi_1 \wedge \psi_2] = f$, and that $v[\psi_1 \wedge \psi_2] \in \mathcal{D}$ otherwise, are like in the proof of Theorem 24. Assume next that $v[\psi_1] = I_n^k$ and $v[\psi_2] \in \{I_n^{k+1}, t_n^{k+1}\}$. Then both $\tilde{\psi}_1$ and $\tilde{\psi}_2$ are in Γ^*, and so $\widetilde{\psi_1 \wedge \psi_2} \in \Gamma^*$. Also, $\psi_1 = \daleth_k\varphi_1$, $\psi_2 = \daleth_{k+1}\varphi_2$ for $\varphi_1, \varphi_2 \in \alpha_n$. It follows that $\psi_2 \sim^S \neg\psi_1$ and $\psi_1 \wedge \psi_2 \sim^S \psi_1 \wedge \neg\psi_1$. By lemma 25-2, $\widetilde{\psi_1 \wedge \psi_2} \sim_L^{dc} \widetilde{\psi_1 \wedge \neg\psi_1}$. By property 7 of Γ^*, $\widetilde{\psi_1 \wedge \neg\psi_1} \in \Gamma^*$, and so $\tilde{\psi}_1, \widetilde{\neg\psi_1} \in \Gamma^*$. This entails that $\widetilde{o\psi_1} \notin \Gamma^*$. Hence schema (1) implies that $\neg(\psi_1 \wedge \neg\psi_1) \notin \Gamma^*$. Hence $v[\psi_1 \wedge \psi_2] \in \mathcal{T}$.

Obviously, $v[\psi] \in \mathcal{D}$ for every $\psi \in \Gamma$, while $v[\psi_0] = f$. Hence $\Gamma \nvdash_{\mathcal{QM}_31} \psi_0$. $\square$

Definition 33. *For* $\mathbf{X} \subseteq Ax$, $\mathcal{QM}_31(\mathbf{X})$ *is obtained from* $\mathcal{QM}_31$ *through the following modifications:*

1. *If* $(\mathbf{i}_1) \in \mathbf{X}$: $a \in \mathcal{F} \Rightarrow \tilde{o}(a) = \mathcal{T}$
2. *If* $(\mathbf{i}_2) \in \mathbf{X}$: $a \in \mathcal{T} \Rightarrow \tilde{o}(a) = \mathcal{T}$
3. *If* $(\mathbf{c}) \in \mathbf{X}$ *or* $(\mathbf{a}_\neg) \in \mathbf{X}$: $\tilde{\neg}f = \mathcal{T}$
4. *If both* $(\mathbf{e})$ *and* $(\mathbf{w})$ *are in* $\mathbf{X}$, *delete all the truth-values in* $\mathcal{I}$. *Otherwise, if* $(\mathbf{e}) \in \mathbf{X}$: $\tilde{\neg}I_i^j = \{I_i^{j+1}\}$. *If* $(\mathbf{w}) \in \mathbf{X}$: $a \in \mathcal{F} \Rightarrow \tilde{\neg}a = \mathcal{T}$ *and* $\tilde{\neg}I_j^i = \{t_j^i\}$
5. *If* $(\mathbf{a}_\wedge) \in \mathbf{X}$: $a \in \mathcal{T}$ *and* $b \in \mathcal{T} \Rightarrow a\tilde{\wedge}b = \mathcal{T}$
6. *If* $(\mathbf{a}_\vee) \in \mathbf{X}$: $a \in \mathcal{T}, b \notin \mathcal{I}$ *or* $b \in \mathcal{T}, a \notin \mathcal{I} \Rightarrow a\tilde{\vee}b = \mathcal{T}$
7. *If* $(\mathbf{a}_\supset) \in \mathbf{X}$: $a \in \mathcal{F}, b \notin \mathcal{I}$ *or* $b \in \mathcal{T}, a \notin \mathcal{I} \Rightarrow a\tilde{\supset}b = \mathcal{T}$
8. *If* $(\mathbf{o}_\wedge) \in \mathbf{X}$: $a \in \mathcal{T}$ *or* $b \in \mathcal{T}$ *and* $a, b \in \mathcal{D} \Rightarrow a\tilde{\wedge}b = \mathcal{T}$
9. *If* $(\mathbf{o}_\vee) \in \mathbf{X}$: $a \in \mathcal{T}$ *or* $b \in \mathcal{T} \Rightarrow a\tilde{\vee}b = \mathcal{T}$
10. *If* $(\mathbf{o}_\supset) \in \mathbf{X}$: $a \in \mathcal{F}$ *or* $b \in \mathcal{T} \Rightarrow a\tilde{\supset}b = \mathcal{T}$
11. *If* $(\mathbf{v}_\wedge) \in \mathbf{X}$: $a, b \in \mathcal{T} \cup \mathcal{I} \Rightarrow a\tilde{\wedge}b = \mathcal{T}$
12. *If* $(\mathbf{v}_\vee) \in \mathbf{X}$: $a \notin \mathcal{F}$ *or* $b \notin \mathcal{F} \Rightarrow a\tilde{\vee}b = \mathcal{T}$
13. *If* $(\mathbf{v}_\supset) \in \mathbf{X}$: $a \in \mathcal{F}$ *or* $b \in \mathcal{T} \cup \mathcal{I} \Rightarrow a\tilde{\supset}b = \mathcal{T}$
14. *If* $(\mathbf{a}_\forall) \in \mathbf{X}$: $H \subseteq \mathcal{T} \Rightarrow \tilde{Q}[H] = \mathcal{T}$
15. *If* $(\mathbf{a}_\exists) \in \mathbf{X}$: $H \subseteq \mathcal{T} \cup \mathcal{F}$ *and* $H \cap \mathcal{T} \neq \emptyset \Rightarrow \tilde{Q}[H] = \mathcal{T}$
16. *If* $(\mathbf{o}_\forall) \in \mathbf{X}$: $H \cap \mathcal{T} \neq \emptyset$ *and* $H \subseteq \mathcal{D} \Rightarrow \tilde{\forall}[H] = \mathcal{T}$
17. *If* $(\mathbf{o}_\exists) \in \mathbf{X}$: $H \cap \mathcal{T} \neq \emptyset \Rightarrow \tilde{Q}[\exists] = \mathcal{T}$
18. *If* $(\mathbf{v}_\forall) \in \mathbf{X}$: $H \subseteq \mathcal{T} \cup \mathcal{I} \Rightarrow \tilde{\forall}[H] = \mathcal{T}$
19. *If* $(\mathbf{v}_\exists) \in \mathbf{X}$: $(H \cap (\mathcal{T} \cup \mathcal{I})) \neq \emptyset \Rightarrow \tilde{\exists}[H] = \mathcal{T}$

The Nmatrices $\mathcal{QM}_3\mathbf{d}(\mathbf{X})$ *and* $\mathcal{QM}_3\mathbf{b}(\mathbf{X})$ *are defined similarly.*

Remark: it is easy to see that for any $\mathbf{X} \subseteq Ax$ and $y \in \{(\mathbf{l}), (\mathbf{d}), (\mathbf{b})\}$, the set of conditions in $\mathbf{X}$ is coherent, the interpretations of the connectives and the quantifiers of $\mathcal{QM}_3y(\mathbf{X})$ never return empty sets and so $\mathcal{QM}_3y(\mathbf{X})$ is well-defined.

Theorem 34. (Soundness and completeness) *Let* $\Gamma \cup \{\psi_0\}$ *be a set of* $\mathcal{L}_C$-*formulas. Let* $\mathbf{X} \subseteq Ax$ *and* $y \in \{\mathbf{l}, \mathbf{d}, \mathbf{b}\}$. *Then* $\Gamma \vdash_{\mathbf{QB}y[\mathbf{X}]} \psi_0$ *iff* $\Gamma \vdash_{\mathcal{Q}\mathcal{M}_3y(\mathbf{X})} \psi_0$.

Proof: It is easy to show that $\mathcal{Q}\mathcal{M}_3y(\mathbf{X})$ is a (simple) refinement of $\mathcal{Q}\mathcal{M}_3(\mathbf{X})$ and so by theorem 1, $\vdash_{\mathcal{Q}\mathcal{M}_3(\mathbf{X})} \subseteq \vdash_{\mathcal{Q}\mathcal{M}_3y(\mathbf{X})}$. It is also easy to check that for any schema in $\mathbf{X}$, the relevant condition guarantees its validity in $\mathcal{Q}\mathcal{M}_3y(\mathbf{X})$, and so soundness follows. The proof of completeness is a straightforward extension of the proof of theorem 32.

Corollary 35. *Let* $\Gamma \cup \psi$ *be a set of* $\mathcal{L}_C$-*formulas, in which* $\circ$ *does not occur. Then* $\Gamma \vdash_{\mathbf{QBlca}} \psi$ *iff* $\Gamma \vdash_{\mathbf{QBlcia}} \psi$.

Proof: It can be easily checked that the only difference between the Nmatrices $\mathcal{Q}\mathcal{M}_3\mathbf{lcia}$ and $\mathcal{Q}\mathcal{M}_3\mathbf{lca}$ is in their interpretation of $\circ$.

Corollary 36. *Let the Nmatrix* $\mathcal{Q}\mathcal{M}_3 C_1^*$ *for* $\mathcal{L}_{\mathrm{cl}}$ *be obtained from the Nmatrix* $\mathcal{Q}\mathcal{M}_3\mathbf{lcia}$ *for* $\mathcal{L}_C$ *(or* $\mathcal{Q}\mathcal{M}_3\mathbf{lca}$*) by discarding the interpretation of* $\circ$. *Then* $\mathcal{Q}\mathcal{M}_3 C_1^*$ *is a characteristic Nmatrix for* C_1^*.

Proof: similar to the proof of theorem 34. (Another alternative is to use a translation of C_1^* to **QBlcia**, similar to the translation of the proof of theorem 107 of [11] for the propositional case.)

Remark: da Costa's C_1 is usually considered to be the $\circ$-free analogue of the propositional fragment of **QBlcia** (called **Cila** in [8,11]). However, from the above corollaries it follows that it is equally justified to identify it with **Cla**, the propositional fragment of **QBlca**. A similar observation applies to C_1^*.

Lemma 37. (Effectiveness) *For every* $\mathbf{X} \subseteq Ax$ *and every* $y \in \{(\mathbf{l}), (\mathbf{d}), (\mathbf{b})\}$, $\mathcal{Q}\mathcal{M}_3\mathbf{y}(\mathbf{X})$ *is effective.*

Proof: This follows from proposition 21, and the suitability of $\mathcal{Q}\mathcal{M}_3\mathbf{y}(\mathbf{X})$ for $\sim_L^{dc}$.

5   Logical Indistinguishability in First-Order LFIs

In this section we apply the framework of Nmatrices and in particular their effectiveness to prove a very important proof-theoretical property of the first-order LFIs investigated here.

Definition 38. *Let* **S** *be a system which includes positive classical logic. Two sentences A and B are logically indistinguishable in* **S** *if* $\varphi(A) \vdash_{\mathbf{S}} \varphi(B)$ *and* $\varphi(B) \vdash_{\mathbf{S}} \varphi(A)$ *for every sentence $\varphi(\psi)$ in the language of* **S**.

Theorem 39. *Let* **S** *be a system over a first-order language L which includes* $\{\neg, \supset\}$, *and assume that* $A \vdash_{\mathbf{S}} B$ *whenever* $A \sim_L^{dc} B$. *If one of the following holds, then two sentences A, B are logically indistinguishable in* **S** *iff* $A \sim_L^{dc} B$:

1. **QBbcia$_\mathbf{p}$wv$_\mathbf{Q}$** *is an extension of* **S**.
2. **QBbcia$_\mathbf{p}$ev$_\mathbf{Q}$** *is an extension of* **S**.
3. **QBbive** *is an extension of* **S**

Proof: For all the parts one direction is trivial: assume that $A \sim_L^{dc} B$. Then since $\sim_L^{dc}$ is a congruence relation, $\psi(A) \sim_L^{dc} \psi(B)$ for every ψ and so A, B are logically indistinguishable by our assumption about S.

For the converse, let A, B be two sentences, such that $A \nsim_L^{dc} B$.

For the first and the second parts, let q be an atomic propositional sentence[5], such that q does not occur in A or B. Let $S = \langle D, I \rangle$ be some L-structure, such that $I[q] = I_0^0$, and for every two closed terms $\mathbf{t}_1 \neq \mathbf{t}_2$ occurring in A and B respectively, $I[\mathbf{t}_1] \neq I[\mathbf{t}_2]$. Let W_S be the minimal set of $L(D)$-sentences closed under subformulas, such that $A, B, q \in W_S$. Let v be some partial S-valuation on W_S, satisfying: $v[q] = I_0^0$, $v[q \supset (B \supset B)] = I_0^0$, $v[\circ(q \supset (B \supset B))] = f$, $v[q \supset (A \supset A)] = t_0^0$, and $v[\circ(q \supset (A \supset A))] = t_0^0$ (such v exists, since both $v[A \supset A]$ and $v[B \supset B]$ are in $\mathcal{D}$, and by lemma 13, $q \supset (A \supset A) \nsim_L^{dc} q \supset (B \supset B)$ iff $q \supset (A \supset A) \nsim^S q \supset (B \supset B)$). It is easy to check that v is legal in $\mathcal{QM}_3\mathbf{bcia_pwv_Q}$ and in $\mathcal{QM}_3\mathbf{bcia_pev_Q}$. By lemma 37 it follows that $\circ(q \supset (A \supset A)) \nvdash_\mathbf{S} \circ(q \supset (B \supset B))$. Hence A and B are not logically indistinguishable in $\mathbf{S}$.

For the third part, assume without a loss in generality that $A \supset A$ is not a subformula of $B \supset B$. Let $S = \langle D, I \rangle$ be an L-structure, such that for every two closed terms $\mathbf{t}_1 \neq \mathbf{t}_2$ occurring in A and B respectively, $I[\mathbf{t}_1] \neq I[\mathbf{t}_2]$. Let W_S be the minimal set of $L(D)$-sentences closed under subformulas, such that $\neg\neg\neg(B \supset B) \in W_S$. Let v be some partial S-valuation on W_S, satisfying: $v[B \supset B] = t_0^0$, $v[\neg(B \supset B)] = f$, $v[\neg\neg(B \supset B)] = I_0^0$, $v[\neg\neg\neg(B \supset B)] = I_0^1$. Extend v to a partial valuation defined also on the subformulas of $\neg\neg\neg(A \supset A)$, which satisfies: $v[A \supset A] = t_0^0$, $v[\neg(A \supset A)] = f$, $v[\neg\neg(A \supset A)] = t_0^0$, $v(\neg\neg\neg(A \supset A)) = f$. Again this is possible since by lemma 13. It is easy to see that v is legal in $\mathcal{QM}_3\mathbf{bive}$. By lemma 37, it follows that $\neg\neg\neg(B \supset B) \nvdash_\mathbf{S} \neg\neg\neg(A \supset A)$. Hence A and B are not logically indistinguishable in $\mathbf{S}$.   □

Remarks:

1. This theorem extends similar theorems from [2] and [20]. In [2] it is proved for propositional systems weaker than the propositional fragments of $\mathbf{QBbcia_pe}$ and $\mathbf{QBbio_pe}$. In [20] a similar theorem for the first-order case is proved for systems weaker than $\mathbf{QBbcia_pe}$. This theorem extends these results in the following aspects:

    - Covering first-order systems stronger than $\mathbf{QBbcia_p}$ and weaker than $\mathbf{QBbcia_pwv_Q}$.
    - Covering first-order systems stronger than $\mathbf{QBbcia_pe}$ and weaker than $\mathbf{QBbcia_pev_Q}$.
    - Extending to the first-order case the propositional results of [2] for systems weaker than $\mathbf{QBbio_pe}$ and generalizing them to systems weaker than $\mathbf{QBbive}$.

---

[5] For simplicity we assume that we have propositional sentences in L, but it is not difficult to replace q by a suitable first-order sentence.

2. Extensions of **QBcio** do not have the property described above. In fact, it can be shown that $\circ(A \supset A)$ and $\circ(B \supset B)$ are logically indistinguishable in **QBcio** for any two sentences A and B (it is shown in [11] for the propositional case).
3. Extensions of **QBiew** also do not have the above property. In fact, it is easy to see that **QBiew** collapses into classical logic, where any two equivalent formulas are logically indistinguishable.

Acknowledgement

This research was supported by THE ISRAEL SCIENCE FOUNDATION (grant No 809-06).

References

1. Avron, A., Lev, I.: Non-deterministic Multi-valued Structures. Journal of Logic and Computation 15, 241–261 (2005)
2. Avron, A.: Non-deterministic semantics for logics with a consistency operator. International Journal of Approximate Reasoning (forthcoming, 2006)
3. Avron, A.: Non-deterministic Matrices and Modular Semantics of Rules. In: Beziau, J.-Y. (ed.) Logica Universalis, pp. 149–167. Birkhäuser Verlag (2005)
4. Avron, A.: Non-deterministic Semantics for Families of Paraconsistent Logics. In: Beziau, J.-Y., Carnielli, W. (eds.) Paraconsistency with no Frontiers (to appear)
5. Avron, A., Zamansky, A.: Quantification in Non-deterministic Multi-valued Structures. In: Proceedings of the 35th IEEE International Symposium on Multiple-Valued Logics, pp. 296–301. IEEE Computer Society Press, Los Alamitos (2005)
6. Batens, D., Mortensen, C., Priest, G., van Bendegem, J.P. (eds.): Frontiers of Paraconsistent Logic, King s College Publications. Studies in Logic and Computation, vol. 8. Research Studies Press (2000)
7. Bremer, M.: An Introduction to Paraconsistent Logics. Peter Lang GmbH (2005)
8. Carnielli, W.A., Marcos, J., de Amo, S.: Formal inconsistency and evolutionary databases. Logic and Logical Philosophy 8, 115–152 (2000)
9. Carnielli, W.A., Coniglio, M.E., D'Ottaviano, I.M.L.: Paraconsistency - the Logical Way to the Inconsistent. Lecture notes in pure and applied mathematics, vol. 228. Marcel Dekker, New York (2002)
10. Carnielli, W.A., Marcos, J.: A Taxonomy of C-systems. [9], 1–94 (2002)
11. Carnielli, W.A., Coniglio, M.E., Marcos, J.: Logics of Formal Inconsistency. In: Gabbay, D., Guenther, F. (eds.) Handbook of Philosophical Logic, 2nd edn., Kluwer Academic Publishers, Dordrecht (to appear)
12. da Costa, N.C.A.: On the theory of inconsistent formal systems. Notre Dame Journal of Formal Logic 15, 497–510 (1974)
13. da Costa, N.C.A., Krause, D., Bueno, O.: Paraconsistent Logics and Paraconsistency: Technical and Philosophical Developments. In: Jacquette, D. (ed.) Philosophy of Logic, pp. 791–911. North-Holland, Amsterdam (2007)
14. van Dalen, D.: Logic and Structure, pp. 109–123. Springer, Heidelberg (1997)
15. Decker, H.: A Case for Paraconsistent Logic as a Foundation of Future Information Systems. In: CAiSE Workshops, vol. 2, pp. 451–461 (2005)

16. Enderton, H.: A Mathematical Introduction to Logic, pp. 65–97. Academic Press, London (1972)
17. Fitting, M.: First-Order Logic and Automated Theorem Proving, pp. 109–123. Springer, Heidelberg (1996)
18. Leblanc, H.: Alternatives to Standard First-order Semantics. In: Handbook of Philosophical Logic, 2nd edn. vol. 2, pp. 53–133. Kluwer Academic Publishers, Dordrecht (2001)
19. Shoenfield, J.R.: Mathematical Logic. Association for Symbolic Logic, 109–123 (1967)
20. Zamansky, A., Avron, A.: Non-deterministic semantics for first-order paraconsistent logics. In: Proceedings of the 10th International Conference on Principles of Knowledge Representation and Reasoning (KR06), pp. 431–440 (2006)
21. Zamansky, A., Avron, A.: Quantification in non-deterministic multi-valued structures. In: Proceedings of the 35th IEEE International Symposium on Multiple-Valued Logic (ISMVL05), pp. 296–301. IEEE Computer Society Press, Los Alamitos (2005)

Note on Conditional Constructivity

Matthias Baaz

Institute of Discrete Mathematics and Geometry, Technical University of Vienna,
Wiedner Hauptstrasse 8-10 / E104, A-1040 Vienna, Austria
baaz@logic.at

Abstract. In this note we provide a straightforward translation $\mathcal{C}_p^\Gamma(T)$ for sets of formulas T and $H_\Gamma(\exists x A(x))$ for existential formulas $\exists x A(x)$ s.t. $\mathcal{C}_p^\Gamma(T) \vdash H_\Gamma(\exists x A(x))$ expresses "$\exists x A(x)$ is derivable constructively from T iff it is derivable at all".

1 Preliminaries

The strength of mathematical logic lies often in its ability to express metamathematical statements on a mathematical level. In this note we deal with conditional constructive provability, i.e. with statements "if $\exists x A(x)$ is provable at all from T then it is constructively provable". In addition, the signature of the witness can be specified arbitrarily.

The idea is to add a variable position x to every atomic formula, let $B^*(x)$ be the transform of B and let $A^*(y, x)$ be the transform of $\exists y A(y)$ after deletion of the outermost existential quantifier. Let T^* be the $\forall$-closure of $\{B^*(x) \mid B \text{ in } T\}$. Then $T^* \vdash \exists x \forall y(A^*(y, x) \supset A^*(x, x))$ expresses the desired statement.

The reasons to express constructive provability and conditional constructive provability using a translation within classical logic are mainly the following:

- It is not possible to characterize classical constructive provability by a so-called constructive logic $\mathcal{L}$ weaker than classical logic: There will be always T and $\exists x A(x)$, such that $T \vdash \exists x A(x)$ non constructively in $\mathcal{L}$ but $T \vdash A(t)$ for some t in classical logic.[1]
- Usual classical models can be used to study classical non-provability in the constructive sense in the presence of provability.
- "$\exists x A(x)$ is constructively provable" can be used as assumption/axiom without extending the framework of classical logic, in case of conditional constructive provability as meaningful assumption/axiom for all extensions of a given theory.

2 $\mathcal{C}_p^\Gamma / \mathcal{C}_c^\Gamma$

Let $\vdash$ denote classical deduction and let $\mathrm{cl}_\exists(A)$ $(\mathrm{cl}_\forall(A))$ be the existential (universal) closure of A.

---

[1] $T \equiv ((Q \vee \neg Q) \supset P(0)) \wedge (P(0) \vee P(1))$ and $\exists x P(x)$ provide an example for any intermediate first-order logic $\mathcal{L}$.

S. Aguzzoli et al.(Eds.): Algebraic and Proof-theoretic Aspects, LNAI 4460, pp. 25–29, 2007.

Let T be a theory, Γ be assigned to $A \equiv \exists y A'(y)$, and assume that all bound variables are different to x.[2]

Define

$\psi_\Gamma^x(z) \equiv z$ (z a bound or free variable)

$\psi_\Gamma^x(c) \equiv c^*(x)$

(c constant, $c \notin \Gamma$, c^* is a new function symbol of arity 1)

$\psi_\Gamma^x(c) \equiv c$ (c constant, $c \in \Gamma$)

$\psi_\Gamma^x(f(t_1,\ldots,t_r)) \equiv f^*(\psi_\Gamma^x(t_1),\ldots,\psi_\Gamma^x(t_r),x)$

($f \notin \Gamma$, f^* a new function symbol of arity $r+1$)

$\psi_\Gamma^x(f(t_1,\ldots,t_r)) \equiv f(\psi_\Gamma^x(t_1),\ldots,\psi_\Gamma^x(t_r))$ ($f \in \Gamma$)

$\psi_\Gamma^x(P(v_1,\ldots,v_n)) \equiv P^*(\psi_\Gamma^x(v_1),\ldots,\psi_\Gamma^x(v_n),x)$

(P^* a new predicate symbol of arity $n+1$)

$\psi_\Gamma^x(\neg A) \equiv \neg\psi_\Gamma^x(A)$

$\psi_\Gamma^x(A \vee B) \equiv \psi_\Gamma^x(A) \vee \psi_\Gamma^x(B)$

$\psi_\Gamma^x(A \wedge B) \equiv \psi_\Gamma^x(A) \wedge \psi_\Gamma^x(B)$

$\psi_\Gamma^x(A \supset B) \equiv \psi_\Gamma^x(A) \supset \psi_\Gamma^x(B)$

$\psi_\Gamma^x(\exists y A) \equiv \exists y \psi_\Gamma^x(A)$

$\psi_\Gamma^x(\forall y A) \equiv \forall y \psi_\Gamma^x(A)$.

$C_p^\Gamma(T) \equiv \{\mathrm{cl}_\forall(\psi_\Gamma^x(B)) \mid B \in T\}$

$C_c^\Gamma(\exists y A(y)) \equiv \exists x \psi_\Gamma^x(A(x))$.[3]

Example 1. Consider $P(0) \vee P(1)$ and $\exists y P(y)$.

$\Gamma = \{0,1\}$

$\psi_\Gamma^x(P(0) \vee P(1)) \equiv P^*(0,x) \vee P^*(1,x)$ $\psi_\Gamma^x(\exists y P(y)) \equiv \exists y P^*(y,x)$

$C_p^\Gamma(P(0) \vee P(1)) \equiv \forall x(P^*(0,x) \vee P^*(1,x))$

$C_c^\Gamma(\exists y P(y)) \equiv \exists x P^*(x,x)$

$\Gamma = \{1\}$

$\psi_\Gamma^x(P(0) \vee P(1)) \equiv P^*(0^*(x),x) \vee P^*(1,x)$ $\psi_\Gamma^x(\exists y P(y)) \equiv \exists y P^*(y,x)$

$C_p^\Gamma(P(0) \vee P(1)) \equiv \forall x(P^*(0^*(x),x) \vee P^*(1,x))$

$C_c^\Gamma(\exists y P(y)) \equiv \exists x P^*(x,x)$

---

[2] Γ is a signature for the specification of terms which are admitted as witnesses.

[3] Note that by duality the translation C_p^Γ / C_c^Γ can be used to control resources, i.e. to a priori limit the number of instances of universal axioms to be used in the proof.

Theorem 1. $T \vdash A(t)$ *for some closed term of the signature of* Γ *iff* $\mathcal{C}_p^\Gamma(T) \vdash \mathcal{C}_c^\Gamma(\exists x A(x))$.

Proof. See [1] or [2], for a more general setting ($\mathcal{C}_p^\Gamma / \mathcal{C}_c^\Gamma$ correspond to $\mathcal{C}_p^\chi / \mathcal{C}_c^\chi$ with $\chi = \left\langle \begin{matrix} 1 \\ \Gamma \end{matrix} \right\rangle$). The proof uses the following property of resolution refutations. For sets of clauses $\{(\neg)L_{i1}(\bar{y}_{i1}, x), \dots, (\neg)L_{ik_i}(\bar{y}_{ik_i}, x)\}$ ground substitutions of refutations must always coincide at the x-position: x stores the term t making the argument constructive. Function symbols not in Γ cannot occur in t as their translation depends on x.

Example 2. $P(0) \vee P(1)$ does not prove $\exists x P(x)$ constructively as

$$\mathcal{C}_p^{\{0,1\}}(P(0) \vee P(1)) \equiv \forall x(P^*(0, x) \vee P^*(1, x)),$$

$$\mathcal{C}_c^{\{0,1\}}(\exists x P(x)) \equiv \exists x P^*(x, x),$$

and $\forall x(P^*(0, x) \vee P^*(1, x)) \not\vdash \exists x P^*(x, x)$.

Example 3. $P(0), P(0) \vee P(1)$ do prove $\exists x P(x)$ constructively. This is not the case if the signature is restricted to 1 as

$$\mathcal{C}_p^{\{1\}}(P(0) \vee P(1)) \equiv \forall x(P^*(0^x(x), x) \vee P^*(1, x)),$$

$$\mathcal{C}_p^{\{1\}}(P(0)) \equiv \forall x P^*(0^x(x), x),$$

$$\mathcal{C}_c^{\{1\}}(\exists x P(x)) \equiv \exists x P^*(x, x),$$

and $\forall x(P^*(0^x(x), x)), \forall x(P^*(0^x(x), x) \vee P^*(1, x)) \not\vdash \exists x P^*(x, x)$.

Example 4. $\exists x P(x)$ does not prove $\exists x P(x)$ constructively ($\Gamma = \{0\}$) as

$$\mathcal{C}_c^{\{0\}}(\exists x P(x)) \equiv \forall x \exists y P^*(x, y),$$

$$\mathcal{C}_c^{\{1\}}(\exists x P(x)) \equiv \exists x P^*(x, x),$$

and $\forall x \exists y P^*(x, y) \not\vdash \exists x P^*(x, x)$.

Example 5. We use a well known example of non-constructivity (cf. [3]). There are irrational numbers a, b such that a^b is rational: consider $\sqrt{2}^{\sqrt{2}}$. If $\sqrt{2}^{\sqrt{2}}$ is rational let $a = b = \sqrt{2}$. If $\sqrt{2}^{\sqrt{2}}$ is irrational let $a = \sqrt{2}^{\sqrt{2}}$ and $b = \sqrt{2}$, where

$$a^b = (\sqrt{2}^{\sqrt{2}})^{\sqrt{2}} = \sqrt{2}^2 = 2.$$

We formalize this argument using the predicate $R(x)$, the constant $\sqrt{2}$, and the function $\exp(x, y)$ (also written as x^y).

Let $T = \neg R(\sqrt{2}), R\left((\sqrt{2}^{\sqrt{2}})^{\sqrt{2}}\right)$ and $\Gamma = \{\sqrt{2}, \exp(x, y)\}$.

$$T \vdash \exists x \exists y(\neg R(x) \wedge \neg R(y) \wedge R(x^y))$$

$$C_p^\Gamma(T) = \forall x \neg R^*(\sqrt{2}, x), \forall x R^*\left((\sqrt{2}^{\sqrt{2}})^{\sqrt{2}}, x\right)$$

$C_c^\Gamma(\exists x \exists y(\neg R(x) \wedge \neg R(y) \wedge R(x^y))) = \exists x \exists y(\neg R^*(x, x) \wedge \neg R^*(y, x) \wedge R^*(x^y, x)).$

The following structure $\langle M, \bar{R}^*, \exp, \sqrt{2} \rangle$ is a model for

$$\forall x \neg R^*(\sqrt{2}, x), \forall x R^*\left((\sqrt{2}^{\sqrt{2}})^{\sqrt{2}}, x\right), \forall x \forall y(R^*(x, x) \vee R^*(y, x) \vee \neg R^*(x^y, x))$$

and consequently a counterexample to

$$C_p^\Gamma(T) \vdash C_c^\Gamma(\exists x \exists y(\neg R^*(x, x) \wedge \neg R^*(y, x) \wedge R^*(x^y, x))).$$

M is the set of terms constructed from $\sqrt{2}$ and $\exp(x, y)$,
$(\sqrt{2}, v) \notin \bar{R}^*$ for all v,
$(\sqrt{2}^{\sqrt{2}}, \sqrt{2}) \notin \bar{R}^*$,
$(u, v) \in \bar{R}^*$ otherwise.
   Therefore there is no term t such that

$$T \vdash \exists y(\neg R(t) \wedge \neg R(y) \wedge R(t^y)).$$

3   Conditional Constructivity

Let $H_\Gamma(\exists y A(y)) \equiv \exists x \forall y(\psi_\Gamma^x(A(y)) \supset \psi_\Gamma^x(A(x))).$

Example 6. $H_\Gamma(\exists x P(x)) \equiv \exists x \forall y(P^*(y, x) \supset P^*(x, x)).$

Proposition 1. $T \vdash A \Leftrightarrow \{\forall x \psi_\Gamma^x(B) \mid B \in T\} \vdash \forall x \psi_\Gamma^x(A).$

Proof. By induction on the proof length.

Theorem 2.

   (i) *$T \vdash A(t)$ for some closed term of the signature of $\Gamma \Rightarrow C_p^\Gamma(T) \vdash H_\Gamma(\exists x\ A(x)).$*

   (ii) *$C_p^\Gamma(T) \vdash H_\Gamma(\exists x A(x)), T \subseteq S, S \vdash \exists x A(x) \Rightarrow S \vdash A(t)$ for some closed term of the signature of Γ.*

Proof.

   (i) $T \vdash A(t)$ for some closed term of the signature of $\Gamma \Rightarrow C_p^\Gamma(T) \vdash \exists x\ \psi_\Gamma^x(A(x))$ by Theorem 1. $\Rightarrow C_p^\Gamma(T) \vdash \exists x \forall y(\psi_\Gamma^x(A(y)) \supset \psi_\Gamma^x(A(x))) \equiv H_\Gamma(\exists y A(y)).$

   (ii) $C_p^\Gamma(T) \vdash H_\Gamma(\exists y A(y)), T \subseteq S, S \vdash \exists x A(x) \Rightarrow C_p^\Gamma(S) \vdash H_\Gamma(\exists y A(y)),$
$C_p^\Gamma(S) \vdash \forall x \exists y \psi_\Gamma^x(A(y)) \Rightarrow C_p^\Gamma(S) \vdash \exists x \psi_\Gamma^x(A(x))$ as
$\vdash H_\Gamma(\exists y A(y)) \supset (\forall x \exists y \psi_\Gamma^x(A(y))) \supset \exists x \psi_\Gamma^x(A(x))$ and $C_p^\Gamma(S) \vdash \forall x\ \exists y$ $\psi_\Gamma^x(A(y))$ by Proposition 1 $\Rightarrow S \vdash A(t)$ for some closed term t in the signature Γ by Theorem 1.
Note that t is already "known" to T as $H_\Gamma(\exists y A(y)) \equiv C_c^\Gamma(\exists x \forall y(A(y) \supset A(x)))$ ($\vdash \exists x \forall y(A(y) \supset A(x))$!).

Example 7. $P(0) \vee P(1)$, $\exists x P(x) \supset P(0)$ prove the conditional constructivity for $\exists y P(y)$, prove $\exists x P(x)$, but do not prove $\exists x P(x)$ constructively.

$$\mathcal{C}_p^{\{0,1\}}(P(0) \vee P(1)) \equiv \forall x (P^*(0,x) \vee P^*(1,x))$$

$$\mathcal{C}_p^{\{0,1\}}(\exists x P(x) \supset P(0)) \equiv \forall x (\exists y P^*(y,x) \supset P^*(0,x))$$

$$H_{\{0,1\}}(\exists y P(y)) \equiv \exists x \forall y (P^*(y,x) \supset P^*(x,x)).$$

Obviously

$$\mathcal{C}_p^{\{0,1\}}(P(0) \vee P(1)), \mathcal{C}_p^{\{0,1\}}(\exists x P(x) \supset P(0)) \vdash H_{\{0,1\}}(\exists y P(y)).$$

4 Conclusion

The establishment of conditional (relative) constructivity is an essential feature of constructive mathematics, as relative constructivity proofs allow for the combination of constructive parts of non-constructive proofs with suitable constructive specializations. The translation presented in this paper makes it possible to use classical models to analyze, why relative constructivity fails.

References

1. Baaz, M.: Note on a translation to characterize constructivity. J. Proc. Steklov Inst. Math. 242, 125–129 (2003)
2. Baaz, M.: Controlling witnesses. Annals of Pure and Applied Logic 136, 22–29 (2005)
3. Troelstra, A., van Dalen, D.: Constructivism in Mathematics, An Introduction, vol. 1. North-Holland, Amsterdam (1988)

Symmetric MV-Algebras

L.P. Belluce[1], Antonio Di Nola[2], and Ada Lettieri[3,*]

[1] Department of Mathematics,
University of British Columbia, Vancouver, B.C. Canada
belluce@math.ubc.ca
[2] Department of Mathematics and Informatics,
University of Salerno, Via Ponte don Melillo , 84084 Fisciano (Sa), Italy
adinola@unisa.it
[3] Dipartimento di Costruzioni e Metodi Matematici in Architettura,
University of Napoli, Federico II, Via Monteoliveto 3, Napoli, Italy
lettieri@unina.it

Abstract. We introduce the class of Symmetric MV-algebras. Such algebras have a suitable behavior with respect to a family of MV-polynomials. It turns out that the class of Symmetric MV-algebras can be characterized as the class of MV-algebras having homomorphic image in the variety generated by a single MV-chain with $p+1$ elements, where $p = 1$ or p is a prime number. Also, using symmetric MV-algebras, we provide a new characterization of the above mentioned varieties.

1 Introduction

In this paper we will be concerned with the problem of characterizing the class of MV-algebras having homomorphic image in the variety generated by a single MV-chain with $p + 1$ elements, where $p = 1$ or p is a prime number, see Theorem 37. Also we provide a new characterization of these varieties.

The characterization of this class of MV-algebras leads to a study of MV-algebras, called *symmetric*, having suitable behavior with respect to a family of MV-polynomials. As consequences of studying symmetric MV-algebras, we obtain results concerning, for a given arbitrary MV-algebras A, the biggest subalgebra $MV_p(A)$ of A which is a member of the subvariety generated by the $p+1$ elements MV-chain, see Theorem 26. Also we show that a suitable condition over a symmetric MV-algebra assures the existence of closed Boolean spaces of the set of the maximal ideals of A.

Let $\mathcal{L}$ be the poset, under $\subseteq$, of subalgebras of the MV-algebra $[0, 1]$. $\mathcal{L}$ then has the greatest element, $[0, 1]$.

$\mathcal{L}$ also contains atoms, that is subalgebras $A \subseteq [0, 1]$ such that $A' \subseteq A$, then $A' = \{0, 1\}$ or $A' = A$. The algebra $\{0, \frac{1}{2}, 1\}$ is such an atom.

Since, for a maximal ideal M of an MV-algebra A, $\frac{A}{M}$ is isomorphic to an element of $\mathcal{L}$, we have a method to refine the structure of the maximal ideal

---

* Partially supported by U.P.I.M.D.S. of Università degli Studi di Napoli Federico II.

S. Aguzzoli et al.(Eds.): Algebraic and Proof-theoretic Aspects, LNAI 4460, pp. 30–49, 2007.
© Springer-Verlag Berlin Heidelberg 2007

space. Heuristically, the "smaller" is the quotient $\frac{A}{M}$, the "larger" is the maximal ideal M. In effect this provides a pre-order on the set of maximal ideals.

Thus, from this point of view, this work is a study of the set of the maximal ideals of "type p", namely maximal ideals M with $\frac{A}{M}$ an atom of $\mathcal{L}$; that is, an MV-chain with $p + 1$ elements, $p = 1$ or p prime number.

Moreover this work will study certain extensions of the Boolean subalgebra of all idempotent elements of an MV-algebra.

The class of MV-polynomials, we call symmetric, will permit us to study the appropriate algebras.

2   Generalities on MV-Algebras

An MV-algebra is an algebraic structure $A = (A,^*, \oplus, 0,)$ satisfying the following axioms:

1. $(x \oplus y) \oplus z = x \oplus (y \oplus z)$;
2. $x \oplus y = y \oplus x$;
3. $x \oplus 0 = x$;
4. $x \oplus 0^* = 0^*$;
5. $(x^*)^* = x$;
6. $(x^* \oplus y)^* \oplus y = (y^* \oplus x)^* \oplus x$.

We define the constant 1 and the operation $\odot$ as follows:

(7) $1 = 0^*$
(8) $x \odot y = (x^* \oplus y^*)^*$

From (8), with $y = 1$, it follows $x^* \oplus x = 1$. We shall adopt the usual conventions for MV-terms: * operation is more binding than any other operation and the $\odot$ operation is more binding than $\oplus$. On A two new operations $\vee$ and $\wedge$ are defined as follows: $x \vee y = (x^* \oplus y)^* \oplus y$ and $x \wedge y = (x^* \odot y)^* \odot y$. The structure $(A, \vee, \wedge, 0, 1)$ is a bounded distributive lattice. We shall write $x \leq y$ iff $x \wedge y = x$.

We say that the MV-algebra A is linearly ordered, if the lattice $(A, \vee, \wedge, 0, 1)$ is linearly ordered. Such an algebra is also called MV-chain. Let α be a cardinal number; we say that the MV-algebra A is α-complete if, for every family $\{x_\beta, \beta < \alpha\} \subseteq A$, $\bigvee_{\beta < \alpha} x_\beta$ exists in A.

An MV-algebra is nontrivial if and only if $0 \neq 1$. In the sequel we will concern exclusively with nontrivial MV-algebras.

MV-algebras, originating from an algebraic analysis of Łukasiewicz many-valued logic, are non-idempotent generalizations of Boolean algebras. Actually, Boolean algebras are just the MV-algebras obeying the additional equation $x \oplus x = x$. Let $B(A) = \{x \in A \mid x \oplus x = x\}$ be the set of all idempotent elements of A. Then, $B(A)$ is a subalgebra of A, which is also a Boolean algebra. Indeed, it is the greatest Boolean subalgebra of A. A remarkable example of MV-algebra is given by the interval $[0, 1]$ of real numbers, where MV-operations are defined as follows:

1. $\{0,1\}$ are the constant elements;
2. $x \oplus y = min\{1, x+y\}$;
3. $x \odot y = max\{0, x+y-1\}$;
4. $x^* = 1 - x$.

Denote by N the set of all the integer positive numbers and set $\mathcal{P} = \{n \in N \mid n \ is \ prime\}$. For every $n \in N$ set $S_n = \{0, \frac{1}{n}, \ldots, \frac{n-1}{n}, 1\}$ and $S_n^\omega = \Gamma(Z \otimes Z, (n,0))$[7], where Z is the totally ordered additive group of integers and $Z \otimes Z$ is the lexicographic product of Z by itself. S_n is a subalgebra of $[0,1]$, while S_n^ω is an infinite MV-chain which is not enclosed in $[0,1]$.

Moreover we shall write nx instead of $x \oplus \cdots \oplus x$ (n-times), x^n instead of $x \odot \cdots \odot x$ (n-times) and we set $0x = 0$. Moreover, to make the notations easier, we will denote the product $a \odot b$ by ab.

A subset $J \neq \emptyset$, of an MV-algebra A, is an ideal of A if it is closed under $\oplus$ and $x \leq y$, $y \in J$ imply $x \in J$. Let $H \subset A$, we will denote by $id\{H\}$ the ideal of A generated by H. An ideal J of an MV-algebra A is called *prime* iff $J \neq A$ and whenever $x \wedge y \in J$, then either $x \in J$ or $y \in J$. An ideal J of A is called *maximal* iff it is proper and no proper ideal of A strictly contains J. Every maximal ideal is prime, but not conversely. J is prime iff $\frac{A}{J}$ is totally ordered. For every ideal J of A, the set $\{a \in A : a^* \in J\}$ shall be denoted by J^*. Moreover we shall denote by $J^\perp$ the ideal $\{a \in A : a \wedge x = 0, \text{ for every } x \in J\}$.

The set of all prime ideals of an MV-algebra A shall be denoted by $SpecA$, while $MaxA$ shall denote the sets of the maximal ideals of A. $SpecA$ endowed with the Stone-Zariski topology turns out to be a spectral space [2]. That is, the sets $U(x) = \{J \in SpecA \mid x \notin J\}$, $x \in A$, generate a topology on $SpecA$. The open sets on $SpecA$ are the sets $U(I) = \{J \in SpecA : I \not\subseteq J\}$, I ideal of A. Moreover we will set $U_c(x) = \{J \in SpecA \mid x \in J\}$ and $U_c(I) = \{J \in SpecA \mid I \subseteq J\} = SpecA \setminus U(I)$.

The intersection of all maximal ideals, the radical of A, will be denoted by $RadA$. An MV-algebra A is called *semisimple* if $RadA = \{0\}$. An ideal I of A is called semisimple if it is the intersection of all maximal ideals that contain it; equivalently, I is semisimple in A iff $\frac{A}{I}$ is a semisimple algebra. Evidently $RadA$ is a semisimple ideal and it is the smaller semisimple ideal of A. For every MV-algebra and $H \subseteq A$, we will denote by $\langle H \rangle$ the subalgebra of A generated by H. It is well known that $\langle RadA \rangle = RadA \cup (RadA)^*$.

The order of an element $x \in A$ is the least integer n such that $nx = 1$. When such integer n exists, we say that x has finite order, in symbols $ordx = n$; otherwise we say that x has infinite order and we write $ordx = \infty$.

Simple MV-algebras are algebras having $\{0\}$ as unique ideal. Simple MV-algebras are, up to isomorphism, exactly all the subalgebras of $[0,1]$ [5]. Thus every simple MV-algebra is totally ordered (MV-chain).

An MV-algebra is simple iff each $x \in A \setminus \{0\}$ has finite order.

Let **MV** be the variety of all MV-algebras. For every $A \in$ **MV**, $V(A)$ denotes the subvariety of MV generated by A. In [7] the authors proved the following:

Lemma 1. *Let A be an MV-algebra. Then, for $n \in N$, there exists the greatest subalgebra A_0 of A, such that $A_0 \in V(S_n)$.*

In the sequel the algebra A_0 of Lemma 1 shall be denote by $MV_n(A)$ and, for $n \in N$, we will denote by $D(n)$ the set of all the divisors of n.

Definition 2. *Let* $n \in N$. *For every MV-algebra* A *and* $M \in MaxA$, M *is called of type n, if* $\frac{A}{M} \cong S_n$.

Let $\mathbb{S}$ denote the family of all MV-algebras A such that the only subalgebras of A are $\{0,1\}$ and A. It is easy to see that the finite MV-chain $S_p \in \mathbb{S}$ if and only if $p \in \mathcal{P}$. However there are algebras in $\mathbb{S}$ which are non simple, such as the Boolean algebra $\{0,1\} \times \{0,1\}$.

In the poset of subalgebras of $[0,1]$, $\{0,1\}$ is the unique minimal element. Indeed $\{0,1\}$ is the smallest element. Moreover each subalgebra S_p with $p \in \mathcal{P}$, is an atom in the poset of subalgebras of $[0,1]$.

We shall focus on maximal ideals of type p, $p \in \mathcal{P} \cup \{1\}$.

Not every MV-algebra A has maximal ideals of type 1, for example $[0,1]$, or less trivially, $[0,1]^X$. Examples of MV-algebras, having some maximal ideals of type 1, can be found in [9], where the class of such MV-algebras is denoted by **BP**. Moreover in [6] is defined the subvariety **BP$_0$** of **MV** equationally defined by $2x^2 = (2x)^2$ and characterized as the class of MV-algebras whose elements are the algebras where all maximal ideals are of type 1. It is proved that the subvariety of the Boolean algebras is strictly contained in **BP$_0$**.

Here we prove that any subvariety which is generated by a single MV-chain S_p or S_p^ω, with $p \in \mathcal{P}$, is characterized by the property that any member of it has all maximal ideals of type p or type 1, see Theorems 33 and 34.

We shall examine topological aspects of the subspace $Max_1A \subseteq MaxA$ of the maximal ideals of A of type 1. For any unexplained notion on MV-algebras see [5].

Now we collect some lemmas and a definition that shall be used in the sequel.

Lemma 3. *Let* A *be an MV-chain and* n *a positive integer. If* $na = nb \neq 1$, *then* $a = b$; *similarly, if* $a^n = b^n \neq 0$, *then* $a = b$.

Proof. Without loss of generality, assume $a < b$. Thus $ba^* > 0$, $b = a \oplus a^*b$ and $nb = na \oplus n(a^*b) < 1$. By [5, Lemma 1.6.1,(iii)] $n(a^*b) = 0$, which is absurd.

The proof of the second part of the lemma is analogous.

Lemma 4. *Let* A *be a MV-algebra and* $a \in A \backslash \{0,1\}$. *If, for some integer* $k > 0$, $ka = a^*$, *then* $S = \{0, a, 2a, ..., (k-1)a, a^*, 1\}$ *is a subalgebra of* A.

Proof. S is clearly closed under $\oplus$.

To show that S is closed under *, we shall prove that $((j+1)a)^* = (k-j)a$, for every j such that $0 < j < k$.

If $j = 1$, we have $(2a)^* = (a^*)^2 = a^*(a \oplus (k-1)a) = a^* \wedge (k-1)a = (k-1)a$. Then we proceed by induction for $j > 1$. By induction hypothesis we have

$((j+1)a)^* = (ja)^*a^* = ((k-j+1)a)a^* = ((k-j)a \oplus a)a^* = a^* \wedge (k-j)a = (k-j)a$.

It follows hence that S is a subalgebra of A.

We note that the subalgebra S above is isomorphic to

$$S_{k+1} = \{0, \frac{1}{k+1}, \frac{2}{k+1}, ..., \frac{k}{k+1}, 1\}.$$

Lemma 5. *Let $p \in N$ and S be a subalgebra of $[0, 1]$, satisfying the following properties:*

(i) for all $x \in S \setminus \{1\}$, $x^p = 0$;
(ii) there is $a \in S \setminus \{0\}$, such that $(a^*)^{p-1} \neq 0$.

Then $S = S_p$.

Proof. By (i), $(a^*)^p = 0$ and $a^* \leq (p-1)a$; consequently

$$(a^*)^{p-1} \leq ((p-1)a)^{p-1}. \tag{1}$$

Now $((p-1)a)^p = ((p-1)a)^{p-1}((p-1)a) = 0$ and so

$$((p-1)a)^{p-1} \leq (a^*)^{p-1}. \tag{2}$$

Thus, from (1) and (2), it follows $(a^*)^{p-1} = ((p-1)a)^{p-1}$ and, by Lemma 3, $a^* = (p-1)a$. Therefore, applying Lemma 4, the subalgebra of S, generated by a, is S_p, where $a = \frac{1}{p}$.

To prove that $S = S_p$, it suffices to show that there is no any element $x \in S$ and $0 < x < \frac{1}{p}$.

Suppose there is an $x \in S$ such that $0 < x < \frac{1}{p}$. Then $(p-1)x \leq \frac{p-1}{p} < 1$ and $1 - \frac{(p-1)}{p} \leq 1 - (p-1)x \leq x$ being, by hypothesis, $1 \leq px$. From this $\frac{1}{p} \leq x$ which is absurd.

Definition 6. *Let I be an ideal of an MV-algebra A. I is called* hyperarchimedean *if*

$$\{J \in SpecA \mid J \supseteq I\} \subseteq MaxA.$$

Obviously every hyperarchimedean ideal is a semisimple ideal.

MV-polynomials, which we concern in the paper are the 1-ary polynomials on the structure of MV-algebra, obeying the classical definition of Universal Algebra. It is well known that, if A and A' are MV-algebras, h a homomorphism from A to A' and W an MV-polynomial, then $h \circ W = W \circ h$.

3   Symmetric MV-Polynomials and Symmetric MV-Algebras

In this section we will show how each finite MV-chain $S_p \subseteq [0, 1]$, $p \in \mathcal{P}$, can be characterized as the zeroset of a certain MV-polynomial W_p, seen as a self-mapping of $[0, 1]$. Moreover we will show that, coupling in a suitable manner certain ideals I of an arbitrary MV-algebra A and the above mentioned polynomials W_p, we can find subalgebras of A, denoted by $Sym_A(W_p, I)$. Such subalgebras include $B(A)$ and satisfy the property of having the quotient $\frac{Sym_A(W_p, I)}{J}$ isomorphic to S_p or to S_1, for every prime ideal $J \supseteq I$.

Definition 7. *An MV-polynomial W shall be called* symmetric *if, for every MV-algebra A and every $a \in A$, $W(a) = W(a^*)$.*

An easy example of a non-trivial (that is non constant) symmetric polynomial is $W(z) = z \wedge z^*$.

Definition 8. *We shall call W stable (resp. strongly stable) if, for any MV-algebra A and every semisimple ideal (resp. ideal) I of A, the following statements hold:*

(i) $W(0) \in I$
(ii) if $W(a), W(b) \in I$, then $W(a \oplus b) \in I$.

The following theorem provides two remarkable examples of symmetric and strongly stable
MV-polynomials. Define,

$$W_1(z) = z \wedge z^*,$$
$$W_2(z) = z \wedge z^* \wedge (z^2 \vee (z^*)^2).$$

Theorem 9. W_1 *and* W_2 *are symmetric and strongly stable.*

Proof. It is plain that W_1 and W_2 are symmetric MV-polynomials. Now we prove that they are strongly stable.

Let A be an arbitrary MV-algebra, I an ideal of A and $W_1(x), W_1(y) \in I$. Since $W_1(x \oplus y) = (x \oplus y) \wedge x^* y^* \leq (x \wedge x^* y^*) \oplus (y \wedge x^* y^*) \leq (x \wedge x^*) \oplus (y \wedge y^*)$, we have $W_1(x \oplus y) \leq W_1(x) \oplus W_1(y) \in I$. So from $W_1(0) = 0$, W_1 is strongly stable. Consider now W_2. Let J be a prime ideal and $I \subseteq J$. Clearly $W_2(0) = 0 \in J$ Suppose that $W_2(a), W_2(b) \in J$.

$$W_2(a \oplus b) = ((a \oplus b)^2 \vee (a^* b^*)^2) \wedge (a \oplus b) \wedge a^* b^*.$$

Therefore necessarily $W_2(a \oplus b) \in J$ in the following cases:

1. $a, b \in J$, or
2. $a^* \in J$, or
3. $b^* \in J$.

Before considering the remaining cases, let us remark that:

(i) $W_2(\frac{a}{J}) = \frac{W_2(a)}{J} = 0$ and $W_2(\frac{b}{J}) = \frac{W_2(b)}{J} = 0$;
(ii) $W_2(\frac{x}{J}) = 0$ iff either $x \in J$ or $x^* \in J$ or $\frac{x}{J} = \frac{x^*}{J}$.

Assume $a, b \notin J$ and $a^*, b^* \notin J$.

Since $\frac{a}{J}, \frac{b}{J} \notin \{0, 1\}$, $\frac{a}{J} = \frac{a^*}{J} = \frac{b}{J} = \frac{b^*}{J}$. Thus, $\frac{a \oplus b}{J} = \frac{1}{J}$ and $a^* b^* \in J$; which implies $W_2(a \oplus b) \in J$.

Assume $a \notin J$, $b \in J$ and $a^*, b^* \notin J$.

In this case $\frac{b}{J} = 0$ and $\frac{a}{J} = \frac{a^*}{J}$. Hence $\frac{a}{J} = \frac{a \oplus b}{J} = \frac{a^*}{J} = \frac{a^* b^*}{J}$ and $\frac{a \oplus b}{J} = \frac{(a \oplus b)^*}{J}$. Therefore $(a \oplus b)^2 \vee ((a \oplus b)^*)^2 \in J$ and it follows that $W_2(a \oplus b) \in J$. By arbitrariety of J the thesis follows.

Let I be an ideal of an MV-algebra A and W an MV- polynomial. Set

$$Sym_A(W, I) = \{a \in A : W(a) \in I\}.$$

Then, with the above notations, we have:

Proposition 10. *Let A be an MV-algebra, W a symmetric and stable (resp. strongly stable) MV-polynomial and I a semisimple ideal (resp. ideal) of A. Then $Sym_A(W, I)$ is a subalgebra of A and I is an ideal of $Sym_A(W, I)$.*

Proof. It is immediate to see that $Sym_A(W, I)$ is a subalgebra of A. Let us now show that $I \subseteq Sym_A(W, I)$. If I is semisimple, then $\{0\} = \{I\}$ is a semisimple ideal of the semisimple MV-algebra $\frac{A}{I}$. Let $a \in I$. Since W is stable, in $\frac{A}{I}$, we have $W(\frac{a}{I}) = W(I) = \frac{W(a)}{I} = I$, which implies $a \in Sym_A(W, I)$. If I is an arbitrary ideal of A, using the strong stability of W in $\frac{A}{I}$, similarly we obtain $I \subseteq Sym_A(W, I)$.

In the sequel, writing $Sym_A(W, I)$ we tacitly assume A to be an MV-algebra, I a semisimple ideal (an ideal) of A and W a symmetric and stable (strongly stable) MV-polynomial.

Remark 11. *Since every semisimple ideal in an MV-algebra is an intersection of maximal ideals, it suffices to check the stable condition only on the maximal ideals. Similarly, it suffices to check the strongly stable condition only on prime ideals.*

Definition 12. *Let $n \in N$ and W an MV-polynomial. Then we say that W has the n-chain property if, for every $a \in S_n$, $W(a) = 0$ and for every MV-chain A, the following holds:*

if $W(a) = 0$, for every $a \in A$, then there is $r \in D(n)$ such that $A \cong S_r$.

Proposition 13. *Let A be an MV-algebra, $n \in N$ and W a symmetric and stable (resp. strongly stable) MV-polynomial having the n-chain property. Then for any MV-algebra A and any semisimple ideal (resp. any ideal) I of A, the subalgebra $Sym_A(W, I)$ satisfies the following conditions:*

(i) *If J is a prime ideal of $Sym_A(W, I)$ and $I \subseteq J$, then there is $r \in D(n)$ such that $\frac{Sym_A(W, I)}{J} \cong S_r$.*

(ii) $\frac{Sym_A(W, I)}{I} \in V(S_n)$.

Proof. (i) Let $\frac{a}{J} \in \frac{Sym_A(W, I)}{J}$. Being $I \subseteq J$, $W(\frac{a}{J}) = \frac{W(a)}{J} = J$ and the thesis follows from the n-chain property of W.

(ii) By Chang's Subdirect Representation Theorem [5, Th.1.3.3.] there is an embedding from $\frac{Sym_A(W,I)}{I}$ to $\Pi_{J \in SpecSym_A(W,I), J \supseteq I} \frac{Sym_A(W,I)}{J}$. Hence the thesis follows from (i).

We will apply this proposition to a class of symmetric and stable MV-polynomials. $Sym_A(W, I)$ shall be called W-symmetric subalgebra of A over I. A will be called a W-symmetric algebra if $A = Sym_A(W, I)$, for some proper ideal I. The concept of W-symmetric algebra extends that of Boolean algebra. Indeed an MV-algebra B is a Boolean algebra, if and only if $B = Sym_B(z \wedge z^*, \{0\})$.

MV-polynomials in one variable correspond to McNaughton functions of one variable.

What the above allows is to prove the following:

Theorem 14. *To each rational number $\frac{k}{p}$, between 0 and 1 there corresponds a wff $W_{\frac{k}{p}}(z)$ such that $W_{\frac{k}{p}}(a) = 0$ iff $a = \frac{k}{p}$ or $a = 1 - \frac{k}{p}$. Moreover $W_{\frac{k}{p}}(z) = W_{\frac{k}{p}}(z^*)$.*

Proof. Without loss of generality we may suppose that $\frac{k}{p} \leq \frac{1}{2}$ and $gcd(k, p) = 1$. Let

$$y_1 = -px + k, \qquad y_2 = px - k, \qquad y_3 = -px + p - k, \qquad y_4 = px + k - p.$$

Consider the function $y(x)$ where

$$y(x) = \begin{cases} min(1, y_1(x)), & \text{if } 0 \leq x \leq \frac{k}{p}, \\ min(1, y_2(x)), & \text{if } \frac{k}{p} \leq x \leq \frac{1}{2}, \\ min(1, y_3(x)), & \text{if } \frac{1}{2} \leq x \leq 1 - \frac{k}{p}, \\ min(1, y_4(x)), & \text{if } 1 - \frac{k}{p} \leq x \leq 1. \end{cases}$$

Then $y(x)$ satisfies the following:

(1) $y(x)$ is piecewise linear and continuous on $[0, 1]$,
(2) $y(a) = 0$ iff $a \in \{\frac{k}{p}, 1 - \frac{k}{p}\}$,
(3) $y(x)$ is symmetric, that is $y(a) = y(1 - a)$, for every $a \in [0, 1]$.

Consequently, since all the coefficients of the linear pieces of y are integers, there is an MV-polynomial W such that $W(a) = 0$ iff $a = \frac{k}{p}$ or $a = 1 - \frac{k}{p}$.

For our purposes it will be useful to explicitly construct the required wff. We note that the class of wff we use is by no means unique.

Definition 15. *We call a wff W of Łukasiewicz logic a nested monomial if it can be generated in the following manner:*

1) $(mz)^n$ is a nested monomial for any $n, m \neq 0$,
2) if $F(z)$ is a nested monomial, so is $(mF(z))^n$ for any $n, m \neq 0$.

It is clear that $F(z)$ is a nested monomial iff there are sequences of positive integers $m_1, ..., m_k$ (called coefficients) and $n_1, ..., n_k$ (called exponents) such that

$$F(z) = (m_k(m_{k-1}(...(m_2(m_1 z)^{n_1})^{n_2})...)^{n_{k-1}})^{n_k}. \qquad (*)$$

Immediately we have:

Lemma 16. *Let $F(z)$ be a nested monomial and A an MV-algebra. Then the following statements hold:*

(i) *If $a \in B(A)$, then $F(a) = a$.*
(ii) *Let A be non Boolean. Then $F(z)$ is the identity map on A iff $m = n = 1$ for all coefficients m and exponents n;*
(iii) *If $a \in RadA$ and for some exponent n, $n > 1$, then $F(a) = 0$.*
(iv) *If If $a \in (RadA)^*$ and for some coefficient m, $m > 1$, then $F(a) = 1$.*

With the notations of $(*)$ we get:

Proposition 17. *Let $\frac{k}{p} \in [0,1]$, $p \in \mathcal{P} \setminus \{2\}$ and $0 < \frac{k}{p} < \frac{1}{2}$. Then there is a nested monomial $F_{k,p}(z)$, with $m_1, n_1 > 1$, defined on $[0,1]$, such that:*

(i) $F_{k,p}(a) = \frac{1}{p}$ *iff $a = \frac{k}{p}$,*
(ii) *for $a \neq 0, 1$, $kF_{k,p}(a) = a$ iff $a = \frac{k}{p}$.*

Proof. (i) For $k=1$, let $F_{1,p}(z) = ((p-1)z)^{p-1}$. Then $F_{1,p}(\frac{1}{p}) = \frac{(p-1)^2 - p(p-2)}{p} = \frac{1}{p}$. Conversely, if $F_{1,p}(a) = \frac{1}{p}$, then $(p-1)^2 a - (p-2) = \frac{1}{p}$, from which we have $a = \frac{1}{p}$. Then we can proceed by induction. For k', $1 \leq k' < k < \frac{p}{2}$ suppose the statement is true. Let $m \geq 2$ be the positive integer such that

$$mk < p < (m+1)k. \qquad (3)$$

By (3), we have

$$\frac{p}{(p-mk)} - \frac{(p-k)}{(p-mk)} = \frac{k}{(p-mk)} > 1.$$

Then we can fix an integer $n > 1$, such that

$$\frac{(p-k)}{(p-mk)} < n < \frac{p}{(p-mk)}. \qquad (4)$$

Consider now the expression $(m(\frac{k}{p}))^n = \frac{p-n(p-mk)}{p} = \frac{k'}{p}$. By (4) we get $0 < k' < k$. By the induction assumption there is a nested wff $F_{k',p}(z)$ such that $F_{k',p}(a) = \frac{1}{p}$ iff $a = \frac{k'}{p}$. Set $F_{k,p}(z) = F_{k',p}((mz)^n)$. Note that $F_{k,p}(z)$ is nested and $(ma)^n = \frac{k'}{p}$ iff $a = \frac{k}{p}$. Hence $F_{k,p}(a) = \frac{1}{p}$ iff $a = \frac{k}{p}$.

(ii) Suppose now that $kF_{k,p}(a) = a$, $a \neq 0, 1$. Each nested monomial is a linear function of the form $y(z) = max(0, rz - s)$ where r, s are positive integers. The function $y(z) = 0$ for $z \leq \frac{s}{r}$ and $y(z) = 1$ for $z \geq \frac{1+s}{r}$. Thus the line $y(z) = z$ intersects $y(z) = rz - s$ in exactly one point different from $0, 1$. Since $kF_{k,p}(\frac{k}{p}) = \frac{k}{p}$ we can infer from $kF(a) = a$ that $a = \frac{k}{p}$.

Let $W'_{k,p}(z) = kF_{k,p}(z)$, $F_{k,p}(z)$ as in Proposition 17. Then for $a \neq 0, 1$, $W'_{k,p}(a) = a$ iff $a = \frac{k}{p}$. Now set, for $p \in \mathcal{P} \setminus \{2\}$ and $0 < \frac{k}{p} < \frac{1}{2}$,

$$W_{k,p}(z) = d(W'_{k,p}(z), z) \wedge d(W'_{k,p}(z^*), z^*), \tag{5}$$

where $d(x, y) = xy^* \vee x^*y = xy^* \oplus x^*y$. With the above notations, by definition, we have:

Lemma 18. *For each $p \in \mathcal{P} \setminus \{2\}$ and $0 < \frac{k}{p} < \frac{1}{2}$, $W_{k,p}(z)$ is symmetric.*

Proposition 19. *Let $a \in [0, 1]$ and k, p positive integers such that $p \in \mathcal{P} \setminus \{2\}$ and $0 < \frac{k}{p} < \frac{1}{2}$. Then $W_{k,p}(a) = 0$ iff $a \in \{0, \frac{k}{p}, \frac{p-k}{p}, 1\}$.*

Proof. Since $W'_{k,p}(z)$ is nested, $W'_{k,p}(0) = 0$ and $W'_{k,p}(1) = 1$. Thus $W_{k,p}(0) = W_{k,p}(1) = 0$. Assume $W_{k,p}(a) = 0$, $a \neq 0, 1$. Then, by (5), either $d(W'_{k,p}(a), a) = 0$ or $d(W'_{k,p}(a^*), a^*) = 0$. The former implies that $W'_{k,p}(a) = a$, which, by Proposition 17(ii), is equivalent to $a = \frac{k}{p}$. The latter implies that $W'_{k,p}(a^*) = a^*$ and so $a^* = \frac{k}{p}$ from which we infer $a = \frac{p-k}{p}$.

Moreover

Proposition 20. *Let A be an MV-chain, $a \in A$ and $a \neq 0, 1$. If $W_{1,p}(a) = 0$, then $(p-1)a = a^*$ or $(p-1)a^* = a$.*

Proof. Suppose first $d(((p-1)a)^{p-1}, a) = 0$. Then $((p-1)a)^{p-1} = a$. Hence $a^* = (p-1)((a^*)^{p-1})$. Thus, $((p-1)a)a^* = ((p-1)a)((a^*)^{p-1} \oplus (p-2)((a^*)^{p-1}))$. From this, $a^* \wedge ((p-2)a) = (p-1)a \wedge (p-2)((a^*)^{p-1})$.

Claim 1: $(p-2)a < a^*$.

Indeed if $a^* \leq (p-2)a$, $1 = (p-1)a$ and $(a^*)^{p-1} = 0$, which implies $a^* = 0$ and $a = 1$. Applying Claim 1, $(p-2)a = (p-1)a \wedge (p-2)((a^*)^{p-1})$.

Claim 2: $(p-2)((a^*)^{p-1}) < (p-1)a$.

Indeed if $(p-1)a \leq (p-2)((a^*)^{p-1})$, we get $(p-1)a = (p-2)a$ which implies $a \in \{0, 1\}$. Applying the Claim 2, $(p-2)(a^*)^{p-1} = (p-2)a < 1$. By Lemma 3, $(a^*)^{p-1} = a$ and so $(p-1)a = a^*$. If $d(((p-1)a^*)^{p-1}, a^*) = 0$ then letting $b = a^*$ we have $(p-1)b = b^*$. That is $(p-1)a = a^*$.

Define,

for $p \in \mathcal{P} \setminus \{2\}$, $W_p(z) = \bigwedge_{1 \leqslant k \leqslant \frac{p-1}{2}} W_{k,p}(z)$.

Proposition 21. *Let $p \in \mathcal{P}$. Then the following statements hold:*

(i) for $a \in [0, 1]$, $W_p(a) = 0$ iff $a \in S_p = \{0, \frac{1}{p}, \frac{2}{p}, ..., \frac{p-1}{p}, 1\}$;

(ii) let $a \in]0, 1[$. $W_p(a) = 0$ iff for exactly one k, $1 \leq k \leq \frac{p-1}{2}$, $W_{k,p}(a) = 0$;

(iii) let A be an MV-algebra. If $a \in MV_p(A)$, then $W_p(a) = 0$; if $a \in \langle RadA \rangle$, then $W_p(a) = a$.

Proof. (i) Let $p = 2$. $W_2(a) = 0$ if $a \in \{0, 1\}$ or if $a^2 \vee (a^*)^2 = 0$. The latter implies that $a^2 = (a^*)^2 = 0$, so $a = a^*$ and $A \cong \{0, \frac{1}{2}, 1\}$. If $p > 2$, the statement follows by Proposition 19.

(ii) It follows by Proposition 19.
(iii) Let $a \in MV_p(A)$. Then, by Chang's Subdirect Representation Theorem [5, Th.1.3.3.], $a = (a_h)_{h \in H}$, where $a_h \in S_p$, for each $h \in H$. Fixed $h \in H$, by (i) we get:

$$(W_p(a))_h = W_p(a_h) = 0;$$

Hence $W_p(a) = 0$. If $a \in \langle RadA \rangle$, then the thesis follows by definitions and Lemma 16(iii),(iv).

Corollary 22. *For any MV-algebra A and $a \in B(A)$, $W_p(a) = 0$.*

Proposition 23. *For every $p \in \mathcal{P}$, W_p has the p-chain property.*

Proof. Let A be an MV-chain and $W_p(a) = 0$ on A. If $a \in RadA$, by Proposition 21(iii), $W_p(a) = a$, which implies $RadA = \{0\}$. Then A is, up to isomorphism, a subalgebra of $[0,1]$. Hence the thesis follows by Proposition 21(i).

Theorem 24. *For every $p \in \mathcal{P}$, W_p is a stable and symmetric MV-polynomial.*

Proof. Let us prove first that W_p is stable. By Remark 11 it suffices to check the stable condition only on the maximal ideals of an MV-algebra A. Let $M \in MaxA$ and $W_p(a), W_p(b) \in M$. Then in $\frac{A}{M}$ we have that $\frac{W_p(a)}{M} = W_p(\frac{a}{M}) = \frac{W_p(b)}{M} = W_p(\frac{b}{M}) = 0$. Hence, by Proposition 21(i), $\frac{a}{M}, \frac{b}{M} \in S_p$, and $\frac{a \oplus b}{M} \in S_p$. Consequently, $W_p(\frac{a \oplus b}{M}) = 0$ and so $W_p(a \oplus b) \in M$. The symmetry of W_p is evident for $p = 2$. For $p > 2$, the statement follows by Lemma 18.

By Theorems 9 and 24, and Proposition 10 we get:

Theorem 25. *Let A be an MV-algebra and I a semisimple ideal of A (or any ideal if $p = 1, 2$). Then $Sym_A(W_p, I)$ is a subalgebra of A and I is and ideal of $Sym_A(W_p, I)$.*

Theorem 26. *Let A be an MV-algebra and I a semisimple ideal of A (or any ideal if $p = 1, 2$). Then the following statements hold:*

(i) $\langle MV_p(A) \cup RadA \rangle \subseteq Sym_A(W_p, I)$;
(ii)) *If J is a prime ideal of $Sym_A(W_p, I)$ and $I \subseteq J$, then there is $r \in \{1, p\}$ such that $\frac{Sym_A(W_p, I)}{J} \cong S_r$;*
(iii) $\frac{Sym_A(W_p, I)}{I} \in V(S_p)$;

Proof. (i) From Proposition 21(iii) it follows that if $a \in MV_p(A) \cup RadA$, then $W_p(a) \in RadA \subseteq I$. Thus $\langle MV_p(A) \cup RadA \rangle \subseteq Sym_A(W_p, I)$.

(ii) and (iii) follow from Proposition 23, Theorems 9 and 24, and Proposition 13(i) and (ii).

As we observed in the introduction, some results about MV-algebras, having maximal ideals of type 1, are quoted in [9], where the class of such algebras is denoted by **BP**. Now we are going to generalize these results to the case $p \in \mathcal{P}$ and to analyze them by using symmetry. Given an MV-algebra A and $p \in \mathcal{P}$, we can consider the ideal $N_A(W_p)$ of A, defined by $N_A(W_p) = id\{W_p(a) \mid a \in A\}$. (We will write $N(W_p)$ for $N_A(W_p)$ when A is understood.) In [9] it is shown that, for any MV-algebra A, the property of having at least a maximal ideal of type 1 turns out to be equivalent to the following: $id\{z \wedge z^*, z \in A\} \neq A$. Here, in our terminology, we get:

Theorem 27. *Let A be an MV-algebra. Then we get:*

(i) If $N_A(W_1) \neq A$, then every prime ideal J, that contains $N_A(W_1)$, is of type 1, that is, $\frac{A}{J} \cong \{0,1\}$.

(ii) If J is a prime ideal of A and $\frac{A}{J} = \{0,1\}$ then J contains $N_A(W_1)$.

A way to generalize Theorem 27 would be to pass from maximal ideals of type 1 to maximal ideals of type p. Indeed we have:

Theorem 28. *Let A be an MV-algebra A and $p \in \mathcal{P}$. Then we get:*

(i) If $N_A(W_p) \neq A$, then every prime ideal J, containing $N_A(W_p)$, there is $r \in \{1,p\}$ such that $\frac{A}{J} \cong S_r$.

(ii) If J is a prime ideal of A and $\frac{A}{J} \cong S_p$, then J contains $N_A(W_p)$.

Proof. Let $N_A(W_p)$ be proper and J a prime ideal including $N_A(W_p)$. For each $a \in A$, $W_p(\frac{a}{J}) = \frac{W_p(a)}{J} = 0$. Since W_p has p-chain property, there is $r \in \{1,p\}$ such that $\frac{A}{J} \cong S_r$. So (i) is proved. In the hypothesis of (ii), by Proposition 21(i) we get, for every $a \in A$, $W_p(\frac{a}{J}) = \frac{W_p(a)}{J} = 0$. Hence $W_p(a) \in J$ and $N_A(W_p) \subseteq J$.

By the above results, in any MV-algebra A, if $N(W_p) \neq A$ ($p \in \mathcal{P} \cup \{1\}$), then every prime ideal containing $N(W_p)$ is a maximal ideal. From this we have:

Corollary 29. *Let A be an MV-algebra and $p \in \mathcal{P} \cup \{1\}$. If $N_A(W_p) \neq A$, then $N_A(W_p)$ is an hyperarchimedean ideal.*

In the sequel we shall use the following lemmas:

Lemma 30. *Let A be MV-algebra and $p \in \mathcal{P}$. Then $N(W_p) \subseteq N(W_1)$.*

Proof. It will be sufficient to show that $W_p(a) \in N(W_1)$, for every $a \in A$. If $N(W_1) = A$, it is trivial. Let $N(W_1) \neq A$, M a maximal ideal containing $N(W_1)$ and $a \in A$. Since $\frac{a}{M} \in \{0,1\}$, $W_p(\frac{a}{M}) = \frac{W_p(a)}{M}) = 0$ and $W_p(a) \in M$. Since M is arbitrary, by Corollary 29 $W_p(a) \in N(W_1)$.

Proposition 31. *Let A be an MV-algebra. If A has a maximal ideal of type p, then A is a W_p-symmetric algebra over each ideal I such that $N(W_p) \subseteq I$.*

Proof. By Theorem 24 and Corollary 25 $N(W_p)$ is a proper semisimple ideal of A. Therefore we can consider $Sym_A(W_p, N(W_p))$ which obviously is A. If $N(W_p) \subseteq I$, then, for every $x \in A$, $W_p(x) \in I$ and $A = Sym_A(W_p, I)$.

Lemma 32. *Let A be an MV-algebra. Then if A is W_p-symmetric over some ideal I of A, then $I \supseteq N(W_p)$.*

Proof. By hypothesis, for every $a \in A$, $W_p(a) \in I$, hence $N(W_p) \subseteq I$.

Proposition 33. *Let A be an MV-algebra, $p \in \mathcal{P} \cup \{1\}$ and I a semisimple ideal (an ideal if p=1,2) of A. Then the following statements hold:*

(i) $MV_p(\frac{A}{I}) = \frac{Sym_A(W_p, I)}{I}$;

(ii) $Sym_A(W_p, I)$ *is the largest subalgebra R of A for which $\frac{R}{I} \in V(S_p)$;*

Proof. (i) Claim:

$$\frac{Sym_A(W_p, I)}{I} \quad \text{is a subalgebra of} \quad \frac{A}{I}.$$

We have to show that, for every $x \in Sym_A(W_p, I)$, the equivalence classes of x with respect to I, considered in $Sym_A(W_p, I)$ or in A, coincide. That is, if $y \in A$ and $d(x, y) \in I$, then $y \in Sym_A(W_p, I)$.

Let $\frac{y}{I} = \frac{x}{I}$ in A. Then $W_p(\frac{y}{I}) = W_p(\frac{x}{I}) = \frac{W_p(x)}{I} = 0$. Hence $W_p(y) \in I$ and $y \in Sym_A(W_p, I)$. From Claim and Theorem 26(iii) $\frac{Sym_A(W_p, I)}{I} \subseteq MV_p(\frac{A}{I})$. To show that $\frac{Sym_A(W_p(z), I)}{I} = MV_p(\frac{A}{I})$, consider $\frac{y}{I} \in MV_p(\frac{A}{I})$. By [5, Th.1.3.3.] $MV_p(\frac{A}{I}) \hookrightarrow \Pi_{j \in J} S_j$, with $j \in \{1, p\}$; Then we have $(W_p(\frac{y}{I}))_j = W_p((\frac{y}{I}))_j) = 0$. Therefore $W_p(\frac{y}{I}) = 0$, $W_p(y) \in I$ and $y \in Sym_A(W_p, I)$.

(ii) Suppose R is a subalgebra of A for which $I \subseteq R$ and $\frac{R}{I} \in V(S_p)$. Let $x \in R$. Then $W_p(\frac{x}{I}) = 0$. Therefore $W_p(x) \in I$ and so $x \in Sym_A(W_p, I)$. That is, $R \subseteq Sym_A(W_p, I)$.

We have observed that $Sym_A(W, I)$ is a generalization of $B(A)$ as the latter is just $Sym_A(W_1, \{0\})$. Indeed the concept of W-symmetric algebra generalizes that one of *p-valued* algebra, with $p \in \mathcal{P}$. Indeed we get:

Theorem 34. *Let A be an MV-algebra. Then the following conditions are equivalent:*

(i) $A \in V(S_p)$;
(ii) $A = Sym_A(W_p, \{0\})$;
(iii) $N(W_p) = \{0\}$.

Proof. If $A \in V(S_p)$, then $\{0\}$ is a semisimple ideal of A. By Proposition 32(i) we have

$$A = MV_p(\frac{A}{\{0\}}) = \frac{Sym_A(W_p, \{0\})}{\{0\}} = Sym_A(W_p, \{0\}).$$

Assume now $A = Sym_A(W_p, \{0\})$. By Theorem 26(iii) $A = \frac{A}{\{0\}} \in V(S_p)$. Thus we proved that (i) and (ii) are equivalent. The equivalence between (ii) and (iii) follows by Lemma 31.

A further generalization is the following:

Theorem 35. *Let A be an MV-algebra. Then the following conditions are equivalent:*

(i) $A \in V(S_p^\omega)$;
(ii) $A = Sym_A(W_p, RadA)$;
(iii) $N(W_p) = RadA$.

Proof. Let us prove first (ii) $\Leftrightarrow$ (iii). Let $A = Sym_A(W_p, RadA)$. Then by Lemma 31 $N(W_p) = RadA$. The other implication is trivial.

Now we show (i) $\Leftrightarrow$ (ii). If $A \in V(S_p^\omega)$, then by [7, Th.18] $\frac{A}{RadA} \in V(S_p)$ and, by Theorem 33, $\frac{A}{RadA} = Sym_{\frac{A}{RadA}}(W_p, \{RadA\})$. Let $a \in A$. $W_p(\frac{a}{RadA}) = \frac{W_p(a)}{RadA} = RadA$. Thus $W_p(a) \in RadA$ and $A = Sym_A(W_p, RadA)$. Assume now $A = Sym_A(W_p, RadA)$ and $a \in A$. Then $W_p(\frac{a}{RadA}) = \frac{W_p(a)}{RadA} = RadA$. Therefore, by Theorem 33 $\frac{A}{RadA} \in V(S_p)$, and by [7, Th.18] $A \in V(S_p^\omega)$.

By the above theorem immediately we have:

Corollary 36. *Let A be an MV-algebra. If $A \in V(S_p^\omega)$, then $RadA$ is an hyperarchimedean ideal.*

Theorem 37. *Let A be an MV-algebra and $p \in \mathcal{P}$. Then the following are equivalent:*

(i) A has maximal ideal of type p or 1;
(ii) $N_A(W_p) \neq A$;
(iii) A is W_p-symmetric with respect to $N(W_p)$.
(iv) A is W_p-symmetric.

Proof. (ii) $\Rightarrow$ (i) follows from Theorem 28.

(i) $\Rightarrow$ (ii). Let M be a maximal ideal of A having type p or 1. If $\frac{A}{M} \cong S_1$, then $N_A(W_1) \neq A$ and the thesis follows from Lemma 30. Let $\frac{A}{M} \cong S_p$ and $a \in A$. By Proposition 21(i), $W_p(\frac{a}{M}) = \frac{W_p(a)}{M} = 0$. Thus $W_p(a) \in M$ and $N_A(W_p) \subseteq M \neq A$.

So we proved (i) $\Leftrightarrow$ (ii).

(ii) $\Rightarrow$ (iii). Corollary 29 allows us to consider the subalgebra $Sym_A(W_p, N_A(W_p))$ of A. As a matter of fact $A = Sym_A(W_p, N_A(W_p))$. Indeed for $a \in A$, $W_p(a) \in N_A(W_p)$.

(iii) $\Rightarrow$ (iv) is trivial.

(iv) $\Rightarrow$ (ii). Assume $A = Sym_A(W_p, I)$, for some semisimple proper ideal I of A. Then $W_p(a) \in I$, for every $a \in A$. Thus $N_A(W_p) \subseteq I \neq A$.

Proposition 38. *Let A be an MV-algebra and $p \in \mathcal{P}$. Then the following statements are equivalent:*

(i) A is W_p-symmetric;
(ii) A has a homomorphic image in the variety $V(S_p)$.

Proof. (i) $\Rightarrow$ (ii) The thesis immediately follows from the implication (iv) $\Rightarrow$ (i) of Theorem 36.

(ii) $\Rightarrow$ (i) By hypothesis there exists an ideal I of A such that $\frac{A}{I} \in V(S_p)$. Let $J \supseteq I$ a prime ideal of A. We get $\frac{\frac{A}{I}}{\frac{J}{I}} \cong \frac{A}{J} \in V(S_p)$. Hence $\frac{A}{J} \cong S_p$ or $\frac{A}{J} \cong S_1$. From that, the thesis again follows from Theorem 36.

Theorem 36 says that if A is W_1-symmetric, then A is W_p-symmetric over $N(W_1)$. This result makes it appear that there is an ambiguity in the notion of W_p-symmetry. To clarify this we have,

Proposition 39. *Let A be an MV-algebra and p, q prime integers. If A is W_p-symmetric over an ideal I of A and W_q-symmetric over I, then either $p = q$ or A is W_1-symmetric over I.*

Proof. Let $p \neq q$. Since $A = Sym_A(W_p, I)$, for any maximal ideal $M \supseteq I$, $\frac{A}{M}$ is either $\{0, 1\}$ or $\frac{A}{M} \cong S_p$. Similarly for q we obtain $\frac{A}{M}$ is either $\{0, 1\}$ or $\frac{A}{M} \cong S_q$. It follows that $\frac{A}{M} = \{0, 1\}$ and thus A has maximal ideals of type 1 and A is W_1-symmetric over I.

Let us observe that if $M \in Max_1 A$, for some MV-algebra A, then M is minimal with respect the property of including $N(W_1)$.

We wish to conclude this paragraph by exhibiting an example of MV-algebra, having a denumerable infinity of different types of maximal ideals, but no having maximal ideals of type 1.

Example 1. Let $A = \prod_{n \in N} S_{p_n}$ where p_n is the nth prime number. Clearly A has maximal ideals of each type p_n, that is $V(N(W_{p_n}))$ is non-empty for each prime integer p_n. However A has no maximal ideals of type 1. Indeed, let $a = (a_n)_{n \in N} \in A$ be the element such that $a_n = \frac{p_n - 1}{2p_n}$, for every $n \in N$. a has order 4. Therefore $a \wedge a^* = a$ has finite order and so $N_A(W_1) = A$.

Example 2. An example of a symmetric MV-algebra having maximal ideals of type belonging to a given family $\{p_1, ..., p_n\}$ of prime numbers and no other maximal ideals is given by $A = S_{p_1}^X \times ... \times S_{p_n}^X$ for some set $X \neq \emptyset$.

4   Maximal Ideals of Type 1

We shall compare some properties of $Sym_A(W_1, I)$ and $B(A)$.

Theorem 40. *If A is α-complete and I is an α-complete ideal, then $Sym_A(W_1, I)$ is α-complete.*

Proof. Suppose A, I are α-complete. Let $x_\beta \in Sym_A(W_1, I)$, $\beta < \alpha$. By α-completeness of A, $x = \bigvee_\beta x_\beta$ exists in A. Now each $x_\beta \wedge x_\beta^* \in I$; hence $x^* \wedge x_\beta \in I$, for each $\beta < \alpha$. Then we have $x^* \wedge x = x^* \wedge \bigvee_\beta x_\beta = \bigvee_\beta (x_\beta \wedge x^*) \in I$, by α-completeness of I. Therefore $x \in Sym_A(W_1, I)$ and so $Sym_A(W_1, I)$ is α-complete.

The above theorem strengthens the following result:

If A is an α-complete MV-algebra, then $B(A)$ is an α-complete subalgebra of A, see [3] and [5, Corollary 6.6.5(i)] . Indeed $B(A) = Sym_A(W_1, \{0\})$.

Proposition 41. *Let A be an MV-algebra, I a semisimple ideal of A and $x, y \in A$. If $x \in Sym_A(W_1, I)$ and $d(x, y) \in Sym_A(W_1, I)$, then $y \in Sym_A(W_1, I)$.*

Proof. We show first that the proposition is true for $B(A)$. Let $x, d(x, y) \in B(A)$ and J be a prime ideal of A. Then $\frac{d(x,y)}{J}$ and $\frac{x}{J}$ are idempotent and so $\frac{d(x,y)}{J}, \frac{x}{J} \in \{0, 1\} \subseteq \frac{A}{J}$.

$$\frac{d(x,y)}{J} = \begin{cases} \frac{y}{J} & \text{if } \frac{x}{J} = 0, \\ \frac{y^*}{J} & \text{if } \frac{x}{J} = 1. \end{cases}$$

From above either $y \in J$ or $y^* \in J$, hence $y \wedge y^* \in J$. Since J is an arbitrary prime ideal, it follows that $y \wedge y^* = 0$ and so $y \in B(A)$. Now let I be a semisimple ideal of A and assume $x, d(x, y) \in Sym_A(W_1, I)$. By Proposition 26(iii) and Claim in the proof of Proposition 32, $\frac{d(x,y)}{I}$ and $\frac{x}{I}$ are idempotents in $\frac{A}{I}$; hence they are in $\frac{B(A)}{I}$. Since $\frac{d(x,y)}{I} = d(\frac{x}{I}, \frac{y}{I})$, $\frac{y}{I} \in B(\frac{A}{I})$. By idempotency $\frac{y}{I} \wedge \frac{y^*}{I} = \frac{y \wedge y^*}{I} = 0$. Therefore $y \wedge y^* \in I$ and we may conclude that $y \in Sym_A(W_1, I)$.

Every ideal in a Boolean algebra, if maximal, is of type 1. On the other hand $A = [0, 1]^X$, $X \neq \emptyset$ has no maximal ideals of type 1. Moreover we have $B(A) \subseteq Sym_A(W_1, I) \subseteq A$ for any ideal I of A. We get that these intermediate subalgebras always have maximal ideals of type 1. Indeed, by Theorem 26(ii), if $Q \in Spec(Sym_A(W_1, I))$, with $N(W_1) \subseteq Q$, then Q is a maximal ideal of type 1 in $Sym_A(W_1, I)$. Since every ideal in an MV-algebra is contained in some prime ideal, it is evident that $Sym_A(W_1, I)\}$ always contains maximal ideals of type 1.

Proposition 42. *Let A be an MV-algebra and $M \in Max A$. Then the following are equivalent:*

(i) *M is of type 1 in A;*
(ii) *for all $x \in A$, $x \in M$ or $x^* \in M$;*
(iii) *for all $x, y \in A$, $xy \in M$ implies $x \in M$ or $y \in M$.*

Proof. The equivalence among (i) and (ii) is trivial.

Since $xx^* = 0$ it is clear that (iii) implies (ii). Assume (ii). Let $xy \in M$ and suppose that $x \notin M$. Then $x^* \in M$ and $x^* \oplus xy = x^* \vee y \in M$ from which we have $y \in M$.

Definition 43. *We call an MV-algebra A Boolean $-$ mixed if A is not Boolean and $A = A' \times B$ where B is a Boolean algebra.*

If $A = A' \times B$, we will denote by π_1 and π_2 the projection of A in A' and B respectively. Then we get:

Definition 44. *We call an MV-algebra A a subdirect algebra of a Boolean $-$ mixed algebra $C = A' \times B$, if A is a subalgebra of C and $\pi_1(A) = A'$ and $\pi_2(A) = B$.*

Proposition 45. *Let A be an MV-algebra. Then the following statements are equivalent:*

(i) A is W_1-symmetric;
(ii) A has a Boolean homomorphic image.

Proof. (i) $\Rightarrow$ (ii) The thesis immediately follows from Theorem 27(i).

(ii) $\Rightarrow$ (i) By hypothesis there exists an homomorphism φ from A onto B. Then for every $M \in MaxB$, we get $\varphi^{-1}(M) \in MaxA$ is of type 1. From that, the thesis again follows from Theorem 27.

Proposition 46. *Let A be an MV-algebra. Then the following statements are equivalent:*

(i) A is a subdirect algebra of a Boolean-mixed algebra;
(ii) A is a non-Boolean W_1-symmetric;
(iii) A is a retract of a Boolean-mixed algebra.

Proof. (i) $\Rightarrow$ (ii) Suppose A is a subdirect subalgebra of $A' \times B$ where A is non-Boolean and B is Boolean. The projection of A on B is an homomorphism from A onto B. Then the proof is completed by Proposition 44.

(ii) $\Rightarrow$ (i) If A is W_1-symmetric, then $N(W_1) \neq A$. Thus we can give a subdirect representation of A by the map $\mu : A \to A \times \frac{A}{N(W_1)}$, given by $\mu(x) = (x, \frac{x}{N(W_1)})$. μ is an injective morphism, that is a subdirect representation. Since A is non-Boolean and $\frac{A}{N(W_1)}$ is Boolean, the equivalence (i) $\Leftrightarrow$ (ii) is proved.

(ii) $\Rightarrow$ (iii) Let $\mu : A \to A \times \frac{A}{N(W_1)}$ the above injective morphism and $\pi : (x, \frac{x}{N(W_1)}) \to x$ the projection of $A \times \frac{A}{N(W_1)}$ on A. Since $\pi \circ \mu = I_A$, the implication is proved.

(iii) $\Rightarrow$ (ii) By hypothesis there are a Boolean-mixed algebra $A' \times B$ (A' non-Boolean and B Boolean MV-algebras), an injective morphism $\mu : A \to A' \times B$ and a surjective homomorphism $\chi : A' \times B \to A$ such that $\chi \circ \mu = I_A$. Thus, up to an isomorphism, A is a subalgebra of $A' \times B$. Therefore the projection of $A \times B$ on B holds on having A a Boolean homomorphic image. By Proposition 44, A is W_1-symmetric.

In [1, Corollary 3.2] is proved that $MaxA$ coincides with the set of all maximal ideals of type 1 iff $Rad(A) = N(W_1)$. An example of such an algebra is $\mathbf{C}^N$, where $\mathbf{C}$ is the perfect algebra with one generator. In the semisimple case this happens iff A is Boolean. Otherwise we get:

Proposition 47. *Let A be a semisimple MV-algebra and $N' = \bigcap\{M \mid M \in MaxA \setminus Max_1A\}$. If $MaxA \neq Max_1A \neq \emptyset$, then, $N' = (N_A(W_1))^{\perp}$.*

Proof. $N' \cap N_A(W_1) \subseteq \bigcap_{M \in MaxA} M = \{0\}$. Then $N' \subseteq (N_A(W_1))^{\perp}$. On other hand if $M \in Max(A) \setminus Max_1A$, then $N_A(W_1) \not\subseteq M$; that implies $(N_A(W_1))^{\perp} \subseteq M$ and so $(N_1)^{\perp} \subseteq N'$.

As an application of Proposition 41 we get a result which strengthens Theorem 3 of [4]. Indeed we have:

Proposition 48. *Let A be an MV-algebra. Then the following statements are equivalent:*

1. *$MaxA = Max_1A$*
2. *$ord(xy) = \infty$ iff $ord(x) = \infty$ or $ord(y) = \infty$.*

5   Topological Issues on Maximal Ideals of Type p

In this section we provide a certain topological characterization of $U_c(N_A(W_p))$. Let A be an MV-algebra. By Lemma 30, $N_A(W_p) \subseteq N_A(W_1)$, for every $p \in \mathcal{P}$. Consequently $U_c(N_A(W_1)) \subseteq U_c(N_A(W_p))$. The main result of this section is that, if A is W_p-symmetric, the subset of $MaxA$, $U_c(N_A(W_p))$, is a closed Boolean subspace of $SpecA$.

Theorem 49. *Let A be a W_p-symmetric MV-algebra over a semisimple ideal I of A. Then $U_c(N_A(W_p))$ is a closed Boolean subspace of $SpecA$.*

Proof. $U_c(N_A(W_p))$ is a closed in $SpecA$ by definition. By Theorem 36 $N_A(W_p) \neq A$. Moreover from Corollary 29 and Theorem 26(iii), $U_c(N_A(W_p)) \subseteq Max(A)$ and $\frac{A}{I} \in V(S_p)$. Hence $Spec\left(\frac{A}{I}\right)$ is a Boolean space. Consider the bijection $h : M \in U_c(N_A(W_p)) \to \frac{M}{I} \in Spec(\frac{A}{I})$. Let J be an ideal of A containing I and $\mathcal{O} = U(\frac{J}{I})$ an open set in $Spec(\frac{A}{I})$. We get $\frac{J}{I} \not\subseteq \frac{M}{I}$ if and only if $J \not\subseteq M$. Consequently $h^{-1}(\mathcal{O}) = U(J)$ and h is a homeomorphism.

Proposition 50. *Let A be an MV-algebra and $p \in \mathcal{P}$. Then the following statements are equivalent:*

1. *$M \in U_c(N_A(W_p)) \setminus U_c(N_A(W_1))$;*
2. *for all $x \in A \setminus M$, $(x^*)^p \in M$ and there exists an $a \in A \setminus M$ such that $(a^*)^{p-1} \notin M$.*

Proof. (1) $\Rightarrow$ (2) Let $M \in U_c(N(W_p)) \setminus U_c(N_A(W_1))$. By Theorems 27 and 28 $\frac{A}{M} \cong S_p$. Let η be such an isomorphism. If $x \notin M$, then $\frac{x}{M} \neq 0$. Since $\eta(\frac{x}{M}) \in S_p$, $\frac{px}{M} = 1$, that is, $(x^*)^p \in M$. Assume $a \in \eta^{-1}(\frac{1}{p})$, then $a \in A \setminus M$. Since $\eta((a^*)^{p-1}) = \frac{1}{p}$, we have $(a^*)^{p-1} \notin M$.

(2) $\Rightarrow$ (1) By Lemma 5 $\frac{A}{M} \cong S_p$, thus $M \in U_c(N_A(W_p)) \setminus U_c(N_A(W_1))$.

In [9] it was proved:

Proposition 51. *Let A be an MV-algebra. Then Max_1A is a closed subspace of $SpecA$.*

We strengthen it by

Proposition 52. *Let A be an MV-algebra. Then Max_1A is a closed Boolean subspace of $SpecA$.*

Proof. Since $SpecA$ is compact, by Proposition 49, Max_1A is compact. Let $M_1, M_2 \in Max_1A$, $M_1 \neq M_2$ and $x \in M_2 \setminus M_1$; so that $x^* \in M_1 \setminus M_2$. Then $M_1 \in U(x)$, $M_2 \in U(x^*)$. As $U(x) \cap U(x^* \cap Max_1A = \emptyset$, we see that

Max_1A is Hausdorff. Clearly the sets $U(x)$ form an open basis for Max_1A; but $U(x) \cap Max_1A = U_c(x^*) \cap Max_1A$. Thus we found a basis of clopen sets. Hence the proposition is proved.

Proposition 53. *Let A be an MV-algebra such that:*

(i) $(N_A(W_1))^{\perp} \neq \{0\}$ and
(ii) $\frac{A}{(N_A(W_1))^{\perp}}$ has no maximal ideals of type 1.

Then Max_1A is a clopen Boolean subspace of $SpecA$.

Proof. By Proposition 51 we have only to show that he set of all maximal ideals of type 1 of A is an open subset of $SpecA$.

Since $\frac{A}{(N_A(W_1))^{\perp}}$ has no maximal ideals of type 1, $N_{\frac{A}{(N(W_1))^{\perp}}}(W_1) = \frac{A}{(N_A(W_1))^{\perp}}$. Thus for some $u \in N_A(W_1)$, $\frac{u}{(N_A(W_1))^{\perp}} = \frac{1}{(N_A(W_1))^{\perp}}$ and $u^* \in (N_A(W_1))^{\perp}$. If $x \in N_A(W_1)$, then $x \wedge u^* = 0$ so $x \leq u$. It follows that $N_A(W_1) = id\{u\}$ and $(N_A(W_1))^{\perp} = id\{u^*\}$.

Claim: $U(u^*) = Max_1A$.

Indeed, let J be a maximal ideal of A of type 1. Since $u \in N_A(W_1)$, we get $u \in J$ and $u^* \notin J$; so $J \in U(u^*)$.

Assume now $J \in U(u^*)$. Then, since $u \wedge u^* = 0$, $u \in J$. From this $N_A(W_1) \subseteq J$ and $J \in Max_1A$. By the Claim the proposition is proved.

Example. Now we will exhibit an example of MV-algebra, satisfying the hypothesis of the previous theorem. Consider the MV-algebra $A' = [0,1]^{N_0}$. Let M be the maximal ideal $M = \{x \in A \mid x_0 = 0\}$ and $A = M \cup M^* = \{0,1\} \times 0,1]^N$. Then $N(W_1) \subseteq M$. We claim that A satisfies the conditions (i) and (ii) of Proposition 52.

Let $e \in A$ defined by $e_0 = 0$, $e_n = 1$, $n > 0$. We get $e \in M$ and $e^* \in (N_A(W_1))^{\perp} \neq \emptyset$.

Let $y \in A$ be defined by $y_0 = 0$, $y_n = \frac{1}{2}$, $n > 0$. Then $y \wedge y^* = y$ and so $y \in N_A(W_1) \subseteq M$. Since $e = y \oplus y = 2(y \wedge y^*) = 2W_1(y)$, we get $e \in N_A(W_1)$. From that

$$\frac{e}{(N_A(W_1))^{\perp}} = \frac{2W_1(y)}{(N_A(W_1))^{\perp}} = 2W_1(\frac{y}{(N_A(W_1))^{\perp}})$$

that means

$$\frac{e}{(N_A(W_1))^{\perp}} \in N_{\frac{A}{(N_A(W_1))^{\perp}}}(W_1).$$

Since $e^* \in (N_A(W_1))^{\perp}$,

$$\frac{e}{(N(W_1))^{\perp}} = \frac{1}{(N(W_1))^{\perp}}.$$

So $\frac{A}{(N_A(W_1))^{\perp}} = N_{\frac{A}{(N_A(W_1))^{\perp}}}(W_1)$ has no maximal ideals of type 1.

References

1. Ambrosio, R., Lettieri, A.: A classification of bipartite MV algebras. Math. Japon 38, 111–117 (1993)
2. Belluce, L.P.: Semisimple algebras of infinite valued logic and bold fuzzy set theory. Canad. J. Math. 38(6), 1356–1379 (1986)
3. Belluce, L.P.: α-complete MV-algebras. In: Höhle, U., Klement, E.P. (eds.) Non Classical Logics and Their Application to Fuzzy Sets, pp. 7–22. Kluwer Academy Publisher, Dordrecht (1992)
4. Cella, C., Lettieri, A.: Preboolean MV-algebras as Bipartire MV-algebras. Stochastica XIII-1, 31–36 (1992)
5. Cignoli, R., D'Ottaviano, I.M.L., Mundici, D.: Algebraic Foundations of many-valued Reasoning. Kluwer Academic Publishers, Dordrecht (2000)
6. Di Nola, A., Lettieri, A.: Perfect MV-algebras are categorically equivalent to abelian ℓ-groups. Studia Logica 53, 417–432 (1994)
7. Di Nola, A., Lettieri, A.: Equational Characterization of All Varieties of MV-algebras. Journal of Algebra 221, 463–474 (1999)
8. Di Nola, A., Lettieri, A.: One Chain Generated Varieties of MV-algebras e. Journal of Algebra 225, 667–697 (2000)
9. Di Nola, A., Liguori, F., Sessa, S.: Using Maximal Ideals In The Classification of MV-algebras. Portugaliae Mathematica 50(1) (1993)

Implicit Operations in MV-Algebras and the Connectives of Łukasiewicz Logic

Xavier Caicedo

Department of Mathematics,
Universidad de los Andes,
A.A. 4976, Bogotá
xcaicedo@uniandes.edu.co

Dedicated to Daniele Mundici

Abstract. It is shown that a conservative expansion of infinite valued Łukasiewicz logic by new connectives univocally determined by their axioms does not necessarily have a complete semantics in the real interval [0,1]. However, such extensions are always complete with respect to valuations in a family of MV-chains. Rational Łukasiewicz logic being the largest one that has a complete semantics in [0,1]. In addition, this logic does not admit expansions by axiomatic implicit connectives that are not already explicit. Similar results are obtained for n-valued Łukasiewicz logic and for the logic of abelian lattice ordered groups. These and related results are obtained by the study of compatible operations implicitly defined by identities in the varieties of MV-algebras and abelian ℓ-groups; the pertaining algebraic results having independent interest.

1 Introduction

Much research effort has been devoted to enrich propositional Łukasiewicz logic with new connectives in order to enhance its geometric expressiveness and algebraic significance. These connectives are usually introduced as new operations in the real interval $[0, 1]$, in consonance with the role of Łukasiewicz logic as one of the basic models of fuzzy logic. We present here a different approach that seems natural from the proof theoretic and algebraic perspectives and may contribute to clarify the possibilities of this quest.

Consider a conservative extension $L(C)$ of an algebraizable deductive calculus $L = (L, \vdash_L)$, by axiom schemes which define univocally a new n-ary connective symbol C. That means that the duplicate system $L(C) \cup L(C')$ deduces $C(p_1...p_n) \leftrightarrow C'(p_1...p_n)$, where $\leftrightarrow$ is the equivalence formula associated to the algebraizability of L. Then we say that C is an (axiomatic) implicit connective of L. If there is a formula $\varphi \in L$ such that $\vdash_{L(C)} C(p_1...p_n) \leftrightarrow \varphi(p_1...p_n)$, we say that C is explicit; otherwise, it is a proper implicit connective of L.

It is shown in [9] that any implicit connective of classical propositional calculus is explicit, but that is not the case for Heyting intuitionistic calculus where one has instead the approximation $\vdash_{Heyt(C)} \neg\neg C(p_1...p_n) \leftrightarrow \varphi(p_1...p_n)$. We do

S. Aguzzoli et al.(Eds.): Algebraic and Proof-theoretic Aspects, LNAI 4460, pp. 50–68, 2007.

not have at the moment a clear picture of the implicit connectives of intuition-istic logic; however, the intermediate calculus G_n given by n-valued Gödel logic possesses a proper implicit connective S such that the extension $G_n(S)$ does not allow proper implicit connectives. Something similar is shown to hold for n-valued Łukasiewicz logic L_n in [8].

We study in this paper the implicit connectives of infinite-valued Łukasiewicz calculus Ł. This logic has infinitely many proper implicit connectives: among others, the division connectives introduced in [3] and utilized in [15] to define Rational Łukasiewicz logic RŁ. The latter logic is complete with respect to its natural interpretation in the real interval $[0, 1]$, according to [15], and it is shown in [3] to satisfy a natural extension of McNaughton's theorem, and to be the minimum extension of Ł having the interpolation property.

Our main results here are the following:

Any implicit connective of RŁ is explicit (Theorem 7).

Thus, RŁ is maximal with respect to extensions by implicit connectives. How-ever, it is not the largest extension of Ł by implicit connectives. We exhibit such extensions which are sound but not complete with respect to values in $[0, 1]$, and thus they can not be interpreted faithfully into RŁ (Theorem 3). On the other hand, we show that any extension of Ł by implicit connectives is complete with respect to a family of MV-chains, thus qualifying as a fuzzy logic in the broad sense (Theorem 2, cf. [13]). Among those, RŁ is the largest one having a complete semantics with values in $[0, 1]$:

Any extension of Ł by implicit connectives having a complete semantics in $[0, 1]$ *has a faithful syntactic interpretation into* RŁ (Theorem 8).

The latter result implies, for example, that the product connective of combined product logic ŁΠ (cf. [20]) is not an implicit connective of Ł since it is not interpretable into RŁ; that is, it can not be characterized univocally by any axiomatization whatsoever.

We review also the case of n-valued Łukasiewicz calculus L_n, showing sim-ilar results, and exhibiting examples of implicit connectives whose logic is not complete with respect to a single MV-chain.

Our main tool are the results of [8] which imply that any extension $L(\mathcal{C})$ of Ł by a family $\mathcal{C}$ of implicit connectives is algebraizable by a variety of enriched MV-algebras, where the operations interpreting the connectives in $\mathcal{C}$ are implic-itly defined by identities and are compatible with all the MV-algebra congru-ences. Therefore, studying implicit connectives of Łukasiewicz logic amounts to studying compatible operations implicitly defined by identities in the variety of MV-algebras. Our main algebraic result in this direction may have independent interest (DMV-algebras are the enriched MV-algebras of RŁ):

Any compatible operation defined implicitly by identities in the variety of DMV-algebras is given by a term of the variety (Theorem 5).

For the variety of lattice ordered abelian groups, related to MV-algebras by Mundici's functor [21], we have:

Any compatible operation defined implicitly by identities in divisible lattice ordered abelian groups is given by a $\mathbb{Q}$-vector lattice term. (Theorem 10).

The last result allows us to prove analogues of the previous results for the Logic of equilibrium introduced in [14].

We refer the reader to [7], [6], and [12] as standard references for the concepts of universal algebra, algebraizable logics, and model theory utilized in this paper.

2   Preliminaries

We start with some general preliminaries on implicit operations in varieties of algebras and their relation to implicit connectives.

Let $\mathbb{V}$ be a variety of algebras of type τ and let $\mathcal{E}(\mathcal{C})$ be (the universal closure of) a set of identities of type $\tau \cup \mathcal{C}$ where $\mathcal{C}$ is a family of new function symbols.

Definition 1. $\mathcal{E}(\mathcal{C})$ *defines implicitly $\mathcal{C}$ in $\mathbb{V}$, if in each algebra $A \in \mathbb{V}$ there is at most one family $\{\nabla^A : A^n \longrightarrow A\}_{\nabla \in \mathcal{C}}$ such that $(A, \nabla^A)_{\nabla \in \mathcal{C}} \models \mathcal{E}(\mathcal{C})$. We say then that $\mathcal{C}$ is an *implicit family of operations of $\mathbb{V}$*, or an *implicit operation* in case it has single member.

The class

$$\mathbb{V}(\mathcal{C}) = \{(A, \nabla^A)_{\nabla \in \mathcal{C}} : A \in \mathbb{V}, \ (A, \nabla^A)_{\nabla \in \mathcal{C}} \models \mathcal{E}(\mathcal{C})\}.$$

is a new variety of type $\tau \cup \mathcal{C}$. The class $Red_{\mathcal{C}}$ of *reducts* of $\mathbb{V}(\mathcal{C})$, that is, those algebras of $\mathbb{V}$ where each $\nabla \in \mathcal{C}$ exists, does not need to be all of $\mathbb{V}$. In case $Red_{\mathcal{C}}$ generates $\mathbb{V}$ then $\mathbb{V}(\mathcal{C})$ is *conservative* over $\mathbb{V}$, that is, any identity of type τ holding in $\mathbb{V}(\mathcal{C})$ already holds in $\mathbb{V}$.

The following lemmas collect some basic facts about implicit operations.

Lemma 1. *Let $\mathcal{C}$ be an implicit family of operations of $\mathbb{V}$. Then*
1. Each $\nabla \in \mathcal{C}$ has an explicit first order definition $\theta_\nabla(\mathbf{x}, y)$ of type τ. That is, for any $A \in Red_{\mathcal{C}}$ and $\mathbf{x}$, y in A

$$y = \nabla^A(\mathbf{x}) \Leftrightarrow A \models \theta_\nabla(y, \mathbf{x}).$$

2. The class $Red_{\mathcal{C}}$ is first order axiomatizable.
3. If each $\nabla \in \mathcal{C}$ exists in A_i for all $i \in I$ then it exists and is computed componentwise in the product $\Pi_i A_i$. The same is true for reduced products $\Pi_i A_i / F$.

Proof. 1. This is a simultaneous form of Beth's definability theorem. Without loss of generality, assume that $\mathcal{E}(\mathcal{C})$ contains the defining identities of $\mathbb{V}$ and $\mathcal{E}(\mathcal{C}')$ is a duplicate of $\mathcal{E}(\mathcal{C})$ with disjoint copies of the symbols in $\mathcal{C}$. Pick $\nabla \in \mathcal{C}$ and fix distinct variables $y, \mathbf{x}$, then $\mathcal{E}(\mathcal{C}) \cup \mathcal{E}(\mathcal{C}') \models \nabla(\mathbf{x}) = \nabla'(\mathbf{x})$ by hypothesis, and $\mathcal{E}(\mathcal{C})$ may be assumed to be a single sentence by compactness of first order logic. Thus, the above may be written $\mathcal{E}(\mathcal{C}) \wedge y = \nabla(\mathbf{x}) \models \mathcal{E}(\mathcal{C}') \rightarrow y = \nabla'(\mathbf{x})$, and Craig's interpolation lemma yields an interpolant $\theta_\nabla(y, \mathbf{x})$ which does not contain the operation symbols in $\mathcal{C}$ or $\mathcal{C}'$. Standard logical manipulations give then $\mathcal{E}(\mathcal{C}) \models y = \nabla(\mathbf{x}) \leftrightarrow \theta_\nabla(y, \mathbf{x})$, which proves the claim.

2. All operations $\nabla \in \mathcal{C}$ exist in A if and only if A satisfies the set of sentences $\{\forall \mathbf{x} \exists! y \theta_\nabla(y, \mathbf{x})\}_{\nabla \in \mathcal{C}} \cup \mathcal{E}(\nabla/\theta_\nabla)_{\nabla \in \mathcal{C}}$, where $\mathcal{E}(\nabla/\theta_\nabla)_{\nabla \in \mathcal{C}}$ is the result of rewriting the identities in $\mathcal{E}(\mathcal{C})$ so that all the occurrences of $\nabla \in \mathcal{C}$ appear in the form $y = \nabla(\mathbf{x})$ and then replacing these by $\theta_\nabla(y, \mathbf{x})$. For example, $\nabla_1(\nabla_1(v, x), x) = \nabla_2 v$ should be rewritten: $\forall y \forall y'[(y = \nabla_1(v, x) \wedge y' = \nabla_2 v) \rightarrow y' = \nabla_1(y, x)]$, and then $\forall u[\theta_{\nabla_1}(y, v, x) \wedge \theta_{\nabla_2}(y', v) \rightarrow \theta_{\nabla_1}(y', y, x)]$.

3. If $(A, \nabla^A)_{\nabla \in \mathcal{C}} \models \mathcal{E}(\mathcal{C})$ for all $i \in I$ then $\Pi_{i/F}(A_i, \nabla^{A_i})_{\nabla \in \mathcal{C}} \models \mathcal{E}(\mathcal{C})$ for any filter F over I because identities are preserved by reduced products. $\qquad \square$

Definition 2. An implicit operation ∇ of $\mathbb{V}$ will be *compatible* if for any $A \in Red_\mathcal{C}$ the congruences of A are congruences of $(A, \nabla^A)_{\nabla \in \mathcal{C}}$.

Not every implicit operation of a variety is compatible. For example, the identities

$$nD_n(x) = x, \quad D_n(nx) = x$$

$(n \geq 2)$ define an implicit operation in the variety of abelian groups, since any other operation f satisfying the second equation must satisfy $f(x) = f(nD_n(x)) = D_n(x)$. It may be seen that D_n exists exactly in the n-divisible abelian groups having no elements of order n, where $D_n(x) = \frac{1}{n}x$ is well defined. But this operation is not compatible because we have $k \equiv 0 \pmod{\mathbb{Z}}$ in the group $(\mathbb{Q}, +, -, 0)$ for any integer k, but $D_n(k) \not\equiv D_n(0) \pmod{\mathbb{Z}}$ if n does not divide k.

Lemma 2. Let $\mathcal{C}$ be an implicit family of compatible operations of $\mathbb{V}$.
1. If $h : A \rightarrow B$ is an onto homomorphism of $\mathbb{V}$ and all $\nabla \in \mathcal{C}$ exist in A then all them exist in B and $h\nabla^A(a_1, .., a_n) = \nabla^B(h(a_1), .., h(a_n))$.
2. Reducts of subdirectly irreducible algebras of $\mathbb{V}(\mathcal{C})$ are subdirectly irreducible in $\mathbb{V}$.

Proof. 1. If $h : A \rightarrow B$ is an onto homomorphism and ∇^A is compatible with $Ker(h)$, then the function $f_\nabla(h(a)) = h(\nabla^A(a))$ is well defined in B. Therefore, $h : (A, \nabla^A)_{\nabla \in \mathcal{C}} \rightarrow (B, f_\nabla)_{\nabla \in \mathcal{C}}$ becomes an homomorphism. As $(A, \nabla^A)_{\nabla \in \mathcal{C}} \models \mathcal{E}(\mathcal{C})$, then $(B, f_\nabla)_{\nabla \in \mathcal{C}} \models \mathcal{E}(\mathcal{C})$ and by definition $f_\nabla = \nabla^B$.
2. Since $(A, \nabla^A)_{\nabla \in \mathcal{C}}$ and A have the same congruences, a monolith of the first structure is a monolith of the second. $\qquad \square$

Our interest in compatible implicit operations is explained by their relation to implicit connectives of algebraizable logics given by Theorem 1 below. We will consider only logics $\mathcal{L}$ which are strongly algebraizable in the sense of Blok and Pigozzi (cf. [6]) with respect to an equivalence formula $\leftrightarrow$ and a constant formula 1 of the calculus. This means that

$$\varphi \vdash_\mathcal{L} \varphi \leftrightarrow 1, \qquad \varphi \leftrightarrow 1 \vdash_\mathcal{L} \varphi \qquad \text{(a)}$$

and there is a variety of algebras $\mathbb{V}$, of the same signature as the logic, such that the following algebraic completeness theorem holds:

$$\{\varphi_i \leftrightarrow \psi_i\}_{i \leq n} \vdash_\mathcal{L} \varphi \leftrightarrow \psi \text{ if and only if } \{\varphi_i = \psi_i\}_{i \leq n} \models_\mathbb{V} \varphi = \psi; \qquad \text{(b)}$$

equivalently, due to (a),

$$\{\varphi_i\}_{i \leq n} \vdash_{\mathcal{L}} \varphi \text{ if and only if } \{\varphi_i = 1\}_{i \leq n} \models_V \varphi = 1, \qquad (c)$$

the usual completeness with respect to valuations in all the algebras of V. Notice that we use, as we will keep on using throughout the paper, the formulas of the calculus as terms of the variety.

Most familiar logics are algebraizable in this sense. By finiteness of the deductions in $\mathcal{L}$ and compactness of first order logic applied to V, (c) holds for infinite theories $\{\varphi_i\}_{i \in I}$. In fact, this *strong algebraic completeness* may be achieved by taking only valuations in the subdirectly irreducible algebras of V:

$$\{\varphi_i\}_{i \in I} \vdash_{\mathcal{L}} \varphi \text{ if and only if } \{\varphi_i = 1\}_{i \in I} \models_{S.I.(V)} \varphi = 1. \qquad (sc)$$

Now, let $\mathcal{L}(\mathcal{C})$ be an extension of $\mathcal{L}$ by a system of axiom schemes $\mathcal{A}(\mathcal{C})$ involving a family of new connective symbols $\mathcal{C}$, and let

$$\mathcal{A}^*(\mathcal{C}) = \{\varphi = 1 : \varphi \in \mathcal{A}(\mathcal{C})\};$$

then we may define the variety

$$V(\mathcal{C}) = \{(A, f_\nabla)_{\nabla \in \mathcal{C}} : A \in V, (A, f_\nabla)_{\nabla \in \mathcal{C}} \models \mathcal{A}^*(\mathcal{C})\}.$$

One has by construction that $\vdash_{\mathcal{L}(\mathcal{C})} \varphi$ implies $\models_{V(\mathcal{C})} \varphi = 1$, but the reciprocal does not necessarily hold. That is, we can not claim that $\mathcal{L}(\mathcal{C})$ is algebraizable by $V(\mathcal{C})$. However, algebraicity is obtained in the following case.

Definition 3. $\mathcal{L}(\mathcal{C})$ *defines implicitly* $\mathcal{C}$ *over* $\mathcal{L}$ *if* $\vdash \nabla\mathbf{p} \leftrightarrow \nabla'\mathbf{p}$ *for each* $\nabla \in \mathcal{C}$, *where* $\mathcal{A}(\mathcal{C}')$ *is a duplicate of* $\mathcal{A}(\mathcal{C})$ *with a new connective symbol* ∇' *replacing each* $\nabla \in \mathcal{C}$.

Theorems 1 and 4 in [8] yield:

Theorem 1. *If* $\mathcal{L}$ *is algebraizable by a variety of algebras* V, *and* $\mathcal{L}(\mathcal{C}) = \mathcal{L} \cup \mathcal{A}(\mathcal{C})$ *defines implicitly a family of connectives* $\mathcal{C}$ *over* $\mathcal{L}$, *then* $\mathcal{A}^*(\mathcal{C})$ *defines an implicit family of compatible operations of* V *(that we denote* $\mathcal{C}$ *also) and* $\mathcal{L}(\mathcal{C})$ *is algebraizable by* $V(\mathcal{C})$, *by means of the same formulas* $\leftrightarrow$ *and* 1 *as* $\mathcal{L}$.

This theorem fails in various ways if the extension does not define implicitly $\mathcal{C}$. It may happen that $\mathcal{L}(\mathcal{C})$ is not algebraizable at all, or that it is algebraizable by algebras not having reducts in V, or that it is algebraizable for algebras with reducts in V but the interpretation of the connectives in $\mathcal{C}$ is not compatible. See [8] for examples.

3   Implicit Connectives of Łukasiewicz Logic

Infinitely valued Łukasiewicz calculus L has the primitive connectives $\rightarrow$, $\neg$, and the following axioms plus the Modus Ponens rule:

$$p \to (q \to p)$$
$$(p \to q) \to ((q \to r) \to (p \to r))$$
$$((p \to q) \to q) \to ((q \to p) \to p)$$
$$(\neg p \to \neg q) \to (q \to p).$$

Its expressive power is better revealed by the use of the following explicitly defined connectives:

$$p \curlyvee q := (p \to q) \to q$$
$$p \curlywedge q := \neg(\neg p \curlyvee \neg q)$$
$$p \leftrightarrow q := (p \to q) \curlywedge (q \to p)$$
$$1 := p \to p$$
$$0 := \neg(p \to p)$$
$$p \oplus q := \neg p \to q$$
$$p \odot q := \neg(p \to \neg q).$$

For each integer $n \geq 2$, the abbreviations:

$$np := \underbrace{p \oplus \ldots \oplus p}_{n} \quad \text{and} \quad p^{n} := \underbrace{p \odot \ldots \odot p}_{n},$$

are unambiguous up to equivalence due to associativity and commutativity of $\oplus$ and $\odot$. The set $\{\oplus, \neg\}$ serves as a complete set of connectives because $\vdash_{\mathrm{L}} (p \to q) \leftrightarrow (\neg p \oplus q)$. We will assume familiarity with this calculus. For a full account we refer the reader to [10].

Utilizing $\{\oplus, \neg, 0\}$ as primitive connectives (0 superfluous but convenient), Łukasiewicz logic is algebraizable with respect to the defined connectives $\leftrightarrow$ and 1 by the variety of MV-*algebras,* $\mathcal{MV}$, variety generated as a quasivariety by the Łukasiewicz algebra

$$[0,1]_{MV} = ([0,1], \oplus, \neg, 0), \qquad x \oplus y = \min\{x + y, 1\}, \qquad \neg x = 1 - x.$$

Any MV-algebra has a natural lattice order defined by $x \leq y$ iff $(x \to y) = 1$, where $\curlyvee, \curlywedge$ become the join and meet, and $0, 1$ become minimum and maximum, respectively. Chang's representation theorem [11] says that the subdirectly irreducible algebras of this variety are MV-*chains* (linearly ordered MV-algebras) and thus any MV-algebra is a subdirect product of MV-chains. Moreover, $[0,1]_{MV}$ generates $\mathcal{MV}$ as a quasivariety and thus we have Chang's completeness theorem: [1]

$$\{\varphi_i\}_{i \leq n} \vdash_{\mathrm{L}} \varphi \text{ if and only if } \{\varphi_i = 1\}_{i \leq n} \models_{[0,1]} \varphi = 1.$$

It is well known that Ł is not strongly complete with respect to $[0,1]_{MV}$; that is, the above does not hold for infinite theories. However, Ł is strongly complete for valuation in all MV-chains, by (sc) in the previous section. In fact, it is enough to take the divisible MV-chains because any MV-chain is embeddable in a divisible one.

---

[1] Chang's theorem is usually stated with an empty set of premises but it is equivalent to the given version because Ł has a form of the Deduction Theorem.

Strong completeness with respect to a family of totally ordered algebras has been proposed as a test for being a 'fuzzy logic' in [13]. Our first observation is that any extension of Łukasiewicz logic by implicit connectives qualifies as a fuzzy logic in this sense.

Theorem 2. *Any extension* $Ł(\mathcal{C})$ *of* $Ł$ *by implicit connectives is strongly complete with respect to the class of* $\mathcal{MV}(\mathcal{C})$-*chains.*

Proof. By Theorem 1, $Ł(\mathcal{C})$ is algebraizable by the variety $\mathcal{MV}(\mathcal{C})$ where $\mathcal{C}$ is an implicit family of compatible operations of $\mathcal{MV}$. Thus, by (sc), $Ł(\mathcal{C})$ is strongly complete with respect to valuations in the subdirectly irreducible algebras of $\mathcal{MV}(\mathcal{C})$, which by Lemma 2-2 have subdirectly irreducible reducts in $\mathcal{MV}$ and thus are chains. □

However, we will see later (Theorem 3) that $Ł(\mathcal{C})$ does not need to be complete, even the less strongly complete, with respect to values in the algebra $[0,1]_{MV}$.

3.1   Division Connectives, Rational Łukasiewicz Logic

For $n \geq 2$, the axiom schemes:

(A1) $n\delta_n p \to p$
(A2) $p \to n\delta_n p$
(A3) $(p \to nq) \to (\delta_n p \to q)$

define an implicit connective δ_n of $Ł$. To see this, assume the same axioms for a different connective symbol λ:

(A1$_\lambda$) $n\lambda p \to p$,   (A2$_\lambda$) $p \to n\lambda p$,   (A3$_\lambda$) $(p \to nq) \to (\lambda p \to q)$.

Then A3 gives $(p \to n\lambda p) \to (\delta_n p \to \lambda p)$ and Modus Ponens with A2$_\lambda$ yields $\delta_n p \to \lambda p$. Similarly, A3$_\lambda$ and A2 give $\lambda p \to \delta_n p$. In sum, $\vdash_{Ł(\delta_n) \cup Ł(\lambda)} \delta_n p \leftrightarrow \lambda p$.

This axiom system is equivalent to the one given in [15] with a different version for the third axiom. These connectives were introduced semantically in [3] and are explicitly definable from the propositional existential quantifier introduced in [1].

According to Theorem 1, $Ł(\delta_n)$ is algebraized by the variety $\mathcal{MV}(\delta_n)$, where δ_n is a compatible operation defined implicitly by the inequalities

$n\delta_n(x) \leq x$
$x \leq n\delta_n(x)$
$(x \to ny) \leq (\delta_n(x) \to y)$.

The reader may verify, after some computation, that these reduce to the single identity:

$$(n-1)\delta_n(x) = x \odot \neg\delta_n(x).$$

This operation exists exactly in the n-*divisible* MV-algebras introduced in [17]. In particular, $\delta_n(x) = \frac{1}{n}x$ in $[0,1]_{MV}$, and it does not exist in any finite non trivial algebra.

The calculus $R\text{Ł} = L(\delta_n)_{n \geq 2}$, obtained by adding the axioms of δ_n to L for all $n \geq 2$, is called *Rational Łukasiewicz logic* in [15], and the corresponding variety $\mathcal{MV}(\delta_n)_{n \geq 2}$, consisting of divisible MV-algebras enriched with all the operations δ_n, is called the variety of DMV-algebras, $\mathcal{DMV}$ for short.

It follows immediately from Lemma 2-2 that each DMV-algebra is a subdirect product of DMV-chains. Moreover, Theorem 2, together with the first order completeness of the theory of non trivial divisible MV-chains (see [17]), yields a quick proof of completeness of RŁ with respect to values in $[0, 1]$:

Proposition 1. (Th 4.3, [15]) $R\text{Ł} = L(\delta_n)_{n \geq 2}$ *is complete with respect to valuations in* $([0, 1]_{MV}, \delta_n)_{n \geq 2}$.

Proof. By Theorem 2, RŁ is algebraically complete with respect to all DMV-chains. But any no trivial divisible MV-chain is elementarily equivalent to $[0, 1]_{MV}$ by first order completeness. By first order definability of the δ_n, this means that all non trivial DMV-chains are elementarily equivalent to $([0, 1]_{MV}, \delta_n)_{n \geq 2}$. Hence, any quasi-identity holds in all DMV chains if and only if it holds in this algebra.   □

3.2   Approximate Division Connectives

We exhibit now a family of implicit connectives whose calculus is sound but not complete for values in $[0, 1]_{MV}$. It is clear from the proof of uniqueness of δ_n in the previous example that the pair of axioms

(B1) $p \to n\delta_n^* p$
(B2) $(p \to nq) \to (\delta_n^* p \to q)$

already define an implicit connective of L. Regarding its algebraic interpretation we have:

Proposition 2. δ_n^* *exist in a MV-chain M if and only if* $\min\{y \in M : ny \geq x\}$ *exists for all* $x \in M$, *in which case* $\delta_n^*(x)$ *is that minimum.*

Proof. The identities defining the variety $\mathcal{MV}(\delta_n^*)$ become:

(E1) $x \leq n\delta_n^* x$,   (E2) $\neg x \oplus ny \leq \neg\delta_n^* x \oplus y$.

Assume they hold in a chain M and $x \leq ny$ there. Then $\neg x \oplus ny = 1$ and thus $\neg\delta_n^* x \oplus y = 1$ by E2, which means $\delta_n^* x \leq y$. Together with E1, this shows $\delta_n^* x = \min\{y : ny \geq x\}$. Reciprocally, assume the function $f(x) = \min\{y : ny \geq x\}$ exists in a chain. Then f satisfies (E1) by definition. For the second equation, consider first $f(x) \leq y$, then $\neg f(x) \oplus y = 1$ and thus E2 holds trivially. Consider now $y < f(x)$, then $ny < x$ by definition of f and thus $u = x \odot \neg ny > 0$. Moreover, $x = ny \oplus u \leq ny \oplus nu = n(y \oplus u)$, which implies $y \oplus u \geq f(x)$. Suppose E2 is false, then $\neg x \oplus ny > \neg f(x) \oplus y$ and taking negations $u = x \odot \neg ny < f(x) \odot \neg y$. Adding y to both sides gives: $y \oplus u < y \oplus (f(x) \odot \neg y) = f(x)$, a contradiction.   □

Therefore, δ_n^* exists in $[0, 1]_{MV}$ where it coincides with $\delta_n(x) = \frac{1}{n}x$, and it exists also in the finite Łukasiewicz chains

$$L_k = (\{0, \tfrac{1}{k-1}, .., 1\}, \oplus, \neg), \qquad k \geq 2,$$

as well as in all finite MV-algebras by Lemma 1 (3), because these are products of L_k's. However, the reader may check that δ_n^* does not exist in any of the Komori algebras K_m, [16]. Observe that if δ_n exists in a MV-algebra M then δ_n^* also exists in M and coincides there with δ_n, because δ_n^M satisfies the defining identities of δ_n^*. With this observation it is easy to show:

Theorem 3. $Ł(\delta_n^*)$ *is sound but not complete for values in* $([0,1]_{MV}, \delta_n^*)$.

Proof. Soundness is clear because δ_n^* exists in $[0,1]_{MV}$. Now, $\nvdash_{Ł(\delta_n^*)} (n-1)\delta_n^*1 \leftrightarrow \neg\delta_n^*1$ because the equation $(n-1)x = \neg x$ does not have solutions in L_n. But $([0,1]_{MV}, \delta_n^*)$ can not refute this because δ_n^* coincides in $[0,1]_{MV}$ with δ_n and $\delta_n 1 = \frac{1}{n}$ satisfies the given equation.   □

We do not know if $Ł(\delta_n^*)$ is complete with respect to a single chain.

4   Lattice-Ordered Abelian Groups and MV-Algebras

Abelian lattice ordered groups, *ℓ-groups* for short, are abelian groups with a lattice order compatible with the group operations. They may be presented as a variety $\ell\mathcal{G}$ in the vocabulary $\{+, -, 0, \curlyvee, \curlywedge\}$ where $-$ represents difference and $\curlyvee, \curlywedge$ represent the join and meet of the lattice order, respectively. The homomorphism must preserve not only the group structure and the order but also $\curlyvee$ and $\curlywedge$. We refer the reader to [5] for full details, but emphasize here the following facts:

Fact 1. ℓ-groups are closed under lexicographic products. We will utilize the notation $G \otimes H$ to denote lexicographic product (left priority).

Fact 2. Linearly ordered abelian groups may be expanded naturally to ℓ-groups. All subdirectly irreducible ℓ-groups are linearly ordered.

Fact 3. Any ℓ-group may be embedded in a divisible abelian ℓ-group, the usual divisible hull of the group with a naturally extended order.

We will need also the following model theoretic fact. Recall that a first order theory has *elimination of quantifiers* if for any formula $\theta(\mathbf{x})$ of the language of the theory there is a quantifier free formula $\psi(\mathbf{x})$ which is equivalent to $\theta(\mathbf{x})$ in all models of the theory (see [12]).

Fact 4. The theory of non trivial linearly ordered divisible groups (or ℓ-groups) is complete and has elimination of quantifiers with respect to the language $\{+, -, 0, <\}$ ([22], [10], Cor. 3.1.17 [18]), also with respect to the language $\{+, -, 0, \curlyvee, \curlywedge\}$ because in the context of total order $x < y$ is equivalent to the formula $x \curlywedge y \neq y$.

Consider now the relation between ℓ-groups and MV-algebras.

Definition 4. A *unital ℓ-group* will be a pair (G, u) where G is an ℓ-group and $u \geq 0$. If for any $x \in G$ there is n such that $nu \geq x$, then u is a *strong unit*.

We will need the following refinement of Fact 4.

Lemma 3. *The theory of linearly ordered divisible unital ℓ-groups (G, u) with $u > 0$ is complete.*

Proof. This theory trivially inherits elimination of quantifiers from the theory of linearly ordered divisible ℓ-groups (Fact 4). Therefore, it is model complete (that is, any embedding between its models is elementary, see [12]). To obtain completeness it is enough to notice that $(\mathbb{Q}, +, -, 0, <, 1)$ is a prime model of the theory (it is embeddable in all other models). Indeed, if $u > 0$, the unique group homomorphism $(\mathbb{Z}, 1) \rightarrow (G, u)$ sending 1 to u is injective and preserves the order, and it may be extended canonically to $\mathbb{Q}$ maintaining the same characteristics.   □

Notice that the previous result does not hold if we add two distinguished constants $0 < u_1 < u_2$ to ℓ-groups since $(\mathbb{Q}, 1, 2) \not\equiv (\mathbb{Q}, 1, 3)$.

Unital ℓ-groups form a variety $\ell\mathcal{G}_*$ whose morphisms are the ℓ-group homomorphism preserving the constant u. The functor $\Gamma : \ell\mathcal{G}_* \rightarrow \mathcal{MV}$ associates to each unital ℓ-group an MV-algebra by generalizing the definition of the Lukasiewicz algebra $[0, 1]_{MV}$:

$$\Gamma(G, u) = ([0, u], \oplus, \neg, 0), \qquad x \oplus y := (x + y) \curlywedge u, \qquad \neg x := u - x$$
$$\Gamma(h) = h \upharpoonright [0, u].$$

Mundici [21] has shown that his functor has a left adjoint

$$\Sigma : \mathcal{MV} \rightarrow \ell\mathcal{G}_*$$

such that $\Gamma \circ \Sigma = I_{\mathcal{MV}}$ and Σ establishes an equivalence of categories between $\mathcal{MV}$ and the subcategory of $\ell\mathcal{G}_*$ where u is a strong unit. In particular, any MV-algebra is of the form $M = \Gamma(\Sigma M)$. The following may be easily verified by construction or in general categorical grounds:

Lemma 4. *Γ and Σ preserve divisibility, linear order, and injectivity of homomorphisms. Hence, for any MV-algebras M, N :*
1. M is divisible iff ΣM is divisible.
2. M is a chain iff ΣM is linearly ordered.
3. $h : M \rightarrow N$ is an injective homomorphism iff $\Sigma h : M \rightarrow N$ is injective.

Clearly, $\Gamma(G, u)$ is first order definable in (G, u). This definability is best expressed by the following translation (cf. [10]). To any first order formula $\theta(\mathbf{x})$ in the language $\{\oplus, \neg, 0\}$ of MV-algebras associate $\theta^*(\mathbf{x}, u)$, in the language $\{+, -, 0, \curlyvee, \curlywedge\}$ of ℓ-groups, by the following substitution of atomic terms

$$0 \longmapsto 0, \qquad x \oplus y \longmapsto (x + y) \curlywedge u, \qquad \neg x \longmapsto u - x,$$

and restriction of quantifiers to the interval $[0, u]$. Then, for any unital ℓ-group (G, u) and any list of parameters $\mathbf{a}$ in $[0, u]$,

$$\Gamma(G, u) \models \theta[\mathbf{a}] \text{ iff } (G, u) \models \theta^*[\mathbf{a}, u].$$

In particular, for any MV-algebra M and choice of parameters $\mathbf{a}$ in M,

$$M \models \theta[\mathbf{a}] \text{ iff } \Sigma M \models \theta^*[\mathbf{a}, 1_M]. \tag{t}$$

The first order theory of non trivial divisible MV-chains was already mentioned to be complete, [17]. This is an immediate consequence of Lemma 3 and the translation (t), and it implies automatically the completeness of the theory of DMV-chains by definability of the δ_n. In fact, these theories inherit also full elimination of quantifiers from divisible linearly ordered ℓ-groups. Since this is not immediate because elimination of quantifiers is sensible to the vocabulary utilized, and we have not seen it mentioned in the literature, we provide a proof utilizing the following criterion:

Lemma 5. (Corollary 3.1.6, [18]) *T has elimination of quantifiers if and only if for any pair of models B, C of T having a common substructure A, not necessarily a model of T, and for any formula $\theta(\mathbf{x}, y)$ and choosing $\mathbf{a}$ of a list of parameters in A, it holds that $B \models \exists y \theta[\mathbf{a}, y]$ implies $C \models \exists y \theta[\mathbf{a}, y]$.*

Theorem 4. *The theory of non trivial divisible MV-chains (DMV-chains) has elimination of quantifiers in the language $\{\oplus, \neg, 0\}$.*

Proof. Let M, N be non trivial divisible MV-chains and A a common MV-subalgebra. By Lemma 4, we have injections $\Sigma A \leq \Sigma M$ and $\Sigma A \leq \Sigma N$ between totally ordered unital ℓ-groups with ΣM and ΣN non trivial and divisible. Now let $\theta(\mathbf{x}, y)$ be any formula of type $\{\oplus, \neg, 0\}$ and $\mathbf{a} \in A^r$, $m \in M$ be such that $M \models \theta[\mathbf{a}, m]$. Then $\Sigma M \models (0 \leq m \leq 1_M) \wedge \theta^*[\mathbf{a}, m, 1_M]$ by (t). Since $\mathbf{a}$ and $1_M = 1_N = 1_A$ belong to ΣA, by Fact 4 and the above criterion (Lemma 5), there is $n \in N$ such that $\Sigma N \models (0 \leq n \leq 1_M) \wedge \theta^*[\mathbf{a}, n, 1_M]$. Thus $N \models \varphi[\mathbf{a}, n]$ by (t) again. Once more by Lemma 5, we conclude that the theory of divisible MV-chains has elimination of quantifiers. The claim about DMV-chains is immediate from the first order definability of the δ_n. $\qquad\square$

5   Implicit Operations of MV-Algebras and Maximality of RŁ

The next result holds for each member of any implicit family of compatible operations. For the sake of simplicity, we consider a single operation only.

Theorem 5. *Any compatible operation implicitly defined by identities in DMV-algebras is given by a term of type $\{\oplus, \neg, \delta_n\}_{n \geq 2}$. Moreover, it exists in all the DMV-algebras or in the trivial algebra only.*

Proof. If such an operation ∇ exists in the trivial algebra only, 0 is the desired term. Assume it exists in a non trivial DMV-algebra M. Then, by compatibility of ∇ (Theorem 1), this operation exists in any non trivial subdirectly irreducible factor of M (Lemma 2-1), which must be a non trivial DMV-chain by Lemma 2-2. By completeness of the theory of these chains and the first order definability of Red_∇ (Lemma 1-2), ∇ exists in all non trivial DMV-chains, in particular in the chain $([0, 1]_{MV}, \delta_n)_n$. Let $\theta(y, \mathbf{x})$ be the explicit first order definition of ∇ given by Lemma 1-1, which we may assume to be given in the language of MV-algebras since the δ_n are first order definable, and let $\theta^*(y, \mathbf{x}, u)$ be its translation to the language of unital ℓ-groups where u is the unit constant. By (t), $\theta^*(y, \mathbf{x}, 1)$ defines $\nabla^{[0,1]} : [0, 1]^n \to [0, 1]$ as a partial function in the unital ℓ-group $(\mathbb{R}, 1)$. Since the join and meet $\curlyvee, \curlywedge$ are interdefinable with the order $<$, we may put $\theta^*(y, \mathbf{x}, 1)$ in the language $\{+, -, 0, <, 1\}$, then in quantifier free form using Fact 4, and finally in full disjunctive normal form $\bigvee_{\alpha} \theta_\alpha(y, \mathbf{x}, 1)$. Each θ_α is a conjunction of atomic formulas $t = 0$, $t < 0$ or their negations, where the term t has the form $k_0 y + \ldots + k_n x_n + k_{n+1}1$, $k_i \in \mathbb{Z}$. Negations may be eliminated because in linearly ordered groups: $t \neq 0 \Leftrightarrow (t < 0 \vee -t < 0)$ and $t \not< 0 \Leftrightarrow (t = 0 \vee -t < 0)$. Separating the atomic formulas where y appears with non zero coefficient, and solving for y, $\theta_\alpha(y, \mathbf{x}, 1)$ becomes equivalent in $(\mathbb{R}, 1)$ to:

$$\bigwedge_i y = t_i(\mathbf{x}, 1) \wedge \bigwedge_j y < s_j(\mathbf{x}, 1) \wedge \bigwedge_k u_k(\mathbf{x}, 1) = 0 \wedge \bigwedge_r v_r(\mathbf{x}, 1) < 0,$$

where some of the conjunctions may be empty and the terms t_i, s_j, u_k, v_r have now rational coefficients.

If the first large conjunction $\bigwedge_i$ is empty and there are values $b \in [0, 1]$, $\mathbf{a} \in [0, 1]^n$, satisfying $\theta_\alpha(b, \mathbf{a}, 1)$, then by density of $<$ in $[0, 1]$ there are infinitely many values $y \in [0, 1]$ satisfying $\theta_\alpha(y, \mathbf{a}, 1)$. This contradicts the functionality of $\theta^*(y, \mathbf{x}, 1)$. Therefore, the first large conjunction is non-empty (or θ_α is unsatisfiable and thus superfluous in the disjunctive normal form). Fixing one equation in the first conjunction, say $y = t_0(\mathbf{x}, 1)$, and substituting the other occurrences of y by t_0 throughout the formula, θ_α becomes

$$y = t_0 \wedge \bigwedge_i t_0 = t_i \wedge \bigwedge_j t_0 < s_j \wedge \bigwedge_k u_k = 0 \wedge \bigwedge_r v_r < 0$$

which may be rearranged to $\psi_\alpha(y, \mathbf{x}, 1)$:

$$y = t_0 \wedge \bigwedge_k u_k = 0 \wedge \bigwedge_r v_r < 0.$$

Thus $\theta^*(y, \mathbf{x}, 1)$ is equivalent in $(\mathbb{R}, 1)$ to a disjunction $\bigvee_{\alpha} \theta'_\alpha(y, \mathbf{x}, 1)$ which describes a definition by cases of $\nabla^{[0,1]}$:

$$\nabla^{[0,1]} \mathbf{x} = \begin{cases} t_0(\mathbf{x}, 1) & \text{if } \bigwedge_k u_{0k}(\mathbf{x}, 1) = 0 \wedge \bigwedge_r v_{0r}(\mathbf{x}, 1) < 0 \\ \vdots \\ t_m(\mathbf{x}, 1) & \text{if } \bigwedge_k u_{mk}(\mathbf{x}, 1) = 0 \wedge \bigwedge_r v_{mr}(\mathbf{x}, 1) < 0 \end{cases} \tag{d}$$

where t_i, u_{ik}, v_{ir} are linear terms with rational coefficients, and the regions R_i defined by the conditions in the right hand side determine a partition of $[0, 1]^n$. This could have been obtained also utilizing the fact that the theory of linearly ordered $\mathbb{Q}$-vector spaces is o-minimal (that is, any definable subset of the universe is a finite union of order intervals), see Corollary 7.6, Chap. 1, in [23].

Our aim now is to show that $\nabla^{[0,1]}$ is continuous. By the initial observations, ∇ exists in the DMV-chain $M = (\Gamma(\mathbb{R} \otimes \mathbb{R}, (1, 1)), \delta_n)_{n \geq 2}$, and it is defined as a partial function $\nabla^M : [(0,0),(1,1)]^n \to [(0,0),(1,1)]$ in the unital ℓ-group $(\mathbb{R} \otimes \mathbb{R},(1,1))$ by the formula $\theta^*(y,\mathbf{x},u)$. Since the latter group is elementarily equivalent to $(\mathbb{R},1)$ by Lemma 3 then it satisfies the sentence

$$\forall y \forall \mathbf{x} \in [0,u]^{n+1}(\theta^*(y,\mathbf{x},u) \leftrightarrow \bigvee_\alpha \theta'_\alpha(y,\mathbf{x},u)),$$

which says precisely that definition (d) by cases holds for $\nabla^M \mathbf{x}$ in $(\mathbb{R} \otimes \mathbb{R},(1,1))$ with the unital constant (1,1) in the place of 1 (notice that being these groups torsion free and divisible, the rational coefficients in the θ'_α are first order definable).

Moreover, the first projection $\pi_1 : (\mathbb{R} \otimes \mathbb{R},(1,1)) \to (\mathbb{R},1)$ is an onto homomorphism of unital ℓ-groups whose restriction to M gives an onto homomorphism $\pi_1 : M \to ([0,1]_{MV}, \delta_n)_n$ of MV-algebras, and a fortiori of DMV-algebras by compatibility of the δ_n.

We are ready to show that $\nabla^{[0,1]}$ is continuous. Suppose that is not the case; then there is a convergent sequence $\mathbf{a}_m \to \mathbf{a}$ in $[0,1]^n$ such that $\nabla^{[0,1]}(\mathbf{a}_n)$ does not converge to $\nabla^{[0,1]}(\mathbf{a})$. We may assume that $\{\mathbf{a}_n\} \subseteq R_i$ for some i because there are finitely many regions. Then $\nabla^{[0,1]}(\mathbf{a}_n) = t_i(\mathbf{a}_n,1) \to t_i(\mathbf{a},1)$ by continuity of t_i and thus

$$\nabla^{[0,1]}(\mathbf{a}) \neq t_i(\mathbf{a},1). \qquad (e)$$

Similarly, $u_{ik}(\mathbf{a},1) = \lim_n u_{ik}(\mathbf{a}_m,1) = 0$ and $v_{ir}(\mathbf{a},1) = \lim_n v_{ir}(\mathbf{a}_m,1) \leq 0$ by continuity of u_{ik} and v_{ir}. Take a point $\mathbf{b} \in R_i$ and consider the point $\mathbf{a} * \mathbf{b} = ((a_1,b_1),...,(a_n,b_n)) \in M^n$ where $\mathbf{a} = (a_1,..,a_n)$, $\mathbf{b} = (b_1,..,b_n)$. Then

$$u_{ik}(\mathbf{a} * \mathbf{b},(1,1)) = (u_{ik}(\mathbf{a},1),u_{ik}(\mathbf{b},1)) = (0,0)$$
$$v_{ir}(\mathbf{a} * \mathbf{b},(1,1)) = (v_{ir}(\mathbf{a},1),v_{ir}(\mathbf{b},1)) \leq_{lex} (0,v_{ir}(\mathbf{b},1)) <_{lex} (0,0)$$

for all k,r. That is, $\mathbf{a} * \mathbf{b}$ belongs to the region R_i in $\mathbb{R} \otimes \mathbb{R}$ and thus by (d)

$$\nabla^M(\mathbf{a} * \mathbf{b}) = t_i(\mathbf{a} * \mathbf{b},(1,1)) = (t_i(\mathbf{a},1),t_i(\mathbf{b},1)).$$

On the other hand, since ∇ is a compatible implicit operation of DMV-algebras and $\pi_1 : M \to ([0,1]_{MV},\delta_n)_n$ is an onto homomorphism then

$$t_i(\mathbf{a},1) = \pi_1 \nabla^M(\mathbf{a} * \mathbf{b}) = \nabla^{[0,1]}(\pi_1(a_1,b_1),...,\pi_1(a_n,b_n))) = \nabla^{[0,1]}(\mathbf{a})$$

by Lemma 2-1, contradicting (e). We conclude, that $\nabla^{[0,1]}$ is continuous.

By the analogue of McNaughton theorem for DMV algebras (Lemma 9 in [3]), $\nabla^{[0,1]}$ must be given by a term φ of type $\{\oplus,\neg,\delta_n\}_{n\geq 2}$. Then the identities in $\mathcal{E}(\nabla)$ are satisfied by φ in all the algebras of the variety generated by $([0,1]_{MV},\delta_n)_{n\in\omega}$, that is, in all the DMV-algebras. This means, by uniqueness, that ∇ exists and is given by φ in all these algebras. $\square$

We may conclude that RŁ does not admit proper implicit connectives:

Theorem 6. *Any implicit connective of Rational Łukasiewicz logic is explicit. More precisely, if $R\text{Ł}(\mathcal{C})$ is an extension of RŁ by implicit connectives then for each $\nabla \in \mathcal{C}$ there is $\varphi \in R\text{Ł}$ such that $\vdash_{R\text{Ł}(\mathcal{C})} \nabla(\mathbf{p}) \leftrightarrow \varphi(\mathbf{p})$.*

Proof. Due to Theorem 1, for any implicit family $\mathcal{C}$ of connectives of Ł, the logic RŁ($\mathcal{C}$) is algebraized by $\mathcal{DMV}(\mathcal{C})$, where $\mathcal{C}$ is an implicit family of compatible operation of DMV-algebras. By Theorem 5, for each $\nabla \in \mathcal{C}$ there is a term φ of DMV algebras such that $\models_{\mathcal{DMV}(\mathcal{C})} \nabla(\mathbf{x}) = \varphi(\mathbf{x})$, and by algebraizability this implies $\vdash_{RŁ(\mathcal{C})} \nabla(\mathbf{p}) \leftrightarrow \varphi(\mathbf{p})$, where $\varphi \in RŁ$. $\qquad\square$

An inspection of the proof of Theorem 5 shows that it actually proves:

Theorem 7. *Any member of a family of compatible operations defined implicitly by identities in MV-algebras is given by a term of type $\{\oplus, \neg, \delta_n\}_{n \geq 2}$ in all DMV-algebras where the family exists (if any).*

This result will allow us to show that RŁ is the largest extension of Ł by implicit connectives having a sound and complete semantics with values in $[0,1]$, module bi-interpretations leaving Ł fixed.

Definition 5. Call a function $T : Ł(\mathcal{C}) \to Ł(\mathcal{D})$ between extensions of Ł by implicit connectives a *faithful translation* over Ł if there are formulas $\varphi_\nabla \in Ł(\mathcal{D})$, $\nabla \in \mathcal{C}$, such that for any $\alpha, \alpha_i \in Ł(\mathcal{C})$,
   1. $T(\alpha) = \alpha(\nabla/\varphi_\nabla)_{\nabla \in \mathcal{C}}$
   2. $\{\alpha_i\}_{i \leq n} \vdash_{Ł(\mathcal{C})} \alpha$ iff $\{T(\alpha_i)\}_{i \leq n} \vdash_{Ł(\mathcal{D})} T(\alpha)$.

This amounts to say that $Ł(\mathcal{C})$ is bi-interpretable with a full fragment of $Ł(\mathcal{D})$ by a translation that fixes Ł.

Theorem 8. *An extension $Ł(\mathcal{C})$ of Ł by implicit connectives is sound and complete with respect to valuations in $([0,1]_{MV}, f_\nabla)_{\nabla \in \mathcal{C}}$ for some interpretation of the connectives in $\mathcal{C}$ if and only if there is a faithful translation $T : Ł(\mathcal{C}) \to RŁ$.*

Proof. For simplicity, we consider a single connective. Assume the hypothesis for $Ł(\nabla)$. By soundness, f_∇ satisfies the identities corresponding to the axioms defining implicitly ∇, and thus $\nabla^{[0,1]} = f_\nabla$ exists in $[0,1]_{MV}$. By Theorem 7, there is a DMV-term φ such that $f_\nabla = \varphi$ in $[0,1]_{MV\delta} = ([0,1]_{MV}, \delta_n)_n$. Hence, we have the following chain of equivalences: $\{\alpha_i\}_{i \leq n} \vdash_{Ł(\nabla)} \alpha$ iff $\{\alpha_i = 1\}_{i \leq n} \models_{([0,1]_{MV}, f_\nabla)} \alpha = 1$ (completeness of $Ł(\nabla)$), iff $\{\alpha_i(\nabla/\varphi) = 1\}_{i \leq n} \models_{[0,1]_{MV\delta}} \alpha(\nabla/\varphi) = 1$ (previous observation), iff $\{\alpha_i(\nabla/\varphi)\}_{i \leq n} \vdash_{RŁ} \alpha(\nabla/\varphi)$ (completeness of RŁ). Therefore, $T(\alpha) := \alpha(\nabla/\varphi)$ is the required translation.

Reciprocally, if there is a faithful translation $T : Ł(\nabla) \to RŁ$ as described, then $\{\alpha_i\}_{i \leq n} \vdash_{Ł(\nabla)} \alpha$ iff $\{\alpha_i(\nabla/\varphi)\}_{i \leq n} \vdash_{RŁ} \alpha(\nabla/\varphi)$ (hypothesis), iff $\{\alpha_i(\nabla/\varphi) = 1\}_{i \leq n} \models_{[0,1]_{MV\delta}} \alpha(\nabla/\varphi) = 1$ (completeness of RŁ), iff $\{\alpha_i(\nabla) = 1\}_{i \leq n} \models_{([0,1]_{MV}, \varphi^{[0,1]})} \alpha(\nabla) = 1$. Thus, $Ł(\nabla)$ is complete with respect to $([0,1]_{MV}, \varphi^{[0,1]})$. $\qquad\square$

By Theorem 3, the previous result implies that the logic $Ł(\delta_n^*)$ of approximate division introduced in Section 3 can not be faithfully embedded in RŁ, even less in $Ł(\delta_n)$, for $n \geq 2$. Therefore, RŁ is not the maximum extension of Ł by implicit connectives.

Observe that $Ł(\delta_n)$ cannot be embedded in $Ł(\delta_n^*)$, even as a weak fragment. Otherwise, the image γ of $\delta_n 1$ by a possible translation would satisfy $\vdash_{Ł(\delta_n^*)}$

$(n-1)\gamma \leftrightarrow \neg\gamma$, which is impossible because the corresponding equation, $(n-1)$ $x = \neg x$ has no solution in L_n. Therefore, $\mathrm{L}(\delta_n^*)$ and $\mathrm{L}(\delta_n)$ are incomparable extensions of Ł with respect to faithful translations.

6   Implicit Connectives of n-Valued ŁUkasiewicz Logic

For $n \geq 2$, Lukasiewicz n-valued calculus $Ł_n$ (cf. [10]) is algebraized by the variety $\mathcal{MV}_n$ of n-valued MV-algebras, generated in turn (as a quasivariety) by the Łukasiewicz chain L_n. By Jónsson's lemma (Th. 6.8, [7]), the subdirectly irreducible algebras of $\mathcal{MV}_n$ are the subalgebras of L_n because this variety is congruence distributive and these algebras are simple. Moreover, they are the only chains of the variety.

For $n \geq 3$, the axiom

$$(n-2)c \leftrightarrow \neg c$$

defines an implicit constant connective of $Ł_n$. In fact, it defines an implicit connective already in Ł because the quasi-identity

$$\forall x \forall y (mx = \neg x \wedge my = \neg y \implies x = y)$$

holds in $[0,1]_{MV}$, and by completeness $mc \leftrightarrow \neg c, mc' \leftrightarrow \neg c' \vdash_{\mathrm{L}} c \leftrightarrow c'$. According to Theorem 6, c is reducible to $\delta_{n-1}(1)$ in RŁ.

Returning to $Ł_n$, c is realized algebraically in L_n as the element $\frac{1}{n-1}$, but it does not exists in any proper subalgebra of L_n. Thus $(L_n, \frac{1}{n-1})$ is the only subdirectly irreducible algebra of the corresponding variety $\mathcal{MV}_n(c)$ by Lemma 2-2, and therefore $Ł_n(c)$ is sound and strongly complete with respect to values in this algebra by Theorem 1.

Theorem 9. *Any implicit connective of $Ł_n(c)$ is explicit.*

Proof. For any implicit extension $Ł_n(c, \nabla)$, the only subdirectly irreducible algebra of $\mathcal{MV}_n(c, \nabla)$ is $(L_n, \frac{1}{n-1}, \nabla^{L_n})$ by Lemma 2-2 and the previous observations, and thus this algebra generates the variety. But $(L_n, \frac{1}{n-1})$ is a primal algebra because it is term equivalent to the basic Post algebra of order n. Then ∇ is a term φ of $\mathcal{MV}_n(c)$ in $(L_n, \frac{1}{n-1})$. The identity $\nabla = \varphi$ is inherited by the variety $\mathcal{MV}_n(c, \nabla)$, and thus $\vdash_{Ł_n(c,\nabla)} \nabla \leftrightarrow \varphi$ by algebraizability. $\square$

It is possible to show, as in Theorem 8, that $Ł_n(c)$ is the largest extension of $Ł_n$ by implicit connectives which is complete with respect to values in the algebra L_n. However, there are such extension that are not complete with respect to L_n, or any single given chain. For example, the axioms

$$nc^*$$
$$np \rightarrow (c^* \rightarrow p)$$

define an implicit connective of $Ł_n$ which is realized in each subalgebra of L_n as the minimum positive element of that subalgebra. Thus $Ł_n(c^*)$ is complete with respect to the family of chains $(L_k, \frac{1}{k-1})$, $(k-1)|(n-1)$. But it is not complete with respect to any particular one of them. We illustrate the case when $n = 5$.

Proposition 3. $L_5(c^*)$ *is a conservative extension of* L_5 *not complete with respect to any single chain.*

Proof. The only chains of $\mathcal{MV}_5(c^*)$ are $(L_5, \frac{1}{4})$ and $(L_3, \frac{1}{2})$. The logic is not complete with respect to the first chain because $\nvdash_{L_5(c_4^*)} 3c^* \leftrightarrow \neg c^*$, which may be falsified only in $(L_3, \frac{1}{2})$, nor is it complete with respect to the second one because $\nvdash_{L_5(c_4^*)} 2c^*$, which may be falsified only in $(L_5, \frac{1}{4})$.   □

7   Implicit Operations of ℓ-Groups and Implicit Connectives of Abelian Logic

For each $n \geq 2$, the single identity

$$nD_n(x) = x$$

defines an implicit operation $D_n(x) = \frac{1}{n}x$ in ℓ-groups because these groups are torsion free. This operation may be seen to be compatible because the congruences of ℓ-groups are determined by their convex subgroups and $\frac{1}{n}x$ belongs to the interval determined by 0 and x. The variety $\ell\mathcal{G}(D_n)_{n\geq 2}$ consists of all divisible ℓ-groups endowed with these operations. This is essentially the variety of $\mathbb{Q}$-*vector lattices* (lattice ordered $\mathbb{Q}$-vector spaces satisfying $r(x \vee y) = rx \vee ry$ for any positive $r \in \mathbb{Q}$). Clearly, there is an analogue of Mundici's functor which sends $\ell\mathcal{G}(D_n)_{n\geq 2}$ onto the variety of DMV-algebras.

The proof of Theorem 5 may be readily adapted to show the following result, which we state for a single operation but holds equally for families.

Theorem 10. *Any compatible operation* ∇ *defined implicitly by identities over the variety* $\ell\mathcal{G}(D_n)_{n\geq 2}$ *is given by a term of the variety.*

Proof. If ∇ exists in a non trivial $G \in \ell\mathcal{G}(D_n)_{n\geq 2}$, then by compatibility it exists in each one of the non trivial subdirectly irreducible factors of a subdirect decomposition of G. From Lemma 2-2 and Fact 2 in Section 4, these are divisible linearly ordered ℓ-groups. By completeness of the theory of these groups (Fact 4) and first order definability of ∇, this operation exists in all non trivial linearly ordered groups of $\ell\mathcal{G}(D_n)_{n\geq 2}$, in particular in $(\mathbb{R}, D_n)_n$. Arguing as in the proof of Theorem 5, the first order definition $\theta(y, \mathbf{x})$ of ∇ takes the form in $\mathbb{R}$:

$$\nabla^{\mathbb{R}}\mathbf{x} = \begin{cases} t_1(\mathbf{x}) & \text{if } \bigwedge_k u_{1k}(\mathbf{x}) = 0 \wedge \bigwedge_r v_{1r}(\mathbf{x}) < 0 \\ \vdots \\ t_m(\mathbf{x}) & \text{if } \bigwedge_k u_{mk}(\mathbf{x}) = 0 \wedge \bigwedge_r v_{mr}(\mathbf{x}) < 0 \end{cases} \tag{q}$$

where t_i, u_{1k}, and v_{1r} are linear expressions with rational coefficients, and the left right conditions determine a partition of $\mathbb{R}$ into disjoint non empty regions R_i.

To prove that $\nabla^{\mathbb{R}}$ is continuous, notice first that ∇ exists and must obey (q) in the group $(\mathbb{R} \otimes \mathbb{R}, D_n)_n$ because this fact is expressible by first order sentences and $(\mathbb{R} \otimes \mathbb{R}, D_n)_n \equiv (\mathbb{R}, D_n)_n$. Moreover, the first projection $\pi_1 : \mathbb{R} \otimes \mathbb{R} \to \mathbb{R}$ is an epimorphism of ℓ-groups which may be seen to preserve the D_n. Thus $\pi_1 : (\mathbb{R} \otimes \mathbb{R}, D_n)_n \to (\mathbb{R}, D_n)_n$ is an epimorphism and it must preserve ∇ by the compatibility hypothesis; that is,

$$\pi_1 \nabla^{\mathbb{R} \otimes \mathbb{R}}((x_1, y_1), ..., (x_n, y_n)) = \nabla^{\mathbb{R}}(x_1, ..., x_n). \tag{r}$$

As in the proof of Theorem 5, were $\nabla^{\mathbb{R}}$ not continuous we could find a region R_i and points $\mathbf{a} \notin R_i$, $\mathbf{b} \in R_i$ in $\mathbb{R}^n$ such that $\nabla^{\mathbb{R}}(\mathbf{a}) \neq t_i(\mathbf{a})$ and $\mathbf{a} * \mathbf{b} = ((a_1, b_1), ..., (a_n, b_n))$ would belong to the region R_i in $(\mathbb{R} \otimes \mathbb{R})^n$. Hence,

$$\nabla^{\mathbb{R} \otimes \mathbb{R}}(\mathbf{a} * \mathbf{b}) = t_i(\mathbf{a} * \mathbf{b}) = (t_i(\mathbf{a}), t_i(\mathbf{b}))$$

and thus $\nabla^{\mathbb{R}}(\mathbf{a}) = \pi_1 \nabla^{\mathbb{R} \otimes \mathbb{R}}(\mathbf{a} * \mathbf{b}) = t_i(\mathbf{a})$, by (r), a contradiction.

We have then a piecewise linear function with rational coefficients. Let m be the common denominator of the coefficients of the $t_i(\mathbf{x}), u_{1k}(\mathbf{x}), v_{1r}(\mathbf{x})$. Then $m\nabla^{\mathbb{R}}(\mathbf{x})$ is a piecewise linear continuous function with integer coefficients in $\mathbb{R}$ and thus it must be given by an ℓ-group term (folklore, see final remark in [4]), say $m\nabla^{\mathbb{R}}(\mathbf{x}) = u(\mathbf{x})$. Hence, $\nabla^{\mathbb{R}}(\mathbf{x}) = \frac{1}{m}u(\mathbf{x}) = D_m u(\mathbf{x})$, a term of $\ell\mathcal{G}(D_n)_{n \geq 2}$. By first order completeness, ∇ is given by $D_m u(\mathbf{x})$ in all subdirectly irreducible algebras of $\ell\mathcal{G}(D_n)_{n \geq 2}$. Therefore, the set of identities $\mathcal{E}(\nabla/D_m u(\mathbf{x}))$ holds in all the algebras of the variety $\ell\mathcal{G}(\nabla, D_n)_{n \geq 2}$ and, by uniqueness, $\nabla(\mathbf{x}) = D_m u(\mathbf{x})$ in $\ell\mathcal{G}(\nabla, D_n)_{n \geq 2}$. $\qquad \square$

A *Logic of equilibrium*, $\mathcal{B}al$, is described in [14] which is algebraizable by the variety of ℓ-groups (being thus a version of so called *Abelian logic*, [19]). It has the axiom schemes:

$$(p \to q) \to ((r \to q) \to (r \to p))$$
$$(p \to (q \to r)) \to (q \to (p \to r)$$
$$((p \to q) \to q) \to p$$
$$((p \to q)^+ \to (q \to p)^+) \to (p \to q)$$
$$p^{++} \to p^+$$

and inference rules

$$p \to q, p \vdash q, \qquad p, q \vdash p \to q, \qquad p \vdash p^+, \qquad (p \to q)^+ \vdash (p^+ \to q^+)^+.$$

The defined connectives

$$0 := p \to p, \qquad -p := q \to 0, \qquad p + q := -p \to q, \qquad p \curlyvee q := (p \to q)^+ + q$$

form a complete set since $p \to q \dashv\vdash -p + q$ and $p^+ \dashv\vdash p \curlyvee 0$, and they allow the interpretation of $\mathcal{B}al$ in ℓ-groups so that we get algebraic completeness:

$$\{\varphi_i\}_{i \leq n} \vdash_{\mathcal{B}al} \varphi \text{ iff } \{\varphi_i = 0\}_{i \leq n} \models_{\ell\mathcal{G}} \varphi = 0.$$

In fact, algebraic completeness holds with respect to values in $\mathbb{Z}$ (or $\mathbb{Q}$, or $\mathbb{R}$), because these groups generate $\ell\mathcal{G}$ as a quasi-variety, [5]. The 'equivalence' and constant formula mediating algebraicity are just $p \to q$ (equivalently, $-q + p$), and thus this connective must satisfy symmetry and transitivity, and $1 := 0$.

Since $p + ... + p = 0 \models_{\ell\mathcal{G}} p = 0$, because all ℓ-groups are torsion free, we have by algebraic completeness: $n\varphi \vdash_{\mathcal{B}al} \varphi$ for any $n \geq 2$. Also, $-np + nq = 0 \models_{\ell\mathcal{G}} n(-p+q) = 0$, which implies $n\varphi \rightarrow n\psi \vdash_{\mathcal{B}al} n(\varphi \rightarrow \psi)$.

It follows easily from the previous observations that the single axiom

$$p \rightarrow nD_np$$

defines implicitly the connective D_n over $\mathcal{B}al$. Indeed:

$$p \rightarrow nD_np, \; p \rightarrow n\lambda p \vdash \; nD_np \rightarrow n\lambda p \vdash \; n(D_np \rightarrow \lambda p) \vdash \; D_np \rightarrow \lambda p.$$

By Theorem 1, the logic $R\mathcal{B}al = \mathcal{B}al(D_n)_{n\geq2}$, that we could call *Rational logic of equilibrium*, is algebraized by the variety $\ell\mathcal{G}(D_n)_{n\geq2}$ introduced above. Together with Theorem 10, this implies:

Corollary 1. *Every implicit connective of $R\mathcal{B}al$ is explicit.*

Note that $R\mathcal{B}al$ is complete with respect to values in $\mathbb{R}$ (or $\mathbb{Q}$). One may show, as in Theorem 8, that it is the largest extension of $\mathcal{B}al$ by implicit connectives with this property:

Theorem 11. *An extension of $\mathcal{B}al$ by implicit connectives is sound and complete with respect to valuations in $(\mathbb{R}, f_\nabla)_\nabla$ for some interpretation f_∇ of the new connectives if and only if it has a faithful translation into $R\mathcal{B}al$.*

8   Final Remarks

We have not considered in this paper extensions of Łukasiewicz logic by connectives implicitly defined by axiom schemes and new inference rules. In this case, the extension is still algebraizable by a (perhaps proper) quasivariety of enriched MV-algebras (Th. 1 in [8]), but the algebraic interpretation of the connectives is not necessarily compatible. For example, the following system:

$$\beta p \curlyvee \neg\beta p$$
$$p \rightarrow \beta p$$
$$q \curlyvee \neg q, (p \rightarrow q) \vdash (\beta p \rightarrow q)$$

defines implicitly a connective β over Ł . It may be shown that the extension Ł(β) is algebraizable by the MV-algebras which support the operation

$$\beta(x) := \text{smallest boolean } y \text{ greater or equal than } x.$$

Thus, β exists in all MV-chains, particularly in $[0,1]$, where it takes the form of the Baaz delta operator, [2]:

$$\beta(x) = \begin{cases} 0 & \text{if } x = 0 \\ 1 & \text{if } x > 0. \end{cases}$$

Clearly, this operation is not compatible in the non-simple MV-chains, and thus, by Theorem 1, β can not be defined implicitly by means of axioms only.

This fact marks a sharp difference with classical propositional calculus, because it may be shown that the latter does not admit new connectives defined implicitly by axiom schemes and inference rules.

References

1. Aguzzoli, S., Mundici, D.: Weirstrass approximation theorem and Łukasiewicz formulas with one quantified variable. In: Fitting, M., Orlowska, E. (eds.) Beyond Two: Theory and Applications of Multiple Valued Logic, pp. 315–335. Physica-Verlag, Springer, Heidelberg (2003)
2. Baaz, M.: Infinite-valued Gödel logics with 0-1-projections and relativizations. In: Hájek, P. (ed.) Proceedings of Gödel 96. Lecture Notes in Logic 6, pp. 23–33. Springer, Heidelberg (1996)
3. Baaz, M., Veith, H.: Interpolation in fuzzy logic. Archive for Mathematical Logic 38, 461–498 (1999)
4. Baker, K.A.: Free vector lattices. Canad. J. Math. 20, 58–66 (1968)
5. Bigard, A., Keimel, K., Wolfenstein, S.: Groupes et Anneaux Réticulés. Lecture Notes in Mathematics, vol. 608. Springer, Heidelberg (1971)
6. Blok, W.J., Pigozzi, D.: Algebraizable logics. Memoirs of the AMS 396 (1989)
7. Burris, S., Sankappanavar, H.P.: A Course in Universal Algebra. Graduate Texts in Mathematics, vol. 78. Springer, Heidelberg (1981)
8. Caicedo, X.: Implicit connectives of algebraizable logics. Studia Logica 78, 155–170 (2004)
9. Caicedo, X., Cignoli, R.: An algebraic approach to intuitionistic connectives. Journal of Symbolic Logic 60, 1620–1636 (2001)
10. Cignoli, R., D'Ottaviano, I.M.L., Mundici, D.: Algebraic Foundations of Many-valued reasoning. Kluwer Academic Publishers, Dordrecht (2000)
11. Chang, C.C.: A new proof of the completeness of Łukasiewicz axioms. Trans. A.M.S. 93, 74–80 (1959)
12. Chang, C.C., Keisler, J.: Model Theory, 3rd edn. North Holland, Amsterdam (1990)
13. Běhounek, L., Cintula, P.: Fuzzy logics as the logics of chains. Fuzzy Sets and Systems 157(5), 604–610 (2006)
14. Galli, A., Lewin, R., Sagastume, M.: The logic of equilibrium and abelian lattice ordered groups. Arch. Math. Logic 43, 141–158 (2004)
15. Gerla, B.: Rational Łukasiewicz logic and DMV-algebras. Neural Networks World 11, 579–584 (2001)
16. Komori, Y.: Super-Łukasiewicz propositional logics. Nagoya Math. J. 84, 119–133 (1981)
17. Lacava, F., Saeli, D.: Sul model-completamento della teoría delle Ł-catene. Bolletino Unione Matematica Italiana 14-A(5), 107–110 (1977)
18. Marker, D.: Model Theory, An Introduction. Springer, Heidelberg (2002)
19. Metcalfe, G., Olivetti, N., Gabbay, D.: Sequent and Hypersequent Calculi for Abelian and Łukasiewicz Logics. ACM Transactions on Computational Logic 6(3), 578–613 (2005)
20. Montagna, F.: An algebraic approach to propositional fuzzy logic. Journal of Logic Language and Information 9, 91–124 (2000)
21. Mundici, D.: Interpretation of AF C-algebras in Łukasiewicz sentential calculus. Journal of Functional Analysis 65, 15–63 (1986)
22. Robinson, A.: Complete theories. North Holland, Amsterdam (1956)
23. Van den Dries, L.: Tame topology and o-minimal structures. Cambridge U. Press, Cambridge (1998)

The Algebras of Łukasiewicz Many-Valued Logic: A Historical Overview*

Roberto Cignoli

Instituto Argentino de Matemática - CONICET,
Saavedra 15, piso 3,
C1083ACA Buenos Aires, Argentina
`cignoli@dm.uba.ar`

To Daniele Mundici on his 60th birthday

Abstract. An outline of the history of the algebras corresponding to Łukasiewicz many-valued logic from the pioneering work by G. Moisil in 1940 until D. Mundici's work in 1986.

1 Łukasiewicz and Post Many-Valued Logics

The three-valued system of propositional calculus was constructed by Jan Łukasiewicz in the year 1920 and described in a lecture given at the Polish Philosophical Society in Lwów. A short paper in Polish, based on his lecture, was published the same year [40].

The n-valued systems, discovered by Łukasiewicz in 1922, were briefly described in a textbook on Mathematical Logic published in 1929 [41]. A joint paper with Alfred Tarski, published in German in 1930 [44], contains, among other things, an account of results obtained by several Polish logicians on n-valued systems of propositional calculi, where n is either an integer ≥ 2 or $n = \aleph_0$. In [42], published in the same year and also in German, Łukasiewicz explains the philosophical ideas about determinism and modalities that leaded him to the construction of the n-valued calculi.

An idea of Łukasiewicz's philosophical motivation for the introduction of many-valued logic can be grasped from the following paragraphs of his Farewell Lecture as Rector of Warsaw University, on March 7, 1918 [10]:

> I have declared a spiritual war upon all coercion that restricts man's creative activity. There are two kinds of coercion. One of them is physical [...].
> The other kind of coercion is logical. We must accept self evident principles and the theorems resulting therefrom. This coercion is much stronger than the physical; there is no hope for liberation. No physical or intellectual force can overcome the principles of logic and mathematics.

---

* This paper is an expanded version of a talk delivered at the INTERNATIONAL CONFERENCE IN HONOUR OF DANIELE MUNDICI ON THE OCCASION OF HIS 60TH BIRTHDAY at Gargnano, Italy, on March 20, 2006.

S. Aguzzoli et al.(Eds.): Algebraic and Proof-theoretic Aspects, LNAI 4460, pp. 69–83, 2007.

That coercion originated with the rise of Aristotelian logic and Euclidean geometry.
The concept was born of science as a system of principles and theorems connected by logical relationship. [...]
In the universe conceived in this way there is no place for a creative act resulting not from a law but from a spontaneous impulse [...].
The creative mind revolts against this concept of science, the universe and life. A brave individual, conscious of his value, does not want to be just a link in the chain of cause, but wants himself affect the course of events. This was always been the background of the opposition between science and art. [...]
He has two paths to choose from: either to submerge himself in scepticism and abandon research, or to come to grips with the concept of science based on Aristotelian logic. I have chose that second path.[...]
In striving to transform the concept of science based on Aristotelian logic I had to forge weapons stronger than that logic. It was symbolic logic that became such a weapon for me.

As the Referee pointed out, it is worthwhile to stress the fact that Łukasiewicz's idea of a third truth-value as a way to 'liberation' from 'the coercion originated with the rise of Aristotelian logic and Euclidean geometry' grew up in the discussions on determinism which took place immediately before World War I among polish scholars (see [70,92]).

In his 1920 thesis at Columbia University [69], Emil Leon Post[1] developed systems of n-valued propositional calculi, for n an integer ≥ 2, as natural generalizations of the truth-table approach to classical propositional calculus.

In contrast with Łukasiewicz, Post had no philosophical motivations.

The following paragraph is taken from the Introduction of the published paper:

Whether these "non-Aristotelian" logics and the general development which includes them will have a direct application we do not know; but we believe that, inasmuch as the theory of elementary propositions is at the base of the complete system of *Principia*, this broadened outlook upon the theory will serve to prepare us for a similar analysis of that complete system, and so ultimately of mathematics.

Other systems of many-valued logic were considered by different authors, even before the publication of [40][2]. Only Post's work is explicitly mentioned because we will see that for each finite $n \geq 2$, Łukasiewicz and Post n-valued logics are strongly related from the algebraic point of view.

---

[1] Although Post was born in Poland, he arrived in the United States when he was seven years old, so had no influence of the Polish philosophical school.

[2] A system of three-valued logic, different from the one of Łukasiewicz was considered by Charles S. Peirce in 1912, see [24]. More than two truth values were used by Paul Bernays in his *Habilitationsschrift* at the University of Göttingen (1918), to give independence proof for postulates of classical propositional calculus. Parts of this work were published eight yeas latter [5] (see [94]).

2 Moisil's Łukasiewicz Algebras

In 1940 Gregorie Moisil introduced in [49] three-valued and four-valued Łukasiewicz algebras. To my knowledge, this was *the first attempt to give algebras corresponding to Łukasiewicz many-valued logic.*

In 1942 Paul C. Rosenbloom [75] introduced Post algebras, the algebras of Post many-valued logics.

Moisil's motivations and aims are clearly established in the following paragraphs, extracted from the Introduction of [49]:

> La logique formelle, en tant que science symbolique indépendante, est en possession de deux méthodes différentes. La première, appelée d'habitude méthode axiomatique est celle qui a été presque unanimement utilisée, celle qu'on trouve, par exemple, dans les traités de MM. Hilbert et Ackermann, de MM. Hilbert et Bernays, dans *Principia Mathematica*. On considère la logique comme un ensemble de *thèses*, en appelant thèse une expression qui est toujours vraie. Les thèses sont déduites d'un certain nombre d'axiomes à l'aide de certains schémas déductifs (tels que le modus ponens ou la règle de substitution). Cette méthode sera appelée *calcul des thèses*.
>
> Une seconde méthode est celle introduite par MM. Gentzen et Jaskowski [...].
>
> A chacune de ces méthodes purement logiques (c'est-à-dire ne supposant pas les Mathématiques constituées) on peut faire correspondre une branche des Mathématiques [...].
>
> Au calcul des thèses correspond ce qu'il convient d'appeler d'Algèbre de la Logique, en donnant à ce terme la signification générale d'étude algébrique des systèmes suggérés par le calcul des thèses. Les systèmes les plus intéressantes sont ceux qui ont été appelés structures (Oystein Ore), lattice (G. Birkhoff), Verbände (F. Klein) ou logiques. Ce sont des systèmes à deux lois de composition. Parmi les structures on a étudié les structures modulaires, distributives, avec éléments complémentaires el les algèbres de Boole.
>
> La relation entre le calcul des thèses et l'Algèbre de la Logique est établie par la méthode des matrices. Un premier problème consiste à définir une matrice telle que le calcul des thèses considéré soit celui qui est remplie ou satisfait par cette matrice (Tarski [84]) . Le calcul des propositions classiques a été définie a l'aide de la matrice L_2 à deux éléments ("le vrai" et "le faux"), celui de M. Heyting pour une matrice infinie (Jaskowski [32]), les logiques de M. Łukasiewicz à l'aide des matrices qui sont des structures simplement ordonnées.
>
> Un second problème qui se pose est celui caractériser algébriquement toutes les matrices qui correspondent à un calcul des thèses donné. Ce problème est résolu pour le calcul des thèses classique auquel correspond l'étude des algèbres de Boole.
>
> MM. Birkhoff [6] et Stone [83] ont montré que toute algèbre de Boole finie est le produit de structures L_2 et que toute algèbre de Boole infinie peut

être représentée comme une algèbre de classes, c'est-à-dire comme une sous-structure de L_2^E, où E est un certain ensemble. C'est là un troisième problème fondamental, celui de la représentation des différentes algèbres suggérés par la logique.

C'est à l'étude de ceux deus derniers problèmes pour les logiques trivalentes et tétravalentes de M. Łukasiewicz qu'est dédié ce Mémoire. Nous avons tout d'abord caractérisé algébriquement ces logiques, en créant un calcul qui les rend très maniables pour l'algorithmiste. En second lieu nous avons démontré que, dans le cas finie, ce calcul est adéquat à ces logiques, toute algèbre qui satisfait ses axiomes étant un produit cartésien de structures L_2, L_3 respectivement L_2, L_3, L_4.

Łukasiewicz built up his logic from the connectives of implication→and negation¬, whose "truth-tables" are defined, for $x, y \in [0,1]$ as

$$\neg x := 1 - x, \tag{2.1}$$

$$x \rightarrow y := \min(1 - x + y, 1). \tag{2.2}$$

When n is an integer ≥ 2, the n-valued calculus is obtained by restricting the values of x, y to

$$L_n := \{0, \frac{1}{n-1}, \frac{2}{n-1} \cdots \frac{n-2}{n-1}, 1\} \subseteq [0,1], \tag{2.3}$$

and for $n = \aleph_0$, x, y are allowed to take any rational value in $[0, 1]$.

Notice that for $x, y \in [0, 1]$,

$$\max(x, y) = (x \rightarrow y) \rightarrow y, \tag{2.4}$$

and

$$\min(x, y) = \neg \max(\neg x, \neg y). \tag{2.5}$$

Thus the order structure of $[0, 1]$ can be recovered from $\neg$ and $\rightarrow$.

The unary operator ∇, defined by the truth-table

$$\nabla x = \begin{cases} 1 & \text{if } x > 0, \\ 0 & \text{if } x = 0, \end{cases} \tag{2.6}$$

can be interpreted as a modal operator of possibility.

Tarski, then a collaborator of Łukasiewicz, observed that ∇ can be defined on L_3 by

$$\nabla x = \neg x \rightarrow x = \min(x + x, 1).$$

Moisil defined three-valued Łukasiewicz algebras as systems

$$\langle A, \vee, \wedge, \neg, \nabla, 0, 1 \rangle$$

such that $\langle A, \vee, \wedge, 0, 1 \rangle$ is a distributive lattice with smallest element 0 and greatest element 1, $\neg$ and ∇ are unary operations that correspond to negation and to possibility, respectively.

L_3, equipped with the natural lattice operations and $\neg$ and ∇ as given respectively by (2.1) and (2.6) is an example of a three-valued Łukasiewicz-algebra, which has L_2, the two-element Boolean algebra, as a subalgebra.

Moisil showed that Łukasiewicz's implication (2.2) is definable in L_3, and that each *finite* three-valued Łukasiewicz algebra is a direct product of algebras L_3 and L_2.

In the subsequent paper [50], Moisil introduced the following example of a three-valued Łukasiewicz algebra: Let B be a Boolean algebra, and let $B^{[2]} := \{(x, y) \in B \times B : x \leq y\}$. Then $B^{[2]}$ with the lattice operations defined pointwise, and $\neg(x, y) := (\neg y, \neg x)$, and $\nabla(x, y) = (y, y)$ is a three-valued Łukasiewicz-algebra.

Then he proved that for each three-valued Łukasiewicz algebra A there is a Boolean algebra B such that A is embedded in $B^{[2]}$, improving a result already obtained in [49]. In this way, and taking into account the results of Stone [83], he obtained a representation of three-valued Łukasiewicz algebras as pairs of sets.

Inspired by the relations discovered by Stone between Boolean algebras and rings [82], Moisil investigated the relations between three-valued Łukasiewicz algebras and rings that are a product of a ring of characteristic 2 and a ring of characteristic 3 [51]. An equational characterization of three-valued Łukasiewicz algebra was given in [52].

On each L_n Moisil considered $n - 1$ unary operations $\nabla_1^n, \ldots, \nabla_{n-1}^n$ defined as follows:

$$\nabla_i^n \left(\frac{j}{n-1} \right) = \begin{cases} 1 & \text{if } i + j \geq n, \\ 0 & \text{if } i + j < n. \end{cases} \tag{2.7}$$

Notice that $\nabla_2^3 = \nabla$ and $\nabla_1^3 = \neg \nabla \neg$.

Moisil considered these operations as generalized modal operators, ∇_1^n, which assigns the value 0 to each $x \neq 1$, correspond to necessity, and ∇_{n-1}^n corresponds to possibility.

In his paper [50] he also introduced n-valued Łukasiewicz algebras for $2 \leq n < \aleph_0$ as bounded distributive lattices equipped with an involutive negation satisfying the De Morgan laws, and $n - 1$ unary operations corresponding to the modal operators (2.7).

Moisil showed that each n-valued Łukasiewicz algebra can be embedded in a product of algebras L_n, and also in $B^{[n]}$, for some Boolean algebra B.

It follows that the modal operations ∇_i^n can be defined on L_n from Łukasiewicz implication and negation, but as was observed by Alan Rose while he was visiting the University of Bahía Blanca in 1965, it is not possible to define Łukasiewicz implication from the lattice operations, the negation and the modal operators when $n \geq 5$. Hence, *for $n \geq 5$ n-valued Łukasiewicz algebras do not correspond to n-valued Łukasiewicz logic.*

A correct algebrization of the n-valued calculus, for $n \geq 5$, can be obtained by adding to the operations of n-valued Łukasiewicz algebras a set of $\frac{n(n-5)+2}{2}$ binary operations satisfying some simple equations. In this way n-valued Łukasiewicz propositional calculus can be considered as an expansion of the intuitionistic calculus. The algebras so expanded are called *proper n-valued Łukasiewicz algebras* [16,17].

It is worthwhile to remark that Dana Scott [81], without reference to Moisil, considered the operators ∇_i^n on L_n as two-valued valuations, and he showed that they are related with n-valued Łukasiewicz implication as follows:

$\nabla_i^n (x \to y) = 1$ iff whenever $i + j \leq k + 1$ and $\nabla_j^n x = 1$, then $\nabla_k^n y = 1$.

Moisil also defined infinite-valued Łukasiewicz algebras, where the modal operators are indexed by a totally ordered set of arbitrary cardinality. But they are not related with Łukasiewicz infinite-valued calculus. Moisil considered these algebras in relation with fuzzy logic.[3]

Three-valued Łukasiewicz algebras were intensively investigated by Antonio Monteiro during the early sixties of the last century. Monteiro's work during that period was mostly shown in his lectures at the University of Bahía Blanca (Argentina), and it is partially summarized in his posthumous paper [56, Chapitre VII].

Besides given a simple equational characterization of three-valued Łukasiewicz algebras [54], he introduced the weak implication $\Rightarrow$ by the formula:

$$x \Rightarrow y := \nabla \neg x \vee y \tag{2.8}$$

and he showed that the Łukasiewicz implication (2.2) and the weak implication are related as follows:

$$x \to y = (x \Rightarrow y) \wedge (\neg y \Rightarrow \neg x),$$

$$x \Rightarrow y = x \to (x \to y).$$

Hence a subset of a three-valued Łukasiewicz algebra containing the greatest element is closed under modus ponens with respect to Łukasiewicz implication if and only if it is closed under modus ponens with respect to weak implication. Hence both implications are equivalent from the point of view of deduction in three-valued Łukasiewicz logic (see [56]).

Let me mention the following important results obtained by Monteiro:

1. Three-valued Łukasiewicz algebras coincide with the semisimple Nelson algebras, i. e., the algebras of the constructive logic with strong negation considered by D. Nelson and A. A. Markov. Consequently, *three-valued Łukasiewicz logic is an axiomatic extension of the constructive logic with strong negation* (see [56,57]).

---

[3] The monograph [9] is the standard reference for Moisil's Łukasiewicz algebras. They are also considered in [1, Chapter XI]. For historical remarks and updated references see [26].

2. It is possible to define from each monadic Boolean algebra A (as defined by Halmos [29]) a three-valued Łukasiewicz algebra $L(A)$, and each three-valued Łukasiewicz algebra is isomorphic to $L(A)$ for a suitable monadic Boolean algebra A (see [55,56]).

As a matter of fact, it turns out that the relation between three-valued Łukasiewicz algebras and monadic Boolean algebras is functorial (see [45]).

Since it was shown by Halmos that monadic Boolean algebras are the algebraic counterpart of classical first order monadic calculus, Monteiro considered that the representation of three-valued Łukasiewicz algebras into monadic Boolean algebras gives a proof of the consistency of Łukasiewicz three-valued logic relative to classical logic.

It is fair to say that Monteiro's results on three-valued Łukasiewicz algebras inspired most of the research done in the theory of Łukasiewicz n-valued Łukasiewicz algebras (see [9] and the references given there).

3   Chang's MV-Algebras

A deep result on Łukasiewicz infinite valued-logic was proved by Robert Mac-Naughton in 1951 [48], characterizing the propositional formulas of n variables, modulo logical equivalence, by means of $[0, 1]$-valued piecewise linear continuous functions on the hypercube $[0, 1]^n$ equipped with the usual product topology.

MacNaughton also characterized the functions from L_n^k into L_n that represent the formulas of Łukasiewicz n-valued propositional calculus.

Łukasiewicz had conjectured that a propositional formula φ is a tautology of the $\aleph_0$-valued calculus if and only if φ can be derived by the rules of detachment and substitution from five formulas that he proposed as axioms (see [44]). Mordechaj Wajsberg, who in 1931 had given an axiomatization of Łukasiewicz three-valued logic, claimed in [91] that he had proved the conjecture, but his proof was never published. Wajsberg was killed during the Second World War.

The first printed proof of Łukasiewicz conjecture, due A. Rose and B. J. Rosser, appeared in 1958 [74]. They use in their proof MacNaughton's theorem.

The same year C. C. Chang [13] introduced MV-algebras, with the intention of proving Łukasiewicz conjecture by algebraic means.

Notice that in the real segment $[0, 1]$ we have that

$$x \oplus y := \min(1, x + y) = \neg x \to y, \tag{3.9}$$

and

$$x \to y = \neg x \oplus y. \tag{3.10}$$

Hence Chang defined MV-algebras essentially in terms of a binary operation $\oplus$ that corresponds to the truncated addition in $[0, 1]$ and the negation $\neg$ that have to satisfy certain equations. Thus MV-algebras form a variety or equational class. (The operation $\odot$ can be defined as $x \odot y = \neg(\neg x \oplus \neg y)$.

If we add to the axioms given by Chang to define MV-algebras the requirement that the operation $\oplus$ be idempotent, $x \oplus x = x$, then we obtain the characterization of Boolean algebras as complemented distributive lattices.

Of course, the segment $[0, 1]$ with truncated addition and Łukasiewicz negation $\neg$ given by (2.1) is an MV-algebra, known as the *standard MV-algebra*.

Moreover, Chang proved that the Lindenbaum-Tarski algebra of Łukasiewicz $\aleph_0$-valued calculus is an MV-algebra, and that a formula φ is provable from Łukasiewicz axioms by detachment and substitution if and only if its equivalence class is the unit of this algebra.

Hence to prove Łukasiewicz conjecture turns out to be equivalent to prove that the standard MV-algebra generates the variety of MV-algebras.

Chang proved that (in the current universal algebra language) the simple MV-algebras are the standard MV-algebra and its subalgebras.

Then one way to prove that the standard MV-algebra generates the whole variety is to prove that all algebras in the variety are semisimple, i. e., subdirect products of subalgebras of the standard MV-algebra $[0, 1]$. Notice that it is the method used by Rasiowa and Sikorski [71] to prove the completeness of some axiomatizations of the classical propositional calculus with respect to two-valued tautologies.

But (fortunately) this is not the case, because Chang constructed an example of a non-semisimple MV-algebra.

As a matter of fact, the paper develops a very sophisticated mathematical theory that ends with some weak applications to Łukasiewicz logic (see [15]).

The next year, Chang published in the same journal another paper [14], where he observed that if u is a positive element of a totally ordered abelian group G, then the segment $[0, u] = \{x \in G : 0 \leq x \leq u\}$ becomes an MV-algebra if we define the operations $\oplus$ and $\neg$ as

$$x \oplus y = \min(u, (x + y)),$$

and

$$\neg x = u - x.$$

Then, given a totally ordered MV-algebra A, he was able to construct a totally ordered abelian group $G(A)$ and $u > 0$ in $G(A)$ such that A is isomorphic to the MV-algebra $[0, u]$.

He also proved that every MV-algebra is a subdirect product of totally ordered MV-algebras. From these results he could prove Łukasiewicz's conjecture by translating it into a problem in the first order theory of totally ordered abelian groups.

In the early sixties Chang and his student Belluce published some papers concerning with the predicate calculus based on Łukasiewicz infinite-valued logic. In particular monadic MV-algebras were considered [4,2].

In 1973 appeared Piero Mangani's paper [46], in which the author derived from a few axioms many important properties of MV-algebras. For instance, he showed that the algebras L_n are quasi-primal.

Mangani's paper was followed by papers by Saeli and Lacava [77,38,35,36,37], all published in Italian, were some interesting results on MV-algebras are obtained. For instance, Lacava [35] observed that if u is a positive element of a lattice ordered abelian group G, then the segment $[0, u] := \{x \in G : 0 \leq x \leq u\}$ becomes an MV-algebra by defining

$$x \oplus y = u \wedge (x + y) \text{ and } \neg x = u - x.$$

Moreover, using the fact that each MV-algebra is a subdirect product of totally ordered MV-algebras together with Chang's results, Lacava embedded each MV-algebra in a segment of a lattice-ordered abelian group. Lacava also characterized the subdirectly irreducible MV-algebras and showed that (lattice) complete MV-algebras are semisimple [36].

In 1977, Revaz Grigolia [28] gave an equational characterization of the subvarieties of the variety of MV-algebras generated by the finite chains L_n, considered as subalgebras of the standard MV-algebra $[0, 1]$. The algebras in such subvarieties were called MV_n-algebras.

Grigolia used MV_n-algebras to give an axiomatization for each n-valued Łukasiewicz calculus.

MV_n-algebras and proper n-valued Łukasiewicz algebras are term-wise equivalent. Besides being defined with just two operations, MV_n-algebras have the advantage that all belong to the same variety, independently of n. This is not the case with proper n-valued Łukasiewicz algebras, because the first order language used to define them depends on n.

On each n-valued Łukasiewicz algebra $\mathbf{A}$ define the operators J_i, for $i = 1, \ldots, n-1$:

$$J_i(x) = \sigma^n_{n-i}(x) \wedge \neg \sigma^n_{n-i-1}(x),$$

where $\sigma^n_0(x) = 0$ and $\sigma^n_n(x) = 1$. Notice that in L_n we have:

$$J_i\left(\frac{j}{(n-1)}\right) = \begin{cases} 1 & \text{if } i = j, \\ 0 & \text{if } i \neq j. \end{cases}$$

Thus for $j = 1, \ldots, n-1$, the sentence

"The proposition p has truth-value $\frac{j}{n-1}$"

can be expressed in Łukasiewicz n-valued logic.

But it follows from the mentioned results of MacNaughton that such kind of operations cannot be defined in the infinite-valued logic. In some cases this kind of operations can be added, as it is the case of the so called Baaz operation.

As I already mentioned, Post algebras of order n, the algebras of n-valued Post logic, have been introduced by Rosenbloom in 1941. They were further investigated during the sixties by G. Epstein [23], T. Traczyk [87,88], G. Rousseau [76] , Ph. Dwinger [22] (see also [1,9] and the references given there). It turned out that they can be characterized as n-valued Łukasiewicz algebras with $n-2$ constants, satisfying some simple equations, added [1,9]. Post algebras were also considered by Dietrich Schwartz [78,79] under the name of *MV-algebras of finite order*. An MV-algebra of order n is an MV-algebra A satisfying the equation $x^{n-1} \oplus x = x$ and endowed with a constant c that satisfies equations that guarantee that the map $\frac{k}{n-1} \mapsto k.c$ is an MV-homomorphism from L_n into A.

The (lattice) complete Post algebras of order n can be characterized as the injective objects in the category of MV_n-algebras.

H. W. Buff [12] considered decidability problems of MV-algebras, and L. P. Belluce [3] gave a functional representation of semi-simple MV-algebras, initiate the study of the prime spectra of MV-algebras, and consider some problems on (lattice) complete MV-algebras.

4   Other Approaches to MV-Algebras

In 1966 Y. Imai and K. Iseki [30] introduced BCK-algebras as a common abstraction of the algebras corresponding to the implicative fragments of several logics existing in the literature, including classical and intuitionistic logic. Since then a lot of papers concerned with these algebras were published.

The bounded commutative BCK-algebras , a class of BCK-algebras defined by K. Iseki and S. Tanaka [31], was intensively investigated by W. H. Cornish [18,19], A. Romanowska and T. Traczyk [72,73] at the end of the seventies and beginning of the eighties. It was proved by Font, Rodríguez and Torrens [25], and independently, by Daniele Mundici [59], that these algebras coincide with MV-algebras. As a consequence, some results on MV-algebras were rediscovered in terms of BCK-algebras.

In particular, relations between a class of bounded commutative BCK-algebras and lattice ordered abelian groups were obtained by Cornish [18], corresponding to the relation between perfect MV-algebras and lattice-ordered abelian groups established by Di Nola and Lettieri [21].

Bruno Bosbach [11] introduced MV-algebras under the name of *symmetric bricks*. He was lead to bricks by his investigations on the algebraic structure of positive cones of (non necessarily abelian) lattice ordered groups. He developed the theory of bricks in an independent way. The paper contains, among other things, representations theorems that generalize the characterization of Boolean algebras as Boolean rings, and results on the structure of complete bricks.

In 1981, Yuichi Komori [34] investigated the axiomatic extensions of infinite-valued Łukasiewicz propositional calculus using algebraic tools. Although Komori was acquainted with the papers [13,14] and in a few places refers to them, his work was rather independent from Chang's. He introduced *CN algebras*, that were presented in the original language of Łukasiewicz, i. e., implication and negation, and with axioms that were straightforward adaptations of the axioms conjectured by Łukasiewicz. Komori made explicit use of the completeness of the first order theory of a special class of totally ordered abelian groups, previously introduced by him in [33]. Komori's CN-algebras are term-wise equivalent to Chang's MV-algebras, hence Komori determined *the lattice of subvarieties of the variety of MV-algebras*.

In his Doctoral Dissertation of 1981 at the University of Barcelona, Antonio Jesús Rodríguez also presented MV-algebras in the original language of Łukasiewicz, and he called the algebras so defined *Wajsberg algebras*. The main parts of the dissertation was published in [25]. Trough this paper Willem Blok became acquainted with the algebras of Łukasiewicz infinite-valued logic, and with his collaborators connected them with the theory of *hoops* [8,7].

A. Torrens [86] started the classification of Wajsberg algebras in terms of Boolean products.

5 Mundici's Work

In the papers described before, the algebras related to Łukasiewicz many-valued logic were considered as interesting algebraic structures that could eventually be applied to obtain some logical results.

A turning point of the theory was the paper [58] by Daniele Mundici *Interpretation of AF C*-Algebras in Łukasiewicz Sentential Calculus* published in the Journal of Functional Analysis in 1986.

It was certainly surprising to see the words "Łukasiewicz sentential calculus" in the title of an article of about fifty pages published in the Journal of Functional Analysis, and even more surprising to see that the paper was communicated by the 1982 Fields Medal Alan Connes.

In that paper it is proved that Chang's MV-algebras are categorically equivalent to lattice-ordered abelian groups with a strong unit. This result allowed Daniele to relate, via dimension groups, countable MV-algebras with A(pproximately) F(inite-dimensional) C*-algebras, an important class of algebras considered in Functional Analysis (see, for instance, [27]). Since MV-algebras are the Lindenbaum algebras of Łukasiewicz propositional calculus modulo a theory, a theory of the calculus is associated with the corresponding AFC*-algebra, and Daniele showed, among other things, that to simple AFC*-algebras correspond finitely axiomatizable theories. Daniele continued these investigations in several papers (see, for instance, [60,61,62,65,66,67]).

In subsequent papers Daniele gave a semantics for MV_n-algebras in terms of Ulam games, paving the way to apply MV-algebras to coding theory [63,64,67]. Moreover, he discovered that deduction in Łukasiewicz logic are related to desingularization of toric varieties [68].

These results stimulated further researches by Daniele and many other people in the theory of MV-algebras and their connections with other mathematical structures. But this is not history, but present. The evolution of these ideas should be consider in the future.

Perhaps another old professor will explain them during the celebration of the 60th birthday of some of the young organizers of this meeting.

Thanks for your attention.

References

1. Balbes, R., Dwinger, P.: Distributive Lattices. University of Missouri, Columbia, Missouri (1974)
2. Belluce, L.P.: Further results on infinite-valued predicate calculus. J. Symb. Logic 29, 69–78 (1964)
3. Belluce, L.P.: Semisimple algebras of infinite valued logic. Can. J. Math. 38, 1356–1379 (1986)
4. Belluce, L.P., Chang, C.C.: A weak completeness theorem for infinite valued first-order logic. J. Symb. Log. 28, 43–50 (1963)
5. Bernays, P.: Axiomatische Untersuchungen des Aussagen-Kalkuls der "Principia Mathematica". Math. Z. 25, 305–320 (1926)
6. Birkhoff, G.: Rings of sets. Duke Math. J. 3, 443–454 (1937)
7. Blok, W.J., Ferreirim, I.M.A.: On the structure of hoops. Algebra Univers. 43, 233–257 (2000)
8. Blok, W.J., Pigozzi, D.: On the structure of varieties with equationally definable principal congruences III. Algebra Univers. 32, 545–608 (1994)
9. Boicescu, V., Filipoiu, A., Georgescu, G., Rudeanu, S.: Łukasiewicz-Moisil Algebras. North-Holland, Amsterdam (1991)
10. Borkowski, L. (ed.): Selected Works of J. Łukasiewicz. North-Holland, Amsterdam (1970)
11. Bosbach, B.: Concerning bricks. Acta Math. Hung. 38, 89–104 (1981)
12. Buff, H.W.: Decidable and undecidable MV-algebras. Algebra Univers. 21, 234–249 (1985)
13. Chang, C.C.: Algebraic analysis of many-valued logics. Trans. Amer. Math. Soc. 88, 467–490 (1958)
14. Chang, C.C.: A new proof of the completeness of the Łukasiewicz axioms. Trans. Amer. Math. Soc. 93, 74–90 (1959)
15. Chang, C.C.: The writing of the MV-algebras. Stud. Log. 61, 3–6 (1998)
16. Cignoli, R.: Proper n-valued Łukasiewicz algebras as S-algebras of Łukasiewicz n-valued propositional calculi. Stud. Log. 41, 4–16 (1982)
17. Cignoli, R.: An algebraic approach to elementary theories based on n-valued Łukasiewicz logics. Z. Math. Logik Grundlagen der Mathematik 30, 87–96 (1984)
18. Cornish, W.H.: Lattice-ordered groups and BCK-algebras. Math. Jap. 25, 471–476 (1980)
19. Cornish, W.H.: On Iséki's BCK-algebras. In: Algebraic structures and applications, pp. 101–122. M. Dekker, New York (1982)
20. Czyzowicz, J., Mundici, D., Pelc, A.: Ulam's searching game with lies. Journal of Combinatorial Theory A(52), 62–76 (1989)
21. Di Nola, A., Lettieri, A.: Perfect MV-algebras are categorically equivalent to abelian ℓ-groups. Stud. Log. 53, 417–432 (1994)
22. Dwinger, P.: A survey of the theory of Post algebras. In: Dunn, J.M., Epstein, E. (eds.) Modern Uses of multiple valued Logics, pp. 53–75. D. Reidel, Dordrecht (1977)
23. Epstein, G.: The lattice theory of Post algebras. Trans. Amer. Math. Soc. 95, 300–317 (1960)
24. Fisch, M., Turquette, A.: Peirce's triadic logic. Trans. Charles S. Peirce Soc. 2, 71–85 (1966)
25. Font, J.M., Rodríguez, A.J., Torrens, A.: Wajsberg algebras. Stochastica 8, 5–31 (1984)

26. Georgescu, G., Iourgulescu, A., Rudeanu, S.: Grigore C. Moisil (1906 - 1973) and his School in Algebraic Logic. International Journal of Computers, Communications & Control 1, 81–99 (2006)
27. Goodearl, K.: Notes on Real and Complex C^*-algebras. Birkhäuser, Boston (1982)
28. Grigolia, R.S.: Algebraic analysis of Łukasiewicz-Tarski's n-valued logical systems. In: Wójcicki, R., Malinowski, G. (eds.) Selected Papers on Łukasiewicz Sentential Calculi, Ossolineum, Wrocław, pp. 81–92 (1977)
29. Halmos, P.: Algebraic Logic I (Monadic Boolean algebras). Compos. Math. 12, 217–249 (1956)
30. Imai, Y., Iséki, K.: On axiom system of propositional calculi XIV. Proc. Japan Acad. 42, 19–22 (1966)
31. Iséki, K., Tanaka, S.: An introduction to the theory of BCK-algebras. Math. Jap. 23, 1–26 (1978)
32. Jaskowski, J.: Recherches sur le systéme de la logique intuitionniste. In: Actes du Congrés International de Philosophie scientifique, VI Philosophie des Mathémtiques, Hermann, Paris, pp. 58–61 (1936)
33. Komori, Y.: Completeness of two theories on ordered abelian groups and embedding relations. Nagoya Math. J. 77, 33–39 (1980)
34. Komori, Y.: Super Łukasiewicz propositional logics. Nagoya Math. J. 84, 119–133 (1981)
35. Lacava, F.: Alcune proprietá delle Ł-algebre e delle Ł-algebre esistenzialmente chiuse. Boll. Unione Mat. Ital. A 16, 360–366 (1979)
36. Lacava, F.: Sulla struttura delle Ł-algebre, Atti. Accad. Naz. Lincei, VIII Ser., Rend. Cl. Sci. Fis. Mat. Nat. 67, 275–281 (1979)
37. Lacava, F.: Sulla classe delle Ł-algebre esistenzialmente chiuse. Atti. Accad. Naz. Lincei, VIII Ser., Rend. Cl. Sci. Fis. Mat. Nat. 68, 319–322 (1980)
38. Lacava, F., Saeli, D.: Proprietà e model-completamento di alcune varietà di algebre di Łukasiewicz, Atti. Accad. Naz. Lincei, VIII Ser., Rend. Cl. Sci. Fis. Mat. Nat. 60, 359–367 (1976)
39. Lacava, F., Saeli, D.: Sul model-completamento della teoria delle Ł-catene. Boll. Unione Mat. Ital. A(5), 107–110 (1977)
40. Łukasiewicz, J.: O logice trójwarkościowej. Ruch Filozoficzny 6, 170–171 (1920) (English translation in [10])
41. Łukasiewicz, J.: Elementy logiki matematycznej. Warzawa (1929) (English translation in [43])
42. Łukasiewicz, J.: Philosophische Bemerkungen zu mehrwertigen Systemen des Aussagenkalküls. C. R. Soc. Sci. Lett. Varsovie, Cl. III 23, 153–178 (1930) (English translation in [10])
43. Łukasiewicz, J.: Elements of Mathematical Logic. Pergamon Press, New York (1964)
44. Łukasiewicz, J., Tarski, A.: Untersuchungen über den Aussagenkalkül. vol. 23, pp. 30–50 (1930) (English translation in [10] and [85])
45. Mayet, R.: Relations entre les anneaux booléens, les anneaux monadiques et les algébres de Łukasiewicz. C. R. Acad. Sci. Paris Ser. A B, 275, A777–A779 (1972)
46. Mangani, P.: Su certe algebre connesse con logiche a piú valori. Boll. Unione Mat. Ital. A(8), 68–78 (1973)
47. McCall, S. (ed.): Polish Logic 1920-1939. Clarendon Press, Oxford (1967)
48. McNaughton, R.: A theorem about infinite-valued sentential logic. J. Symb. Log. 16, 1–13 (1951)
49. Moisil, G.: Recherches sur les logiques nonchrysippiènnes. Ann. Sci. Univ. Jassy 26, 431–436 (1940) (reprinted in [53], pp. 195–232)

50. Moisil, G.: Notes sur les logiques nonchrysippiènnes. Ann. Sci. Univ. Jassy 27, 86–98 (1941) (reprinted in [53], pp. 233–243)
51. Moisil, G.: Sur les anneaux de caracteristique 2 ou 3 et leur applications, Bull. De l'École Polytech. Bucharest 12, 66–90 (1941) (reprinted in [53], pp. 259–282)
52. Moisil, G.: Sur les idéaux des algébres Lukasiewicziennes trivalentes. Ann. Univ. "C. I. Parhon" Bucuresti. Ser. Acta Logica 3, 83–93 (1960) (reprinted in [53], pp. 244–258)
53. Moisil, G.: Essays sur les Logiques Nonchrysippiènnes. Académie de la République Socialiste de Roumanie, Bucharest (1972)
54. Monteiro, A.: Sur la Définition des Algèbres de Łukasiewicz trivalentes, Universidad Nacional del Sur, Bahía Blanca (1964)
55. Monteiro, A.: Construction des Algèbres de Łukasiewicz trivalentes dans les Algèbres de Boole Monadiques-I. Math. Jap. 12, 1–23 (1967)
56. Monteiro, A.: Sur les algèbres de Heyting symétriques. Port. Math. 39, 1–237 (1980)
57. Monteiro, A.: Unpublished papers, I, Notas Log. Mat., vol. 40, Bahía Blanca (1996)
58. Mundici, D.: Interpretation of AF C^*-algebras in Łukasiewicz sentential calculus. J. Funct. Anal. 65, 15–63 (1986)
59. Mundici, D.: MV-algebras are categorically equivalent to bounded commutative BCK-algebras. Math. Jap. 31, 889–894 (1986)
60. Mundici, D.: The Turing complexity of AF C^*-algebras with lattice-ordered K_0. In: Börger, E. (ed.) Computation Theory and Logic. LNCS, vol. 270, pp. 256–264. Springer, Heidelberg (1987)
61. Mundici, D.: Farey stellar subdivisions, ultrasimplicial groups and K_o of AF C^*-algebras. Adv. Math. 68, 23–39 (1988)
62. Mundici, D.: The C^*-algebras of three-valued logics. In: Ferro, R., Bonotto, C., Valentini, S., Zanardo, A. (eds.) Logic Colloquium 1988, Padova, pp. 61–77. North-Holland, Amsterdam (1989)
63. Mundici, D.: Complexity of adaptive error-correcting codes. In: Schönfeld, W., Börger, E., Kleine Büning, H., Richter, M.M. (eds.) CSL 1990. LNCS, vol. 533, pp. 300–307. Springer, Heidelberg (1991)
64. Mundici, D.: The logic of Ulam's game with lies. In: Bicchieri, C., Dalla Chiara, M.L. (eds.) Knowledge, Belief and Strategic Interaction, pp. 275–284. Cambridge University Press, Cambridge (1992)
65. Mundici, D.: Turing complexity of the Behncke-Leptin C^*-algebras with a two-point dual. Ann. Math. Artif. Intell. 26, 287–294 (1992)
66. Mundici, D.: Logic of infinite quantum systems. Int. J. Theoret. Phys. 32, 1941–1955 (1993)
67. Mundici, D.: Ulam's game, Łukasiewicz logic and AF C^*-algebras. Fundamenta Informaticae 18, 151–161 (1993)
68. Mundici, D.: Łukasiewicz normal forms and toric desingularizations. In: Hodges, W., et al. (eds.) Proceedings of Logic Colloquium 1993, Keele, England, pp. 401–423. Oxford University Press, Oxford (1996)
69. Post, E.L.: Introduction to a general theory of elementary propositions. Amer. J. Math. 43, 163–185 (1921)
70. Rand, R.: Prolegomena to Three-valued Logic. The Polish Review 13, 3–61 (1968)
71. Rasiowa, H., Sikorski, R.: The Mathematics of Metamathematics, Państowe Wydawnictwo Naukowe, Warsaw (1963)
72. Romanowska, A., Traczyk, T.: On commutative BCK-algebras. Math. Jap. 24, 567–583 (1980)
73. Romanowska, A., Traczyk, T.: Commutative BCK-algebras: subdirectly irreducible algebras and varieties. Math. Jap. 27, 35–48 (1982)

74. Rose, A., Rosser, J.B.: Fragments of many-valued statement calculi. Trans. Amer. Math. Soc. 87, 1–53 (1958)
75. Rosenbloom, P.C.: Post algebras, I: postulates and general theory. Amer. J. Math. 64, 167–188 (1942)
76. Rousseau, G.: Post algebras and pseudo-Post algebras. Fund. Math. 67, 133–145 (1970)
77. Saeli, D.: Problemi di decisione per algebre connesse a logiche a più valori, Atti. Accad. Naz. Lincei, VIII Ser., Rend. Cl. Sci. Fis. Mat. Nat. 59, 219–223 (1975)
78. Schwartz, D.: Das Homomorphietheorem für MV-Algebren endlicher Ordnung. Z. Math. Logik Grundlagen Math. 22, 141–148 (1976)
79. Schwartz, D.: Aritmetische Theorie der MV-Algebren endlicher Ordung. Math. Nachr. 77, 65–75 (1977)
80. Schwartz, D.: Polyadic MV-algebras. Z. Math. Logik Grundlagen der Mathematik 26, 561–564 (1980)
81. Scott, D.: Completeness and axiomatizability in many-valued logic. In: Tarski Symposium. Amer Math. Soc., Providence, Rh. I., pp. 411–435 (1974)
82. Stone, M.H.: Subsumption of Boolean algebras under the theory of rings. Proc. Natl. Acad. Sci. USA 21, 103–105 (1935)
83. Stone, M.H.: The theory of representations for Boolean algebras. Trans. Amer. Math. Soc. 40, 37–111 (1936)
84. Tarski, A.: Der Aussagenkalkul und die Topologie. Fund. Math. 31, 103–134 (1938) (English transltion in [85])
85. Tarski, A.: Logic, Semantics, Metamathematics. Clarendon Press, Oxford (1956) (reprinted Hackett, Indianapolis, 1983)
86. Torrens, A.: W-algebras which are Boolean products of members of SR[1] and CW-algebras. Stud. Log. 46, 263–272 (1987)
87. Traczyk, T.: Axioms and some properties of Post algebras. Colloq. Math. 10, 193–209 (1963)
88. Traczyk, T.: A generalization of the Loomis-Sikorski Theorem. Colloq. Math. 12, 155–161 (1964)
89. Traczyk, T.: On the variety of bounded commutative BCK-algebras. Math. Jap. 24, 238–292 (1979)
90. Traczyk, T.: Free bounded commutative BCK-algebra, with one free generator. Demonstr. Math. 16, 1049–1105 (1983)
91. Wajsberg, M.: Beiträge zum Metaaussagenkalkül I. Mh. Math. Phys. 42, 221–242 (1935) (English translation in: Surma 1977)
92. Wolénski, J.: Logic and Philosophy in the Łvov - Warsaw School. Kluwer, Dordrecht (1989)
93. Yutani, H.: On a system of axioms of commutative BCK-algebras. Math. Seminar Notes Kobe Univ. 5, 255–256 (1977)
94. Zach, R.: Completeness before Post: Bernays, Hilbert, and the development of propositional logic. Bull. Symb. Log. 5, 331–366 (1999)

Reversibility and Irreversibility in Quantum Computation and in Quantum Computational Logics*

Maria Luisa Dalla Chiara[1], Roberto Giuntini[2], and Roberto Leporini[3]

[1] Dipartimento di Filosofia,
Università di Firenze,
Via Bolognese 52, I-50139 Firenze, Italy
`dallachiara@unifi.it`
[2] Dipartimento di Scienze Pedagogiche e Filosofiche,
Università di Cagliari,
Via Is Mirrionis 1, I-09123 Cagliari, Italy
`giuntini@unica.it`
[3] Dipartimento di Matematica, Statistica, Informatica e Applicazioni,
Università di Bergamo,
Via dei Caniana 2, I-24127 Bergamo, Italy
`roberto.leporini@unibg.it`

Abstract. A characteristic feature of quantum computation is the use of *reversible* logical operations. These correspond to *quantum logical gates* that are mathematically represented by unitary operators defined on convenient Hilbert spaces. Two questions arise: 1) to what extent is quantum computation bound to the use of reversible logical operations? 2) How to identify the logical operations that admit a *quantum computational simulation* by means of appropriate gates? We introduce the notion of *quantum computational simulation* of a binary function defined on the real interval $[0, 1]$, and we prove that for any binary Boolean function there exists a unique fuzzy extension admitting a quantum computational simulation. As a consequence, the Łukasiewicz conjunction and disjunction do not admit a quantum computational simulation.

1 Introduction

A characteristic feature of quantum computation is the use of *reversible* logical operations. These correspond to *quantum logical gates* (briefly, *gates*) that are mathematically represented by unitary operators defined on convenient Hilbert spaces. From the physical point of view, any gate (which transforms systems of qubits into systems of qubits) describes a possible time-evolution of a physical system that carries a given amount of quantum information. On this basis, one can say that gates represent some special logical connectives that have an intrinsic *reversible* and *dynamic* behavior.

---

* We warmly thank Francesco Paoli for his stimulating comments on the paper.

S. Aguzzoli et al.(Eds.): Algebraic and Proof-theoretic Aspects, LNAI 4460, pp. 84–106, 2007.

Quantum computational logics are new forms of quantum logic, that arise as a natural logical abstraction from the theory of gates in quantum computation. In these logics, formulas denote quantum information quantities (systems of qubits, or, more generally, mixtures of systems of qubits), while the logical connectives are interpreted as logical operations defined in terms of special gates.

Two interesting questions arise in this framework: 1) to what extent is quantum computation bound to the use of reversible logical operations? 2) How to identify the logical operations that admit a *quantum computational simulation* by means of appropriate gates?

2   Qubits, Quregisters, Qumixes

Let us first sum up some basic notions of quantum computation. Consider the two-dimensional Hilbert space $\mathbb{C}^2$, where any vector $|\psi\rangle$ is represented by a pair of complex numbers. Let $\mathcal{B}^{(1)} = \{|0\rangle, |1\rangle\}$ be the *canonical orthonormal basis* for $\mathbb{C}^2$ such that $|0\rangle = (0, 1)$; $|1\rangle = (1, 0)$.

Definition 1. *Qubit*
A qubit is a unit vector $|\psi\rangle$ of the space $\mathbb{C}^2$.

Hence, any qubit has the following form:

$$|\psi\rangle = a_0 |0\rangle + a_1 |1\rangle \quad (\text{ where } a_0, a_1 \in \mathbb{C} \text{ and } |a_0|^2 + |a_1|^2 = 1).$$

From an intuitive point of view, a qubit can be regarded as a quantum variant of the classical notion of bit: a kind of "quantum perhaps". In this framework, the two basis-elements $|0\rangle$ and $|1\rangle$ represent the two classical bits 0 and 1, respectively. From a physical point of view, a qubit represents a *state* of a single particle, carrying an atomic piece of quantum information. In order to carry the information stocked by n qubits, we need of course a compound system, consisting of n particles.

Definition 2. *Quregister*
*An n-qubit system (also called n-*quregister*) is a unit vector in the n-fold tensor product Hilbert space $\otimes^n \mathbb{C}^2 := \underbrace{\mathbb{C}^2 \otimes \ldots \otimes \mathbb{C}^2}_{n-times}$ (where $\otimes^1 \mathbb{C}^2 := \mathbb{C}^2$).*

We will use $x, y, \ldots$ as variables ranging over the set $\{0, 1\}$. At the same time, $|x\rangle, |y\rangle, \ldots$ will range over the basis $\mathcal{B}^{(1)}$. Any factorized unit vector $|x_1\rangle \otimes \ldots \otimes |x_n\rangle$ of the space $\otimes^n \mathbb{C}^2$ will be called a *classical register*. We will also write $|x_1, \ldots, x_n\rangle$ instead of $|x_1\rangle \otimes \ldots \otimes |x_n\rangle$, and $|\psi_1\rangle \ldots |\psi_n\rangle$ instead of $|\psi_1\rangle \otimes \ldots \otimes |\psi_n\rangle$. The set $\mathcal{B}^{(n)}$ of all classical registers is an orthonormal basis for the space $\otimes^n \mathbb{C}^2$.

Quregisters are *pure states*: maximal pieces of information about the particles under consideration. Both in quantum theory and in quantum information, one can also consider *mixed states* (or *mixtures*), which represent pieces of information that are not maximal. In the framework of quantum computation, mixed states (mathematically represented by density operators of an appropriate Hilbert space) are also called *qumixes*.

Definition 3. *Qumix*
A qumix is a density operator of $\otimes^n \mathbb{C}^2$ (where $n \geq 1$).

Needless to say, quregisters correspond to particular qumixes that are *pure states* (i.e. projections onto one-dimensional closed subspaces of a given $\otimes^n \mathbb{C}^2$). We will indicate by $\mathfrak{D}(\otimes^n \mathbb{C}^2)$ the set of all density operators of $\otimes^n \mathbb{C}^2$. Hence the set $\mathfrak{D} = \bigcup_{n=1}^{\infty} \mathfrak{D}(\otimes^n \mathbb{C}^2)$ will represent the set of all possible qumixes.

Apparently, the elements of the computational basis of $\otimes^n \mathbb{C}^2$ can be labelled by binary strings such as: $|\underbrace{011 \ldots 10}_{n-times}\rangle$. Since any string of this kind represents a natural number $i \in [0, 2^n - 1]$ in binary notation, any unit vector of $\otimes^n \mathbb{C}^2$ can be briefly expressed as a *superposition* having the following form: $\sum_{i=0}^{2^n - 1} a_i |i\rangle$, where $|i\rangle$ is the (classical) register corresponding to the number i.

For any $n \in \mathbb{N}^+$, we define the following two sets of coefficients:

$$C_1^n := \{i \, : \, |i\rangle = |x_1, \ldots, x_n\rangle \text{ and } x_n = 1\};$$

$$C_0^n := \{i \, : \, |i\rangle = |x_1, \ldots, x_n\rangle \text{ and } x_n = 0\}$$

(when no confusion is possible, we will omit the index n in C_1^n, C_0^n). As one can easily see, every n-quregister $|\psi\rangle$ has the form

$$\sum_{i \in C_0} a_i |i\rangle + \sum_{j \in C_1} b_j |j\rangle \text{ (where } \sum_{i \in C_0} |a_i|^2 + \sum_{j \in C_1} |b_j|^2 = 1).$$

For semantic aims, it is useful to distinguish the *true* from the *false* registers in any space $\otimes^n \mathbb{C}^2$. We assume the following convention (which is a natural generalization of classical semantics): any classical register corresponds to a classical truth-value that is determined by its last element. Hence, in particular, the bit $|1\rangle$ corresponds to the truth-value *Truth*, while the bit $|0\rangle$ corresponds to the truth-value *Falsity*.

Definition 4. *True and false registers*
Let $|i\rangle$ be a register of $\otimes^n \mathbb{C}^2$.

- *$|i\rangle$ is called* true *iff $i \in C_1^n$;*
- *$|i\rangle$ is called* false *iff $i \in C_0^n$.*

On this basis, we can identify, in any space $\otimes^n \mathbb{C}^2$, two special projection-operators ($P_1^{(n)}$ and $P_0^{(n)}$) that represent, in this framework, the *Truth-property* and the *Falsity-property*, respectively. The projection $P_1^{(n)}$ is determined by the closed subspace spanned by the set of all true registers, while $P_0^{(n)}$ is determined by the closed subspace spanned by the set of all false registers. As is well known, in quantum theory, projections have the role of *mathematical representatives* of possible physical properties of the quantum objects under investigation. Hence, it turns out that *Truth* and *Falsity* behave here as special cases of physical properties.

As a consequence, one can naturally apply the *Born rule* that determines *the probability-value that a quantum system in a given state satisfies a given property.* Consider any qumix ρ, which represents a possible state of a quantum system in the space $\otimes^n \mathbb{C}^2$. By applying the Born rule, we obtain that the probability-value that a physical system in state ρ satisfies the *Truth-property* $P_1^{(n)}$ is the number $\mathrm{tr}(P_1^{(n)}\rho)$ (where tr is the *trace functional*). This suggests the following natural definition of the notion of *probability* of a given qumix.

Definition 5. *Probability of a qumix*
For any qumix $\rho \in \mathfrak{D}(\otimes^n \mathbb{C}^2)$:

$$\mathbf{p}(\rho) := \mathrm{tr}(P_1^{(n)}\rho).$$

From an intuitive point of view, $\mathbf{p}(\rho)$ represents the probability that the information stored by the qumix ρ is true. In the particular case where ρ corresponds to the qubit

$$|\psi\rangle = a_0 |0\rangle + a_1 |1\rangle,$$

we obtain that $\mathbf{p}(\rho) = |a_1|^2$.

Given a quregister $|\psi\rangle$, we will also write $\mathbf{p}(|\psi\rangle)$ instead of $\mathbf{p}(P_{|\psi\rangle})$, where $P_{|\psi\rangle}$ is the density operator represented by the projection onto the one-dimensional subspace spanned by the vector $|\psi\rangle$.

An interesting relation connects qumixes with the real numbers in the interval $[0,1]$. For any $n \in \mathbb{N}^+$, any real number $\lambda \in [0,1]$ uniquely determines a qumix $\rho_\lambda^{(n)}$:

$$\rho_\lambda^{(n)} := (1 - \lambda)k_n P_0^{(n)} + \lambda k_n P_1^{(n)}$$

(where k_n is a normalization coefficient). From an intuitive point of view, $\rho_\lambda^{(n)}$ represents a *mixture of pieces of information* that might correspond to the *Truth* with probability λ.

Lemma 1. *Let $|\psi\rangle = \sum_{i=0}^{2^n-1} a_i |i\rangle$ be an n-quregister. Then,*

$$\mathbf{p}(|\psi\rangle) = \sum_{i \in C_1} |a_i|^2.$$

3   Gates

As mentioned in the Introduction, *gates* are unitary operators that transform quregisters into quregisters. Being unitary, gates represent characteristic *reversible logical operations.* The canonical gates (which are studied in the literature) can be naturally generalized to qumixes. We will consider here the following gates: the *negation*, the *Petri-Toffoli gate* and the *square root of the negation*.

Let us first describe these gates in the framework of quregisters.

Definition 6. *The negation*
For any $n \geq 1$, the negation on $\otimes^n \mathbb{C}^2$ is the linear operator $\mathsf{Not}^{(n)}$ such that for every element $|x_1, \ldots, x_n\rangle$ of the basis $\mathcal{B}^{(n)}$:

$$\mathsf{Not}^{(n)}(|x_1, \ldots, x_n\rangle) := |x_1, \ldots, x_{n-1}\rangle \otimes |1 - x_n\rangle.$$

In other words, $\mathsf{Not}^{(n)}$ inverts the value of the last element of any basis-vector of $\otimes^n \mathbb{C}^2$.

Definition 7. *The Petri-Toffoli gate*
For any $m \geq 1$ and any $n \geq 1$ the Petri-Toffoli gate is the linear operator $\mathsf{T}^{(m,n,1)}$ defined on $\otimes^{m+n+1} \mathbb{C}^2$ such that for every element $|x_1, \ldots, x_m\rangle \otimes |y_1, \ldots, y_n\rangle \otimes |z\rangle$ of the basis $\mathcal{B}^{(m+n+1)}$:

$$\mathsf{T}^{(m,n,1)}(|x_1, \ldots, x_m\rangle \otimes |y_1, \ldots, y_n\rangle \otimes |z\rangle) := |x_1, \ldots, x_m\rangle \otimes |y_1, \ldots, y_n\rangle \otimes |x_m y_n \boxplus z\rangle,$$

where $\boxplus$ represents the sum modulo 2.

One can easily show that both $\mathsf{Not}^{(n)}$ and $\mathsf{T}^{(m,n,1)}$ are unitary operators.

Consider now the set $\mathfrak{R}$ of all quregisters $|\psi\rangle$ "living" in $\otimes^n \mathbb{C}^2$, for some $n \geq 1$. The gates Not and T can be uniformly defined on this set in the expected way:

$$\mathsf{Not}(|\psi\rangle) := \mathsf{Not}^{(n)}(|\psi\rangle), \qquad \text{if } |\psi\rangle \in \otimes^n \mathbb{C}^2$$

$$\mathsf{T}(|\psi\rangle \otimes |\varphi\rangle \otimes |\chi\rangle) := \mathsf{T}^{(m,n,1)}(|\psi\rangle \otimes |\varphi\rangle \otimes |\chi\rangle),$$
$$\text{if } |\psi\rangle \in \otimes^m \mathbb{C}^2, \ |\varphi\rangle \in \otimes^n \mathbb{C}^2 \text{ and } |\chi\rangle \in \mathbb{C}^2.$$

On this basis, a conjunction And and a disjunction Or can be defined for any pair of quregisters $|\psi\rangle$ and $|\varphi\rangle$:

$$\mathsf{And}(|\psi\rangle, |\varphi\rangle) := \mathsf{T}(|\psi\rangle \otimes |\varphi\rangle \otimes |0\rangle);$$

$$\mathsf{Or}(|\psi\rangle, |\varphi\rangle) := \mathsf{Not}(\mathsf{And}(\mathsf{Not}(|\psi\rangle), \mathsf{Not}(|\varphi\rangle))).$$

Clearly, $|0\rangle$ represents an "ancilla" in the definition of And.

The gates we have considered so far are, in a sense, "semiclassical". A quantum logical behaviour only emerges in the case where our gates are applied to (proper) superpositions. When restricted to classical registers, such operators turn out to behave as classical (reversible) truth-functions. We will now consider an important example of a *genuine quantum gate* that transforms classical registers (elements of $\mathcal{B}^{(n)}$) into quregisters that are superpositions. This gate is the *square root of the negation*.

Definition 8. *The square root of the negation*
For any $n \geq 1$, the square root of the negation on $\otimes^n \mathbb{C}^2$ is the linear operator $\sqrt{\mathsf{Not}}^{(n)}$ such that for every element $|x_1, \ldots, x_n\rangle$ of the basis $\mathcal{B}^{(n)}$:

$$\sqrt{\mathsf{Not}}^{(n)}(|x_1, \ldots, x_n\rangle) := |x_1, \ldots, x_{n-1}\rangle \otimes \frac{1}{2}((1+i)|x_n\rangle + (1-i)|1 - x_n\rangle),$$

where $i := \sqrt{-1}$.

One can easily show that $\sqrt{\mathtt{Not}}^{(n)}$ is a unitary operator. The basic property of $\sqrt{\mathtt{Not}}^{(n)}$ is the following:

$$\text{for any } |\psi\rangle \in \otimes^n \mathbb{C}^2, \ \sqrt{\mathtt{Not}}^{(n)}(\sqrt{\mathtt{Not}}^{(n)}(|\psi\rangle)) = \mathtt{Not}^{(n)}(|\psi\rangle).$$

In other words, applying twice the square root of the negation means negating.

From a logical point of view, $\sqrt{\mathtt{Not}}^{(n)}$ can be regarded as a "tentative partial negation" (a kind of "half negation") that transforms *precise pieces of information* into *maximally uncertain* ones. For, we have:

$$\mathtt{p}(\sqrt{\mathtt{Not}}^{(1)}(|1\rangle)) = \frac{1}{2} = \mathtt{p}(\sqrt{\mathtt{Not}}^{(1)}(|0\rangle)).$$

As expected, also $\sqrt{\mathtt{Not}}$ can be uniformly defined on the set $\mathfrak{R}$ of all quregisters.

Interestingly enough, the gate $\sqrt{\mathtt{Not}}$ seems to represent a genuine *quantum logical operation* that does not admit any counterpart either in classical logic or in standard fuzzy logics (see [4]).

The gates considered so far can be naturally generalized to qumixes [9]. When our gates will be applied to density operators, we will write: NOT, $\sqrt{\mathtt{NOT}}$, $\mathbb{T}$, AND, OR (instead of Not, $\sqrt{\mathtt{Not}}$, T, And, Or).

Definition 9. *The negation*
For any qumix $\rho \in \mathfrak{D}(\otimes^n \mathbb{C}^2)$,

$$\mathtt{NOT}^{(n)}(\rho) := \mathtt{Not}^{(n)} \rho \, \mathtt{Not}^{(n)}.$$

Definition 10. *The square root of the negation*
For any qumix $\rho \in \mathfrak{D}(\otimes^n \mathbb{C}^2)$,

$$\sqrt{\mathtt{NOT}}^{(n)}(\rho) := \sqrt{\mathtt{Not}}^{(n)} \rho \, \sqrt{\mathtt{Not}}^{(n)*},$$

where $\sqrt{\mathtt{Not}}^{(n)*}$ is the adjoint of $\sqrt{\mathtt{Not}}^{(n)}$.

It is easy to see that for any $n \in \mathbb{N}^+$, both $\mathtt{NOT}^{(n)}(\rho)$ and $\sqrt{\mathtt{NOT}}^{(n)}(\rho)$ are qumixes of $\mathfrak{D}(\otimes^n \mathbb{C}^2)$.

Definition 11. *The Petri-Toffoli gate*
Let $\rho \in \mathfrak{D}(\otimes^m \mathbb{C}^2)$, $\sigma \in \mathfrak{D}(\otimes^n \mathbb{C}^2)$ and $\tau \in \mathfrak{D}(\mathbb{C}^2)$.

$$\mathbb{T}^{(m,n,1)}(\rho, \sigma, \tau) := T^{(m,n,1)}(\rho \otimes \sigma \otimes \tau)T^{(m,n,1)}.$$

On this basis, the conjunction AND is defined as follows:

Definition 12. *The conjunction*
Let $\rho \in \mathfrak{D}(\otimes^m \mathbb{C}^2)$ and $\sigma \in \mathfrak{D}(\otimes^n \mathbb{C}^2)$.

$$\mathtt{AND}^{(m,n,1)}(\rho, \sigma) := \mathbb{T}^{(m,n,1)}(\rho, \sigma, P_0^{(1)}).$$

Furthermore, the disjunction OR is defined via the the de Morgan law.

Like in the quregister-case, the gates NOT, $\sqrt{\text{NOT}}$, $\mathbb{T}$, AND, OR can be uniformly defined on the set $\mathfrak{D}$ of all qumixes.

An interesting preorder relation can be defined on the set $\mathfrak{D}$ of all qumixes.

Definition 13. *Preorder*
$\rho \preceq \sigma$ *iff the following conditions hold:*

(i) $\mathrm{p}(\rho) \leq \mathrm{p}(\sigma)$;
(ii) $\mathrm{p}(\sqrt{\text{NOT}}(\sigma)) \leq \mathrm{p}(\sqrt{\text{NOT}}(\rho))$.

One immediately shows that $\preceq$ is reflexive and transitive, but not antisymmetric (counterexamples can be easily found in $\mathfrak{D}(\mathbb{C}^2)$). From an intuitive point of view, $\rho \preceq \sigma$ means that the information σ is "closer to the truth" than the information ρ.

An equivalence relation can be then defined on $\mathfrak{D}$ as follows.

Definition 14. *Equivalence*
$\sigma \equiv \tau$ *iff* $\sigma \preceq \tau$ *and* $\tau \preceq \sigma$.

One can prove that $\equiv$ is a congruence relation with respect to the operations AND, NOT, $\sqrt{\text{NOT}}$. On this basis, we introduce two structures: the *reversible quantum computational structure* and its quotient, the *contracted reversible quantum computational structure*.

Definition 15. *The reversible quantum computational structure*
The structure
$$(\mathfrak{D}, \text{AND}, \text{NOT}, \sqrt{\text{NOT}}, P_0^{(1)}, P_1^{(1)}, \rho_{1/2}^{(1)}),$$
where $P_0^{(1)}, P_1^{(1)}, \rho_{1/2}^{(1)}$ *represent respectively the* Falsity, *the* Truth *and the* indeterminate truth-value, *is called the* reversible quantum computational structure.

Definition 16. *The contracted reversible quantum computational structure*
The structure
$$([\mathfrak{D}]_\equiv, \text{AND}, \text{NOT}, \sqrt{\text{NOT}}, [P_0^{(1)}]_\equiv, [P_1^{(1)}]_\equiv, [\rho_{1/2}^{(1)}]_\equiv),$$
where the operations AND, NOT, $\sqrt{\text{NOT}}$ *are defined on the equivalence classes belonging to the quotient* $[\mathfrak{D}]_\equiv$ *in the expected way, is called the* contracted reversible quantum computational structure.

4   Quantum Computational Formulas and Quantum Circuits

In the standard semantics of *quantum computational logics*, formulas denote qumixes, while the logical connectives correspond to some special gates. We consider first a *minimal quantum computational language* $\mathcal{L}$ that contains a privileged atomic formula $\mathbf{f}$ (whose intended interpretation is the *Falsity*). Molecular formulas are built by means of the following primitive connectives: the *negation* ($\neg$), the *square root of the negation* ($\sqrt{\neg}$), a ternary *conjunction* $\bigwedge$ (which corresponds to the Petri-Toffoli gate). For any formulas α and β, the expression $\bigwedge(\alpha, \beta, \mathbf{f})$ is a formula of $\mathcal{L}$. In this framework, the usual conjunction $\alpha \wedge \beta$ is dealt with as a metalinguistic abbreviation for the ternary conjunction $\bigwedge(\alpha, \beta, \mathbf{f})$. We will use the following metavariables: $\mathbf{q}, \mathbf{r} \dots$ for atomic formulas and $\alpha, \beta, \dots$ for formulas. The connective disjunction ($\vee$) is supposed to be defined via the *de Morgan law* ($\alpha \vee \beta := \neg(\neg\alpha \wedge \neg\beta)$).

Any formula α of $\mathcal{L}$ describes a *quantum circuit* that can be applied to an input, represented by a qumix living in a Hilbert space whose dimension depends on the linguistic form of α. Let us first introduce some useful syntactical notions. By *atomic complexity* of a formula α (indicated by $At(\alpha)$) we mean the number of occurrences of atomic formulas in α. For instance, $At(\neg \bigwedge(\mathbf{q}, \neg\mathbf{q}, \mathbf{f})) = 3$. Since the atomic complexity of α determines the dimension of the Hilbert space where a qumix representing information about α should live, the space $\otimes^{At(\alpha)}\mathbb{C}^2$ will be also called the *semantic space* of α. We will briefly write $\mathcal{H}^\alpha$, instead of $\otimes^{At(\alpha)}\mathbb{C}^2$.

Any formula α can be naturally decomposed into its parts, giving rise to a special configuration called the *syntactical tree* of α (indicated by $STree^\alpha$).

Roughly, $STree^\alpha$ can be represented as a sequence of *levels*:

$$Level_k(\alpha)$$

$$\dots$$

$$Level_1(\alpha),$$

where:

- each $Level_i(\alpha)$ (with $1 \le i \le k$) is a sequence of subformulas of α;
- the *bottom level* ($Level_1(\alpha)$) consists of α;
- the *top level* ($Level_k(\alpha)$) is the sequence of all atomic occurrences in α;
- for any i (with $1 \le i < k$), $Level_{i+1}(\alpha)$ is the sequence obtained by dropping the *principal connective* in all molecular formulas occurring in $Level_i(\alpha)$, and by repeating all the atomic formulas that possibly occur in $Level_i(\alpha)$.

As an example, consider the following formula: $\alpha = \mathbf{q} \wedge \neg\mathbf{q} = \bigwedge(\mathbf{q}, \neg\mathbf{q}, \mathbf{f})$. The syntactical tree of α is the following configuration:

$$Level_3(\alpha) = (\mathbf{q}, \mathbf{q}, \mathbf{f});$$
$$Level_2(\alpha) = (\mathbf{q}, \neg\mathbf{q}, \mathbf{f});$$
$$Level_1(\alpha) = (\bigwedge(\mathbf{q}, \neg\mathbf{q}, \mathbf{f})).$$

By *Height* of α (indicated by $Height(\alpha)$) we mean the number of levels of the syntactical tree of α. For instance, $Height(\bigwedge(\mathbf{q}, \neg\mathbf{q}, \mathbf{f})) = 3$.

The syntactical tree of α (which represents a purely syntactical object) uniquely determines a sequence of gates that are all defined on the semantic space of α. We will call this sequence of gates the *qubit tree* of α.

Consider a formula α such that $At(\alpha) = t$ and $Height(\alpha) = k$. Let $Level_i^j(\alpha)$ represent the j-th *node* of $Level_i(\alpha)$. Each $Level_i^j(\alpha)$ (where $1 \le i < Height(\alpha)$) can be naturally associated to a unitary operator Op_i^j, according to the following *operator-rule*:

$$Op_i^j := \begin{cases} I^{(1)} & \text{if } Level_i^j(\alpha) \text{ is an atomic formula;} \\ \text{Not}^{(r)} & \text{if } Level_i^j(\alpha) = \neg\beta \text{ and } At(\beta) = r; \\ \sqrt{\text{Not}}^{(r)} & \text{if } Level_i^j(\alpha) = \sqrt{\neg}\beta \text{ and } At(\beta) = r; \\ \text{T}^{(r,s,1)} & \text{if } Level_i^j(\alpha) = \bigwedge(\beta,\gamma,\mathbf{f}), At(\beta) = r \text{ and } At(\gamma) = s, \end{cases}$$

where $I^{(1)}$ is the identity operator of $\mathbb{C}^2$.

On this basis, one can associate a gate G_i^α to each $Level_i(\alpha)$ (such that $1 \le i < Height(\alpha)$):

$$G_i^\alpha := \bigotimes_{j=1}^{|Level_i(\alpha)|} Op_i^j,$$

where $|Level_i(\alpha)|$ is the length of the sequence $Level_i(\alpha)$.

Being a tensor product of unitary operators, every G_i^α turns out to be a unitary operator. One can easily show that all G_i^α's are defined on the same space, $\mathcal{H}^\alpha$.

Definition 17. *The qubit tree of α*
The qubit tree of α *(denoted by $QTree^\alpha$) is the sequence of gates*

$$(G_1^\alpha, \ldots, G_{Height(\alpha)-1}^\alpha)$$

that is uniquely determined by the syntactical tree of α.

As an example, consider again the formula: $\alpha = \bigwedge(\mathbf{q}, \neg\mathbf{q}, \mathbf{f})$.

In order to build the qubit tree of α, let us first determine the operators Op_i^j corresponding to each node of $Stree^\alpha$. We obtain:

- $Op_1^1 = \text{T}^{(1,1,1)}$, because $\bigwedge(\mathbf{q}, \neg\mathbf{q}, \mathbf{f})$ is connected with $(\mathbf{q}, \neg\mathbf{q}, \mathbf{f})$ (at $Level_2(\alpha)$);
- $Op_2^1 = I^{(1)}$, because $\mathbf{q}$ is connected with $\mathbf{q}$ (at $Level_3(\alpha)$);
- $Op_2^2 = \text{Not}^{(1)}$, because $\neg\mathbf{q}$ is connected with $\mathbf{q}$ (at $Level_3(\alpha)$);
- $Op_2^3 = I^{(1)}$, because $\mathbf{f}$ is connected with $\mathbf{f}$ (at $Level_3(\alpha)$).

The qubit tree of α is represented by the sequence of gates (G_1^α, G_2^α), where:

$$G_1^\alpha = Op_1^1 = \text{T}^{(1,1,1)};$$
$$G_2^\alpha = Op_2^1 \otimes Op_2^2 \otimes Op_2^3 = I^{(1)} \otimes \text{Not}^{(1)} \otimes I^{(1)}.$$

As we have seen, qubit trees consist of unitary operators (which can be applied to quregisters). The notion of qubit tree can be naturally generalized to qumixes. In such a case we will speak of *qumix trees*, and we will call *quantum tree* either a qubit tree or a qumix tree. Let $(G_1^\alpha, \ldots, G_{k-1}^\alpha)$ be the qubit tree of α. We can define the following sequence of functions on the set $\mathfrak{D}(\mathcal{H}^\alpha)$:

$$^\mathfrak{D}G_1^\alpha(\rho) = G_1^\alpha \, \rho \, G_1^{\alpha*}$$

$$\ldots$$

$$^\mathfrak{D}G_{k-1}^\alpha(\rho) = G_{k-1}^\alpha \, \rho \, G_{k-1}^{\alpha*}.$$

One can easily prove that, for any $\rho \in \mathfrak{D}(\mathcal{H}^\alpha)$ and for any i $(1 \leq i \leq k-1)$, $^\mathfrak{D}G_i^\alpha(\rho)$ is a density operator of $\mathfrak{D}(\mathcal{H}^\alpha)$. The sequence

$$QumTree^\alpha = (^\mathfrak{D}G_1^\alpha, \ldots, {}^\mathfrak{D}G_{k-1}^\alpha)$$

will be called the *qumix tree* of α, while the elements of a qumix tree will be called *qumix gates*. Apparently, qubit trees and qumix trees consist of different kinds of mathematical objects: the elements of a qubit tree are unitary operators, while the elements of a qumix tree are special bijections that transform density operators into density operators. Both qumix trees and qubit trees represent reversible information processes.

Consider now a formula α and let $(^\mathfrak{D}G_1^\alpha, \ldots, {}^\mathfrak{D}G_{k-1}^\alpha)$ be the qumix tree of α. Any choice of a qumix ρ in $\mathcal{H}^\alpha$ determines a sequence $(\rho_k, \ldots, \rho_1)$ of qumixes of $\mathcal{H}^\alpha$, where:

$$\rho_k = \rho$$

$$\rho_{k-1} = {}^\mathfrak{D}G_{k-1}^\alpha(\rho_k)$$

$$\ldots$$

$$\rho_1 = {}^\mathfrak{D}G_1^\alpha(\rho_2)$$

Since $Level_k(\alpha)$ is the sequence of all occurrences of atomic formulas in α and $Level_1(\alpha) = \alpha$, the qumix ρ_k can be regarded as a possible *input-information* concerning the atomic parts of α, while ρ_1 represents the *output-information* about α, given the input-information ρ_k. Each ρ_i corresponds to an intermediate result of the computation (representing the *information* about $Level_i(\alpha)$, given the input-information ρ_k).

How to determine an information about the parts of α under a given input? It is natural to apply the standard quantum-theoretic rule that determines the *states of the parts of a compound system*.

Suppose that:

$$Level_i(\alpha) = \beta_{i_1}, \ldots \beta_{i_r}.$$

We have:

$$\mathcal{H}^\alpha = \mathcal{H}^{\beta_{i_1}} \otimes \ldots \otimes \mathcal{H}^{\beta_{i_r}}.$$

We know that $QumTree^\alpha$ and the choice of an input ρ_k (in $\mathcal{H}^\alpha$) determine a sequence of qumixes:

$$\rho_k \rightsquigarrow Level_k(\alpha) = (\mathbf{q}_1, \ldots, \mathbf{q}_t)$$

$$\ldots$$

$$\rho_i \leadsto Level_i(\alpha) = (\beta_{i_1}, \dots, \beta_{i_r})$$

$$\dots$$

$$\rho_1 \leadsto Level_1(\alpha) = (\alpha)$$

Consider $red^j(\rho_i)$, the *reduced state of ρ_i with respect to the j-th subsystem.*[1] From a semantic point of view, this state can be regarded as a *contextual information* about β_{i_j} (the subformula of α occurring at the j-th position at $Level_i(\alpha)$) under the input ρ_k. Apparently, a contextual information about a subformula is generally a mixture.

An interesting situation arises when the qumix ρ_k, representing a global information about the atomic parts of α, is an *entangled* pure state.[2]

As an example, consider the formula $\alpha = \neg \bigwedge(\mathbf{q}, \neg\mathbf{q}, \mathbf{f})$ (which represents an example of the *noncontradiction principle* formalized in the quantum computational language). The input-information might be the following entangled state:

$$|\psi_4\rangle = \frac{1}{\sqrt{2}} |110\rangle + \frac{1}{\sqrt{2}} |000\rangle \leadsto Level_4(\alpha) = (\mathbf{q}, \mathbf{q}, \mathbf{f})$$

The reduced states of $|\psi_4\rangle$ turn out to be the following:

$red^1(\frac{1}{\sqrt{2}}|110\rangle + \frac{1}{\sqrt{2}}|000\rangle) = \frac{1}{2}P_0^{(1)} + \frac{1}{2}P_1^{(1)}$

$red^2(\frac{1}{\sqrt{2}}|110\rangle + \frac{1}{\sqrt{2}}|000\rangle) = \frac{1}{2}P_0^{(1)} + \frac{1}{2}P_1^{(1)}$

$red^3(\frac{1}{\sqrt{2}}|110\rangle + \frac{1}{\sqrt{2}}|000\rangle) = P_0^{(1)}$

Hence, the contextual information about both occurrences of $\mathbf{q}$ is the (proper) mixture

$$\frac{1}{2}P_0^{(1)} + \frac{1}{2}P_1^{(1)}.$$

At the same time, the contextual information about $\mathbf{f}$ is projection $P_0^{(1)}$ (representing the *Falsity*).

Quantum trees can be naturally regarded as examples of quantum circuits that compute outputs under given inputs. Since both qubit trees and qumix trees are determined by the syntactical tree of a given formula, one can also say that any formula α of the quantum computational language plays the role of an intuitive and "economical" description of a quantum circuit (which gives

---

[1] We recall that $red^j(\rho_i)$ is the unique density operator that satisfies the following condition: for any self-adjoint operator A^j of $\mathcal{H}^{\beta_j}$,

$$\mathbf{tr}(red^j(\rho_i)A^j) = \mathbf{tr}(\rho_i(I^1 \otimes \dots \otimes I^{j-1} \otimes A^j \otimes I^{j+1} \otimes \dots \otimes I^r)),$$

(where I^h is the identity operator of $\mathcal{H}^{\beta_h}$). As a consequence, ρ_i and $red^j(\rho_i)$ are statistically equivalent with respect to the j-th subsystem of the compound system described by ρ_i.

[2] The basic features of an *entangled state* $|\psi\rangle$ are the following: 1) $|\psi\rangle$ is a maximal information (a pure state) that describes a compound physical system S; 2) the pieces of information determined by $|\psi\rangle$ about the parts of S are, generally, non-maximal (proper mixtures). Hence, the information about the *whole* is more precise than the information about the *parts*.

rise to a reversible information process). Notice that, in spite of its superficial appearance, the structure of a quantum circuit is deeply parallel: in fact, any proper qubit (which is a superposition of the two classical bits) determines a branching.

5   Compositional and Holistic Quantum Computational Semantics

Two kinds of quantum computational semantics have been investigated: a *compositional* and a *holistic* semantics (see [4] and [5]). In the *compositional* semantics, the meaning of a molecular formula is determined by the meanings of its parts (like in classical logic). In this framework, the input-information about the top level of the syntactical tree of a formula α is always associated to a factorized state $\rho_1 \otimes \ldots \otimes \rho_t$, where t is the atomic complexity of α and $\rho_1, \ldots, \rho_t$ are qumixes of $\mathbb{C}^2$. As a consequence, the meaning of a molecular α cannot be a pure state, if the meanings of some atomic parts of α are proper mixtures.

The *holistic quantum compositional semantics*[3] is based on a more "liberal" assumption: the input information about the top-level of the syntactical tree of α can be represented by any qumix "living" in the semantic space of α. As a consequence, the meanings of all levels of $STree^\alpha$ are not, generally, factorized states.

Suppose that:

$$Level_i(\alpha) = (\beta_1, \ldots, \beta_r).$$

As we have seen, the space $\mathcal{H}^\alpha$ can be naturally regarded as the Hilbert space of a compound physical system consisting of r parts (mathematically represented by the spaces $\mathcal{H}^{\beta_1}, \ldots, \mathcal{H}^{\beta_r}$), where each part may be compound. On this basis, for any qumix ρ_i (associated to $Level_i(\alpha)$) and for any node $Level_i^j(\alpha)$, we can consider the *reduced state* $red^j(\rho_i)$ with respect to the j-th subsystem of the system described by ρ_i. As we have seen, according to the formalism of quantum theory, the state $red^j(\rho_i)$ describes the j-th subsystem on the basis of the *global* information ρ_i (about the total system). Since $Level_i(\alpha) = (\beta_1, \ldots, \beta_r)$, the qumix $red^j(\rho_i)$ (which is a density operator of the space $\mathcal{H}^{\beta_j}$) represents a *possible meaning* of the sentence β_j.

We can now introduce the basic definitions of the holistic semantics. The main concept is the notion of *holistic quantum computational model*: a function Hol that assigns to any formula α of the quantum computational language a *global meaning*, which cannot be generally inferred from the meanings of the parts of α. Of course (like in the standard semantic approaches), the function Hol shall preserve the logical form of α (by interpreting the logical connectives as the corresponding qumix gates).

In order to define the concept of *holistic quantum computational model*, we will first introduce the notions of *atomic holistic model* and of *tree holistic model*.

---

[3] In [4] we have presented a weaker version of the holistic semantics.

Definition 18. *Atomic holistic model*
An atomic holistic model *is a map* Hol^{At} *that associates a qumix to any formula* α *of* $\mathcal{L}$ *, satisfying the following conditions:*

(1) $\mathrm{Hol}^{At}(\alpha) \in \mathfrak{D}(\mathcal{H}^{\alpha})$;
(2) Let $At(\alpha) = n$ *and* $Level_{Heigth(\alpha)} = \mathbf{q}_1, \ldots, \mathbf{q}_n$. *Then,*

   (2.1) if $\mathbf{q}_j = \mathbf{f}$, *then* $red^j(\mathrm{Hol}^{At}(\alpha)) = P_0^{(1)}$;
   (2.2) if $\mathbf{q}_j$ *and* $\mathbf{q}_h$ *are two occurrences in* α *of the same atomic formula, then* $red^j(\mathrm{Hol}^{At}(\alpha)) = red^h(\mathrm{Hol}^{At}(\alpha))$.

Apparently, $\mathrm{Hol}^{At}(\alpha)$ represents a *global interpretation* of the atomic formulas occurring in α. At the same time, $red^j(\mathrm{Hol}^{At}(\alpha))$, the *reduced state* of the compound system (described by $\mathrm{Hol}^{At}(\alpha)$) with respect to the j-th subsystem, represents a *contextual meaning* of $\mathbf{q}_j$ with respect to the *global meaning* $\mathrm{Hol}^{At}(\alpha)$. Conditions (2.1) and (2.2) guarantee that $\mathrm{Hol}^{At}(\alpha)$ is well behaved. For, the contextual meaning of $\mathbf{f}$ is always the *Falsity*, while two different occurrences (in α) of the same atomic formula have the same contextual meaning.

The map Hol^{At} (which assigns a meaning to the top-level of the syntactical tree of any sentence α) can be naturally extended to a map Hol^{Tree} that assigns a meaning to each level of the syntactical tree of any α, following the prescriptions of the qumix tree of α.

Consider a formula α such that:

$$QumTree^{\alpha} = ({}^{\mathfrak{D}}G_1^{\alpha}, \ldots, {}^{\mathfrak{D}}G_{Heigth(\alpha)-1}^{\alpha}).$$

The map Hol^{Tree} is defined as follows:

$$\mathrm{Hol}^{Tree}(Level_{Heigth(\alpha)}) = \mathrm{Hol}^{At}(\alpha)$$

$$\mathrm{Hol}^{Tree}(Level_i(\alpha)) = {}^{\mathfrak{D}}G_i^{\alpha}(\mathrm{Hol}^{Tree}(Level_{i+1}(\alpha))$$

(where $Heigth(\alpha) > i \geq 1$).

On this basis, one can naturally define the notion of *holistic (quantum computational) model* of $\mathcal{L}$.

Definition 19. *Holistic model*
A map Hol *that assigns to any formula* α *a qumix of the space* $\mathcal{H}^{\alpha}$ *is called a* holistic (quantum computational) model *of* $\mathcal{L}$ *iff there exists an atomic holistic model* Hol^{At} *s.t.:*

$$\mathrm{Hol}(\alpha) = \mathrm{Hol}^{Tree}(Level_1(\alpha)),$$

where Hol^{Tree} *is the extension of* Hol^{At}.

Given a formula γ, Hol determines the *contextual meaning*, with respect to the context $\mathrm{Hol}(\gamma)$, of any occurrence of a subformula β in γ.

Definition 20. *Contextual meaning of a node*
Let β be a subformula of γ occurring at the $j-th$ position of the $i-th$ level of the syntactical tree of γ. We indicate by $\beta[^i_j]$ the node of $STree^\gamma$ corresponding to such occurrence. The contextual meaning of $\beta[^i_j]$ with respect to the context $\mathrm{Hol}(\gamma)$ is defined as follows:

$$\mathrm{Hol}^\gamma(\beta[^i_j]) = red^j(\mathrm{Hol}^{Tree}(Level_i(\gamma))).$$

Hence, we have:

$$\mathrm{Hol}^\gamma(\gamma) = \mathrm{Hol}^{Tree}(Level_1(\gamma)) = \mathrm{Hol}(\gamma).$$

Suppose that $\beta[^i_j]$ and $\beta[^h_k]$ are two nodes of the syntactical tree of γ, representing two occurrences of the same subformula β. One can show that:

$$\mathrm{Hol}^\gamma(\beta[^i_j]) = \mathrm{Hol}^\gamma(\beta[^h_k]).$$

In other words, two different occurrences of one and the same subformula in a formula γ receive the same contextual meaning with respect to the context $\mathrm{Hol}(\gamma)$.

On this basis, one can define the *contextual meaning* of a subformula β of γ, with respect to the context $\mathrm{Hol}(\gamma)$:

$$\mathrm{Hol}^\gamma(\beta) := \mathrm{Hol}^\gamma(\beta[^i_j]),$$

where $\beta[^i_j]$ is any occurrence of β at a node of $STree^\gamma$.

Apparently, Hol^γ is a partial function that is only defined for the subformulas of γ. For any formula γ, we call the partial function Hol^γ (which assigns a meaning to each subformula of γ with respect to the context $\mathrm{Hol}(\gamma)$) a *contextual holistic model* of the language.

Suppose now that β is a subformula of two different formulas γ and δ. Generally, we have:

$$\mathrm{Hol}^\gamma(\beta) \neq \mathrm{Hol}^\delta(\beta).$$

In other words, formulas may receive different contextual meanings in different contexts![4]

In this framework, compositional models can be described as particular cases of holistic models.

Definition 21. *Compositional model*
A model Hol is called compositional *iff the following condition is satisfied for any formula α: $\mathrm{Hol}^{At}(\alpha) = \mathrm{Hol}(\mathbf{q}_1) \otimes \ldots \otimes \mathrm{Hol}(\mathbf{q}_t)$, where $\mathbf{q}_1, \ldots, \mathbf{q}_t$ are the atomic formulas occurring in α.*

---

[4] As an example, consider the following situation (which is possible in the framework of the holistic semantics): $\gamma = \mathbf{q}$, $\delta = \neg\mathbf{q}$, $\mathrm{Hol}^{At}(\gamma) = P_1^{(1)}$, $\mathrm{Hol}^{At}(\delta) = P_1^{(1)}$. Hence: $\mathrm{Hol}^\gamma(\mathbf{q}) = \mathrm{Hol}^{At}(\mathbf{q}) = P_1^{(1)}$. At the same time, $\mathrm{Hol}^\delta(\mathbf{q}) = red^1(\mathrm{Hol}^{At}(\delta)) = \mathrm{Hol}^{At}(\delta) = P_0^{(1)}$.

As expected, unlike holistic models, compositional models are context-independent. Suppose that β is a subformula of two different formulas γ and δ. We have:

$$\text{Hol}^\gamma(\beta) = \text{Hol}^\delta(\beta) = \text{Hol}(\beta).$$

The notion of logical consequence in the framework of the holistic quantum computational semantics represents a reasonable variant of the standard notions of logical consequence.

Let us first define the notion of *consequence in a given contextual model*.

Definition 22. *Consequence in a given contextual model* Hol^γ
A formula β is a consequence of a formula α in a given contextual model Hol^γ
$(\alpha \models_{\text{Hol}^\gamma} \beta)$ *iff*

1. α *and* β *are subformulas of* γ;
2. $\text{Hol}^\gamma(\alpha) \preceq \text{Hol}^\gamma(\beta)$ *(where $\preceq$ is the preorder relation defined in 13).*

Definition 23. *Logical consequence (in the holistic semantics)*
A formula β is a logical consequence of a formula α (in the holistic semantics) iff for any formula γ such that α and β are subformulas of γ and for any Hol,

$$\alpha \models_{\text{Hol}^\gamma} \beta.$$

We call **HQCL** the logic that is semantically characterized by the logical consequence relation we have just defined. Hence, $\alpha \models_{\textbf{HQCL}} \beta$ iff for any formula γ such that α and β are subformulas of γ and for any Hol,

$$\alpha \models_{\text{Hol}^\gamma} \beta.$$

At the same time, by *compositional quantum computational logic* (**CQCL**) we mean the logic that is semantically characterized by the class of all compositional quantum computational models. Hence, $\alpha \models_{\textbf{CQCL}} \beta$ iff for any compositional model Hol,

$$\alpha \models_{\text{Hol}} \beta.$$

Although the basic ideas of the holistic and of the compositional quantum computational semantics are quite different, one can prove that **HQCL** and **CQCL** are the same logic (see [5]). In other words, for any formulas α and β,

$$\alpha \models_{\textbf{HQCL}} \beta \text{ iff } \alpha \models_{\textbf{CQCL}} \beta.$$

This means that the logics (formalized in our "poor" sentential languages) are not able to capture the difference between an analytical and a holistic semantic procedure.

Since **HQCL**= **CQCL**, we will simply speak of *quantum computational logic* (denoted by **QCL**). One is dealing with a nonstandard form of *unsharp quantum logic*, where the noncontradiction principle breaks down ($\nvDash_{\textbf{QCL}} \neg(\alpha \wedge \neg\alpha)$), while conjunction is not idempotent ($\alpha \nvDash_{\textbf{QCL}} \alpha \wedge \alpha$). Interestingly enough, distributivity is here violated "in the wrong direction" with respect to orthodox quantum logic. For, $\alpha \wedge (\beta \vee \gamma) \models_{\textbf{QCL}} (\alpha \wedge \beta) \vee (\alpha \wedge \gamma)$, but not the other way around!

6   Irreversible Logical Operations

Is it reasonable to deal also with *irreversible logical operations* in quantum computation? And what might be the computational and the physical meaning of such operations?

We will first restrict our analysis to the set $\mathfrak{D}(\mathbb{C}^2)$ of all qumixes living in the two-dimensional space $\mathbb{C}^2$. In order to define an *irreversible conjunction* on $\mathfrak{D}(\mathbb{C}^2)$, it is expedient to recall an important property that holds for the reversible conjunction AND.

Lemma 2. *For any qumixes σ and τ, $\mathrm{p}(\mathrm{AND}(\sigma, \tau)) = \mathrm{p}(\sigma) \cdot \mathrm{p}(\tau)$ (see [4]).*

Apparently, the quantum computational conjunction shows a quite nonstandard behavior with respect to classical probability theory. Qumixes always behave as *independent events*: the probability of a conjunction is the product of the probabilities of the two members.

On this basis, one can naturally define an irreversible conjunction (indicated by IAND) as follows:

Definition 24. *For any qumixes σ and τ of $\mathfrak{D}(\mathbb{C}^2)$,*

$$\mathrm{IAND}(\sigma, \tau) := \rho^{(1)}_{\mathrm{p}(\sigma) \cdot \mathrm{p}(\tau)}$$

(where $\rho^{(1)}_{\mathrm{p}(\sigma) \cdot \mathrm{p}(\tau)}$ is the qumix of $\mathbb{C}^2$ that is uniquely determined by the real number $\mathrm{p}(\sigma) \cdot \mathrm{p}(\tau)$).

One can prove that

$$\mathrm{IAND}(\sigma, \tau) = red^3(\mathrm{AND}(\sigma, \tau)) = red^3(\mathbb{T}(\sigma, \tau, P_0^{(1)})).$$

In other words, $\mathrm{IAND}(\sigma, \tau)$ represents the reduced state of $\mathrm{AND}(\sigma, \tau)$ on the third subsystem.

An interesting situation arises when both σ and τ are pure states. For instance, suppose that:

$$\sigma = P_{|\psi\rangle} \quad \text{and} \quad \tau = P_{|\varphi\rangle},$$

where $|\psi\rangle$ and $|\varphi\rangle$ are proper qubits. Then,

$$\mathrm{AND}(\sigma, \tau) = P_{\mathbb{T}^{(1,1,1)}(|\psi\rangle \otimes |\varphi\rangle \otimes |0\rangle)},$$

which is a pure state. At the same time, we have

$$\mathrm{IAND}(\sigma, \tau) = red^3(P_{\mathbb{T}^{(1,1,1)}(|\psi\rangle \otimes |\varphi\rangle \otimes |0\rangle)}),$$

which is a proper mixture. Apparently, when considering only the properties of the third subsystem we lose some information. As a consequence, we obtain a final state that does not represent maximal knowledge. From an intuitive point of view, one can say that whenever we restrict our attention to the qumixes living in $\mathbb{C}^2$ and to some irreversible operations (defined on $\mathfrak{D}(\mathbb{C}^2)$) we are only concerned with the results, ignoring the "history" of our computation.

In this perspective, we can now introduce the notion of *irreversible quantum computational structure*.

Definition 25. *The irreversible quantum computational structure*
The structure

$$(\mathfrak{D}(\mathbb{C}^2), \text{IAND}, \text{NOT}, \sqrt{\text{NOT}}, P_0^{(1)}, P_1^{(1)}, \rho_{1/2}^{(1)}),$$

where IAND *is the irreversible conjunction defined above, is called the* irreversible quantum computational structure.

On this basis an *irreversible (compositional) quantum computational semantics* for the language $\mathcal{L}$ can be developed in the expected way.

Interestingly enough, one can prove that the irreversible and the reversible quantum computational semantics characterize the same logic (see [4]). Hence, we can conclude that there is no way to distinguish between reversible and irreversible logical operations in the framework of our logics, formalized in the "poor" language $\mathcal{L}$.

Are there other interesting irreversible operations that might be considered in quantum computation? Some natural candidates are represented, for instance, by a Łukasiewicz-like conjunction and a Łukasiewicz-like disjunction.

Definition 26. *The Łukasiewicz conjunction and disjunction.*
For any qumixes σ and τ of $\mathfrak{D}(\mathbb{C}^2)$,

$$- \text{ŁAND}(\sigma, \tau) := \rho_{\text{p}(\sigma) \odot \text{p}(\tau)}^{(1)}$$
$$- \text{ŁOR}(\sigma, \tau) := \rho_{\text{p}(\sigma) \oplus \text{p}(\tau)}^{(1)},$$

where $\oplus$ and $\odot$ are the truncated sum and its dual, defined on the real interval $[0, 1]$. In other words: $x \oplus y := min\{1, x + y\}$; $x \odot y := max\{0, x + y - 1\}$, for any $x, y \in [0, 1]$.

A de Morgan relation holds between ŁAND and ŁOR (like in fuzzy logics).

$$\text{ŁAND}(\sigma, \tau) = \text{NOT}\{\text{ŁOR}[\text{NOT}(\sigma), \text{NOT}(\tau)]\};$$

$$\text{ŁOR}(\sigma, \tau) = \text{NOT}\{\text{ŁAND}[\text{NOT}(\sigma), \text{NOT}(\tau)]\}.$$

On this basis, our irreversible quantum computational structure can be enriched as follows:

Definition 27. *The Łukasiewicz quantum computational structure*
The structure

$$(\mathfrak{D}(\mathbb{C}^2), \text{IAND}, \text{ŁAND}, \text{NOT}, \sqrt{\text{NOT}}, P_0^{(1)}, P_1^{(1)}, \rho_{1/2}^{(1)})$$

is called the Łukasiewicz quantum computational structure.

One can prove that the equivalence relation $\equiv$ (see Def. 14) is a congruence with respect to the Łukasiewicz conjunction ŁAND. As a consequence, we are entitled to introduce the *contracted Łukasiewicz quantum computational structure*:

Definition 28. *The contracted Łukasiewicz quantum computational structure*
The structure

$$([\mathfrak{D}]_{\equiv}, \text{AND}, \oplus, \text{NOT}, \sqrt{\text{NOT}}, [P_0^{(1)}]_{\equiv}, [P_1^{(1)}]_{\equiv}, [\rho_{1/2}^{(1)}]_{\equiv})$$

(where the operations are defined in the expected way) is called the contracted
Łukasiewicz quantum computational structure.

Both the irreversible conjunction and the Łukasiewicz operations can be extended to the whole set $\mathfrak{D}$ of all possible qumixes. Let us first define the irreversible conjunction IAND on the cartesian product $\mathfrak{D} \times \mathfrak{D}$.

Definition 29. *For any $\sigma \in \mathfrak{D}(\otimes^m \mathbb{C}^2)$ and any $\tau \in \mathfrak{D}(\otimes^n \mathbb{C}^2)$,*

$$\text{IAND}(\sigma, \tau) := \rho_{\text{p}(\sigma) \cdot \text{p}(\tau)}^{(m+n)}$$

We know that the reversible conjunction AND has been defined in terms of the
Petri-Toffoli gate (recall that for any $m, n > 0$, $\text{T}^{(m,n,1)}$ is a unitary operator of
$\otimes^{m+n+1} \mathbb{C}^2$). In a similar way, we can reasonably define an irreversible conjunction $\text{IAND}^{(m,n)}$ on the set of all qumixes living in $\mathfrak{D}(\otimes^{m+n} \mathbb{C}^2)$.
Let $\rho \in \mathfrak{D}(\otimes^{m+n} \mathbb{C}^2)$. We have:

$$\otimes^{m+n} \mathbb{C}^2 = (\otimes^m \mathbb{C}^2) \otimes (\otimes^n \mathbb{C}^2).$$

Of course, the qumix ρ can be regarded as the state of a compound system
consisting of two parts: the state of the first subsystem (indicated by $red^{\otimes^m \mathbb{C}^2}(\rho)$)
lives in $\otimes^m \mathbb{C}^2$, while the state of the second subsystem (indicated by $red^{\otimes^n \mathbb{C}^2}(\rho)$)
lives in $\otimes^n \mathbb{C}^2$. On this basis, we can now define the irreversible conjunction
$\text{IAND}^{(m,n)}$ on the whole set $\mathfrak{D}(\otimes^{m+n} \mathbb{C}^2)$.

Definition 30. *The irreversible conjunction.*
For any $\sigma \in \mathfrak{D}(\otimes^{m+n} \mathbb{C}^2)$,

$$\text{IAND}^{(m,n)}(\sigma) := \text{IAND}(red^{\otimes^m \mathbb{C}^2}(\sigma), red^{\otimes^n \mathbb{C}^2}(\sigma)).$$

In the particular case where $\sigma = \tau_1^{(m)} \otimes \tau_2^{(n)}$, we will obtain:

$$red^{\otimes^m \mathbb{C}^2}(\sigma) = \tau_1^{(m)} \text{ and } red^{\otimes^n \mathbb{C}^2}(\sigma) = \tau_2^{(n)}.$$

Hence,
$$\text{IAND}^{(m,n)}(\sigma) = \text{IAND}(\tau_1^{(m)}, \tau_2^{(n)}).$$

In a similar way, we can define the Łukasiewicz operations LAND (on $\mathfrak{D} \times \mathfrak{D}$)
and $\text{ŁAND}^{(m,n)}$ (on $\mathfrak{D}(\otimes^{m+n} \mathbb{C}^2)$), *mutatis mutandis*.

We call *qumix operation* on $\mathfrak{D}(\otimes^n \mathbb{C}^2)$ any total function on $\mathfrak{D}(\otimes^n \mathbb{C}^2)$. Apparently, both $\text{IAND}^{(m,n)}$ and $\text{ŁAND}^{(m,n)}$ are examples of qumix operations. Needless
to say, qumix operations are generally irreversible. Of course, any qumix-gate $^{\mathfrak{D}}G$
defined on $\mathfrak{D}(\otimes^n \mathbb{C}^2)$ is a particular case of a qumix operation that corresponds
to a reversible function.

Qumix operations can be combined by means of a product (indicated by $\times$).

Definition 31. *The product of qumix operations*
Let $Q_1^{(m)}$ and $Q_2^{(n)}$ be two qumix operations defined on $\mathfrak{D}(\otimes^m\mathbb{C}^2)$ and $\mathfrak{D}(\otimes^n\mathbb{C}^2)$, respectively. The product $Q_1^{(m)} \times Q_1^{(n)}$ is defined for any $\sigma \in \mathfrak{D}(\otimes^{(m+n)}\mathbb{C}^2)$ as follows:

- $[Q_1^{(m)} \times Q_1^{(n)}](\sigma) := {}^{\mathfrak{D}}(G_1 \otimes G_2)(\sigma)$, *if there exist a gate G_1 of $\otimes^m\mathbb{C}^2$ and a gate G_2 of $\otimes^n\mathbb{C}^2$ such that $Q_1^{(m)} = {}^{\mathfrak{D}}G_1$ and $Q_2^{(n)} = {}^{\mathfrak{D}}G_2$.*
- $[Q_1^{(m)} \times Q_2^{(n)}](\sigma) := Q_1^{(m)}(red^{\otimes^m\mathbb{C}^2}(\sigma)) \otimes G_2^{(n)}(red^{\otimes^n\mathbb{C}^2}(\sigma))$, *otherwise.*

On this basis, we can now extend our notion of *quantum tree*, introducing the concept of *possibly irreversible quantum tree*. Let us first consider a richer quantum computational language $\mathcal{L}^I$ which contains at the same time the reversible connectives $\neg$, $\sqrt{\neg}$, $\wedge$ and the irreversible conjunctions $\wedge_I$ and $\wedge_L$ (corresponding to the qumix operations IAND and ŁAND, respectively). The notion of *syntactical tree* for the formulas of this language is then defined like in the case of the language $\mathcal{L}$. As happens for $\mathcal{L}$, the syntactical tree of any formula α of $\mathcal{L}^I$ determines a sequence of qumix operations $Q_1^\alpha, \ldots, Q_{Height(\alpha)-1}^\alpha$. We will call such a sequence the *possibly irreversible quantum tree* of α. Clearly, any quantum tree is a particular case of a possibly irreversible quantum tree (a case, where all the qumix operations occurring in the tree are reversible).

What might be the physical and the computational interest of possibly irreversible quantum circuits? As is well known, any reversibility-breaking in quantum computation is generally connected with a failure of *quantum coherence*, which may be determined by different "causes" (a noise, a measurement, and so on). Hence, the theory of possibly irreversible quantum circuits might provide a general framework to describe a number of practical situations.

7   Quantum Computational Simulations

Some of the reversible and irreversible qumix operations we have considered so far are naturally correlated with some fuzzy functions, defined on the the real interval $[0, 1]$. In fact, an important property of the operations NOT, AND, IAND and ŁAND is a *probabilistic truth-functional* behavior. We have:

- $p(NOT(\sigma)) = 1 - p(\sigma)$;
- $p(AND(\sigma, \tau)) = p(\sigma) \cdot p(\tau)$;
- $p(IAND(\sigma, \tau)) = p(\sigma) \cdot p(\tau)$;
- $p(ŁAND(\sigma, \tau)) = p(\sigma) \odot p(\tau) = max\{0, p(\sigma) + p(\tau) - 1\}$.

Notice that not all gates and qumix gates turn out to behave truth-functionally (an important counterexample is, for instance, the gate $\sqrt{Not}$, see [4]).

The fuzzy functions f_{NOT}, f_{AND}, f_{IAND}, $f_{ŁAND}$ (corresponding to NOT, AND, IAND, ŁAND) are naturally defined as follows (for any $x, y \in [0, 1]$):

- $f_{NOT}(x) = 1 - x$;
- $f_{AND}(x, y) = x \cdot y$;

- $f_{\text{IAND}}(x, y) = x \cdot y;$
- $f_{\text{LAND}}(x, y) = x \odot y.$

An interesting question arises: how to go back from the world of the fuzzy (generally irreversible) functions to the world of the (reversible) gates? Is it possible to characterize the fuzzy functions that, in a sense, admit a *quantum computational simulation* by means of appropriate (reversible) gates? Definition 33 and Theorem 1 give an answer to this question.

Definition 32. *Fuzzy extension of a Boolean function*
Let $f : \{0, 1\}^2 \to \{0, 1\}$ be a binary Boolean function. A fuzzy extension *of f is any function $g : [0, 1]^2 \to [0, 1]$ such that*

$$\forall x, y \in \{0, 1\} : \quad g(x, y) = f(x, y).$$

Of course, the fuzzy extension of a binary Boolean function is generally not unique. Given a Boolean function $f : \{0, 1\}^2 \to \{0, 1\}$, define the function $g_f : [0, 1]^2 \to [0, 1]$ as follows:

$$\forall x, y \in [0, 1] : \quad g_f(x, y) = x_0 y_0 f(0, 0) + x_0 y_1 f(0, 1) + x_1 y_0 f(1, 0) + x_1 y_1 f(1, 1),$$

where: $x_0 = 1 - x$; $x_1 = x$; $y_0 = 1 - y$; $y_1 = y$. Clearly, $\sum_{i,j=0}^{1} x_i y_j = 1$. Being the extension to the real interval $[0, 1]$ of the normal disjunctive form of the Boolean function f, the function g_f is a fuzzy extension of f.

Definition 33. *Quantum computational simulation*
A function $g : [0, 1]^2 \to [0, 1]$ is said to admit a quantum computational simulation *iff for some natural number $n \geq 1$, there exist a unitary operator $U_g : \otimes^{n+2}\mathbb{C}^2 \to \otimes^{n+2}\mathbb{C}^2$ and a quregister $|\chi\rangle \in \otimes^n\mathbb{C}^2$ (playing the role of an ancilla) such that for any pair $|\psi\rangle, |\varphi\rangle$ of qubits in $\mathbb{C}^2$ (playing the role of control-qubits[5]), the following condition is satisfied:*

$$p(U_g(|\psi\rangle \, |\varphi\rangle \, |\chi\rangle)) = g(p(|\psi\rangle), p(|\varphi\rangle)).$$

Theorem 1. *Let $f : \{0, 1\}^2 \to \{0, 1\}$ be a Boolean function. Then, the function g_f is the unique fuzzy extension of f admitting a quantum computational simulation.*

Proof. We already know that g_f is a fuzzy extension of f. We first prove that g_f admits a quantum computational simulation.
    Put $|\chi\rangle = |0\rangle$. Let $x, y, z \in \{0, 1\}$. Define $U_{g_f} : \otimes^3\mathbb{C}^2 \to \otimes^3\mathbb{C}^2$:

$$U_{g_f}(|x\rangle \, |y\rangle \, |z\rangle) = |x\rangle \, |y\rangle \, |f(x, y) \boxplus z\rangle,$$

where $\boxplus$ is the sum modulo 2. Take the linear extension of U_{g_f} (still denoted by U_{g_f}). An easy computation shows that U_{g_f} is unitary and that for any pair $|\psi\rangle, |\varphi\rangle$ of qubits in $\mathbb{C}^2$ the following condition is satisfied:

$$p(U_{g_f}(|\psi\rangle \, |\varphi\rangle \, |0\rangle)) = g_f(p(|\psi\rangle), p(|\varphi\rangle)).$$

---

[5] The *control-qubits* represent the "genuine arguments" of a gate, while the *ancilla-qubit* guarantees reversibility.

We will now prove that g_f is unique. In other words: if $h : [0,1]^2 \to [0,1]$ is a fuzzy extension of f that admits a quantum computational simulation, then $h = g_f$. Let $h : [0,1]^2 \to [0,1]$ be a fuzzy extension of f that admits a quantum computational simulation. By definition, we have:

$$\forall x, y \in \{0,1\}: \quad h(x,y) = f(x,y) = g_f(x,y).$$

Moreover, for some $m \geq 1$, there exist a unitary operator $U_h : \otimes^{m+2}\mathbb{C}^2 \to \otimes^{m+2}\mathbb{C}^2$ and an m-quregister $|\delta\rangle$ such that for any pair $|\psi\rangle, |\varphi\rangle$ of qubits in $\mathbb{C}^2$, the following condition is satisfied:

$$\mathrm{p}(U_h(|\psi\rangle |\varphi\rangle |\delta\rangle)) = h(\mathrm{p}(|\psi\rangle), \mathrm{p}(|\varphi\rangle)).$$

We want to show that $\forall x, y \in [0,1]$: $h(x,y) = g_f(x,y)$.
Let $x, y \in [0,1]$. Then, there exist two qubits $|\psi\rangle, |\varphi\rangle$ such that

$$|\psi\rangle = \sqrt{x_0}\,|0\rangle + \sqrt{x_1}\,|1\rangle \quad \text{and} \quad |\varphi\rangle = \sqrt{y_0}\,|0\rangle + \sqrt{y_1}\,|1\rangle,$$

where $x_0 := 1 - x$, $x_1 := x$, $y_0 := 1 - y$, $y_1 := y$. Hence, $x = \mathrm{p}(|\psi\rangle)$ and $y = \mathrm{p}(|\varphi\rangle)$. Accordingly (by hypothesis and by linearity of U_h), we obtain:

$$\begin{aligned}
h(x,y) = \mathrm{p}(&\sqrt{x_0 y_0}\,U_h(|00\rangle |\delta\rangle) + \sqrt{x_0 y_1}\,U_h(|01\rangle |\delta\rangle) \\
&+ \sqrt{x_1 y_0}\,U_h(|10\rangle |\delta\rangle) + \sqrt{x_1 y_1}\,U_h(|11\rangle |\delta\rangle)).
\end{aligned}$$

We will now show that $\mathrm{p}(U_h(|\psi\rangle |\varphi\rangle |\delta\rangle)) = g_f(x,y)$. Hence, $h(x,y) = g_f(x,y)$. We have $\forall x, y \in \{0,1\}$:

$$\mathrm{p}(U_h(|x\rangle |y\rangle |\delta\rangle)) = h(x,y) = f(x,y) = g_f(x,y).$$

Therefore,

$$U_h(|x\rangle |y\rangle |\delta\rangle) = \sum_{i \in C_0} a_i^{xy}(1 - f(x,y))\,|i\rangle + \sum_{i \in C_1} b_i^{xy} f(x,y)\,|i\rangle,$$

where

$$\sum_{i \in C_0} |a_i^{xy}|^2 (1 - f(x,y)) = 1 - f(x,y)$$

and

$$\sum_{i \in C_1} |b_i^{xy}|^2 f(x,y) = f(x,y).$$

A simple computation shows that $\mathrm{p}(U_h(|\psi\rangle |\varphi\rangle |\delta\rangle))$ is equal to

$$p\left(\sum_{r,s=0}^{1}\left(\sum_{i\in C_0}\sqrt{x_r y_s}a_i^{rs}(1-f(r,s))\,|i\rangle + \sum_{i\in C_1}\sqrt{x_r y_s}b_i^{rs}f(r,s)\,|i\rangle\right)\right)$$
$$= \left|\left|\sum_{r,s=0}^{1}\sum_{i\in C_1}\sqrt{x_r y_s}b_i^{rs}f(r,s)\,|i\rangle\right|\right|^2.$$

Now, for any choice of $u,v,\overline{u},\overline{v}\in\{0,1\}$ such that $(u,v)\neq(\overline{u},\overline{v})$, the quregisters $|u\rangle\,|v\rangle\,|\delta\rangle$ and $|\overline{u}\rangle\,|\overline{v}\rangle\,|\delta\rangle$ are orthogonal. Since U_h is unitary, we obtain that

$$\sum_{i\in C_1}\sqrt{x_u y_v}\,b_i^{uv}f(u,v)\,|i\rangle \quad\text{is orthogonal to}\quad \sum_{i\in C_1}\sqrt{x_{\overline{u}}\,y_{\overline{v}}}\,b_i^{\overline{u}\,\overline{v}}f(\overline{u},\overline{v})\,|i\rangle.$$

Thus, we have:

$$p(U_h(|\psi\rangle\,|\varphi\rangle\,|\delta\rangle))) = \sum_{r,s=0}^{1}\left|\left|\sum_{i\in C_1}\sqrt{x_r y_s}\,b_i^{rs}f(r,s)\,|i\rangle\right|\right|^2.$$

Consequently,

$$h(x,y) = p(U_h(|\psi\rangle\,|\varphi\rangle\,|\delta\rangle)))$$
$$= \sum_{r,s=0}^{1}\sum_{i\in C_1}x_r y_s |b_i^{rs}|^2 f(r,s)$$
$$= \sum_{r,s=0}^{1}x_r y_s f(r,s)$$
$$= g_f(x,y).$$

Hence, we can conclude that $\forall x,y\in[0,1]:\ h(x,y)=g_f(x,y)$.

Corollary 1

(i) *There exist exactly 16 functions that are fuzzy extensions of the 16 binary Boolean functions, admitting a quantum computational simulation;*

(ii) *the function $f:[0,1]^2\to[0,1]$ such that $f(x,y)=xy$ is the unique extension of the Boolean conjunction admitting a quantum computational simulation;*

(iii) *the MYCIN sum $f:[0,1]^2\to[0,1]$ such that $f(x,y)=x+y-xy$ is the unique fuzzy extension of the Boolean disjunction admitting a quantum computational simulation;*

(iv) *the function $f:[0,1]^2\to[0,1]$ such that $f(x,y)=x+y-2xy$ is the unique extension of the Boolean exclusive disjunction admitting a quantum computational simulation.*

Corollary 2

– *The Łukasiewicz conjunction ($x\odot y:=max\{0,x+y-1\}$), which is a fuzzy extension of the Boolean conjunction, and the Łukasiewicz disjunction ($x\oplus y:=min\{x+y,1\}$), which is a fuzzy extension of the Boolean disjunction, do not admit a quantum computational simulation.*

References

1. Birkhoff, G., von Neumann, J.: The logic of quantum mechanics. Annals of Mathematics 37, 823–843 (1936)
2. Dalla Chiara, M.L., Giuntini, R., Leporini, R.: Quantum Computational Logics. A Survey. In: Hendricks, V., Malinowski, J. (eds.) Trends in Logic. 50 Years of Studia Logica, pp. 229–271. Kluwer, Dordrecht (2003)
3. Dalla Chiara, M.L., Giuntini, R., Leporini, R.: Quantum computational logics and Fock space semantics. International Journal of Quantum Information 2, 1–8 (2004)
4. Dalla Chiara, M.L., Giuntini, R., Leporini, R.: Logics from quantum computation. International Journal of Quantum Information 3, 293–337 (2005)
5. Dalla Chiara, M.L., Giuntini, R., Leporini, R.: A holistic quantum computational semantics. Natural Computing 5, 1–20 (2006)
6. Dalla Chiara, M.L., Giuntini, R.: Quantum logics. In: Gabbay, G., Guenthner, F. (eds.) Handbook of Philosophical Logic, vol. VI, pp. 129–228. Kluwer, Dordrecht (2002)
7. Dalla Chiara, M.L., Giuntini, R., Greechie, R.: Reasoning in Quantum Theory. Kluwer, Dordrecht (2004)
8. Deutsch, D., Ekert, A., Lupacchini, R.: Machines, logic and quantum physics. Bulletin of Symbolic Logic 3, 265–283 (2000)
9. Gudder, S.: Quantum computational logic. International Journal of Theoretical Physics 42, 39–47 (2003)
10. Nielsen, M.A., Chuang, I.L.: Quantum Computation and Quantum Information. Cambridge Univ. Press, Cambridge (2000)

Cantor–Bernstein Property for MV-Algebras

Antonio Di Nola[1] and Mirko Navara[2]

[1] Department of Mathematics and Informatics, University of Salerno
via S. Allende, 84081 Baronissi, Salerno, Italy
adinola@unisa.it
[2] Center for Machine Perception, Department of Cybernetics
Faculty of Electrical Engineering, Czech Technical University
Technická 2, 166 27 Praha, Czech Republic
navara@cmp.felk.cvut.cz

Abstract. Generalizations of the Cantor–Bernstein theorem have been proved for different types of algebras, starting from σ-complete orthomodular lattices and σ-complete MV-algebras and continuing with more general structures, including (pseudo) effect algebras and (pseudo) BCK-algebras. E.g., for σ-complete MV-algebras a version of the Cantor–Bernstein theorem has been proved which assumes that the bounds of isomorphic intervals are boolean.

There is another direction of research which has been paid less attention. We ask which algebras satisfy the Cantor–Bernstein theorem in the same form as for σ-complete boolean algebras, without any additional assumption. In the case of orthomodular lattices, it has been proved that this class is rather large. E.g., every orthomodular lattice can be embedded as a subalgebra or expressed as an epimorphic image of a member of this class. On the other hand, also the complement of this class is large in the same sense. We study the analogous question for MV-algebras and we find out interesting examples of MV-algebras which possess or do not possess this property. This contributes to the investigations of the scope of validity of the Cantor–Bernstein theorem in its original form.

1 Introduction

The classical Cantor–Bernstein theorem says that two sets X, Y which admit injective mappings $X \to Y$ and $Y \to X$ have the same cardinality. The history of this theorem is rather strange: It was conjectured by Cantor in 1895, and proved by Bernstein in 1898. However, it was proved by Dedekind already in 1887, but his proof has remained unnoticed [24, p. 85]. Sikorski [30] and Tarski [31] proved the following generalization of the (Dedekind)-Cantor-Bernstein theorem: For any two σ-complete boolean algebras A and B and elements $a \in A$ and $b \in B$, if B is isomorphic to the interval $[0, a]_A$ and A is isomorphic to $[0, b]_B$, then A and B are isomorphic. To obtain the classical Cantor–Bernstein theorem, it suffices to assume that A and B are the powersets of X and Y, respectively, with the natural set-theoretic boolean operations.

S. Aguzzoli et al.(Eds.): Algebraic and Proof-theoretic Aspects, LNAI 4460, pp. 107–118, 2007.
© Springer-Verlag Berlin Heidelberg 2007

Our work is inspired by generalizations of the Cantor–Bernstein theorem which appeared recently. It has been generalized to σ-complete orthomodular lattices (mathematical structures obtained naturally as event structures of quantum systems) and to σ-complete MV-algebras (which form the basis for the semantics of the Łukasiewicz logic). Numerous further generalizations to more general structures (including effect algebras as a common generalization of orthomodular lattices and MV-algebras) followed—see the bibliography at the end of this paper. In all these algebras, additional assumptions on the σ-homomorphisms are necessary to satisfy the Cantor–Bernstein theorem.

There is another line of research, initiated in [5]. Here the question is which algebras satisfy the Cantor–Bernstein theorem in its original form for boolean algebras, without any additional condition.

Definition 1. *Let L be an ordered algebra such that each interval $[p,q]_L = \{x \in L \mid p \leq x \leq q\}$ forms an algebra of the same type. Then L is said to satisfy the Cantor–Bernstein property if the following holds: If there is an interval $[p,q]_L$ isomorphic to L, then L is isomorphic to $[r,s]_L$ for all $r \leq p$ and $s \geq q$ $(r,s \in L)$.*

The Cantor–Bernstein property has been first introduced in [5] for σ-complete orthomodular lattices. (Originally, such an algebra was called *interval homogeneous*.) The main conclusion of [5,6] is that there are many σ-complete orthomodular lattices satisfying the Cantor–Bernstein property.

Our aim in this paper is to find analogies in MV-algebras. We ask which MV-algebras satisfy the Cantor–Bernstein theorem without any additional conditions. We collect several observations showing that the Cantor–Bernstein property has non-trivial consequences in MV-algebras, too. In contrast to [5], we do not require σ-completeness; there are interesting examples of non-σ-complete algebras having the Cantor–Bernstein property.

2   Motivation from Orthomodular Lattices

In this section we briefly summarize the main results obtained in [5,6] for orthomodular lattices. They are presented only for inspiration, thus the reader not acquainted with orthomodular lattices may skip this section. In the following sections, we shall look for analogies of these results for MV-algebras. For more details on orthomodular lattices, we refer to [1,19,27].

In the sequel, we denote $\mathbb{N} = \{1,2,3,\ldots\}$ and $\mathbb{N}_0 = \mathbb{N} \cup \{0\}$. If two algebras L, M are isomorphic, we denote it by $L \cong M$.

An *orthomodular lattice* (OML) is a lattice L with bounds $0,1$ and with a unary operation $\neg\colon L \to L$ (*orthocomplementation*) such that

$$a \leq b \Longrightarrow \neg b \leq \neg a\,,$$
$$\neg\neg a = a\,,$$
$$a \vee \neg a = 1\,,$$
$$a \vee b = a \vee (\neg a \wedge (a \vee b))\,.$$

(The latter equation is called the *orthomodular law.*) For $a, b \in L$, $a < b$, the interval $[a, b]_L = \{x \in L \mid a \leq x \leq b\}$ constitutes, with the operations naturally inherited from L, an OML (see [27]). Every orthomodular lattice is a union of boolean subalgebras [7]. Elements $a, b \in L$ are *compatible* if they are contained in a boolean subalgebra of L (equivalently, if $b = (b \wedge a) \vee (b \wedge \neg a)$). We say that a is *central* if it is compatible to all other elements; in this case, L is isomorphic to the direct product of intervals $[0, a]_L \times [0, \neg a]_L$. The *center*, $C(L)$, of L is the set of all central elements. It is a boolean subalgebra of L. (The center in OMLs corresponds to the *boolean skeleton* in MV-algebras.) Papers [5,6] deal only with σ-complete OMLs (σ-OMLs), i.e., with those OMLs which are closed under the formation of countable suprema and infima. Their centers are σ-complete boolean algebras and intervals are σ-OMLs (see [27]).

A *σ-homomorphism* between two σ-OMLs L and M is any mapping $f : L \to M$ which preserves the orthocomplementation and the countable lattice operations. If, moreover, it is surjective, we call it a *σ-epimorphism*. By an *isomorphism* between L and M we mean a bijective mapping $f : L \to M$ such that both f and f^{-1} are OML σ-homomorphisms.

3   Cantor–Bernstein Property for Orthomodular Lattices

For OMLs, Definition 1 can be rephrased in a slightly simplified form:

Proposition 1. *[5] For an OML L, the Cantor–Bernstein property is equivalent to the following condition: If, for some $a \in L$, the interval $[0, a]_L$ is isomorphic to the entire L, then L is isomorphic to the interval $[0, b]_L$ for each $b \geq a$ ($b \in L$).*

The relation of this notion to the Cantor–Bernstein theorem can be expressed as follows:

Proposition 2. *[5] A σ-OML L has the Cantor–Bernstein property iff it satisfies the following condition: If there is a σ-OML M isomorphic to an interval $[0, a]_L$ and L is isomorphic to an interval $[0, b]_M$, then M is isomorphic to L.*

It is shown in [5] that there are OMLs which do not satisfy the Cantor–Bernstein property:

Proposition 3. *The class of σ-OMLs satisfying the Cantor–Bernstein property is not closed under the formation of products.*

There are even boolean algebras which do not satisfy the Cantor–Bernstein property. According to [12,21], there is a boolean algebra A such that $A \not\cong A^2$, but $A \cong A^3$. Such a boolean algebra cannot be σ-complete. This situation is excluded in σ-complete orthomodular lattices, too:

Proposition 4. *Let L be a σ-complete OML. If $L \not\cong L^2$, then $L \not\cong L^n$ for any $n \in \mathbb{N}$, $n > 1$.*

The richness of the class of σ-OMLs satisfying the Cantor–Bernstein property is demonstrated by the following result:

Theorem 1. *Every σ-OML is a σ-epimorphic image of a σ-OML satisfying the Cantor–Bernstein property.*

The proof is based on the following deep fact:

Lemma 1. *[32,20] There is a proper class of mutually non-isomorphic OMLs of height 3 which are not reducible to non-trivial horizontal sums.*

On the other hand, the class of σ-OMLs *not* satisfying the Cantor–Bernstein property is also large:

Theorem 2. *Every σ-OML is a σ-epimorphic image of a σ-OML not satisfying the Cantor–Bernstein property.*

Similar conclusions have been obtained for subalgebras:

Theorem 3. *Every σ-OML is a sub-σ-OML of a σ-OML satisfying the Cantor–Bernstein property.*

Theorem 4. *Every σ-OML is a sub-σ-OML of a σ-OML not satisfying the Cantor–Bernstein property.*

4   MV-Algebras

We refer to [2], [3], and [26] for basic information on MV-algebras.

An *MV-algebra* $M = (M, 0, \oplus, \neg)$ is an algebra where the operation $\oplus \colon M \times M \to M$ is associative and commutative with 0 as the neutral element, the operation $\neg \colon M \to M$ satisfies the identities $\neg\neg x = x$ and $x \oplus \neg 0 = \neg 0$, and, in addition,

$$y \oplus \neg(y \oplus \neg x) = x \oplus \neg(x \oplus \neg y). \tag{1}$$

Example 1. The real unit interval $[0,1]$ equipped with the Łukasiewicz operations $x \oplus y = \min(1, x+y)$ and $\neg x = 1 - x$ is an MV-algebra called the *standard MV-algebra*.

Following common usage, for any elements x, y of an MV-algebra and $n \in \mathbb{N}$, we use the abbreviations $1 = \neg 0$, $x \odot y = \neg(\neg x \oplus \neg y)$, $x \ominus y = x \odot \neg y$, and $n.x = x \oplus \cdots \oplus x$ (n times). We shall denote by $(M, \vee, \wedge)$ the underlying distributive lattice of M, where $x \vee y = x \oplus \neg(x \oplus \neg y)$ and $x \wedge y = x \odot \neg(x \odot \neg y)$.

An MV-algebra M is *σ-complete* (resp., *complete*) iff every sequence (resp., every family) of elements of M has a supremum in M with respect to the underlying order of M.

As shown by Chang, boolean algebras coincide with MV-algebras satisfying the equation $x \oplus x = x$. In this case the operation $\oplus$ coincides with $\vee$, and the operation $\odot$ coincides with $\wedge$.

Let us recall that an element a in an MV-algebra M is called *boolean* iff $a \oplus a = a$. We let $\mathbf{B}(M)$ denote the set of all boolean elements of M (the *boolean skeleton*). It is not hard to see that the operations of M make $\mathbf{B}(M)$ into a boolean algebra. If M is a σ-complete MV-algebra, then $\mathbf{B}(M)$ is a σ-complete boolean algebra, and the σ-infinitary operations of $\mathbf{B}(M)$ agree with the restrictions of the corresponding operations of M.

A *homomorphism* between two MV-algebras is a map that sends zero to zero, and preserves the operations $\oplus$ and $\neg$. A one-to-one surjective homomorphism is called an *isomorphism*.

For an MV-algebra $M = (M, 0, \oplus, \neg)$ and elements $a, b \in M$, $a \leq b$, we define the *interval* $I = [a, b]_M$ by

$$[a, b]_M = \{x \in M \mid a \leq x \leq b\}.$$

It can be considered an MV-algebra $(I, \oplus_I, \neg_I, 0)$ if the operations $\neg_I \colon I \to I$ and $\oplus_I \colon I \times I \to I$ are defined by

$$\neg_I x = (b \ominus x) \oplus a, \tag{2}$$

$$x \oplus_I y = ((x \ominus a) \oplus y) \wedge b. \tag{3}$$

We always assume these operations on an interval and we call it briefly an MV-algebra $[a, b]_M$.

Proposition 5. *Let M be an MV-algebra and $b \in \mathbf{B}(M)$. Then:*

1. *The interval $[0, b]_M$ (as well as the interval $[0, \neg b]_M$) is an ideal of M;*
2. *The map $h_b \colon x \mapsto x \wedge b$ is a homomorphism of M onto $[0, b]_M$ whose kernel coincides with $[0, \neg b]_M$;*
3. *The MV-algebra $[0, b]_M$ is isomorphic to the quotient MV-algebra $M/[0, \neg b]_M$.*

If in a boolean algebra B we denote by I be the principal ideal generated by $\neg b$, then $I = [0, \neg b]_B$, and the algebra $[0, b]_B$ is isomorphic to B/I via the map $x \mapsto x/I$. Condition 3 is a generalization of this fact to MV-algebras.

If a is not a boolean element of an MV-algebra M, then $[0, a]_M$ need not be a homomorphic image of M. For $n \in \mathbb{N}$, we denote by $S_n = \{0, 1/n, 2/n, \dots, 1\}$ the MV-chain with $n + 1$ elements (with the Łukasiewicz operations). Then

$$[0, 1/n]_{S_n} = \{0, 1/n\}$$

is not a homomorphic image of S_n, because S_n has no other proper ideals than $\{0\}$.

On the other hand, the existence of a homomorphism of M onto $[0, a]_M$ need not imply that a is a boolean element of M. As a matter of fact, in the standard MV-algebra $[0, 1]$, multiplication by $1/2$ is a homomorphism of $[0, 1]$ onto the interval MV-algebra $[0, 1/2]$, but the element $1/2$ is not boolean in $[0, 1]$.

Lemma 2. *Let L and M be MV-algebras and let $\varphi \colon L \to M$ be an isomorphism of L onto M. For any $a \in L$, the restriction of the map φ to the interval $[0, a]_L$ is an isomorphism of the MV-algebra $[0, a]_L$ onto the interval $[0, \varphi(a)]_M$.*

Corollary 1. *For each $a \in \mathbf{B}(M)$, the mapping $x \mapsto (x \wedge a, x \wedge \neg a)$ is an isomorphism of M onto the product MV-algebra $[0, a]_M \times [0, \neg a]_M$.*

5   Cantor–Bernstein Theorems for MV-Algebras

The following version of the Cantor-Bernstein theorem has been proved in [4]:

Theorem 5. *Let L and M be σ-complete MV-algebras. Let $a \in \mathbf{B}(L)$, $b \in \mathbf{B}(M)$, such that $L \cong [0, b]_M$ and $M \cong [0, a]_L$. Then $L \cong M$.*

(Here $\cong$ denotes the MV-algebraic isomorphism, preserving all MV-algebraic operations, as well as their lattice structure.)

In [13], Jakubík proved a different form of Cantor-Bernstein theorem for MV-algebras which follows. A *lattice isomorphism* between two MV-algebras L and M is a one-to-one map of L onto M that preserves the underlying lattice structure of L and M (not necessarily all MV-algebraic operations). We say that L and M are *lattice isomorphic* iff there is a lattice isomorphism between L and M. The existence of a lattice isomorphism is a necessary, but not sufficient, condition for the isomorphism of two MV-algebras. To show this, let us denote by $\mathbb{Q}_2$ the set of all dyadic rationals, i.e., rational numbers whose denominators are integer powers of 2. The MV-chains $\mathbb{Q} \cap [0, 1]$ and $\mathbb{Q}_2 \cap [0, 1]$ are lattice isomorphic (as denumerable, densely ordered chains with two endpoints) but they are not isomorphic MV-algebras. Indeed, $\mathbb{Q} \cap [0, 1]$ contains an element $x = 1/3$ satisfying $\neg x = x \oplus x$, but there is no such element in $\mathbb{Q}_2 \cap [0, 1]$.

Theorem 6. *[13] Let L and M be complete MV-algebras satisfying the following condition:*

(∗)   *If $a \in L$ and $[0, a]_L$ is a boolean algebra, then $a \in \mathbf{B}(L)$.*

Suppose that for some $a \in L$, $b \in M$, L is lattice isomorphic to $[0, b]_M$ and M is lattice isomorphic to $[0, a]_L$. Then L and M are isomorphic as MV-algebras.

Many generalizations have followed (see the bibliography). However, all of them require some additional conditions. In Theorem 5, the added assumptions are that the MV-algebras are σ-complete and that the bounds of intervals, a and b, are boolean. (Analogous assumptions are made in most of the generalizations, they concentrate on some σ-complete boolean subalgebra.) In Theorem 6, condition (∗) and completeness of the MV-algebras is assumed. (On the other hand, only lattice isomorphisms are assumed instead of MV-algebraic isomorphisms.) In the sequel we ask in which MV-algebras all these conditions are unnecessary.

6   Cantor–Bernstein Property for MV-Algebras

Also MV-algebras admit to rephrase Definition 1 in a slightly simplified form:

Proposition 6. *For an MV-algebra M, the Cantor–Bernstein property is equivalent to the following condition: If, for some $a \in M$, the interval $[0, a]_M$ is isomorphic to the entire M, then M is isomorphic to the interval $[0, b]_M$ for each $b \geq a$.*

Proof. It suffices to take in Definition 1 $a = q \ominus p$, $b = s \ominus r$.

For an MV-algebra M, we define

$$\mathcal{A}(M) = \{a \in M \mid [0, a]_M \cong M\}.$$

The Cantor–Bernstein property is equivalent to the condition that $\mathcal{A}(M)$ is an order filter (not necessarily an MV-algebraic filter).

It may happen that an MV-algebra does not contain a proper isomorphic subinterval; then we say that it *satisfies the Cantor–Bernstein property trivially.* Otherwise, we say that it *satisfies the Cantor–Bernstein property non-trivially.* If M is an MV-algebra, $a \in M \setminus \{1\}$, and there is an isomorphism $\varphi \colon M \to [0, a]_M$, then $\mathcal{A}(M)$ contains not only $a = \varphi(1)$, but also a strictly decreasing sequence $\varphi^2(1) = \varphi(a)$, $\varphi^3(1), \ldots$. Thus all finite MV-algebras satisfy the Cantor–Bernstein property trivially. Nevertheless, infinite MV-algebras may satisfy the Cantor–Bernstein property trivially or non-trivially.

7   MV-Chains with Cantor–Bernstein Property

In this section we present non-trivial examples of MV-chains with the Cantor–Bernstein property.

There is only one infinite σ-complete MV-chain, $[0, 1]$. The σ-completeness condition used in Theorem 5 was introduced because of an analogy with boolean algebras. Nevertheless, it is not necessary and weaker conditions may be sufficient. What we need is the σ-completeness of the boolean skeleton, but MV-chains which are not σ-complete need not be excluded. However, then the Cantor–Bernstein property may be more complex. We first discuss the case of MV-chains which are hyperarchimedean, then others.

Definition 2. *An element x of an MV-algebra L is said to be* archimedean *iff there is an integer $n \geq 1$ such that $n.x$ is boolean. An MV-algebra L is said to be* hyperarchimedean *iff all its elements are archimedean.*

7.1   Hyperarchimedean MV-Chains

Hyperarchimedean MV-chains are subalgebras of $[0, 1]$ [3, Theorem 3.5.1]. Nevertheless, even in this restricted context we find interesting examples related to the Cantor–Bernstein property.

Example 2. The standard MV-algebra $[0, 1]$ and the MV-chain $\mathbb{Q} \cap [0, 1]$ possess the Cantor–Bernstein property.

We see that σ-completeness of the chain is not necessary for the Cantor–Bernstein property. However, density (in the sense used for ordered sets) is necessary.

Theorem 7. *Let M be a subalgebra of $[0, 1]$. If M satisfies the Cantor–Bernstein property non-trivially, then it contains $\mathbb{Q} \cap [0, 1]$.*

Proof. The non-triviality assumption implies that there is an a, $0 < a < 1$ and an isomorphism $\varphi \colon M \to [0, a]_M$. The set $\mathcal{A}(M)$ contains arbitrarily small non-zero elements of the form $\varphi^k(1)$, $k \in \mathbb{N}$. Their sums generate a dense subset of $[0, 1]$. As any isomorphism between intervals in M preserves sums and ordering, it has to be linear, thus only a multiplication by a constant. According to the Cantor–Bernstein property, $\mathcal{A}(M) = M \setminus \{0\}$. For each $n \in \mathbb{N}$, we can find $b \in \mathcal{A}(M)$ such that $n.b < 1$. There is an isomorphism $\psi \colon M \to [0, n.b]_M$. Thus $\psi^{-1}(n.b) = 1$ and $\psi^{-1}(b) = 1/n$. Hence M contains $1/n$ for all $n \in \mathbb{N}$ and all rational numbers from $[0, 1]$.

The following examples show that density is not sufficient for the Cantor–Bernstein property.

Example 3. The MV-chain $M = \mathbb{Q}_2 \cap [0, 1]$ has not the Cantor–Bernstein property. Indeed, $[0, 1/2]_M \cong M$, while $[0, 3/4]_M$ is not isomorphic to M. Similar examples may be constructed for any other base instead of 2.

   This example also demonstrates another property of homomorphisms: If $a, b \in M$, $a \leq \neg b$, and $M \cong [0, a]_M \cong [0, b]_M$, then $[0, a \oplus b]_M$ need not be isomorphic to M. From isomorphisms $\varphi \colon M \to [0, a]_M$ and $\psi \colon M \to [0, b]_M$, we may construct a homomorphism $\chi \colon M \to [0, a \oplus b]_M$, $\chi(x) = \varphi(x) \oplus \psi(x)$. However, χ need not be an isomorphism. As a counterexample, we may take M as above, $a = 1/2$, $b = 1/4$ and use the same argument as before.

Example 4. Let us take an irrational number r, $0 < r < 1$. Then $M = \{cr + d \in [0, 1] \mid c, d \in \mathbb{Q}\}$ is an MV-algebra which does not satisfy the Cantor–Bernstein property. Indeed, the multiplication by a rational constant b, $0 < b < r$, is an isomorphism $M \to [0, b]_M$. Suppose that there is an isomorphism $\psi \colon M \to [0, r]_M$. We may express r as a limit of rational numbers, $r = \lim_{i \to \infty} a_i$. Then $\psi(r) = \lim_{i \to \infty} \psi(a_i) = \lim_{i \to \infty} ra_i = r^2 \notin M$, a contradiction. Thus $[0, r]_M \not\cong M$.

There are also dense subsets of $[0, 1]$ which satisfy the Cantor–Bernstein property trivially:

Example 5. Let P be the set of all rational numbers from $[0, 1]$ whose denominators are prime numbers. Then P is an MV-algebra. It is not isomorphic to any proper subinterval. Indeed, for each prime p, P contains the element $x = 1/p$ with the property $\neg x = (p - 1).x$. There is no such element in an interval $[0, q/p]_P$, $q \in \{1, \ldots, p - 1\}$ because $q/p^2 \notin P$.

7.2   MV-Chains Which Are Not Hyperarchimedean

In hyperarchimedean MV-chains, the only homomorphisms with intervals are multiplications by constants. We can find other homomorphisms in MV-chains which are not hyperarchimedean.

Example 6. The Chang MV-algebra $S_{\infty,1}$ is isomorphic to the interval $[(0,0), (1,0)]_L$ in the lexicographic product $\text{Lex}(\mathbb{Z},\mathbb{Z})$. Using the Mundici functor Γ, $S_{\infty,1} \cong \Gamma(\text{Lex}(\mathbb{Z},\mathbb{Z}),(1,0))$. It has the Cantor–Bernstein property and $\mathcal{A}(S_{\infty,1}) = \{(1,-n) \mid n \in \mathbb{N}_0\}$.

The above example appears to be exceptional among MV-chains: The MV-algebra $S_{\infty,k} \cong \Gamma(\text{Lex}(\mathbb{Z},\mathbb{Z}),(k,0))$ has the Cantor–Bernstein property iff $k = 1$. This result can be generalized:

Theorem 8. *Let $k \in \mathbb{N}$, $k > 1$, let G be a commutative ordered group, and let M_k be the MV-algebra of the form $\Gamma(\text{Lex}(\mathbb{Z},\mathbb{Z},G),(k,0,0))$. (We use the same symbol 0 for the neutral elements of $\mathbb{Z}$ and G.) Then M_k does not have the Cantor–Bernstein property.*

Proof. Let $a = (k,-kn,0)$, $n \in \mathbb{N}_0$. There is an isomorphism $\varphi \colon M_k \to [0,a]_{M_k}$, $\varphi((x,y,z)) = (x,y-nx,z)$. If $b = (k,-1,0)$, $n \in \mathbb{N}_0$, then $M_k \not\cong [0,b]_{M_k}$, because M_k contains an element $x = (1,0,0)$ satisfying $\neg x = (k-1).x$, but there is no such element in $[0,b]_{M_k}$. (In the interval $[0,a]_{M_k}$, the element $(1,-n,0)$ played this role.)

8   Direct Products and the Cantor–Bernstein Property

The following example shows that there are many σ-complete MV-algebras which satisfy the Cantor–Bernstein property non-trivially.

Example 7. Let $X_1,\ldots,X_j$ be a finite sequence of disjoint sets of strictly decreasing infinite cardinalities. Let M be the direct product

$$M = S_1^{X_1} \times \ldots \times S_k^{X_k} = \prod_{i=1}^{k} S_i^{X_i}. \tag{4}$$

We view the elements of M as functions $a \colon \bigcup_{i \leq k} X_i \to [0,1]$. Suppose that the interval $[0,a]_M$ is isomorphic to M. This is possible only if $\text{card}(a^{-1}(1) \cap X_1) = \text{card } X_1$ because the factors $S_i^{X_i}$, $i > 1$, admit intervals isomorphic to S_1^ω, but only for cardinalities $\omega < \text{card } X_1$. Similarly, we obtain

$$\text{card}(a^{-1}(1) \cap X_i) = \text{card } X_i \quad \text{for all} \quad i = 1,\ldots,k. \tag{5}$$

Condition (5) is necessary and sufficient for $[0,a]_M \cong M$. If it is satisfied for some $a \in M$, than it holds for all $b \in [a,1]_M$, thus M satisfies the Cantor–Bernstein property. The isomorphism between $[0,a]_M$ and M may be non-trivial in the sense that we may admit $a(x) = i/k < 1$ for some $x \in X_k$; then the factor of $[0,a]_M$ corresponding to $x \in X_k$ is isomorphic to $S_i \not\cong S_k$, i.e., to some factor S_i corresponding to $y \in X_i$.

Ex. 7 can be further generalized so that we admit also finite cardinalities.

Example 8. Let $X_1, \ldots, X_k$ be a sequence of disjoint sets and $j \leq k$ such that $X_1, \ldots, X_{j-1}$ have strictly decreasing infinite cardinalities and $X_j, \ldots, X_k$ be finite. Let M be the direct product (4). Then condition (5) is necessary and sufficient for $[0, a]_M \cong M$. Thus M satisfies the Cantor–Bernstein property.

In this example, if $[0, a]_M \cong M$, then $a \upharpoonright \bigcup_{i=j}^k X_i = 1$ and the isomorphism has to coincide with the identity on the factors $\prod_{i=j}^k S_i^{X_i}$.

If $j = 1$, then all sets $X_1, \ldots, X_k$ are finite, so M is finite and satisfies the Cantor–Bernstein property trivially.

In the previous examples, it was necessary to have strictly decreasing infinite cardinalities. We show that non-strict inequalities do not suffice:

Example 9. Let X_1, Y, Z be disjoint sets of the countable infinite cardinality and let $X_2 = Y \cup Z$. Let M be the direct product

$$M = S_1^{X_1} \times S_2^Y \times S_2^Z = S_1^{X_1} \times S_2^{X_2}.$$

We define $a \in M$ by

$$a(x) = \begin{cases} 1 & \text{if } x \in Z, \\ \frac{1}{2} & \text{if } x \in Y, \\ 0 & \text{if } x \in X_1. \end{cases}$$

Then $[0, a]_M \cong S_1^Y \times S_2^Z \cong M$. We define $b \in [a, 1]_M$ by

$$b(x) = \begin{cases} 1 & \text{if } x \in X_2 = Y \cup Z, \\ 0 & \text{if } x \in X_1. \end{cases}$$

Then $[0, b]_M \cong S_2^{X_2} \not\cong M$, because $[0, b]_M$ has no factor isomorphic to S_1. Thus M does not satisfy the Cantor–Bernstein property.

Remark 1. The only important property of S_i in these examples was that S_i is isomorphic to an interval in S_j for $i \leq j$. Other MV-algebras may be used.

Despite the above examples, there seems to be little chance to prove analogies of Ths. 1, 3 for MV-algebras. The reason is that the results in orthomodular lattices relied on complex constructions which do not have counterparts in MV-algebras. In particular, a proper class of non-isomorphic OMLs with given properties is constructed following the method of [20,31,32]. Using them, a product is constructed from non-isomorphic OMLs. In MV-algebras, the selection of such tools is rather limited [3].

Acknowledgements. This research was supported by the grant 201/07/1136 of the Czech Science Foundation.

References

1. Beran, L.: Orthomodular Lattices. Algebraic Approach. Academia, Praha and D. Reidel, Dordrecht (1984)
2. Cignoli, R., Mundici, D.: An invitation to Chang's MV-algebras. In: Droste, M., Göbel, R. (eds.) Advances in Algebra and Model Theory, pp. 171–197. Gordon and Breach Publishing Group, Reading, UK (1997)
3. Cignoli, R., D'Ottaviano, I.M.L., Mundici, D.: Algebraic Foundations of Many-valued Reasoning. In: Trends in Logic, vol. 7, Kluwer Academic Publishers, Dordrecht (1999)
4. De Simone, A., Mundici, D., Navara, M.: A Cantor–Bernstein theorem for σ-complete MV-algebras. Czechoslovak Math. J. 53(128), 437–447 (2003)
5. De Simone, A., Navara, M., Pták, P.: On interval homogeneous orthomodular lattices. Comment. Math. Univ. Carolin. 42, 23–30 (2001)
6. De Simone, A., Navara, M.: On the permanence properties of interval homogeneous orthomodular lattices. Math. Slovaca 54, 13–21 (2004)
7. Dichtl, M.: Astroids and pastings. Algebra Universalis 18, 380–385 (1981)
8. Dvurečenskij, A.: Central elements and Cantor–Bernstein theorem for pseudo-effect algebras. J. Austral. Math. Soc. 74, 121–143 (2003)
9. Freytes, H.: An algebraic version of the Cantor–Bernstein–Schröder Theorem. Czechoslovak J. Math. 54, 609–621 (2004)
10. Goodearl, K.R.: Partially Ordered Abelian Groups with Interpolation. AMS, Providence, RI (1986)
11. Grätzer, G.: General Lattice Theory, 2nd edn. J. Wiley, Basel (1998)
12. Hanf, W.: On some fundamental problems concerning isomorphism of boolean algebras. Math. Scand. 5, 205–217 (1957)
13. Jakubík, J.: Cantor–Bernstein theorem for MV-algebras. Czechoslovak Math. J. 49(124), 517–526 (1999)
14. Jakubík, J.: On orthogonally σ-complete lattice ordered groups. Czechoslovak Math. J. 52(127), 881–888 (2002)
15. Jakubík, J.: A theorem of Cantor–Bernstein type for orthogonally σ-complete pseudo MV-algebras. Tatra Mt. Math. Publ. 22, 91–103 (2002)
16. Jakubík, J.: Convex mappings of archimedean MV-algebras. Math. Slovaca 51(4), 383–391 (2001)
17. Jakubík, J.: Cantor–Bernstein theorem for lattices. Math. Bohem. 127(3), 463–471 (2002)
18. Jenča, G.: A Cantor–Bernstein type theorem for effect algebras. Algebra Univers. 48, 399–411 (2002)
19. Kalmbach, G.: Orthomodular Lattices. Academic Press, London (1983)
20. Kallus, M., Trnková, V.: Symmetries and retracts of quantum logics. Int. J. Theor. Phys. 26, 1–9 (1987)
21. Ketonen, J.: The structure of countable Boolean algebras. Ann. Math. 108, 41–89 (1978)
22. Kinoshita, S.: A solution to a problem of Sikorski. Fund. Math. 40, 39–41 (1953)
23. Kühr, J.: Cantor–Bernstein theorem for pseudo-BCK-algebras (preprint)
24. Levy, A.: Basic Set Theory. Perspectives in Mathematical Logic. Springer, Heidelberg (1979)
25. Monk, J.D., Bonnet, R.: Handbook of Boolean Algebras I. North Holland Elsevier Science Publisher B.V., Amsterdam (1989)

26. Mundici, D.: Interpretation of AF C^*-algebras in Łukasiewicz sentential calculus. J. Functional Analysis 65, 15–63 (1986)
27. Pták, P., Pulmannová, S.: Orthomodular Structures as Quantum Logics. Kluwer, Dordrecht, Boston, London (1991)
28. Riečan, B., Mundici, D.: Probability on MV-algebras. In: Pap, E. (ed.) Handbook of Measure Theory, North-Holland, Amsterdam (2001)
29. Sikorski, R.: Boolean Algebras. Ergebnisse Math. Grenzgeb. Springer, Heidelberg (1960)
30. Sikorski, R.: A generalization of a theorem of Banach and Cantor–Bernstein. Colloquium Math. 1, 140–144, 242 (1948)
31. Tarski, A.: Cardinal Algebras. Oxford University Press, New York (1949)
32. Trnková, V.: Automorphisms and symmetries of quantum logics. Int. J. Theor. Physics 28, 1195–1214 (1989)

A Note on
Representing and Interpreting MV-Algebras

Costas A. Drossos and Panagis Karazeris

Department of Mathematics
University of Patras
GR-26500 Patras, Greece
cdrossos@{math.upatras.gr,upatras.gr,otenet.gr}
pkarazer@upatras.gr

Abstract. We try to make a distinction between the idea of representing and that of interpreting a mathematical structure. We present a
slight generalization of Di Nola's Representation Theorem as to incorpo-
rate this point of view. Furthermore, we examine some preservation and
functorial aspects of the Boolean power construction.

1 Introduction

There are mathematical objects which are inherently and naturally 'nonstandard'. Examples include, the Itô integral, the Schwartz distributions, etc. We
can add to this list the MV-algebras of many-valued logic, since their representation theorem refers to the nonstandard interval $^*[0,1]$.

Nonstandard methods (infinitesimal, Boolean-valued, topos-theoretic) rely on
the existence of at least two levels of viewing mathematical objects, and the
reduction of higher type standard objects to lower type non-standard ones. For
example, equivalence classes of sequences are reduced to real numbers in a model
of infinitesimal analysis, self-adjoint operators are reduced to real numbers in a
Boolean model of set theory, continuous functions to a space are reduced to
spaces in the topos of sheaves over that space.

The existence of a huge amount of nonstandard models implies that the structure of MV-algebras (alongside with many other first-order structures) can have
many nonstandard interpretations. Although the aim of this note is not such a
study, we try to make clear the distinction between representation and interpretation but also to indicate the interplay between the two.

The Boolean power construction is an important tool for representations of
first-order structures. Its importance for the study of many-valued logic is even
bigger as the construction constitutes a functorial passage from the algebras of
classical logic to those of many-valued logic. We examine here some preservation property of that construction (preservation of hyperarchimedeaness) and
discuss possible adjunctions in which this functor participates. We close with
some questions arising from our discussion.

S. Aguzzoli et al.(Eds.): Algebraic and Proof-theoretic Aspects, LNAI 4460, pp. 119–126, 2007.
© Springer-Verlag Berlin Heidelberg 2007

2 Representations and Interpretations

First we would like to state that the main difference between representation and interpretation is that the former is usually seen within a specific model, whereas interpretations involve two, usually different, universes. The idea of interpretation obtains its most general form in category theory, where theories are represented by small categories with suitable structure and interpretations of them become structure-preserving functors into categories with the same structure.

Thus one may interpret the notion of an MV-algebra (like any equationally defined structure) in an arbitrary category with finite products (in particular in an arbitrary topos). The interplay with familiar representations of MV-algebras begins when restricting to interpretations in universes of Boolean-valued or Heyting-valued sets. Then a representation of the MV-algebra usually involves an embedding of it in the global sections of such a "set". For example the familiar ([20]) representation of hyperarchimedean MV-algebras as Boolean products of subalgebras of $[0, 1]$ is an instance of such an approach. When it comes to arbitrary MV-algebras the most general representation known is Di Nola's embedding of an algebra in a power of an ultrapower of $[0, 1]$. Of course Di Nola's representation constitutes a form of a Boolean ultraproduct representation over a special form of Boolean algebra (a powerset). We indicate how this representation can be extended to a more general one over a, possibly, more interesting Boolean algebra.

2.1 Boolean Ultrapowers and Di Nola's Representation Theorem

The next theorem is the Boolean analogue to Frayne's Lemma ([16, Thm. 2.16, p. 42]), and it is the result needed for such a generalization:

Theorem 1. *For structures* $\mathscr{A} := \langle A, ... \rangle, \mathscr{B} := \langle B, ... \rangle$, *then* $\mathscr{A} \equiv \mathscr{B}$ *if and only if* $\mathscr{B}$ *is elementary embeddable in some Boolean ultrapower* $\mathscr{A}\,_U^{(\mathbb{B})}$ *of* $\mathscr{A}$. *The Boolean* $\mathbb{B}$ *can be chosen as a minimal completion of the boolean algebra* $F(\mathscr{A}, A \cup B)/ \approx Th(\mathscr{A}, A)$. *The latter denotes the Boolean algebra of formulae in the language of* $\mathscr{A}$ *with constants from* A *and* B, *modulo the theory of* $\mathscr{A}$.

The ultrafilter U *can be chosen so that as including* $Th(\mathscr{B}, B)/ \approx Th(\mathscr{A}, A)$.

(Recall here that Boolean ultrapowers $\mathscr{A}\,_U^{(\mathbb{B})}$ are just isomorphic to direct limits of ordinary ultrapowers.)

Using the above Theorem we give a proof of the generalization by reproducing the steps of a proof given by Di Nola ([3]):

Theorem 2 (Boolean generalization of Di Nola's Representation Theorem). *For any MV-algebra* A *there is a Boolean ultrapower* $[0, 1]_U^{(\mathbb{B})}$ *of the MV-algebra* $[0, 1]$ *such that* A *can be embedded into* $([0, 1]_U^{(\mathbb{B})})^{Spec(A)}$, *i.e. there exists:*

$$i : A \lhook\joinrel\longrightarrow ([0, 1]_U^{(\mathbb{B})})^{Spec(A)}$$

Proof. Let A be an MV-algebra. By Chang's Representation Theorem, A can be embedded into the direct product

$$\prod \{A/P \mid P \in \mathrm{Spec}(A)\}.$$

If $P \in \mathrm{Spec}(A)$ then A/P is an MV-chain, so A/P can be embedded into a divisible MV-chain D_p. Next, we consider the set $\mathcal{F} := \{D_P \mid P \in \mathrm{Spec}(A)\}$. It is also known that any pair of MV-algebras from $\mathcal{F}$ are elementarily equivalent. But we know that there exists an MV-algebra D such that D_P can be elementarily embedded in D for any $P \in \mathrm{Spec}(A)$. It follows that D is also elementarily equivalent with the MV-algebras of $\mathcal{F}$. But $[0,1]$ is also elementarily equivalent with the MV-algebras of $\mathcal{F}$. It follows that D is also elementarily equivalent with $\mathcal{F}$, since $[0,1]$ is a divisible MV-chain. Thus, by the Boolean analog of Frayne's Lemma 1, D is elementarily embeddable in some Boolean ultrapower $[0,1]_U^{(\mathbb{B})}$. For any $P \in \mathrm{Spec}(A)$ we get

$$A/P \hookrightarrow D_P \hookrightarrow D \hookrightarrow [0,1]_U^{(\mathbb{B})}$$

with i_P the composite arrow.

Hence, if we define

$$i : A \hookrightarrow \left([0,1]_U^{(\mathbb{B})}\right)^{\mathrm{Spec}(A)} \quad /\!/ \quad a \mapsto i(a) : \{i_P(a) : P \in \mathrm{Spec}(A)\},$$

we get the desired embedding for the MV-algebra A. $\square$

2.2   Some Further Remarks on Interpretations

The following theorem ([9, p. 212]) exemplifies the feature of reduction of type, mentioned above.

Gordon's Theorem: *Every universally complete vector lattice is an interpretation of the reals in an appropriate Boolean-valued model.*

The Boolean-valued interpretation of the reals have been introduced by Takeuti ([17]). Choosing as the Boolean algebra a Boolean algebra of projections in a Hilbert space, we get as interpreted reals self-adjoint operators, whereas if we choose a probability algebra we get correspondingly random variables as reals (an idea originally due to D. Scott). In general, appropriate Boolean-valued interpretations of the real and complex numbers give operator algebras (see e.g., [13,14,15]).

Let $\mathbb{B}$ be a complete Boolean algebra, and V a standard model of set theory. Let also $V^{(\mathbb{B})}$ be the Boolean valued model of V with respect to $\mathbb{B}$. We define the embedding

$$(\check{\cdot}) : V \hookrightarrow V^{(\mathbb{B})} \quad /\!/ \quad a \mapsto \check{a}$$

where $\breve{a} : \mathrm{dom}(a) \to \mathbb{B}$ is defined as follows:

$$\mathrm{dom}(a) := \{\breve{x} \mid x \in a\} \quad \text{and} \quad \breve{a}(\breve{x}) = 1, \quad x \in a.$$

For $u \in V^{(\mathbb{B})}$ we define

$$\hat{u} := \{x \in V^{(\mathbb{B})} \mid [\![x \in u]\!] = 1\}.$$

The important property for Boolean powers with respect to a Boolean-valued model $V^{(\mathbb{B})}$ is that *the Boolean power $A^{(\mathbb{B})} \equiv A[\mathbb{B}]$ is isomorphic to* $(\breve{A})$.

Following a theorem in [4] there is a cryptic statement that "MV-algebras are the non-commutative generalization of Boolean algebras". We would like to phrase this as: In the interpretation of Boolean and MV-algebras in the framework of C*-algebras, the later is a non-commutative generalization of the first.

Remark 1. The Theorem 2 holds true for *some* Boolean algebra. On the other hand the reals $\mathbb{R}$ can be interpreted in every Boolean-valued model as $\mathbb{R}^{(\mathbb{B})}$. More precisely, let $V^{(\mathbb{B})}$ be a Boolean-valued model such that the reals in it capture a complete vector lattice. Regarding the $\mathbb{B}$-reals as a $\mathbb{B}$-lattice order group we obtain a $\mathbb{B}$-interpretation of the MV-algebra $[0,1]$, by applying the gamma-functor inside $V^{(\mathbb{B})}$, i.e.

$$[\![\Gamma(\mathbb{R}, 1) = [0,1]]\!] = 1_{\mathbb{B}}.$$

Varying the Boolean algebra $\mathbb{B}$ appropriately, we essentially get Boolean valued interpretations-representations of the MV-algebra $[0,1]$. In each $V^{(\mathbb{B})}$ the interpreted MV-algebra $[0,1]^{(\mathbb{B})}$ $\mathbb{B}-$generates the variety of MV-algebras in $V^{(\mathbb{B})}$. This shows that by varying the Boolean algebra $\mathbb{B}$ we get various interpretations of the structure of MV-algebra. In this sense the above Boolean generalization of Di Nola's Representation theorem, holds for every Boolean algebra. Thus choosing appropriately the Boolean algebra $\mathbb{B}$ we may have various $\mathbb{B}$-representations of MV-algebras. For example choosing $\mathbb{B}$ to be a probability Boolean algebra we get $\mathbb{B}$-representations of MV-algebras in terms of stochastic processes $(f_t)_{t \in \mathrm{Spec}(A)}$, where f_t is a point free stochastic fuzzy set. Similarly, by choosing $\mathbb{B}$ as a projection Boolean algebra in a Hilbert space, we get a $\mathbb{B}$-representations of MV-algebras in terms of families of adjoint operators indexed by $\mathrm{Spec}(A)$, (see also [17,18,13,14,15]).

The above Boolean Representation Theorem initiates the study of the exact relationships between MV-algebras and C*-algebras, see also ([18,7]). Another interesting result, connected with this, is the following, ([19, p. 18]):

Proposition. *Let $\mathcal{U}$ be a free ultrafilter on $\mathbb{N}$. If $^*(\cdot) : V(\mathbb{R}) \hookrightarrow V(^*\mathbb{R})$ is the bounded ultrapower embedding over $\mathcal{U}$, then the C*-algebras $S(\mathfrak{A})$ for $\mathfrak{A}$ hyperfinite dimensional internal C*-algebra are exactly the ultraproducts over $\mathcal{U}$ of finite dimensional C*-algebras. ($S(\mathfrak{A})$ is the infinitesimal hull of $\mathfrak{A}$.)*

3   The Boolean Power Functor

We first state some known results for Boolean powers. By Boolean power we mean constantly "bounded Boolean power" (otherwise most of what follows holds for unbounded Boolean powers over complete separable Boolean algebras).

Theorem 3. ([1])

(i) $\mathfrak{A}[\mathbf{2}] \cong \mathfrak{A}$;

(ii) For any diagram $D\colon I \to \mathbf{BAlg}$ in the category of Boolean algebras with limit $\lim_i B_i$, $\mathfrak{A}[\lim_i B_i] \cong \lim_{i \in I} \mathfrak{A}[\mathbb{B}_i]$. In particular,

(iii) $\mathfrak{A}[\prod_{i \in I} \mathbb{B}_i] \cong \prod_{i \in I} \mathfrak{A}[\mathbb{B}_i]$.

Theorem 4. ([8, Th. 9.7.2 (c), p. 468]) Let $\mathfrak{A}$ be a non-empty $\mathscr{L}$-structure. Then the Boolean power $\mathfrak{A}[-]$ defines a functor

$$\mathfrak{A}[-] : \mathbf{BAlg} \to \mathscr{M},$$

where $\mathscr{M}$ is the category of $\mathscr{L}$-structures and homomorphisms; this functor preserves filtered colimits.

We also have:

Theorem 5. ([4])

(i) For every MV-algebra A, the Boolean power $A[\mathbb{B}]$ is an MV-algebra;

(ii) Given a Boolean algebra $\mathbb{B}$, the center of the MV-algebra $[0,1][\mathbb{B}]$ is isomorphic to $\mathbb{B}$.

(iii) For every semisimple MV-algebra A, and every Boolean algebra $\mathbb{B}$, $A[\mathbb{B}]$ is semisimple.

Recall that a hyperarchimedean MV-algebra is an MV-algebra in which every element x has a power x^n which is idempotent. In particular $[0,1]$ is a hyperarchimedean MV-algebra.

Theorem 6. Let M be a hyperarchimedean MV-algebra. Then the Boolean power $M[B]$ is hyperarchimedean as well.

Proof. For an $f \in M[B]$ one has

$$(f \odot f)(a) = \bigvee \{f(x) \wedge f(y) \mid x \odot y = a\}$$

and since f is a partition the above becomes

$$(f \odot f)(a) = \bigvee \{f(x) \mid x \odot x = a\},$$

so eventually

$$f^n(a) = \bigvee \{f(x) \wedge f(y) \mid x^n = a\}$$

Suppose that f takes m distinct non-zero values $f(x_1), ..., f(x_m)$ and (since M is hyperarchimedean) that $x_1^{n_1}, ..., x_m^{n_m}$ are idempotents.

Then

$$(f^{n_1 \cdots n_m} \odot f^{n_1 \cdots n_m})(a) = \bigvee \{f(x) \mid x^{n_1 \cdots n_m} \odot x^{n_1 \cdots n_m} = a\}$$

$$= \bigvee \{f(x) \mid x^{n_1 \cdots n_m} = a\}$$

$$= f^{n_1 \cdots n_m}(a)$$

so whenever the function $f^{n_1 \cdots n_m}$ takes non-zero values they have to be idempotent. This means that $f^{n_1 \cdots n_m}$ is itself an idempotent element of $M[B]$.   □

Corollary 1. *The Boolean power* $[0,1][B]^*$ *is a hyperarchimedean MV-algebra.*

Specializing Theorem 3.2, we know that for a fixed MV-algebra M the Boolean power construction is functorial, defining a functor $M[-] \colon \textbf{BAlg} \to \textbf{MVAlg}$, from the category of Boolean algebras to that of MV-algebras. On the other hand the center of an MV-algebra also depends functorially on the MV-algebra, thus defining a functor $C(-) \colon \textbf{MVAlg} \to \textbf{BAlg}$. As pointed out in Theorem 3.3(ii), for any Boolean algebra B, the center of the MV-algebra $[0,1][B]$ is isomorphic to B. Thus any MV-homomorphism $M \to [0,1][B]$ determines a Boolean homomorphism $C(M) \to B$ and this fact indicates a possibility to investigate an adjunction between the Boolean power functor $[0,1][-]$ and the center functor $C(-)$. The other direction of a correspondence though wouldn't work: One may not expect to extend a Boolean homomorphism $C(M) \to B$ to an MV-homomorphism $M \to [0,1][B]$. This can be made precise with the aid of Gluschankof's characterization of algebras $\mathscr{C}(X, [0,1]_d)$ of continuous functions from a Stone space to the unit interval equipped with its discrete topology (i.e Boolean powers of $[0,1]$). In particular ([6], Cor. 3.5) such an MV-algebra is injective iff X is finite. Now $C(-)$ preserves monomorphisms (as a matter of fact all limits, being right adjoint to the inclusion of Boolean algebras into MV-algebras) so if it were left adjoint to $[0,1][-]$, by a standard categorical argument, $[0,1][-]$ would have to preserve injective objects. Since there are more injective Boolean algebras than just the finite ones we conclude that there is no such adjunction:

Theorem 7. *The Boolean power construction* $[0,1][-] \colon \textbf{BAlg} \to \textbf{MVAlg}$ *is not a right adjoint to the center construction* $C(-) \colon \textbf{MVAlg} \to \textbf{BAlg}$.

4   Final Remarks

It is well known that there is a connection between fuzzy sets and semisimple MV-algebras. On the other hand cubes of the form $[0,1]^n$ play a vital role in

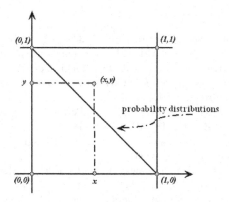

both fuzzy sets and MV-algebras. We consider a simple example: If $X := \{x_1, x_2\}$ then the following square depicts classical and fuzzy sets:

The classical subsets of $\{x_1, x_2\}$ are $\{\emptyset, \{x_1\}, \{x_2\}, \{x_1, x_2\}\}$ and these are represented using indicator functions as:

$$(I_{\{x_2\}}(x_1), I_{\{x_2\}}(x_2)) = (0,1) \qquad (I_{\{x_1,x_2\}}(x_1) I_{\{x_1,x_2\}}(x_2)) = (1,1)$$

$$(I_{\emptyset}(x_1), I_{\emptyset}(x_2)) = (0,0) \qquad (I_{\{x_1\}}(x_1) I_{\{x_1\}}(x_2)) = (1,0)$$

Fuzzy sets on the diagonal $(0,1), (1,0)$ represent probability distributions. All other points represent fuzzy sets.

It appears that *classical sets are the extreme points of non classical sets, or that non classical sets constitute the convex hull of classical sets.*

It would be desirable to have a formal way that expresses this relationship, that is a concrete connection between the two worlds: Boolean algebras and classical logic and MV-algebras and many-valued logic. One such way is through Boolean powers.

First we notice that semisimple MV-algebras are represented using $[0,1]$-valued functions, whereas Boolean algebras are represented using $2 := \{0,1\}$-valued functions.

Using 3 we see that, $[0,1][2] = [0,1]$ and $[0,1][2^n] = [0,1]^n$, $n \in \mathbb{N}$. In this way the Boolean power functor $[0,1][-]$ indeed gives the convex hull of the corresponding Cantor cubes. It would be interesting to investigate the passage from Boolean functions to McNaughton functions but unfortunately the Boolean power functor doesn't help in this direction.

In addition one can prove that the sets 2^ω and $[0,1]$ are isomorphic by choosing in $[0,1]$ the non-terminating expansions. For a set with the power of continuum we may represent its subsets by using hyperfinite cubes 2^H, where H is a hyperfinite natural number. The nonstandard study of hypercubes and MV-algebras seems to be promising in finding an equivalent formulation for MV-algebra problems, avoiding the heavy algebraic geometric formulations.

References

1. Burris, S.: Boolean powers. Algebra Univ. 5, 341–360 (1975)
2. Cignoli, R.L.O., D'Ottaviano, I.M.L., Mundici, D.: Algebraic Foundations of Many-valued Reasoning. Kluwer Acad. Publ., Dordrecht, Boston, London (2000)
3. Di Nola, A.: Representation and reticulation by quotients of MV-algebras. Ricerche di Matematica 40, 291–297 (1991)
4. Drossos, C.A., Karazeris, P.: Coupling an MV-algebra with a Boolean algebra. Internat. J. Approx. Reason. 18, 231–238 (1998)
5. Gispert, J., Mundici, D.: MV-algebras: a variety for magnitudes with archimedean units. Algebra Univ. 53, 7–43 (2005)
6. Gluschankof, D.: Prime deductive systems and injective objects in the algebras of Łukasiewicz infinite valued logic. Algebra Univ. 29, 354–377 (1992)
7. Henson, C.W., Iovino, J.: Ultraproducts in Analysis. In: Henson, C.W., Iovino, J., Kechris, A.S., Odell, E. (eds.) Analysis and Logic, pp. 1–114. Cambridge University Press, Cambridge (2003)
8. Hodges, W.: Model Theory. Cambridge University Press, Cambridge (1993)
9. Kusraev, A.G., Kutateladze, S.S.: Boolean valued analysis. Kluwer Acad. Publ., Dordrecht, Boston, London (1999)
10. Lawvere, F.W.: Categories of Space and of Quantity. In: Echeveria, J., et al. (eds.) The Space of Mathematics: Philosophical, Epistemological and Historical Explorations (International Symposium on Structures in Mathematical Theories. San Sebastian, Spain 1990), de Gruyter, Berlin, pp. 14–30 (1992)
11. Mansfield, R.: The theory of Boolean ultrapowers. Ann. Math. Logic 2, 297–323 (1971)
12. Mundici, D.: Interpretation of AF C^*-algebras in Łukasiewicz sentential calculus. Journal of Functional Analysis 65, 15–63 (1986)
13. Ozawa, M.: Boolean valued interpretation of Hilbert space theory. J. Math. Soc. Japan 35, 609–627 (1983)
14. Ozawa, M.: Boolean valued analysis and type I AW*-algebras. Proc. Japan Acad. 59A, 368–371 (1983)
15. Ozawa, M.: Boolean valued interpretation of Banach space theory and module structures of von Neumann algebras. Nagoya Math. J. 117, 1–36 (1990)
16. Potthoff, K.: Boolean ultrapowers. Arch. math. Logik 16, 37–48 (1974)
17. Takeuti, G.: Two applications of logic to mathematics. Princeton University Press, Princeton, NJ (1978)
18. Takeuti, G.: C^*-algebras and Boolean valued analysis. Japan J. Math. 9, 207–245 (1983)
19. Thayer, F.J.: Quasidiagonal C^*-algebras and nonstandard analysis, Arxiv preprint math.OA/0209292 (2002)
20. Torrens, A.: W-algebras which are Boolean products of members of $SR[1]$ and CW-algebras. Studia Logica 46, 265–274 (1987)

Towards the Generalization of Mundici's Γ Functor to IMTL Algebras: The Linearly Ordered Case

Francesc Esteva and Lluís Godo

Institut d'Investigació en Intel·ligència Artificial (IIIA)
Consejo Superior de Investigaciones Científicas (CSIC)
{esteva|godo}@iiia.csic.es

Dedicated to the Renaissance man, great scientist and good friend Daniele Mundici on the occasion of his 60th anniversary

Abstract. Mundici's Γ functor establishes a categorical equivalence between MV-algebras and lattice-ordered Abelian groups with a strong unit. In this short note we present a first step towards the generalization of such a relationship when we replace MV-algebras by weaker structures obtained by dropping the divisibility condition. These structures are the so-called involutive monoidal t-norm based algebras, IMTL-algebras for short. In this paper we restrict ourselves to linearly ordered IMTL-algebras, for which we show a one-to-one correspondence with a kind of ordered grupoid-like structures with a strong unit. A key feature is that the associativity property in such a new structure related to a IMTL-chain is lost as soon the IMTL-chain is no longer a MV-chain and the strong unit used in Mundici's Γ functor is required here to have stronger properties. Moreover we define a functor between the category of such structures and the category of IMTL algebras that is a generalization of Mundici's functor Γ and, restricted to their linearly ordered objects, a categorical equivalence.

1 Introduction

Completeness results for Łukasiewicz infinitely-valued logic have been obtained by Rose and Rosser and by Chang in the fifties. But it was Chang who gave in [4] an algebraic proof based on the study of the MV-algebras, that constitute the algebraic counterpart of the logic. Chang construction [3] associates to each linearly ordered MV-algebra a linearly ordered Abelian group with strong order unit and conversely. Mundici generalized this early result in [11] to a categorical equivalence (given by what is known as the Γ functor) between the category of MV-algebras and the category of lattice ordered Abelian groups with a strong unit. This categorical equivalence has also been extended by Dvurečenski in [6] to non-commutative MV-algebras (called pseudo-MV-algebras) and arbitrary lattice ordered groups with a strong unit, and even it has been further extended

S. Aguzzoli et al.(Eds.): Algebraic and Proof-theoretic Aspects, LNAI 4460, pp. 127–137, 2007.

by Galatos and Tsinakis in [8] in a very general context of non-integral, non-commutative and unbounded residuated lattices.

In this note our aim is to study the extension of Chang-Mundici's construction in the algebraic setting of t-norm based fuzzy logics, whose biggest variety is the one of MTL-algebras, i.e. of integral, bounded, commutative and pre-linear residuated lattices. Actually, one of the key points in the Chang-Mundici construction is the fact that MV-algebras have an involutive negation, which allows to define a addition-like operation (strong disjunction) as the De Morgan dual of the monoidal operation (strong conjunction). In fact MV-algebras can be axiomatized using only the negation and the strong conjunction. Therefore it seems reasonable, in order to generalize the Γ functor, to try to do it in the frame of (bounded, integral, commutative) residuated lattices with an involutive negation (hence including MV-algebras) and so, having a non-trivial strong disjunction. Moreover, as a first step and for the sake of simplicity, in this paper we shall also restrict ourselves to linearly ordered structures.

Indeed, after reviewing some basic facts about involutive residuated lattices in the next section, and following Chang's construction, in Section 3 we first introduce a type of (possibly) non-associative group-like structures linked to linearly ordered involutive MTL algebras, IMTL-chains for short, and after we show that there exists a one-to-one correspondence between these two classes of algebraic structures that particularizes to Chang-Mundici construction when restricted to linearly ordered MV-chains (in other words, to divisible IMTL-chains). Moreover we define a functor between the category of such algebraic structures and the category of IMTL algebras extending the Γ functor, and when restricted to the subcategories of the corresponding linearly ordered structures provides a categorical equivalence.

2   About Involutive Residuated Lattices

In this paper, following [10], by *residuated lattice* we shall mean a lattice ordered residuated commutative integral monoid, as it is defined next.

Definition 1. *An structure* $\mathcal{A} = \langle A, \wedge, \vee, *, \rightarrow, 0, 1 \rangle$ *is a residuated lattice if:*

(L) $\langle A, \wedge, \vee, 0, 1 \rangle$ *is a bounded lattice,*
(M_*) $\langle A, *, 1 \rangle$ *is a commutative monoid with neutral element 1,*
(R) *Residuation:* $*$ *and* $\rightarrow$ *form an adjoin pair, i.e.,* $x \rightarrow y \geq z$ *if and only if* $x * z \leq y$,

In residuated lattices, a negation operation $\neg$ can be defined as usual by stipulating $\neg x = x \rightarrow 0$.

Residuated lattices form a variety, and the subvarieties we are interested in are those of *involutive residuated lattices*, that is, residuated lattices whose negation operation $\neg$ is involutive, hence satisfying the following condition:

(INV) $\neg\neg x = x$.

Having an involutive negation allows us to define in an involutive residuated lattice a strong disjunction operation $\oplus$ as the dual of the monoidal operation (or strong conjunction) with respect to $\neg$, i.e. $x \oplus y = \neg(\neg x * \neg y)$. Distinguished subvarieties of involutive residuated lattices are:

- the full variety of involutive residuated lattices **IRL**, whose algebras will be denoted IRL-algebras[1];
- the variety **IMTL** of involutive monoidal t-norm based algebras (IMTL-algebras for short) introduced in [7],
- the variety **MV** of MV-algebras, and
- the variety **B** of Boolean algebras.

Note that IMTL-algebras are IRL-algebras satisfying the prelinearity condition

(PL) $(x \rightarrow y) \vee (y \rightarrow x) = 1$,

while MV-algebras are IMTL-algebras verifying the divisibility condition

(DV) $x * (x \rightarrow y) = x \wedge y$.[2]

Finally, Boolean algebras are MV-algebras satisfying the excluded middle law $x \vee \neg x = 1$.

Remark 1. An easy computation shows that all linearly ordered IRL-algebras satisfy the prelinearity condition and thus they are in fact IMTL-algebras. Moreover in [7] it is proved that all IMTL-algebras are subdirect product of linearly ordered IMTL-algebras. Therefore the varieties **IRL** and **IMTL** have the same linearly ordered algebras and hence **IMTL** is the variety generated by linearly ordered IRL-algebras.

It is well known that the **B** and **MV** varieties can be (term-wise) equivalently defined using the operations $\oplus$, $\neg$ and 0. Analogously, IRL and IMTL-algebras can be alternatively defined using the operations $\wedge$, $\vee$, $\oplus$, $\neg$ and 0. Next propositions provide such axiomatizations.[3]

Proposition 1. $\mathcal{A} = \langle A, \wedge, \vee, *, \rightarrow, 0, 1 \rangle$ *is a IRL-algebra if, and only if, the following conditions and equations hold:*

(SL) $\langle A, \wedge, 0, 1 \rangle$ *is a bounded $\wedge$-semilattice,*
(M$_\oplus$) $\langle A, \oplus, 0 \rangle$ *is a commutative monoid with neutral element 0,*
(OW) $x \oplus (y \wedge z) = (x \oplus y) \wedge (x \oplus z)$,
(INV) $\neg\neg x = x$,

---

[1] Called *Girard Monoids* in [10] and proved in [1] to be equivalent to the so-called *Grising algebras* as defined in [9].
[2] Or equivalently, verifying the equation $x \vee y = (x \rightarrow y) \rightarrow y$.
[3] The authors are indebted to Roberto Cignoli for pointing us property (C) that is the key property in this axiomatization and which was also used in [1] to axiomatize the $\{*, \neg\}$-fragment of **IRL**.

(C) $x \oplus \neg(x \oplus y) \geq \neg y$.

where the new operations are defined as follows:
$$\neg x \quad = x \to 0$$
$$x \oplus y = \neg(\neg x * \neg y).$$

Conversely, a structure $\mathcal{A}' = \langle A, \wedge, \vee, \oplus, \neg, 0, 1 \rangle$ satisfies the above conditions and equations if, and only if, $\mathcal{A} = \langle A, \wedge, \vee, *, \to, 0, 1 \rangle$ is a IRL-algebra, where the new operations are defined as follows:
$$x * y \quad = \neg(\neg x \oplus \neg y),$$
$$x \to y = \neg x \oplus y \ .$$

Proof. On the one hand, any IRL-algebra defining $\oplus$ as the dual of $*$ wrt $\neg$ satisfies the set properties of this proposition. The fulfillment of (SL), (M$_\oplus$), (OW) and (INV) is obvious. To prove (C) first observe that $x \oplus y = 1$ if and only if $y \geq \neg x$. Then, simply the following equivalences hold: $y \geq \neg x$ is equivalent to $\neg y \leq \neg\neg x = \neg x \to 0$, and by residuation, it is equivalent to $\neg y * \neg x = 0$, and thus it is also equivalent to $x \oplus y = \neg(\neg x * \neg y) = \neg 0 = 1$. From this equivalence, property (C) is an obvious consequence of the following equality: $y \oplus (x \oplus \neg(x \oplus y)) = (x \oplus y) \oplus \neg(x \oplus y) = 1$.

On the other hand, if $\mathcal{A}' = \langle A, \wedge, \vee, \oplus, \neg, 0 \rangle$ satisfies (SL), (M$_\oplus$), (OW), (INV) and (C), we will prove that the set A with the lattice operations plus $*$, $\to$ and the constants 0 and 1 is an IRL-algebra. The (L) and (M$_*$) conditions are obviously satisfied. Notice that by condition (OW) the operation $\oplus$ is monotone with respect to the order. To prove the residuation property (R), first we prove that $x \oplus y = 1$ if and only if $x \geq \neg y$. To this end we will follow the proof in [1] with the obvious modification. From $x \oplus y = 1$ and condition (C) we obtain $x \oplus \neg 1 = x \geq \neg y$. Suppose now that $y \geq \neg x$. Then $x \oplus y \geq (x \oplus y) \wedge (x \oplus \neg x) = x \oplus (y \wedge \neg x) = x \oplus \neg x = x \oplus \neg(0 \oplus x) \geq \neg 0 = 1$. From this property and definition of $\to$, residuation is easy since, $x \to y \geq z = \neg\neg z$ is equivalent then to $\neg z \oplus (\neg x \oplus y) = 1$, and by associativity and commutativity, it is equivalent to $(\neg x \oplus \neg z) \oplus y = 1$, that is, by definition of $*$, equivalent to $\neg(x * z) \oplus y = 1$, and finally by condition (C), this is equivalent to $y \geq x * z$.

Corollary 1. *An structure $\mathcal{A} = \langle A, \wedge, \vee, *, \to, 0, 1 \rangle$ is a IMTL algebra if, and only if, besides of (M$_\oplus$), (OW), (INV) and (C), the following condition and equation hold:*

(DL) $\langle A, \vee, \wedge, 0, 1 \rangle$ is a bounded distributive lattice,
(OV) $x \oplus (y \vee z) = (x \oplus y) \vee (x \oplus z)$,

Conversely, a structure $\mathcal{A}' = \langle A, \wedge, \vee, \oplus, \neg, 0, 1 \rangle$ satisfies the above properties if, and only if, $\mathcal{A} = \langle A, \wedge, \vee, *, \to, 0, 1 \rangle$ is a IRL-algebra, where the new operations are defined as in Proposition 1.

Proof. Proposition 2.3 in [10] proves that in any integral, residuated, commutative l-monoid, the property (PL) of prelinearity is equivalent to the distributivity of $*$ with respect to $\wedge$, or equivalently to the distributivity of $\oplus$ with respect to $\vee$. Since IMTL-algebras are prelinear IRL-algebras, the proof is completed.

As a consequence of these characterizations, in the rest of the paper we shall indistinctly refer to IRL- and IMTL-algebras as structures in the language $(\wedge, \vee, *, \rightarrow)$ or in the language $(\wedge, \vee, \oplus, \neg)$.

Remark 2. In the above definitions of IRL and IMTL algebras we have used the two lattice operations $\wedge$ and $\vee$ and the two constants 0 and 1. In fact only one operation and one constant would be actually needed since the other ones could be defined from those two using the negation.

3   Chang's Construction and IMTL Chains

Mundici's Γ functor (see [11] for the original paper and [5] for a nice proof of the Γ-functor) is a well known functor that gives a categorical equivalence between the category of MV-algebras and the category of lattice ordered Abelian groups with a strong unit. In fact, it is a deep generalization of a Chang result associating to each MV chain a linearly ordered abelian group (see [3,4]).

In this section we generalize Chang's construction to linearly ordered IRL- (or IMTL-) algebras. In fact we shall work in the IMTL setting, i.e. using the properties of IMTL-algebras given in Corollary 1, because it seems more natural and a generalization to the non-linearly ordered case seems more plausible for **IMTL** than for **IRL**. The latter appears to be more difficult since the **IRL** variety is not generated by its linearly ordered members, moreover in a IRL-algebra the lattice may be not distributive and the $\oplus$ operation may not be a morphism with respect to $\vee$. From now on, the linearly ordered IMTL-algebras will be called IMTL-chains for short.

3.1   The Partially Associative Structure Defined by an IMTL Chain

Extending Chang's construction for MV-chains, we will associate to each IMTL-chain an algebraic structure, which is partially non-associative in the general case.

Definition 2. *Let $\mathcal{A} = \langle A, \wedge, \vee, \oplus, \neg, 0_A, 1_A \rangle$ be a linearly ordered IMTL-algebra. The linearly ordered algebraic structure associated to $\mathcal{A}$ is the structure $\mathcal{S}(\mathcal{A}) = \langle S(\mathcal{A}), +, -, (0, 0_A), \leq \rangle$ of type (2,1,0) where:*

- $S(\mathcal{A}) = \{ (m, x) \mid m \in \mathbb{Z}, x \in A - \{1_A\} \}$
- $(m, x) + (n, y) = \begin{cases} (m + n, x \oplus y), & \text{if } x \oplus y < 1_A \\ (m + n + 1, x * y), \text{otherwise} \end{cases}$
- $-(m, x) = \begin{cases} (-m, 0_A), & \text{if } x = 0_A \\ (-(m + 1), \neg x), \text{otherwise} \end{cases}$
- $\leq$ *is the lexicographic order, that is, $(n, x) \leq (m, y)$ if and only if $n < m$ or $n = m$ and $x \leq y$.*

From this definition it is easy to prove the following properties of $\mathcal{S}(\mathcal{A})$, where we use $\wedge$ and $\vee$ to denote the glb and lub with respect to the lexicographic order $\leq$.

Proposition 2. *If A is a linearly ordered IMTL-algebra, the linearly ordered algebraic structure $S(A) = \langle S(A), +, -, (0, 0_A), \leq \rangle$ satisfies the following properties:*

1) *$+$ is commutative, monotone w.r.t. the order and $(0, 0_A)$ is neutral,*
2) *$(S(A), \wedge, \vee)$ is a distributive lattice,*
3) *$+$ is distributive with respect to $\vee$ and $\wedge$,*
4) *$-(n, x)$ is the inverse element of (n, x) with respect to $+$,*
5) *$-$ is involutive, i.e. $-(-(n, x)) = (n, x)$, and is a morphism with respect to $+$, i.e. $-((n, x) + (k, y)) = -(n, x) + (-(k, y))$,*
6) *for all $k \in \mathbb{Z}$, $(k, 0_A)$ is an associative element, i.e. for any $a, b, c \in S(A)$ it holds that $a + (b + c) = (a + b) + c$ whenever at least one of a, b and c is of the form $(k, 0_A)$.*
7) *for all $x, y \in A$, $(0, x) + [(1, 0_A) + (-((0, x) + (0, y)))] \geq (1, 0_A) + (-(0, y))$, i.e. property (C)*
8) *for all $x, y, z \in A$, $[(0, x) + ((0, y) + (0, z))] \wedge (1, 0_A) = [((0, x) + (0, y)) + (0, z)] \wedge (1, 0_A)$,*
9) *$(1, 0_A)$ is a strong unit in the following sense: for any $(m, x) > (0, 0_A)$ there is a natural k such that $k(1, 0_A) > (m, x)$ where $k(1, 0_A) = (1, 0_A) + \overset{k}{\cdots} + (1, 0_A)$.*

These properties are straightforward consequences of the properties of the IMTL chains given in Corollary 1.

Remark 3. The algebraic ordered structure $S(A)$ is not associative in general. In fact, as it is known, it is associative if, and only if, the initial IMTL-algebra A is a MV-algebra. As an example of non-associativity, take A as the linearly ordered NM-algebra defined by the nilpotent minimum and its residuum over the real interval $[0, 1]$. Recall that in that case, $*$ and $\oplus$ are defined as follows:

$$x * y = \begin{cases} \min(x, y), & \text{if } x > 1 - y \\ 0, & \text{otherwise} \end{cases}$$

$$x \oplus y = \begin{cases} \max(x, y), & \text{if } x < 1 - y \\ 1, & \text{otherwise} \end{cases}$$

Then, if we take $\beta > \alpha > \frac{1}{2}$, we have, for any $m, n, k \in \mathbb{Z}$,

$$((m, \alpha) + (n, 1 - \alpha)) + (k, \beta) = (m + n + 1, 0) + (k, \beta) = (m + n + k + 1, \beta)$$

while

$$(m, \alpha) + ((n, 1 - \alpha) + (k, \beta)) = (m, \alpha) + (n + k + 1, 1 - \alpha) = (m + n + k + 2, 0)$$

Remark 4. Another important property that is lost in the above algebraic ordered structure associated to an IMTL-chain (related to non-associativity) is the cancellation law. For example, taking the standard NM chain (the same as in the previous remark), it is clear that $(m, \alpha) + (n, \beta) = (m, \alpha) + (n, \gamma)$ for $\gamma < \beta \leq 1 - \alpha$.

The initial IMTL-algebra $\mathcal{A}$ can indeed be recovered from the structure $\mathcal{S}(\mathcal{A})$. Actually, it can be identified with the interval $[(0,0),(1,0)]$ of the structure $\mathcal{S}(\mathcal{A})$ with suitably adapted operations.

Proposition 3. *Let $\mathcal{S}(\mathcal{A})$ be the algebraic ordered structure associated to the linearly ordered IMTL-algebra $\mathcal{A}$, and let $\Phi(\mathcal{S}(\mathcal{A})) = \langle A^+, \oplus, \neg, \min, \max, (0, 0_A),$ $(1, 0_A)\rangle$ be the algebra defined by:*

1) $A^+ = \{(m, x) \mid (0, 0_A) \leq (m, x) \leq (1, 0_A)\}$
2) for all $(m, x), (n, y) \in A^+$, $(m, x) \oplus (n, y) = ((m, x) + (n, y)) \wedge (1, 0_A)$, that is, $\oplus$ is the bounded sum.
3) for all $(n, x) \in A^+$, $\neg(n, x) = (1, 0_A) + (-(n, x))$
4) the order is the restriction to A^+ of the order on $\mathcal{S}(\mathcal{A})$.

Then $\Phi(\mathcal{S}(\mathcal{A}))$ is a IMTL-chain which is isomorphic to the initial IMTL-algebra $\mathcal{A}$.

Proof. An easy computation shows that the mapping $f : A^+ \longrightarrow A$ defined by $f(0, x) = x$ and $f(1, 0_A) = 1_A$ is an isomorphism of IMTL-algebras.

3.2   Representation Theorem

We have seen in the previous subsection how to associate to each linearly ordered IMTL-algebra $\mathcal{A}$ the pair $(\mathcal{S}(\mathcal{A}), (1, 0))$ formed by the algebraic ordered structure associated to $\mathcal{A}$ and the element $(1, 0)$. Conversely, given a *suitable* pair formed by an ordered algebraic structure with a distinguished element (not necessarily linearly ordered), we show next that we can build a IMTL-algebra generalizing what Chang did for linearly ordered Abelian groups with a strong unit (see, for example [4]). Inspired in the results of previous section, first we need to introduce the definition of an algebraic structure generalizing the notion of Abelian groups with strong unit.

Definition 3. *A pair $(\mathcal{G}, u)$ formed by an algebra $\mathcal{G} = (G, \wedge, \vee, +, -, 0_G)$ of type $(2,2,2,1,0)$ and by an element $u \in \mathcal{G}$ is called a (lattice ordered) partially associative Abelian groupoid with strong associative unit u if the following properties are satisfied :*

i) $(G, \wedge, \vee)$ *is a distributive lattice*
ii) $(G, +, 0)$ *is an Abelian grupoid with neutral element 0_G,*
iii) For all $x \in G$, $+_x : G \to G$ defined by $+_x(y) = x + y$ is a lattice morphism,
iv) For each $a \in G$, $-a$ is the inverse of a, i.e. $a + (-a) = 0_G$,
v) $-$ *is involutive and a morphism with respect to $+$,*
vi) the strong associative unit $u \in G$ satisfies the following conditions:

(a) for all $x, y \in G$, $u + (x + y) = (u + x) + y$ (u is an associative element),
(b) for all $x, y, z \in G$, $[x^* + (y^* + z^*)] \wedge u = [(x^* + y^*) + z^*] \wedge u$, where $x^* = (x \wedge u) \vee 0_G$,
(c) for all $x, y \in G$, $[x^* + (u + (-((x^* + y^*) \wedge u)))] \wedge u \geq u + (-y^*)$, where x^* is defined as in the previous item ,

(d) *for any $x > 0_G$ there is a natural k such that $ku > x$, where $ku = u + ..k.. + u$ (strong unit).*

It easily follows from the previous definition that any partially associative Abelian groupoid with strong associative unit $(\mathcal{G}, u)$ fulfills the next three properties:

1) u is a cancellative element;
2) any triple containing an element of the form ku, for some $k \in \mathbb{Z}$, is associative;
3) $-$ is an order-reversing lattice isomorphism of $(G, \min, \max)$;

Moreover, it is easy to check that, for any IMTL-chain $\mathcal{A}$, the pair $(\mathcal{S}(\mathcal{A}), (1, 0_A))$ is indeed a linearly ordered partially associative grupoid with strong associative unit.

We can show now that the interval $[0_G, u]$ of a lattice ordered partially associative Abelian groupoid with strong associative unit $(\mathcal{G}, u)$ can be endowed with a structure of IMTL-algebra.

Theorem 1. *Let $(\mathcal{G}, u)$ be a lattice ordered partially associative abelian groupoid with strong associative unit u. Then $\Phi(\mathcal{G}, u) = ([0_G, u], \wedge, \vee, \oplus, \neg, 0)$ is a IMTL-algebra where the lattice operation are the restriction of the lattice operation of $\mathcal{G}$, $\oplus$ is the bounded sum defined by $x \oplus y = (x + y) \wedge u$ and $\neg x = u + (-x)$ for all $x \in [0_G, u]$.*

Proof. We have to prove that $\Phi(\mathcal{G}, u) = \langle [0_G, u], \wedge, \vee, \oplus, \neg, 0_G, u \rangle$ satisfies the properties of Corollary 1. Property (DL) is obvious and (OW) and (OV) are consequences of the fact that $+_x$ is a lattice morphism ((iii) of definition 3). Moreover using ii), v) and (vi-a) from Definition 3, $\neg\neg(x) = u + (-(u + (-x))) = u + ((-u) + x) = (u + (-u)) + x = x$. Finally property (C) is an easy consequence of condition $(vi - c)$ of the strong associative unit u according to Definition 3, taking into account that $x^* = x$ for any $x \in [0_G, u]$.

Finally, for linearly ordered structures we can complete the representation with the following theorem.

Theorem 2. *The following statements hold:*

(i) *Any linearly ordered IMTL-algebra $\mathcal{A}$ is isomorphic to $\Phi(\mathcal{S}(\mathcal{A}), (1, 0_A))$*
(ii) *Any linearly ordered partially associative Abelian groupoid with strong associative unit $(\mathcal{G}, u)$ is isomorphic to $(\mathcal{S}(\Phi(\mathcal{G}, u)), (1, 0_G))$.*

Proof. (i) is proved in Proposition 3. To prove (ii), we define the following mapping:

$$f : \mathcal{G} \to \mathcal{S}(\Phi(\mathcal{G}, u))$$

by $f(x) = (k_x, x^*)$, where k_x is the integer such that $x^* = x + (-k_x u) \in [0_G, u]$. By construction, the mapping is well defined since, for any $x \in \mathcal{G}$, k_x exists and it is unique. Moreover f is a morphism with respect to $+$ since:

1. If $x^* + y^* < u$ then $k_{x+y} = k_x + k_y$, and thus obviously $f(x) + f(y) = (k_x, x^*) + (k_y, y^*) = (k_x + k_y, x^* + y^*) = f(x + y)$.
2. If $x^* + y^* \geq u$ then $k_{x+y} = k_x + k_y + 1$, since $x^* + y^* < 2u$. Thus,
$$f(x + y) = (k_{x+y}, (x + y)^*) = (k_x + k_y + 1, (x + y)^*)$$
and
$$f(x) + f(y) = (k_x, x^*) + (k_y, y^*) = (k_x + k_y + 1, x^* *_{\Phi(G)} y^*).$$
Both expressions actually coincide because
$$x^* *_{\Phi(G)} y^* = \neg_{\Phi(G)}(\neg_{\Phi(G)} x \oplus_{\Phi(G)} (\neg_{\Phi(G)} y)) = u - ((u - x) \oplus (u - y)),$$
and taking into account that $(u - x) \oplus (u - y) = (u - x) + (u - y) < u$, this is equal to $u - ((u - x) + (u - y)) = (x + y) - u = (x + y)^*$.

Obviously f is also morphism for $-$ and clearly $f(u) = (1, 0_G)$. Finally notice that f is a bijection. Indeed, if $f(x) = f(y)$ then $k_x = k_y$ and $x^* = y^*$, and thus $x = k_x u + x^* = y$ as well. And for any $(m, x) \in S(\Phi(G, u))$, a simple computation shows that $f(y) = (m, x)$ for $y = mu + x \in G$.

Summarizing, we have seen that each IMTL-chain can be seen as an interval algebra of some l.o. partially associative Abelian groupoid with an associative strong unit, and conversely, each of such structures can be generated by a suitable IMTL-chain.

4   Towards the Generalization of the Mundici's Functor Γ

Let us consider the category $\mathcal{PAG}$ where the objects are (lattice ordered) partially associative Abelian groupoids with strong associative unit $(\mathcal{G}, u)$, and given two objects $(\mathcal{G}, u)$ and $(\mathcal{G}', u')$, a homomorphism $\varphi : (\mathcal{G}, u) \to (\mathcal{G}', u')$ is a morphism of groupoids $\varphi : \mathcal{G} \to \mathcal{G}'$ such that $\varphi(u) = u'$. The category of IMTL-algebras $\mathcal{IMTL}$ is defined in the obvious way, i.e. the objects are IMTL-algebras and the homomorphisms are the IMTL-algebra morphisms.

Then, as in the MV case, the mapping Φ defined in Theorem 1 actually defines a functor from the category $\mathcal{PAG}$ into the category $\mathcal{IMTL}$. Indeed, over objects, Φ is defined as in Theorem 1, i.e. if $\mathcal{G} = (G, \wedge, \vee, +, -, 0_G)$ is a (lattice ordered) partially associative Abelian groupoid with strong associative unit u, then $\Phi(\mathcal{G}, u) = ([0_G, u], \wedge, \vee, \oplus, \neg, 0)$ with $x \oplus y = (x + y) \wedge u$ and $\neg x = u + (-x)$ for all $x \in [0_G, u]$. Now, given a homomorphism $\varphi : (\mathcal{G}, u) \to (\mathcal{G}', u')$ of $\mathcal{PAG}$, we define $\Phi(\varphi) : \Phi(\mathcal{G}, u) \to \Phi(\mathcal{G}', u')$ as the restriction of φ to $[0_G, u]$. So, defined, it is easy to prove that Φ is a functor from the category $\mathcal{PAG}$ into the category $\mathcal{IMTL}$. To this end we have to check the following two conditions:

(A) Φ transforms homomorphisms of $\mathcal{PAG}$ into homomorphisms of $\mathcal{IMTL}$.
(B) Φ preserves the composition and the identities.

In fact, taking into account that operations of in the IMTL-algebra $\Phi(\mathcal{G}, u)$ are defined from the operations of $\mathcal{G}$, it is not difficult to prove condition (A). Moreover since Φ restricts grupoid morphisms, condition (B) is also easily proved.

To conclude, observe that if $\mathcal{G}$ is a lattice-ordered Abelian group, then $\Phi(\mathcal{G}, u)$ is an MV-algebra since an easy computation shows that $\Phi(\mathcal{G}, u) = \Gamma(\mathcal{G}, u)$.

Therefore, the functor Φ is actually a generalization of the functor Γ. Finally, Theorem 2 shows that the functor Φ provides a categorical equivalence between the subcategories of linearly ordered objects of the categories $\mathcal{PAG}$ and $\mathcal{IMTL}$.

5   Concluding Remarks

This paper contains some initial ideas towards the generalization of Mundici's functor Γ to functor Φ from the categories of (lattice ordered) partially associative lattice abelian groupoids to the category of IMTL-algebras. The interest of the deep result by Mundici is to relate MV-algebras to a very well known and studied class of algebraic structures such as lattice-ordered Abelian groups. This is not the case for IMTL-algebras since the algebraic structures that can be associated to them are not well known and till now we have not proved that Φ is a categorical equivalence. Actually, the algebraic structures associated to IMTL-algebras which are not MV-algebras are necessarily non associative. The interest of this research, if any, would probably be in the converse sense, that is, available results about IMTL-algebras can perhaps help in knowing something more about some particular (partially) non-associative structures. To prove or disprove that Φ is a categorical equivalence is left to be accomplished in future work.

Acknowledgments

The authors acknowledge partial support of the Spanish project MULOG TIN2004-07933-C03-01. The authors are also indebted for the helpful comments provided by an anonymous referee.

References

1. Bou, F., Garcia-Cerdaña, A., Verdú, V.: On some Substructural Aspects of t-Norm Based Logics. In: Proc. of IPMU'04, Perugia (Italy), pp. 545–552 (2004)
2. Bou, F., Garcia-Cerdaña, A., Verdú, V.: On two fragments with negation and without implication of the logic of residuated lattices. Archive for Mathematical Logic 45, 615–647 (2006)
3. Chang, C.C.: Algebraic analysis of many-valued logics. Transactions of the American Mathematical Society 88, 467–490 (1958)
4. Chang, C.C.: A new proof of the completeness of the Łukasiewicz axioms. Transactions of the American Mathematical Society 93, 74–90 (1959)
5. Cignoli, R., D'Ottaviano, I.M.L., Mundici, D.: Algebraic Foundations of Many-valued Reasoning. Kluwer, Dordrecht (2000)
6. Dvurečenskij, A.: Pseudo MV-algebras are intervals in l-groups. J. Austr. Math. Soc. 72(3), 427–445 (2002)
7. Esteva, F., Godo, L.: Monoidal t-norm based Logic: Towards a logic for left-continuous t-norms. Fuzzy Sets and Systems 124, 271–288 (2001)
8. Galatos, N., Tsinakis, C.: Generalized MV-algebras. Journal of Algebra 283, 254–291 (2005)

9. Grišin, V.N.: Predicate and set theoretic calculi on logic without contraction. Math. USSR Izv. 18(1), 42–59 (1982)
10. Höhle, U.: Commutative, residuated l-monoids. In: Höhle, U., Klement, E.P. (eds.) Non-Classical Logics and Their Applications to Fuzzy Subsets, pp. 53–106. Kluwer Acad. Publ., Dordrecht (1995)
11. Mundici, D.: Interpretation of AF C*-algebras in Łukasiewicz sentential calculus. Journal of Functional Analysis 65, 15–63 (1968)

Verification by Parallelization of Parametric Code[*]

Tobias Gedell and Reiner Hähnle

Department of Computer Science and Engineering
Chalmers University of Technology
412 96 Göteborg, Sweden
{gedell,reiner}@chalmers.se

Abstract. Loops and other unbound control structures constitute a major bottleneck in formal software verification, because correctness proofs over such control structures generally require user interaction: typically, induction hypotheses or invariants must be found or modified by hand. Such interaction involves expert knowledge of the underlying calculus and proof engine. We show that one can replace interactive proof techniques, such as induction, with automated first-order reasoning in order to deal with parallelizable loops. A loop can be parallelized, whenever the execution of a generic iteration of its body depends only on the step parameter and not on other iterations. We use a symbolic dependence analysis that ensures parallelizability. This guarantees soundness of a proof rule that transforms a loop into a universally quantified update of the state change information effected by the loop body. This rule makes it possible to employ automatic first-order reasoning techniques to deal with loops. The method has been implemented in the KeY verification tool. We evaluated its applicability with representative case studies from the JAVA CARD domain.

1 Introduction

The context of this paper is formal software verification of object-oriented programs. The target programs are executable JAVA programs (not abstract programs) and we want to prove complex functional properties of these. There are a number of software verification systems that target JAVA and related programming languages [2,4,10,18,22,26]. All of these systems are semi-automatic at best. The reason is that the emergence of undecidable predicates is typical when proving correctness for the combination of data structures of unbounded size and of control structures that can lead to an unbounded number of execution steps. Typical examples of the former include integers, lists (arrays), trees. The

---

[*] This work was funded in part by a STINT institutional grant and by the IST programme of the EC, Future and Emerging Technologies under the IST-2005-015905 MOBIUS project. This article reflects only the author's views and the Community is not liable for any use that may be made of the information contained therein. This paper is an extended and revised version of [13].

S. Aguzzoli et al.(Eds.): Algebraic and Proof-theoretic Aspects, LNAI 4460, pp. 138–159, 2007.
© Springer-Verlag Berlin Heidelberg 2007

most important representatives of the latter are loops, recursive method calls, and concurrent processes. All of them are present in JAVA-like languages.

If we do not want to abstract away from real JAVA programs as in software model checking [15] or trade off verification for mere bug finding [12], then the inherent limitations of computability do not allow a complete, uniform deduction system for program verification. Even though it seems that the calculi used for program verification are practically complete in the sense that complex, realistic examples can be handled [4,8,16] without encountering incompleteness phenomena, this is not enough. To see why, let us look at an example.

Example 1 (Array reversal).
The following loop reverses the elements of the int array a:

```
int half = a.length / 2 - 1;
for (int i = 0; i <= half; i++) {
  int tmp = a[i];
  a[i] = a[a.length - 1 - i];
  a[a.length - 1 - i] = tmp;
}
```

A formal specification can be given in first-order logic as follows:

Precondition: a $\neq$ null
Postcondition: $\forall j.(0 \leq j < $ a.length $\rightarrow$ a$[j] \doteq$ \old(a)[a.length $- 1 - j])$

The keyword \old indicates that the value a had before the execution is referred to.   □

What are the options to prove total correctness of this loop with respect to its contract? Finite unwinding is impossible and abstraction has difficulties to record that the value a.length depends on a. The standard approach is to use one of two general-purpose mechanisms for dealing with unbounded control structures, *invariants* or *induction*. In the first case, one would establish that the loop preserves a suitable invariant property I, which must be strong enough to imply the postcondition. Termination of the loop is proven separately (and is trivial for this example). Alternatively, an induction argument over i would typically establish that the loop reverses all array positions. The problem is that both, a suitable invariant and a suitable induction hypothesis, are not straightforward to derive from the postcondition: it is necessary to introduce a new variable k for the index up to which the array has been reversed already, k must have appropriate bounds, the precondition must be included, etc. In general, the postcondition might not be given (for example, if the task is to derive the specification from the code). In this case, it is even more difficult to come up with a suitable invariant or induction hypothesis. In addition, loop rules in realistic imperative languages [6] are very complex. User interaction involves a high amount of technical knowledge and is thus extremely expensive.

There is a large body of work on heuristically guided inductive theorem proving, but most of it is done in the context of functional programming [7,9]. Existing work on automatic synthesis of loop invariants in imperative programs [17,23] is defined only for an abstract while-language. A recent divide-and-conquer technique for decomposition of induction proofs [20] works for a larger fragment of JAVA, but it is targeted at simplifying user interaction rather than eliminating it.

1.1 Main Contributions

The contribution of this paper is to present a new verification technique that relies neither on abstraction, nor on invariants, nor on induction. It is *complementary* to the work cited above in so far as our goal is to recognize situations where complex invariants can be avoided altogether.

The key insight (illustrated by means of Example 1) is that the swap operations realized in the loop body can be executed independently of each other: the assignment to a[i] and the value of a[a.length - 1 - i] do not depend on any a[j] and a[a.length - 1 - j] with i ≠ j provided that i and j are within the bounds specified in the guard of the loop.

Now, a new way to prove correctness of the loop goes as follows: first compute the effect of a generic iteration of the loop body parameterized with i; second, prove that there are no dependencies between different iterations in the loop range; third, generalize the effect of the loop body over all values that the parameter i takes on in the loop range; and fourth, prove that the postcondition is implied by the loop. Importantly, the last step involves no induction, but automatable first-order search stratagems such as quantifier elimination and term rewriting.

Obviously, verification by parallelization of parametric code is an *incomplete* verification technique for loops, because not all loops are parallelizable. On the other hand, it is not an exotic special case either: from an analysis of the *unchanged* code of several real JAVA CARD programs we concluded that parallelizable loops occur naturally and relatively frequently, see Section 10. As we show in Section 11, verification by parallelization is not restricted to loops, but can be applied whenever a non-linear program is composed of parametric pieces of code, for example, in recursive calls and concurrent processes. In addition, the current trend towards multi-core processors will result in more code being written in such a way that it is parallelizable. Therefore, verification by parallelization is a *relevant* technique for increasing the degree of automation in software verification.

The most important aspect of verification by parallelization is that it is a *highly automatable* verification technique. First, because the computation of the effect (i.e., the strongest postcondition relative to a given precondition) $\mathcal{U}(\texttt{i})$ of a piece of code p(i) parameterized by i is done automatically. Even the choice of the parameter i is automatic and guided by heuristics. The details are given in Sections 4 and 5. Second, the effect of some non-linear parameterized code (such as a loop with body p(i)) is represented in form of a universally quantified state update, say, \for int I; {i := I}{$\mathcal{U}(\texttt{i})$}. Therefore, it can be further processed during the remaining verification proof by employing first-order reasoning, see Section 8.

Soundness of the universal quantification step is ensured by an automatic symbolic dependence analysis described in Sections 6 and 7. This analysis is executed not directly on the code p(i), but on the simplified and normalized effect $\mathcal{U}(i)$ computed by symbolic execution before. This feature makes our approach *robust*, because the success of the dependence analysis does not rely on any syntactic restrictions of p(i). A further robustness feature is that our dependence analysis does not simply fail in case when dependencies are detected, but yields a symbolic constraint that is sufficient for dependencies not to occur and that can be used elsewhere in the verification attempt, see Section 9.

In the following section, we collect a number of technical notions needed later on. In Section 3, we walk informally through the method guided by an example. The remaining sections then give the technical details.

2   Basic Definitions

The platform for our experiments is the KeY tool [4], which features an interactive theorem prover for formal verification of sequential JAVA programs.

2.1   Dynamic Logic for JAVA CARD

In KeY the target program to be verified and its specification are both modeled in an instance of a dynamic logic (DL) [14] calculus called JAVA DL [3]. JAVA DL extends other variants of DL used for theoretical investigations or verification purposes, because it handles such phenomena as side effects, aliasing, object types, exceptions, and finite integer types. JAVA DL fully axiomatizes the JAVA CARD programming language [27] which contains all JAVA features minus multi-threading, floating point types, and dynamic class loading. It has also some features that JAVA does not have, but they are not addressed in this article.

Deduction in the JAVA DL calculus is based on symbolic program execution and simple program transformations and so is close to a programmer's understanding of JAVA. It can be seen as a modal logic with a modality ⟨p⟩ for every program p, where ⟨p⟩ refers to the final state (if p terminates normally) that is reached after executing p.

The *program formula* ⟨p⟩ ϕ expresses that the program p terminates in a state in which ϕ holds without throwing an exception. A formula $\phi \rightarrow$ ⟨p⟩ ψ is valid if for every state S satisfying precondition ϕ a run of the program p starting in S terminates normally, and in the terminating state the postcondition ψ holds.

The programs occurring in JAVA DL formulas are executable JAVA code. Each rule of the JAVA DL calculus specifies how to execute symbolically one particular statement, possibly with additional restrictions. When a loop or a recursive method call is encountered, it is in general necessary to perform induction over a suitable data structure. In this paper we show how induction can be avoided in the case of parallelizable loops.

2.2   State Updates

In JAVA (as in other object-oriented programming languages), different object type variables may refer to the same object. This phenomenon, called aliasing, causes difficulties for the handling of assignments in a calculus for JAVA DL. For example, whether or not the formula o1.f $\doteq$ 1 holds after (symbolic) execution of the assignment o2.f = 2;, depends on whether o1 and o2 refer to the same object. Therefore, JAVA assignments cannot be symbolically executed by syntactic substitution without causing excessive branching. In the JAVA DL calculus a different solution is used, based on the notion of (state) *updates*.

Definition 1. Atomic updates *are of the form* loc:= val, *where* val *is a logical term without side effects and* loc *is either (i) a program variable* v, *or (ii) a field access* o.f, *or (iii) an array access* a[i]. *Updates may appear in front of any formula, where they are surrounded by curly brackets for easy parsing. The semantics of* { loc:= val}ϕ *is the same as that of* $\langle$loc=val;$\rangle$ ϕ.

Changes of the computation state can be represented with the help of updates. For example, the update {loc := val}ϕ represents all states in which the formula ϕ holds after the value of loc has been changed to val. In a somewhat loose manner we use updates to represent states, for example, the update {loc := val} is used to represent an arbitrary state, where the value of loc is val.

Definition 2. *General* updates *are defined inductively based on atomic updates. If* $\mathcal{U}$ *and* $\mathcal{U}'$ *are updates then so are: (i)* $\mathcal{U}, \mathcal{U}'$ *(parallel composition), (ii)* $\mathcal{U};\mathcal{U}'$ *(sequential composition), (iii)* \if *(b)* {$\mathcal{U}$}, *where b is a quantifier-free formula (conditional execution), (iv)* \for *T* s; $\mathcal{U}(s)$, *where s is a variable over a well-ordered type* T *and* $\mathcal{U}(s)$ *is an update with occurrences of s (quantification), (v)* {$\mathcal{U}$}$\mathcal{U}'$ *application.*

The semantics of sequential, conditional, and application updates is obvious; the meaning of a parallel update is the simultaneous application of all its constituent updates except when two left hand sides refer to the same location: in this case the syntactically later update wins. This models natural program execution flow. The semantics of \for *T* s; $\mathcal{U}(s)$ *is the parallel execution of all updates in* $\bigcup_{x \in T}${$s := x; \mathcal{U}(s)$}. *As for parallel updates, a last-win clash-semantics is in place: the maximal[1] update with respect to the well-order on* T *and the syntactic order within each* $\mathcal{U}(s)$ *wins.*

The restriction that right-hand sides of updates must be side effect-free is not essential: by introducing fresh local variables and symbolic execution of complex expressions the JAVA DL calculus rules normalize arbitrary assignments so that they meet the restrictions of updates. A full formal treatment of updates is in [24], see also [4].

Sequential composition of updates is automatically transformed into parallel composition in KeY and we will therefore mostly not consider it further.

---

[1] Well-orders are usually defined with respect to minimal elements. We use the dual definition here, because it is more natural in our setting.

3   Outline of the Approach

Let us look at the following example:

```
for (int i = 1; i < a.length; i++)
    if (c != 0) a[i] = b[i+1];
    else a[i] = b[i-1];
```

In a first step, the loop initialization expression is transformed out of the loop and symbolically executed. The reason is that the initialization expression might be complex and have side effects. This results in a state $\mathcal{S} = \{i := 1\}$. The remaining loop now has the form: **for** (; i < a.length; i++)...

We proceed to symbolically execute the loop body, the step expression, and the guard for a generic value of i. In order to do this correctly, we must eliminate from the current state all locations that can potentially be modified in the body, step, or guard. In Section 4 we describe an algorithm that approximates such a set of locations rather precisely. Applied to the present example we obtain i and a[i] as modifiable locations. Consequently, generic execution of the loop body, step, and guard starts in the empty state. Note that the set of modifiable locations does not include, for example, c. This is important, because if $\mathcal{S}$ contains, say, c := 1, we would start the execution in the state $\{c := 1\}$ and the resulting state would be much simplified.

In our example, symbolic execution of one loop iteration starting in the empty state gives $\mathcal{S}' = \{i := i + 1, \text{ \if } (c \neq 0) \{a[i] := b[i+1]\}, \text{ \if } (c \doteq 0) \{a[i] := b[i-1]\}\}$, where the step and guard expressions were executed as well.

The next step is to check whether the state update $\mathcal{S}'$ resulting from the execution of the generic iteration contains dependencies that make it impossible to represent the effect of the loop as a quantified update. For $\mathcal{S}'$ this is the case if and only if c is 0 and a and b are the same array. In this case, the body amounts to the statement a[i] = a[i-1] which contains a data dependence that cannot be parallelized. All other dependencies can be captured by parallel execution of updates with last-win clash-semantics. The details of the dependence analysis are explained in Section 6 and Section 7. In the example it results in a logical constraint $\mathcal{C}$ that, among other things, contains the disjunction of $c \neq 0$ and $a \neq b$. A further logical constraint $\mathcal{D}$ strengthening $\mathcal{C}$ is computed which, in addition, ensures that the loop terminates normally. In the example, normal termination is ensured by a and b not being **null** and b having enough elements, that is, b.length > a.length.

At this point the proof is split into two cases using cut formula $\mathcal{D}$. Under the assumption $\mathcal{D}$ the loop can be transformed into a quantified update. If $\mathcal{D}$ is not provable, then the loop must be also tackled with a conventional induction rule, but one may use the additional assumption $\neg\mathcal{D}$, which may well simplify the proof.

For the sake of illustration assume now $\mathcal{S}$ and $\mathcal{S}'$ both contain $\{c := 1\}$ and the termination constraint in $\mathcal{D}$ holds. In this case, we can additionally simplify $\mathcal{S}'$ to $\{c := 1, i := i + 1, a[i] := b[i+1]\}$.

In the final step we synthesize from (i) the initial state $\mathcal{S}$, (ii) the effect of a generic execution of an iteration $\mathcal{S}'$ and (iii) the guard, a state update, where the loop variable i is universally quantified. The details are explained in Section 8. The result for the example in somewhat simplified manner is as follows:

\for int n;
$$\{\texttt{i} := n+1\}\{\texttt{\textbackslash if } (\texttt{i} \geq 1 \land \texttt{i} < \texttt{a.length})\, \{\texttt{c} := 1,\, \texttt{i} := \texttt{i}+1,\, \texttt{a[i]} := \texttt{b[i+1]}\}\}$$

Here we make use of an update applied to an update. The variable n holds the iteration number, i.e., 0 for the first iteration, 1 for the second, and so on. For each iteration we need to assign the loop variable its value. This is done by the update $\{\texttt{i} := n+1\}$. We apply this update to the guarded update which has the effect that all occurrences of i in non-update positions (guard, arguments, right-hand sides) are replaced by $n+1$. The resulting update is:

\for int n;
$$\{\texttt{\textbackslash if } (n+1 \geq 1 \land n+1 < \texttt{a.length})\, \{\texttt{c} := 1,\, \texttt{i} := n+2,\, \texttt{a[}n+1\texttt{]} := \texttt{b[}n+2\texttt{]}\}\}$$

The for-expression is a universal first-order quantifier whose scope is an update that contains occurrences of the variable n (see Def. 2 and [24]). Subexpressions are first-order terms that are simplified eagerly while symbolic execution proceeds. first-order quantifier elimination rules based on skolemization and instantiation are applicable, for example, for any positive value j such that $j < \texttt{a.length}$ we obtain immediately the update $\texttt{a[}j\texttt{]} := \texttt{b[}j\texttt{+1]}$ by instantiation. Proof search is performed by the usual first-order strategies without user interaction.

4   Computing the Effect of a Generic Loop Iteration

In this section we describe how we compute the state modifications performed by a generic loop iteration. As a preliminary step we move the initialization out of the loop and execute it symbolically, because the initialization expression may contain side-effects. We are left with a loop consisting of a guard, a step expression, and a body:

$$\texttt{for (; guard; step) body} \tag{1}$$

We want to compute the state modifications performed by a generic iteration of the loop. A single loop iteration consists of executing the body, evaluating the step expression, and testing the guard expression. This behavior is captured in the following compound statement where dummy is needed, because JAVA expressions are not statements.

$$\texttt{body; step; boolean dummy = guard;} \tag{2}$$

We proceed to symbolically execute the compound statement (2) for a generic value of the loop variable. This is quite similar to computing the strongest post condition of a given program. Platzer [21] has worked out the details of how to compute the strongest post condition in the specific JAVA program logic that we use and our methods are based on the same principles. Our method handles the fragment of JAVA that the symbolic execution machinery of KeY handles, which is JAVA CARD [27].

Let p be the code in (2). The main idea is to try to prove validity of the program formula $\mathcal{S}\langle p \rangle$ *fin*, where *fin* is an arbitrary, but unspecified non-rigid predicate that signifies when to stop symbolic execution. Complete symbolic execution of p starting in state $\mathcal{S}$ eventually yields a proof tree whose open leaves are of the form $\Gamma \rightarrow \mathcal{U}$ *fin* for some update expression $\mathcal{U}$. The predicate *fin* cannot be shown to be true or false in the program logic. Therefore, after all instructions in p have been executed, symbolic execution is stuck. At this stage we extract two vectors $\vec{\Gamma}$ and $\vec{\mathcal{U}}$ consisting of corresponding Γ and $\mathcal{U}$ from all open leaf nodes. Different leaves correspond to different execution paths in the loop body.

Example 2. Consider the following statement p:

```
if (i > 2) a[i] = 0 else a[i] = 1; i = i + 1;
```

After the attempt to prove $\langle p \rangle$ *fin* becomes stuck there are two open leaves:

$$V \wedge i > 2 \rightarrow \{\texttt{a[i]} := 0, \ \texttt{i} := \texttt{i} + 1\} \textit{fin}$$
$$V \wedge i \not> 2 \rightarrow \{\texttt{a[i]} := 1, \ \texttt{i} := \texttt{i} + 1\} \textit{fin}$$

where V stands for $\texttt{a} \neq \textbf{null} \wedge i \geq 0 \wedge \texttt{i} < \texttt{a.length}$. We extract the following vectors:

$$\vec{\Gamma} \equiv \langle V \wedge i > 2, V \wedge i \not> 2 \rangle$$
$$\vec{\mathcal{U}} \equiv \langle \{\texttt{a[i]} := 0, \ \texttt{i} := \texttt{i} + 1\}, \{\texttt{a[i]} := 1, \ \texttt{i} := \texttt{i} + 1\} \rangle \tag{3}$$

□

Symbolic execution can become stuck at a leaf containing a program in three ways:

1. The program has been fully executed and only an update and the formula *fin* remain. This is what we call a *success leaf*. The effect of the program was successfully transformed into a state update. Success leaves are always of the form $\Gamma \rightarrow \mathcal{U}$ *fin*.
2. Abrupt termination caused by, for example, a thrown exception. In this case the program cannot be transformed into a state update. We call this a *failed leaf*.
3. The strategies for automatic symbolic execution were not strong enough to execute all instructions in the program. This could possibly be remedied by enabling more powerful and expensive strategies and restart symbolic execution. If they are still not strong enough, we count the leaf as a failed leaf.

If a failed leaf can be reached from the initial state, then our method cannot handle the loop. We must, therefore, make sure that our method is only applied to loops for which we have proven that no failed leaf can be reached. We construct the vector $\vec{\mathcal{F}}$ consisting of the path conditions Γ of all failed leaves and let the negation of $\vec{\mathcal{F}}$ become a condition that needs to be proven when applying our method.

Example 3. In Example 2 we only showed the success leaves. When symbolic execution becomes stuck, there are, in addition to the success leaves, failed leaves of the following form:

$$
\begin{aligned}
\texttt{a} \doteq \textbf{null} &\rightarrow \dots \textit{fin} \\
\texttt{a} \neq \textbf{null} \wedge \texttt{i} < 0 &\rightarrow \dots \textit{fin} \\
\texttt{a} \neq \textbf{null} \wedge \texttt{i} \not< \texttt{a.length} &\rightarrow \dots \textit{fin}
\end{aligned}
$$

The first leaf corresponds to the case where a is **null** and using a throws a null pointer exception. The second and third leaves correspond to the case where i is outside a's bounds and accessing a[i] throws an index out of bounds exception. From the failed leaves we extract the following vector:

$$\vec{\mathcal{F}} \equiv \langle \texttt{a} \doteq \textbf{null}, \texttt{a} \neq \textbf{null} \wedge \texttt{i} < 0, \texttt{a} \neq \textbf{null} \wedge \texttt{i} \not< \texttt{a.length} \rangle \qquad \square$$

Note that symbolic execution discards any code that cannot be reached. As a consequence, an exception that occurs at a code location that cannot be reached from the initial state will not occur in the leaves of the proof tree. This means that our method is not restricted to code that cannot throw any exception, which would be very restrictive.

So far we said nothing about the state in which we start a generic loop iteration. Choosing a suitable state requires some care, as the following example shows.

Example 4. Consider the following code:

```
c = 1;
i = 0;
for (; i < a.length; i++) {
    if (c != 0) a[i] = 0;
    b[i] = 0; }
```

At the beginning of the loop we are in state $\mathcal{S}_{\text{init}} = \{\texttt{c} := 1, \texttt{i} := 0\}$. It is tempting, but wrong, to start the generic loop iteration in this state. The reason is that i has a specific value, so one iteration would yield $\{\texttt{a[0]} := 0, \texttt{b[0]} := 0, \texttt{i} := 1\}$, which is the result after the *first* iteration, not a generic one. The problem is that $\mathcal{S}_{\text{init}}$ contains information that is not invariant during the loop. Starting the loop iteration in the empty state is sound, but suboptimal. In the example, we would get $\{\texttt{\textbackslash if } (\texttt{c} \neq 0) \{\texttt{a[i]} := 0\}, \texttt{b[i]} := 0, \texttt{i} := \texttt{i}+1\}$, which is unnecessarily imprecise, since we know that c is equal to 1 during the entire execution of the loop. $\qquad \square$

We want to use as much information as possible from the state $\mathcal{S}_{\text{init}}$ at the beginning of the loop and only remove those parts that are not invariant during all iterations of the loop. Executing the loop in the largest possible state corresponds to performing dead code elimination. When we reach a loop of the form (1) in state S_{init} we proceed as follows:

1. Execute **boolean dummy** = **guard**; in state S_{init} and obtain S. We need to evaluate the guard since it may have side effects. Evaluation of the guard might cause the proof to branch, in which case we apply the following steps to *each* branch. If our method cannot be applied to one of the branches we backtrack to state S_{init} and use the standard rules to prove the loop. If the guard evaluates to false, we skip the loop and proceed using the standard rules.
2. Compute the vectors $\vec{\Gamma}, \vec{\mathcal{U}}$ and $\vec{\mathcal{F}}$ from (2) starting in state S.
3. Obtain S' by removing from S all those locations that are modified in a success leaf. This is done as follows: for each modified location in S, add an update of the location to itself in parallel to the updates in S. They are added syntactically after all updates in S and, therefore, the clash-semantics of updates ensures that the previous assignments to the modified locations in S are canceled. More formally, S' is defined as follows: $S' = S, \bigcup_{l \in mod(\vec{\mathcal{U}}, S)}\{l := l\}$, where $mod(\vec{\mathcal{U}}, S)$ is the set of locations in S whose assigned term in $\vec{\mathcal{U}}$ differs from its assigned term in S. How to compute this set is discussed below.
4. If $S' = S$ then stop; otherwise let S become S' and goto Step 2.

The algorithm terminates since the number of locations that can be removed from the initial state is bound both by the textual size of the loop[2] and, in case the state does not contain any quantified update, the size of the state itself. The final state of this algorithm is a greatest fixpoint containing as much information as possible from the initial state S. Let us call this final state S_{iter}.

Example 5. Example 4 yields the following sequence of states:

Round	Start state	State modifications	New state	Remark
1	$\{c := 1, i := 0\}$	$\{a[0] := 0, b[0] := 0, i := 1\}$	$\{c := 1, i := i\}$[3]	
2	$\{c := 1, i := i\}$	$\{a[i] := 0, b[i] := 0, i := i+1\}$	$\{c := 1, i := i\}$	Fixpoint

□

Computing the set $mod(\vec{\mathcal{U}}, S)$ can be difficult. Assume S contains $a[c] := 0$ and $\vec{\mathcal{U}}$ contains $a[i] := 1$. If i and c can have the same value then $a[c]$ should be removed from S, otherwise it is safe to keep it. In general it is undecidable whether two variables can assume the same value. A similar situation occurs when S contains $a.f := 0$ and $\vec{\mathcal{U}}$ contains $b.f := 1$. If a and b are references to the same object then $a.f$ must be removed from the new state. These issues are handled by using a dependence analysis to compute $mod(\vec{\mathcal{U}}, S)$. The details of how this is done are described in Section 7.

---

[2] Including the size of any method called by the loop.
[3] The new state that gets computed is $\{c := 1, i := 0, i := i\}$ but is simplified to $\{c := 1, i := i\}$.

5   Loop Variable and Loop Range

For the dependence analysis and for creating the quantified state update we need to identify a loop variable and the loop range. The requirement we have on a loop variable is that it must, in each success leaf, be updated with the same step function by an unguarded update.

When deciding whether a particular variable i is a possible loop variable, we look for a function $step$ such that $i := step(i)$ is found in each update $\mathcal{U} \in \vec{\mathcal{U}}$. Remember that $\vec{\mathcal{U}}$ contains the updates from all success leaves. In KeY, finding such a function is often not possible due to eager simplification performed on updates. If, for example, for a specific leaf, the path condition contains $i \doteq 0$ the update $i := i + c$ will be simplified to $i := c$. This means that even if $i := i + c$ is the step function of the loop it will not be found in all leaves. To handle this we must take the path condition Γ into account. For each success leaf with path condition Γ and update $\mathcal{U}$ we require that under the path condition, $step(i)$ is equal to the expression assigned to i by $\mathcal{U}$. Formally, this is expressed by $\Gamma \rightarrow step(i) \doteq \mathcal{U}i$.

The step function describes the execution order of the loop iterations and expresses how the loop variable changes between each loop iteration. For constructing the quantified state update we need to know the value that the loop variable has in each iteration of the loop, that is, we need to have a function from the number of an iteration to the value of the loop variable in that iteration. This function is defined as $iter(n) = step^n(start)$ where n is the number of the iteration and $start$ the initial value of the loop variable. In JAVA DL we cannot write recursive expressions directly, so we have to rewrite the body of $iter$ into a non-recursive expression. This is in general hard, but whenever the loop variable is incremented or decremented with a constant value in each iteration, it is easy to do. At present we impose this as a restriction: the step function must have the form i + e, where i is the loop variable and e is invariant during loop execution. Then one obtains the following definition: $iter(n) = start + n * e$. It would be possible to let the user provide the definition of $iter$ allowing for more complicated step functions to be handled. It would, however, come at the price of making the method less automatic.

To identify the loop variable, we start with the set of variables occurring in the loop and remove all those for which a step function cannot be found. After this we might be left with more than one variable. Since we cannot, currently, handle more than one loop variable we need to eliminate the other candidates. If they are not eliminated they would cause data flow-dependencies that could not be handled by our method. A candidate is eliminated by transforming its expression into one which is not dependent on the candidate location. For example, the candidate l, introduced by the assignment l = l + c;, can be eliminated by transforming the assignment into l = init + n * c;, where init is the initial value of l and n the number of the iteration.

To make the identification of loop variables more efficient we use a heuristic that favors variables that occur in the loop guard (as loop variables often do) and that are syntactically small (for example, i is considered smaller than a[l]).

Example 6. Consider the code in Example 2 which gives the vector in (3). The only variable for which a step function can be found is `i`. It is, therefore, identified as the loop variable. □

To determine the loop range we begin by computing the specification of the guard in a similar way as we computed the state modifications of a generic iteration in the previous section. We attempt to prove ⟨**boolean** `dummy` = `guard;`⟩ *fin*. From the open leaves of the form $\Gamma \rightarrow$ {`dummy` := `e`, ...} *fin*, we create the formula GS which characterizes when the guard is true. Formally, GS is defined as $\bigvee_\Gamma (\Gamma \wedge$ `e` $\doteq$ **true**). The formula GF characterizes when the guard is *not* successfully evaluated. We let GF be the disjunction of all Γ' from the open leaves that are not of the form above.

Example 7. Consider the following guard `g` ≡ `i` < `a.length`. When all instructions in the formula ⟨**boolean** `dummy` = `g;`⟩ *fin* have been symbolically executed, there are two success leaves:

$$\text{a} \not\doteq \textbf{null} \ \wedge \ \text{i} < \text{a.length} \rightarrow \{\text{dummy} := \textbf{true}\} \, \textit{fin}$$
$$\text{a} \not\doteq \textbf{null} \ \wedge \ \text{i} \not< \text{a.length} \rightarrow \{\text{dummy} := \textbf{false}\} \, \textit{fin}$$

From these we extract the following formula GS:

$$(\text{a} \not\doteq \textbf{null} \ \wedge \ \text{i} < \text{a.length} \ \wedge \ \textbf{true} \doteq \textbf{true}) \ \vee$$
$$(\text{a} \not\doteq \textbf{null} \ \wedge \ \text{i} \not< \text{a.length} \ \wedge \ \textbf{false} \doteq \textbf{true})$$

After simplification of GS we obtain:

$$\text{a} \not\doteq \textbf{null} \ \wedge \ \text{i} < \text{a.length} \quad .$$

When the instructions have been symbolically executed, there is also a failed leaf containing `a` $\doteq$ **null** $\rightarrow$ ... *fin*. From it we extract the formula $GF \equiv \text{a} \doteq \textbf{null}$. □

The formula GR_n characterizes when the iteration number n is within the loop range. The following definition expresses that there exists an iteration where the loop variable has the value $iter(n)$ and, moreover, this iteration can be reached:

$$GR_n \equiv n \geq 0 \ \wedge \ \{\text{i} := iter(n)\}GS \ \wedge \ \forall m.\ 0 \leq m < n \rightarrow \{\text{i} := iter(m)\}GS$$

It is important that the loop terminates, otherwise, our method would be unsound. We, therefore, create a termination constraint GT that needs to be proven when applying our method. The termination constraint expresses that there exists a number n of iterations after which the guard formula evaluates to false. The constraint GT is defined as:

$$GT \equiv \exists n.\ n \geq 0 \wedge \{\text{i} := iter(n)\}\neg GS$$

6   Dependence Analysis

Transforming a loop into a quantified state update is only possible when the iterations of the loop are independent of each other. Two loop iterations are independent of each other if the execution of one iteration does not affect the execution of the other. According to this definition, the loop variable clearly causes dependence, because each iteration both reads its current value and updates it. We will, however, handle the loop variable by quantification. Therefore, it is removed from the update before the dependence analysis is begun. The problem of loop dependencies was intensely studied in loop vectorization and parallelization for program optimization on parallel architectures. Some of our concepts are based on results in this field [1,28].

6.1   Classification of Dependencies

In our setting we encounter three different kinds of dependence; *data flow-dependence*, *data anti-dependence*, and *data output-dependence*.

Example 8. It is tempting to assume that it is sufficient for independence of loop iterations that the final state after executing a loop is independent of the order of execution, but the following example shows this to be wrong:

```
for (int i = 0, sum = 0; i < a.length; i++) sum += a[i];
```

The loop computes the sum of all elements in the array a which is independent of the order of execution, however, running all iterations in parallel gives the wrong result, because reading and writing of sum collide.   □

Definition 3. *Let S_J be the final state after executing a generic loop iteration over variable i during which it has value J and let $<$ be the order on the type of i.*

There is a data input-dependence *between iterations $K \neq L$ iff S_K writes to a location (i.e., appears on the left-hand side of an atomic update) that is read (appears on the right hand side of an atomic update or as an argument or in a guard of an update) in S_L. We speak of* data flow-dependence *when $K < L$ and of* data anti-dependence, *when $K > L$.*

There is data output-dependence *between iterations $K \neq L$ iff S_K writes to a location that is overwritten in S_L.*

Example 9. When executing the second iteration of the following loop, the location a[1], modified by the first iteration, is read, indicating data flow-dependence:

```
for (int i = 1; i < a.length; i++) a[i] = a[i - 1];
```

The following loop exhibits data output-dependence:

```
for (int i = 1; i < a.length; i++) last = a[i];
```

Each iteration assigns a new value to last. When the loop terminates, last has the value assigned to it by the last iteration.   □

Loops with data flow-dependencies cannot be parallelized, because each iteration must wait for a preceding one to finish before it can perform its computation.

In the presence of data anti-dependence swapping two iterations is unsound, but parallel execution is possible provided that the generic iteration acts on the original state before loop execution begins. In our translation of loops into quantified state updates in Section 8 below, this is ensured by simultaneous execution of all updates. Thus, we can handle loops that exhibit data anti-dependence. The final state of such loops depends on the order of execution, so independence of the order of executions is not only insufficient (Example 8) but even unnecessary for parallelization.

Even loops with data output-dependence can be parallelized by assigning an ordinal to each iteration. An iteration that wants to write to a location first ensures that no iteration with higher ordinal has already written to it. This requires a total order on the iterations. From the step function we extracted the function *iter*, so this order can easily be constructed. The order is used in the quantified state update together with a last-win clash-semantics to obtain the desired behavior.

6.2   Comparison to Traditional Dependence Analysis

Our dependence analysis is different from most existing analyses for loop parallelization in compilers [1,28]. The major difference is that these analyses must not be expensive in terms of computation time, because the user waits for the compiler to finish. Traditionally, precision is traded off for lower cost. Here we use dependence information to avoid using induction which comes with an extremely high cost, because it typically requires user interaction. In consequence, we strive to make the dependence analysis as precise as possible as long as it is still fully automatic. In particular, our analysis can afford to try several algorithms that work well for different classes of loops.

A second difference to traditional dependence analysis is that we do not require a definite answer. When used during compilation to a parallel architecture, a dependence analysis must give a Boolean answer as to whether a given loop is parallelizable or not. In our setting it is useful to know that a loop is parallelizable relative to satisfaction of a symbolic constraint. Then we can let a theorem prover validate or refute this constraint, which typically is a much easier problem than proving the original loop.

7   Implementation of the Dependence Analysis

Our dependence analysis analyzes a loop and symbolically computes a *constraint* that characterizes when the loop is free of dependencies. The advantage of the constraint-based approach is that we can avoid to deal with a number of very hard problems such as aliasing: for example, locations a[i] and b[i] are the same iff a and b are references to the same array, which can be difficult to determine. Our analysis side-steps the aliasing problem simply by generating a constraint saying that *if* a is not the same array as b *then* there is no dependence. The validity of the generated constraint will then be decided by a theorem prover.

When looking for dependencies in the loop we do not analyze the loop itself but the state updates computed from the generic loop iteration. The dependence analysis is, therefore, defined over updates. The binary function δ defined in Table 1 takes two updates as arguments and computes a constraint that characterizes the absence of data flow-dependence among its arguments. In the definitions, we let *locs(t)* be the set of locations occurring in the term t and *slocs(loc)* the set of locations occurring as arguments in loc as defined below:

$$\begin{aligned} slocs(\mathtt{v}) &= \emptyset \\ slocs(\mathtt{o.f}) &= locs(o) \\ slocs(\mathtt{a[i]}) &= locs(a) \cup locs(i) \end{aligned}$$

Table 1. Computing dependence constraints among updates

Atomic updates

$$\mathtt{v := val}\ \delta\ \mathtt{loc := val'}\quad = \begin{cases} \mathbf{true} & \text{when } \mathtt{v} \notin (locs(\mathtt{val'}) \cup slocs(\mathtt{loc})) \\ \mathbf{false} & \text{otherwise} \end{cases}$$

$$\mathtt{o1.f := val}\ \delta\ \mathtt{loc := val'} = \neg(\bigvee\nolimits_{o2.f \in (locs(\mathtt{val'}) \cup slocs(\mathtt{loc}))}\ o1 \doteq o2)$$

$$\mathtt{a[i] := val}\ \delta\ \mathtt{loc := val'} = \neg(\bigvee\nolimits_{b[j] \in (locs(\mathtt{val'}) \cup slocs(\mathtt{loc}))} (a \doteq b \wedge i \doteq j))$$

General updates

$$\begin{aligned} \mathcal{U}\ \delta\ \backslash\mathtt{if}\ (b)\ \{\mathcal{U}'\} &= \neg b \vee \mathcal{U}\ \delta\ \mathcal{U}' \\ \backslash\mathtt{if}\ (b)\ \{\mathcal{U}\}\ \delta\ \mathcal{U}' &= \neg b \vee \mathcal{U}\ \delta\ \mathcal{U}' \\ \mathcal{U}\ \delta\ \backslash\mathtt{for}\ T\ s; \mathcal{U}'(s) &= \forall s.\ \mathcal{U}\ \delta\ \mathcal{U}'(s) \\ \backslash\mathtt{for}\ T\ s; \mathcal{U}(s)\ \delta\ \mathcal{U}' &= \forall s.\ \mathcal{U}(s)\ \delta\ \mathcal{U}' \\ \mathcal{U}_0, \ldots, \mathcal{U}_m\ \delta\ \mathcal{U}'_0, \ldots, \mathcal{U}'_n &= \bigwedge\nolimits_{i,j} \mathcal{U}_i\ \delta \mathcal{U}'_j \end{aligned}$$

The computation of the dependence constraint of a loop uses the vectors $\vec{\Gamma}$ and $\vec{\mathcal{U}}$ extracted from the success leaves during symbolic execution of the loop body. They were obtained as the result of a generic loop iteration in Section 4. If the preconditions of two leaves are true for two different loop iterations we need to ensure that the updates of the leaves are data flow-independent of each other (Def. 3). Formally, if there exist two distinct iteration numbers k and l and (possibly identical) leaves r and s, for which $k < l$, $\{\mathtt{i} := iter(k)\}\Gamma_r$ and $\{\mathtt{i} := iter(l)\}\Gamma_s$ are true, then we need to ensure independence of $\mathcal{U}_r$ and $\mathcal{U}_s$.

We do this for all pairs of leaves and define the dependence constraint for the entire loop as follows where GR is the loop range predicate and $\mathcal{I}_{r,s,k,l}$ is defined as $\{\mathtt{i} := iter(k)\}\mathcal{U}_r\ \delta\ \{\mathtt{i} := iter(l)\}\mathcal{U}_s$.

$$\mathcal{C} \equiv \bigwedge_{r,s} \forall k, l.\ \left(k < l \wedge \left(\begin{array}{c} GR_k \wedge GR_l \wedge \\ \{\mathtt{i} := iter(k)\}\Gamma_r \wedge \{\mathtt{i} := iter(l)\}\Gamma_s \end{array} \right) \right) \to \mathcal{I}_{r,s,k,l}$$

The condition $k < l$ ensures that we only capture data flow-dependence and not data anti-dependence.

Example 10. Consider the loop from the array reversal Example 1. When computing the effect of the generic loop iteration, we get one success leaf with the following update: $\{$tmp $:=$ a[i], a[i] $:=$ a[a.length - 1 - i], a[a.length - 1 - i] $:=$ a[i]$\}$.

The dependence constraint $I_{0,0,k,l}$ is false only if a.length - 1 - $iter(l) \doteq iter(k)$ holds. In the example we have $iter(n) = n$, so this can be simplified to a.length - 1 $\doteq k + l$.

In order for $\mathcal{C}$ to be true we need to show that there are no iteration numbers k and l, such that the above equality holds. From the guard specification we obtain that the maximum iteration number is a.length / 2 - 1. The maximum value of $k + l$ is, therefore, a.length - 3 which is not equal to a.length - 1. This makes $\mathcal{C}$ true and means that the loop does not contain any dependencies that cannot be handled by our method.   □

7.1   Computing $mod(\vec{\mathcal{U}}, \mathcal{S})$

In Section 4 we used $mod(\vec{\mathcal{U}}, \mathcal{S})$ to compute the set of those locations in $\mathcal{S}$ whose assigned term in $\mathcal{U}$ differs from its assigned term in $\mathcal{S}$. This is very similar to an output dependence analysis. If a location is assigned a different term in $\mathcal{U}$ and $\mathcal{S}$ there will be an output dependence between them. Similarly as above, we define in Table 2 a function δ^o that gives the set of locations, where the terms in its two update arguments differ. The fourth case in the part for atomic updates in Table 2 is the default that is used when none of the other cases applies.

Table 2. Computing output dependence constraints

Atomic updates

v $:=$ val δ^o v $:=$ val$'$	$= \{$v$\}$ **when** val $\not\doteq$ val$'$
o.f $:=$ val δ^o o$'$.f $:=$ val$'$	$= \{$o$'$.f$\}$ **when** o $\doteq$ o$'$ $\wedge$ val $\not\doteq$ val$'$
a[i] $:=$ val δ^o b[j] $:=$ val$'$	$= \{$b[j]$\}$ **when** a $\doteq$ b $\wedge$ i $\doteq$ j $\wedge$ val $\not\doteq$ val$'$
_ δ^o _	$= \emptyset$

General updates

$\mathcal{U}$ δ^o \if (b) $\{\mathcal{U}'\}$	$= \mathcal{U}$ δ^o $\mathcal{U}'$ **when** b
\if (b) $\{\mathcal{U}\}$ δ^o $\mathcal{U}'$	$= \mathcal{U}$ δ^o $\mathcal{U}'$ **when** b
$\mathcal{U}$ δ^o \for T s; $\mathcal{U}'(s)$	$= \bigcup_s \mathcal{U}$ δ^o $\mathcal{U}'(s)$
\for T s; $\mathcal{U}(s)$ δ^o $\mathcal{U}'$	$= \bigcup_s \mathcal{U}(s)$ δ^o $\mathcal{U}'$
$\mathcal{U}_0, \dots, \mathcal{U}_m$ δ^o $\mathcal{U}'_0, \dots, \mathcal{U}'_n$	$= \bigcup_{i,j} \mathcal{U}_i$ $\delta^o \mathcal{U}'_j$

It is sometimes not possible to decide the **when** side conditions in Table 2. In this case we approximate conservatively and assume they are true. Possibly, we remove too much information this way, but the method remains sound. If the second argument is a quantified update, the set of locations could potentially be very large which would make the computation of δ^o very expensive. This can, however, not happen since quantified updates cannot occur in the updates computed for the generic loop iteration.

Another possibility when a side condition cannot be decided would be to compute two different results, one result for when the condition is true and one for when it is false. A problem with this approach is that it potentially doubles the number of returned results each time a side condition cannot be decided. The returned result is used for the computation of the generic loop iteration and, therefore, returning many results would lead to many different generic loop iterations where each needs to be analyzed by the dependence analysis.

Further details on the implementation of the dependence analysis are in [25].

8   Constructing the State Update

If we can show that the iterations of a loop are independent of each other (i.e., the constraint C defined in the previous section holds), we can capture all state modifications of the loop in one update. Concretely, we use the following quantified update (GR_n, Γ_r, $iter$, and $\mathcal{U}_r$ were defined in Sections 4 and 5):

$$\mathcal{U}_{loop} \equiv \text{\textbackslash for int } n; \{\text{\textbackslash if } (GR_n) \{\{\mathtt{i} := iter(n)\} \bigcup_r \text{\textbackslash if } (\Gamma_r) \{\mathcal{U}_r\}\}\} \quad (4)$$

The innermost conditional update in (4) corresponds to one loop iteration, where the loop variable i has the value $iter(n)$. In each state only one Γ_r can be true so we do not need to ensure any particular order of the updates $\vec{\mathcal{U}}$.

The guard GR ensures that the iteration number n is within the loop range. We must take care when using last-win clash-semantics to handle data output-dependence. The iteration with the highest iteration number should have priority over all other iterations. This is ensured by the standard well-order on the JAVA integer type.

9   Using the Analysis in a Correctness Proof

When we encounter a loop during symbolic execution we analyze it for paralleliz-ability as described above and compute the dependence constraint. We replace the loop by (4) if no failed leaves for the iteration statement or the guard expression can be reached (see Section 4), the loop terminates (formula GT, see Section 5), and the dependence constraint C in Section 7 is valid. Taken together, this yields:

$$\mathcal{D} \equiv (\bigwedge_{\mathcal{F} \in \vec{\mathcal{F}}} \neg(\exists n.GR_n \wedge \{i := iter(n)\}\mathcal{F})) \wedge$$
$$\neg(\exists n.GR_n \wedge \{i := iter(n)\}GF) \wedge GT \wedge C$$

If $\mathcal{D}$ does not hold, we fall back to the standard rules to verify the loop (usually induction). In many cases it is not trivial to immediately validate or refute $\mathcal{D}$. Then we perform a cut on $\mathcal{D}$ in the proof and replace the loop by the quantified state update $\mathcal{U}_{loop}$ (4) in the proof branch where $\mathcal{D}$ is assumed to hold. The general outline of a proof using a cut on $\mathcal{D}$ is as follows:

$$\cfrac{\cfrac{\text{If not } \Gamma \Rightarrow \mathcal{D},}{\text{use standard induction}}{\Gamma \Rightarrow \mathcal{U}\langle\text{for } \ldots ; \ldots\rangle\phi, \mathcal{D}} \quad \cfrac{\Gamma, \mathcal{D} \Rightarrow \mathcal{U}\mathcal{U}_{loop}\langle\ldots\rangle\phi}{\Gamma, \mathcal{D} \Rightarrow \mathcal{U}\langle\text{for } \ldots ; \ldots\rangle\phi}}{\Gamma \Rightarrow \mathcal{U}\langle\text{for } \ldots ; \ldots\rangle\phi} \; cut$$

$$\vdots$$

If we can validate or refute $\mathcal{D}$ we can close one of the two branches. Typically, this involves to show that there is no aliasing between the variables occurring in the dependence constraint. Even when it is not possible to prove or to refute $\mathcal{D}$ our analysis is useful, because $\mathcal{D}$ in the succedent of the left branch can make it easier to close.

10 Evaluation

We evaluated our method with three representative JAVA CARD programs [19]: DeMoney, SafeApplet and IButtonAPI that together consist of ca. 2200 lines of code (not counting comments). These programs contain 17 loops. Out of these, our method can be applied to five (sometimes, a simple code transformation like v += e to v = v0 + i * e is required). Additionally, four loops can be handled if we allow object creation in the quantified updates (which is currently not realized). The remaining eight loops cannot be handled because they contain abrupt termination and irregular step functions. The results are summarized in Table 3.

Table 3. Parallelizable loops in some representative JAVA CARD programs

	DeMoney	SafeApplet	IButtonAPI	Total
LoC	1633	514	102	2249
Size (kB)	182	22	3	207
# loops	10	6	1	17
handled	4	0	1	5
with ext.	3	1	0	4
remaining	3	5	0	8

All loops in the row "handled" are detected automatically as parallelizable and are transformed into quantified updates. The evaluation shows that a considerable number of loops in realistic legacy programs can be formally verified without resorting to interactive and, therefore, expensive techniques such as induction. Interestingly, the percentage of loops that can be handled differs drastically among the three programs. A closer inspection reveals that the reason is not that, for example, all the loops in SafeApplet are inherently not parallelizable. Some of them could be rewritten so that they become parallelizable. This suggests to develop programming guidelines (just as they exist for compilation on parallel architectures) that ensure parallelizability of loops.

11 Future Work

The coverage of our verification method can be improved in various ways. One example is the function from the iteration number to the value of the loop variable (see Section 5). In addition, straightforward automatic program transformations that reduce the amount of dependencies (for example, v += e; into v = vInit + i * e;) could be derived by looking at the updates computed from a generic loop iteration. Recent work on automatic termination analysis [11] could be tried in the present setting for proving the termination constraint in Section 5.

We intend to develop general programming guidelines that ensure parallelizability of loops. The current trend towards multi-core processors will result in more code being written in such a way that it is parallelizable and will for sure rekindle the interest in parallelizability.

Critical dependencies exhibited during dependence analysis are likely to cause complications even in a proof attempt based on a more general proof method such as invariants or induction. Hence, one could try to use the information obtained from the dependence analysis to guide the generalization of, for example, loop invariants.

At the moment we take into account JAVA integer semantics only by checking for overflow. The integer model could be made more precise by computing all integer operators modulo the size of the underlying integer type. This would require changes only in the dependence analysis; the JAVA DL calculus covers full JAVA integer semantics already [5].

So far our verification method has been worked out and implemented for loop structures, however, it can be seen as a particular instance of a modular approach to proving correctness of non-linear programs composed of code pieces p(i) parameterized by some i:

1. Compute automatically the effect $\mathcal{U}_p(i)$ of p(i) with respect to a given precondition.
2. Using the dependence analysis on $\mathcal{U}_p(i)$, compute a sufficient condition $\mathcal{C}$ under which the code p(i) can be seen as *modular* with respect to different iterations of the parameter i.
3. The result of the analysis can be used in non-linear composition of p(i) as done here for iterative control structures. The idea is just as well applicable for recursive method calls and concurrent processes as is illustrated by the following example:

```
int [] a = new int [n];
for (int i = 0; i < n; i++) {
  new MyThread (i,a).start ();
}
```

If we assume that the run() method of the class MyThread updates exactly position i of the array a, then the effect can be easily captured by an update obtained from executing `run()` in the instance created by **new MyThread(i,a);**. One difference to loops is that in the context of threads one would probably exclude data output-dependence (see Section 6.1) unless assumptions about the scheduler can be made. Otherwise, the inherently parallel structure of state updates is well suited to model concurrent threads.

In this paper we do not discuss in detail what happens after a loop has been transformed into a quantified update. This is outside the scope of the present work. So far, the KeY theorem prover has limited capabilities for automatic reasoning over first-order quantified updates. Since quantified updates occur in many other scenarios [24] it is worth to spend more effort on that front.

12   Conclusion

We presented a method for formal verification of loops that works by transforming loops into automatable first-order constructs (quantified updates) instead of interactive methods such as invariants or induction. The approach is restricted to loops that can be parallelized, but an analysis of representative programs from the JAVA CARD domain shows that such loops occur frequently. The method can be applied to most initialization and array copy loops but also to more complex loops as witnessed by Example 1.

The method relies on the capability to represent state change information effecting from symbolic execution of imperative programs explicitly in the form of syntactic updates [3,24]. With the help of updates the effect of a generic loop iteration is represented so that it can be analyzed for the presence of data dependencies. Ideas for the dependency analysis are taken from compiler optimization for parallel architectures, but the analysis is not merely static. Loops that are found to be parallelizable are transformed into first-order quantified updates to be passed on to an automated theorem prover.

A main advantage of our method is its robustness in the presence of syntactic variability in the target programs. This is achieved by performing symbolic execution before doing the dependence analysis. The method is also fully automatic whenever it is applicable and gives useful results in the form of symbolic constraints even if it fails.

Acknowledgments

Many thanks to Richard Bubel whose help with the prototypic implementation was invaluable. Max Schröder did the final implementation [25] which is the basis for Section 7. Thanks are also due to Philipp Rümmer for many inspiring discussions. The valuable comments of the anonymous reviewer led to several improvements.

References

1. Banerjee, U., Chen, S.-C., Kuck, D.J., Towle, R.A.: Time and parallel processor bounds for Fortran-like loops. IEEE Trans. Computers 28(9), 660–670 (1979)
2. Barnett, M., Leino, K.R.M., Schulte, W.: The Spec# programming system: an overview. In: Barthe, G., Burdy, L., Huisman, M., Lanet, J.-L., Muntean, T. (eds.) CASSIS 2004. LNCS, vol. 3362, pp. 49–69. Springer, Heidelberg (2005)
3. Beckert, B.: A dynamic logic for the formal verification of Java Card programs. In: Attali, I., Jensen, T. (eds.) JavaCard 2000. LNCS, vol. 2041, pp. 6–24. Springer, Heidelberg (2001)
4. Beckert, B., Hähnle, R., Schmitt, P.H. (eds.): Verification of Object-Oriented Software. LNCS (LNAI), vol. 4334. Springer, Heidelberg (2007)
5. Beckert, B., Schlager, S.: Software verification with integrated data type refinement for integer arithmetic. In: Boiten, E.A., Derrick, J., Smith, G.P. (eds.) IFM 2004. LNCS, vol. 2999, pp. 207–226. Springer, Heidelberg (2004)
6. Beckert, B., Schlager, S., Schmitt, P.H.: An improved rule for while loops in deductive program verification. In: Lau, K.-K., Banach, R. (eds.) ICFEM 2005. LNCS, vol. 3785, Springer, Heidelberg (2005)
7. Boyer, R.S., Moore, J S.: A Computational Logic Handbook. Academic Press, London (1988)
8. Breunesse, C.-B.: On JML: Topics in Tool-assisted Verification of Java Programs. PhD thesis, Radboud University of Nijmegen (2006)
9. Bundy, A., Basin, D., Hutter, D., Ireland, A.: Rippling: Meta-Level Guidance for Mathematical Reasoning. Cambridge Tracts in Theoretical Computer Science, vol. 56. Cambridge University Press, Cambridge (June 2005)
10. Burdy, L., Requet, A., Lanet, J.-L.: Java applet correctness: a developer-oriented approach. In: Araki, K., Gnesi, S., Mandrioli, D. (eds.) FME 2003. LNCS, vol. 2805, pp. 422–439. Springer, Heidelberg (2003)
11. Cook, B., Podelski, A., Rybalchenko, A.: Termination proofs for systems code. In: Schwartzbach, M.I., Ball, T. (eds.) Proc. ACM SIGPLAN Conf. on Programming Language Design and Implementation, Ottawa, Canada, pp. 415–426. ACM Press, New York (2006)
12. Flanagan, C., Leino, K.R.M., Lillibridge, M., Nelson, G., Saxe, J.B., Stata, R.: Extended static checking for Java. In: Proc. ACM SIGPLAN 2002 Conf. on Programming Language Design and Implementation, Berlin, pp. 234–245. ACM Press, New York (2002)
13. Gedell, T., Hähnle, R.: Automating verification of loops by parallelization. In: Hermann, M., Voronkov, A. (eds.) LPAR 2006. LNCS (LNAI), vol. 4246, pp. 332–346. Springer, Heidelberg (2006)
14. Harel, D., Kozen, D., Tiuryn, J.: Dynamic Logic. MIT Press, Cambridge (2000)
15. Holzmann, G.J.: Software analysis and model checking. In: Brinksma, E., Larsen, K.G. (eds.) CAV 2002. LNCS, vol. 2404, pp. 1–16. Springer, Heidelberg (2002)
16. Jacobs, B., Marché, C., Rauch, N.: Formal verification of a commercial smart card applet with multiple tools. In: Rattray, C., Maharaj, S., Shankland, C. (eds.) AMAST 2004. LNCS, vol. 3116, pp. 241–257. Springer, Heidelberg (2004)
17. Leino, K.R.M., Logozzo, F.: Loop invariants on demand. In: Yi, K. (ed.) APLAS 2005. LNCS, vol. 3780, pp. 119–134. Springer, Heidelberg (2005)
18. Marché, C., Paulin-Mohring, C.: Reasoning about Java programs with aliasing and frame conditions. In: Hurd, J., Melham, T. (eds.) TPHOLs 2005. LNCS, vol. 3603, pp. 179–194. Springer, Heidelberg (2005)

19. Mostowski, W.: Formalisation and verification of Java Card security properties in dynamic logic. In: Cerioli, M. (ed.) FASE 2005. LNCS, vol. 3442, pp. 357–371. Springer, Heidelberg (2005)
20. Olsson, O., Wallenburg, A.: Customised induction rules for proving correctness of imperative programs. In: Beckert, B., Aichernig, B. (eds.) Proc. Software Engineering and Formal Methods (SEFM), Koblenz, Germany, pp. 180–189. IEEE Press, Los Alamitos (2005)
21. Platzer, A.: Using a program verification calculus for constructing specifications from implementations. Master's thesis, Univ. Karlsruhe, Dept. of Computer Science (2004)
22. Poetzsch-Heffter, A., Müller, P.: A Programming Logic for Sequential Java. In: Swierstra, S.D. (ed.) ESOP 1999 and ETAPS 1999. LNCS, vol. 1576, pp. 162–176. Springer, Heidelberg (1999)
23. Rodríguez-Carbonell, E., Kapur, D.: Program verification using automatic generation of invariants. In: Liu, Z., Araki, K. (eds.) ICTAC 2004. LNCS, vol. 3407, pp. 325–340. Springer, Heidelberg (2005)
24. Rümmer, P.: Sequential, parallel, and quantified updates of first-order structures. In: Hermann, M., Voronkov, A. (eds.) LPAR 2006. LNCS (LNAI), vol. 4246, pp. 422–436. Springer, Heidelberg (2006)
25. Schroeder, M.: Using a symbolic dependence analysis for verification of programs containing loops. Master's thesis, Department of Computer Science, University of Karlsruhe (2007)
26. Stenzel, K.: Verification of Java Card Programs. PhD thesis, Fakultät für angewandte Informatik, University of Augsburg (2005)
27. Sun Microsystems, Inc.: Santa Clara, California, USA. JAVA CARD 2.2.1 Application Programming Interface (October 2003)
28. Wolfe, M.J.: Optimizing Supercompilers for Supercomputers. MIT Press, Cambridge (1989)

Finitely Presented Abelian Lattice-Ordered Groups

A.M.W. Glass[1] and Françoise Point[2]

[1] DPMMS
Wilberforce Road
Cambridge CB3 OWB, England
amwg@dpmms.cam.ac.uk
[2] Institut de Mathématique
Université de Mons-Hainaut, Le Pentagone
6, avenue du Champ de Mars, B-7000 Mons, Belgium
point@logique.jussieu.fr

To Daniele Mundici on his 60th birthday.

Abstract. We give necessary and sufficient conditions for the first-order theory of a finitely presented abelian lattice-ordered group to be decidable. We also show that if the number of generators is at most 3, then elementary equivalence implies isomorphism. We deduce from our methods that the theory of the free MV-algebra on at least 2 generators is undecidable.

1 Introduction

Throughout, let n be a fixed positive integer and $FA\ell(n)$ be the free abelian lattice-ordered group on n generators. Let $\mathcal{L}$ be the language $\{+, \wedge, \vee, 0\}$ for this structure.

The additive group C of all continuous functions from $\mathbb{R}^n$ to $\mathbb{R}$ is a lattice-ordered group under the pointwise ordering. The sublattice subgroup of C generated by the standard n projections $\pi_i : \mathbb{R}^n \to \mathbb{R}$ mapping $(x_1, \cdots, x_n)$ to x_i $(i = 1, \ldots, n)$ is (isomorphic to) the free abelian lattice-ordered group $FA\ell(n)$ on n generators ([1]).

For $f \in FA\ell(n)$, let $Z(f)$ be the zero set of f and $\langle f \rangle_{cl}$ be the principal ℓ-ideal of $FA\ell(n)$ generated by f. There is a one-to-one correspondence between the closed integral simplicial cones (see Definition 2.1) and the zero-sets of elements of $FA\ell(n)$. One can use this to interpret the lattice of zero-sets of the elements of $FA\ell(n)$ by first-order formulae. This played a central role in the proofs of the results obtained in [6]. We first showed that $FA\ell(2) \not\equiv FA\ell(n)$ for any $n > 2$. Then, using induction and a duality result due to Beynon [3], we proved that $FA\ell(m) \not\equiv FA\ell(n)$ if $m \neq n$. As a consequence of our proof and an undecidability result due to A. Grzegorczyk for some topological theories [8], we derived that the theory of $FA\ell(n)$ is undecidable if $n > 2$. In contrast, the first-order theory of the free abelian group on any finite number of generators is decidable.

S. Aguzzoli et al.(Eds.): Algebraic and Proof-theoretic Aspects, LNAI 4460, pp. 160–193, 2007.

W. M. Beynon generalised K. Baker's characterisation of projective vector lattices on a finite number of generators ([1]) and showed that finitely generated projective abelian lattice-ordered groups are precisely the finitely presented abelian lattice-ordered groups ([3] Theorem 3.1). These in turn are the quotients of $FA\ell(n)$ by principal ℓ-ideals. D. Mundici asked whether one could generalise the results in [6] and also classify the theories of finitely generated projective abelian lattice-ordered groups. This seems intractable. However, we will prove:

Theorem 1. *Let $m, n \leq 3$, $f \in FA\ell(m)$ and $g \in FA\ell(n)$. Then $FA\ell(m)/\langle f \rangle_{cl}$ and $FA\ell(n)/\langle g \rangle_{cl}$ are elementarily equivalent iff they are isomorphic.*

Theorem 2. *The first-order theory of $FA\ell(n)/\langle f \rangle_{cl}$ is decidable iff the dimension of $Z(f)$ is at most 2.*

Note that we are not concerned here with decidability questions concerning isomorphisms. Undecidability results in group theory can be converted into algorithmic insolubility statements in topology. For instance, in dimension 5, it is known that there is no algorithm for deciding whether a compact piecewise linear manifold is piecewise linearly equivalent to a standard piecewise linear sphere ([10] page 22). A.M.W. Glass and J. J. Madden used similar facts to show that the isomorphism problem for projective abelian lattice-ordered groups on 10 generators is undecidable (see [7]).

2   Projective Finitely Generated Abelian ℓ-Groups

We recall some notation and basic results from [1], [2], [3], and [5] Chapter 5.

First, $FA\ell(n) := \{f = \bigwedge_i \bigvee_j f_{ij} : f_{ij} \in Hom(\mathbb{Z}^n, \mathbb{Z})\}$, and any $g \in Hom(\mathbb{Z}^n, \mathbb{Z})$ is equal to $\sum_{i=1}^n m_i.\pi_i$, where $m_i := g(e_i) \in \mathbb{Z}$ for all $i \in \{1, \ldots, n\}$.

Definition 1. A subspace $\sum_{i=1}^n m_i x_i = 0$ (with all $m_i \in \mathbb{Z}$) will be called an *integral hyperspace*, and the corresponding n-dimensional subsets $\sum_{i=1}^n m_i x_i > 0$, $\sum_{i=1}^n m_i x_i < 0$, $\sum_{i=1}^n m_i x_i \geq 0$ and $\sum_{i=1}^n m_i x_i \leq 0$ (with all $m_i \in \mathbb{Z}$) will be called *integral half spaces*. A *cone* in $\mathbb{R}^n$ is a subset which is invariant under multiplication by elements of $\mathbb{R}^+$. A *closed cone* is a cone which is closed in the standard topology of $\mathbb{R}^n$; the vertex is the origin. We will always confine ourselves to such cones defined by integral half spaces. A closed (or open) *integral simplicial cone* is a cone obtainable by finite unions and intersections from closed (or open) integral half spaces. It is convex if it is obtained using only intersections. Note that on each ray contained in such a cone and containing a point with rational coordinates, there is a unique non-zero point p with integral coordinates such that the open line segment $(0, p)$ contains no point with integral coordinates. Following [3] Section 2, we will call such a point *the initial integer lattice point* on this ray.

Definition 2. For $f \in FA\ell(n)$, let $Z(f)$ be the zero set of f; *i.e.*,

$$Z(f) = \{x \in \mathbb{R}^n : f(x) = 0\}.$$

Let $S(f)$ be the support of f; *i.e.*,

$$S(f) = \{x \in \mathbb{R}^n : f(x) \neq 0\}.$$

Let $\mathcal{K}$ be a subset of $\mathbb{R}^n$; then $S_\mathcal{K}(f)$ is the support of f on $\mathcal{K}$ ($=\{x \in \mathcal{K} : f(x) \neq 0\}$). In the special case that $\mathcal{K}$ is the $(n-1)$-sphere $S^{(n-1)}$, we write $\mathcal{S}(f)$ for $S_\mathcal{K}(f)$ and $\mathcal{Z}(f)$ for $Z(f) \cap S^{(n-1)}$. Note that $f(rx) = rf(x)$ for all $x \in S^{(n-1)}$ and $r \in \mathbb{R}_+$. Hence $\mathcal{Z}(f)$ completely determines $Z(f)$ and $\mathcal{S}(f)$ completely determines $S(f)$.

As mentioned in the introduction, there is a one-to-one correspondence between the closed integral simplicial cones and the zero-sets of the elements of $FA\ell(n)$. Let $f \in FA\ell(n)$. We define the *dimension* of a zero set $Z(f)$ to be k if it contains the positive span of k $\mathbb{R}$-linearly independent vectors in $\mathbb{R}^n$ (but not $(k+1)$ such).

As is standard, we will write ℓ-*group* as a shorthand for lattice-ordered group.

Given an element $f \in FA\ell(n)$, let $|f| = f \vee -f$; then $|f| \in FA\ell(n)^+ := \{g \in FA\ell(n) : g(x) \geq 0 \text{ for all } x \in \mathbb{R}^n\}$. If $f \neq 0$, then $|f| \in FA\ell(n)_+ := FA\ell(n)^+ \setminus \{0\}$. Note that $f_1 = 0 \ \& \ \ldots \ \& \ f_m = 0$ iff $|f_1| \vee \cdots \vee |f_m| = 0$. Hence every finitely presented abelian ℓ-group can be written in the form $FA\ell(n)/\langle f \rangle_{cl}$ for some $n \in \mathbb{Z}_+$ and $f \in FA\ell(n)_+$, where $\langle f \rangle_{cl}$ is the ℓ-ideal of $FA\ell(n)$ generated by f; *i.e.*, $\langle f \rangle_{cl}$ is the subgroup of $FA\ell(n)$ generated by all elements g with $|g| \leq m.f$, for some $m \in \mathbb{N}$. Then $\mathcal{S}(f) = \mathcal{S}(g)$ iff $\langle f \rangle_{cl} = \langle g \rangle_{cl}$ (see [1]).

Since $FA\ell(m)/\langle f \rangle_{cl} \cong FA\ell(m+k)/\langle f' \rangle_{cl}$ where $f' = f \vee |\pi_{m+1}| \vee \cdots \vee |\pi_{m+k}|$, we may assume that $m = n$ in Theorem 1 and that $f, g \in FA\ell(n)^+$. We will consider the two cases $m = n = 2$ and $m = n = 3$ separately. These are proved in Sections 5 and 9, respectively.

Let $\mathcal{K}$ be a closed simplicial cone in $\mathbb{R}^n$. A map $h : \mathcal{K} \to \mathbb{R}^k$ is *piecewise homogeneous linear* if h is continuous and there is a finite subdivision $\{\mathcal{K}_s : s = 1, \ldots, m\}$ of $\mathcal{K}$ and a finite set of homogeneous linear functions $h_1, \cdots, h_m : \mathbb{R}^n \to \mathbb{R}^k$ such that $h(x) = h_s(x)$ for all $x \in \mathcal{K}_s$ ($s = 1, \ldots, m$). If there is a retract r from $\mathbb{R}^n$ to $\mathcal{K}$ such that the composite $h \circ r$ is a piecewise homogeneous linear map from $\mathbb{R}^n$ to $\mathbb{R}^k$, then h can be expressed as $h = \bigwedge_i \bigvee_j g_{ij}$ where each g_{ij} is some h_s, $s = 1, \ldots, m$ (see Theorem 3.1 in [2]). We call such a piecewise homogeneous linear map an ℓ-*map*. If we restrict ourselves to rational closed simplicial cones $\mathcal{K} \subseteq \mathbb{R}^n$, any ℓ-map from $\mathcal{K}$ to $\mathbb{R}^k$ with integer coefficients is called an *integral ℓ-map*; it has the form $(u_1(x), \cdots, u_k(x))$ with $u_1, \cdots, u_k \in FA\ell(n)$ (see Corollary 1 to Theorem 3.1 in [3]).

Let $f \in FA\ell(m)^+$ and $g \in FA\ell(n)^+$. We say that $Z(f)$ and $Z(g)$ are ℓ-*equivalent* if there is an ℓ-map $\theta : Z(f) \to Z(g)$ with inverse $\tau : Z(g) \to Z(f)$ which is also an ℓ-map. If the ℓ-maps are integral, we also say that $\mathcal{Z}(f)$ and $\mathcal{Z}(g)$ are *integrally ℓ-equivalent* and write

$$\mathcal{Z}(f) \sim_\ell \mathcal{Z}(g).$$

Let $\theta : \mathbb{R}^n \to \mathbb{R}^m$ be an integral ℓ-map mapping $Z(g)$ onto $Z(f)$; say, $\theta(x) = (u_1(x), \cdots, u_m(x))$ with $u_1, \cdots, u_m \in FA\ell(n)$. Let $T(\theta)$ be the induced map from $FA\ell(m)$ to $FA\ell(n)$; i.e., $T(\theta) : h \mapsto h \circ \theta$. We identify $h \circ \theta$ with $h|_{Z(f)}$. The kernel of $T(\theta)$ is the ℓ-ideal $\langle f \rangle_{cl}$. For convenience we will denote the image $T(\theta)(h)$ by h^θ and write $T^*(\theta)$ for the induced ℓ-isomorphism between $FA\ell(m)/\langle f \rangle_{cl}$ and $FA\ell(n)/\langle g \rangle_{cl}$ (see Corollary 5.2.2 in [5]).

The Baker-Beynon Duality (see Corollary 2 of Theorem 3.1 in [2]) is

Theorem 3. *Let $f \in FA\ell(m)_+$ and $g \in FA\ell(n)_+$. Then $FA\ell(m)/\langle f \rangle_{cl} \cong FA\ell(n)/\langle g \rangle_{cl}$ (as $\mathcal{L}$-structures) iff $\mathcal{Z}(f) \sim_\ell \mathcal{Z}(g)$.*

As a consequence, one obtains ([3], Theorem 3.1)

Theorem 4. *The class of finitely generated projective abelian ℓ-groups is precisely the class of finitely presented abelian ℓ-groups; each has the form $FA\ell(n)/\langle f \rangle_{cl}$ for some $n \in \mathbb{Z}_+$ and $f \in FA\ell(n)_+$.*

Theorems 3 and 4 give a correspondence between equivalence classes of zero-sets modulo the relation $\sim_\ell$ and equivalence classes of finitely presented abelian ℓ-groups under isomorphism.

Remarks: Let $f, g \in FA\ell(n)^+$.

1. Suppose that $\mathcal{Z}(f) \sim_\ell \mathcal{Z}(g)$. Then the integral ℓ-map $\theta : \mathbb{R}^n \to \mathbb{R}^n$ realising this equivalence and mapping $Z(f)$ to $Z(g)$ need not be a homeomorphism of $\mathbb{R}^n$. (See for instance [10], Annex C.1).
2. If $Z(f)$ and $Z(g)$ are *simplicially equivalent*, then $\mathcal{Z}(f) \sim_\ell \mathcal{Z}(g)$.

We elaborate on (2). Recall that a (rational) simplicial cone $Z(f)$ can be presented as a union of (rational) convex simplicial cones belonging to a complex $\mathcal{K}$ (Lemma 0.1 in [3]). Subdivide this presentation into a primitive rational simplicial one and denote this simplicial presentation of $\mathcal{K}$ by $\mathcal{S}$ — if two rational closed simplicial cones have isomorphic subdivisions into closed simplicial convex cones, then they have isomorphic subdivisions into primitive rational convex simplicial cones (Corollary 3 in Section 2 of [3]).

We will occasionally pass without mention from a simplicial complex in $\mathbb{R}^n$ to its domain and view it as a subset of $\mathbb{R}^n$.

Let $0x_1, \cdots, 0x_r$ be the 1-dimensional simplicial cones in $\mathcal{S}$ emanating from the origin. Choose initial integer lattice points $p_1, \cdots, p_r$ on these rays. Let $P(f)$ be the (rational) simplicial cone associated with $\mathcal{S}$ and let $_sP(f)$ be the image of this simplicial cone on $S^{(n-1)}$ obtained by taking the intersection with $S^{(n-1)}$ of all rays from 0 to the simplicial cone $P(f)$; we will call such a simplicial complex an $\mathcal{S}$-*simplicial complex*. Let $\{u_i : i = 1, \ldots, r\}$ be the Schauder hats associated with $\mathcal{S}$. That is, they are the continuous functions that are linear on each cone of $\mathcal{S}$ with $u_i(p_j) = \delta_{ij}$ $(i, j = 1, \ldots, r)$. Let I be the ℓ-ideal generated by $\pi_1 \vee 0, \cdots, \pi_r \vee 0$, $\bigvee_{j=1}^t (\bigwedge_{k \in X_j} \pi_k)$, where $X_1, \cdots, X_t$ are the subsets of $\{1, \cdots, r\}$ for which the corresponding subsets of $\{p_1, \cdots, p_r\}$ do not span a simplex of $\mathcal{S}$. Then $FA\ell(n)/\langle f \rangle_{cl}$ is isomorphic to $FA\ell(r)/I$ by the map $T(\theta)$ where $\theta : \mathbb{R}^r \to \mathbb{R}^n$ is the integral ℓ-map sending $Z(f)$ to $Z(I)$ (see Corollary 2, Section 2 in [3]).

Let f, $g \in FA\ell(n)$. Then $Z(f)$ and $Z(g)$ are rational closed simplicial cones in $\mathbb{R}^n$. If $P(f)$ and $P(g)$ are simplicially equivalent (by integral ℓ-maps), then $\mathcal{Z}(f) \sim_\ell \mathcal{Z}(g)$ by Corollary 3, Section 3 in [3] and Corollary 2 to Theorem 4.1 in [2]. Hence $FA\ell(n)/\langle f \rangle_{cl} \cong FA\ell(n)/\langle g \rangle_{cl}$.

For further background and more details, see the survey article [9].

We next consider first-order theories. In our proof of the undecidability result of $FA\ell(n)$ for $n \geq 3$ (see Theorem 4.8 in [6]), we showed how to express in $\mathcal{L}$ that two elements f, $g \in FA\ell(n)$ had the same zero-sets (or equivalently the same supports). (The formula depended on n.) We first showed how to express in $\mathcal{L}$ the notion of "dimension" of a zero-set by induction. Let $\psi_{n,k}(x)$ be such formulae ($k = -1, \ldots, n-1$). That is, for each $k \in \{-1, \ldots, n-1\}$,

$$FA\ell(n) \models \psi_{n,k}(f) \quad \text{iff} \quad dim(\mathcal{Z}(f)) = k.$$

This allowed us to express that a zero-set is empty, and then to interpret the lattice of zero-sets of the elements of $FA\ell(n)$. This last result implies that for any $f \in FA\ell(n)$, the structure $FA\ell(n)/\langle f \rangle_{cl}$ is first-order interpretable in $FA\ell(n)$.

We will frequently implicitly use

Lemma 1. *Let $g \in FA\ell(n)$. Then $FA\ell(n) \models \psi_{n,k}(|f| \vee |g|)$ iff the zero-set of the restriction of g to $\mathcal{Z}(f)$ has dimension k.*

3   Components

In this section we reduce determining elementary equivalence to $FA\ell(n)/\langle f \rangle_{cl}$ to the special case that $\mathcal{Z}(f)$ has a single connected component. We will show

Proposition 1. *Let f, $g \in FA\ell(n)^+$. If $FA\ell(n)/\langle f \rangle_{cl} \equiv FA\ell(n)/\langle g \rangle_{cl}$, then $\mathcal{Z}(f)$ and $\mathcal{Z}(g)$ have the same number of connected components.*

We first consider connectedness for supports and zero-sets of elements of a finitely presented abelian ℓ-group. Since we can only use definable open (respectively closed) subsets and their restrictions to the zero-set of a distinguished element, we will use the term definably connected.

Example A. Let $g, h \in FA\ell(3)_+$ with $\mathcal{S}(g)$ the northern hemisphere, and $\mathcal{S}(h) = \mathcal{S}(g) \setminus (\{X\} \cup A)$, where X is the north pole and A is an arc in the northern hemisphere. Now $k \perp g$ iff $k \perp h$ (in either case, $\mathcal{S}(k)$ is contained in the southern hemisphere). Then $\mathcal{S}(g)$ and $\mathcal{S}(h)$ are connected and differ by a set with empty interior; and $\mathcal{Z}(g)$ is connected, but $\mathcal{Z}(h)$ is not.

Recall the formulae we used in [6] for $FA\ell(n)$.

We expressed that the support $\mathcal{S}(h)$, of an element $h > 0$, is *definably connected* by the formula $\theta_S(h)$ given by

$$(h > 0) \ \& \ \neg((\exists h_1, h_2 > 0)(h_1 \perp h_2 \ \& \ h_1 \vee h_2 = h)),$$

where $h \perp g$ is a shorthand for $h \wedge g = 0$ (equivalently that $\mathcal{S}(h) \subseteq \mathcal{Z}(g)$).

[We have used the subscript S on θ to make clear that we are dealing with support.]

That is, $FA\ell(n) \models \theta_S(h)$ iff $\mathcal{S}(h)$ is connected.

More generally, if $g, h \in FA\ell(n)^+$, write $g \sim h$ as a shorthand for

$$(\forall k > 0)(k \perp g \leftrightarrow k \perp h).$$

So

Lemma 2. $FA\ell(n) \models g \sim h$ iff the interior of the symmetric difference of $\mathcal{Z}(g)$ and $\mathcal{Z}(h)$ is empty.

Caution. In Example A, if $\mathcal{Z}(f) = \{X\} \cup B$ where B is any closed disc in the northern hemisphere disjoint from A with $X \notin B$, then $g \sim h$ but $FA\ell(3)/\langle f \rangle_{cl} \models \theta_S(h + \langle f \rangle_{cl})$ & $\neg\theta_S(g + \langle f \rangle_{cl})$.

Let $h \in FA\ell(n)_+$ and $\mathcal{Z}(h)$ be such that for each $x \in \mathcal{Z}(h)$, there is a neighbourhood $N(x)$ of x such that $N(x) \cap \mathcal{Z}(h)$ contains the support of a non-zero element. We expressed that $\mathcal{Z}(h)$ is connected by the formula $\theta_Z(h)$ given by

$$(\exists k > 0)(k \perp h) \ \& \ (\forall k > 0) \left[(k \perp h) \rightarrow (\exists g \geq k)(\theta_S(g) \ \& \ g \perp h) \right].$$

[We have used the subscript Z on θ to make clear that we are dealing with zero sets. The first conjunct has been included for when we relativise to $\mathcal{Z}(f)$ later.]

Lemma 3. Let $h \in FA\ell(n)_+$ satisfy the above hypothesis. Then $FA\ell(n) \models \theta_Z(h)$ iff $\mathcal{Z}(h)$ is connected.

More generally, if $g \in FA\ell(n)_+$, we say that $\mathcal{Z}(g)$ is *definably connected* if $g \sim h$ for some $h \in FA\ell(n)_+$ with h as above $\mathcal{Z}(h)$ connected.

Caution. Let $f \in FA\ell(n)_+$ and consider the above formula in $FA\ell(n)/\langle f \rangle_{cl}$. It is possible to have that both $FA\ell(n)/\langle f \rangle_{cl} \models \theta_Z(0 + \langle f \rangle_{cl})$ and $FA\ell(n) \models \neg\theta_Z(f)$. Such an example is provided by letting $\mathcal{Z}(f)$ be two closed discs on $S^{(2)}$ whose intersection is a single point.)

Let $\mathcal{S}$ be a simplicial complex in $S^{(n-1)}$. If the rays from the origin to the vertices of $\mathcal{S}$ all contain initial integral lattice points, then we say that the simplicial complex is *rationally determined*. If P_1, P_2 are non-empty disjoint open simplicial complexes whose union contains $\mathcal{Z}(f)$ ($f \in FA\ell(n)_+$), then by the density of $\mathbb{Q}^n$ in $\mathbb{R}^n$, we may choose open rationally determined simplicial complexes $P'_j \subseteq P_j$ ($j = 1, 2$) so that $\mathcal{Z}(f) \subseteq P'_1 \cup P'_2$. We will always do this.

Lemma 4. $FA\ell(n)/\langle f \rangle_{cl} \models \theta_Z(0 + \langle f \rangle_{cl})$ iff whenever there are two disjoint open simplicial complexes P_1, P_2 in $S^{(n-1)}$ with $P_1 \cup P_2 \supseteq \mathcal{Z}(f)$, the intersection of one of them with $\mathcal{Z}(f)$ is trivial.

Proof: Suppose that P_1, P_2 are non-empty disjoint open simplicial complexes in $S^{(n-1)}$ with $P_1 \cup P_2 \supseteq \mathcal{Z}(f)$. As just remarked, we may assume that P_j is rationally determined ($j = 1, 2$). Hence there are $h_j \in FA\ell(n)_+$ with $\mathcal{S}(h_j) = P_j$

$(j = 1, 2)$. Let $g \geq h_1 \vee h_2$. If $P_j \cap \mathcal{Z}(f) \neq \emptyset$ $(j = 1, 2)$, then g witnesses that $FA\ell(n)/\langle f \rangle_{cl} \models \neg \theta_Z(0 + \langle f \rangle_{cl})$.

Conversely, suppose that $FA\ell(n)/\langle f \rangle_{cl} \models \neg \theta_Z(0 + \langle f \rangle_{cl})$. Let $k \in FA\ell(n)_+$ be such that $k \perp h$ and for all $g \geq k$ we have $FA\ell(n)/\langle f \rangle_{cl} \models \neg \theta_S(g + \langle f \rangle_{cl})$. By replacing k by an element g of possibly greater support if necessary, we may assume that $\mathcal{S}(k) \supseteq \mathcal{Z}(f)$. Write $k = k_1 \vee \cdots \vee k_m$ with $k_1, \ldots, k_m$ pairwise disjoint each having connected support and $\mathcal{S}(k_i) \cap \mathcal{Z}(f) \neq \emptyset$ $(i = 1, \ldots, m)$. Thus $m \geq 2$. Then $P_1 = \mathcal{S}(k_1)$ and $P_2 = \bigcup_{i=2}^{r} \mathcal{S}(k_i)$ are the desired simplicial complexes. $\square$

By the same technique one can prove

Lemma 5. Let $f, h \in FA\ell(n)_+$. Then $FA\ell(n)/\langle f \rangle_{cl} \models \theta_S(h + \langle f \rangle_{cl})$ iff $\mathcal{S}(h) \cap \mathcal{Z}(f)$ is connected.

We next wish to write $FA\ell(n)/\langle f \rangle_{cl}$ as a direct sum which cannot be further decomposed into non-trivial direct summands. We do this by decomposing $\mathcal{Z}(f)$ into maximal simplices. These are the connected components of $\mathcal{Z}(f)$.

As above, we observe that if $\mathcal{Z}(h_j) \subseteq \mathcal{Z}(f)$ $(j = 1, 2)$ and there does not exist any $k \in FA\ell(n)_+$ with $\mathcal{S}(k) \cap \mathcal{Z}(f)$ contained in the symmetric difference of $\mathcal{Z}(h_1)$ and $\mathcal{Z}(h_2)$, then one cannot hope to distinguish between $\mathcal{Z}(h_1)$ and $\mathcal{Z}(h_2)$ in $FA\ell(n)/\langle f \rangle_{cl}$. In this case we write $\mathcal{Z}(h_1) \sim_f \mathcal{Z}(h_2)$; i.e.,

$$FA\ell(n)/\langle f \rangle_{cl} \models (\forall k \geq 0)(k \perp h_1 + \langle f \rangle_{cl} \leftrightarrow k \perp h_2 + \langle f \rangle_{cl}).$$

We can now express in $\mathcal{L}$ that $\mathcal{Z}(g)$ is a *definably connected component* of $\mathcal{Z}(f)$; that is, $\mathcal{Z}(g)$ is a maximal connected subset of $\mathcal{Z}(f)$ to within $\sim_f$.

Lemma 6. Let $f, g \in FA\ell(n)_+$. The formula

$$(\exists h > 0)[\theta_S(h) \ \& \ (\forall k > 0)(k \perp g \rightarrow k \not\perp h) \ \& \ (\forall h' > h)(h' \not\perp g \rightarrow \neg \theta_S(h'))]$$

holds in $FA\ell(n)/\langle f \rangle_{cl}$ at $g + \langle f \rangle_{cl}$ iff $\mathcal{Z}(g)$ is $\sim_f$-equivalent to a connected component of $\mathcal{Z}(f)$.

Proof: Let $f, f_1, \cdots, f_m \in FA\ell(n)_+$, with $\mathcal{Z}(f_1), \cdots, \mathcal{Z}(f_m)$ the pairwise disjoint non-empty connected components of $\mathcal{Z}(f)$; so $\mathcal{Z}(f) = \bigcup_{j=1}^{m} \mathcal{Z}(f_j)$.

If $\mathcal{Z}(g) \sim_f \mathcal{Z}(f_1)$, there is an open rationally determined simplicial complex in $S^{(n-1)}$ with $P \supseteq \mathcal{Z}(f_1)$ and $P \cap \mathcal{Z}(f_j) = \emptyset$ for $j = 2, \ldots, m$. So there is $h \in FA\ell(n)_+$ with $\mathcal{S}(h) = P$. Then the first two conjuncts of the formula clearly hold in $FA\ell(n)/\langle f \rangle_{cl}$ by considering $h + \langle f \rangle_{cl}$. If $h' > h$ with $h' \not\perp g$ on $\mathcal{Z}(f)$, then $\mathcal{S}(h') \cap \mathcal{S}(g) \cap \mathcal{Z}(f) \neq \emptyset$; so $\mathcal{S}(h') \cap \mathcal{Z}(f_j) \neq \emptyset$ for some $j \in \{2, \ldots, m\}$. By Lemma 5, the formula holds.

Conversely, assume that the formula holds in $FA\ell(n)/\langle f \rangle_{cl}$. We may assume that $\mathcal{Z}(g)$ is minimal to within $\sim_f$. The satisfaction of the first conjunct implies that $\mathcal{Z}(g) \cap \mathcal{Z}(f)$ is definably connected in $\mathcal{Z}(f)$. We may assume that $\mathcal{Z}(g) \cap \mathcal{Z}(f) \subseteq \mathcal{Z}(f_1)$, say. If $\mathcal{Z}(g) \cap \mathcal{Z}(f) \neq \mathcal{Z}(f_1)$, then $\mathcal{Z}(f_1) \backslash \mathcal{Z}(g)$ is a non-empty open subset of $\mathcal{Z}(f_1)$. Hence there is $p \in \mathcal{Z}(f_1) \backslash \mathcal{Z}(g)$ and a simplex neighbourhood

P of p in $S^{(n-1)}$ such that $P \cap \mathcal{Z}(g) = \emptyset$. Let $h' \in FA\ell(n)_+$ with $\mathcal{S}(h') \subseteq P$. Then $h' \vee h$ witnesses that the formula fails to hold in $FA\ell(n)/\langle f \rangle_{cl}$.   □

The following is well known.

Lemma 7. *Let $f_j \in FA\ell(n)_+$ $(j = 1, 2)$ with $\mathcal{Z}(f_1) \cap \mathcal{Z}(f_2) = \emptyset$. Then*

$$FA\ell(n)/\langle (f_1 \vee f_2) \rangle_{cl} \cong FA\ell(n)/\langle f_1 \rangle_{cl} \times FA\ell(n)/\langle f_2 \rangle_{cl}.$$

We now use Lemma 6 to provide a sentence of $\mathcal{L}$ that counts the number of connected components of $FA\ell(n)/\langle f \rangle_{cl}$. Let $f, f_1, \cdots, f_m \in FA\ell(n)_+$ with $\mathcal{Z}(f_1), \cdots, \mathcal{Z}(f_m)$ the disjoint definably connected components of $\mathcal{Z}(f)$; so $\mathcal{Z}(f) = \bigcup_{i=1}^m \mathcal{Z}(f_i)$. That is,

$$FA\ell(n)/\langle f \rangle_{cl} \cong FA\ell(n)/\langle f_1 \rangle_{cl} \times \cdots \times FA\ell(n)/\langle f_m \rangle_{cl}.$$

Let

$$\rho_m := (\exists h_1, \ldots, h_m > 0) \, [\bigwedge_{1 \leq i < j \leq m} h_i \perp h_j \, \& \, \bigwedge_{1 \leq i \leq m} \theta_S(h_i) \, \& $$

$$(\forall h_i' \geq h_i)[(\exists k > 0)(k \leq h_i' \, \& \, k \perp h_i) \rightarrow \neg \theta_S(h_i')]].$$

By the previous lemmata

Lemma 8

$$FA\ell(n)/\langle f \rangle_{cl} \models \rho_m \quad \text{iff} \quad \mathcal{Z}(f) \text{ has at least } m \text{ connected components.}$$

Thus we have

Lemma 9. *Let $f \in FA\ell(n)^+$. Then $\mathcal{Z}(f)$ has exactly m connected components iff $FA\ell(n)/\langle f \rangle_{cl} \models \rho_m \, \& \, \neg \rho_{m+1}$.*

Proposition 1 follows.   □

We now generalise Lemma 4.

Lemma 10. *Let $f \in FA\ell(n)_+$ and $\mathcal{Z}(f)$ have connected components $\mathcal{Z}(f_1), \ldots, \mathcal{Z}(f_m)$. Let $h \in FA\ell(n)_+$ be such that for all $j \in \{1, \ldots, m\}$, either $\mathcal{Z}(h) \cap \mathcal{Z}(f_j)$ is empty or all the connected components of $\mathcal{Z}(h) \cap \mathcal{Z}(f_j)$ have the same dimension as $\mathcal{Z}(f_j)$. Then $FA\ell(n)/\langle f \rangle_{cl} \models \theta_Z(h + \langle f \rangle_{cl})$ iff $\mathcal{Z}(h) \cap \mathcal{Z}(f)$ is connected.*

Proof: By the assumption on h, $FA\ell(n)/\langle f \rangle_{cl} \models \neg \theta_Z(h + \langle f \rangle_{cl})$ if the intersection of $\mathcal{Z}(h)$ with more than one connected component of $\mathcal{Z}(f)$ is non-empty. So we may assume that $\mathcal{Z}(h) \cap \mathcal{Z}(f_j) = \emptyset$ for $j = 2, \ldots, m$. If $\mathcal{Z}(h) \cap \mathcal{Z}(f_1)$ is not connected, then there are disjoint open rationally determined simplicial complexes P_1 and P_2 in $S^{(n-1)}$ with $P_i \cap \mathcal{Z}(h) \cap \mathcal{Z}(f_1) \neq \emptyset$ $(i = 1, 2)$. Hence there are $h_i \in FA\ell(n)_+$ with $\mathcal{S}(h_i) = P_i$ $(i = 1, 2)$. Let $g \geq h_1 \vee h_2$ with $g \perp f$. This witnesses that $FA\ell(n)/\langle f \rangle_{cl} \models \neg \theta_Z(h + \langle f \rangle_{cl})$.

The other direction is trivial.   □

Putting $h = f$ in Lemma 10, we see

Corollary 1. *Let* $f \in FA\ell(n)_+$. *Then* $FA\ell(n)/\langle f \rangle_{cl} \models \theta_Z(0 + \langle f \rangle_{cl})$ *iff* $Z(f')$ *is connected for some* $f' \sim f$.

Note that the hypothesis on h in Lemma 10 can be expressed by an $\mathcal{L}$-formula to within $\sim_f$: Let $Z(h)$ be a definably connected subset of $Z(f)$. Then for any open set of the form $S(k)$, there exists k' with $S(k') \supseteq S(k)$ such that $S(k') \cap Z(h)$ is relatively connected in $Z(h)$. The $\mathcal{L}$-expressibility now follows from Lemma 6.

4   Further Formulae

We next express that the restriction of the support of an element $h > 0$ to the zero-set of an element f consists of one ray; *i.e.*, $S(h) \cap Z(f)$ consists of a single point. We will use the formula $\theta_1(h)$ given by

$$\theta_S(h) \ \& \ (\forall g_1, g_2 > 0)(g_1 \vee g_2 \le h \ \to \ g_1 \not\perp g_2).$$

[The subscript 1 on θ is to make clear that we are dealing with a single point.]

Lemma 11. $FA\ell(n)/\langle f \rangle_{cl} \models \theta_1(h + \langle f \rangle_{cl})$ *iff* $Z(f) \cap S(h)$ *consists of a single isolated point.*

Proof: If $Z(f) \cap S(h) = \{p\}$, then as $0 < g_j \le h$, we must have $g_j(p) > 0$ $(j = 1, 2)$. So $FA\ell(n)/\langle f \rangle_{cl} \models \theta_1(h + \langle f \rangle_{cl})$.

Conversely, if $FA\ell(n)/\langle f \rangle_{cl} \models \theta_S(h + \langle f \rangle_{cl})$, then $Z(f) \cap S(h)$ is connected. If it is not a single point, let $p_1, p_2 \in Z(f) \cap S(h)$ be distinct. Let $P_j \subseteq S(h)$ be a simplicial complex in $S^{(n-1)}$ containing p_j $(j = 1, 2)$ with $P_1 \cap P_2 = \emptyset$. Let $h_j \in FA\ell(n)_+$ with $S(h_j) \subseteq P_j$ $(j = 1, 2)$. Then $g_j = h_j \wedge h$ $(j = 1, 2)$ witness that $FA\ell(n)/\langle f \rangle_{cl} \models \neg\theta_1(h + \langle f \rangle_{cl})$. $\square$

We will use the formula $\theta_2(h)$ to express that the support of an element h when restricted to $Z(f)$ is connected and strictly contains the support of two non-zero elements with disjoint supports. Again the subscript has been chosen according to the intended meaning. Let $\theta_2(h)$ be the formula:

$$\theta_S(h) \ \& \ (\exists g_1, g_2 > 0)(g_1 \vee g_2 \le h \ \& \ g_1 \perp g_2).$$

The following lemma follows easily by the same proof as used above.

Lemma 12. $FA\ell(n)/\langle f \rangle_{cl} \models \theta_2(h + \langle f \rangle_{cl})$ *iff* $Z(f) \cap S(h)$ *is connected and strictly contains the support of two non-zero elements with disjoint supports.*

If $Z(f) \cap S(h)$ does not consist of an isolated point, we can express in $\mathcal{L}$ that $S(h)$ covers a maximal connected subset of $Z(f)$. Define $\theta_2^*(h)$ to be

$$\theta_2(h) \ \& \ (\forall g \ge h)(\theta_S(g) \to (\forall u > 0)[u \perp g \leftrightarrow u \perp h]).$$

By essentially the same proofs

Lemma 13. *Let* $f \in FA\ell(n)_+$. *Then* $FA\ell(n)/\langle f \rangle_{cl} \models \theta_2^*(h + \langle f \rangle_{cl})$ *iff* $\mathcal{S}(h)$ *covers a unique connected component of* $\mathcal{Z}(f)$.

Let f, $h \in FA\ell(n)_+$ and assume that $\mathcal{S}(h) \subseteq \mathcal{Z}(f)$. Then $\mathcal{S}(h)$ differs from $\mathcal{Z}(f)$ by a set which does not have relative maximal dimension in $S^{(n-1)}$ if

$$FA\ell(n) \models h \perp f \ \& \ \forall g > 0 \ (g \perp f \rightarrow g \not\perp h).$$

We will denote *any* such element h by $f^\#$. That is,

$$FA\ell(n) \models f^\# \perp f \ \& \ (\forall g > 0)(g \perp f \rightarrow g \not\perp f^\#).$$

It is not unique.

Let k, $h \in FA\ell(n)_+$. If

$$FA\ell(n)/\langle f \rangle_{cl} \models h \perp k \ \& \ (\forall g > 0)(g \perp k \rightarrow g \not\perp h),$$

then we will write $k^\#$ for any such element h. This is equivalent to $\mathcal{S}(k^\#) \cap \mathcal{Z}(f) \subseteq \mathcal{Z}(k) \cap \mathcal{Z}(f)$ and $\mathcal{S}(k^\#) \cap \mathcal{Z}(f)$ differs from $\mathcal{Z}(k) \cap \mathcal{Z}(f)$ by a set which does not have (locally) relative maximal dimension. It is not unique.

5   Quotients of $FA\ell(2)$

Our purpose in this section is to prove

Theorem 5. *Let* f, $g \in FA\ell(2)^+$. *Then*

$$FA\ell(2)/\langle f \rangle_{cl} \equiv FA\ell(2)/\langle g \rangle_{cl} \ \textit{iff} \ FA\ell(2)/\langle f \rangle_{cl} \cong FA\ell(2)/\langle g \rangle_{cl}.$$

To achieve this, we need three lemmata.

Lemma 14. *Let* $f \in FA\ell(2)_+$ *and* $\mathcal{Z}(f)$ *consist of one or more arcs. Then*

$$FA\ell(2)/\langle f \rangle_{cl} \not\equiv FA\ell(2).$$

Proof: If $\mathcal{Z}(f_1)$ is a proper arc of $S^{(1)}$ which is maximal in $\mathcal{Z}(f)$, let $h_1, h_2, h_3 \in FA\ell(2)_+$ all have support contained in $Z(f_1)$ with $\mathcal{S}(h_j)$ a single arc $(j = 1, 2, 3)$, the arc for h_3 being between that of h_1 and h_2 in $\mathcal{Z}(f_1)$. Under the natural interpretation, the following formula is satisfied in $FA\ell(2)/\langle f \rangle_{cl}$ but not in $FA\ell(2)$:

$$(\exists h_1, h_2, h_3 > 0)[\bigwedge_{i=1}^{3} \theta_S(h_i) \ \& \ h_3 \perp (h_1 \vee h_2) \ \& \ h_1 \perp h_2 \ \&$$

$$(\forall h)[(h > (h_1 \vee h_2) \ \& \ \theta_S(h)) \rightarrow (h \not\perp h_3)]].$$

□

Lemma 15. *Let* $f, g \in FA\ell(2)_+$ *with* $\mathcal{Z}(f)$ *comprising* n_1 *disjoint arcs and* n_2 *isolated points, and* $\mathcal{Z}(g)$ *comprising* n_1' *disjoint arcs and* n_2' *isolated points, with* $(n_1, n_2) \neq (n_1', n_2')$. *Then*

$$FA\ell(2)/\langle f \rangle_{cl} \not\equiv FA\ell(2)/\langle g \rangle_{cl}.$$

Proof: Assume first that $n_1 \neq n_1'$; say $n_1 > n_1'$. Let ϕ_{n_1} be the sentence

$$(\bigwedge_{i \in n_1} \exists h_i > 0)(\theta_2^*(h_i) \ \& \ (\bigwedge_{i, \, i' \in n_1, \, i \neq i'} h_i \perp h_{i'}) \ \& \ [\forall h > 0] \, [\theta_2(h) \ \rightarrow \ h \wedge (\bigvee_i h_i) \neq 0]).$$

Then $FA\ell(2)/\langle f \rangle_{cl}$ satisfies ϕ_{n_1} but $FA\ell(2)/\langle g \rangle_{cl}$ does not.

Now assume that $n_1 = n_1'$ and $n_2 > n_2'$. Let ϕ_{n_1,n_2} be the sentence

$$[\bigwedge_{i \in n_1} (\exists h_i > 0)(\theta_2^*(h_i) \ \& \bigwedge_{i, \, i' \in n_1, \, i \neq i'} h_i \perp h_{i'}) \ \& \ (\bigwedge_{j \in n_2} \exists u_j > 0)(\theta_1(u_j) \ \&$$

$$(\bigwedge_{i=1}^n u_j \perp h_i) \ \& \bigwedge_{j, \, j' \in n_2, \, j' \neq j} (u_j \perp u_{j'}) \ \& \ (\forall h > 0) \, (h \wedge (\bigvee_{i \in n_1} h_i \vee \bigvee_{j \in n_2} u_j) \neq 0)].$$

Clearly ϕ_{n_1,n_2} holds in $FA\ell(2)/\langle f \rangle_{cl}$ but not in $FA\ell(2)/\langle g \rangle_{cl}$. □

Lemma 16. (Beynon, [3], p.262) *Let $f \in FA\ell(2)_+$. Then,*

$$FA\ell(2)/\langle f \rangle_{cl} \cong (FA\ell(2)/\langle \pi_2 \vee 0 \rangle_{cl})^{n_1} \times \mathbb{Z}^{n_2},$$

where n_1 is the number of pairwise disjoint maximal arcs in $\mathcal{Z}(f)$ and n_2 is the number of isolated points in $\mathcal{Z}(f)$.

We can now prove Theorem 5.

Proof: Suppose that $FA\ell(2)/\langle f \rangle_{cl} \equiv FA\ell(2)/\langle g \rangle_{cl}$. If f and g are both non-zero, then by Lemma 15, the number of connected pieces of the zero sets of f and g of the same dimensions are the same. By Lemma 16, the ℓ-groups are isomorphic.

If $g = 0$ and $f \neq 0$, then by Lemma 14, $FA\ell(2)/\langle f \rangle_{cl} \not\equiv FA\ell(2)$ whenever $\mathcal{Z}(f)$ contains an arc. If $\mathcal{Z}(f)$ comprises n isolated points, then the sentence that there are $n+1$ pairwise perpendicular strictly positive elements holds in $FA\ell(2)$ but not in $FA\ell(2)/\langle f \rangle_{cl}$. □

6 Decidability of Quotients of $FA\ell(2)$

In this section we prove a special case of Theorem 2:

Theorem 6. *Let $f \in FA\ell(2)^+$. Then $FA\ell(2)/\langle f \rangle_{cl}$ is decidable.*

We will use our previous result on the decidability of $FA\ell(2)$ (see Corollary 3.5 in [6]).

Lemma 17. *Given any formula ξ, we can construct a formula ξ^r such that:*

$$FA\ell(2)/\langle \pi_2 \vee 0 \rangle_{cl} \models \xi(\bar{h} + \langle \pi_2 \vee 0 \rangle_{cl}) \ iff \ FA\ell(2) \models \xi^r(\bar{h}, \pi_2 \vee 0),$$

where $\bar{h} \subset FA\ell(2)$.

Proof: We define ξ^r by induction on the complexity of the formula ξ. For an atomic formula $\xi(\bar{x}) := (t(\bar{x}) = 0)$, we define $\xi^r(\bar{x}, y)$ as $R(t(x), y)$, where the latter is the formula $(\forall h > 0)(h \perp y \to h \perp t(\bar{x}))$. For a quantifier-free formula $\xi(\bar{x})$ (*i.e.*, a Boolean combination of atomic formulae $\xi_i(\bar{x}) := t_i(\bar{x}) = 0$), we define $\xi^r(\bar{x}, y)$ to be the same Boolean combination of $\xi_i^r(\bar{x}, y)$. Finally, if $\xi(\bar{x})$ is in prenex normal form $Q(\bar{z})\xi(\bar{z}, \bar{x})$, where $Q(\bar{z})$ is a block of quantifiers, define $\xi^r(\bar{x}, y)$ as $Q(\bar{z})\xi^r(\bar{z}, \bar{x}, y)$.

We now prove (by induction on the complexity of the formula) that for any $\bar{h} \subset FA\ell(2)$,

$$FA\ell(2)/\langle \pi_2 \vee 0 \rangle_{cl} \models \xi(\bar{h} + \langle \pi_2 \vee 0 \rangle_{cl}) \quad \text{iff} \quad FA\ell(2) \models \xi^r(\bar{h}, \pi_2 \vee 0).$$

It suffices to prove it for atomic formulae. This is immediate as $t(\bar{h} + \langle \pi_2 \vee 0 \rangle_{cl}) = 0$ iff $t(\bar{h}) \in \langle \pi_2 \vee 0 \rangle_{cl}$ iff $t(\bar{h})|_{Z(\pi_2 \vee 0)} = 0$ iff $Z(t(\bar{h})) \supseteq Z(\pi_2 \vee 0)$, and the last of the equivalent conditions holds iff $R(t(\bar{h}), \pi_2 \vee 0)$. $\quad\square$

Corollary 2. *The ℓ-group $FA\ell(2)/\langle \pi_2 \vee 0 \rangle_{cl}$ has decidable theory.*

Proof: Apply Lemma 17 and Corollary 3.5 in [6]. $\quad\square$

Theorem 6 now follows from Theorem 5, Lemma 16, Corollary 3.5 in [6], the decidability of Presburger arithmetic, and the Feferman-Vaught Theorem on direct products. $\quad\square$

7   Decidability Results for 2-Dimensional Zero-Sets

In this section we generalise Theorem 6 to allow arbitrary $n \in \mathbb{Z}_+$.

Theorem 7. *Let $n \in \mathbb{Z}_+$ and $f \in FA\ell(n)_+$. If $dim(Z(f)) \leq 2$, then the theory of $FA\ell(n)/\langle f \rangle_{cl}$ is decidable.*

Proof: By Proposition 1 and the Feferman-Vaught Theorem, we may assume that $\mathcal{Z}(f)$ is connected.

If $dim(Z(f)) = 0$, then $\mathcal{Z}(f) = \emptyset$ and $FA\ell(n)/\langle f \rangle_{cl} \cong \{0\}$, which has decidable theory.

If $dim(Z(f)) = 1$, then $\mathcal{Z}(f)$ is a single point and $FA\ell(n)/\langle f \rangle_{cl} \cong \mathbb{Z}$. By Presburger's Theorem, $Th(\mathbb{Z}, +, \leq)$ is decidable. The theory of $FA\ell(n)/\langle f \rangle_{cl}$ is therefore decidable if $dim(Z(f)) = 1$.

If $Z(f)$ has dimension 2, then $\mathcal{Z}(f)$ comprises a finite number of arcs or a circle. If $n = 2$, we have already shown that the theory is decidable if $\mathcal{Z}(f)$ is a single arc or the entire 1-sphere (see Section 6 and [6]). So assume that $n \geq 3$.

Let $f \in FA\ell(n)_+$ with $dim(\mathcal{Z}(f)) = 1$. Let $_SP(f)$ be the $\mathcal{S}$-simplicial complex associated with the primitive simplicial presentation $\mathcal{S}$ of $\mathcal{Z}(f)$ on $S^{(n-1)}$ (see Section 2).

Let $0x_1, \cdots, 0x_k$ be the rays emanating from the origin to the vertices of $\mathcal{S}$ and $u_1, \cdots, u_k$ be the Schauder hats associated with $\mathcal{S}$. Let $p_1, \cdots, p_k$ be the intersection of these cones with $S^{(n-1)}$.

Let r be a piecewise homogeneous linear retract from $\mathbb{R}^n$ to $Z(f)$. We map each simplicial cone $Z(u_i) \subseteq Z(f)$ by a piecewise homogeneous integral linear map $\theta_i : \mathbb{R}^n \to \mathbb{R}^2$ mapping $S^{(n-1)}$ to $S^{(1)}$ so that

(*) $\bigwedge_{1 \leq i \leq i' \leq k} \theta_i(p_j) = \theta_{i'}(p_j)$ $(j = 1, \dots, k)$,   and
        $\bigwedge_{1 \leq j < j' \leq k} \theta_i(p_j) \neq \theta_i(p_{j'})$ $(i = 1, \dots, k)$.

Let $\tilde{u}_i \in \overline{FA\ell(2)}$ be such $Z(\tilde{u}_i) = \theta_i(Z(u_i))$ $(i = 1, \dots, k)$.

Let τ_i be a piecewise homogeneous integral linear map from $\mathbb{R}^2$ to $\mathbb{R}^n$ mapping $Z(\tilde{u}_i)$ to $Z(u_i)$ so that $\tau_i \circ \theta_i$ is the identity on $Z(u_i)$ and $\theta_i \circ \tau_i$ is the identity on $Z(\tilde{u}_i)$.

Any finite conjunction of atomic formulae is equivalent to a single atomic formula (since $w_1 = 0$ & $\dots$ & $w_s = 0$ iff $|w_1| \vee \dots \vee |w_s| = 0$). So any open formula is equivalent to the conjunction of a single atomic formula ϕ and negations of a finite set of atomic formulae ψ_t $(t \in T)$. We partition T into subsets $T_1, \dots T_k$, where we allow some of these T_m to be empty. We claim that (1) and (2) are equivalent, where (1) is:

$$FA\ell(n)/\langle f \rangle_{cl} \models \exists g \, (\phi(g, \bar{a} + \langle f \rangle_{cl}) \; \& \bigwedge_{t \in T} \neg \psi_t(g, \bar{a} + \langle f \rangle_{cl}))$$

and (2) is:

$$\bigvee_{k-\text{partitions of } T} \bigwedge_{1 \leq i \leq k} \exists f_i \in FA\ell(2) \bigwedge_{1 \leq i \leq i' \leq k} \bigwedge_{j=1}^{k} f_i(\theta_i(p_j)) = f_{i'}(\theta_{i'}(p_j)) \quad \text{and}$$

$$FA\ell(2)/\langle \tilde{u}_i \rangle_{cl} \models \gamma_i(f_i + \langle \tilde{u}_i \rangle_{cl}),$$

where $\gamma_i(x)$ is given by $\gamma_i(x) := \phi(x, \bar{a} \circ \tau_i) \; \& \bigwedge_{t \in T_i} \neg \psi_t(x, \bar{a} \circ \tau_i)$.

For suppose that $FA\ell(2)/\langle \tilde{u}_i \rangle_{cl} \models \gamma_i(f_i + \langle \tilde{u}_i \rangle_{cl})$ for all $i \in \{1, \dots, k\}$. Define $g_i(\bar{x}) = f_i \circ \theta_i \circ r(\bar{x})$ $(i = 1, \dots, k)$. By (*), this is well-defined since $r(\bar{x}) \in Z(f) = \bigcup_{i=1}^{k} Z(u_i)$. Hence (1) follows.

Conversely, suppose that (1) holds. Define $f_i(\bar{x}) = g \circ \tau_i(\bar{x})$ $(i = 1, \dots, k)$. Then $FA\ell(2)/\langle \tilde{u}_i \rangle_{cl} \models \gamma_i(f_i + \langle \tilde{u}_i \rangle_{cl})$ for all $i \in \{1, \dots, k\}$.

The proof is completed as in [6] Lemma 3.5 using the Feferman-Vaught Theorem and the decidablility of Presburger Arithmetic.   □

8   Interlude

Let $f, \, g \in FA\ell(n)^+$. To prove a general version of Theorem 1, we need only show that if $FA\ell(n)/\langle f \rangle_{cl} \equiv FA\ell(n)/\langle g \rangle_{cl}$, then $P(f)$ and $P(g)$ are simplicially equivalent. For this, it is enough to show that $P(f)$ and $P(g)$ have isomorphic simplicial subdivisions S_f and S_g, respectively (S_f and S_g would then have isomorphic subdivisions into primitive rational cones — see Corollary 3 in [3]). We will succeed with this approach when $n = 3$.

In Section 3 we expressed (in $\mathcal{L}$) the notion of a component of a zero-set $Z(f)$, where $f \in FA\ell(n)_+$. We can therefore count the number of components of $\mathcal{Z}(f)$ and so reduce to the case that $Z(f)$ and $Z(g)$ each have a single component. Hence it is enough to show that $P(f)$ and $P(g)$ have isomorphic simplicial subdivisions in this case.

We will denote the set of all simplices of dimension at most i by $\mathcal{S}_f^i$; namely, those corresponding to finite union of simplicial convex cones generated by at most $i + 1$ linearly independent elements.

Consider two examples of connected simplicial complexes on $S^{(2)}$. Both comprise two "filled in" triangles T_1 and T_2. In the first case $T_1 \cap T_2 = \{p\}$, a single shared vertex. In some sense, $T_1 \cup T_2$ is connected with two basic constituents, T_1 and T_2. On the other hand, if $T_1 \cap T_2$ has dimension 1 or 2, then $T_1 \cup T_2$ comprises just one basic constituent. With these ideas in mind, we now define a basic constituent of $\mathcal{Z}(f)$. We give a description and construction as both will be used later.

Given a connected zero set $\mathcal{Z}(f)$, we want to express in $\mathcal{L}$ that this set can be decomposed into closed simplicial cones $\mathcal{Z}(f_j)$ ($j \in J$) such that the intersection of any two of them $\mathcal{Z}(f_{j_1})$ and $\mathcal{Z}(f_{j_2})$ (of respective dimensions m_1, m_2) is of dimension at most $m_1 - 1$ if $m_1 < m_2$, and at most $m_1 - 2$ if $m_1 = m_2$. We also regard $\mathcal{Z}(f_{j_1})$ and $\mathcal{Z}(f_{j_2})$ as distinct constituents if $m_1 = m_2 = 1$, $\mathcal{Z}(f_{j_1}) \cap \mathcal{Z}(f_{j_2})$ is a single point $\{p\}$ and there is at least one other $\mathcal{Z}(f_{j_3})$ whose intersection with $\mathcal{Z}(f_{j_1})$ is a finite set of points including $\{p\}$. The simplicial complexes in $S^{(n-1)}$ associated with these zero sets will constitute the *basic constituents* of a component of a zero set.

A word needs to be added concerning this last case. If one of these one dimensional zero sets is a circle, we regard it as a looped arc instead of a circle if there are no other points p of this sort on the circle; if there are other such points, let $p_1, \ldots, p_m$ be an enumeration of them in a clockwise direction, we regard the circle as being made up of arcs (p_i, p_{i+1}) ($i = 1, \ldots, m$ with $p_{m+1} := p_1$) each of which will be a basic constituent.

To obtain such a decomposition of a connected zero set $\mathcal{Z}(f)$ into basic constituents, we divide $\mathcal{Z}(f)$ into basic constituents (with $dim(\mathcal{Z}(f)) = m > 1$), as follows. Determine if there are two subsets $\mathcal{Z}(f_1)$ and $\mathcal{Z}(f_2)$ of $\mathcal{Z}(f)$ each of dimension m with $\mathcal{Z}(f_1) \cup \mathcal{Z}(f_2) = \mathcal{Z}(f)$ and $\mathcal{Z}(f_1) \cap \mathcal{Z}(f_2)$ a set of dimension at most $m-2$. If so, repeat with $\mathcal{Z}(f_1)$ and $\mathcal{Z}(f_2)$. If one cannot find such sets $\mathcal{Z}(f_1)$ and $\mathcal{Z}(f_2)$ but, say $\mathcal{Z}(f_2)$ has dimension less than m, $\mathcal{Z}(f_1) \cup \mathcal{Z}(f_2) = \mathcal{Z}(f)$, and $\mathcal{Z}(f_1) \cap \mathcal{Z}(f_2)$ has dimension strictly less than the dimension of $\mathcal{Z}(f_2)$, then repeat the process with each of $\mathcal{Z}(f_1)$ and $\mathcal{Z}(f_2)$. Of course, one must consider the case that the set $\mathcal{Z}(f_1) \cap \mathcal{Z}(f_2)$ is disconnected, but it is clear what to do in that case. Eventually, we will be unable to go further with any of the $\mathcal{Z}(f_{i,j,k,...})$ obtained except those with dimension 1. We do the special case decomposition as above until we can go no further. Once the process stops, the $\mathcal{Z}(g)$ obtained are the basic constituents. This decomposition is unique.

For example, if $\mathcal{Z}(f)$ is the union of two non-disjoint closed "discs" on the 2-sphere, then it has two basic constituents if the two discs intersect in a point, and has a single basic constituent if the intersection of the discs has dimension 1 or 2.

If $\mathcal{Z}(f)$ is the union of a closed disc and an arc emiting once from the disc (on the 2-sphere), then $\mathcal{Z}(f)$ has two basic constituents, the disc and that part of the arc not in the interior of the disc.

If $\mathcal{Z}(f)$ is the union of three closed arcs A_i on the 2-sphere with endpoints p and p_i and $A_i \cap A_j = \{p\}$ ($i, j \in \{1, 2, 3\}$ with $i \neq j$), then $\mathcal{Z}(f)$ has three basic constituents.

9   Quotients of $FA\ell(3)$

Our goal in this section is to prove the analogue of Theorem 5; *i.e.,*

Theorem 8

$$FA\ell(3)/\langle f \rangle_{cl} \equiv FA\ell(3)/\langle g \rangle_{cl} \;\; iff \;\; FA\ell(3)/\langle f \rangle_{cl} \cong FA\ell(3)/\langle g \rangle_{cl}. \;\; (*)$$

By the remarks in Section 2 and the interlude, this is equivalent to proving that

$$FA\ell(3)/\langle f \rangle_{cl} \equiv FA\ell(3)/\langle g \rangle_{cl} \text{ implies that}$$

$$\mathcal{Z}(f) \text{ and } \mathcal{Z}(g) \text{ have equivalent simplicial subdivisions } (**).$$

By Proposition 1, we may assume that $\mathcal{Z}(f)$ and $\mathcal{Z}(g)$ each have a single connected component.

We can use $\theta_1(x)$ to determine (in $\mathcal{L}$) iff $\mathcal{Z}(f)$ has dimension 0; $(**)$ holds if it does. The formula $\exists x \theta_2(x)$ holds in $FA\ell(n)/\langle f \rangle_{cl}$ iff $\mathcal{Z}(f)$ has a non-singleton component. So we will assume that $\mathcal{Z}(f)$ has dimension 1 or 2.

9.1   Basic Constituents I

We begin this subsection by showing how to determine (in $\mathcal{L}$) the dimension of a basic constituent of $\mathcal{Z}(f)$ ($f \in FA\ell(3)_+$).

There are two types of basic constituents of dimension 1, namely proper arcs and simple closed curves ("circles"). The difference between them is that given any three disjoint subarcs (or three distinct points) of any proper arc, one of them is between the other two. This fails if $\mathcal{Z}(f) \cap \mathcal{S}(h)$ is a closed curve. If $\mathcal{Z}(f) \cap \mathcal{S}(h)$ has dimension 2, then there are pairwise disjoint closed rationally determined 2-simplices P_1, P_2, P_3 in the interior of $\mathcal{Z}(f) \cap \mathcal{S}(h)$. By taking $f_j \in FA\ell(3)_+$ with connected support contained in P_j ($j = 1, 2, 3$), we see that this also fails in this case.

Let $\mu_a(h)$ be the $\mathcal{L}$-formula

$$\theta_S(h) \;\&\; \neg\theta_1(h) \;\&$$

$$(\forall f_1, f_2, f_3 > 0)([\,(f_1 \vee f_2 \vee f_3) \leq h \,\&\, f_1 \vee f_2 \perp f_3 \,\&\, f_1 \perp f_2 \,\&\, \bigwedge_{i=1}^{3} \theta_S(f_i)] \rightarrow$$

$$\bigvee_{\{i,j,k\}=\{1,2,3\}} (\forall g > 0)([\theta_S(g) \,\&\, g \geq (f_i \vee f_j)] \rightarrow g \wedge f_k \neq 0)).$$

From the above discussion,

Lemma 18. $FA\ell(3)/\langle f\rangle_{cl} \models \mu_a(h + \langle f\rangle_{cl})$ iff $\mathcal{Z}(f) \cap \mathcal{S}(h)$ is a proper arc.

To express in $\mathcal{L}$ that $\mathcal{Z}(f)$ contains a closed arc $(\mathcal{Z}(g))$ which is not contained in a 2-dimensional subset of $\mathcal{Z}(f)$, we can similarly use:

$$\bar{\mu}_a(g) := (\forall h > 0)[(h \perp g \,\&\, \theta_S(h)) \rightarrow \mu_a(h)].$$

By the above remarks,

Lemma 19

(1) $FA\ell(3)/\langle f\rangle_{cl} \models \mu_a(g + \langle f\rangle_{cl})$ iff $\mathcal{Z}(f) \cap \mathcal{S}(g)$ is an arc not contained

in any 2-dimensional subset of $\mathcal{Z}(f)$,   and

(2) $FA\ell(3)/\langle f\rangle_{cl} \models \bar{\mu}_a(g + \langle f\rangle_{cl})$ iff $\mathcal{Z}(f) \cap \mathcal{Z}(g)$ is a closed arc not

contained in any 2-dimensional subset of $\mathcal{Z}(f)$.

(3) The closed arc is maximal in $\mathcal{Z}(f)$ iff $FA\ell(3)/\langle f\rangle_{cl} \models \nu_a(g + \langle f\rangle_{cl})$,

where $\nu_a(g) := \bar{\mu}_a(g) \,\&\, (\forall k \leq g)\,(k > 0 \rightarrow [\bar{\mu}_a(k) \leftrightarrow (\forall x > 0)(x \perp k \leftrightarrow x \perp g)])$.

We can also provide $\mathcal{L}$-formulae to determine whether two such maximal arcs are the same or not and their number.

On the other hand, by the above lemma, there is an $\mathcal{L}$-formula $\lambda(h)$ expressing that $\mathcal{S}(h) \cap \mathcal{Z}(f)$ comprises two disjoint arcs not contained in any 2-dimensional subset of $\mathcal{Z}(f)$. Let $\mu_c(h)$ be the $\mathcal{L}$-formula

$$\theta_S(h) \,\&\, \neg\mu_a(h) \,\&\, (\exists h_1, h_2 > 0)[h_1 \not\perp h_2 \,\&\, \lambda(h_1 \wedge h_2) \,\&\,$$

$$(\forall g)\,(g \perp h \leftrightarrow g \perp h_1 \vee h_2)].$$

Lemma 20. Let $f \in FA\ell(3)_+$. Then $\mathcal{Z}(f)$ contains a simple closed curve in the form $\mathcal{S}(h)$ (which is not contained in a 2-dimensional subset of $\mathcal{Z}(f)$) iff

$$FA\ell(3)/\langle f\rangle_{cl} \models \mu_c(h + \langle f\rangle_{cl}).$$

Proof: $FA\ell(3)/\langle f\rangle_{cl} \models \mu_c(h + \langle f\rangle_{cl})$ iff $\mathcal{S}(h) \cap \mathcal{Z}(f)$ is not an arc but is the union of two arcs $\mathcal{S}(h_1) \cap \mathcal{Z}(f)$ and $\mathcal{S}(h_2) \cap \mathcal{Z}(f)$. Since the intersection of $\mathcal{S}(h_1) \cap \mathcal{Z}(f)$ and $\mathcal{S}(h_2) \cap \mathcal{Z}(f)$ is non-empty and open in $\mathcal{Z}(f)$, the connected set $\mathcal{S}(h) \cap \mathcal{Z}(f)$ is 1-dimensional. It is therefore a simple closed curve. $\qquad\square$

Corollary 3. *If* $f, g \in FA\ell(3)_+$ *and* $FA\ell(3)/\langle f \rangle_{cl} \equiv FA\ell(3)/\langle g \rangle_{cl}$, *then* $dim(\mathcal{Z}(f)) = 1$ *iff* $dim(\mathcal{Z}(g)) = 1$.

This corollary could also have been deduced from Lemma 18: $dim(Z(f)) = 1$ iff

$$FA\ell(3)/\langle f \rangle_{cl} \models (\forall g > 0)([\theta_S(g) \ \& \ \neg\theta_1(g)] \rightarrow (\exists h > 0)[h \leq g \ \& \ \mu_a(h)]).$$

Note: If $\mathcal{Z}(g_1)$ is an arc, $\mathcal{Z}(g_2)$ is a simple closed curve and $\{x_0\} = \mathcal{Z}(g_1) \cap \mathcal{Z}(g_2)$, then the formula $\mu_c(x)$ fails at $g_2 + \langle f \rangle_{cl}$ since for any $h \in FA\ell(3)$ with $h(x_0) > 0$ we have $FA\ell(3) \models \neg\mu_a(h + \langle f \rangle_{cl})$.

9.2 $dim(\mathcal{Z}(f)) = 1$

We can now complete the proof of Theorem 8 in the special case that $dim(\mathcal{Z}(f)) = 1$. That is,

Proposition 2. *Let* $f, g \in FA\ell(3)^+$ *with* $dim(\mathcal{Z}(f)) = 1$. *If* $FA\ell(3)/\langle f \rangle_{cl} \equiv FA\ell(3)/\langle g \rangle_{cl}$, *then* $dim(\mathcal{Z}(g)) = 1$ *and* $FA\ell(3)/\langle f \rangle_{cl} \cong FA\ell(3)/\langle g \rangle_{cl}$.

As before, we may assume that $\mathcal{Z}(f)$ is connected.

If $\mathcal{Z}(f)$ is a simple closed curve, then $FA\ell(3)/\langle f \rangle_{cl} \models (\exists h > 0)\mu_c(h + \langle f \rangle_{cl})$. So the same holds for $FA\ell(3)/\langle g \rangle_{cl}$, whence Proposition 2 holds in this case.

So assume that $\mathcal{Z}(f)$ is a connected set of arcs. As we can count the number of distinct maximal arcs (using ν_a), we can describe (first-order) the number of arcs comprising the component of $\mathcal{Z}(f)$ if it has dimension 1. We now need to consider incidence between arcs.

Call a point of $\mathcal{Z}(f)$ a *vertex* if it either

(i) has at least two maximal closed arcs containing it, or
(ii) is the endpoint of a unique maximal closed arc.

Maximal closed arcs between vertices will be called *edges*.

Thus we get a *connected graph* $\Gamma(f)$ with the property that every vertex of type (i) has valency at least three.

We can use $\nu_a(x)$, etc., to express (in $\mathcal{L}$) the existence of a vertex of type (i) in $\mathcal{Z}(f)$. We form the sentence that there is a vertex of type (i) with minimal valency (among type (i) vertices), say $m_1 > 1$: *i.e.*, there is a vertex incident to m_1 edges, but no type (i) vertex in $\mathcal{Z}(f)$ is incident to fewer than m_1 edges. This is achieved by an element $h \in FA\ell(3)_+$ with connected support which intersects exactly m_1 distinct edges, and any $h' \in FA\ell(3)_+$ with connected support which intersects at least two distinct distinct edges must intersect at least m_1 distinct edges.

Moreover, we can count the number of minimal valency type (i) vertices in $\Gamma(f)$ and then proceed to the next largest valency m_2, the length of the paths between vertices of valencies (m, m'), *etc.*

Thus we can determine these properties in $\mathcal{L}$ and hence the properties of the finite planar graph $\Gamma(f)$. Consequently, we can determine (in $\mathcal{L}$) if $\mathcal{Z}(f)$ is 1-dimensional and, if it is, the first-order properties of the finite connected planar graph $\Gamma(f)$.

This is enough to determine $\Gamma(f)$ up to isomorphism. So we have

$$FA\ell(3)/\langle f\rangle_{cl} \equiv FA\ell(3)/\langle g\rangle_{cl} \rightarrow \Gamma(f) \equiv \Gamma(g) \rightarrow \Gamma(f) \cong \Gamma(g).$$

Conversely, $\Gamma(f) \cong \Gamma(g)$ implies that $Z(f) \sim_{\ell} Z(g)$.
So (∗∗) holds if $\mathcal{Z}(f)$ is 1-dimensional.
This completes the proof of Proposition 2.   □

9.3 Basic Constituents II

Let $f \in FA\ell(3)_+$ and p be a point of $\mathcal{Z}(f)$. We call p a *separating point* if for every open disc B with centre p and small enough positive radius, $\mathcal{Z}(f) \cap B$ contains a 2-dimensional open subset but $(\mathcal{Z}(f) \cap B) \setminus \{p\}$ is not connected.

Example B. In each part of this example, the word "triangle" will refer to the inside as well as to the triangle itself. So our triangles will be closed 2-dimensional sets.

(i) Let T_1, T_2 be two triangles with intersection a common vertex p. Let $\mathcal{Z}(f) = T_1 \cup T_2$ with $\mathcal{Z}(f_j) = T_j$ $(j = 1, 2)$; so $\mathcal{S}(f_i)$ is the interior of $\mathcal{Z}(f_j)$ $(i \neq j, i, j \in \{1, 2\})$. Then p is a separating point of $\mathcal{Z}(f)$. The same would be true if we replaced T_2 by an arc A whose intersection with T_1 is p, an endpoint of A.

(ii) Let T_1, T_2, T_3 be triangles whose pairwise intersection is a common vertex p. Let $\mathcal{Z}(f) = T_1 \cup T_2 \cup T_3$ with $\mathcal{Z}(f_1) = T_1$ and $\mathcal{Z}(f_2) = T_2 \cup T_3$. So $\mathcal{S}(f_2)$ is the interior of T_1 and is connected but $\mathcal{S}(f_1)$ is the union of the interiors of T_2 and T_3 (and so is not connected). Again, p is a separating point of $\mathcal{Z}(f)$ but it has "valency" 3.

(iii) Let T be a triangle with midpoints p_1, p_2, p_3. Remove the interior of the triangle formed from p_1, p_2, p_3 so that the result is the union of three triangles T_1, T_2, T_3 where $T_i \cap T_j = \{p_k\}$ $(\{i, j, k\} = \{1, 2, 3\})$. If $\mathcal{Z}(f) = T_1 \cup T_2 \cup T_3$, then p_1, p_2, p_3 are separating points of valency 2 (use the same f_1, f_2 for T_1, T_2, T_3 as in (ii)).

(iv) Let T_1, T_2, T_3 be three triangles with one edge on a common line. Suppose that $T_1 \cap T_3 = \emptyset$, $T_1 \cap T_2 = \{p\}$, a common vertex (on the line) and $T_2 \cap T_3 = \{q\}$, a common vertex (on the line). Again let $\mathcal{Z}(f) = T_1 \cup T_2 \cup T_3$. Then $\mathcal{Z}(f)$ has 2 separating points of valency 2. However, in both (iii) and (iv), $\mathcal{Z}(f)$ has three basic constituents. So the valency and number of basic constituents is not sufficient to count the number of points of intersection.

(v) Let S_1 be the union of two overlapping triangles sharing a common side. Let p_1, p_2 be the vertices not on this side. Let S_2 be the union of two overlapping triangles sharing a common side. Let the vertices not on this side also be p_1, p_2. Suppose further that $S_1 \cap S_2 = \{p_1, p_2\}$. Then p_1, p_2 are separating points for $\mathcal{Z}(f)$ (take $\mathcal{Z}(f_j) = S_j$).

Example C. Consider $\Delta \subseteq S^{(2)}$ a rectangle (together with its inside) and let p be an interior point. Let T_1, T_2 be two triangles (again including the inside) in the interior of Δ with common vertex p such that $T_1 \cap T_2 = \{p\}$. Let $(T_1 \cup T_2)^o$

denote the interior of $(T_1 \cup T_2)$, and set $\Delta_0 := \Delta \setminus (T_1 \cup T_2)^\circ$. Then Δ_0 is the zero set of some $f \in FA\ell(3)_+$. So $\mathcal{Z}(f)$ has a single basic constituent of dimension 2 but is not a manifold. Note that p is a separating point.

We can modify the example in several ways. We can take a finite set $\{T_j : j \in J\}$ of triangles in the interior of Δ with pairwise intersection $\{p\}$, and remove $(\bigcup_{j \in J} T_j)^\circ$ from Δ. Alternatively, we can let p be on the boundary of Δ. In all cases, the result is a single basic constituent that is not a manifold. We can obviously extend this to allow a finite number of points p some interior to Δ and some not.

The points in these examples are somewhat different from those in Example B. Those in Examples B are "bridge" points, whereas those in Examples C are not (see below). These simple examples will illustrate the need for what we do in this subsection.

We show how to define separating points and then how to distinguish between those of the sorts typified in the examples.

We begin by showing how to express in $\mathcal{L}$ that two connected sets $\mathcal{Z}(f_1)$ and $\mathcal{Z}(f_2)$ (at least one of which is 2-dimensional) intersect in a single point.

By Corollary 3, there is an $\mathcal{L}$-formula $\psi_2(x)$ such that

$$FA\ell(3)/\langle f \rangle_{cl} \models \psi_2(h + \langle f \rangle_{cl}) \quad \text{iff} \quad dim(\mathcal{S}(h)) = 2.$$

Let f_1, $f_2 \in FA\ell(3)_+$ and

$$\Phi_{sep}(f_1, f_2) := \theta_Z(f_1 \wedge f_2) \,\&\, f_1^\# \perp f_2^\# \,\&\, \psi_2(f_1^\#) \,\&\, \bigwedge_{j=1}^{2} \theta_S(f_j^\#)$$

$$\&\, (\exists h > 0)(\theta_S(h) \,\&\, h \not\perp f_1^\# \,\&\, h \not\perp f_2^\#) \,\&\,$$

$$(\forall h_1, h_2 > 0)([\bigwedge_{i=1}^{2} \theta_S(h_i) \,\&\, (\forall g_1, g_2 > 0)([\theta_Z(g_1 \wedge g_2) \,\&\,$$

$$\bigwedge_{j=1}^{2}(g_j \geq f_j \,\&\, \theta_S(g_j^\#))] \to (h_i \not\perp g_1^\# \,\&\, h_i \not\perp g_2^\#)] \to [h_1 \not\perp h_2]).$$

Lemma 21. *Let $f \in FA\ell(3)_+$ with $\mathcal{Z}(f)$ connected of dimension 2. Then $FA\ell(3)/\langle f \rangle_{cl} \models \Phi_{sep}(f_1 + \langle f \rangle_{cl}, f_2 + \langle f \rangle_{cl})$ iff $dim(\mathcal{Z}(f_1) \cap \mathcal{Z}(f)) = 2$, and the intersection of $\mathcal{Z}(f_1) \cap \mathcal{Z}(f)$ and $\mathcal{Z}(f_2) \cap \mathcal{Z}(f)$ consists of a single point of $\mathcal{Z}(f)$.*

Proof: Suppose that $FA\ell(3)/\langle f \rangle_{cl} \models \Phi_{sep}(f_1 + \langle f \rangle_{cl}, f_2 + \langle f \rangle_{cl})$. Since $f_j^\# \perp f_j$, the relative interior (in $\mathcal{Z}(f)$) of $\mathcal{Z}(f_j) \cap \mathcal{Z}(f)$ is non-empty ($j = 1, 2$). Also, $\mathcal{Z}(f_1) \cap \mathcal{Z}(f)$ has dimension 2 since $\psi_2(f_1^\#)$. Since $\theta_Z(f_1 \wedge f_2)$, we deduce that $\mathcal{Z}(f_1) \cup \mathcal{Z}(f_2)$ is connected. The remaining part of the formula ensures that if we shrink the connected set $\mathcal{Z}(f_1) \cup \mathcal{Z}(f_2)$ so that it remains connected, then $\mathcal{Z}(g_1) \cap \mathcal{Z}(g_2)$ is still a single point.

The converse direction is obvious.   □

Corollary 4. *Let $f \in FA\ell(3)_+$ with $\mathcal{Z}(f)$ connected of dimension 2. Then $FA\ell(3)/\langle f \rangle_{cl} \models (\exists f_1, f_2 > 0)\ \Phi_{sep}(f_1 + \langle f \rangle_{cl}, f_2 + \langle f \rangle_{cl})$ iff $\mathcal{Z}(f)$ contains a separating point.*

Corollary 5. *Let $f \in FA\ell(3)_+$ with $\mathcal{Z}(f)$ connected of dimension 2. Then there is an $\mathcal{L}$-sentence Φ_{sep,M_0} such that $FA\ell(3)/\langle f \rangle_{cl} \models \Phi_{sep,M_0}$ iff $\mathcal{Z}(f)$ contains exactly M_0 separating points.*

Proof: We can take the conjunction of

$$\{\Phi_{sep}(f_{2m-1}, f_{2m}) : m = 1, \ldots, M\}, \qquad \bigwedge_{1 \leq i < j \leq 2M} f_i^\# \perp f_j^\#, \text{ and}$$

$$(\exists h_1, \ldots, h_M > 0)(\bigwedge_{i=1}^{M} \theta_S(h_i) \ \& \ h_i \not\perp f_{2i-1}^\# \ \& \ h_i \not\perp f_{2i}^\# \ \& \ \bigwedge_{j \neq i}(h_i \perp f_{2j-1}^\# \ \& \ h_i \perp f_{2j}^\#).$$

It witnesses that $\mathcal{Z}(f)$ has at least M separating points. (The second line of the formula is necessary as a separating point might have valency greater than 2.) The existential sentence formed is satisfied in $FA\ell/\langle f \rangle_{cl}$ iff $\mathcal{Z}(f)$ has at least M separating points. The negation of the corresponding sentence with $M + 1$ in place of M holds in $FA\ell/\langle f \rangle_{cl}$ iff $\mathcal{Z}(f)$ does not have $M + 1$ separating points. The corollary follows. $\qquad\square$

Let $f_1, \ f_2 \in FA\ell(3)_+$ and

$$\Psi_1(f_1, f_2) := \theta_Z(f) \ \& \ f_1 \perp f_2 \ \& \ (\forall h > 0)(h \not\perp f_1 \vee f_2) \ \& \ \Phi_{sep}(f_1, f_2).$$

The proof of Lemma 21 shows

Lemma 22. *Let $f \in FA\ell(3)_+$ with $\mathcal{Z}(f)$ connected of dimension 2. Then $FA\ell(3)/\langle f \rangle_{cl} \models \Psi_1(f_1 + \langle f \rangle_{cl}, f_2 + \langle f \rangle_{cl})$ iff $\mathcal{S}(f_1) \cup \mathcal{S}(f_2)$ is dense in $\mathcal{Z}(f)$, $dim(\mathcal{Z}(f_1) \cap \mathcal{Z}(f)) = 2$, and the intersection of $\mathcal{Z}(f_1) \cap \mathcal{Z}(f)$ and $\mathcal{Z}(f_2) \cap \mathcal{Z}(f)$ consists of a single point of $\mathcal{Z}(f)$.*

We can clearly modify the $\mathcal{L}$-formula to express that the basic constituent $\mathcal{Z}(f_1)$ intersects the remaining basic constituents in exactly $M \geq 2$ points ($M \in \mathbb{N}$).

$$\Psi_M(f_1, f_2) := \theta_Z(f) \ \& \ f_1 \perp f_2 \ \& \ \psi_2(f_1) \ \& \ \psi_2(f_2) \ \&$$

$$(\forall h > 0)(h \not\perp f_1 \vee f_2) \ \& \ (\exists h_1, \ldots, h_M > 0)(\bigwedge_{i=1}^{M} \theta_S(h_i) \ \& \ h_i \not\perp f_1 \ \& \ h_i \not\perp f_2) \ \&$$

$$\bigwedge_{j \neq i} h_j \perp h_i \ \& \ [(\forall g > 0)([\theta_S(g) \ \& \ g \not\perp f_1 \ \& \ g \not\perp f_2] \to [\bigvee_{i=1}^{M} g \not\perp h_i])].$$

Lemma 23. *Let $f \in FA\ell(3)_+$ with $\mathcal{Z}(f)$ connected of dimension 2 and $M \geq 2$. Then $FA\ell(3)/\langle f \rangle_{cl} \models \Psi_M(f_1 + \langle f \rangle_{cl}, f_2 + \langle f \rangle_{cl})$ iff $\mathcal{S}(f_1) \cup \mathcal{S}(f_2)$ is dense in $\mathcal{Z}(f)$, $dim(\mathcal{Z}(f_j) \cap \mathcal{Z}(f)) = 2$ $(j=1,2)$, and the intersection of $\mathcal{Z}(f_1) \cap \mathcal{Z}(f)$ and $\mathcal{Z}(f_2) \cap \mathcal{Z}(f)$ consists of exactly M points of $\mathcal{Z}(f)$.*

Proof: The proof is a trivial modification of the proof of Lemma 22.   □

We call a separating point p a *bridge* if it is a separating point between at least two distinct basic constituents. That is, there are basic constituents $\mathcal{Z}(f_1)$ and $\mathcal{Z}(f_2)$ of $\mathcal{Z}(f)$ such that $\mathcal{Z}(f_1) \cap \mathcal{Z}(f_2)$ is a finite set of points including p. If $\mathcal{Z}(f)$ is a "pinched annulus", then $\mathcal{Z}(f)$ has a single basic constituent; so the pinch point is a separating point that is not a bridge. One can capture the difference between separating points that are bridges and those that are not. If $f_1^{\#}$ and $f_2^{\#}$ give witness to a separating point p, then there is $h \geq f_1^{\#} \vee f_2^{\#}$ such that $\mathcal{S}(h)$ is connected and contains no separating point iff p is not a bridge point. All of this can be expressed in $\mathcal{L}$ by the preceding lemmata. Hence

Corollary 6. *Let $f \in FA\ell(3)_{+}$. Then there are $\mathcal{L}$-formulae $\Phi_{bridge}(x_1, x_2)$ and $\Phi_{\neg bridge}(x_1, x_2)$ such that $FA\ell(3)/\langle f \rangle_{cl} \models \Phi_{bridge}(f_1 + \langle f \rangle_{cl}, f_2 + \langle f \rangle_{cl})$ iff $\mathcal{Z}(f_1), \mathcal{Z}(f_2)$ determine a bridge point; and $FA\ell(3)/\langle f \rangle_{cl} \models \Phi_{\neg bridge}(f_1 + \langle f \rangle_{cl}, f_2 + \langle f \rangle_{cl})$ iff $\mathcal{Z}(f_1), \mathcal{Z}(f_2)$ determine a separating non-bridge point.*

As in Corollary 5, we can modify the $\mathcal{L}$-formulae to obtain

Proposition 3. *If $f, g \in FA\ell(3)^{+}$ and $FA\ell(3)/\langle f \rangle_{cl} \equiv FA\ell(3)/\langle g \rangle_{cl}$ with $\mathcal{Z}(f)$ connected, then $\mathcal{Z}(f)$ and $\mathcal{Z}(g)$ have the same number of separating points and bridge points, and the same number of basic constituents of the same dimensions. Corresponding bridge points have the same valency with attached basic constituents having the same dimensions. Corresponding non-bridge separating points also have the same valency. Moreover, the bijection between the basic constituents of $\mathcal{Z}(f)$ and $\mathcal{Z}(g)$ preserves the number of separating points between the corresponding pairs.*

Consequently, it suffices to prove Theorem 8 in the special case that $\mathcal{Z}(f)$ (and so $\mathcal{Z}(g)$) has a single basic constituent.

9.4 $dim(\mathcal{Z}(f)) = 2$

We assume throughout this subsection that $\mathcal{Z}(f)$ has dimension 2 which is a basic constituent. By a trivial modification of Corollary 6, we can determine (in $\mathcal{L}$) if $\mathcal{Z}(h) \subseteq \mathcal{Z}(f)$ has a separating point; so we can determine if $\mathcal{S}(h^{\#})$ (for such $\mathcal{Z}(h)$) is a 2-dimensional manifold. Let $\mu_2(x)$ be an $\mathcal{L}$-formula such that

Lemma 24. *Let $f, h \in FA\ell(3)_{+}$ with $FA\ell(3)/\langle f \rangle_{cl} \models \psi_2(h^{\#} + \langle f \rangle_{cl})$. Then*

$$FA\ell(3)/\langle f \rangle_{cl} \models \mu_2(h + \langle f \rangle_{cl}) \quad \text{iff} \quad \mathcal{S}(h^{\#}) \cap \mathcal{Z}(f) \text{ is a 2-dimensional manifold.}$$

Note that if $\mathcal{S}(f^{\#})$ is a 2-dimensional manifold, then it is homotopic to the entire 2-sphere, an open "disc" (*i.e.*, the inside of a triangle) or "a band with m handles" which we will call an *m-band* ($m \in \mathbb{N}$). Such a homotopy can clearly be realised by a piecewise linear integral function.

To prove Theorem 8, we will take advantage of the fact that the 2-dimensional basic constituent $\mathcal{Z}(f)$ can be triangulated.

We will need to be able to recognise (in $\mathcal{L}$) an *interior cutting arc* $\mathcal{Z}(g)$ of $\mathcal{Z}(f') \subseteq \mathcal{Z}(f)$. We will express it by a formula $\iota(g, f')$ which we now develop. The key is that an interior cutting arc cannot be the support of any element of $FA\ell(3)$ restricted to $\mathcal{Z}(f)$ as it is not open in $\mathcal{Z}(f)$, but it does cut $\mathcal{Z}(f')$ in two.

Let $\rho(g)$ be the conjunction of (i) and (ii) given by
(i) $(\forall h > 0)$ $(h \not\perp g)$ and
(ii) $\neg \theta_S(g)$.
Clearly

Lemma 25. *Let* $f, g \in FA\ell(3)_+$ *with* $\mathcal{Z}(g) \subseteq \mathcal{Z}(f)$. *Then the interior of* $\mathcal{Z}(g)$ *in* $\mathcal{Z}(f)$ *is empty and* $\mathcal{S}(g) \cap \mathcal{Z}(f)$ *is not connected in* $\mathcal{Z}(f)$ *iff* $FA\ell(3)/\langle f \rangle_{cl} \models \rho(g + \langle f \rangle_{cl})$.

Let $\lambda(g, g_1, g_2, f')$ be the conjunction of (iii), (iv) and (v) defined by

(iii) $g = g_1 \vee g_2$ & $\theta_Z(g_1 \wedge g_2)$,
(iv) $\bigwedge_{i=1}^{2}(g_i > 0$ & $\mu_2(g_i^{\#})$ & $\theta_S(g_i^{\#}))$,   and
(v) $g_1^{\#} \perp g_2^{\#}$ and $0 < g_j^{\#} \perp f'$ $(j = 1, 2)$.

Since $g_1^{\#} \perp g_2^{\#}$, $\mathcal{Z}(g)$ has dimension at most 1. Hence, clearly

Lemma 26. *Let* $f, f', g \in FA\ell(3)_+$ *with* $FA\ell(3)/\langle f \rangle_{cl} \models \mu_2(f' + \langle f \rangle_{cl})$. *If* $\mathcal{Z}(g) \subseteq \mathcal{Z}(f')$, *then* $\mathcal{Z}(g)$ *has dimension 1 and is the intersection of two zero sets of dimension 2 (whose union is* $\mathcal{Z}(f')$ *and whose interiors are disjoint) iff*

$$FA\ell(3)/\langle f \rangle_{cl} \models (\exists g_1, g_2)[\lambda(g + \langle f \rangle_{cl}, g_1, g_2, f' + \langle f \rangle_{cl}) \ \& \ (\forall h \perp g_1 \wedge g_2)(h \perp f' + \langle f \rangle_{cl})].$$

Note that if $\mathcal{Z}(g) \subseteq \mathcal{Z}(f')$ and $g + \langle f \rangle_{cl}$ satisfies $\rho(x)$ & $(\exists y, z)\lambda(g + \langle f \rangle_{cl}, y, z, f' + \langle f \rangle_{cl})$ in $FA\ell(3)/\langle f \rangle_{cl}$, then $\mathcal{Z}(g)$ has dimension exactly 1 as $\mathcal{Z}(g)$ divides the 2-dimensional subset $\mathcal{Z}(f')$ of $\mathcal{Z}(f)$ into two disjoint sets. Indeed, $\mathcal{Z}(g)$ comprises a single "cutting arc or circle" that divides $\mathcal{Z}(f')$ in two and, possibly, a union of a finite set of "non-cutting" arcs and isolated points. It cannot include two cutting arcs as both $\mathcal{S}(g_j^{\#})$ $(j = 1, 2)$ are connected.

Caution. (1) The "cutting arc" could be an arc on the sphere whose restriction to $\mathcal{Z}(f)$ is a finite union of disjoint arcs (*e.g.*, if $\mathcal{Z}(f)$ is an annulus and the arc is a diameter of the external circle).

(2) The additional arcs could intersect the "cutting arc or circle". So the "cutting arc" (respectively, "cutting circle") is an arc (respectively, circle) in the usual sense of the word, but is a union of arcs in our previous sense of the word.

We next express (in $\mathcal{L}$) that $\mathcal{S}(k) \cap \mathcal{Z}(f')$ surrounds the "cutting" part of $\mathcal{Z}(g) \cap \mathcal{Z}(f')$. Consider the $\mathcal{L}$-formula $\sigma_0(k, g, f')$ given by:

(vi) $\rho(g)$ & $\theta_S(k)$ & & $(\exists g_1, g_2)$ $\lambda(g, g_1, g_2, f')$ &

$$(\forall g_1, g_2)(\lambda(g, g_1, g_2, f') \rightarrow [\bigwedge_{i=1}^{2} k \not\perp g_i^{\#} \ \& \ \theta_S(k \wedge g_i^{\#})]\,) \ \&$$

$$(\forall h > 0)([\theta_S(h) \ \& \ (\forall g_1, g_2)(\lambda(g, g_1, g_2, f') \rightarrow \bigwedge_{i=1,2} h \not\perp g_i^{\#})] \rightarrow h \not\perp k).$$

Lemma 27. *Let $f, f', g, k \in FA\ell(3)_+$ with $\mathcal{Z}(f')$ as in the previous lemma and $\mathcal{Z}(g) \subseteq \mathcal{Z}(f')$. Then $\mathcal{Z}(g)$ has dimension 1, cuts $\mathcal{Z}(f')$ and its cutting arc (or circle) is contained in $S(k) \cap \mathcal{Z}(f)$ iff $FA\ell(3)/\langle f \rangle_{cl} \models \sigma_0(k + \langle f \rangle_{cl}, g + \langle f \rangle_{cl}, f' + \langle f \rangle_{cl})$.*

Proof: Suppose that $FA\ell(3)/\langle f \rangle_{cl} \models \sigma_0(k + \langle f \rangle_{cl}, g + \langle f \rangle_{cl}, f' + \langle f \rangle_{cl})$. By Lemmata 25 and 26, $\mathcal{Z}(g)$ has dimension 1 and includes an arc or circle that divides $\mathcal{Z}(f')$ into two disjoint sets of dimension 2. Indeed, we may assume that $\mathcal{Z}(g)$ is a single such arc or circle as nothing is affected by removing either any non-cutting arcs or any isolated points. The universal conjuncts imply that, for every pair of elements g_1, g_2 associated with $\mathcal{Z}(g)$, $S(k)$ cannot be disjoint from the connected support of any element whose support intersects $S(g_1^{\#})$ and $S(g_2^{\#})$. Thus (the cutting part of) $\mathcal{Z}(g)$ is contained in $S(k) \cap \mathcal{Z}(f)$. The converse follows from the same considerations and lemmata. □

We can alternatively express that $\mathcal{Z}(g) \cap \mathcal{Z}(f)$ is not a singleton:

(vii) $\psi(g, f') := (\exists a_1, a_2 > 0)[a_1 \perp a_2 \ \& \ \forall k > 0 \,(\sigma_0(k, g, f') \rightarrow a_i \not\perp k)]$.

To summarise the lemmata, (i) rules out that $\mathcal{Z}(g) \cap \mathcal{Z}(f)$ has relative maximal dimension in $\mathcal{Z}(f)$. That is, it cannot have dimension $n - 1 \ (= 2)$ or include an arc which is not a subset of some 2-dimensional subset of $\mathcal{Z}(f)$. Thus (i) implies that $\mathcal{Z}(g) \cap \mathcal{Z}(f')$ is a finite set of arcs and circles all contained in 2-dimensional subsets of $\mathcal{Z}(f)$, and a finite set of points. By (ii), $S(g) \cap \mathcal{Z}(f')$ is not connected. By (iii), (iv) and (v), $\mathcal{Z}(g) \cap \mathcal{Z}(f')$ is the intersection of two zero sets of dimension 2 whose interiors are disjoint. By (vi), $S(k)$ is connected as is its restriction to $S(g_1^{\#})$ and $S(g_2^{\#})$ whenever g_1, g_2 satify conditions (iii)-(v). So $S(k)$ cannot "pinch" $\mathcal{Z}(g)$ if $\mathcal{Z}(g)$ is a single arc or circle. Moreover, $S(k)$ cannot be decomposed into two disjoint supports one of which is included in $S(g_1^{\#})$. So (vi) ensures that $S(k)$ cannot be essentially shrunk. By (vii), $\mathcal{Z}(g) \cap \mathcal{Z}(f')$ is not a single point and the same is true when this is intersected with any connected $S(k)$ that is not disjoint from the support of both $g_1^{\#}$ and $g_2^{\#}$. Thus $\mathcal{Z}(g) \cap \mathcal{Z}(f')$ is the union of (either a cutting circle or a cutting arc) and a finite set of arcs and points.
    Let

$$\sigma(g, g_1, g_2, k, f') := \rho(g) \ \& \ \lambda(g, g_1, g_2, f') \ \& \ \psi(g, f') \ \& \ \sigma_0(k, g, f').$$

By the above lemmata, we obtain

Corollary 7. *With the above notation,*

$$FA\ell(3)/\langle f \rangle_{cl} \models \sigma(g + \langle f \rangle_{cl}, g_1 + \langle f \rangle_{cl}, g_2 + \langle f \rangle_{cl}, k + \langle f \rangle_{cl}, f' + \langle f \rangle_{cl}) \quad \textit{iff}$$

$g = g_1 \vee g_2$ *with all the above properties for* g_1, g_2,

$\mathcal{Z}(g) \subseteq \mathcal{Z}(f')$ has dimension 1 and includes exactly one cutting arc or circle Γ contained in the interior of $\mathcal{Z}(f')$,
$(\mathcal{Z}(g) \cap \mathcal{Z}(f')) \setminus \Gamma$ is a finite set of points and arcs,
and the restriction of $\mathcal{S}(k)$ to $\mathcal{Z}(f)$ surrounds Γ.

We next want to recognise interior cutting circles in $\mathcal{Z}(f')$. The idea is easy. If we take three pairwise disjoint connected supports $\mathcal{S}(a_j)$ ($j = 1, 2, 3$) each intersecting the cutting arc in $\mathcal{Z}(f')$, then we can find a surrounding $\mathcal{S}(k)$ such that removing the middle $\mathcal{S}(a_j)$ from $\mathcal{S}(k)$ results in a disconnected set. In the case of a cutting circle, we can "just go round the back of the circle".

Let $\iota_0(g, f')$ be the $\mathcal{L}$-formula:

$$(\exists g_1, g_2 > 0)(g_1 \vee g_2 = g \ \& \ (\exists k > 0)\sigma(g, g_1, g_2, k, f') \ \& \ \gamma(g, g_1, g_2, f')),$$

where $\gamma(g, g_1, g_2, f')$ is given by:

$$(\forall a_1, a_2, a_3 > 0)([\bigwedge_{i=1,2,3} \theta_S(a_i) \ \& \ a_i \not\perp g_1^{\#} \ \& \ a_i \not\perp g_2^{\#} \ \& \ \bigwedge_{j \neq i} a_j \perp a_i] \rightarrow$$

$$[(\exists k > 0)(\ \sigma(g, g_1, g_2, k, f') \ \&$$

$$\bigvee_{\{i_1, i_2, i_3\} = \{1,2,3\}} (\forall h > 0)([h \leq k \ \& \ h \not\perp a_{i_1} \ \& \ h \not\perp a_{i_3} \ \& \ \theta_S(h)] \rightarrow h \not\perp a_{i_2})]).$$

Let $\iota_1(g, f')$ be the $\mathcal{L}$-formula:

$$(\exists g_1, g_2 > 0)(g_1 \vee g_2 = g \ \& \ (\exists k > 0) \ \sigma(g, g_1, g_2, k, f') \ \& \ \neg\gamma(g, g_1, g_2, f')),$$

By our preceding remarks

Lemma 28. *With the previous notation,*
   $FA\ell(3)/\langle f \rangle_{cl} \models \iota_0(g, f')$ *iff* $\mathcal{Z}(g) \cap \mathcal{Z}(f')$ *contains a single cutting arc of* $\mathcal{Z}(f')$ *(and possibly a finite set of arcs and points); and*
$FA\ell(3)/\langle f \rangle_{cl} \models \iota_1(g, f')$ *iff* $\mathcal{Z}(g) \cap \mathcal{Z}(f')$ *contains a single interior cutting circle of* $\mathcal{Z}(f')$ *(and possibly a finite set of non-cutting arcs and points).*

Note that a cutting arc with ends joined by an arc entirely in the boundary of $\mathcal{Z}(f')$ falls under the first clause of the lemma, not the second.
   We next remove the extraneous interior arcs. If there were a non-cutting arc A in the interior of $\mathcal{Z}(f')$, then it would occur as a subset of $\mathcal{Z}(g_1)$ or $\mathcal{Z}(g_2)$. We assume the former. If necessary, by replacing $g_1^{\#}$ by $g_1' \leq g_1^{\#}$ whose support has boundary including $\mathcal{Z}(g)$, we may also assume that $\mathcal{S}(g_1^{\#})$ is a 2-dimensional manifold. Then there would be $h \geq g_1^{\#}$ with $h \perp g_1$ such that $\mathcal{Z}(h) = A$. Let $h_1, h_2 > 0$ be such that $h_j^{\#} \geq g_1^{\#}$ with $dim(\mathcal{S}(h_j^{\#})) = 2$ ($j = 1, 2$) and $\mathcal{Z}(h_1) \cap \mathcal{Z}(h_2) = A$. Then A cuts $\mathcal{Z}(h_1 \wedge h_2) \cap \mathcal{Z}(g_1)$ in two. Since $h \geq g_1^{\#}$,

the only arcs which occur as subsets of $\mathcal{Z}(h)$ inside $\mathcal{S}(g_1^{\#})$ must be subsets of $\mathcal{Z}(g)$. Thus we can recognise (in $\mathcal{L}$) if $\mathcal{Z}(g)$ includes interior non-cutting arcs. Therefore there is an $\mathcal{L}$-formula $\iota(g, f')$ that holds in $FA\ell(3)/\langle f \rangle_{cl}$ iff $\mathcal{Z}(g)$ has no such arcs but has a single interior arc that cuts $\mathcal{Z}(f')$ in two. Similarly, there is an $\mathcal{L}$-formula $\iota_c(g, f')$ that holds in $FA\ell(3)/\langle f \rangle_{cl}$ iff $\mathcal{Z}(g)$ has no such arcs but has an interior circle that cuts $\mathcal{Z}(f')$ in two. Hence

Proposition 4. *Let* $f, f', g \in FA\ell(3)$ *with* $\mathcal{Z}(f') \subseteq \mathcal{Z}(f)$ *and* $\mathcal{S}(f'^{\#})$ *a 2-dimensional manifold. Then there are $\mathcal{L}$-formulae $\iota(g, f')$ and $\iota_c(g, f')$ such that*

$FA\ell(3)/\langle f \rangle_{cl} \models \iota(g + \langle f \rangle_{cl}, f' + \langle f \rangle_{cl})$ *iff* $\mathcal{Z}(g) \cap \mathcal{Z}(f')$ *is a single cutting arc (and possibly a finite set of points, and a finite set of arcs in the boundary of f') of $\mathcal{Z}(f')$, and*

$FA\ell(3)/\langle f \rangle_{cl} \models \iota_c(g + \langle f \rangle_{cl}, f' + \langle f \rangle_{cl})$ *iff* $\mathcal{Z}(g) \cap \mathcal{Z}(f')$ *is a single interior circle (and possibly a finite set of points, and a finite set of arcs in the boundary of f') of $\mathcal{Z}(f')$.*

We now have the tools to complete the triangulation of $\mathcal{Z}(f)$. To do so, we first show how to recognise (from $\mathcal{L}$) that a zero set is piecewise integer linear homeomorphic to a filled-in triangle.

Proposition 5. *Let* $f, f' \in FA\ell(3)_+$ *with* $\mathcal{Z}(f') \subseteq \mathcal{Z}(f)$ *and* $\mathcal{S}(f'^{\#})$ *a 2-manifold.*

(I) $FA\ell(3)/\langle f \rangle_{cl} \models (\forall g) \neg \iota(g, f' + \langle f \rangle_{cl})$ *iff* $\mathcal{Z}(f')$ *is the 2-sphere.*

(II) *For each* $m \in \mathbb{N}$, *there is an $\mathcal{L}$-formula $\iota'_m(g, f')$ such that*
$FA\ell(3)/\langle f \rangle_{cl} \models (\exists g) \iota'_m(g, f' + \langle f \rangle_{cl})$ *iff* $\mathcal{Z}(f')$ *is a closed m-band.*

(III) *There is an $\mathcal{L}$-formula $\iota''(f')$ such that*
$FA\ell(3)/\langle f \rangle_{cl} \models \iota''(f' + \langle f \rangle_{cl})$ *iff* $\mathcal{Z}(f')$ *is piecewise integer linear homeomorphic to a closed triangle (including inside).*

Proof: (I) If $\mathcal{Z}(f')$ is the entire 2-sphere, then there is no cutting arc (it must be a circle); indeed, f' must be 0. If $\mathcal{Z}(f')$ is a band (possibly with handles) or a triangle, there is a cutting arc. Hence (I) follows from Proposition 4.

(II) and (III) The key idea in the remainder of the proof is that if 4 points lie on a line, then one can join the first and third on one side of the line and the second and fourth on the other side (so that the joining lines do not cross). However, this cannot be done without crossing if one confines the joining to be on the same side of the line. We will modify this idea to code it into our language.

Let $\mathcal{Z}(f')$ be a multiband with $m \in \mathbb{N}$ handles. Let R be a filled-in rectangle and $\{T_j : j \in J\}$ be a finite set of pairwise disjoint closed triangles in the interior of R where $|J| = m + 1$. Let I_j be the interior of T_j ($j \in J$). Then $\mathcal{Z}(f')$ is piecewise integer linear homeomorphic to $R \setminus \bigcup_{j \in J} I_j$. There is an arc A on the sphere that passes though each I_j ($j \in J$) and cuts $\mathcal{Z}(f')$ in two. Let $g \in FA\ell(3)_+$ be such that $\mathcal{Z}(g) = A \cap \mathcal{Z}(f')$. So $\mathcal{Z}(g)$ is a union of $m + 1$ disjoint arcs and $g = g_1 \vee g_2$ with g_1, g_2 as before. Let $k \in FA\ell(3)_+$ be such that $\mathcal{S}(k)$ surrounds $\mathcal{Z}(g)$. By definition, $\mathcal{S}(k)$ must "go round" each T_j. Fix $j_0 \in J$ and let $\{x_i : i = 1, 2, 3, 4\}$ be a set of distinct points on the boundary of T_{j_0} in order x_1, x_2, x_3, x_4 progressing clockwise around the boundary of T_{j_0}.

Let $a_1, a_2, a_3, a_4 \in FA\ell(3)_+$ be pairwise orthogonal with connected supports so that $a_i \leq k \wedge f'^{\#}$ and x_i is in the closure of $\mathcal{S}(a_i) \cap \mathcal{Z}(f')$ ($i = 1, 2, 3, 4$). Suppose that for each $\{i, i'\} \subseteq \{1, 2, 3, 4\}$, there are $h_{i,i'} \leq k$ in $FA\ell(3)_+$, each with connected support, such that $\mathcal{S}(h_{i,i'}) \cap \mathcal{S}(a_{i''}) \neq \emptyset$ iff $i'' \in \{i, i'\}$. We do not want the supports of the $\mathcal{S}(a_i)$ to cut $\mathcal{S}(g_1^{\#} \wedge k)$ in two so we further require that if $a_i, a_{i'} \not\perp g_1^{\#}$, then there is such an $h_{i,i'} \leq g_1^{\#} \wedge k$. Similarly with $g_2^{\#}$ in place of $g_1^{\#}$. Then there do not exist orthogonal $h_1, h_2 \leq k \cap f'^{\#}$ in $FA\ell(3)_+$ with $h_1 \perp (a_2 \vee a_4)$, $h_2 \perp (a_1 \vee a_3)$ and $h_1 \not\perp a_1$, $h_1 \not\perp a_3$, $h_2 \not\perp a_2$ and $h_2 \not\perp a_4$. By our previous results, all this is expressible in $\mathcal{L}$. We can take the finite conjunction over all $j_0 \in J$. Let the resulting $\mathcal{L}$-formula be $\underline{\iota}'_m(x, y)$. Thus $FA\ell(3)/\langle f \rangle_{cl} \models (\exists g)\, \underline{\iota}'_m(g, f' + \langle f \rangle_{cl})$ if $\mathcal{Z}(f')$ is a closed m'-band for some $m' \geq m$. We can therefore obtain an $\mathcal{L}$-formula $\iota'_m(x, y)$ from $\underline{\iota}'_m(x, y)$ that is satisfied in $FA\ell(3)/\langle f \rangle_{cl}$ if $\mathcal{Z}(f)$ is an m-band but not an m'-band if $m' \neq m$.

On the other hand, if $\mathcal{Z}(f')$ is a closed triangle, let A be any cutting arc. Let k be such that $\mathcal{S}(k)$ surrounds $\mathcal{Z}(g) = A$ but contains no points on the boundary of $\mathcal{Z}(f')$. Then we can find orthogonal h_1, h_2 whenever a_1, a_2, a_3, a_4 satisfy the above hypotheses by letting $h_1 \leq g_1^{\#}$ and $h_2 \leq g_2^{\#}$ where g_1, g_2 are such that $\mathcal{Z}(g_1) \cap \mathcal{Z}(g_2) = \mathcal{Z}(g)$, $\mathcal{Z}(f') = \mathcal{Z}(g_1) \cup \mathcal{Z}(g_2)$, $g_1^{\#} \perp g_2^{\#}$ and $\mathcal{S}(g_i^{\#})$ are connected and 2-dimensional (with the obvious modifications to these restrictions on h_1, h_2 if any a_{2i+j} is orthogonal to $g_j^{\#}$ ($i = 0, 1$; $j = 1, 2$). Thus $FA\ell(3)/\langle f \rangle_{cl} \models (\exists g)(\iota(g, f' + \langle f \rangle_{cl})$ & $(\forall g' > 0)(\neg \underline{\iota}'_2(g', f' + \langle f \rangle_{cl}))$ if $\mathcal{Z}(f')$ is a closed triangle.

This completes the proof of (II) and (III).   □

We can now complete the proof of Theorem 8.

Proof: Let $\mathcal{Z}(f)$ have dimension 2. By Proposition 3, we can determine the number of basic constituents of $\mathcal{Z}(f)$ of dimensions $0, 1$, and 2, their number and how they fit together. We can also determine the ones that have separating non-bridge points, their number and the valency of each such point. We can write each such basic constituent as a minimal union of ($\sim_\ell$) triangles any pair of which intersect in a single point or a single arc. By Proposition 5, we can recognise ($\sim_\ell$) triangles in $\mathcal{L}$. By Corollary 6, we can determine the former and by Proposition 4 we can also determine the latter. Now every 2-dimensional basic constituent of $\mathcal{Z}(f)$ can be triangulated and we can recognise triangles with inside (in $\mathcal{L}$) by Proposition 4. We can therefore determine how the triangulation is sewn together by sentences in $\mathcal{L}$. Therefore, the same triangulation must occur for $\mathcal{Z}(g)$ if $FA\ell(3)/\langle f \rangle_{cl} \equiv FA\ell(3)/\langle g \rangle_{cl}$. By Whittlesey's classification of 2-complexes [11], (∗∗) holds. Consequently, Theorem 8 is proved.   □

10   Basic Constituents in $FA\ell(n)/\langle f \rangle_{cl}$

We would like to prove that if $FA\ell(n)/\langle f \rangle_{cl} \equiv FA\ell(n)/\langle g \rangle_{cl}$, then $\mathcal{Z}(f)$ and $\mathcal{Z}(g)$ have the same number of components (respectively basic constituents) of the *same* type and of the same dimension and that in each component, the corresponding intersections of the various constituents are the same.

Assume that $\mathcal{Z}(f)$ has only one component, having basic constituents $\mathcal{Z}(f_1)$, ..., $\mathcal{Z}(f_m)$. We would like to show that this is $\mathcal{L}$-expressible. Unfortunately, there is no classification of simplicial complexes in general which is suitable for our purposes. We therefore confine our attention to "special" $\mathcal{Z}(f)$ in the following lemmata and provide $\mathcal{L}$-expressibility only in such $FA\ell(n)/\langle f \rangle_{cl}$. This will allow us to adapt the ideas of [6], and will suffice for our applications in the following two sections. We first establish

Lemma 29. *Let* $n \in \mathbb{Z}_+$ *and* $f \in FA\ell(n)_+$ *with* $Z(f)$ *integrally ℓ-equivalent to a closed convex cone of dimension n_1. Then for each $j \in \{-1, 0, , \ldots, n_1 - 1\}$, there is a formula* $\psi^*_{n_1, j}(x)$ *such that*

$$FA\ell(n)/\langle f \rangle_{cl} \models \psi^*_{n_1, j}(h + \langle f \rangle_{cl}) \text{ iff } dim(\mathcal{Z}(f) \cap \mathcal{Z}(h)) = j.$$

Proof: Without loss of generality, we may assume that $Z(f)$ is a closed convex cone of dimension n_1. Let $\psi_{n,j}(x)$ be the formula from [6] (Definition 4.1) whose validity in $FA\ell(n)$ is equivalent to $dim(\mathcal{Z}(x)) = j$, where $j \in \{-1, 0, \ldots, n-1\}$.

We prove the lemma by induction on $j < n_1$. This is clear for $j = k := n_1 - 1$ as $\psi_{k,k-1}(h) := (\exists g > 0)(g \perp h)$. In [6], $\phi_{k,k-1}(h)$ denoted the following formula:

$$\psi_{k,k-1}(h) \ \& \ (\forall g > 0)(g \perp f \rightarrow (\exists k)(k \perp f \ \& \ \theta_S(k))).$$

Now consider $\psi_{k,j}(h)$ with $j < k - 1$, from [6]. This formula was defined using the auxiliary formula:

$$\chi(a) := (\exists a_1, a_2 > 0) \ \chi(a, a_1, a_2), \quad \text{where}$$

$$\chi(a, a_1, a_2) := a > 0 \ \& \ a = a_1 \vee a_2 \ \& \ \neg\psi_{n,n-1}(a) \ \& \ \bigwedge_{i=1}^{2} \phi_{n,n-1}(a_i) \ \& \ a_1 \perp a_2.$$

Then $\psi_{k,j}(h) := \exists a \ (\chi(a) \ \& \ \psi^r_{k-1,j}(h, a))$.

Let $\pi^{(n_1)} = (\pi_1 \vee 0) \vee \cdots \vee (\pi_{n_1} \vee 0)$. Since $FA\ell(n)/\langle f \rangle_{cl} \cong FA\ell(n_1)/\langle \pi^{(n_1)} \rangle_{cl}$, we get that

$$FA\ell(n)/\langle f \rangle_{cl} \models \psi_{n_1, j}(h + \langle f \rangle_{cl})$$

$$\text{iff}$$

$$FA\ell(n_1)/\langle \pi^{(n_1)} \rangle_{cl} \models \psi_{n_1, j}(h + \langle \pi^{(n_1)} \rangle_{cl}).$$

So we need only show that this latter holds iff $dim(\mathcal{Z}(h) \cap \mathcal{Z}(\pi^{(n_1)})) = j$.

If $n_1 = n$, we can replace the formulae $\psi_{n,j}(x)$ by $\psi_{n,j}(x \vee \pi^{(n_1)})$ $(j = 0, \ldots, n-1)$. So assume that $n_1 < n$.

The key is that as $Z(\pi^{(n_1)})$ is a convex cone of dimension strictly less than n, there is $a \in FA\ell(n)_+$ satisfying $\chi(x)$ such that its zero-set includes the zero-set of $\pi^{(n_1)}$. If $I(a) := \langle a \rangle_{cl} \subseteq FA\ell(n)$, then

$$FA\ell(n)/\langle \pi^{(n_1)}_{cl} \rangle \cong (FA\ell(n)/I(a))/\langle \pi^{(n_1)} + I(a) \rangle_{cl};$$

and the latter is isomorphic to $FA\ell(n-1)/\langle\pi_a\rangle_{cl}$, where π_a is the restriction of $\pi^{(n_1)}$ to the zero-set of a (viewed as a subset of $\mathbb{R}^{n-1}$). Moreover,

$$FA\ell(n-1)/\langle\pi_a\rangle_{cl} \cong (FA\ell(n)/I(a))/\langle\pi^{(n_1)}+I(a)\rangle_{cl}.$$

By induction, there are formulae $\psi^*_{n_1,j}(x)$ such that

$$FA\ell(n-1)/\langle\pi_a\rangle_{cl} \models \psi^*_{n_1,j}(h+\langle\pi_a\rangle_{cl}) \quad \text{iff} \quad dim(\mathcal{Z}(\pi_a)\cap\mathcal{Z}(h)) = j$$

$(j=-1,\ldots,n_1-1)$. So, for such j, we have

$$FA\ell(n)/\langle\pi^{(n_1)}\rangle_{cl} \models \psi^*_{n_1,j}(h+\langle\pi_a\rangle_{cl}) \quad \text{iff} \quad dim(\mathcal{Z}(\pi^{(n_1)})\cap\mathcal{Z}(h)) = j,$$

as desired.   □

We next consider the case when $\mathcal{Z}(f)$ is definably connected.

Lemma 30. *Let* $n \in \mathbb{Z}_+$ *and* $f \in FA\ell(n)_+$ *with* $\mathcal{Z}(f)$ *definably connected. Suppose that* $f_1,\cdots,f_m \in FA\ell(n)_+$ *with* $Z(f) = \bigcup_{i=1}^m Z(f_i)$ *where each* $Z(f_i)$ *is integrally ℓ-equivalent to a closed convex cone of dimension* $n_i \le n$ *and assume that this decomposition is minimal such. Let* $n_0 = max\{n_1,\ldots,n_m\}$. *Then for each* $j \in \{-1,0,,\ldots,n_0-1\}$, *there is a formula* $(\psi^*_{n_i,j})^z(x,y)$ *with* $n_i \ge j$ *such that*

$$FA\ell(n)/\langle f\rangle_{cl} \models \bigvee_{1\le i\le m}(\psi^*_{n_i,j})^z(h+\langle f\rangle_{cl}, f_i+\langle f\rangle_{cl}) \quad \text{iff} \quad dim(\mathcal{Z}(f)\cap\mathcal{Z}(h)) \ge j.$$

Proof: We first show that for any formula γ, we can construct a formula γ^z such that for any $\bar{h} \subset FA\ell(n)$,

$$FA\ell(n)/\langle f_i\rangle_{cl} \models \gamma(\bar{h}+\langle f_i\rangle_{cl}) \quad \text{iff} \quad FA\ell(n)/\langle f\rangle_{cl} \models \gamma^z(\bar{h}, f_i).$$

We proceed as in Lemma 4.6 in [6] by induction on the complexity of γ.

It suffices to define γ^z when γ is an atomic formula; *i.e.*, of the form $t(\bar{h}) = 0$, where $t(\bar{x})$ is a term. Then $t(\bar{h}+\langle f_i\rangle_{cl}) = 0$ iff $t(\bar{h}) \in \langle f_i\rangle_{cl}$ iff the restriction of $t(\bar{h})$ to $Z(f_i)$ is equal to 0 iff $Z(f_i) \subseteq Z(t(\bar{h}))$ iff $(\forall k>0)(k \perp f_i \rightarrow k \perp t(\bar{h}))$.

Let $h > 0$ be such that $dim(\mathcal{Z}(f)\cap\mathcal{Z}(h)) = j$.

This implies that $dim(\mathcal{Z}(f_i)\cap\mathcal{Z}(h)) = j$ for some $i \in \{1,\ldots,m\}$.

By Lemma 29, there is a formula $\psi^*_{n_i,j}(x)$ such that

$$FA\ell(n)/\langle f_i\rangle_{cl} \models \psi^*_{n_i,j}(h+\langle f_i\rangle_{cl}) \quad \text{iff} \quad dim(\mathcal{Z}(f_i)\cap\mathcal{Z}(h)) = j.$$

Now, by the above,

$$FA\ell(n)/\langle f_i\rangle_{cl} \models \psi^*_{n_i,j}(h+\langle f_i\rangle_{cl}) \quad \text{iff}$$

$$FA\ell(n)/\langle f\rangle_{cl} \models (\psi^*_{n_i,j})^z(h+\langle f\rangle_{cl}, f_i+\langle f\rangle_{cl}).$$

Conversely, assume that for some $1 \le i \le m$, there exists $0 \le j \le n_i$ such that

$$FA\ell(n)/\langle f\rangle_{cl} \models (\psi^*_{n_i,j})^z(h+\langle f\rangle_{cl}, f_i+\langle f\rangle_{cl}).$$

By the above,

$$FA\ell(n)/\langle f_i \rangle_{cl} \models \psi^*_{n_i,j}(h + \langle f_i \rangle_{cl}).$$

By Lemma 29,

$$dim(\mathcal{Z}(f_i) \cap \mathcal{Z}(h)) = j.$$

Therefore,

$$dim(\mathcal{Z}(f) \cap \mathcal{Z}(h)) \geq j.$$

□

Proposition 6. *Let* $f \in FA\ell(n)$ *and suppose that* $\mathcal{Z}(f)$ *is definably connected of dimension* $n-1$ *and satisfies the hypotheses of the previous lemma. Then* $FA\ell(n)/\langle f \rangle_{cl} \not\equiv FA\ell(n)$.

Proof: First assume that $Z(f)=Z(\pi_n \vee 0)$. View $FA\ell(n-1)$ as generated by $\pi_2, \cdots, \pi_n$. Then

$$(FA\ell(n)/\langle \pi_n \vee 0 \rangle_{cl})/\langle \pi_1 \rangle_{cl} \cong FA\ell(n-1)/\langle \pi_n \vee 0 \rangle_{cl}.$$

By the induction hypothesis, there is a sentence τ that holds in $FA\ell(n-1)/\langle \pi_n \vee 0 \rangle_{cl}$ but not in $FA\ell(n-1)$.

By Lemma 4.6 in [6], given any sentence σ one can construct a *relativized* formula $\sigma^r(\pi_1)$ such that $FA\ell(n-1) \models \sigma$ iff $FA\ell(n) \models \sigma^r(\pi_1)$.

We need the corresponding result for $FA\ell(n-1)/\langle \pi_n \vee 0 \rangle_{cl}$; *i.e.*, given any sentence σ,

$$FA\ell(n-1)/\langle \pi_n \vee 0 \rangle_{cl} \models \sigma \quad \text{iff} \quad FA\ell(n)/\langle \pi_n \vee 0 \rangle_{cl} \models \sigma^r(\pi_1).$$

To define an $\mathcal{L}$-sentence $\bar{\tau}$ which distinguishes the ℓ-groups, we use the formula $\chi(x)$ defined in Lemma 4.5 in [6] (see the proof of Lemma 29 above).

Recall that if $f \in FA\ell(n)_+$ and $FA\ell(n) \models \chi(f)$, then there is $f' \geq f$ such that $FA\ell(n) \models \chi(f')$ and an isomorphism $\vartheta : FA\ell(n)/\langle f' \rangle_{cl} \cong FA\ell(n-1)$. Moreover, this element f' satisfies the minimality condition that for any $g \in FA\ell(n)_+$ with $Z(g) \subsetneq Z(f')$, we have $FA\ell(n) \models \neg\chi(g)$. Additionally, for $j \in \{-1, 0, \ldots, n-1\}$

$$dim\mathcal{Z}(\vartheta(h+ < f' >_{cl})) = j \quad \text{iff} \quad dim(\mathcal{Z}(h) \cap \mathcal{Z}(f')) = j.$$

Consequently, the sentence $\bar{\tau}$ is given by

$$(\exists h > 0) \, (\chi(h) \, \& \, (\forall h' \geq h)(\chi(h') \rightarrow \, \tau^r(h)).$$

Indeed, $FA\ell(n)/\langle \pi_n \vee 0 \rangle_{cl} \models \bar{\tau}$ since we may choose $h = \pi_1$. On the other hand, by way of contradiction, suppose that for some element $h \in FA\ell(n)_+$, we have $FA\ell(n) \models \chi(h) \, \& \, (\forall h' \geq h)(\chi(h') \rightarrow \, \tau^r(h))$. Choose $h' \geq h$ to be a π_1-like element; this implies that $FA\ell(n) \models \tau^r(h')$. Therefore, $FA\ell(n)/\langle h' \rangle_{cl} \cong FA\ell(n-1) \models \tau$, which contradicts the induction hypothesis.

Now consider the general case. Without loss of generality, we may assume that $Z(f)$ includes $Z((-\pi_1 \vee 0) \vee (-\pi_2 \vee 0) \vee \cdots \vee (-\pi_n \vee 0))$. Now

$$FA\ell(n)/\langle \pi_1 - \pi_2 \rangle_{cl} \cong FA\ell(n-1),$$

and $(FA\ell(n)/\langle f \rangle_{cl})/\langle \pi_1 - \pi_2 \rangle_{cl} \cong FA\ell(n-1)/\langle f' \rangle_{cl}$ for some $f' \in FA\ell(n-1)_+$, where $Z(f')$ contains $Z((-\pi_2 \vee 0) \vee \cdots \vee (-\pi_n \vee 0))$.

We may therefore apply the induction hypothesis: there is a sentence τ that holds in $FA\ell(n-1)/\langle f' \rangle_{cl}$ but not in $FA\ell(n-1)$.

The same proof as above shows that the sentence $\bar\tau$ distinguishes $FA\ell(n)/\langle f \rangle_{cl}$ from $FA\ell(n)$. $\quad\square$

Proposition 7. *Let $f, g \in FA\ell(n)_+$ with $Z(f), Z(g)$ satisfying the hypotheses of Lemma 30. Then $FA\ell(n)/\langle f \rangle_{cl} \not\equiv FA\ell(n)/\langle g \rangle_{cl}$ if $dim(Z(f)) \neq dim(Z(g))$.*

Proof: Let $dim(Z(g)) = n_2 < dim(Z(f)) = n_1 \leq n$. In $FA\ell(n)/\langle f \rangle_{cl}$ we can find $n_1 + 1$ strictly positive elements $h_0, h_1, \cdots, h_{n_1}$ such that $dim(Z(f) \cap Z(h_i)) = i$, for $0 \leq i \leq n_1$. $\quad\square$

Using the previous results in this section, we can generalise (the proof of) Lemmata 14 and 15.

Let $f \in FA\ell(n)_+$ and $f_1, \cdots, f_m \in FA\ell(n)$ with $Z(f_i)$ non-trivial convex cones such that $Z(f) = \cup_{i=1}^m Z(f_i)$ and this decomposition is the minimal such. For each $j = -1, 0, \ldots, n-1$, let $c(f, j)$ be the number of elements in $D_j := \{i \in \{1, \ldots, m\} : dim(Z(f_i)) = j\}$. Let $C(f) = (c(f, -1), c(f, 0), \ldots, c(f, n-1)) \in \mathbb{N}^{n+1}$.

Lemma 31. *Let $f, g \in FA\ell(n)_+$. Then $FA\ell(n)/\langle f \rangle_{cl} \equiv FA\ell(n)/\langle g \rangle_{cl}$ implies $C(f) = C(g)$.*

As noted in Example B, the converse is false. We need to be able to detect different types of subsets of $S^{(n-1)}$ of dimension j and different types of simplices. This is where the lack of a classification of such types is a crucial obstacle.

11   Undecidability

In this section we complete the proof of Theorem 2.

Theorem 9. *Let $n \in \mathbb{Z}_+$ and $f \in FA\ell(n)_+$. If $dim(Z(f)) > 2$, then the theory of $FA\ell(n)/\langle f \rangle_{cl}$ is undecidable.*

We first recall Grzegorczyk's conditions on a topological theory that imply undecidability.

The topological space is Hausdorff, connected and is normal (*i.e.*, two disjoint closed sets are contained in disjoint open sets); it has a countable basis, and every non-empty closed subset contains a closed subset that is minimal. Further, if A and B are two finite closed subsets, then

(i) if $A \cap B = \emptyset$ and $A \cup B$ is included in a connected open subset E, then there exist two connected open sets $C \supseteq A$ and $D \supseteq B$ such that $C \cap D = \emptyset$ and $C \cup D \subseteq E$; and

(ii) if there exists a bijection between A and B, then there exists a closed set C such that $A \cup B \subseteq C$ and every component D of C contains exactly one point of A and one point of B. (Recall that a component is the union of all connected subsets of C containing a given element of C.)

We now prove Theorem 9.

Proof: We first establish the result when $n = 3$.

By the Feferman-Vaught Theorem and the proof of Theorem 8, it is enough to prove the result for $\mathcal{Z}(f)$ a single connected component which is a "disc" (if $\mathcal{Z}(f)$ is the entire 2-sphere, then $FA\ell(3)/\langle f \rangle_{cl} \cong FA\ell(3)$, which has undecidable theory [6]; and if $\mathcal{Z}(f)$ is not the entire 2-sphere, we can recognise a triangle ($\sim_\ell$ disc) in it.) We therefore assume that $\mathcal{Z}(f)$ is the closed upper half sphere $S_+^{(2)}$.

We wish to use the same technique as in [6]. The difficulty is that $\mathcal{Z}(f)$ no longer satisfies Grzegorczyk's conditions as condition (i) fails for A, B two element subsets of the equator each intersecting every equatorial arc containing the other. So we need to slightly modify our proof from [6].

Consider a latitudinal circle L in C which is disjoint from the equator. This is recognisable using $\iota_c(x)$ (see Section 9.4). Although we have been unable to recognise L from its union with a finite set of points and arcs in $S_+^{(2)}$ (the arcs all lying on the equator), the $\mathcal{L}$-formula does provide elements $g_1^\#$ and $g_2^\#$ whose supports are respectively the points in $S_+^{(2)}$ above L and those below. Now the analysis given in the proof of (II) and (III) of Proposition 5 applies: given 4 points on L we can always join them in pairs (in $S_+^{(2)}$) without crossing, and we can convert this into an $\mathcal{L}$-formula as in the proof of Proposition 5. The proof applies not just to a_i with the closure of their supports containing points of L but also to arbitrary $a_i \leq g_1^\#$ (satisfying the hypotheses in that proof) whose supports are contained in $\mathcal{S}(g_1^\#)$, provided we let one of h_1 and h_2 have support intersecting $\mathcal{S}(g_2^\#) \subseteq \mathcal{Z}(f)$. However, it fails for $\mathcal{S}(g_2^\#)$ if we take the a_i to have supports whose closure includes equatorial points. Thus we can distinguish $g_1^\#$ from $g_2^\#$ in $\mathcal{L}$. Now $\mathcal{S}(g_1^\#) \subseteq \mathcal{Z}(f)$ is the set of points in $S_+^{(2)}$ above L (modulo a finite set of points). It satisfies *all* of Grzegorczyk's conditions *when viewed inside* $\mathcal{Z}(f)$ provided that we consider the open subsets of the whole upper half sphere.

We can interpret this sublattice of zero-sets using the dimension formulae $\psi_{3,j}$ (see Lemma 30). By Grzegorczyk's result, it follows that $FA\ell(3)/\langle f \rangle_{cl}$ has undecidable theory. Thus the theorem holds if $n = 3$ and $Z(f)$ has dimension at least 3.

We now extend the analysis when $n \geq 4$. Again, by the Feferman-Vaught Theorem, we may assume that $\mathcal{Z}(f)$ is connected. If Grzegorczyk's condition (i) holds, all his conditions are satisfied and the result is proved. We therefore assume that his condition (i) fails in $\mathcal{Z}(f)$.

The analysis of formula $\sigma(g, g_1, g_2, k)$ given in Section 9.4 applies for $n \geq 4$ with minor variations. Firstly, the conditions imply that $\mathcal{Z}(g) \cap \mathcal{Z}(f)$ cannot have relative maximal dimension ℓ in any basic constituent of dimension ℓ, and that $\mathcal{S}(g) \cap \mathcal{Z}(f)$ is not the union of two disjoint sets each of the form $\mathcal{S}(g') \cap \mathcal{Z}(f)$ for some $g' \in FA\ell(n)_+$. Furthermore, by (iii), (iv) and (v), $\mathcal{Z}(g) \cap \mathcal{Z}(f)$ is the intersection of two zero sets (with disjoint non-empty interiors), the intersection of either with a basic constituent of $\mathcal{Z}(f)$ being either empty or of the dimension of that basic constituent. Again, by (vii), $\mathcal{Z}(g) \cap \mathcal{Z}(f)$ is not a single point and the same is true when this is intersected with any connected $\mathcal{S}(k)$ that is not disjoint from the support of both $g_1^\#$ and $g_2^\#$. Thus $\mathcal{Z}(g) \cap \mathcal{Z}(f)$ is a finite union of sets (each of dimension at least 1) and each d dimensional constituent lying in a d'-dimensional subset of $\mathcal{Z}(f)$ with $d' > d$. By (vi), $\mathcal{S}(k)$ is connected as is its restriction to $\mathcal{S}(g_1^\#)$ and $\mathcal{S}(g_2^\#)$. So $\mathcal{S}(k)$ cannot "pinch" $\mathcal{Z}(g)$ if $\mathcal{Z}(g)$ is a single connected set. The condition also ensures that $\mathcal{S}(k)$ cannot be "essentially" shrunk.

Next consider the formula $\iota_c(g)$ from the proof of Proposition 4 in Section 9.4. The support of any element k which features in the formula has dimension greater than that of $\mathcal{Z}(g)$. If $dim(\mathcal{Z}(g)) > 1$, then $dim(\mathcal{S}(k)) \geq 3$. Hence there is $h \geq a_1 \vee a_2$ with $\theta_S(h \wedge k)$ and $h \perp a_3$ as we have the necessary "degrees of freedom" to move inside k and avoid a_3 when the $\mathcal{S}(a_j)$ are balls of sufficiently small radius inside $\mathcal{S}(k)$. This contradicts the conjunct $\iota_1(g, f)$ of $\iota_c(g, f)$. Therefore, $dim(\mathcal{Z}(g)) = 1$.

Since $\mathcal{Z}(g)$ cuts $\mathcal{Z}(f)$, it follows that $\mathcal{Z}(g) \cap \mathcal{Z}(f')$ includes an "interior circle" Γ inside a basic constituent $\mathcal{Z}(f')$ of $\mathcal{Z}(f)$ (where $dim(\mathcal{Z}(f')) = 2$); indeed, $\mathcal{Z}(g) \cap \mathcal{Z}(f')$ is Γ together with, possibly, a finite set of arcs and points, all arcs being contained in the boundary of $\mathcal{Z}(f')$. We may again distinguish $g_1^\#$ from $g_2^\#$ and assume that $\mathcal{S}(g_1^\#)$ is the set of points inside Γ (modulo a finite set of points). We can again relativise and specialise, just as in the $n = 3$ case. Hence the proof of the undecidability of $Th(FA\ell(3)/\langle f \rangle_{cl})$ when $dim(\mathcal{Z}(f)) = 2$ applies equally to $Th(FA\ell(n)/\langle f \rangle_{cl})$. This completes the proof of the theorem.

$\square$

12 MV-Algebras

Let $n \in \mathbb{Z}_+$ and f be a piecewise linear continuous function from $[0, 1]^n$ to $[0, 1]$; i.e., there is a finite cover $X_1, \ldots, X_m$ of $[0, 1]^n$ into closed connected subsets with pairwise dijoint interiors and linear functions $f_1, \cdots, f_m$, such that $f(x) = f_j(x)$ for all $x \in X_j$ ($j = 1, \ldots, m$). Note that each f_j has the form: $\sum_{1 \leq i \leq n} a_i \pi_i + b_i$, where $\pi_i(x_1, \cdots, x_n) = x_i$ and $a_i, b_i \in \mathbb{Z}$. This set of functions, $\mathcal{M}c_n$ (the set of McNaughton functions), is closed under the operations: $f^* = 1 - f$, $f_1 \oplus f_2 = min(1, f_1 + f_2)$, and $f_1.f_2 = max(0, f_1 + f_2 - 1)$. One can easily check that $\mathcal{M}c_n := (M, \oplus, ^*, 0)$ is an MV-algebra (see Definition 1.1.1 in [4]). Indeed, $\mathcal{M}c_n$ is isomorphic to FMV_n, the free MV-algebra on n generators. (see Theorem 9.1.5 in [4].)

Let G be an abelian ℓ-group and $u \in G_+$. Then u is said to be a *strong order unit* of G if for all $g \in G$ there is $n = n(g) \in \mathbb{N}$ such that $g \leq nu$. In this case, let $[0, u]$ be the set $\{g \in G : 0 \leq g \leq u\}$. For $x, y \in G$, let $x \oplus y := u \wedge (x + y)$ and $x^* := u - x$. Then $\Gamma(G, u) := (G, \oplus, ^*, 0)$ is an MV algebra (see Proposition 2.1.2 in [4]).

The application $\Gamma : (G, u) \rightarrow \Gamma(G, u)$ defines a functor from the category of abelian ℓ-groups with strong order units to the category of MV-algebras.

Theorem 10.   *1. FMV_1 is decidable.*
2. FMV_n with $n \geq 2$ is undecidable.

Proof: (1) We can interpret FMV_1 in $FA\ell(2)$ which is decidable [6], the constant 1 being interpreted by $|\pi|_1 \vee |\pi_2|$.

(2) Let $\pi^{(n+1)} = (\pi_1 \vee 0) \vee \cdots \vee (\pi_{n+1} \vee 0)$. The theory of $FA\ell(n+1)/\langle \pi^{(n+1)} \rangle_{cl}$ is undecidable by Theorem 9 and Lemma 30. The same proof shows that the theory of the ℓ-group $(FA\ell(n+1)/\langle \pi^{(n+1)} \rangle_{cl}, u + \langle \pi^{(n+1)} \rangle_{cl})$ with distinguished element $u + \langle \pi^{(n+1)} \rangle_{cl}$ has undecidable theory whenever u is an element with trivial zero-set in $FA\ell(n + 1)$. But FMV_n is bi-interpretable with $\Gamma(FA\ell(n + 1)/\langle \pi^{(n+1)} \rangle_{cl}, u + \langle \pi^{(n+1)} \rangle_{cl})$. Consequently, its theory is also undecidable.   □

Acknowledgements. This work began during a conference in Irkusk in August 2004; we would like to thank Vasily Bludov for inviting us and for his hospitality. It continued in Cambridge during a program in Model Theory and its Applications at the Isaac Newton Institute (January-June 2005). We are most grateful to Dennis Barden, W. B. R. Lickorish and Burt Totaro (DPMMS, Cambridge) for thoughts, references and valuable suggestions during that period. Finally, we wish to thank Vincenzo Marra for further helpful discussions at the 2nd Vienna-Florence Logic Conference in Florence in November 2005.

References

1. Baker, K.A.: Free vector lattices. Canad. J. Math. 20, 58–66 (1968)
2. Beynon, W.M.: Duality theorems for finitely generated vector lattices. Proc. London Math. Soc. 31(3), 114–128 (1975)
3. Beynon, W.M.: Applications of duality in the theory of finitely generated lattice-ordered abelian groups. Can. J. Math. 29(2), 243–254 (1977)
4. Cignoli, R., d'Ottaviano, I., Mundici, D.: Algebraic foundations of many-valued reasoning. Trends in Logic, vol. 7. Kluwer Academic publishers, Dordrecht (2000)
5. Glass, A.M.W.: Partially ordered groups. Series in Algebra, vol. 7. World Scientific Pub. Co., Singapore (1999)
6. Glass, A.M.W., Macintyre, A.J., Point, F.: Free abelian lattice-ordered groups. Annals of Pure and Applied Logic 134, 265–283 (2005)
7. Glass, A.M.W., Madden, J.J.: The word problem versus the isomorphism problem. J. London Math. Soc. 30(1), 53–61 (1984)
8. Grzegorczyk, A.: Undecidability of some topological theories. Fund. Math. 38, 137–152 (1951)

9. Marra, V., Mundici, D.: Combinatorial fans, lattice-ordered groups, and their neighbours: a short excursion. Séminaire Lotharingien de Combinatoire 47, B47 (2002)

10. Semmes, S.: Real analysis, quantitative topology and geometric complexity. Publicacions matematiques (Barcelona) 45, 3–67, 265–333 (2001)

11. Whittlesey, E.F.: Classification of finite 2-complexes. Proc. Amer. Math. Soc. 9, 841–845 (1958)

On Fuzzy Theories with Crisp Sentences[*]

Petr Hájek

Institute of Computer Science
Academy of Sciences of the Czech Republic
182 07 Prague, Czech Republic
hajek@cs.cas.cz

Abstract. If T is a consistent theory over a fuzzy predicate logic with Gödel negation (e.g. Gödel logic, product logic) then T remains consistent after adding the schema tertium non datur ($\varphi \vee \neg\varphi$) for sentences (closed formulas). We prove and discuss this.

1 Introduction

For fuzzy logics given by continuous t-norms see [4] and/or the survey papers [3] (propositional logics) and [1] (predicate logics). Recall Łukasiewicz's, Gödel's and the product t-norms Also recall the Mostert-Shields representation of each continuous t-norm as the ordered sum of isomorphic copies of the just named t-norms. Each continuous t-norm $*$ defines a t-norm algebra $[0,1]_*$ on the real unit interval with the lattice operations min, max, the operation $*$ and its residuum $\Rightarrow$.

Now t-norm algebras are particular BL-algebras (the variety of BL-algebras is generated by t-norm algebras). Each BL-algebra serves as algebra of truth functions of conjunction & and implication $\Rightarrow$. BL is the propositional logic of all BL-algebras and, at the same time of all linearly ordered BL algebras and of all t-norm algebras.

Particular continuous t-norms define stronger logics (notably Łukasiewicz, Gödel, product) and subvarieties of BL-algebras. Negation is defined as $\neg\varphi$ being $\varphi \to \bar{0}$ (φ implies falsity). Łukasiewicz logic proves the double negation axiom $\varphi \equiv \neg\neg\varphi$ and over $[0,1]$, $\neg x = 1 - x$. Gödel negation over $[0,1]$ is $\neg 0 = 1$, $\neg x = 0$ for $x > 0$. This is the negation of Gödel logic, product logic and in general of each continuous t-norm logic except t-norms whose first component in the Mostert-Shields representation is Łukasiewicz. The logic with Gödel negation SBL is BL extended by the schema $\neg(\varphi \& \psi) \to (\neg\varphi \vee \neg\psi)$ (see [2]). (SBL stands for strict basic logic.) Recall that $(\varphi \wedge \psi)$ is $\varphi \& (\varphi \to \psi)$, $(\varphi \vee \psi)$ is $((\varphi \vee \psi) \to \psi) \wedge ((\psi \to \varphi) \to \varphi)$.

For each predicate language and each BL-algebra **A** one defines safe **A** interpretations of the language; for a natural system BL$\forall$ of axioms and deduction rules we have *strong general completeness* saying that for any theory T and formula φ, T proves φ over BL$\forall$ iff for every linearly ordered BL-algebra **L**, φ has

---

[*] The author was partly supported by grant A100300503 of the Grant Agency of the Academy of Sciences of the Czech Republic and partly by the Institutional Research Plan AV0Z10300504.

S. Aguzzoli et al.(Eds.): Algebraic and Proof-theoretic Aspects, LNAI 4460, pp. 194–200, 2007.
© Springer-Verlag Berlin Heidelberg 2007

value 1 in each safe **A** interpretation which is a model of T. This gives analogous completeness theorems for logics given by a particular continuous t-norm and the corresponding variety, thus e.g. Ł$\forall$, G$\forall$, $\Pi\forall$, SBL$\forall$, etc.

In his [7], Turunen proves two remarkable Theorems 5 and 6 on locally finite BL-algebras (a BL-algebra **A** is locally finite if for each $x \in A$ different from 1 there is a natural n such that $a^n = 0, a^n$ being $A * \cdots * a, n$ times). They can be immediately paraphrased as speaking on (propositional) theories over a given fuzzy logic (BL or its schematic extension).

Theorem 1. *(Turunen interpreted) Let T be a maximal consistent theory over a propositional fuzzy logic $\mathcal{L}$; then T proves each instance of the double negation schema $\neg\neg\varphi \equiv \varphi$, thus T proves all tautologies of Łukasiewicz logic.*

Now SBL (and each logic with Gödel negation) proves the schema $\neg\varphi \vee \neg\neg\varphi$ so that if a propositional theory over such logic extends also Łukasiewicz then it proves $\varphi \vee \neg\varphi$ and hence all tautologies of classical (Boolean) logic.

Our main topic si to see what consequences this result has for fuzzy predicate logics, in particular for logics with Gödel negation.

In Sect. 2 we prove a variant of Turunen's result for predicate calculus(just his proof).

For theories over predicate logics we get provability of the schema of double negation for *closed* formulas and we shall discuss consequences of it. In particular, for logics with Gödel negation we are led to the negation of *theories with crisp sentences*, i.e. proving $\varphi \vee \neg\varphi$ for each *sentence* φ. In Sect. 3 we give some examples and formulate some open problems.

2   Maximal Consistent Theories

Assume a predicate fuzzy logic (schematic extension of BL$\forall$) to be given. *Sentences* are closed formulas.

Definition 1. *(1) A theory T over $\mathcal{L}$ is consistent if $T \nvdash \overline{0}$ (equivalently, if there is a sentence unprovable in T).*
(2) T is maximal consistent if T is consistent and for each sentence φ unprovable in T, $T \cup \{\varphi\}$ is inconsistent.
(3) T is locally finite if for each sentence φ unprovable in T there is in $n \geq 1$ such that $T \vdash \varphi^n \to \overline{0}$ (φ^n being $\varphi \& \ldots \& \varphi$, n copies).

Lemma 1. *If T is a maximal consistent theory then T is locally finite.*

Proof. If $T \nvdash \varphi$ (φ a sentence) then $T \cup \{\varphi\}$ is inconsistent (due to maximality), hence $T \cup \{\varphi\} \vdash \overline{0}$, thus, by the deduction theorem (cf. [4] 5.1.23), there is an n such that $T \vdash \varphi^n \to \overline{0}$, i.e. $T \vdash \neg(\varphi^n)$.

Lemma 2. *If T is locally finite, $T \nvdash \varphi$, and $T \nvdash \neg\varphi$ (φ a sentence) then $T \nvdash \neg\neg\varphi$.*

Proof. Assume $T \nvdash \varphi, T \nvdash \neg\varphi$. Let n be minimal such that $T \vdash \varphi^n \to \overline{0}$; since $T \nvdash \varphi \to \overline{0}$, we get $n > 1$. Take a minimal such n. Then $T \vdash (\varphi^{n-1}\&\varphi) \to \overline{0}$, thus $T \vdash \varphi^{n-1} \to \neg\varphi$, hence $T \nvdash \neg\varphi \to \overline{0}$ (otherwise we would get $T \vdash \varphi^{n-1} \to \overline{0}$), which is $T \nvdash \neg\neg\varphi$.

Lemma 3. *For a consistent locally finite T and a sentence φ, $T \vdash \varphi$ iff $T \vdash \neg\neg\varphi$.*

Proof. If $T \vdash \varphi$ then trivially $T \vdash \neg\neg\varphi$. Assume $T \vdash \neg\neg\varphi$, then $T \nvdash \neg\varphi$, T being consistent. But then $T \nvdash \varphi$ would get $T \nvdash \neg\neg\varphi$ by the preceding lemma, thus $T \vdash \varphi$.

Lemma 4. *A locally finite T proves $\neg\neg\varphi \to \varphi$ for each sentence φ.*

Proof. By the preceding lemma, it is enough to show that propositional BL proves $\neg\neg(\neg\neg\varphi \to \varphi)$. A direct (rather complicated) proof may be extracted from [7], proof of Theorem 5; alternatively, you may use completeness of propositional BL and show that the formula in question is a tautology in each $[0,1]_*$ (distinguishing $*$ with Gödel negation, Łukasiewicz t-norm and a t-norm whose first component is Ł).

Theorem 2. *Each consistent theory T (over a given predicate logic $\mathcal{L}$) has a consistent extension $T' \supseteq T$ with the same language proving the double negation schema $\varphi \equiv \neg\neg\varphi$ for all **sentences** φ.*

Furthermore, T' may be taken complete as a fuzzy theory (for each pair φ, ψ of sentences, $T' \vdash (\varphi \to \psi)$ or $T' \vdash (\psi \to \varphi)$.)

Proof. Just take a maximal consistent extension T' of T (in the same language); it proves double negation schema for sentences by the lemmas above and is complete thanks to maximality: if $T' \nvdash \varphi \to \psi$ and $T' \nvdash \psi \to \varphi$ then $(T', \varphi \to \psi) \vdash \overline{0}$ and $(T', \psi \to \varphi) \vdash \overline{0}$, hence $T' \vdash \overline{0}$ by the usual proof.

Corollary 1. *Let $\mathcal{L}\forall$ be SBL$\forall$ or its schematic extension (e.g. Gödel or product predicate logic). Each consistent theory T over $\mathcal{L}\forall$ has a consistent (complete) extension T' with the same language proving the schema tertium non datur, $\varphi \lor \neg\varphi$, for each **sentence** φ.*

This is because SBL extended by the schema of double negation is equivalent to classical logic and so is BL extended by tertium non datur.

Indeed, evidently SBL$\vdash \neg(\varphi\&\varphi) \to \neg\varphi$, which is [4] 4.1.3(2). Thus SBL$\vdash \neg\varphi \lor \neg\neg\varphi$ (see the proof of [4] 4.1.3(3) using only BL and 4.1.3(2)). If you add $\neg\neg\varphi \equiv \varphi$ you get tertium non datur and BL with tertium non datur is classical propositional logic ([4] 4.3). (We use throughout the obvious fact that if one substitutes to a proof in propositional logic closed predicate formulas for propositional variables we get a proof in the predicate calculus.)

Remark 1. Note that if T' is maximal consistent over SBL$\forall$ (or over its schematic extension) then T' is also complete in the classical sense: for each sentence φ, either $T' \vdash \varphi$ or $T' \vdash \neg\varphi$. Indeed, if $T' \nvdash \varphi, T' \nvdash \neg\varphi$, then (T', φ) is inconsistent, hence $T' \vdash (\varphi^n) \to \bar{0}$ but $T' \vdash \varphi^n \equiv \varphi$ (since T' proves all closed predicate intences of tautologies of the classical propositional calculus); thus $T' \vdash \varphi \to \bar{0}$, analogously $T' \vdash (\neg\varphi) \to \bar{0}$, hence $T' \vdash (\varphi \vee \neg\varphi) \to \bar{0}$, T' is inconsistent which is a contradiction.

3 Discussion

We discuss theories over $\mathcal{L}\forall$ where $\mathcal{L}$ is a schematic extension of SBL, thus $\mathcal{L}\forall$ is a predicate logic with Gödel negation.

Definition 2. *A theory T has crisp sentences if it proves tertium non datur $\varphi \vee \neg\varphi$ for all sentences φ.*

Then in each model $\mathbf{M}$ of T the truth value of each sentence is 1 or 0. Our result says that if T is consistent then its extension by the schema tertium non datur for sentences is consistent and has crisp sentences.

First let us make clear that a model of a theory with crisp sentences need not be crisp, i.e. truth values of formulas with variables need not be 0 or 1. Moreover, a theory with crisp sentences consistent over our logic $\mathcal{L}$ may be inconsistent as a theory over classical logic, as the following example shows.

Example 1. In the sequel, $T^{\#}$ is the theory having just one unary predicate P and two axioms,

$$\neg(\forall x)P(x), \neg(\exists x)\neg P(x).$$

Clearly $T^{\#}$ is consistent over SBL. Let $M = N$ and for each $n \in N$, let the value of P for n be $r_P(n) = 1/(n+1)$. Call this model $M^{\#}$. Then for any continuous t-norm $*$ with Gödel negation $\|(\forall x)P(x)\|^*_{\mathbf{M}^{\#}} = 0$ and $\|(\exists x)\neg P(x)\|^*_{\mathbf{M}^{\#}} = 0$, thus $\mathbf{M}^{\#}$ is a $*$-model of $T^{\#}$. (Note that a linearly ordered BL-algebra is an SBL-algebra iff it has Gödel negation, see [2] Lemma 1.) Thus in particular, $T^{\#}$ is consistent over $G\forall$ and $\varPi\forall$. But of course $T^{\#}$ is inconsistent over classical logic and even over $\text{Ł}\forall$ (since $\text{Ł}\forall \vdash \neg(\exists x)\neg P(x) \equiv (\forall x)P(x)$). $T^{\#}$ does not have crisp sentences: modify our model such that $\|(\exists x)P(x)\| = \frac{1}{2}$. Let $\hat{T}^{\#} \supseteq T^{\#}$ be a (consistent) theory with crisp sentences; then $\hat{T}^{\#}$ is an example of a consistent theory (over SBL$\forall$, $G\forall$, $\varPi\forall$,...) with crisp sentences having no crisp model. We have shown:

Fact 1. *There exist consistent theories with crisp sentences (over SBL$\forall$, $G\forall$, $\varPi\forall$ etc.) that are classically inconsistent.*

Would it be reasonable to investigate the logic resulting from our logic $\mathcal{L}\forall$ (where $\mathcal{L}$ is a schematic extension of SBL) by the schema tertium non datur for *sentences*?

Definition 3. $\mathcal{L}\forall(EM)$ *is the extension of the logic $\mathcal{L}\forall$ by the schema of axioms $\varphi \vee \neg\varphi$ (excluded middle alias tertium non datur) for all closed sentences.*

Warning: Such a logic is *not* a predicate calculus given by a schematic extension of SBL in the sense of [4] 5.1.7: there one demands that formulas resulting by substituting *any* predicate formulas for propositional variables of any instance of the schema are axioms. Thus theorems on predicate logics given by a schematic extension of BL do not automatically apply to $\mathcal{L}\forall$(EM). But we easily get completeness:

Theorem 3. *Let T be a predicate theory. T proves a sentence φ over $\mathcal{L}\forall$(EM) iff φ is true in all $\mathbf{L}$-models $\mathbf{M}$ of T with crisp sentences (i.e. for each sentence $\alpha, \|\alpha\|_{\mathbf{M}}^{\mathbf{L}} = 1$ or $= 0$) for any $\mathcal{L}$-algebra $\mathbf{L}$.*

Proof. If $T \vdash_{\mathcal{L}\forall(\text{EM})} \varphi$ then clearly φ is true in each such model. Conversely, if T does not prove φ over $\mathcal{L}\forall$(EM) then let T' be the extension of T by all closed instances of tertium non datur: then T' does not prove φ over $\mathcal{L}\forall$ (we have made the logical tertium non datur axioms of $\mathcal{L}\forall$(EM) to axioms of T'). Thus by completeness of $\mathcal{L}\forall$, there is a model $\mathbf{M}$ of T (over $\mathcal{L}\forall$) in which φ is not true; but since $\varphi \vee \neg\varphi$ is true $\mathbf{M}$, $\neg\varphi$ is true in $\mathbf{M}$ (everything in the sense of an $\mathcal{L}$-algebra). Then $T \cup \{\neg\varphi\}$ is consistent over $\mathcal{L}\forall$ and hence over $\mathcal{L}\forall$(EM) by a corollary above. This completes the proof.

As an example of something where $\mathcal{L}\forall$(EM) might possibly differ from logics given by schematic extensions of BL let us discuss witnessing existential formulas. Recall that if T is a theory over $\mathcal{L}\forall$, T proves a closed formula $(\exists x)\psi(x)$ and c is a new constant, then $(T, \psi(c))$ is a conservative extension of T (over $\mathcal{L}\forall$).[1] Does this hold for theories over $\mathcal{L}\forall$(EM)?

Problem 1. *Let T be a theory over $\mathcal{L}\forall$(EM) proving a sentence $(\exists x)\varphi(x)$, let c be a constant not in the language of T, let T' be the extension of T by the axiom $\varphi(c)$ (and of its language by c). Over $\mathcal{L}\forall$(EM), is T' a conservative extension of T?*

Over $\mathcal{L}\forall$ we can formulate the problem as follows: Let T be a theory with crisp sentences proving $(\exists x)\varphi(x)$. Is there a theory T' with crisp sentences (with the language extended by the constant c) which proves $\varphi(c)$ and extends T conservatively? (If yes then T extended by $\varphi(c)$ and all closed instances of the schema $\alpha(c) \vee \neg\alpha(c)$ is such a T'. Clearly, this T' is consistent of T is.)

The problem is left open; we add some comments.

Lemma 5. *Over $\mathcal{L}\forall$ the fact that T is a theory with crisp sentences proving $(\exists x)\varphi(x)$ and T_1 is $T \cup \{\varphi(c)\}$ (c a new constant) does not always imply that T_1 is a theory with crisp sentences.*

Proof. Take the theory $\hat{T}^{\#}$ as above and extend it by a unary predicate Q and the axiom $(\forall x)Q(x)$. This is our new T^*; each model of $\hat{T}^{\#}$ trivially expands to a model of T^*. Also obviously T^* has crisp sentences since each sentence of T^* is

---

[1] See [4] 5.4.17 – the proof works for any predicate logic $\mathcal{L}\forall$ for $\mathcal{L}$ being a standard extension of BL. (Caution: the proof in 5.2.15(2) is defective.)

provably equivalent to a sentence not containing Q (just replace each occurrence of $Q(x)$ by $\bar{1}$) and $\hat{T}^{\#}$ proves excluded middle for the modified formula.

Now T^* proves $(\exists x)Q(x)$; let T_1^* be T^* plus $Q(c)$. T_1^* does not have crisp sentences: in each model (over an algebra $\mathbf{L}$) of T^*, all $\mathbf{L}$-values of $P(x)$ are positive and their infimum is $0_{\mathbf{L}}$. Thus in such a model $\mathbf{M}$, any element $m \in M$ can be taken to be the interpretation of c, giving a model of T_1^*. Hence $T_1^* \not\vdash Q(c) \vee \neg Q(c)$.

We present a partial solution of the problem.

Lemma 6. *If T is maximal consistent over $\mathcal{L}\forall$ then the answer to the problem is positive.*

Proof. Let T be given and let T' be $T \cup \{\varphi(c)\}$. Then T' is consistent over $\mathcal{L}\forall$ by the classical proof. Extend T' to a consistent theory T'' in the enriched language, T'' having crisp sentences. T'' proves $(\exists x)\varphi(x)$ (over $\mathcal{L}\forall$) and extends T conservatively: let $T'' \vdash \alpha$, α being a sentence in the language of T. Then $T \vdash \alpha$ or $T \vdash \neg\alpha$ (T being maximal consistent!) but $T \vdash \neg\alpha$ would make T'' inconsistent. Thus $T \vdash \alpha$.

Definition 4. *(see [6]). A theory T is $\exists$-Henkin if for each sentence $(\exists x)\varphi(x)$ provable in T there is a constant c (in the language of T) such that $T \vdash \varphi(c)$. A theory is $\forall$-Henkin if for each sentence $(\forall x)\varphi(x)$ unprovable in T there is a constant c (in the language of T) such that $\varphi(c)$ is unprovable in T.*

Theorem 4. *Each consistent theory over $\mathcal{L}\forall$ with crisp sentences has a consistent complete $\exists$-Henkin extension with crisp sentences.*

Proof. Let T_0 be the theory given. Given T_n, first extend it to the consistent theory T_n' having for each T_n-sentence $(\exists x)\varphi(x)$ a new constant c_φ such that $T_n' \vdash \varphi(c_\varphi)$; then get T_{n+1} by extending T_n' to a maximal consistent theory in the language of T_n' (thus T_{n+1} has crisp sentences). Let $T_\infty = \bigcup_n T_n$; T_∞ is the required theory.

Remark 2. An analogous statement for $\forall$-Henkin seems to be false. At least you cannot extend each consistent theory over $\mathcal{L}\forall$ with crisp sentences to a consistent complete theory with crisp sentences which is both $\exists$-Henkin and $\forall$-Henkin. Assume you can and let $\hat{T}^{\#}$ be as above and let $\hat{T}_{He}^{\#}$ be a complete consistent theory with crisp sentences which is both $\exists$-Henkin and $\forall$-Henkin. Then the corresponding canonical model (whose object are the constants and $\|P(c_1 \ldots)\|$ is the class $[P(c_1 \ldots)]$ in the Lindenbaum algebra of $\hat{T}_{He}^{\#}$) would be crisp since the algebra is just the two-element Boolean algebra). But $\hat{T}^{\#}$ and hence any extension of $\hat{T}^{\#}$ has no crisp models as we have seen.

Several notions concerning fuzzy theories could be investigated w.r.t. the logic $\mathcal{L}\forall$(EM) (or, equivalently, w.r.t. models with crisp sentences). For example:

Problem 2. *Characterize model-theoretically conservative extension of theories and existence of witnessed models over the logic $\mathcal{L}\forall$(EM)(see [1,6,5]).*

4 Conclusion

The notion of a theory with crisp sentences (over a predicate logic with Gödel negation) appears to be a new notion with surprising properties. Hopefully it will contribute to our understanding of logics with Gödel negation. This paper brings only first analysis and leaves several things unsolved or even untouched. Any comments are welcome.

References

1. Cintula, P., Hájek, P.: Triangular norm based fuzzy predicate logics. In: Proc. 2005 Linz conference on fuzzy logic (to appear)
2. Esteva, E., Godo, L., Hájek, P., Navara, M.: Residuated fuzzy logics with involutive negation. Arch. Math. Logic 39, 103–124 (2000)
3. Gottwald, S., Hájek, P.: Triangular norm based mathematical fuzzy logics. In: Mesiar, K. (ed.) Logical, algebraic, analytic and probabilistic aspects of triangular norms, pp. 275–299. Elsevier, Amsterdam (2005)
4. Hájek, P.: Metamathematics of fuzzy logic. Kluwer, Dordrecht (1998)
5. Hájek, P.: On witnessed models in fuzzy logic. Math. Logicv Quatrly 53, 66–77 (2007)
6. Hájek, P., Cintula, P.: On theories and models in fuzzy predicate logics. The Journal of Symbolic Logic 71, 863–888 (2006)
7. Turunen, E.: Metamathematics behind fuzzy logic. Physica Verlag, Heidelberg, New York (1999)

Proof Transformations and
Structural Invariance[*]

Stefan Hetzl and Alexander Leitsch

Institute of Computer Languages (E185),
Vienna University of Technology, Favoritenstraße 9,
1040 Vienna, Austria
{hetzl,leitsch}@logic.at

Abstract. In this paper we define the concept of a profile, which is a characteristic clause set, corresponding to an **LK**-proof in first-order logic, which is invariant under rule permutations. It is shown (via cut-elimination) that the profile is even invariant under a large class of proof transformations (called "simple transformations"), which includes transformations to negation normal form. As proofs having the same profile show the same behavior w.r.t. cut-elimination (which can be formally defined via the method CERES), proofs obtained by simple transformations can be considered as equal in this sense. A comparison with related results based on proof nets is given: in particular it is shown that proofs having the same profile define a larger equivalence class than those having the same proof net.

1   Introduction

Cut-elimination introduced by Gerhard Gentzen [7] is the most prominent form of proof transformation in logic and plays an important role in automating the analysis of mathematical proofs. The removal of cuts corresponds to the elimination of intermediate statements (lemmas) from proofs resulting in a proof which is analytic in the sense, that all statements in the proof are subformulas of the result. Therefore, the proof of a combinatorial statement is converted into a purely combinatorial proof. Cut-elimination is therefore an essential tool for the analysis of proofs, especially to make implicit parameters explicit.

In [3] the cut-elimination method CERES has been defined that works by employing the resolution technique from automated theorem proving. It has been shown in [4] that it can be considered as a generalization of the usual reductive cut-elimination methods. The main proof-theoretic tool of CERES is the *characteristic clause set* which gives a concise representation of the logical material that is used to build the cut-formulas. From the fact that two proofs have the same characteristic clause set one can deduce that they basically have the same set of cut-free proofs under the CERES-method.

In this paper we define the *profile* of a proof as an improved version of the characteristic clause set that, among others, has the property of being invariant

---

[*] Supported by the Austrian Science Fund (project no. P17995-N12).

S. Aguzzoli et al.(Eds.): Algebraic and Proof-theoretic Aspects, LNAI 4460, pp. 201–230, 2007.
© Springer-Verlag Berlin Heidelberg 2007

under arbitrary rule permutations. This implies that two proofs having the same proof net (in the sense of [10]) also have the same profile.

The central part of this paper is an investigation of a certain class of proof transformations, so called simple transformations, containing as a special case for example the transformation of formulas into negation-normal-form. We show that the profile is invariant under application of simple transformations to cut formulas. This result means that proofs differing only by such a transformation show the same behavior w.r.t. cut-elimination (by the method CERES).

1.1 Related Work

In [5] Danos, Joinet and Schellinx give an elegant formulation of a class of confluent and strongly terminating cut-elimination procedures for classical logic. In [6] they build on this work to show that the normal forms are not changed after application of transformations called computational isomorphisms. Our work is similar to [6] in its conceptual aims: to isolate a class of transformations that have no effect on the cut-elimination of a proof. However, the frameworks in which these analyses are carried out are very different: [6] builds on the confluence (and termination) result established in [5] to show that *the normal form is preserved*. In this paper, we isolate a *structural invariant*, the proof profile whose preservation induces the equality of the *set of normal forms* of the cut-elimination method CERES. The former can be considered a restriction, the latter an extension of Gentzen's original cut-elimination procedure. In contrast to [6] however, we have to restrict the application of our transformations to the parts of a proof that go into cuts. We conjecture that our result also holds without this restriction, but proving this will be more difficult because the profile changes in a more complicated way.

2 Sequent Calculus

In order to distinguish different occurrences of the same formula in a sequent without having to introduce exchange rules to the calculus, we formally use sequents of indexed formulas.

Definition 1 (indexed formula). *An indexed formula is pair consisting of a formula and an index from some countable infinite index set $\mathcal{I}$.*

A sequent is a pair of multisets of formulas. An indexed sequent is a pair of sets of indexed formulas.

We distinguish countable sets of *free* and *bound* variables.

We use the following variant of sequent calculus for classical first-order logic:

Definition 2 (LK-proof). *An **LK**-proof φ is a tree. The nodes of φ are labelled with indexed sequents, the edges are labelled with rules and the leaves are axiom sequents. Furthermore each formula index occurs at most once in a proof.*

1. *Axiom sequents are of the form*

$$A \vdash A \quad \text{for an atomic formula } A$$

2. *Logical Rules*
   (a) Conjunction

$$\frac{\Gamma \vdash \Delta, A \quad \Pi \vdash \Lambda, B}{\Gamma, \Pi \vdash \Delta, \Lambda, A \wedge B} \ \wedge : r \qquad \frac{A, B, \Gamma \vdash \Delta}{A \wedge B, \Gamma \vdash \Delta} \ \wedge : l$$

   (b) Disjunction

$$\frac{A, \Gamma \vdash \Delta \quad B, \Pi \vdash \Lambda}{A \vee B, \Gamma, \Pi \vdash \Delta, \Lambda} \ \vee : l \qquad \frac{\Gamma \vdash \Delta, A, B}{\Gamma \vdash \Delta, A \vee B} \ \vee : r$$

   (c) Implication

$$\frac{\Gamma \vdash \Delta, A \quad B, \Pi \vdash \Lambda}{A \rightarrow B, \Gamma, \Pi \vdash \Delta, \Lambda} \ \rightarrow: l \qquad \frac{A, \Gamma \vdash \Delta, B}{\Gamma \vdash \Delta, A \rightarrow B} \ \rightarrow: r$$

   (d) Negation

$$\frac{\Gamma \vdash \Delta, A}{\neg A, \Gamma \vdash \Delta} \ \neg : l \qquad \frac{A, \Gamma \vdash \Delta}{\Gamma \vdash \Delta, \neg A} \ \neg : r$$

   (e) Universal Quantification

$$\frac{A\{x \leftarrow t\}, \Gamma \vdash \Delta}{(\forall x)A, \Gamma \vdash \Delta} \ \forall : l \qquad \frac{\Gamma \vdash \Delta, A\{x \leftarrow \alpha\}}{\Gamma \vdash \Delta, (\forall x)A} \ \forall : r$$

   For the variable α and the term t the following must hold:
   i. t must not contain bound variables,
   ii. α is a free variable, called eigenvariable, *which must not occur in*
   $\Gamma \cup \Delta \cup \{A\}$ *(eigenvariable condition).*
   (f) Existential Quantification

$$\frac{\Gamma \vdash \Delta, A\{x \leftarrow t\}}{\Gamma \vdash \Delta, (\exists x)A} \ \exists : r \qquad \frac{A\{x \leftarrow \alpha\}, \Gamma \vdash \Delta}{(\exists x)A, \Gamma \vdash \Delta} \ \exists : l$$

   The restrictions on α and t are the same as for universal quantification.
3. *Structural Rules*
   (a) Weakening

$$\frac{\Gamma \vdash \Delta}{\Gamma \vdash \Delta, A} \ w : r \qquad \frac{\Gamma \vdash \Delta}{A, \Gamma \vdash \Delta} \ w : l$$

   (b) Contraction

$$\frac{A, A, \Gamma \vdash \Delta}{A, \Gamma \vdash \Delta} \ c : l \qquad \frac{\Gamma \vdash \Delta, A, A}{\Gamma \vdash \Delta, A} \ c : r$$

   (c) Cut

$$\frac{\Gamma \vdash \Delta, A \quad A, \Pi \vdash \Lambda}{\Gamma, \Pi \vdash \Delta, \Lambda} \ cut$$

Definition 3 (pseudo-LK-proof). *A pseudo-**LK**-proof (also called an **LKps**-proof) is an **LK**-proof where the following rules are replaced:*

1. *Contraction by pseudo-contraction:*

$$\frac{A, B, \Gamma \vdash \Delta}{A, \Gamma \vdash \Delta} \; psc:l \qquad \frac{\Gamma \vdash \Delta, A, B}{\Gamma \vdash \Delta, A} \; psc:r$$

   if A and B are logically equivalent (in first-order logic).
2. *Cut by pseudo-cut:*

$$\frac{\Gamma \vdash \Delta, A \quad B, \Pi \vdash \Lambda}{\Gamma, \Pi \vdash \Delta, \Lambda} \; pscut$$

   if A and B are logically equivalent (in first-order logic).

We need the technical notion of pseudo-LK-proofs, as many useful proof transformations destroy the proof property in intermediary steps, but keep this of a pseudo-proof. Moreover the analysis of proofs via profiles and characteristic clause sets (see [3] and Section 3) can be generalized to pseudo-proofs without any problems.

Definition 4. *An **LKps**-proof is called* regular *if all eigenvariables are different from each other.*

Definition 5 (main and auxiliary occurrence). *Let φ be an **LK**-proof and let ρ be a rule in φ. The formula occurrence whose main symbol has been introduced by ρ in the sequent immediately below ρ is called the* main *occurrence of ρ. The formula occurrence(s) that has/have been used to compose the main occurrence of ρ is/are called* auxiliary *occurrence(s) of ρ.*

Definition 6 ($\rightarrow_G$). *We define the Gentzen-style cut-elimination as the reduction relation $\rightarrow_G$ on regular **LK**-proofs which is the union of the reduction relations $\rightarrow_{G_p}, \rightarrow_{G_q}, \rightarrow_{G_a}, \rightarrow_{G_w}, \rightarrow_{G_c}, \rightarrow_{G_r}$ defined as follows:*
*Let φ be an **LK**-proof of the form:*

$$\frac{\stackrel{(\varphi_1)}{\Gamma \vdash \Delta, A} \quad \stackrel{(\varphi_2)}{A, \Pi \vdash \Lambda}}{\Gamma, \Pi \vdash \Delta, \Lambda} \; cut$$

1. *Reduction of propositional rules $\rightarrow_{G_p}$:*
   The cut formula is introduced by propositional rules on both sides immediately above the cut.
   (a) $A = B \wedge C$, $\varphi =$

$$\frac{\dfrac{\stackrel{(\varphi_1')}{\Gamma_1 \vdash \Delta_1, B} \quad \stackrel{(\varphi_1'')}{\Gamma_2 \vdash \Delta_2, C}}{\Gamma_1, \Gamma_2 \vdash \Delta_1, \Delta_2, B \wedge C} \wedge:r \quad \dfrac{\stackrel{(\varphi_2')}{B, C, \Pi \vdash \Lambda}}{B \wedge C, \Pi \vdash \Lambda} \wedge:l}{\Gamma_1, \Gamma_2, \Pi \vdash \Delta_1, \Delta_2, \Lambda} \; cut$$

then $\varphi \to_{G_p} \varphi' :=$

$$\dfrac{\dfrac{(\varphi_1'') }{\Gamma_2 \vdash \Delta_2, C} \qquad \dfrac{\dfrac{(\varphi_1')}{\Gamma_1 \vdash \Delta_1, B} \quad \dfrac{(\varphi_2')}{B, C, \Pi \vdash \Lambda}}{C, \Gamma_1, \Pi \vdash \Delta_1, \Lambda} \; cut}{\Gamma_1, \Gamma_2, \Pi \vdash \Delta_1, \Delta_2, \Lambda} \; cut$$

(b) $A = B \vee C$: *symmetric to case 1a.*

(c) $A = B \to C$, $\varphi =$

$$\dfrac{\dfrac{(\varphi_1')}{B, \Gamma \vdash \Delta, C}}{\Gamma \vdash \Delta, B \to C} \to : r \quad \dfrac{\dfrac{(\varphi_2')}{\Pi_1 \vdash \Lambda_1, B} \quad \dfrac{(\varphi_2'')}{C, \Pi_2 \vdash \Lambda_2}}{B \to C, \Pi_1, \Pi_2 \vdash \Lambda_1, \Lambda_2} \to : l}{\Gamma, \Pi_1, \Pi_2 \vdash \Delta, \Lambda_1, \Lambda_2} \; cut$$

then $\varphi \to_{G_p} \varphi' :=$

$$\dfrac{\dfrac{\dfrac{(\varphi_2')}{\Pi_1 \vdash \Lambda_1, B} \quad \dfrac{(\varphi_1')}{B, \Gamma \vdash \Delta, C}}{\Pi_1, \Gamma \vdash \Lambda_1, \Delta, C} \; cut \qquad \dfrac{(\varphi_2'')}{C, \Pi_2 \vdash \Lambda_2}}{\Gamma, \Pi_1, \Pi_2 \vdash \Delta, \Lambda_1, \Lambda_2} \; cut$$

(d) $A = \neg B$, $\varphi =$

$$\dfrac{\dfrac{\dfrac{(\varphi_1')}{B, \Gamma \vdash \Delta}}{\Gamma \vdash \Delta, \neg B} \neg : r \quad \dfrac{\dfrac{(\varphi_2')}{\Pi \vdash \Lambda, B}}{\neg B, \Pi \vdash \Lambda} \neg : l}{\Gamma, \Pi \vdash \Delta, \Lambda} \; cut$$

then $\varphi \to_{G_p} \varphi' :=$

$$\dfrac{\dfrac{(\varphi_2')}{\Pi \vdash \Lambda, B} \quad \dfrac{(\varphi_1')}{B, \Gamma \vdash \Delta}}{\Gamma, \Pi \vdash \Delta, \Lambda} \; cut$$

2. *Reduction of quantifier rules* $\to_{G_q}$:
   The cut formula is introduced by quantifier rules on both sides immediately above the cut.
   (a) $A = (\forall x)B$, $\varphi =$

$$\dfrac{\dfrac{(\varphi_1')}{\Gamma \vdash \Delta, B\{x \leftarrow \alpha\}}}{\Gamma \vdash \Delta, (\forall x)B} \forall : r \quad \dfrac{\dfrac{(\varphi_2')}{B\{x \leftarrow t\}, \Pi \vdash \Lambda}}{(\forall x)B, \Pi \vdash \Lambda} \forall : l}{\Gamma, \Pi \vdash \Delta, \Lambda} \; cut$$

then $\varphi \to_{G_q} \varphi' :=$

$$\dfrac{\dfrac{(\varphi_1'\{\alpha \leftarrow t\})}{\Gamma \vdash \Delta, B\{x \leftarrow t\}} \quad \dfrac{(\varphi_2')}{B\{x \leftarrow t\}, \Pi \vdash \Lambda}}{\Gamma, \Pi \vdash \Delta, \Lambda} \; cut$$

(b) $A = (\exists x)B$: *symmetric to case 2a.*

3. *Reduction of axioms* $\to_{G_a}$:

   The cut formula is introduced by an axiom on (at least) one of the two sides immediately above the cut.

   (a) φ_1 *is an axiom sequent,* $\varphi =$

$$
\frac{A \vdash A \quad \overset{(\varphi_2)}{A, \Pi \vdash \Lambda}}{A, \Pi \vdash \Lambda} \; cut
$$

   then $\varphi \to_{G_a} \varphi_2$

   (b) φ_2 *is an axiom sequent, then* $\varphi \to_{G_a} \varphi_1$

4. *Reduction of weakening* $\to_{G_w}$:

   The cut formula is introduced by weakening on (at least) one of the two sides immediately above the cut.

   (a) φ_1 *ends with* $w : r$, $\varphi =$

$$
\frac{\dfrac{\overset{(\varphi_1')}{\Gamma \vdash \Delta}}{\Gamma \vdash \Delta, A} \; w : r \quad \overset{(\varphi_2)}{A, \Pi \vdash \Lambda}}{\Gamma, \Pi \vdash \Delta, \Lambda} \; cut
$$

   then $\varphi \to_{G_w} \varphi' :=$

$$
\frac{\overset{(\varphi_1')}{\Gamma \vdash \Delta}}{\Gamma, \Pi \vdash \Delta, \Lambda} \; w : *
$$

   (b) φ_2 *ends with* $w : l$: *symmetric to case 3b.*

5. The cut formula is introduced by a contraction on (at least) one of the two sides immediately above the cut.

   (a) φ_1 *ends with* $c : r$, $\varphi =$

$$
\frac{\dfrac{\overset{(\varphi_1')}{\Gamma \vdash \Delta, A, A}}{\Gamma \vdash \Delta, A} \; c : r \quad \overset{(\varphi_2)}{A, \Pi \vdash \Lambda}}{\Gamma, \Pi \vdash \Delta, \Lambda} \; cut
$$

   then $\varphi \to_{G_c} \varphi' :=$

$$
\frac{\dfrac{\overset{(\varphi_1')}{\Gamma \vdash \Delta, A, A} \quad \overset{(\varphi_2)}{A, \Pi \vdash \Lambda}}{\Gamma, \Pi \vdash \Delta, \Lambda, A} \; cut \quad \overset{(\varphi_2')}{A, \Pi \vdash \Lambda}}{\dfrac{\Gamma, \Pi, \Pi \vdash \Delta, \Lambda, \Lambda}{\Gamma, \Pi \vdash \Delta, \Lambda} \; c : *} \; cut
$$

   where φ_2' *is a variant of* φ_2, *defined by renaming all eigenvariables in* φ_2 *by fresh ones (in order to keep the regularity of the proof).*

   (b) φ_2 *ends with* $c : l$: *symmetric to case 5a*

6. *rank-reduction* $\to_{G_r}$:
   The cut formula is not *introduced immediately above the cut on (at least) one of the two sides.*
   (a) on the right side
     i. φ_2 *ends with a unary rule,* $\varphi =$

$$
\cfrac{(\varphi_1)}{\Gamma \vdash \Delta, A} \quad \cfrac{\cfrac{(\varphi_2')}{A, \Pi' \vdash \Lambda'}}{A, \Pi \vdash \Lambda} \; r}{\Gamma, \Pi \vdash \Delta, \Lambda} \; cut
$$

   Then $\varphi \to_{G_r} \varphi' :=$

$$
\cfrac{\cfrac{(\varphi_1)}{\Gamma \vdash \Delta, A} \quad \cfrac{(\varphi_2')}{A, \Pi' \vdash \Lambda'}}{\cfrac{\Gamma, \Pi' \vdash \Delta, \Lambda'}{\Gamma, \Pi \vdash \Delta, \Lambda}} \; cut}{} \; r
$$

   which is a valid **LK***-proof. Note that regularity ensures that the eigen-variable condition cannot be violated.*
     ii. φ_2 *ends with a binary rule* μ
         A. *the ancestor of A is in the left premise of* μ, $\varphi =$

$$
\cfrac{(\varphi_1)}{\Gamma \vdash \Delta, A} \quad \cfrac{\cfrac{(\varphi_2')}{A, \Pi_1' \vdash \Lambda_1'} \quad \cfrac{(\varphi_2'')}{\Pi_2' \vdash \Lambda_2'}}{A, \Pi \vdash \Lambda} \; r}{\Gamma, \Pi \vdash \Delta, \Lambda} \; cut
$$

   Then $\varphi \to_{G_r} \varphi' :=$

$$
\cfrac{\cfrac{\cfrac{(\varphi_1)}{\Gamma \vdash \Delta, A} \quad \cfrac{(\varphi_2')}{A, \Pi_1' \vdash \Lambda_1'}}{\Gamma, \Pi_1' \vdash \Delta, \Lambda_1'} \; cut \quad \cfrac{(\varphi_2'')}{\Pi_2' \vdash \Lambda_2'}}{\Gamma, \Pi \vdash \Delta, \Lambda}}{} \; r
$$

   which is a valid **LK***-proof.*
         B. *the ancestor of A is in the right premise of* μ: *symmetric to the previous case.*
   (b) on the left side: symmetric to case 6a

   The reduction relation $\to_{G_r}$ can be carried over to **LKps**-proofs; however $\to_{G_r}$ is not capable of eliminating all cuts in **LKps**-proofs (in contrast to the CERES-method [3] which also eliminates pseudo-cuts).

3 The Profile

The profile of an **LKps**-proof is a set of labelled clauses. In order to give the definition of the profile, we first explain labelled clause logic.

3.1   Labelled Clauses

We use $\mathcal{L}$ to denote a countable infinite set of labels (e.g. $\mathcal{L} = \mathbb{N}$).

Definition 7 (clause). *A clause is a sequent consisting only of atomic formulas. A labelled clause is a clause that is assigned a non-empty set of labels from $\mathcal{L}$. For a clause c we write $\mathcal{L}(c)$ to denote this set.*

We will use the notation $A_1, \ldots, A_n \vdash^{\{l_1, \ldots, l_k\}} B_1, \ldots, B_m$ for the clause $A_1, \ldots, A_n \vdash B_1, \ldots, B_m$ with the set of labels $\{l_1, \ldots, l_k\}$. For the sake of readability we will sometimes omit the curly braces.

Definition 8 (merge, product). *Let $c = \Gamma \vdash^{L_1} \Delta$ and $d = \Pi \vdash^{L_2} \Lambda$ be labelled clauses. We define the merge of c and d as $c \circ d := \Gamma, \Pi \vdash^{L_1 \cup L_2} \Delta, \Lambda$. Let C, D be sets of labelled clauses. We define the product of C and D as $C \times D := \{c \circ d \mid c \in C, d \in D\}$.*

The labels will be used in order to describe subsets of sets of labelled clauses as follows: For a clause c and a set of labels L we will say that c *is an L-clause* if there exists a label l that is both in L and $\mathcal{L}(c)$.

Definition 9 (clause selection based on labels). *Let C be a set of labelled clauses. Let F, G be propositional formulas built up from label sets $L, L_1, L_2, \ldots$ as atoms and the connectives $\wedge, \vee, \neg$. We define C^F as follows:*

1. $C^L := \{c \in C \mid c$ *is an L-clause$\}$*
2. $C^{\neg F} := C \setminus C^F$
3. $C^{F \wedge G} := C^F \cap C^G$
4. $C^{F \vee G} := C^F \cup C^G$

Example 1. Let $C := \{\vdash^1 P \,; \, P \vdash^{2,3} R \,; \, R \vdash^3 \,; \, P \vdash^{2,3,4} Q \,; \, Q \vdash^{3,4}\}$. Then

$$C^{\{4\} \vee \neg \{3\}} = C^{\{4\}} \cup (C \setminus C^{\{3\}}) = \{\vdash^1 P \,; \, P \vdash^{2,3,4} Q \,; \, Q \vdash^{3,4}\}$$

Definition 10 (restricted product). *Let C, D be sets of labelled clauses and L be a set of labels. We define the operation $\times_L$ as*

$$C \times_L D := (C^L \times D^L) \cup C^{\neg L} \cup D^{\neg L}$$

Example 2. Let $C = \{P \vdash^1 \,; \, Q \vdash^2\}, D = \{\vdash^3 P \,; \, \vdash^4 Q\}$. Then

$$C \cup D = \{P \vdash^1 \,; \, Q \vdash^2 \,; \, \vdash^3 P \,; \, \vdash^4 Q\}$$
$$C \times D = \{P \vdash^{1,3} P \,; \, P \vdash^{1,4} Q \,; \, Q \vdash^{2,3} P \,; \, Q \vdash^{2,4} Q\}$$
$$C \times_{\{1,4\}} D = \{P \vdash^{1,4} Q \,; \, Q \vdash^2 \,; \, \vdash^3 P\}$$

The reader can easily convice himself that - under the usual interpretation of a clause set as a universally quantified conjunctive normal form - the logical meaning of the union ($\cup$) is conjunction, the meaning of the product ($\times$) is disjunction and that the restricted product is in-between in the sense that $C \cup D$ implies $C \times_L D$, which in turn implies $C \times D$, for all $L \subseteq \mathcal{L}$.

Lemma 1. *Let C, D, E be sets of labelled clauses and $L, L_1, L_2 \subseteq \mathcal{L}$. Then*

1. $C \times_L D = D \times_L C$
2. *If C contains no L_2-clauses and E contains no L_1-clauses then*

$$C \times_{L_1} (D \times_{L_2} E) = (C \times_{L_1} D) \times_{L_2} E$$

Proof. 1. follows easily from commutativity of $\times$ and $\cup$

2. We start with the left-hand side of the equation:

$$C \times_{L_1} (D \times_{L_2} E) = (C^{L_1} \times ((D^{L_2} \times E^{L_2}) \cup D^{\neg L_2} \cup E^{\neg L_2})^{L_1}) \cup$$
$$C^{\neg L_1} \cup ((D^{L_2} \times E^{L_2}) \cup D^{\neg L_2} \cup E^{\neg L_2})^{\neg L_1}$$

by definition. Note that $(X \cup Y)^L = X^L \cup Y^L$ for all sets of labelled clauses X, Y and all label sets L, so we have:

$$(C^{L_1} \times ((D^{L_2} \times E^{L_2})^{L_1} \cup D^{L_1 \wedge \neg L_2} \cup E^{L_1 \wedge \neg L_2})) \cup$$
$$C^{\neg L_1} \cup (D^{L_2} \times E^{L_2})^{\neg L_1} \cup D^{\neg L_1 \wedge \neg L_2} \cup E^{\neg L_1 \wedge \neg L_2}$$

Distributing $\times$ over $\cup$ we get:

$$(C^{L_1} \times (D^{L_2} \times E^{L_2})^{L_1}) \cup (C^{L_1} \times D^{L_1 \wedge \neg L_2}) \cup (C^{L_1} \times E^{L_1 \wedge \neg L_2}) \cup$$
$$C^{\neg L_1} \cup (D^{L_2} \times E^{L_2})^{\neg L_1} \cup D^{\neg L_1 \wedge \neg L_2} \cup E^{\neg L_1 \wedge \neg L_2}$$

As E contains no L_1-clauses we can write $(D^{L_2} \times E^{L_2})^{L_1} = D^{L_1 \wedge L_2} \times E^{L_2}$ and $(D^{L_2} \times E^{L_2})^{\neg L_1} = D^{\neg L_1 \wedge L_2} \times E^{L_2}$ and obtain:

$$(C^{L_1} \times (D^{L_1 \wedge L_2} \times E^{L_2})) \cup (C^{L_1} \times D^{L_1 \wedge \neg L_2}) \cup (C^{L_1} \times E^{L_1 \wedge \neg L_2}) \cup$$
$$C^{\neg L_1} \cup (D^{\neg L_1 \wedge L_2} \times E^{L_2}) \cup D^{\neg L_1 \wedge \neg L_2} \cup E^{\neg L_1 \wedge \neg L_2}$$

As E does not contain L_1-clauses, i.e. $E^{L_1} = \emptyset$ also $C^{L_1} \times E^{L_1 \wedge \neg L_2} = \emptyset$. Furthermore we can write $E = E^{\neg L_1}$ and - as C does not contain L_2-clauses - also $C = C^{\neg L_2}$. We obtain

$$(C^{L_1 \wedge \neg L_2} \times (D^{L_1 \wedge L_2} \times E^{\neg L_1 \wedge L_2})) \cup$$
$$(C^{L_1 \wedge \neg L_2} \times D^{L_1 \wedge \neg L_2}) \cup (D^{\neg L_1 \wedge L_2} \times E^{\neg L_1 \wedge L_2}) \cup$$
$$C^{\neg L_1 \wedge \neg L_2} \cup D^{\neg L_1 \wedge \neg L_2} \cup E^{\neg L_1 \wedge \neg L_2}$$

The right-hand side can be rewritten to the same expression in an analogous way.

q.e.d.

3.2   Definition of the Profile

In addition to labelled clauses we will consider labelled **LKps**-proofs to define the profile of a proof.

Definition 11 (labelled LKps-proof). *A labelled **LKps**-proof is a pseudo-proof where each axiom is assigned a unique label from $\mathcal{L}$. Furthermore each formula occurrence μ is assigned a set of labels in the following way:*

1. *If μ occurs in an axiom its set of labels is the singleton set containing the axiom label.*
2. *If μ does not occur in an axiom its set of labels is the union of the sets of labels of its immediate ancestor formula occurrences.*

So the set of labels of a formula occurrence describes the set of axioms that were used to build up this formula occurrence. For a formula occurrence μ in a labelled **LKps**-proof we write $\mathcal{L}(\mu)$ for its set of labels. For a rule ρ in a labelled **LK**-proof $\mathcal{L}(\rho)$ denotes the union of the label sets of the auxiliary formula occurrences of ρ. The cut-elimination rules defined in Definition 6 can be carried over to labelled **LK**-proofs with only minor modifications: in case of contraction elimination ($\rightarrow_{G_c}$) the renaming of eigenvariables has to be extended to the renaming of labels.

From now on we consider only proofs with skolemized end-sequents; skolem-ization is necessary for cut-elimination based on profiles and characteristic clause sets [3]. Note that every proof can be transformed into a skolemized version [2].

Let Ω denote the set of all formula occurrences which are ancestors of pseudo-cut formulas. A rule with auxiliary formulas in Ω is called an Ω-rule, with auxiliary formulas not in Ω a Σ-rule. For a sequent occurrence ν and a set of formula occurrences M, let $\mathrm{S}(\nu, M)$ denote the sub-sequent of the sequent at ν that contains only the formulas whose occurrences are in M.

Definition 12 (proof profile). *Let φ be a regular labelled **LKps**-proof. We define the profile $\mathrm{P}(\varphi)$ of φ by induction on a position ν in φ.*

1. *If ν is an axiom:*
$$\mathrm{P}(\varphi).\nu := \{\mathrm{S}(\nu, \Omega)\}.$$

2. *If ν is a unary rule with ancestor rule μ, then:*
$$\mathrm{P}(\varphi).\nu := \mathrm{P}(\varphi).\mu$$

3. *If ν is a binary rule with ancestor rules μ_1, μ_2 then*
   (a) If ν is an Ω-rule:
$$\mathrm{P}(\varphi).\nu := \mathrm{P}(\varphi).\mu_1 \cup \mathrm{P}(\varphi).\mu_2$$

   (b) If ν is a Σ-rule:
$$\mathrm{P}(\varphi).\nu := \mathrm{P}(\varphi).\mu_1 \times_{\mathcal{L}(\nu)} \mathrm{P}(\varphi).\mu_2$$

Note that this definition of a proof profile does not depend on syntactic details of the sequent calculus variant. Exactly the same definition can be used for example for additive calculi or for a calculus with arbitrary atomic axiom sequents, etc. Another important feature of the proof profile is that for the CERES method [3] it can be used instead of the characteristic clause set and will always yield cut-free proofs that are at most as long as those corresponding to the characteristic clause set.

3.3 Compatibility

Lemma 2 (compatibility of P). *Let $\chi[\varphi]_\mu$ be an* **LKps**-*proof, let φ' be another* **LK**-*proof with the same end-sequent as φ. Let $\sigma_1, \ldots, \sigma_n$ be the formula occurrences in the end-sequent of φ and let $\sigma'_1, \ldots, \sigma'_n$ be the corresponding formula occurrences in the end-sequent of φ'. Let θ be a substitution whose domain is included in the set of eigenvariables of φ. We write χ' for $\chi[\varphi']_\mu$. If*

1. *$P(\chi').\mu = (P(\chi).\mu)\theta$ and*
2. *for $i = 1, \ldots, n : \mathcal{L}(\sigma'_i) = \mathcal{L}(\sigma_i)$*

then

$$P(\chi') = P(\chi)\theta$$

Proof. Let ν be a formula occurrence in χ that is not in φ, let ν' be the corresponding formula occurrence in χ'. If ν is not on the path between μ and the end-sequent then we clearly have $\mathcal{L}(\nu') = \mathcal{L}(\nu)$. If it is then by induction on the length of this path and by using 2 we have $\mathcal{L}(\nu') = \mathcal{L}(\nu)$.

Now, using $\mathcal{L}(\nu') = \mathcal{L}(\nu)$ we proceed by induction on the length of the path between μ and the end-sequent. If the last rule is unary then the induction step obviously extends to give $P(\chi') = P(\chi)\theta$. If the last rule is binary, observe that θ cannot change variables of the part that does not contain μ because its domain is restricted to the eigenvariables of φ and the proof is regular, so also $P(\chi') = P(\chi)\theta$ q.e.d.

3.4 Permutation of Independent Rules

It is a well-known fact about the sequent calculus that the order of rule applications can be permuted up to a high degree (see e.g. [8]). In this section we will formally define these rule permutations and show that the proof profile is not changed by permuting rules.

Definition 13 (adjacent). *Two rules in an* **LKps**-*proof are said to be* adjacent *if one occurs immediately above the other.*

Definition 14 (independent). *Two adjacent rules in an* **LKps**-*proof are said to be* independent *if neither*

1. *the main occurrence of the upper rule is an auxiliary occurrence of the lower rule, nor*
2. *the lower rule is unary with two auxiliary occurrences that are split by the binary upper rule, nor*
3. *the lower rule is a strong quantifier rule and the upper rule is a weak quantifier rule introducing a term that contains the eigenvariable of the lower rule*

Definition 15 (permutation of independent rules). *Let φ be an* **LKps**-*proof whose last two rules are independent. Let φ' be the proof that differs from φ only by swapping the order of the last two rules. Then we write $\varphi \sim_\pi \varphi'$.*

We will denote with $\approx_\pi$ the reflexive, transitive and compatible closure of the rule swapping relation $\sim_\pi$.

Lemma 3 (invariance under $\approx_\pi$). *Let χ, χ' be two **LKps**-proofs with $\chi \approx_\pi \chi'$. Then*

$$P(\chi') = P(\chi)$$

Proof. By transitivity of $=$, it suffices to show the invariance of P for a single rule swapping. Let μ be the position in χ where the rule swapping occurs, so we have $\varphi \sim_\pi \varphi'$ with $\chi = \chi[\varphi]_\mu$ and $\chi' = \chi[\varphi']_\mu$.

We will first show $P(\chi').\mu = P(\chi).\mu$.

If both swapped rules are unary rules, then we simply have

$$P(\chi).\mu = C = P(\chi').\mu$$

For some set of labelled clauses C.

If one of the swapped rules is a unary rule and one a binary rule, we have

$$P(\chi).\mu = C \circ D$$

where $\circ = \cup$ or $\circ = \times_{\mathcal{L}(\rho)}$ where ρ is the binary rule. In both cases also

$$P(\chi').\mu = C \circ D$$

because $\mathcal{L}(\rho)$ clearly is not changed by the swapping of two rules.

If both rules are binary then the last rules ρ_1 and ρ_2 of φ, φ' have the form (omitting the sequents and concrete rule types):

$$\cfrac{\cfrac{(\varphi_1, C) \quad (\varphi_2, D)}{}\rho_1 \quad (\varphi_3, E)}{}\rho_2 \qquad \text{and} \qquad \cfrac{(\varphi_1, C) \quad \cfrac{(\varphi_2, D) \quad (\varphi_3, E)}{}\rho_2}{}\rho_1$$

From the existence of the left proof one can deduce that E does not contain any clauses with labels from $\mathcal{L}(\rho_1)$ because all labels in E refer to axioms in φ_3 and $\mathcal{L}(\rho_1)$ cannot contain any labels from axioms in φ_3 because it is parallel to it. Symmetrically from the right proof one can deduce that C does not contain any clauses with labels from $\mathcal{L}(\rho_2)$.

For the profiles at μ we have

$$P(\chi).\mu = (C \circ_1 D) \circ_2 E \qquad \text{and} \qquad P(\chi').\mu = C \circ_1 (D \circ_2 E)$$

for operators $\circ_1, \circ_2$ associated to the rules ρ_1 and ρ_2.

If both $\circ_1 = \cup$ and $\circ_2 = \cup$ then $P(\chi).\mu = P(\chi').\mu$ follows from associativity of $\cup$. If $\circ_1 = \times_{\mathcal{L}(\rho_1)}$ and $\circ_2 = \times_{\mathcal{L}(\rho_2)}$ then with the observation above we can apply Lemma 1 to obtain $P(\chi).\mu = P(\chi').\mu$.

Now, let $\circ_1 = \times_{\mathcal{L}(\rho_1)}$ and $\circ_2 = \cup$. Then – abbreviating $\mathcal{L}(\rho_1)$ as L – we have

$$C \times_L (D \cup E) = (C^L \times (D \cup E)^L) \cup C^{\neg L} \cup (D \cup E)^{\neg L}$$
$$= (C^L \times (D^L \cup E^L)) \cup C^{\neg L} \cup D^{\neg L} \cup E^{\neg L}$$

but as E does not contain labels from L we know that $E^L = \emptyset$ and $E^{\neg L} = E$ and so

$$= (C^L \times D^L) \cup C^{\neg L} \cup D^{\neg L} \cup E$$
$$=^{p.d.} (C \times_L D) \cup E$$

If $\circ_1 = \cup$ and $\circ_2 = \times_{\mathcal{L}(\rho_2)}$ the proof proceeds analogously using the observation that C does not contain labels from $\mathcal{L}(\rho_2)$.

Condition 2 of Lemma 2 is fulfilled, because rule swappings do not change the ancestor relation in the proof, so we can apply Lemma 2 and conclude $P(\chi') = P(\chi)$ q.e.d.

In [10] E. Robinson defines proof nets for classical propositional logic and shows ([10], proposition 6.2):

Proposition 1. *Two* **LK**-*proofs* φ *and* φ' *(for classical propositional logic) induce isomorphic proof nets iff* $\varphi \approx_\pi \varphi'$.

Building on this and Lemma 3 we can easily conclude

Corollary 1. *If two* **LK**-*proofs* φ *and* φ' *(for classical propositional logic) induce isomorphic proof nets then* $P(\varphi) = P(\varphi')$.

R. McKinley defines in his PhD thesis [9] an extension of Robinson's proof nets to first-order classical logic by treating quantifiers with boxes. We conjecture that the result of Corollary 1 also extends to this notion of proof net.

4   The Profile and Cut-Elimination

In [4] an analysis of the behavior of the original characteristic clause sets under Gentzen's cut-elimination procedure has been given. It has been shown that, if φ is reduced to φ' by cut-elimination steps, the characteristic clause set of φ subsumes that of φ'. The subsumption relation consists of the three basic parts of 1) duplication of clauses (including variable renaming), 2) instantiation of clauses and 3) deletion of clauses. However, due to the nature of this cut-elimination procedure and the characteristic clause sets these three parts occur in a mixed fashion at different cut-elimination steps.

In this section we carry out an analogous analysis but with the important difference that we move from Gentzen's original calculus (which is a mixture of multiplicative and additive rules) to the purely multiplicative calculus **LKps** and from the original characteristic clause sets to the proof profiles defined in this paper. This allows to carry out the analysis of [4] in a much "cleaner" fashion which will make it possible to use the lemmas in the analysis of the effect of transformations defined by cut-elimination (as done in Section 5). We will now show that

1. duplication of clauses arises iff a contraction rule is eliminated, that
2. instantiation of clauses arises iff a quantifier rule is eliminated and that
3. deletion of clauses arises iff a weakening rule is eliminated.

In all other cases the profile remains unchanged.

Lemma 4 (rank-reduction)

$$\chi \to_{G_r} \chi' \implies P(\chi') = P(\chi)$$

Proof As rank-reduction $\to_{G_r}$ is contained in the permutation of adjacent independent rules $\approx_\pi$, we can apply Lemma 3. q.e.d.

Lemma 5 (propositional reduction)

$$\chi \to_{G_p} \chi' \Longrightarrow P(\chi') = P(\chi)$$

Proof Let μ be the position where the reduction is applied, so $\chi = \chi[\varphi]_\mu$ and $\chi' = \chi[\varphi']_\mu$. We first show $P(\chi').\mu = P(\chi).\mu$ by case distinction on the main connective of the cut at μ:

1. Conjunction: Then φ has the form:

$$\cfrac{\cfrac{(\varphi_1, C) \quad (\varphi_2, D)}{\Gamma \vdash \Delta, A \quad \Pi \vdash \Lambda, B}{\Gamma, \Pi \vdash \Delta, \Lambda, A \wedge B} \wedge : r \qquad \cfrac{(\varphi_3, E)}{A, B, \Theta \vdash \Sigma}{A \wedge B, \Theta \vdash \Sigma} \wedge : l}{\Gamma, \Pi, \Theta \vdash \Delta, \Lambda, \Sigma} cut$$

and φ' has the form:

$$\cfrac{(\varphi_2, D) \quad \cfrac{(\varphi_1, C) \quad (\varphi_3, E)}{\Gamma \vdash \Delta, A \quad A, B, \Theta \vdash \Sigma}{B, \Gamma, \Theta \vdash \Delta, \Sigma} cut}{\Pi \vdash \Lambda, B \qquad \qquad \qquad \qquad \qquad}{\Gamma, \Pi, \Theta \vdash \Delta, \Lambda, \Sigma} cut$$

So we have

$$P(\chi).\mu = (C \cup D) \cup E$$

and

$$P(\chi').\mu = D \cup (C \cup E)$$

which are equal by commutativity and associativity of $\cup$.
2. Disjunction: analogous: by commutativity and associativity of $\cup$
3. Implication: analogous: by commutativity and associativity of $\cup$
4. Negation: analogous: by commutativity and associativity of $\cup$

Also condition 2 of Lemma 2 is fulfilled because $\to_{G_p}$ does not change the ancestor axioms of the formula occurrences in the end-sequent of the rewritten part. So we can use Lemma 2 to conclude $P(\chi') = P(\chi)$ q.e.d.

Lemma 6 (quantifier reduction). *Let χ be a regular* **LKps**-*proof and let*

$$\chi \to_{G_q} \chi'$$

where the substitution $\{\alpha \leftarrow t\}$ is applied to the reduced sub-proof of χ. Then

$$P(\chi') = P(\chi)\{\alpha \leftarrow t\}$$

Proof. Let μ be the position where the reduction is applied, so $\chi = \chi[\varphi]_\mu$ and $\chi' = \chi[\varphi']_\mu$. We will show this only for the universal quantifier, for the existential quantifier the proof is analogous:

Then φ has the form

$$\frac{\dfrac{(\varphi_1, C)}{\Gamma \vdash \Delta, B\{x \leftarrow \alpha\}} \; \forall : r}{\dfrac{\Gamma \vdash \Delta, (\forall x)B}{\Gamma, \Pi \vdash \Delta, \Lambda}} \qquad \dfrac{\dfrac{(\varphi_2, D)}{B\{x \leftarrow t\}, \Pi \vdash \Lambda} \; \forall : l}{(\forall x)B, \Pi \vdash \Lambda}$$
$$cut$$

and φ' has the form

$$\frac{\dfrac{(\varphi_1\{\alpha \leftarrow t\}, C\{\alpha \leftarrow t\})}{\Gamma \vdash \Delta, B\{x \leftarrow t\}} \qquad \dfrac{(\varphi_2, D)}{B\{x \leftarrow t\}, \Pi \vdash \Lambda}}{\Gamma, \Pi \vdash \Delta, \Lambda} \; cut$$

So we have

$$P(\chi).\mu = C \cup D$$

and

$$P(\chi').\mu = C\{\alpha \leftarrow t\} \cup D$$

but α does not occur in D so

$$P(\chi').\mu = (P(\chi).\mu)\{\alpha \leftarrow t\}$$

And as the label sets of the formula occurrences in the sequent at μ do not change we can apply Lemma 2. q.e.d.

The reduction of a weakening rule deletes a sub-proof and - by introducing new weakening rules - makes some formula occurrences further down in the proof weak that have not been weak before. This may have the result that an auxiliary formula of a binary rule, that goes into the end-sequent, becomes weak and thus this binary rule becomes superfluous (because it could be replaced by a weakening). The effect of this transformation on the profile is that of deletion of certain clauses: All clauses from the deleted sub-proof as well as all clauses that share a label with a superfluous binary rule are deleted.

Lemma 7 (weakening reduction). *Let χ be an **LKps**-proof and μ a position in χ of a cut that can be reduced by $\rightarrow_{G_w}$. Then*

$$\chi[\varphi]_\mu \rightarrow_{G_w} \chi[\varphi']_\mu$$

We write χ' for $\chi[\varphi']_\mu$. Let D be the set of axiom labels of the sub-proof deleted by this $\rightarrow_{G_w}$-step. Let furthermore $\sigma_1, \ldots, \sigma_n$ be those binary Σ-rules on the path between μ and the end-sequent of χ that each have an auxiliary occurrence $\alpha_1, \ldots, \alpha_n$ with $\mathcal{L}(\alpha_i) \subseteq D$. Let $\beta_1, \ldots, \beta_n$ be the other auxiliary formula occurrences of these rules and abbreviate $L_i := \mathcal{L}(\beta_i)$. Then

$$P(\chi') = P(\chi)^{\neg D \wedge \neg L_1 \wedge \ldots \wedge \neg L_n}$$

Proof. Let ν be a formula occurrence in χ but not in φ and let ν' be the corresponding formula occurrence in χ'. Then one can easily show by induction on the length l of the path between μ and the end-sequent of χ that:

$$(\star) \quad \mathcal{L}(\nu') = L(\nu) \setminus D$$

We abbreviate $D^* := \neg D \wedge \neg L_1 \wedge \ldots \wedge \neg L_n$ and show $\mathrm{P}(\chi') = \mathrm{P}(\chi)^{D^*}$ again by induction on the length l of the path between μ and the end-sequent.

If $l = 0$ then $n = 0$. Furthermore, $\mathrm{P}(\chi) = X \cup Y$ for sets of labelled clauses X and Y and $\mathrm{P}(\chi') = X$. But X contains no labels from D while Y contains only labels from D, so $\mathrm{P}(\chi') = X = (X \cup Y)^{\neg D} = \mathrm{P}(\chi)^{\neg D}$.

If $l > 0$ we make a case distinction according to the type of the last rule ρ in χ: If ρ is unary then the result follows immediately from (IH). If ρ is a binary Ω-rule then $\mathrm{P}(\chi) = X \cup Y$ and $\mathrm{P}(\chi') = X^{D^*} \cup Y$, but Y contains no labels from D nor any from $L_1, \ldots, L_n$, so $Y = Y^{D^*}$ and thus $\mathrm{P}(\chi') = X^{D^*} \cup Y = X^{D^*} \cup Y^{D^*} = (X \cup Y)^{D^*} = \mathrm{P}(\chi)^{D^*}$. If ρ is a binary Σ-rule, let α be the auxiliary occurrence on the path between μ and the root. We distinguish two cases:

1. $\mathcal{L}(\alpha) \subseteq D$, i.e. α becomes weak after the reduction, so $\alpha = \alpha_{n+1}$, the other auxiliary occurrence is β_{n+1} and its labels $\mathcal{L}(\beta_{n+1}) = L_{n+1}$. We have $\mathrm{P}(\chi) = X \times_{\mathcal{L}(\alpha) \cup L_{n+1}} Y$ and by $(\star)$ and (IH) that $\mathrm{P}(\chi') = X^{D^*} \times_{L_{n+1}} Y$. By algebraic manipulations one shows that $\mathrm{P}(\chi') = (X \cup Y)^{D^* \wedge \neg L_{n+1}}$ and $\mathrm{P}(\chi)^{D^* \wedge \neg L_{n+1}} = X^{\neg \mathcal{L}(\alpha) \wedge D^* \wedge \neg L_{n+1}} \cup Y^{D^* \wedge \neg L_{n+1}}$. By our case assumption $\mathcal{L}(\alpha) \subseteq D$, so $\neg \mathcal{L}(\alpha) \wedge D^*$ can be simplified to D^* because $\neg D$ is contained in D^* and thus $\mathrm{P}(\chi)^{D^* \wedge \neg L_{n+1}} = X^{D^* \wedge \neg L_{n+1}} \cup Y^{D^* \wedge \neg L_{n+1}} = (X \cup Y)^{D^* \wedge \neg L_{n+1}}$.

2. $\mathcal{L}(\alpha) \not\subseteq D$: In this case we have $\mathrm{P}(\chi) = X \times_L Y$ for a set of labels L, and by $(\star)$ and (IH) that $\mathrm{P}(\chi') = X^{D^*} \times_{L \setminus D} Y$. Writing $L \setminus D$ as $L \wedge \neg D$, using algebraic manipulations and simplifying $D^* \wedge L \wedge \neg D$ to $D^* \wedge L$ gives $\mathrm{P}(\chi') = (X^L \times Y^L)^{D^*} \cup X^{D^* \wedge \neg(L \wedge \neg D)} \cup Y^{\neg(L \wedge \neg D)}$. By further simplifications one shows that $\mathrm{P}(\chi') = (X^L \times Y^L)^{D^*} \cup (X^{\neg L})^{D^*} \cup (Y^{\neg L})^{D^*} = \mathrm{P}(\chi)^{D^*}$ q.e.d.

Corollary 2. *Let χ be an* **LKps***-proof and μ a position in χ of a cut that can be reduced by $\to_{\mathrm{G_w}}$. Let D be the set of axiom labels of the sub-proof deleted by this $\to_{\mathrm{G_w}}$-step. If all formula occurrences in the deleted sub-proof are ancestors of cut formulas then*

$$\mathrm{P}(\chi') = \mathrm{P}(\chi)^{\neg D}$$

Proof. By applying Lemma 7 and observing that in this case there can be no binary Σ-rule with an auxiliary formula α s.t. $\mathcal{L}(\alpha) \subseteq D$, thus $n = 0$ and $\mathrm{P}(\chi') = \mathrm{P}(\chi)^{\neg D}$ q.e.d.

Lemma 8 (contraction reduction). *Let χ be an* **LKps***-proof and μ a position in χ of a cut that can be reduced by $\to_{\mathrm{G_c}}$. Then*

$$\chi[\varphi]_\mu \to_{\mathrm{G_c}} \chi[\varphi']_\mu$$

Let D be the set of axiom labels of the sub-proof duplicated by this $\to_{\mathrm{G_c}}$-step and let π be the permutation on labels and variables applied to the new copy of the duplicated sub-proof. We write χ' for $\chi[\varphi']_\mu$. Then

$$\mathrm{P}(\chi') = \mathrm{P}(\chi) \cup \mathrm{P}(\chi)^D \pi$$

Proof. Let ν be a formula occurrence in χ but not in φ and let ν' be the corresponding formula occurrence in χ'. Then one can show by induction on the length l of the path between μ and the end-sequent of χ that:

$$(\star) \quad \mathcal{L}(\nu') = \mathcal{L}(\nu) \cup (\mathcal{L}(\nu) \cap D)\pi$$

We show $P(\chi') = P(\chi) \cup P(\chi)^D \pi$ again by induction on the length l of the path between μ and the end-sequent. If $l = 0$ then $P(\chi) = X \cup Y$ and $P(\chi') = X \cup X\pi \cup Y$ but as $(X \cup Y)^D = X$ we obtain $P(\chi)^D \pi = X\pi$. If $l > 0$ we make a case distinction according to the type of the last rule ρ: If ρ is a unary rule then the result holds immediately by (IH). If ρ is a binary Ω-rule then $P(\chi) = X \cup Y$ and by (IH): $P(\chi') = X \cup X^D \pi \cup Y$ but as Y contains no labels from D we have $P(\chi)^D \pi = X^D \pi$.

If ρ is a binary Σ-rule then $P(\chi) = X \times_L Y$ and by (IH) and $(\star)$: $P(\chi') = (X \cup X^D \pi) \times_{L \cup (L \cap D)\pi} Y$. By observing that neither X nor Y contain any labels from the image of π and that thus for $Z \in \{X, Y\}$ and any label sets M, N: $Z^{M \vee N\pi} = Z^M$ and $Z^{\neg(M \vee N\pi)} = Z^{\neg M}$ one shows that

$$P(\chi') = P(\chi) \cup ((X^D \pi)^{L \vee (L \wedge D)\pi} \times Y^L) \cup (X^D \pi)^{\neg(L \vee (L \wedge D)\pi)}$$

So it remains to show

$$P(\chi)^D \pi = ((X^D \pi)^{L \vee (L \wedge D)\pi} \times Y^L) \cup (X^D \pi)^{\neg(L \vee (L \wedge D)\pi)}$$

As Y cannot contain any labels from D, we have

$$P(\chi)^D \pi = ((X^L \times Y^L)^D \cup X^{\neg L \wedge D})\pi = (X^{L \wedge D} \pi \times Y^L) \cup X^{\neg L \wedge D} \pi$$

By algebraic manipulations concerning the variable and label permutation π one shows the remaining equations:

$$X^{L \wedge D} \pi = (X^D \pi)^{L \vee (L \wedge D)\pi} \text{ and } X^{\neg L \wedge D} \pi = (X^D \pi)^{\neg(L \vee (L \wedge D)\pi)}$$

q.e.d.

5 A General Invariance Property

Definition 16. *Let A and B be formulas. Then any cut-free proof of $A \vdash B$ is called a* transformation *of A to B (generally denoted by $\tau_{A,B}$).*

We define the effect of transformations on proofs via cut-elimination. To this aim we define a refinement of $\rightarrow_G$ and corresponding normal forms:

Definition 17. *Let $\tau_{A,B}$ be a transformation, φ be a proof of a sequent $\Gamma \vdash \Delta, A$ and ψ be a proof of a sequent $B, \Pi \vdash \Lambda$. We consider the proofs $T(\varphi, \tau_{A,B})$:*

$$\frac{\overset{\varphi}{\Gamma \vdash \Delta, A} \quad \overset{\tau_{A,B}}{A \vdash B}}{\Gamma \vdash \Delta, B} \; cut$$

and $T(\tau_{A,B}, \psi)$:

$$\frac{\overset{\tau_{A,B}}{A \vdash B} \quad \overset{\psi}{B, \Pi \vdash \Lambda}}{A, \Pi \vdash \Lambda} \; cut$$

We mark in $T(\varphi, \tau_{A,B})(T(\tau_{A,B}, \psi))$ *all ancestors of the final cut and refine* $\to_G$ *to* $\to_{G_t}$ *by the following restrictions:*

(1) apply the reduction rules only cuts whose auxiliary formulas are marked.
(2) apply the elimination rules for axioms only if all other $\to_G$*-reduction rules on marked formulas fail.*
(3) Eliminate a cut between two (atomic) axioms by eliminating the axiom coming from $\tau_{A,B}$ *(i.e. the axiom with the labels coming from* $\tau_{A,B}$*). In more detail: replace the subproof*

$$\frac{B^{\{i\}} \vdash B^{\{i\}} \quad B^{\{j\}} \vdash B^{\{j\}}}{B^{\{i\}} \vdash B^{\{j\}}} \; cut$$

(where i is a label in the φ*-part (in the* ψ*-part) and j is a label in the* $\tau_{A,B}$*-part) by*

$$B^{\{i\}} \vdash B^{\{i\}}.$$

Then by $\tau_{A,B}(\psi)((\varphi)\tau_{A,B})$ *we denote the set of all* $\to_{G_t}$*-normal forms of* $T(\tau_{A,B}, \psi)$ ($T(\varphi, \tau_{A,B})$).

Remark 1. Note that Gentzen normal forms of proofs are not unique in general. Therefore the elimination of the cut with the transformation $\tau_{A,B}$ may yield different proofs. So any element from the set $(\varphi)\tau_{A,B}$ can be considered as the transformed proof.

Below we investigate a class of transformations $\tau_{A,B}$ where A is logically equivalent to B:

Definition 18. *Two formulas* A, B *are called* V*-equivalent if they contain the same variables.*

Definition 19. *Let* τ *be a transformation* $\tau_{A,B}$ *and let* A, B *be* V*-equivalent. Moreover let* $x_1, \ldots, x_n$ *be the bound variables in* A *(respectively in* B*). Then* τ *is called* Q*-simple if*

(a) For every variable x_i *there are exactly two quantifier introductions in* τ.
(b) If $\{x_i \leftarrow \alpha_i\}$ *is a substitution corresponding to a strong quantifier introduction on an ancestor of* A *then* $\{x_i \leftarrow \alpha_i\}$ *is also a substitution corresponding to a weak quantifier introduction on an ancestor of* B.
(c) If $\{x_i \leftarrow \alpha_i\}$ *is a substitution corresponding to a strong quantifier introduction on an ancestor of* B *then* $\{x_i \leftarrow \alpha_i\}$ *is also a substitution corresponding to a weak quantifier introduction on an ancestor of* A.

Remark 2. In a Q-simple transformation the strong substitutions for A are the weak ones for B and vice versa. In particular, all quantifier introductions have variable substitutions.

Example 3. The following transformation τ is Q-simple:

$$
\cfrac{\cfrac{\cfrac{\cfrac{\cfrac{\cfrac{P(\alpha_1,\alpha_2) \vdash P(\alpha_1,\alpha_2)}{\vdash \neg P(\alpha_1,\alpha_2), P(\alpha_1,\alpha_2)}\ \neg:r}{\vdash \neg P(\alpha_1,\alpha_2), (\exists y)P(\alpha_1,y)}\ \exists:r}{\vdash (\forall y)\neg P(\alpha_1,y), (\exists y)P(\alpha_1,y)}\ \forall:r}{\vdash (\exists x)(\forall y)\neg P(x,y), (\exists y)P(\alpha_1,y)}\ \exists:r}{\vdash (\exists x)(\forall y)\neg P(x,y), (\forall x)(\exists y)P(x,y)}\ \forall:r}{\neg(\forall x)(\exists y)P(x,y) \vdash (\exists x)(\forall y)\neg P(x,y)}\ \neg:l
$$

No transformation with end-sequent $(\forall x)Q(x) \vdash (\exists x)Q(x)$ is Q-simple.

Definition 20. *A transformation $\tau_{A,B}$ is called simple if it is Q-simple and does not contain structural rules.*

Example 4. The transformation τ defined in Example 3 is simple. Moreover the identical transformation I is simple. I can be defined in the following way:

If A is an atom then $I(A) = A \vdash A$. If A contains logical operators, then $I(A)$ can be defined inductively. We consider the cases $A \equiv B \to C$ and $A \equiv (\forall x)B$, the others are straightforward.

$$
I(B \to C) = \cfrac{\cfrac{\cfrac{I(B)\quad I(C)}{B \vdash B \quad C \vdash C}}{\cfrac{B, B \to C \vdash C}{B \to C \vdash B \to C}\ \to:r}\ \to:l}{}
\qquad
I((\forall x)B) = \cfrac{\cfrac{\cfrac{I(B\{x \leftarrow \alpha\})}{B\{x \leftarrow \alpha\} \vdash B\{x \leftarrow \alpha\}}}{\cfrac{(\forall x)B \vdash B\{x \leftarrow \alpha\}}{(\forall x)B \vdash (\forall x)B}\ \forall:r}\ \forall:l}{}
$$

Definition 21. *Two formulas A, B are called strongly equivalent (notation $A \sim_s B$) if there exist simple transformations $\tau_{A,B}$ and $\tau_{B,A}$.*

Remark 3. Note that, in contrast to full logical equivalence, it is decidable whether two formulas are strongly equivalent. This is clear as the number of inferences in a simple transformation $\tau_{A,B}$ is bounded by the logical complexity of $A \vdash B$.

Example 5. Note that the existence of a simple transformation from A to B does not imply the existence of a simple transformation from B to A. Let $P(x)$ and Q be atom formulas. Then there is a simple transformation from $(\forall x)P(x) \wedge Q$ to $(\forall x)(P(x) \wedge Q)$:

$$
\cfrac{\cfrac{\cfrac{\cfrac{P(\alpha) \vdash P(\alpha) \quad Q \vdash Q}{P(\alpha), Q \vdash P(\alpha) \wedge Q}\ \wedge:r}{(\forall x)P(x), Q \vdash P(\alpha) \wedge Q}\ \forall:l}{(\forall x)P(x) \wedge Q \vdash P(\alpha) \wedge Q}\ \wedge:l}{(\forall x)P(x) \wedge Q \vdash (\forall x)(P(x) \wedge Q)}\ \forall:r
$$

But there is no simple transformation from $(\forall x)(P(x) \wedge Q)$ to $(\forall x)P(x) \wedge Q$.

Definition 22. *A binary relation $\triangledown$ on formulas is called* compatible *if, for all formulas A and B, $A \triangledown B$ implies $C[A]_\lambda \triangledown C[B]_\lambda$ for any formula context $C[\ ]_\lambda$.*

Proposition 2. $\sim_s$ *is a compatible equivalence relation on formulas.*

Proof. reflexivity: Define $\tau_{A,A}$ as $I(A)$; $I(A)$ is simple for all A.

symmetry: immediate by definition.

transitivity:
Assume $A \sim_s B$ and $B \sim_s C$. Then there exist simple transformations $\tau_{A,B}$ and $\tau_{B,C}$; we may assume w.l.o.g. that $\tau_{A,B}$ and $\tau_{B,C}$ do not share eigenvariables. By $V(X)$ we denote the set of variables in X.

By definition of $\sim_s$ we have $V(A) = V(B)$, $V(B) = V(C)$ and thus $V(A) = V(C)$. We consider the proof η_{AC}:

$$\frac{\overset{\tau_{A,B}}{A \vdash B} \quad \overset{\tau_{B,C}}{B \vdash C}}{A \vdash C} \ cut$$

As $\tau_{A,B}$ and $\tau_{B,C}$ do not contain weakening and contractions, the same holds for η_{AC} as well. Clearly η_{AC} is not a transformation; but it is enough to show that any cut-elimination sequence Ψ on η_{AC} yields a transformation which is also simple.

Let $\eta_{AC} \to_G^* \xi$. Then, by definition of the reduction rules for $\to_G$, ξ does not contain weakenings and/or contractions (indeed no additional weakenings and contractions are introduced by the cut-reduction rules). So let Ψ be a cut-elimination sequence on η_{AC}; then its result is a transformation $\tau_{A,C}$ which is weakening- and contraction-free. It remains to show that $\tau_{A,C}$ is also Q-simple.

Let us assume that $X: \{x_1, \ldots, x_n\}$ are the bound variables in A, B, C. As $\tau_{A,B}$ is simple, X can be partitioned into two sets

$$\{y_1, \ldots, y_m\} \quad \{z_1, \ldots, z_k\}$$

s.t. the y_i are the strong variables of quantifier introductions on ancestors of A, and the z_j are the weak variables of quantifier introductions on ancestors of A. Moreover, as $\tau_{A,B}$ is Q-simple, the y_i are the weak variables of quantifier introductions on ancestors of B, and the z_j are the strong variables of quantifier introductions on ancestors of B. Now let us list the vectors of variables in the following order:

(1) strong, ancestor of A, (2) weak, ancestor of A,
(3) strong, ancestor of B, (4) weak, ancestor of B.

This way we obtain a tuple

$$X_{AB}: \ < (y_1, \ldots, y_m), (z_1, \ldots, z_k), (z_1, \ldots, z_k), (y_1, \ldots, y_m) > .$$

Now consider the tuple X_{AB} under substitution of the bound variables by the quantifier substitutions. Then we obtain the *quantifier-introduction vector* for $\tau_{A,B}$:

$$Y_{AB}: \ < (\alpha_1, \ldots, \alpha_m), (\beta_1, \ldots, \beta_k), (\beta_1, \ldots, \beta_k), (\alpha_1, \ldots, \alpha_m) > .$$

For $\tau_{B,C}$ we obtain (replacing A by B, B by C in the tuple notation)

$$X_{BC}: \; < (y_1, \ldots, y_m), (z_1, \ldots, z_k), (z_1, \ldots, z_k), (y_1, \ldots, y_m) > .$$

and the quantifier introduction vector

$$Y_{BC}: \; < (\beta_1', \ldots, \beta_m'), (\gamma_1, \ldots, \gamma_k), (\gamma_1, \ldots, \gamma_k), (\beta_1', \ldots, \beta_m') > .$$

Note that η_{AC} is regular and so the β_i' are different from the β_j.

Now let Ψ be a cut-elimination sequence on η_{AC}. According to the cut-reduction rules for quantifiers, strong variables are replaced by weak terms. As the proofs in Ψ do not contain weakenings and contractions, Ψ contains *exactly* $m + k \; (= n)$ quantifier-elimination steps. Therefore these steps can be characterized by the single substitution

$$\{\beta_1' \leftarrow \alpha_1, \ldots, \beta_m' \leftarrow \alpha_m, \; \beta_1 \leftarrow \gamma_1, \ldots, \beta_k \leftarrow \gamma_k\}.$$

Hence the quantifier introduction vector for the result $\tau_{A,C}$ of Ψ is

$$Y_{AC}: \; < (\alpha_1, \ldots, \alpha_m), (\gamma_1, \ldots, \gamma_k), (\gamma_1, \ldots, \gamma_k), (\alpha_1, \ldots, \alpha_m) > .$$

But this quantifier introduction vector is that of a Q-simple transformation. Therefore $\tau_{A,C}$ is simple.

It remains to show that $\sim_s$ is compatible.

We proceed by induction on the logical complexity of the context. The case of the empty context is trivial.

(IH) Let $C[A]_\lambda \sim_s C[B]_\lambda$ whenever $A \sim_s B$, for any C of complexity $\leq n$ and any position λ in C.

Now let C be of complexity $n + 1$. Then C is of one of the following forms

(a) $C \equiv C_1 \wedge C_2$, (b) $C \equiv C_1 \vee C_2$, (c) $C \equiv C_1 \rightarrow C_2$,

(d) $C \equiv \neg C'$, \qquad (e) $C \equiv (\forall x)C'$, \quad (f) $C \equiv (\exists x)C'$.

We only show the cases c,d,e, the others are analogous.

(c) We consider the formulas $(C_1 \rightarrow C_2)[A]_\mu$ and $(C_1 \rightarrow C_2)[B]_\mu$. There are two possibilities:

(c1) μ is an occurrence in C_1, and

(c2) μ is an occurrence in C_2.

(c1) There exists a position λ in C_1 (corresponding to μ in C) s.t.

$$C[A]_\mu = C_1[A]_\lambda \rightarrow C_2, \; C[B]_\mu = C_1[B]_\lambda \rightarrow C_2.$$

We define a transformation τ transforming $C_1[A]_\lambda \rightarrow C_2$ into $C_1[B]_\lambda \rightarrow C_2$ (the other direction can be obtained by exchanging A and B).

$$\frac{\dfrac{\overset{\tau'}{C_1[B]_\lambda \vdash C_1[A]_\lambda} \quad \overset{I(C_2)}{C_2 \vdash C_2}}{\dfrac{C_1[B]_\lambda, C_1[A]_\lambda \rightarrow C_2 \vdash C_2}{C_1[A]_\lambda \rightarrow C_2 \vdash C_1[B]_\lambda \rightarrow C_2} \;\; \rightarrow: r}}{} \;\; \rightarrow: l$$

By (IH) a simple τ' exists, and $I(C_2)$ is simple; obviously τ itself is simple.

(c2) symmetric to (c1).

(d) We have to show $(\neg C')[A]_\mu \sim_s (\neg C')[B]_\mu$. Again there exists a position λ in C' with $\neg C'[A]_\lambda = (\neg C')[A]_\mu$ (the same for B). The desired transformation τ is

$$\frac{\dfrac{\tau'}{C'[B]_\lambda \vdash C'[A]_\lambda}}{\dfrac{\neg C'[A]_\lambda, C'[B]_\lambda \vdash}{\neg C'[A]_\lambda \vdash \neg C'[B]_\lambda}\ \neg : r}\ \neg : l$$

By (IH) such a simple transformation τ' exists. Clearly τ is also simple. The transformation from $\neg C'[B]_\lambda$ into $\neg C'[A]_\lambda$ can be obtained by exchanging A and B.

(e) We have to prove $((\forall x)C')[A]_\mu \sim_s ((\forall x)C')[B]_\mu$. Again there must be a position λ s.t. $((\forall x)C')[A]_\mu = (\forall x)C'[A]_\lambda$ (the same for B). We define τ as

$$\frac{\dfrac{\tau'}{C'[A]_\lambda\{x \leftarrow \alpha\} \vdash C'[B]_\lambda\{x \leftarrow \alpha\}}}{\dfrac{(\forall x)C'[A]_\lambda \vdash C'[B]_\lambda\{x \leftarrow \alpha\}}{(\forall x)C'[A]_\lambda \vdash (\forall x)C'[B]_\lambda}\ \forall : r}\ \forall : l$$

A simple transformation τ' exists by (IH).

Let $A' = A\{x \leftarrow \alpha\}$, $B' = B\{x \leftarrow \alpha\}$. Then

$$C'\{x \leftarrow \alpha\}[A']_\lambda = C'[A]_\lambda\{x \leftarrow \alpha\}, \ C'\{x \leftarrow \alpha\}[B']_\lambda = C'[B]_\lambda\{x \leftarrow \alpha\}.$$

Clearly the complexity of $C'\{x \leftarrow \alpha\}$ is that of C' itself. It remains to show that $A' \sim_s B'$: consider a simple transformation $\tau_{A,B}$. Either x is a free variable in A and B or it does not occur in both of them. As α is a variable not occurring in A and B, the transformation $\tau_{A,B}\{x \leftarrow \alpha\}$ is also simple. Therefore the transformation τ above is simple as well q.e.d.

Example 6. $\neg(\forall x)(\exists y)P(x,y) \sim_s (\exists x)(\forall y)\neg P(x,y)$:

we have shown in Example 3 that there exists a simple transformation of $\neg(\forall x)(\exists y)P(x,y)$ to $(\exists x)(\forall y)\neg P(x,y)$. It is easy to construct a simple transformation of $(\exists x)(\forall y)\neg P(x,y)$ to $\neg(\forall x)(\exists y)P(x,y)$.

We give an example of logically equivalent formulas which are not strongly equivalent:

$$(\forall x)P(x) \to Q(a) \not\sim_s (\exists x)(P(x) \to Q(a)).$$

Indeed, all transformations of $(\forall x)P(x) \to Q(a)$ to $(\exists x)(P(x) \to Q(a))$ require the use of contractions and thus are not simple. In fact, the quantifier $(\forall x)$ in

$$S: \ (\forall x)P(x) \to Q(a) \vdash (\exists x)(P(x) \to Q(a)).$$

is strong in S and thus (going from the end-sequent to the axioms) must be eliminated prior to $(\exists x)$ (which is weak in S). We see that, in general, the quantifier shifting principles go beyond strong equivalence.

Definition 23. *A formula A is in* negation normal form *(NNF) if it does not contain $\rightarrow$ and $\neg$ occurs only immediately above atoms (i.e. for any subformula $\neg C$ of A, C is an atom).*

Lemma 9. *A formula is in negation normal from iff it is a normal form under the rewrite rules $\mathcal{R}$ (applied to arbitrary occurrences of subformulas):*

> (1) $\neg\neg A \Rightarrow A$, (2) $\neg(A \wedge B) \Rightarrow \neg A \vee \neg B$, (3) $\neg(A \vee B) \Rightarrow \neg A \wedge \neg B$,
>
> (4) $A \rightarrow B \Rightarrow \neg A \vee B$, (5) $\neg(\forall x)A \Rightarrow (\exists x)\neg A$, (6) $\neg(\exists x)A \Rightarrow (\forall x)\neg A$.

Moreover all formulas A can be transformed to a NNF B via $\mathcal{R}$ (we say that B is the NNF of A).

Proof. In [1], proposition 4.6.

Proposition 3. *A formula A is strongly equivalent to its negation normal form.*

Proof. It is enough to show that, for the rewrite rules defined in Lemma 9, the left and right sides are strongly equivalent. Then the result follows from Lemma 9 and the fact that $\sim_s$ is compatible and transitive (Proposition 2).

We give the simple transformations corresponding to the rules in $\mathcal{R}$:

(1) $\neg\neg A \sim_s A$:

$$
\cfrac{\cfrac{\cfrac{I(A)}{A \vdash A}}{\cfrac{\vdash A, \neg A}{\neg\neg A \vdash A}\ \neg:l}\ \neg:r}{}
\qquad
\cfrac{\cfrac{\cfrac{I(A)}{A \vdash A}}{\cfrac{\neg A, A \vdash}{A \vdash \neg\neg A}\ \neg:r}\ \neg:l}{}
$$

(2) $\neg(A \wedge B) \sim_s \neg A \vee \neg B$:

$$
\cfrac{\cfrac{\cfrac{\cfrac{\cfrac{I(A)\quad I(B)}{\cfrac{A \vdash A \quad B \vdash B}{A, B \vdash A \wedge B}\ \wedge:r}}{A, B, \neg(A \wedge B) \vdash}\ \neg:l}{A, \neg(A \wedge B) \vdash \neg B}\ \neg:r}{\neg(A \wedge B) \vdash \neg A, \neg B}\ \neg:r}{\neg(A \wedge B) \vdash \neg A \vee \neg B}\ \vee:r
\qquad
\cfrac{\cfrac{\cfrac{\cfrac{I(A)}{\cfrac{A \vdash A}{A, \neg A \vdash}\ \neg:l}\quad \cfrac{I(B)}{\cfrac{B \vdash B}{B, \neg B \vdash}\ \neg:l}}{A, B, \neg A \vee \neg B \vdash}\ \vee:l}{A \wedge B, \neg A \vee \neg B \vdash}\ \wedge:l}{\neg A \vee \neg B \vdash \neg(A \wedge B)}\ \neg:r
$$

(3) $\neg(A \vee B) \sim_s \neg A \wedge \neg B$: symmetric to (2).

(4) $A \rightarrow B \sim_s \neg A \vee B$:

$$
\cfrac{\cfrac{\cfrac{\cfrac{I(A)\quad I(B)}{\cfrac{A \vdash A \quad B \vdash B}{A, A \rightarrow B \vdash B}\ \rightarrow:l}}{A \rightarrow B \vdash \neg A, B}\ \neg:r}{A \rightarrow B \vdash \neg A \vee B}\ \vee:r}{}
\qquad
\cfrac{\cfrac{\cfrac{\cfrac{I(A)}{\cfrac{A \vdash A}{A, \neg A \vdash}\ \neg:l}\quad \cfrac{I(B)}{B \vdash B}}{A, \neg A \vee B \vdash B}\ \vee:l}{\neg A \vee B \vdash A \rightarrow B}\ \rightarrow:r}{}
$$

(5) $\neg(\forall x)A \sim_s (\exists x)\neg A$:

$$
\cfrac{\cfrac{\cfrac{\cfrac{\cfrac{I(A\{x \leftarrow \alpha\})}{A\{x \leftarrow \alpha\} \vdash A\{x \leftarrow \alpha\}}}{\vdash \neg A\{x \leftarrow \alpha\}, A\{x \leftarrow \alpha\}} \ \neg:r}{\vdash (\exists x)\neg A, A\{x \leftarrow \alpha\}} \ \exists:r}{\vdash (\exists x)\neg A, (\forall x)A} \ \forall:r}{\neg(\forall x)A \vdash (\exists x)\neg A} \ \neg:l
$$

$$
\cfrac{\cfrac{\cfrac{\cfrac{\cfrac{I(A\{x \leftarrow \alpha\})}{A\{x \leftarrow \alpha\} \vdash A\{x \leftarrow \alpha\}}}{A\{x \leftarrow \alpha\}, \neg A\{x \leftarrow \alpha\} \vdash} \ \neg:l}{(\forall x)A, \neg A\{x \leftarrow \alpha\} \vdash} \ \forall:l}{(\forall x)A, (\exists x)\neg A \vdash} \ \exists:l}{(\exists x)\neg A \vdash \neg(\forall x)A} \ \neg:r
$$

(6) $\neg(\exists x)A \sim_s (\forall x)\neg A$: symmetric to (5).

q.e.d.

The following lemma is the technical key to the main result. It shows that simple transformations applied to ancestors of cuts do not change the proof profile modulo variable renaming. In particular, this holds for the transformation to negation normal form.

Lemma 10. *Let φ' be a subproof of an **LKps**-proof φ s.t. φ' is an **LK**-proof of a sequent $\Gamma \vdash \Delta, A$ at node ν, and A is an ancestor of a pseudo-cut. Let $\tau_{A,B}$ be a simple transformation. Then, for any proof ψ in $(\varphi')\tau_{A,B}$, $P(\varphi[\psi]_\nu) = P(\varphi)\pi$, where π is a permutation of eigenvariables.*

Remark 4. Note that, in general, $\varphi[\psi]_\nu$ is a pseudo-proof, even if φ is a proof, as the substitution of ψ for φ' may violate cut- and contraction rules. But note that φ' must be an **LK**-proof!

Proof. We proceed by cut-elimination on the proof $T(\varphi', \tau_{A,B})$:

$$
\cfrac{\overset{\varphi'}{\Gamma \vdash \Delta, A} \quad \overset{\tau_{A,B}}{A \vdash B}}{\Gamma \vdash \Delta, B} \ cut
$$

The profile at the node ν is of the form

$$P(\varphi).\nu = C' \cup D, \quad \text{where } D = \{A_1 \vdash^{l_1} A_1, \ldots, A_m \vdash^{l_n} A_m\}$$

for a set of atoms A_i and labels l_i. Note that all binary inferences in $\tau_{A,B}$ work on ancestors of a cut, so D is the union of all axiom sequents in $\tau_{A,B}$.

Moreover we obtain

$$P(\varphi) = C \cup D$$

For a clause set C, because – on successors of B (which goes into a pseudo-cut) – only unions are performed in the construction of the proof profile.

We apply cut-elimination based on $\rightarrow_{G_t}$ in two phases (as defined in Definition 17): in the first step we eliminate all marked cuts without applying the elimination rule for axioms. In a second step we eliminate the atomic cuts between axioms.

In every phase of cut-elimination by $\rightarrow_{G_t}$ we distinguish a φ'-part (i.e. the part labelled by F, the original label set of φ) and a $\tau_{A,B}$-part. Indeed, every cut appearing in a proof χ obtained by cut-elimination is of the form ξ:

$$\frac{\overset{\rho}{\Pi \vdash \Lambda, C} \quad \overset{\sigma}{C, \Pi' \vdash \Lambda'}}{\Pi, \Pi' \vdash \Lambda, \Lambda'} \; cut$$

where ρ is an (possibly instantiated) subproof of φ', and σ one of $\tau_{A,B}$. For simplicity we assume that the φ'-part is to the left and the $\tau_{A,B}$-part to the right (in fact the sides my change by elimination on negated formulas).

We prove that for all χ with $(\varphi')\tau_{A,B} \rightarrow^*_{G_t} \chi$,we have

$$(\star) \; P(\varphi[\chi]_\nu) = C\pi \cup D^*,$$

where π is a permutation of eigenvariables and D^* is a set of instances of clauses (modulo label renaming) in D.

We know by Lemmas 4 and 5 that $\rightarrow_{G_r}$ and $\rightarrow_{G_p}$ do not change the profile, so we may assume that the cut in ξ is introduced (1) by weakening, or (2) by contraction, or (3) by quantifier introductions on both sides. Let us furthermore assume inductively that $(\star)$ holds for χ.

(1) ξ is of the form

$$\frac{\dfrac{\overset{\rho'}{\Pi \vdash \Lambda}}{\Pi \vdash \Lambda, C} \; w:r \quad \overset{\sigma}{C, \Pi' \vdash \Lambda'}}{\Pi, \Pi' \vdash \Lambda, \Lambda'} \; cut$$

Indeed, weakening can only appear in the φ'-part, not in the $\tau_{A,B}$-part (as $\tau_{A,B}$ is simple). According to the rules of $\rightarrow_{G_t}$, ξ reduces to ξ' for $\xi' =$

$$\frac{\overset{\rho'}{\Pi \vdash \Lambda}}{\Pi, \Pi' \vdash \Lambda, \Lambda'} \; w^*$$

From now on (for the remaining part of the proof) let us assume that the root node of ξ is μ and $\chi' = \chi[\xi']_\mu$. Then, as Π' and Λ' contain only ancestors of a cut, we may apply Corollary 2 and obtain

$$P(\varphi[\chi']_\mu) = C\pi \cup D',$$

where D' is a subset of D^*.

(2) contraction: as in (1) contractions can only occur in the φ'-part, not in the $\tau_{A,B}$-part. So ξ is of the form

$$\frac{\dfrac{\overset{\rho'}{\Pi \vdash \Lambda, C, C}}{\Pi \vdash \Lambda, C} \; c:r \quad \overset{\sigma}{C, \Pi' \vdash \Lambda'}}{\Pi, \Pi' \vdash \Lambda, \Lambda'} \; cut$$

Then $\xi \to_{G_t} \xi'$ for $\xi' =$

$$
\cfrac{\cfrac{\overset{\rho'}{\Pi \vdash \Lambda, C, C} \quad \overset{\sigma}{C, \Pi' \vdash \Lambda'}}{\Pi, \Pi' \vdash \Lambda, \Lambda', C} \; cut \quad \overset{\sigma'}{C, \Pi' \vdash \Lambda'}}{\cfrac{\Pi, \Pi', \Pi' \vdash \Lambda, \Lambda', \Lambda'}{\Pi, \Pi' \vdash \Lambda, \Lambda'} \; c^*} \; cut
$$

where σ' is σ after renaming of eigenvariables and labels. Again, let $\chi' = \chi[\xi']_\mu$. Then, by Lemma 8,

$$
P(\varphi[\chi']_\nu) = C\pi \cup D^* \cup D',
$$

where D' is a set of instances of clauses in D^*.

(3) Elimination of a quantifier:

(3a) $\xi =$

$$
\cfrac{\cfrac{\overset{\rho'}{\Pi \vdash \Lambda, A\{x \leftarrow t\}}}{\Pi \vdash \Lambda, (\exists x)A} \; \exists : r \quad \cfrac{\overset{\sigma'}{A\{x \leftarrow \alpha\}, \Pi' \vdash \Lambda'}}{(\exists x)A, \Pi' \vdash \Lambda'} \; \exists : l}{\Pi, \Pi' \vdash \Lambda, \Lambda'} \; cut
$$

Then $\xi \to_{G_t} \xi'$ for $\xi' =$

$$
\cfrac{\overset{\rho'}{\Pi \vdash \Lambda, A\{x \leftarrow t\}} \quad \overset{\sigma'\{\alpha \leftarrow t\}}{A\{x \leftarrow t\}, \Pi' \vdash \Lambda'}}{\Pi, \Pi' \vdash \Lambda, \Lambda'} \; cut
$$

Then, by Lemma 6,

$$
P(\varphi[\chi']_\nu) = C\pi \cup D^*\{\alpha \leftarrow t\}.
$$

Note that α does not occur in $C\pi$! Again, the φ'-part remains unchanged, and the $\tau_{A,B}$-part is instantiated.

(3b) $\xi =$

$$
\cfrac{\cfrac{\overset{\rho'}{\Pi \vdash \Lambda, A\{x \leftarrow \alpha\}}}{\Pi \vdash \Lambda, (\forall x)A} \; \forall : r \quad \cfrac{\overset{\sigma'}{A\{x \leftarrow \beta\}, \Pi' \vdash \Lambda'}}{(\forall x)A, \Pi' \vdash \Lambda'} \; \forall : l}{\Pi, \Pi' \vdash \Lambda, \Lambda'} \; cut
$$

As σ' is a $\tau_{A,B}$-part, the quantifier substitution for $\forall : l$ is of the form $\{x \leftarrow \beta\}$ where β is an eigenvariable in the proof $\varphi[\xi]_\nu$. Note that no substitution of an eigenvariable in the $\tau_{A,B}$-part (see case (3a)) can change the weak quantifier substitutions in this part, because $\tau_{A,B}$ is simple. Now $\xi \to_{G_t} \xi'$ for $\xi' =$

$$
\cfrac{\overset{\rho'\{\alpha \leftarrow \beta\}}{\Pi \vdash \Lambda, A\{x \leftarrow \beta\}} \quad \overset{\sigma'}{A\{x \leftarrow \beta\}, \Pi' \vdash \Lambda'}}{\Pi, \Pi' \vdash \Lambda, \Lambda'} \; cut
$$

Again, by Lemma 6, we obtain

$$P(\varphi[\chi']_\nu) = C\pi\{\alpha \leftarrow \beta\} \cup D^*.$$

We know that β is a variable. But β cannot occur in $C\pi$ (i.e. in the φ'-part of the proof) as β is an eigenvariable in $\tau_{A,B}$-part and the proof χ is regular. So we obtain

$$C\pi\{\alpha \leftarrow \beta\} = C\pi\{\alpha \leftarrow \beta, \ \beta \leftarrow \alpha\}$$

where $\pi\{\alpha \leftarrow \beta, \ \beta \leftarrow \alpha\}$ is a permutation of eigenvariables.

We have seen that in all cases (1), (2), (3) the property $(\star)$ is preserved. Thus it holds after the first phase of cut-elimination, before the axioms are eliminated. It remains to investigate the elimination of the axioms. Let χ^* be the normal form of $T(\varphi', \tau_{A,B})$ under the first phase of cut-elimination. Then

$$P(\varphi[\chi^*]_\nu) = C\pi \cup D^*.$$

where π is a permutation and

$$D^* = \{B_1 \vdash^{j_1} B_1, \ldots, B_r \vdash^{j_r} B_r\}.$$

Now the only cuts left in χ^* are of the form $\xi =$

$$\frac{B^{\{i\}} \vdash B^{\{i\}} \quad B^{\{j\}} \vdash B^{\{j\}}}{B^{\{i\}} \vdash B^{\{j\}}} \ cut$$

Where i is a label in the φ'-part and j is a label in the $\tau_{A,B}$-part. According to the definition of $\rightarrow_{G_t}$ (Definition 17), ξ is replaced by $\xi' =$

$$B^{\{i\}} \vdash B^{\{i\}}.$$

Let μ be the node of this cut and $\chi' = \chi^*[\xi']$. Then

$$P(\varphi[\chi']_\nu) = C\pi \cup D^* - \{B \vdash^j B\}.$$

This procedure is repeated till all the clauses in the set D^* are used up. Let us call the resulting proof ψ, which does not contain any marked cuts. Then

$$P(\varphi[\psi]_\nu) = C\pi.$$

q.e.d.

Corollary 3. *Let φ' be a subproof of an **LKps**-proof φ s.t. φ' is a proof of a sequent $B, \Gamma \vdash \Delta$ at node ν, and B is an ancestor of a pseudo-cut. Let $\tau_{A,B}$ be a simple transformation. Then, for any proof ψ in $\tau_{A,B}(\varphi')$, $P(\varphi[\psi]_\nu) = P(\varphi)\pi$, where π is a permutation of eigenvariables.*

Proof. completely symmetric to the proof of Lemma 10.

Lemma 11. *Let φ be an* **LK***-proof and σ be a subproof of φ (at node ν) of the form*

$$\frac{\begin{array}{cc} \sigma_1 & \sigma_2 \\ \Gamma \vdash \Delta, A & A, \Pi \vdash \Lambda \end{array}}{\Gamma, \Pi \vdash \Delta, \Lambda} \; cut$$

and let A be strongly equivalent to B. Then there exists an **LK***-proof ψ of the form*

$$\frac{\begin{array}{cc} \psi_1 & \psi_2 \\ \Gamma \vdash \Delta, B & B, \Pi \vdash \Lambda \end{array}}{\Gamma, \Pi \vdash \Delta, \Lambda} \; cut$$

and a permutation of eigenvariables π s.t. $\varphi[\psi]_\nu$ is an **LK***-proof and $P(\varphi[\psi]_\nu) = P(\varphi)\pi$.*

Proof. Apply Lemma 10 to the subproof σ_1 with the transformation $\tau_{A,B}$. The result is a pseudo-proof $\varphi_1 \colon \varphi[\rho]_\nu$ with $P(\varphi_1) = P(\varphi)\pi_1$ for a permutation π_1 and for $\rho =$

$$\frac{\begin{array}{cc} \psi_1 & \sigma_2 \\ \Gamma \vdash \Delta, B & A, \Pi \vdash \Lambda \end{array}}{\Gamma, \Pi \vdash \Delta, \Lambda} \; pscut$$

Then apply Corollary 3 to σ_2 (within φ_1) and obtain a pseudo-proof φ_2, for $\varphi_2 = \varphi_1[\psi]_\nu$, with $P(\varphi_2) = P(\varphi_1)\pi_2$ for a permutation π_2 and for $\psi =$

$$\frac{\begin{array}{cc} \psi_1 & \psi_2 \\ \Gamma \vdash \Delta, B & B, \Pi \vdash \Lambda \end{array}}{\Gamma, \Pi \vdash \Delta, \Lambda} \; cut$$

Then

$$P(\varphi_2) = P(\varphi[\psi]_\nu) = P(\varphi)\pi_1\pi_2.$$

Clearly $\pi_1\pi_2$ is a variable permutation. Moreover φ_2 is not only a pseudo-proof but also a proof (note that ψ is a proof and has the same end-sequent as σ) q.e.d.

The following theorem shows that we can transform the cuts in an **LK**-proof into arbitrary strongly equivalent form without changing the proof profile (indeed, variants that differ only by variable permutations can be considered as equal). All these forms can thus be considered as equivalent w.r.t. cut-elimination.

Theorem 1. *Let φ be an* **LK***-proof with cut formulas $A_1, \ldots, A_n$ and $B_1 \sim_s A_1, \ldots, B_n \sim_s A_n$. Then there exists a proof ψ with cut formulas $B_1, \ldots, B_n$ and $P(\psi) = P(\varphi)\pi$ for a variable permutation π.*

Proof. We iterate the construction defined in Lemma 11, by transforming the cuts with $A_1, \ldots, A_n$ successively into cuts with $B_1, \ldots, B_n$. This way we obtain a proof ψ and permutations $\pi_1, \ldots, \pi_n$ with

$$P(\psi) = P(\varphi)\pi_1 \ldots \pi_n.$$

But $\pi_1 \ldots \pi_n$ is also a permutation q.e.d.

Corollary 4. *Let φ be a proof with cut formulas $A_1, \ldots, A_n$. Then there exists a proof ψ with cut formulas $B_1, \ldots, B_n$, where the B_i are the negation normal forms of the A_i and $P(\psi) = P(\varphi)\pi$ for a permutation π.*

Proof. By Proposition 3 and Theorem 1.

Corollary 4 does not hold for prenex normal from in place of NNF. This is based on the fact, that quantifier shifting does not preserve strong equivalence in general (see Example 6); so Theorem 1 is not applicable in case of prenex normal forms. Moreover, a proof transformation to prenex form, under preservation of cut-homomorphism, is impossible in principle (see [2]).

In Section 3.4 we have shown that profiles define equivalence classes of proofs at least as large as proof nets. Theorem 1 proves that the equivalence classes defined by profiles are in fact larger, due to the strong abstraction from the syntax of cuts.

6   Summary

We have shown that proofs with strongly equivalent cut-formulas (obtained via simple transformations) have the same profile (under variable renaming) and thus can be considered as equal w.r.t. cut-elimination. We did *not* prove that the profile remains the same when the whole proof (i.e. also the formulas in the end-sequent) undergoes simple transformations. We conjecture that even this stronger result holds (e.g. it is easy to show that it holds for transformations to negation normal form), but it is much harder to prove: indeed, if we apply a transformation to a formula which goes to the end-sequent, the original formula changes its status (as it now goes to the cut with the transformation), and the whole profile changes in a more complicated way.

We defined profiles as sets of *labelled* clauses, i.e. two clauses that differ only in their labels are treated as two different clauses. If profiles are defined as sets of clauses (dropping the labels after generation of the profile), the class of equivalent proofs becomes even larger while still having the same set of normal forms of the CERES method. Then, however, cut-elimination on propositional proofs would not increase the profile (it can only shrink by weakening), and thus would not express the duplication of subproofs.

Furthermore, it is possible to apply redundancy-elimination techniques from automated theorem proving like tautology-deletion and subsumption to the profile which results in a smaller and thus more readable version of it. While these transformations formally change the set of normal forms, the logical meaning of them is preserved. On the other hand we clearly can regard profiles as equal if they are equivalent w.r.t. variable renaming. Moreover we believe that the analysis can be carried over to **LK**-proofs in second-order logic.

References

1. Baaz, M., Egly, U., Leitsch, A.: Normal Form Transformations. In: Handbook of Automated Reasoning, pp. 273–333 (2001)
2. Baaz, M., Leitsch, A.: Cut normal forms and proof complexity. Annals of Pure and Applied Logic 97, 127–177 (1999)
3. Baaz, M., Leitsch, A.: Cut-elimination and Redundancy-elimination by Resolution. Journal of Symbolic Computation 29(2), 149–176 (2000)
4. Baaz, M., Leitsch, A.: Towards a Clausal Analysis of Cut-Elimination. Journal of Symbolic Computation 41, 381–410 (2006)
5. Danos, V., Joinet, J.-B., Schellinx, H.: A New Deconstructive Logic: Linear Logic. Journal of Symbolic Logic 62(3), 755–807 (1997)
6. Danos, V., Joinet, J.-B., Schellinx, H.: Computational isomorphisms in classical logic. Theoretical Computer Science 294(3), 353–378 (2003)
7. Gentzen, G.: Untersuchungen über das logische Schließen. Mathematische Zeitschrift 39, 405–431 (1934–1935)
8. Kleene, S.C.: Permutability of Inferences in Gentzen's Calculi LK and LJ. Memoirs of the American Mathematical Society 10, 1–26 (1952)
9. McKinley, R.: Categorical Model for First-Order Classical Proofs. PhD thesis, University of Bath (2006)
10. Robinson, E.: Proof Nets for Classical Logic. Journal of Logic and Computation 13(5), 777–797 (2003)

Rényi-Ulam Game Semantics for Product Logic and for the Logic of Cancellative Hoops

Sándor Jenei[1,*] and Franco Montagna[2]

[1] Institute of Mathematics and Informatics
University of Pécs
Ifjúság u. 6, H–7624 Pécs, Hungary
jenei@ttk.pte.hu
[2] Department of Mathematics and Computer Science
University of Siena
Pian dei Mantellini 44, 53100 Siena, Italy
montagna@unisi.it

1 Introduction

Connections between games and logic are quite common in the literature: for example, to every analytic proof system with the subformula property (hence admitting cut-elimination) one can associate a game in which a player tries to find a cut-free proof and his opponent can attack parts of the proof constructed since then. Along these lines, formulas correspond to games and proofs correspond to winning strategies. A first connection between many-valued logic and games was discovered by Giles in [9]. A variant of such semantics was used in [4] in order to obtain a uniform proof system with a game-theoretical interpretation for Łukasiewicz, product and Gödel logics. The above mentioned papers are extremely interesting, but we would say that the interest of this game semantics is more proof-theoretical than game-theoretical.

A game semantics for Łukasiewicz logic with a clear game theoretical interest, in view also of its connections with the treatment of uncertain information and with error-correcting codes, has been discovered by Daniele Mundici [14]. The game in question is the Rényi-Ulam game, see [17], [18], and the logic is Łukasiewicz logic.

Given a finite set Ω of cardinality N (called *the search space,* we can suppose without loss of generality that $\Omega = \{1, 2..., N\}$) and a natural number e, the Rényi-Ulam game $G(N, e)$ is the following: a player, called *Responder*, chooses an element of Ω called *the secret*. The other player, called *Questioner*, has to guess the secret on the ground of binary questions. Responder has to answer all of them with a maximum of e lies. The connections between this game and Łukasiewicz logic are the following: the information contained in a sequence σ of questions-answers (called *record* in the sequel) can be coded by means of the function m_σ from Ω into $[0, 1]$, called *the truth-value function corresponding to* σ, defined as follows.

---

* Supported by the Bolyai János Research Grant and by the Hungarian-American Enterprise Scholarship Fund (HAESF).

S. Aguzzoli et al.(Eds.): Algebraic and Proof-theoretic Aspects, LNAI 4460, pp. 231–246, 2007.
© Springer-Verlag Berlin Heidelberg 2007

Say that a pair (Q, A), of questions-answers, where Q is *Is the secret in X?* with $X \subseteq \Omega$, and $A \in \{YES, NO\}$ *falsifies* x if either $x \in X$ and $A = NO$ or $x \notin X$ and $A = YES$.

Let for every $x \in \Omega$, h_x^σ be the number of questions-answers in σ which falsify x (counting repetitions!).

Then m_σ is defined, for every $x \in \Omega$, by

$$m_\sigma(x) = \frac{e + 1 - h_x^\sigma}{e + 1}. \tag{1}$$

Note that it is possible that $\sigma \neq \tau$ and $m_\sigma = m_\tau$, but this can only occur if σ and τ have the same informational content (this happens e.g. if τ is obtained from σ after a permutation of the questions-answers, preserving repetitions). As observed by Mundici, the truth-value function m_τ corresponding to the juxtaposition τ of two records σ and ρ is the pointwise Łukasiewicz conjunction $m_\sigma \odot m_\rho$ of m_σ and m_ρ.

Moreover truth-value functions can be partially ordered by the pointwise order $\preceq$: $m_\sigma \preceq m_\rho$ iff for $x = 1, ..., N$, $m_\sigma(x) \leq m_\rho(x)$. (Intuitively, $m_\sigma \preceq m_\rho$ iff the record σ is more informative than ρ). Finally, we can introduce the constantly zero function $\bar{0}$, which corresponds to an inconsistent record, i.e., a record in which every element of the search spaces is falsified by more than e answers, and the constantly 1 function $\bar{1}$, which corresponds to the empty record.

Given a truth-value function m_σ, there is a maximum truth-value function m_ρ such that $m_\sigma \odot m_\rho = \bar{0}$, or equivalently, there exists the less informative record ρ which added to σ produces the inconsistent information. Such a function, called *the complement of m_σ* and denoted by $\neg m_\sigma$, is defined by $\neg m_\sigma = 1 - m_\sigma$. (Łukasiewicz negation). Of course, one can also define an implication $m_\sigma \to m_\rho$ as $\neg(m_\sigma \odot \neg m_\rho)$, and it turns-out that such implication corresponds to the weakest information which added to σ gives an information at least as strong as ρ.

Summing-up, truth-value functions have a logic, which is precisely the $e + 2$-valued Łukasiewicz logic if e is the upper bound to the number of lies allowed by the game. Moreover, if one considers the logic of all truth-value functions corresponding to all Rényi-Ulam games with an arbitrary number e of lies, then the underlying logic is just the infinite-valued Łukasiewicz logic.

One may wonder if similar games can be found for other many-valued logics. A positive answer for the case of Hájek's Basic Logic BL was given by Cicalese and Mundici in [5]. There the authors propose a multichannel variant of the Rényi-Ulam game and prove that such variant constitutes a complete game semantics for BL. A game semantics for Gödel logic can be obtained as a particular case, so what still remains open is a game semantics for product logic. A first attempt to obtain a game semantics for product logic is introduced in [13], where the authors propose a multichannel variant of Pelc's game [15]. It turns-out that for some values of the probability parameter p one obtains a finitely strongly complete game semantics for product logic.

In this paper we explore an alternative game semantics which is closer to that given by the Rényi-Ulam game. The basic idea is that, as observed by Hájek in [11] Wajsberg algebras, the algebras of Łukasiewicz logic, can be presented as truncations of product algebras. More precisely, given a product chain $\mathcal{A}$ and an element $a > 0$, define $\mathcal{A} \searrow a$ to be the algebra whose domain is $\{x \in \mathcal{A} : x \geq a\}$, whose residual and whose lattice operations are the restrictions to $\mathcal{A} \searrow a$ of the analogous operations on $\mathcal{A}$, and whose product $\cdot_a$ is $x \cdot_a y = (x \cdot y) \vee a$. Then it is readily seen that $\mathcal{A} \searrow a$ is a Wajsberg algebra. A similar construction can be performed starting from any (possibly not totally ordered) product algebra and an element a such that $\neg a = 0$, still getting a Wajsberg algebra. It can be shown that every Wajsberg algebra can be obtained in this way from a product algebra.

Taking truncations by lower and lower elements, we obtain better and better approximations of the product algebra we started from by means of Wajsberg algebras. This observation suggests the investigation of a game semantics for product logic consisting of Rényi-Ulam games with larger and larger number of lies. This game, denoted by $G(N, ?)$, is investigated in Section 3 of the present paper. However, in this way we don't obtain a game semantics for product logic, but rather for the logic CH corresponding to cancellative hoops. In order to obtain a game semantics for product logic, we introduce a multichannel game semantics along the lines of [5]: here the first channel is more expensive but completely reliable, whereas along the second and cheaper channel a fixed but unknown number of lies are possible. The game obtained in this way is introduced in Section 4, and is denoted by $G^*(N, ?)$. In Section 4 we show that $G^*(N, ?)$ constitutes a finitely strongly complete algebraic semantics for product logic. Finally, in Section 5 we investigate some probabilistic variants of the games $G(N, ?)$ and $G^*(N, ?)$, having some game-theoretical interest.

2 Preliminaries

Definition 1. *A commutative, integral, bounded residuated lattice (see [12]) (c.i.b. residuated lattice for short) is a system* $\mathbf{L} = \langle L, \&, \rightarrow, \vee, \wedge, 0, 1 \rangle$ *where* $\langle L, \&, 1 \rangle$ *is a commutative monoid,* $\langle L, \vee, \wedge, 0, 1 \rangle$ *is a lattice with minimum* 0 *and maximum* 1, *and the residuation property holds:*

(res)   For all $x, y, z \in L$, $x \leq y \rightarrow z$ iff $x \& y \leq z$.

Sometimes, the symbol $\&$ will be omitted or denoted by $\cdot$. Moreover, we define $\neg x = x \rightarrow 0$, $x \leftrightarrow y = (x \rightarrow y) \& (y \rightarrow x)$.

Definition 2. *A c.i.b. residuated lattice* $\mathcal{A}$ *is said to be* divisible *iff it satisfies the condition* $x(x \rightarrow y) = x \wedge y$, *and* prelinear *iff it satisfies the condition* $(x \rightarrow y) \vee (y \rightarrow x) = 1$.

A BL-algebra *[11] is a divisible and prelinear c.i.b. residuated lattice. A Wajsberg algebra is a BL-algebra satisfying* $\neg\neg x = x$.

Letting in any Wajsberg algebra $\mathcal{W}$ $\neg x = x \rightarrow 0$ and $x \oplus y = \neg x \rightarrow y$, we obtain an *MV-algebra* [6]. MV-algebras and Wajsberg algebras are term-equivalent, and we will identify them in the sequel.

Definition 3. *A* product algebra *is a BL-algebra satisfying* $\neg x \vee ((x \rightarrow (xy)) \rightarrow y) = 1$, *and a* Gödel algebra *is a BL-algebra satisfying* $x \cdot x = x$.

Examples of MV-algebras are: (a) $[0,1]_{MV} = ([0,1], \&_{MV}, \rightarrow_{MV}, \max, \min, 0, 1)$ with $x\&_L y = \max\{x + y - 1, 0\}$ and $x \rightarrow_{MV} y = \min\{1 - x + y, 1\}$; (b) the MV-chain with $e + 2$ elements, that is, the subalgebra of $[0,1]_{MV}$ with domain $\{0, \frac{1}{e+1}, \frac{2}{e+1}, ..., 1\}$.

An example of product algebra is $[0,1]_\Pi = ([0,1], \&_\Pi, \rightarrow_\Pi, \max, \min, 0, 1)$ where $\&_\Pi$ is ordinary product on $[0,1]$ and

$$x \rightarrow_\Pi y = \begin{cases} \frac{y}{x} & \text{if } x > y \\ 1 & \text{otherwise} \end{cases}$$

Note that in any BL-algebra lattice operations may be defined in terms of the monoid operation and its residual: $x \wedge y = x(x \rightarrow y)$, and $x \vee y = ((x \rightarrow y) \rightarrow y) \wedge ((y \rightarrow x) \rightarrow x)$.

Definition 4. *A* hoop *[1] is a subreduct (subalgebra of a reduct) of a divisible c.i.b. residuated lattice in the language* $\{\&, \rightarrow, 1\}$. *A* basic hoop *is a hoop which is a subreduct of a BL-algebra. A basic hoop is said to be* bounded *if it has minimum element, and* Wajsberg *iff it is a subreduct of a Wajsberg algebra.*

In [8] it is shown that every a linearly ordered Wajsberg hoop is bounded iff it is a reduct of a Wajsberg algebra. Moreover, any unbounded totally ordered Wajsberg hoop is *cancellative*, that is, $xy = xz$ implies $y = z$.

We now consider a basic propositional language **L** containing parentheses, propositional variables, the propositional constants 0 and 1, and the binary connectives $\&$, $\rightarrow$, $\vee$ and $\wedge$. For every two formulas A and B, $\neg A$ and $A \leftrightarrow B$ are abbreviations for $A \rightarrow 0$ and for $(A \rightarrow B)\&(B \rightarrow A)$ respectively.

Definition 5. *Let* $\mathcal{A}$ *be a c.i.b. residuated lattice. An* evaluation *of* **L** *in* $\mathcal{A}$ *is just a homomorphism* v *from the algebra of propositional formulas into* $\mathcal{A}$.

Definition 6. *Let* **K** *be a class of c.i.b. residuated lattices, let* Γ *be a set of propositional formulas of* **L**, *and let A be a formula of* **L**. *We say that A is a* semantic consequence *of* Γ *in* **K** *(and we write* $\Gamma \models_\mathbf{K} A$*) iff for every* $\mathcal{A} \in \mathbf{K}$ *and for every evaluation* v *in* $\mathcal{A}$ *if* $v(B) = 1$ *for all* $B \in \Gamma$, *then* $v(A) = 1$.

We write $\models_\mathbf{K} A$, *for* $\emptyset \models_\mathbf{K} A$, *($\emptyset \models_\mathbf{K1} A$ respectively), and in this case we say that A is* valid *in* **K**.

Let **F** *be a propositional formal system for the language* **L**, *and let* **K** *be a class of c.i.b. residuated lattices. We say that* **F** *is* strongly complete *(finitely strongly complete, complete respectively) with respect to* **K** *iff for every set* $\Gamma \cup \{A\}$ *of sentences (for every finite set* $\Gamma \cup \{A\}$ *of sentences, for* $\Gamma = \emptyset$ *and A any sentence respectively) one has:* $\Gamma \models_\mathbf{K} A$ *iff A is derivable from* Γ *in* **F**.

Definition 7. *BL (see [11]) is the logic on the language* **L** *whose axioms are:*

(A1) $(A \rightarrow B) \rightarrow ((B \rightarrow C) \rightarrow (A \rightarrow C))$
(A2) $(A\&B) \rightarrow A$

(A3) $(A\&B) \rightarrow (B\&A)$
(A4) $(A\&(A \rightarrow B)) \rightarrow (B\&B \rightarrow A)$
(A5) $(A \rightarrow (B \rightarrow C)) \rightarrow ((A\&B) \rightarrow C)$
(A6) $((A\&B) \rightarrow C) \rightarrow (A \rightarrow (B \rightarrow C))$
(A7) $((A \rightarrow B) \rightarrow C) \rightarrow (((B \rightarrow A) \rightarrow C) \rightarrow C)$
(A11) $0 \rightarrow A$
(A12) $A \rightarrow 1$

The only rule of BL is Modus Ponens:

$$(MP) \quad \frac{A \quad A \rightarrow B}{B}.$$

Łukasiewicz Logic L is BL plus

(¬¬) $\quad \neg\neg A \rightarrow A.$

Product logic Π is BL plus

(π) $\quad (\neg A) \vee ((A \rightarrow (A\&B)) \rightarrow B),$

Gödel logic G is BL plus

(id) $\quad A \rightarrow (A\&A).$

The following proposition summarizes the main known results about BL and its principal extensions, as well as their first-order versions:

Proposition 1. *Let L be any of BL, Π, G, L. Then L is strongly complete with respect to both the class of BL (product, Gödel, Wajsberg respectively) algebras as well as to the class of BL (product, Gödel, Wajsberg respectively) chains, [11].*

3   A Variant of the Rényi-Ulam Game and the Logic of Cancellative Hoops

Before introducing our first variant, we start with a different, although equivalent, game-theoretic interpretation of Łukasiewicz logic. We still refer to the Rényi-Ulam game with e lies, but we change the definition of truth-value function. More precisely, with reference to the notation from the introduction, given a record σ, for $x \in \Omega$ we simply define, $k_\sigma(x)$ as the "truncated counting of falsifications" as follows:

$$k_\sigma(x) = \min\{h_x^\sigma, e + 1\}. \tag{2}$$

Then it is easy to prove that the set of truth values of all records, including the inconsistent one, is the set of all functions form Ω into $\{0, 1, \ldots, e+1\}$. Note that $\{0, 1, \ldots, e+1\}$ becomes an MV-algebra with top 0 and bottom $e+1$ (thus the order is the inverse of the natural order), letting $x \odot y = \min\{x + y, e + 1\}$ and $\neg x = e + 1 - x$. This MV-algebra is isomorphic to the MV-chain $\mathcal{MV}_{e+2}$ with $e + 2$ elements. Thus the set of all truth value functions (in our new sense) becomes an MV-algebra isomorphic to $(\mathcal{MV}_{e+2})^N$ with respect to the operations

$(k_\sigma \odot k_\tau)(x) = \min\{k_\sigma(x) + k_\tau(x), e + 1\}$ and $(\neg k_\sigma)(x) = e + 1 - k_\sigma(x)$. Note that the truth-value function of the juxtaposition of two records τ and σ is the product of k_τ and k_σ in $\mathcal{MV}^N_{e+2}$. Moreover the induced order $\preceq$ is the inverse of the pointwise order, and its intuitive interpretation is $k_\sigma \preceq k_\tau$ if σ is at least as informative as τ. The top of the algebra corresponds to the inconsistent information, and the bottom corresponds to the null information. Responder wins the game after a record σ iff $k_\sigma(x) = e + 1$ for all elements of Ω except one, which is necessarily the secret.

Of course this semantics is not new, it is just Mundici's semantics (see (1)) upside-down and without normalization. However, it is easier to extend it to a game semantics for the logic of cancellative hoops and for product logic, using the idea that MV-algebras can be regarded as truncations of cancellative hoops or of product algebras. The intuitive idea is the following: if e is the maximum number of lies allowed, then we identify two records σ and τ when for every $x \in \Omega$ either $h^\sigma_x = h^\tau_x$ or $h^\sigma_x > e + 1$ and $h^\tau_x > e + 1$. In other words, we truncate our information to the value $e + 1$, identifying all values above $e + 1$ as *too many*. Letting e larger and larger, our truth-value functions give us a better and better information about the number of answers which falsify each element of Ω. (In particular, the information is complete if the total number of questions in σ does not exceed $e + 1$). Thus our idea is that Rényi-Ulam games are truncations of a more general game in which the number of lies is unbounded, or simply fixed, but unknown to Responder.

This variant, denoted by $G(N, ?)$ is as follows:

1. The first player, called *Responder*, chooses a natural number $x \in \Omega$ (called *the secret*).
2. Another natural number e, representing the maximum number of lies allowed, is selected at random.
3. Whilst $\Omega = \{1, \dots, N\}$ is known to both players, both the secret and the selected number e of lies are known only to Responder.
4. Questioner has to guess the secret by a sequence of binary questions.
5. Responder has to answer all questions and can lie at most e times.

Clearly, in this game Questioner has no winning strategy. In the last section, we will consider a game-theoretically more interesting variant in which the number of lies is chosen at random with a distribution μ which known to Questioner. In this variant, there are strategies which lead Questioner to a win with high probability. Note that the game semantics of $G(N, ?)$ and the enriched game are the same.

In this section we investigate the logic corresponding to $G(N, ?)$. To this purpose, we code any record σ along the lines of our variant of Mundici's construction. The main difference here is that, since the number of lies is unknown to Questioner, we have to consider truth-functions corresponding to *any* number of lies. Thus a natural choice is to define g_σ to be the sequence of truth-value functions corresponding to σ in all Rényi-Ulam games with search space $\Omega = \{1, \dots, N\}$ and with number e of lies respectively equal to $0, 1, \dots$, etc. In other words, denoting as usual the number of questions-answers in σ that falsify x by h_x^σ, the record σ may be coded by the function

$$g_\sigma = (g_\sigma^e : e \in \omega), \tag{3}$$

where g_σ^e is defined, for $x \in \Omega$, by

$$g_\sigma^e(x) = \min\{h_x^\sigma, e+1\},$$

where min is meant with respect to the natural order. The function g_σ is a coding with "truncated counting of falsifications, taking into account *all* possible truncations" (compare with (2)).

Our next coding by f_σ (see (4)) corresponds to the Rényi-Ulam game with an unbounded number of lies, whereas the coding by g_σ corresponds to the collection of all Rényi-Ulam game with e lies when e ranges over all natural numbers. We first consider the coding of σ by means of f_σ. In the last part of the section we will compare this coding with the coding by g_σ, and we will emphasize the relation between these different codings and the construction of $\mathcal{A} \searrow a$ with smaller and smaller a.

Definition 8. *For every record σ in the game $G(N, ?)$, the truth-value function of σ is defined as the function from Ω into ω defined, for each $x \in \Omega$, by*

$$f_\sigma(x) = h_x^\sigma. \tag{4}$$

This is simply "counting falsifications" without truncation (compare with (2)).

Lemma 1. *The set $T(N, ?)$ of all truth value functions f_σ of records σ in the game $G(N, ?)$ coincides with the set ω^N of all sequences of natural numbers with length N.*

Proof. That $T(N, ?) \subseteq \omega^N$ is clear from the definition of f_σ. Conversely, given $\tau = (\tau_1, \ldots, \tau_N) \in \omega^N$, let for $x \in \Omega$, σ_x be the sequence consisting of τ_x questions of the form: *Is the secret equal to x?* with answer NO. Finally, let σ be the juxtaposition of all $\sigma_x : x \in \Omega$. It is readily seen that $\tau = f_\sigma$. ∎

We will use Lemma 1 in order to interpret logical connectives in $T(N, ?)$.

First of all, we interpret conjunction. The idea is that if σ and ρ are records, then, as in the Rényi-Ulam game, the conjunction $f_\sigma \& f_\rho$ of f_σ and f_ρ should be given by the truth-value function of the juxtaposition $\sigma * \rho$ of σ and ρ. In other words, we define: $f_\sigma \& f_\rho = f_{\sigma * \rho}$. Now it is clear that for all $x \in \Omega$ we have that $h_x^{\sigma * \rho} = h_x^\sigma + h_x^\rho$. Therefore, composition is coded by pointwise sum. Now let 0^N denote the sequence $(0, \ldots, 0) \in \omega^N$. Clearly 0^N corresponds to the null information and is the neutral element with respect to the sum.

Next we introduce an order in $T(N, ?)$. As in the Rényi-Ulam game, such an order corresponds to the information content of the sequences: $\tau \preceq \eta$ iff τ is at least as informative as η, that is, if for $x = 1, \ldots, N$ one has $\eta_x \leq \tau_x$. Then one can define a residuum $\Rightarrow$ letting $\tau \Rightarrow \sigma$ be the greatest sequence ρ

(according to $\preceq$) such that $\rho + \tau \preceq \sigma$. It is easily seen that $\tau \Rightarrow \sigma$ is defined by $(\tau \Rightarrow \sigma)(x) = \max\{\sigma(x) - \tau(x), 0\}$.

Now consider the structure $\mathcal{N} = \{\omega, +, 0, \rightarrow\}$, where $x \rightarrow y = \max\{y - x, 0\}$. We know ([8]), that $\mathcal{N}$ has the structure of a cancellative hoop, in which the order $\leq_{\mathcal{N}}$ is the inverse of the natural order and is definable in terms of $\rightarrow$, by $x \leq_{\mathcal{N}} y$ iff $x \rightarrow y = 0$. Moreover $\mathcal{N}$ generates the whole variety of cancellative hoops as a quasivariety [8].

Next, we denote by $\mathcal{N}^N$ the product of $N = Card(\Omega)$ copies of $\mathcal{N}$, with $0^N = (0, ..., 0)$ and with sum $+^N$, order $\leq^N$ and residual $\rightarrow^N$ defined pointwise.

Now consider the structure $T(N, ?) = (T(N, ?), \&, \preceq, \overline{0}, \Rightarrow)$. We have:

Theorem 1. *The structure* $T(N, ?)$ *coincides with* $\mathcal{N}^N$

Now cancellative hoops are the equivalent algebraic semantics (in the sense of [2]) of the logic CH defined as follows, c.f. [10]:

Definition 9. CH *is the logic, in the propositional language with connectives* $\&$ *and* $\rightarrow$, *whose axioms are:*
(a) All the axioms of BL, except from $0 \rightarrow \alpha$.
(b) The axiom $(\alpha \rightarrow (\alpha \& \beta)) \rightarrow \beta$,
and whose only rule is Modus Ponens.

Since any finite consequence relation $\vdash_{CH}$ in CH is translated by a quasi equation of cancellative hoops and valid quasi equations in $(T(N, ?), \&, \overline{0}, \preceq, \Rightarrow)$ are preserved by taking the generated quasivariety, it follows:

Theorem 2. CH *is finitely strongly complete with respect to the structure* $T(N, ?)$, *that is, for any finite set $\Gamma \cup \{\alpha\}$ of formulas of CH we have: $\Gamma \vdash_{CH} \alpha$ iff for every evaluation v in $T(N, ?)$ such that $v(\beta) = 1$ for all $\beta \in \Gamma$ one has $v(\alpha) = 1$.* ∎

We now investigate the alternative way of coding a record σ, by means of the previously defined function g_σ. One moment's reflection shows that the composition of records is coded by the function $g_{\sigma*\tau}^e(x) = \min\{g_\sigma^e(x) + g_\tau^e(x), e + 1\}$. In other words, for e fixed, the operation $\&_g$ corresponding to juxtaposition of records is the Łukasiewicz conjunction $\&_{e+1}$ arising from the truncation of $\mathcal{N}^N$ at $(e + 1, ..., e + 1)$ (remind that the order in $\mathcal{N}^N$ is the inverse of the natural order, so the join in this structure corresponds to the pointwise minimum). We show that in this way the truth values of all records form a cancellative hoop isomorphic to $\mathcal{N}^N$. This is a consequence of a more general result.

Let $\mathcal{C}$ be a cancellative hoop, and let for each $a \in \mathcal{C}$, $\cdot_a$ denote the realization of multiplication in $\mathcal{C} \setminus a$, that is, $x \cdot_a y = (x \cdot y) \vee a$. Now let $A \subseteq \mathcal{C}$ be such that for every $c \in \mathcal{C}$ there is an $a \in A$ with $a \leq c$. Let for all $x \in \mathcal{C}$ x^A denote the function defined, for all $a \in A$, by $x^A(a) = x \vee a$, and let $\mathcal{C}^A = \{x^A : x \in \mathcal{C}\}$. On $\mathcal{C}^A$, define

$$(x^A \cdot^A y^A)(a) = x^A(a) \cdot_a y^A(a) = (x^A(a) \cdot y^A(a)) \vee a.$$

Moreover let the order $\leq^A$ on C^A be defined pointwise, i.e., $x^A \leq^A y^A$ iff for all $a \in A$, $x^A(a) \leq y^A(a)$. Let C^A denote the resulting ordered monoid, and let us define, for $x \in C$, $\Phi(x) = x^A$. Then:

Theorem 3. *Φ is an isomorphism of the ordered monoid reduct of C onto C^A.*

Proof. That Φ is onto follows from the definition of C^A. We show that Φ is one-one. If $x \neq y$, then for any $a \in A$ with $a \leq x \wedge y$ (such an a exists by our assumption on A), we have $x \vee a = x \neq y = y \vee a$, therefore $x^A \neq y^A$. That Φ preserves the order is clear. Finally we show that Φ preserves product: We have

$$(x \vee a) \cdot_a (y \vee a) = (x \cdot y) \vee (x \cdot a) \vee (y \cdot a) \vee a^2 \vee a = (x \cdot y) \vee a.$$

Therefore,

$$\Phi(x \cdot y)(a) = (x \cdot y)^A(a) = (x \cdot y) \vee a = (x \vee a) \cdot (y \vee a) \vee a = x^A(a) \cdot_a y^A(a),$$

and finally $(x \cdot y)^A = x^A \cdot^A y^A$. This ends the proof.   ∎
It follows immediately:

Corollary 1. *Φ induces on C^A a residuation $\to^A$ (defined by $\Phi(x) \to^A \Phi(y) = \Phi(x \to y)$), which makes C^A a cancellative hoop isomorphic to C.*   ∎

A quite natural guess would be that for all $a \in C$ one has $(x^A \to^A y^A)(a) = x^A(a) \to x^A(a)$. However, this is not true in general (the equality fails for instance if $a > x > y$). This is not in contradiction with Corollary 1, because in general the function z defined by $z(a) = (x \vee a) \to (y \vee a)$ is not an element of C^A.

Now consider $\mathcal{N}^N$. Let A be the set of all elements of $\mathcal{N}^N$ of the form $(e + 1, \dots, e + 1)$. Then for all $f_\sigma \in \mathcal{N}^N$, we have that $g_\sigma = (f_\sigma)^A$. Moreover, $\Phi(f_\sigma \& f_\tau) = f^A_{\sigma * \tau} = g_{\sigma * \tau} = g_\sigma \&_g g_\tau$. It follows:

Theorem 4. *The set of truth value functions of records in the game $G(N, ?)$, coded by the functions g_σ and equipped with the operations $\cdot^A$ and $\to^A$, is a cancellative hoop isomorphic to $\mathcal{N}^N$, and therefore also with this new coding the game $G(N, ?)$ constitutes a complete game semantics for the logic CH.*   ∎

4   The Game $G^*(N, ?)$ and Product Logic

We have just seen that $G(N, ?)$ does not constitute a game semantics for product logic, but rather a game semantics for the logic CH corresponding to cancellative hoops. The reason for this is that, since the number of lies is unknown, there is no record corresponding to the inconsistent information. The multichannel semantics by Cicalese and Mundici [5] suggests to us the introduction of a multichannel variant of $G(N, ?)$, denoted by $G^*(N, ?)$, which will constitute a game semantics for product logic.

Let a positive integer N be given. The game $G^*(N, ?)$ is as follows:

1. The first player, called *Responder*, chooses a natural number x between 1 and N (called *the secret*).

2. Another natural number e is selected at random. Whilst N is known to both players, both the secret and the selected number e of lies are known only to Responder.
3. Questioner has to guess the secret by a sequence of binary questions.
4. For each question, Questioner can ask the answer to be sent either by an expensive but absolutely reliable channel C_1 or by a cheaper but noisy channel C_2. It is stipulated that all answers along C_1 must be truthful, whereas at most e answers can be false (or distorted) when they are sent along the noisy channel C_2.

We want to code records in the game $G^*(N, ?)$ by means of functions in analogy with the game $G(N, ?)$. Note that in this case a record should take account also of the channel used. Thus in $G^*(N, ?)$ a record consists of a finite sequence σ of triples question-channel-answer. As in the case of the game $G(N, ?)$, we consider two different codings. For the first coding, we imagine that the number of lies through the channel C_2 is unbounded. Thus let for every x, h_x^σ denote the number of questions-answers which falsify x if none of them is given through the reliable channel C_1, and let $h_x^\sigma = \infty$ if x is falsified by at least one answer through C_1. Define, for $x = 1, ..., N$:

$$f_\sigma^*(x) = h_x^\sigma.$$

The second way of coding takes into consideration all possible games with e lies through channel C_2. Thus we code each record σ by $g_\sigma^* = (g_\sigma^{*e} : e \in \omega)$, where for $x \in \Omega$, $g_\sigma^{*e}(x) = \min\{f_\sigma(x), e+1\}$ (of course, we agree that ∞ is the maximum, therefore we set $\min\{\infty, x\} = x$).

We start from the first type of coding. Let $T^*(N, ?) = \{f_\sigma^* : \sigma \text{ a record}\}$. Note that in $T^*(N, ?)$ we have a truth value function, denoted by $\overline{\infty}$ which is constantly equal to ∞. This function corresponds to the inconsistent record constituted by the triple (Q, C_1, A) with $Q :=$ is the secret in Ω? and answer NO. Such a triplet cannot be produced if Responder is fair. We can prove a lemma analogous to Lemma 1.

Lemma 2. Let $\omega^* = \omega \cup \{\infty\}$. Then $T^*(N, ?) = (\omega^*)^N$.

Proof. (a). Let $\tau = (\tau_1, ..., \tau_N) \in (\omega^*)^N$. Let $Z = \{x \in \Omega : \tau_x = \infty\}$. Then consider the record σ consisting of:

 – The question: is the secret in Z? on channel C_1 with answer NO.
 – For each $x \in \{1, ..., N\} \setminus Z$, a sequence of τ_x questions of the form: Is the secret equal to x? on channel C_2 with answer NO.

It is readily seen that $\tau = f_\sigma^*$.   ∎

In analogy with the game $G(N, ?)$, we want to interpret connectives and order in $T^*(N, ?)$. As usual, conjunction is interpreted as the operation $\&^*$ which codes the operation of juxtaposition of records. Thus we define: $(f_\sigma^* \&^* f_\rho^*) = f_{\sigma*\rho}^*$. Moreover we introduce an order which translates the relation being more *informative than.* Thus we define for $\tau, \rho \in (\omega^*)^\Omega$, $\tau \preceq^* \rho$ iff for all $x \in \Omega$, $\tau_x \geq \rho_x$, where we assume $x \leq \infty$ for all $x \in \omega^*$). We want to describe the structure $\mathcal{T}^*(N, ?) = (T^*(N, ?), \&, \preceq^*, \overline{\infty}, \overline{0})$, where $\overline{0}$ denotes the constantly zero function on Ω. To this purpose, we introduce the structure $(\omega^*, +^*, \leq^*, \infty, 0)$, where:

- For $x, y \in \omega^*$, $x +^* y = \begin{cases} x + y \text{ if } x, y \neq \infty \\ \infty \qquad \text{otherwise} \end{cases}$
- $x \leq^* y$ iff either $x = \infty$ or $x, y \in \omega$ and $y \leq x$.

Then the following lemma is almost immediate:

Lemma 3. *The structure* $\mathcal{T}^*(N, ?)$ *coincides with* $(\omega^*, +^*, \leq^*, \infty, 0)^N$. ■

Next consider the structure $\mathcal{N}^* = (\omega^*, +^*, 0, \infty, \leq^*, \rightarrow^*)$ where $\rightarrow^*$ is defined by

$$x \rightarrow^* y = \begin{cases} y - x \text{ if } x >_{\mathcal{N}^*} y >_{\mathcal{N}^*} \infty \\ 0 \qquad \text{if } x \leq_{\mathcal{N}^*} y \\ \infty \qquad \text{otherwise} \end{cases}.$$

It is easily seen that $\mathcal{N}^*$ is a totally ordered product algebra, which generates the full variety of product algebras. This follows from a result of [7], stating that every infinite totally ordered product algebra generates the full variety of product algebras. Next consider the algebra $(\mathcal{N}^*)^N$. Its operations and order will be denoted by the superscript ^{*N}. Then:

Theorem 5. *In* $\mathcal{T}^*(N, ?)$ *we can define (in a unique way) a residuum* $\rightarrow^{*N}$ *which makes it coincident with* $(\mathcal{N}^*)^N$. ■

Let $\mathcal{T}^*(N, ?)^+$ denote $\mathcal{T}^*(N, ?)$ equipped with $\rightarrow^{*N}$. Then:

Theorem 6. $\mathcal{T}^*(N, ?)^+$ *is a product algebra which generates the variety of product algebras as a quasivariety.*

Proof. $\mathcal{T}^*(N, ?)^+$ coincides with $\mathcal{N}^{*N}$. Moreover $\mathcal{N}$ generates the variety of product algebras as a quasivariety, and since $\mathcal{N}^*$ embeds into $(\mathcal{N}^*)^N$ and $(\mathcal{N}^*)^N$ is a product of N copies of $\mathcal{N}^*$, the two structures generate the same quasivariety, that is, the quasivariety (in fact, the variety) of product algebras. This ends the proof. ■

It is well-known [11] that product algebras constitute the equivalent algebraic semantics of product logic Π. Thus in analogy with Theorem 2, we obtain:

Theorem 7. *Product logic* Π *is finitely strongly complete with respect to the structure* $\mathcal{T}^*(N, ?)^+$. ■

As in the case of the game $G(N, ?)$, we can code records taking account of all possibilities about the number of lies. That, is, we can code a record σ by the previously defined function g_σ^*. Then we may define a monoid operation $\cdot^*$ on truth value functions representing juxtaposition of records (thus letting $g_\sigma^* \cdot^* g_\tau^* = g_{\sigma*\tau}^*$ (therefore, $(g_\sigma^* \cdot^* g_\tau^*)^e(x) = \min\{g_\sigma^{*e}(x) + g_\tau^{*e}(x), e + 1\}$, where

$x + \infty = \infty + x = \infty$. We can also define an order according to the relation *being more informative than*; thus, $g_\sigma^* \preceq^* g_\tau^*$ iff for all $e \in \omega$ and for all $x \in \Omega$, $g_\sigma^{*e}(x) \leq g_\tau^{*e}(x)$. As in the case of the game $G(N, ?)$, in this way we get a structure isomorphic to $\mathcal{T}^*(N, ?)$. The proof is similar to the one given for the game $G(N, ?)$ with some exceptions, for which we need some more facts concerning product algebras.

First of all, every product algebra $\mathcal{A}$ can be represented as a subdirect product of totally ordered product algebras $\mathcal{A}_i : i \in I$. Thus every element of $\mathcal{A}$ can be represented as a sequence $(a_i : i \in I)$ with $a_i \in \mathcal{A}_i$. For all $a \in \mathcal{A}$, we have $\neg a = 0$ iff for all $i \in I$, $a_i > 0_i$, where 0_i is the bottom element of $\mathcal{A}_i$. It is readily seen that the set $\{x \in \mathcal{A} : \neg x = 0\}$ forms a subalgebra of the zero-free reduct of $\mathcal{A}$, which is also a cancellative hoop. We denote this cancellative hoop by $\mathcal{A}^+$.

Lemma 4. *With reference to the previous notation, for every $x \in \mathcal{A}$ and for every $i \in I$, if $x_i > 0_i$, then there is an $a \in \mathcal{A}^+$ such that $a_i < x_i$.*

Proof. Let $a = x^4 \to x^2$. We prove that $a \in \mathcal{A}^+$. Let $j \in I$. If $x_j > 0_j$, then $(x^4 \to x^2)_j = x_j^2 > 0_j$. If $x_j = 0_j$, then $(x^4 \to x^2)_j = 1_j > 0_j$. Thus $a_j > 0_j$ for all $j \in I$, therefore $a \in \mathcal{A}^+$. Moreover, since $x_i > 0_i$, we have $(x^4 \to x^2)_i = x_i^2 < x_i$, and the lemma is proved. ∎

With reference to the previous notation, let $A \subseteq \mathcal{A}^+$ be such that for all $x \in \mathcal{A}^+$, there is $a \in A$ such that $a \leq x$. Let for all $x \in \mathcal{A}$, $x^A = (x \vee a : a \in A)$, and $\mathcal{A}^A = \{x^A : x \in \mathcal{A}\}$. On $\mathcal{A}^A$ define $(x^A \cdot^A y^A) = ((x \cdot y) \vee a : a \in A)$, and $x^A \leq^A y^A$ iff for all $a \in A$, $x \vee a \leq y \vee a$. Then:

Theorem 8. *The map Φ defined for all $x \in \mathcal{A}$, by $\Phi(x) = x^A$, is an isomorphism from the ordered monoid reduct of $\mathcal{A}$ onto $\mathcal{A}^A$. Thus in $\mathcal{A}^A$ we can uniquely define a residuum which makes $\mathcal{A}^A$ a product algebra isomorphic to $\mathcal{A}$ via Φ.*

Proof. The argument is analogous to that of Theorem 3, except from the proof that Φ is one-one. Now assume $x \neq y$. Then there is an $i \in I$ such that $x_i \neq y_i$. Since $\mathcal{A}_i$ is totally ordered, we can assume without loss of generality that $x_i < y_i$. By Lemma 4, there is a $b \in \mathcal{A}^+$ such that $b_i < y_i$. Moreover there is an $a \in A$ such that $a \leq b$. Thus $(x \vee a)_i < (y \vee a)_i$, and $x^A \neq y^A$. This completes the proof. ∎

Now with reference to the product algebra $\mathcal{T}^*(N, ?)^+$, consider the set $A = (e + 1, \ldots, e + 1) : e \in \omega$. It is readily seen that A satisfies the conditions of Theorem 8. Moreover for any record σ we have $g_\sigma^* = (f_\sigma^*)^A$. Finally, $(f_\sigma^* \&^* f_\tau^*)^A = g_\sigma^* \cdot^* g_\tau^* = (f_\sigma^*)^A \cdot^* (f_\tau^*)^A$. It follows:

Theorem 9. *The set of truth value functions of records in the game $G^*(N, ?)$, coded by the functions g_σ^* and equipped with the operations $\cdot^*$ and by its residuum, is a product algebra isomorphic to $(\mathcal{N}^*)^N$, and therefore also with this new coding the game $G^*(N, ?)$ constitutes a complete game semantics for product logic.* ∎

5   Making the Games $G(N,?)$ and $G^*(N,?)$ More Interesting

Although they constitute a complete game semantics for the logic CH and for product logic respectively, the games $G(N,?)$ and $G^*(N,?)$ do not have a clear game-theoretical interest. Indeed, in $G(N,?)$ there is no guessing strategy for Questioner, as the number of allowed lies is unknown to him, and in $G^*(N,?)$ the only guessing strategy consists of a binary search using channel C_1 only. Thus we will consider probabilistic variants which seem to be more interesting from a game-theoretical point of view, and which lead to the same logics (CH and Π respectively). We start from a probabilistic variant of $G(N,?)$.

5.1   The Game $G(N,\mu)$

Let a positive integer N and a σ-additive measure μ on the set ω of natural numbers be given. The game $G(N,\mu)$ is as follows:

1. The first player, called *Responder*, chooses a natural number x between 1 and N (called *the secret*).
2. Another natural number e, representing the maximum number of lies admitted, is selected at random according to the distribution μ. We assume that N and μ are known to both players, whereas the secret and the selected number e of lies are known only to Responder.
3. Questioner has to guess the secret by a sequence of binary questions.
4. Responder has to answer all of them, and e lies at most are allowed.

A probabilistic guessing strategy for $G(N,\mu)$.

For every natural number x, let us write $\mu(x)$ for $\mu(\{x\})$. Then for all $A \subseteq \omega$ we have $\mu(A) = \sum_{i \in A} \mu(i)$, therefore μ is uniquely determined by the numbers $\mu(i) : i \in \omega$. Then for any $0 < q < 1$, Questioner can guess the correct number with probability $\geq q$ using the following strategy:

- Let n_0 be the minimum natural number such that $\sum_{i=0}^{n_0} \mu(i) \geq q$.
- Play the Rényi-Ulam game with n_0 lies and guess the number obtained according to a winning strategy (if you wish, according to the best strategy) for this game.

It is clear that the number obtained in this way is the correct number with probability $\sum_{i=0}^{n_0} \mu(i) \geq q$.

Thus if Questioner just needs an answer which is reliable with probability at least q, then the game $G(N,\mu)$ can be somehow reduced to the traditional Rényi-Ulam game. However, Questioner may want more and more reliable guesses. In this case, unless $\mu(i) = 0$ for almost all natural numbers, he needs to consider Rényi-Ulam games with larger and larger number of lies. In particular if there is no upper bound $q_M < 1$ to the reliability parameter q, then Questioner has to consider all the Rényi-Ulam games with search space $\{1, ..., N\}$ and with number of lies $0, 1, 2, ...,$ etc.. It follows that the codes of records of $G(N, \mu)$ are the same as the codes of records of $G(N, ?)$, therefore they lead to the same logic CH.

5.2   The Game $G^*(N, \mu, n)$

We now consider a probabilistic variant $G^*(N, \mu, n)$ of the game $G^*(N, ?)$.

1. Two positive natural numbers N and $n < \log(N)$ and a σ-additive measure μ on ω are given.
2. The first player, called *Responder*, chooses a natural number x between 1 and N (called *the secret*).
3. Another natural number e, representing the maximum number of lies admitted, is selected at random according to the distribution μ. Once again, N and μ are known to both players, whereas the secret and the selected number e of lies are known only to Responder.
4. Questioner has to guess the secret by a sequence of binary questions. For each question, Questioner may ask Responder to answer either by means of the reliable channel C_1 or by means of the noisy channel C_2. However, a maximum of n questions can be answered through C_1.
5. Responder has to answer all the questions. At most e lies through the channel C_2 are allowed, but no lie at all is permitted through the reliable channel C_1.

Winning strategies for $G^*(N, \mu, n)$.

Although we don't investigate the game $G^*(N, \mu, n)$ in full details, we describe three strategies for Questioner.

- Strategy 1. Questioner uses first n questions through the channel C_1 in order to do a binary search, thus reducing the cardinality of the search space to $M = \frac{N}{2^n}$. Then he plays the game $G(M, \mu)$ using the channel C_2 only. Since the cardinality of the search space is decreased, Questioner may either use a smaller number of questions in order to make a correct guess with probability q, or use the same number of question and obtain a more reliable answer. In any case, with this strategy, Questioner never obtains a completely reliable answer.
- Strategy 2. Choose a $q < 1$ sufficiently close to 1. Let n_0 be the minimum natural number such that $\sum_{i=0}^{n_0} \mu(i) \geq q$. Play the Rényi-Ulam game with n_0 lies, using channel C_2, and consider the number x_0 obtained according to the best strategy for this game. Then ask, using channel C_1, the following question: *is the secret equal to x_0?* If the answer is YES, then x_0 is the secret

(note that in this case the answer is absolutely reliable); otherwise, continue the game with q replaced by $\frac{1+q}{2}$ and with x_0 deleted from the search space. Note that, also with this strategy, there is a little chance that Questioner never obtains a completely reliable guess.

- Strategy 3. Use the first $n-1$ questions through the channel C_1 in order to reduce the cardinality of the search space to $\frac{N}{2^{n-1}}$. Then choose a $q < 1$ sufficiently close to 1. Let n_0 be the minimum natural number such that $\sum_{i=0}^{n_0} \mu(i) \geq q$. With reference to the reduced search space, play the Rényi-Ulam game with n_0 lies, using channel C_2, and consider the number x_0 obtained according to the best strategy for this game. Then ask, using channel C_1, the following question: *is the secret equal to x_0?* If the answer is YES, then x_0 is the secret, and the solution is absolutely reliable. If the answer is NO, then it is no longer possible to use channel C_1, therefore the only possible strategy is the following: take q_1, n_1 such that $q < q_1 < 1$ and $\sum_{i=0}^{n_1} \mu(i) \geq q_1$; then update the search space by deleting x_0, and play the Rényi-Ulam game with n_1 lies, using channel C_2. Guess the number $x_1 \neq x_0$ obtained in this way. Clearly in this case the guess is not completely reliable.

Also in the case of $G^*(N, \mu, n)$, if Questioner wants more and more reliable guesses, then he must take all number of lies into account, therefore the codes of records of $G^*(N, \mu, n)$ are the same as the codes of $G^*(N, ?)$, and they lead to the same logic Π.

6   Conclusions

We have found game semantics for CH and for product logic Π respectively. In both cases, the proposed semantics has the following desirable properties:

- Records are coded by functions which faithfully represent the information contained in them.
- A monoid operation, corresponding to juxtaposition of records, and an order relation corresponding to the relation *being more informative than* can be introduced.
- The ordered monoid obtained in this way is residuated and the residual has an interesting interpretation in terms of records. Moreover, the ordered monoid mentioned above together with such residuum becomes a cancellative hoop (a product algebra, respectively).
- The games introduced in the paper are a complete game semantics for CH (for product logic, respectively).
- There are probabilistic variants of the above mentioned games with some game-theoretical interest.

Roughly speaking, Łukasiewicz logic corresponds to counting (falsifications) with truncation. The logic CH corresponds either to simply counting (without truncation) or to counting with truncation but taking into account all possible truncations. Product logic Π corresponds to a two-channel variant of the previous point where one of the channels is completely reliable.

References

1. Blok, W.J., Ferreirim, I.M.A.: On the structure of hoops. Algebra Universalis 43, 233–257 (2000)
2. Blok, W.J., Pigozzi, D.: Algebraizable Logics. Mem. Amer. Math. Soc., 396, vol.77, Amer. Math. Soc., Providence (1989)
3. Burris, S., Sankappanavar, H.P.: A course in Universal Algebra. Graduate texts in Mathematics. Springer, Heidelberg (1981)
4. Ciabattoni, A., Fermüller, C., Metcalfe, G.: Uniform Rules and Dialogue Games for Fuzzy Logics. In: Baader, F., Voronkov, A. (eds.) LPAR 2004. LNCS (LNAI), vol. 3452, pp. 496–510. Springer, Heidelberg (2005)
5. Cicalese, F., Mundici, D.: Recent developements of feedback coding, and its relations with many-valued logic. In: van Benthem, J., Parikh, R., Ramanujam, R., Gupta, A. (eds.) Proceedings of the First Indian Conference on Logic and its Applications (FICL 2005), Bombay, India, January 2005 (to appear)
6. Cignoli, R., D'Ottaviano, I.M.L., Mundici, D.: Algebraic foundations of many-valued reasoning. Kluwer, Dordrecht (2000)
7. Cignoli, R., Torrens, A.: An algebraic analysis of product logic. Mult. Val. Logic 5, 45–65 (2000)
8. Ferreirim, I.M.A.: On varieties and quasi varieties of hoops and their reducts, PhD thesis, University of Illinois at Chicago (1992)
9. Giles, R.: A non-classical logic for phisics. Studia Logica 4(33), 399–417 (1974)
10. Esteva, F., Godo, L., Hájek, P., Montagna, F.: Hoops and fuzzy logic. Journal of Logic and Computation 13, 531–555 (2003)
11. Hájek, P.: Metamathematics of Fuzzy Logic. Trends in Logic-Studia Logica Library, vol. 4. Kluwer Academic Publ., Dordercht (1998)
12. Jipsen, P., Tsinakis, C.: A survey on residuated lattices. In: Martinez, J. (ed.) Ordered Algebraic structures, pp. 19–56. Kluwer, Dordrecht (2002)
13. Marini, C., Montagna, F., Simi, G.: Product logic and probabilistic Rényi-Ulam games. In: Fuzzy Sets and Systems (preprint 2005, to appear)
14. Mundici, D.: The logic of Ulam's game with lies. In: Knowledge, Belief and Strategic Interaction, Cambridge Studies in Probability, Induction, and Decision Theory, pp. 275–284 (1992)
15. Pelc, A.: Searching with known error probability. Theoretical Computer Science 63, 185–202 (1989)
16. Pelc, A.: Searching games with errors - fifty years of coping with liars. Theoretical Computer Science 270, 71–109 (2002)
17. Rényi, A.: Napló az információelméletről, Gondolat, Budapest (1976) (English translation: A diary on Information Theory. J. Wiley and Sons, New York (1984))
18. Ulam, S.M.: Adventures of a Mathematician. Scribner's, New York (1976)

Notes on Strong Completeness in Łukasiewicz, Product and BL Logics and in Their First-Order Extensions

Franco Montagna

University of Siena
Department of Mathematics and Computer Science
Pian dei Mantellini 44
53100 Siena (Italy)
montagna@unisi.it

Abstract. In this paper we investigate the problem of characterizing infinite consequence relation in standard BL-algebras by the adding of new rules. First of all, we note that finitary rules do not help, therefore we need at least one infinitary rule. In fact we show that one infinitary rule is sufficient to obtain strong standard completeness, also in the first-order case. Similar results are obtained for product logic and for Łukasiewicz logic. Finally, we show some applications of our results to probabilistic logic over many-valued events and to first-order many-valued logic. In particular, we show a tight bound to the complexity of BL first-order formulas which are valid in the standard semantics.

1 Foreword

This paper is dedicated to Daniele Mundici for his 60th birthday. It is inspired by his very interesting paper [24]. Unfortunately, we did not reach the original goal, that is, finding a complete logical system for the treatment of probability over many-valued events. The main results of this paper refer to the complexity of first-order many-valued logics, a field that probably Daniele does not like so much. However, I hope that he will appreciate the techniques used. In any case, Daniele was able to stimulate my interest in probability over many-valued events, and I promise to him that first of all I will improve my knowledge in this subject, and then I try to obtain better contributions to this field.

2 Introduction

The logic BL was introduced by Hájek in [11] as a common fragment of the three most prominent fuzzy logics, Łukasiewicz logic, Gödel logic and product logic (these logics will be defined in the next section). In [14], Hájek conjectured that BL is the logic of all continuous t-norms and their residuals. In order to explain this conjecture, we recall [18] that a *t-norm* is a binary operation $*$ on $[0,1]$ such that $([0,1], *, \leq, 1)$ is a totally ordered commutative monoid with unit

S. Aguzzoli et al.(Eds.): Algebraic and Proof-theoretic Aspects, LNAI 4460, pp. 247–274, 2007.

1. Of course, a t-norm is said to be *continuous* iff it is a continuous function with respect to the usual topology on the reals. A continuous t-norm $*$ induces a *residuum*, i.e., a binary operation $\rightarrow_*$ on $[0,1]$ such that for all $x, y, z \in [0,1]$, one has: $x \leq y \rightarrow_* z$ iff $x * y \leq z$. Now consider a propositional language **L** built-up from propositional variables, the propositional constants 0 and 1, and the connectives $\&, \vee, \wedge$ and $\rightarrow$. Given a continuous t-norm $*$, a $*$-*evaluation* is defined to be a homomorphism from the algebra of formulas of **L** into the algebra $[0,1]_* = ([0,1], *, \max, \min, \rightarrow_*)$. Models built-up from continuous t-norms constitute a privileged semantics for many-valued logics, in the same way as the model of natural numbers constitutes the most natural semantics for arithmetic. For this reason, algebras of the form $([0,1], *, \max, \min, \rightarrow_*)$ are called *standard*.

Given a set K of continuous t-norms, a logic L in the language **L**, and a set $\Gamma \cup \{A\}$ of propositional formulas, we write $\Gamma \models_K A$ (and we say that A is a semantic consequence of Γ in K) to express that for every $* \in K$ and for every $*$-evaluation e, if $e(B) = 1$ for all $B \in \Gamma$, then $e(A) = 1$. We say that A is *valid in K* iff $\emptyset \models_K A$, and that a set Γ of formulas is *satisfiable in K* if $\Gamma \not\models_K 0$. A logic L is said to be *strongly standard complete* with respect to K iff for any set Γ of propositional formulas and for every formula A one has that $\Gamma \vdash A$ iff $\Gamma \models_K A$. We say that L is *finitely strongly standard complete* (*standard complete* respectively) with respect to K iff the above condition holds for finite Γ (for $\Gamma = \emptyset$ respectively). Finally, we denote by K_{TN} the class of all continuous t-norms.

The most important continuous t-norms are: the *Gödel t-norm* $*_G$, defined by $x *_G y = \min\{x, y\}$, the Łukasiewicz t-norm $*_L$, defined by $x *_L y = \max\{x + y - 1, 0\}$ and the product t-norm $*_\pi$, defined by $x *_\pi y = xy$ (ordinary product). The corresponding algebras will be denoted by $[0,1]_G$, $[0,1]_L$ and $[0,1]_\pi$ instead of $[0,1]_{*_G}$, $[0,1]_{*_L}$ and $[0,1]_{*_\pi}$ respectively. Moreover, we write $\models_L$ ($\models_\pi$, $\models_G$ respectively) for $\models_{\{*_L\}}$, ($\models_{\{*_\pi\}}$, $\models_{\{*_G\}}$ respectively). In [11] it is shown that: (a) Gödel logic is strongly standard complete with respect to $\{*_G\}$; (b) Łukasiewicz logic is finitely strongly standard complete, but not strongly standard complete, with respect to $\{*_L\}$; (c) product logic is finitely strongly standard complete, but not strongly standard complete, with respect to $\{*_\pi\}$. Moreover, Hájek formulated the following conjecture:

Conjecture: BL is standard complete with respect to K_{TN}.

The correctness of this conjecture was shown in [4]. There, it is implicitly proved that BL is in fact finitely strongly standard complete with respect to K_{TN}. However, it is easy to prove that BL is not strongly standard complete with respect to K_{TN}. Moreover, there is a recursive set Γ of formulas such that the set of all formulas A such that $\Gamma \models_{K_{TN}} A$ is not recursively enumerable, and the same result is true with $\models_{K_{TN}}$ replaced by $\models_L$ or by $\models_\pi$, [12] and [13]. Hence for $K \in \{K_{TN}, \{*_L\}, \{*_\pi\}\}$, there is no formal system **F** (with a recursive set of axioms and of finitary rules) such that for every set $\Gamma \cup \{A\}$ of formulas, one has: $\Gamma \models_K A$ iff $\Gamma \vdash_{\mathbf{F}} A$.

The situation is even worse for first-order logics. For every class K of continuous t-norms, one can define in a natural way the first-order analogue $\models_{K1}$ of $\models_K$ (cf Section 3 for details). Then, whilst the first-order version of Gödel logic is strongly complete with respect to $\{*_G\}$, for the other logics one has the following negative result:

Proposition 1. *(cf [27], [15], [20]). The set of first-order formulas A such that $\models_{K_{TN}1} A$ ($\models_{L1}$, $\models_{\pi 1}$ respectively) is not recursively enumerable, therefore it cannot be the set of theorems of any formal system with a decidable set of axioms and finitary rules.*

It follows that if we want to formalize any of $\models_{K_{TN}1}$, $\models_{L1}$ or $\models_{\pi 1}$, we need either a non-recursive set of axioms and rules (e.g., one might take the set of all valid formulas as axiom set) or infinitary rules. But for infinite consequence relation we absolutely need infinitary rules: since BL, Łukasiewicz and product logics are finitely strongly standard complete but not strongly standard complete, semantic consequence in standard algebras is not a compact relation, therefore it cannot be formalized by means of any set of finitary rules.

In this paper we exhibit an infinitary rule (R) which allows us to derive all semantic consequences of any set Γ of sentences, both in the propositional case and in the first-order case. The rule is expressed by means of an additional operator $*$ introduced in [21]. In the case of Łukasiewicz and product logics, $*$ coincides with the Baaz operator Δ, cf [11]; moreover, the rule (R) can be replaced by a rule (R') which does not involve Δ.

Our characterization also offers a general method for showing standard completeness of theories T over BL: it is sufficient to show that T is closed under the usual rules and under (R). Other applications are described in the last section. For instance, the results of this paper offer a syntactic characterization of satisfiability of (finite or infinite) sets of probabilistic formulas over Łukasiewicz logic. Moreover, our completeness result allows us to obtain a rather tight bound to the complexity of the set of first-order formulas of product and of BL logics, as well as of Łukasiewicz logic with Δ, which are valid in the standard semantics: in [20] and [16] it is shown that their complexity is at least $\mathbf{0}^\omega$, the complexity of the set of true formulas of arithmetic. In this paper we show that all these sets are recursively enumerable in $\mathbf{0}^\omega$, therefore their complexity does not exceed $\mathbf{0}^{\omega+1}$.

3 Preliminaries

Definition 1. *A commutative, integral, bounded residuated lattice (c.i.b. residuated lattice for short) is a system $\mathbf{L} = \langle L, \&, \rightarrow, \vee, \wedge, 0, 1 \rangle$ where $\langle L, \&, 1 \rangle$ is a commutative monoid, $\langle L, \vee, \wedge, 0, 1 \rangle$ is a lattice with minimum 0 and maximum 1, and the residuation property holds:*

(res)   *For all $x, y, z \in L$, $x \leq y \rightarrow z$ iff $x \& y \leq z$.*

In a longstanding tradition, we will mainly use the symbol $\&$ in a logical context. When dealing with c.i.b. residuated lattices the symbol $\&$ will be often omitted or denoted by $\cdot$, or even by $*$. Moreover, we define $\neg x = x \to 0$, $x \leftrightarrow y = (x \to y)\&(y \to x)$, $x \oplus y = (\neg x) \to y$, and $x \ominus y = \neg(x \to y)$ (the symbols $\oplus$ and $\ominus$ will be only used with reference to Łukasiewicz logic and with its algebraic semantics, the MV-algebras). We also inductively define: $x^0 = 1$; $x^{n+1} = x^n x$; $0x = 0$; $(n+1)x = nx \oplus x$.

The residuation property implies the *left continuity* of the monoid operation: if $\mathcal{A}$ is a c.i.b. residuated lattice and X is a subset of $\mathcal{A}$ such that $\sup X$ exists, then for all $a \in \mathcal{A}$, $a \sup X = \sup(aX)$, where aX denotes the set $\{ax : x \in X\}$.

Definition 2. *A c.i.b. residuated lattice $\mathcal{A}$ is said to be* divisible *iff it satisfies the condition $x(x \to y) = x \wedge y$, and* prelinear *iff it satisfies the condition $(x \to y) \vee (y \to x) = 1$.*

A BL-algebra *is a divisible and prelinear c.i.b. residuated lattice. A* Wajsberg algebra *or* MV-algebra *is a BL-algebra satisfying $\neg\neg x = x$. A* product algebra *is a BL-algebra satisfying $\neg x \vee ((x \to (xy)) \to y) = 1$, and a* Gödel algebra *is a BL-algebra satisfying $xx = x$.*

A BL-algebra *(a* Wajsberg algebra*, a* product algebra *respectively, a* Gödel algebra*) is said to be* standard *iff its lattice reduct is $([0,1], \max, \min)$.*

Note that in any BL-algebra lattice operations may be defined in terms of $\cdot$ and $\to$: $x \wedge y = x(x \to y)$, and $x \vee y = ((x \to y) \to y) \wedge ((y \to x) \to x)$. Note also that, whilst all standard Wajsberg (product, Gödel respectively) algebras are isomorphic to $[0,1]_{\text{L}}$ ($[0,1]_\pi$, $[0,1]_G$ respectively), there is a continuum of mutually non-isomorphic standard BL-algebras: for every $s \in 2^\omega$, consider an ordinal sum $\star_s$ of ω components $\star_n : n \in \omega$, where $\star_n$ is a Łukasiewicz component if $s(n) = 0$ and a product component if $s(n) = 1$. Then it is easy to prove that if $s \neq s'$ then $\star_s$ and $\star_{s'}$ are not isomorphic.

Definition 3. *A* basic hoop *[2] is a zero-free subreduct (subalgebra of a reduct) of a BL-algebra. A basic hoop is said to be* bounded *if it has minimum element, and* Wajsberg *iff it is a subreduct of a Wajsberg algebra.*

In [8] it is shown that every a linearly ordered Wajsberg hoop is bounded iff it is a reduct of a Wajsberg algebra. Moreover, any unbounded totally ordered Wajsberg hoop is *cancellative*, that is, $xy = xz$ implies $y = z$.

Definition 4. *Let $\langle I, \leq \rangle$ be a totally ordered set with minimum i_0. For all $i \in I$, let $\mathcal{A}_i$ be a basic hoop such that for $i \neq j$, $\mathcal{A}_i \cap \mathcal{A}_j = \{1\}$, and assume that $\mathcal{A}_{i_0}$ is bounded. Then $\bigoplus_{i \in I} \mathcal{A}_i$ (the* ordinal sum *of the family $(\mathcal{A}_i)_{i \in I}$) is the structure whose base set is $\bigcup_{i \in I} \mathcal{A}_i$, whose bottom is the minimum of $\mathcal{A}_{i_0}$, whose top is 1, and whose operations are*

$$x \to y = \begin{cases} x \to^{\mathcal{A}_i} y & \text{if } x, y \in \mathcal{A}_i \\ y & \text{if } \exists i > j(x \in \mathcal{A}_i \text{ and } y \in \mathcal{A}_j) \\ 1 & \text{if } \exists i < j(x \in \mathcal{A}_i \setminus \{1\} \text{ and } y \in \mathcal{A}_j) \end{cases}$$

$$x \cdot y = \begin{cases} x \cdot^{\mathcal{A}_i} y & \text{if } x, y \in \mathcal{A}_i \\ x & \text{if } \exists i < j(x \in \mathcal{A}_i, y \in \mathcal{A}_j \setminus \{1\}) \\ y & \text{if } \exists i < j(y \in \mathcal{A}_i, x \in \mathcal{A}_j \setminus \{1\}) \end{cases}$$

In [1] the following is proved:

Theorem 1. *Every linearly ordered BL-algebra $\mathcal{A}$ is (termwise equivalent to) the ordinal sum of an indexed family $\langle \mathcal{W}_i : i \in I \rangle$ of Wajsberg hoops, where I is a linearly ordered set with minimum i_0, and $\mathcal{W}_{i_0}$ is bounded.*

In the sequel, the Wajsberg hoops $\mathcal{W}_i$ in Theorem 1 will be called *the Wajsberg components of $\mathcal{A}$.*

We now consider a basic propositional language $\mathbf{L}$ containing parentheses, propositional variables, the propositional constants 0 and 1, and the binary connectives $\&$, $\rightarrow$, $\vee$ and $\wedge$. Sometimes we will also consider expansions of $\mathbf{L}$ by additional connectives. For every two formulas A and B, $\neg A$, $A \leftrightarrow B$, $A \oplus B$ and $A \ominus B$ are abbreviations for $A \rightarrow 0$, $(A \rightarrow B)\&(B \rightarrow A)$, $(\neg A) \rightarrow B$ and $\neg(A \rightarrow B)$ respectively. Moreover we inductively define, for any formula A and natural number n, $A^0 = 1$; $A^{n+1} = A^n \& A$, $0A = 0$, $(n+1)A = nA \oplus A$.

We also consider the *first-order extension* $\mathbf{L}_1$ of $\mathbf{L}$, which is built from parentheses, individual variables, symbols of predicates (of all arities), the propositional constants 0 and 1, the binary connectives $\&$, $\rightarrow$, $\vee$ and $\wedge$, and the quantifiers $\exists$ and $\forall$. Sometimes we also use constant symbols, but preferably not function symbols. Sometimes we will also consider expansions of $\mathbf{L}_1$ by additional connectives.

Formulas of $\mathbf{L}$ and formulas of $\mathbf{L}_1$ are defined by induction in the obvious way.

Definition 5. *Let $\mathcal{A}$ be a c.i.b. residuated lattice. A propositional evaluation of $\mathbf{L}$ in $\mathcal{A}$ is just a homomorphism e from the algebra of propositional formulas into $\mathcal{A}$.*

Let D be a non-empty set. A first-order structure on $\mathcal{A}$ with domain D is a map $\mathcal{M}$ from the set of closed atomic formulas with parameters in D into $\mathcal{A}$ such that $\mathcal{M}(0) = 0$ and $\mathcal{M}(1) = 1$. (By abuse of language, when there is no danger of confusion, we denote by the same symbol a connective or logical constant and its corresponding operation or constant in $\mathcal{A}$; moreover we identify any element of D with the constant symbol which represents it; if the language $\mathbf{L}_1$ has individual constants, then we must interpret them as elements of D).

Given a c.i.b. residuated lattice $\mathcal{A}$ and a first-order structure $\mathcal{M}$ on it with domain D, we define, for every closed formula A with parameters in D, the value $\|A\|_{\mathcal{A},\mathcal{M}}$ of A in $\mathcal{M}$ by induction as follows:

> *If A is atomic, then $\|A\|_{\mathcal{A},\mathcal{M}} = \mathcal{M}(A)$;*
> *For any connective $\circ$, if $A = B \circ C$, then $\|A\|_{\mathcal{A},\mathcal{M}}$ is defined iff both $\|B\|_{\mathcal{A},\mathcal{M}}$ and $\|C\|_{\mathcal{A},\mathcal{M}}$ are defined, and in this case $\|A\|_{\mathcal{A},\mathcal{M}} = \|B\|_{\mathcal{A},\mathcal{M}} \circ \|C\|_{\mathcal{A},\mathcal{M}}$.*
> *If $A = \forall x B$, then $\|A\|_{\mathcal{A},\mathcal{M}}$ is defined iff for all $d \in D$, $\|B(d)\|_{\mathcal{A},\mathcal{M}}$ is defined and $\inf\{\|B(d)\|_{\mathcal{A},\mathcal{M}} : d \in D\}$ exists in $\mathcal{A}$. In this case, $\|A\|_{\mathcal{A},\mathcal{M}} = \inf\{\|B(d)\|_{\mathcal{A},\mathcal{M}} : d \in D\}$.*
> *If $A = \exists x B$, then $\|A\|_{\mathcal{A},\mathcal{M}}$ is defined iff for all $d \in D$, $\|B(d)\|_{\mathcal{A},\mathcal{M}}$ is defined and $\sup\{\|B(d)\|_{\mathcal{A},\mathcal{M}} : d \in D\}$ exists in $\mathcal{A}$. In this case, $\|A\|_{\mathcal{A},\mathcal{M}} = \sup\{\|B(d)\|_{\mathcal{A},\mathcal{M}} : d \in D\}$.*

A first-order structure $\mathcal{M}$ on $\mathcal{A}$ is is said to be safe if $\|A\|_{\mathcal{A},\mathcal{M}}$ is defined on all closed formulas with parameters in D.

Remark 1. We recall that in [11], a first-order structure on $\mathcal{A}$ with domain D is defined to be a map $\mathcal{M}$ associating for every n-ary predicate symbol P a map $P^{\mathcal{M}}$ from D^n to $\mathcal{A}$. Letting for every atomic formula $P(d_1, ..., d_n)$, $\mathcal{M}(P(d_1, ..., d_n)) = P^{\mathcal{M}}(d_1, ..., d_n)$, the two definitions become completely equivalent.

Definition 6. *Let* **K** *be a class of c.i.b. residuated lattices, let* Γ *be a set of propositional formulas of* **L**, *and let* A *be a formula of* **L**. *We say that* A *is a semantic consequence of* Γ *in* **K** *(and we write* $\Gamma \models_{\mathbf{K}} A$) *iff for every* $\mathcal{A} \in \mathbf{K}$ *and for every evaluation* e *in* $\mathcal{A}$ *if* $e(B) = 1$ *for all* $B \in \Gamma$, *then* $e(A) = 1$.

Let Γ *be a set of closed formulas of* $\mathbf{L_1}$, *let* A *be a formula of* $\mathbf{L_1}$, *and let* **K** *be a class of c.i.b. residuated lattices. We say that* A *is a semantic first-order consequence of* Γ *in* **K** *(and we write* $\Gamma \models_{\mathbf{K1}} A$) *iff for every* $\mathcal{A} \in \mathbf{K}$, *for every* $D \neq \emptyset$, *for every safe structure* $\mathcal{M}$ *over* $\mathcal{A}$ *with domain* D, *if* $\|B\|_{\mathcal{A},\mathcal{M}} = 1$ *for all* $B \in \Gamma$, *then* $\|A\|_{\mathcal{A},\mathcal{M}} = 1$.

We write $\models_{\mathbf{K}} A$, *(*$\models_{\mathbf{K1}} A$ *respectively) for* $\emptyset \models_{\mathbf{K}} A$, *(*$\emptyset \models_{\mathbf{K1}} A$ *respectively), and in this case we say that* A *is valid in* **K**.

Let **F** *be a propositional formal system for the language* **L**, *and let* **K** *be a class of c.i.b. residuated lattices. We say that* **F** *is* strongly complete *(finitely strongly complete, complete respectively) with respect to* **K** *iff for every set* $\Gamma \cup \{A\}$ *of sentences (for every finite set* $\Gamma \cup \{A\}$ *of sentences, for* $\Gamma = \emptyset$ *and* A *any sentence respectively) one has:* $\Gamma \models_{\mathbf{K}} A$ *iff* A *is derivable from* Γ *in* **F**. *Similar definition for the predicate case (we need to replace* **L** *by* $\mathbf{L_1}$ *and* $\models_{\mathbf{K}}$ *by* $\models_{\mathbf{K1}}$).

The following questions are quite natural:

(a) Let **K** denote the class of all BL-algebras (of Gödel algebras, of Wajsberg algebras and of product algebras respectively); is there a formal system **F** (with a decidable set of axioms and of finitary rules) which is strongly complete with respect to **K**?

(b) Same question as (a), but with **K** denoting the class of all totally ordered BL-algebras (Gödel algebras, Wajsberg algebras and product algebras respectively), also called *BL-chains* (*Gödel chains, Wajsberg chains, product chains* respectively).

(c) Same question with **K** denoting the class of all standard BL-algebras (standard Gödel algebras, standard Wajsberg algebras and standard product algebras respectively; thus $\models_{\mathbf{K}}$ must be replaced by $\models_{K_{TN}}$, $\models_G$, $\models_{\mathbf{L}}$ and $\models_\pi$ respectively).

(d) Same question as in (c), but with *strongly complete* replaced by *finitely strongly complete* or by *complete*.

(a'), (b'), (c') and (d'): similar to (a), (b), (c) and (d) respectively, but with first-order closed formulas instead of propositional formulas, and with $\models_{\mathbf{K1}}$ instead of $\models_{\mathbf{K}}$.

It has been shown ([11], [4], [15], [20]) that questions (a), (a'), (b), (b') and (d) have a positive answer, whilst questions (c), (c') and (d') have a positive answer only for standard Gödel algebras, and a negative answer for standard BL-algebras, for standard Wajsberg algebras and for standard product algebras. In order to clarify the situation, we need some important definitions.

Definition 7. BL [11] is the logic on the language **L** whose axioms are:

(A1) $(A \to B) \to ((B \to C) \to (A \to C))$
(A2) $(A\&B) \to A$
(A3) $(A\&B) \to (B\&A)$
(A4) $(A\&(A \to B)) \to (B\&(B \to A))$
(A5) $(A \to (B \to C)) \to ((A\&B) \to C)$
(A6) $((A\&B) \to C) \to (A \to (B \to C))$
(A7) $((A \to B) \to C) \to (((B \to A) \to C) \to C)$
(A11) $0 \to A$
(A12) $A \to 1$

The only rule of BL is Modus Ponens:

(MP) $\quad \dfrac{A \quad A \to B}{B}.$

Łukasiewicz Logic Ł is BL plus

(¬¬) $\quad \neg\neg A \to A.$

Product logic Π is BL plus

(π) $\quad \neg(A) \vee ((A \to (A\&B)) \to B),$

Gödel Logic G is BL plus contraction:

(contr) $\quad A \to (A\&A).$

Definition 8. Let L be any of the logics listed above. The predicate logic $L\forall^-$ is the logic in the language $\mathbf{L}_1$ axiomatized by the axioms of L (extended to all formulas of $\mathbf{L}_1$) plus the following ones:

($\forall 1$) $\forall x A \to A(v/x)$ (v substitutable for x in A).
($\forall 2$) $\forall x(A \to B) \to (A \to \forall x B)$ (x not free in A).
($\exists 1$) $A(v/x) \to \exists x A$ (v substitutable for x in A).
($\exists 2$) $\forall x(A \to B) \to ((\exists x A) \to B)$ (x not free in B).

and whose rules are *(MP)* and *(Gen)*: $\dfrac{A}{\forall x A}.$

The logic $L\forall$ is $L\forall^-$ plus the axiom:

($\forall 3$) $\forall x(A \vee B) \to (A \vee \forall x B)$ (x not free in A).

The following proposition summarizes the main known results about BL and its principal extensions, as well as their first-order versions:

Proposition 2. *(i)* Let L be any of BL, Π, Ł or G. Then L is strongly complete with respect to both the class of BL (product, Wajsberg and Gödel respectively) algebras as well as to the class of BL (product, Wajsberg and Gödel respectively) chains, [11].
(ii) If L is as in (i), then $L\forall^-$ is strongly complete with respect to the class of the corresponding algebras, [7], and $L\forall$ is strongly complete with respect to the class of the corresponding chains.

(iii) G is strongly complete with respect to the class of standard Gödel algebras. Π, L and BL are finitely strongly complete, but not strongly complete, with respect to the class of standard product (Wajsberg, BL respectively) algebras.

(iv) G∀ is strongly complete with respect to the class of standard Gödel algebras. None of L∀, Π∀ or BL∀ is complete with respect to the class of first-order structures on standard Wajsberg (product, BL respectively) algebras. Moreover the set of sentences of L∀, Π∀ or BL∀ which are valid in all standard Wajsberg (product, BL respectively) algebras is not recursively enumerable, therefore it cannot be the set of theorems of a formal system with a decidable set of axioms and finitary rules.

We conclude this section with a description of the Baaz operator Δ, which will be used in the sequel.

Definition 9. *Let L be a propositional (first-order respectively) logic extending BL (BL∀ respectively). The extension of L by Δ is the logic L_Δ whose language is that of L plus the unary operator Δ, whose rules are those of L plus Necessitation:*
$$\frac{A}{\Delta(A)},$$ *and whose axioms are those of L (extended to the formulas in the language with Δ) plus the following ones:*

(1) $\Delta(A \to B) \to (\Delta(A) \to \Delta(B))$
(2) $\Delta(A) \vee \neg\Delta(A)$
(3) $\Delta(A) \to A$.
(5) $\Delta(A) \to \Delta(\Delta(A))$.
(4) $\Delta(A \vee B) \to (\Delta(A) \vee \Delta(B))$.

In any BL-chain, the operator Δ is interpreted as the unary operation δ defined for every x, by $\delta(x) = \begin{cases} 1 & \text{if } x = 1 \\ 0 & \text{otherwise} \end{cases}$

Both the positive and the negative results on standard completeness extend to logics with Δ, with just one difference: the set of first-order formulas of Łukasiewicz logic which are valid in $\{*_L\}$ is Π_2-complete [27], whereas the set of first-order formulas of Łukasiewicz logic plus Δ which are valid in $\{*_L\}$ is non-arithmetical [16].

4   Some Algebraic Results

We start from Hölder's theorem, cf [10], which will be stated here below. Recall that an ordered group is *archimedean* iff for all $a, b > 0$ there is a positive integer n such that $na > b$. Then Hölder's theorem says the following:

Proposition 3. *Any totally ordered archimedean group $\mathcal{G}$ can be embedded into the additive group $\mathcal{R}$ of the reals by a complete embedding (i.e., one which preserves existing suprema and infima).*

Proof. The embedding Φ is defined as follows: first of all, let $\Phi(e) = 0$, where e denotes the neutral element of $\mathcal{G}$. Now fix $u > e$. Let for every $a \in \mathcal{G}$ with $a > e$, $\Phi(a) = \sup\{\frac{n}{m} : a^m \geq u^n\}$ (it can be shown that such a supremum exists, cf [10]), and let for $a < e$, $\Phi(a) = -\Phi(a^{-1})$. That the embedding Φ is complete can be proved as follows: suppose first $e < a = \sup\{a_n : n \in \omega\}$, where, without loss of generality, we can assume $a > a_{n+1} > a_n > e$ for every n. Let $r_n = \Phi(a_n)$, let $r = \sup\{r_n : n \in \omega\}$, and let $s = \Phi(a)$. Clearly, $s \geq r$. Suppose, by the way of contradiction, $s > r$. Let $\frac{n}{m}$ be a rational such that $r < \frac{n}{m} < s$. Hence $a_i^m < u^n$ for every i, and $a^m > u^n$. But product in an abelian ℓ-group commutes with infinite joins and meets, therefore $a^m = \sup\{a_i^m : i \in \omega\}$, and a contradiction has been reached. The case $a \leq e$ is similar (taking the inverse elements and recalling that the group operation commutes with existing infima). Thus Φ preserves existing joins. The proof that it preserves existing (finite or infinite) meets is quite similar. $\qquad\square$

Let $\mathcal{A}$ be either a product chain or an MV-chain. Then $\mathcal{A}$ is said to be *archimedean* iff for every $x, y \in \mathcal{A} \setminus \{0, 1\}$ there is a positive integer n such that $x^n < y$. A totally ordered cancellative hoop $\mathcal{C}$ is said to be archimedean iff for every $x, y \in \mathcal{C} \setminus \{1\}$ there is a positive integer n such that $x^n < y$. Using Mundici's functor Γ [22] for the case of MV-algebras and [6] for product algebras, Hölder's theorem immediately gives:

Proposition 4. *An MV-chain (a product chain respectively) is archimedean iff it can be embedded in the MV-algebra (product algebra respectively) on $[0, 1]$ by a complete embedding. A totally ordered cancellative hoop is archimedean iff it can be embedded into the algebra $((0, 1], \cdot, \to_\pi, 1)$ by a complete embedding, where $\cdot$ and $\to_\pi$ denote product and residuum of product respectively.*

Definition 10. *A totally ordered BL-algebra $\mathcal{A}$ is said to be* weakly archimedean *iff all its Wajsberg components are archimedean, and* weakly saturated *iff all its Wajsberg components have a greatest lower bound which is an idempotent.*

Definition 11. *A BL-algebra with storage [21] is a BL-algebra $\mathcal{B}$ with a unary operation * such that for every $a \in \mathcal{B}$, a^* is the greatest idempotent z such that $z \leq a$. A BL-algebra with storage is said to be* representable *iff it is isomorphic to a subdirect product of BL-chains with storage.*

Clearly, any BL-algebra $\mathcal{B}$ arising from a continuous t-norm is (a reduct of) a representable BL-algebra with storage: for any $a \in \mathcal{B}$, $a^* = a$ if a is an idempotent, and a^* is the infimum of the Wajsberg component which a belongs to otherwise.

BL-algebras with storage are axiomatized by the following axioms:

(s0) The axioms of BL-algebras.
(s1) $a^* = a(a^*)^2$.
(s2) $(b \to (ab^2))^* \to (b \to a^*)$.

Representable BL-algebras with storage are axiomatized (s0), (s1) and (s2) plus:

(s3) $(a \vee b)^* \leftrightarrow (a^* \vee b^*)$.

Lemma 1. *Let A be a BL-chain. The following are equivalent:*
(a) A is weakly archimedean and weakly saturated.
*(b) On A we can define an operation * making it a BL-algebra with storage satisfying the additional condition:*
(+) if $x \leq y^n$ for every n, then $x \leq y^*$.

Proof. (a) $\Rightarrow$ (b). Let for every $x \in A$, x^* denote the infimum of the Wajsberg component which x belongs to. Then x^* is also the greatest idempotent below x, therefore A becomes a BL-algebra with storage. Moreover, the condition (+) is clearly satisfied if x and y are not in the same component; if they are in the same component W, then either $x = y = 1$, or x must be the minimum of W, as W is archimedean. But the minimum of W is an idempotent, as A is weakly saturated. Hence $x = y^*$.

   (b) $\Rightarrow$ (a). Let A be any BL-chain with a storage operator satisfying (+). We prove first that A is weakly saturated. Let W be any Wajsberg component of A, and let $x \in W$, $x < 1$. It suffices to prove that x^* is the infimum of W. Suppose not. Then since x^* is an idempotent, it cannot be in W (otherwise W would have an idempotent different from its maximum and its minimum), therefore there would be a lower bound z of W such that $x^* < z$. But then we would have $z \leq x^n$ for all n, and $x^* < z$, thus invalidating (+). We now prove that A is weakly archimedean. Let $x, y < 1$ be in the same Wajsberg component W of A. We claim that it is impossible that $x < y^n$ for every n. Indeed, in that case, by (+) we would get $x \leq y^*$, therefore $x = y^*$ would be the minimum of W. Hence W would be a reduct of a Wajsberg algebra with minimum $x = y^*$. Now let $z = y \rightarrow y^*$. Then clearly $zy = y^*$, and since $y^n > x = y^*$ for every n, we also have $y^{n+1} > y^*$, and therefore $y^n > y \rightarrow y^* = z$. By (+), this would imply $z \leq y^*$, and therefore $z \rightarrow y^* = (y \rightarrow y^*) \rightarrow y^* = 1$. On the other hand, using equations valid in every Wajsberg hoop, we get: $z \rightarrow y^* = (y \rightarrow y^*) \rightarrow y^* = y$, and a contradiction has been reached. $\square$

Now let A be weakly saturated. We group any maximal set of consecutive two-element components (i.e., any maximal convex set consisting of idempotent elements, added with the top element 1) into a single algebra which will be called a *Gödel component*. Note that any such algebra is a zero-free subreduct of a Gödel algebra.

   Then we group any cancellative component and its infimum (which is an idempotent as A is weakly saturated) into a single algebra, which is a zero-free reduct of a product algebra and will be called a *product component*.

   In this way A is decomposed into components which are MV-algebras, called MV-components, components which are product algebras, called *product components*, components which are subreducts of Gödel algebras, called *Gödel components* and idempotent elements which do not belong to MV or product or Gödel components, but are infima of endpoints of a family of such components.

   We say that a BL-algebra is *saturated* iff for every Gödel, product or MV component C in it, $C \setminus \{1\}$ has a supremum and a minimum which are both idempotents. Note that if C is a Wajsberg component of a weakly saturated

BL-algebra, then $\mathcal{C} \setminus \{1\}$ might either fail to have a supremum or have a supremum which is not an idempotent.

Lemma 2. *cf [14]. Any BL-chain $\mathcal{A}$ embeds into a saturated BL-chain. If in addition $\mathcal{A}$ is weakly saturated and every Gödel component in $\mathcal{A}$ has a minimum, then there is a saturated BL-chain $\mathcal{B}$ such that $\mathcal{A}$ embeds in $\mathcal{B}$ by a complete embedding (i.e., by an embedding preserving existing suprema and infima).*

Proof. Whenever a component $\mathcal{C}$ is such that $\mathcal{C} \setminus \{1\}$ has no supremum (no minimum respectively), add a new idempotent element M_C (m_c respectively), and stipulate that: if x is an upper bound of $\mathcal{C} \setminus \{1\}$, then $M_C x = M_C \wedge x = M_C$, $M_C \vee x = x$, $M_C \to x = 1$, $x \to M_C = M_C$; otherwise, $M_C x = M_C \wedge x = x$, $M_C \vee x = M_C$, $M_C \to x = x$, and $x \to M_C = 1$.

In a similar fashion, stipulate that: if x is a lower bound of $\mathcal{C} \setminus \{1\}$, then $m_C x = m_C \wedge x = x$, $m_C \vee x = m_C$, $m_C \to x = x$ and $x \to m_C = 1$; otherwise, $m_C x = m_C \wedge x = m_C$, $m_C \vee x = x$, $m_C \to x = 1$, and $x \to m_C = m_C$.

Let $\mathcal{C}$ be the algebra obtained in this way. It is clear that $\mathcal{B}$ is a saturated BL-chain that extends $\mathcal{A}$.

Assume now that $\mathcal{A}$ is weakly saturated and every Gödel component in $\mathcal{A}$ has a minimum. First note that if $\mathcal{C}$ is a Gödel or product or MV component of $\mathcal{A}$ and $\mathcal{C} \setminus \{1\}$ has a supremum a in $\mathcal{A}$, then either $a \in \mathcal{C}$ or a is an idempotent. In particular, if $\mathcal{C}$ is a Gödel component, then a is an idempotent and $a \in \mathcal{C}$. To see this, assume first that $\mathcal{C}$ is a Gödel component. Suppose, by the way of contradiction, $a \notin \mathcal{C}$. Thus a is a proper supremum, and since the monoid operation distributes over (possibly infinite) suprema, $a^2 = \sup \{b^2 : b < a\} = \sup \{b : b < a\} = a$. Thus $a \in \mathcal{C}$, and a contradiction has been reached. Now assume that $\mathcal{C}$ is a product or an MV component. If $a \notin \mathcal{C}$, by the definition of ordinal sum we obtain that $a^2 > c$ for all $c \in \mathcal{C} \setminus \{1\}$. Since $a^2 \leq a = \sup(\mathcal{C} \setminus \{1\})$, we must have $a = a^2$, and a must be an idempotent.

Next note that every product or MV component in $\mathcal{A}$ has clearly a minimum and every Gödel component $\mathcal{C}$ of $\mathcal{A}$ has a minimum by hypothesis. It follows that when we construct $\mathcal{B}$ as in the first part of the proof, we do not add minima of any component. Moreover, if we add a new upper bound M_C of $\mathcal{C} \setminus \{1\}$, then either $\mathcal{C} \setminus \{1\}$ has no supremum (therefore we do not change existing suprema), or $\mathcal{C} \setminus \{1\}$ has a supremum a which is not an idempotent. But in this case, $a \in \mathcal{C} \setminus \{1\}$, therefore $a < M_C$, and there is no z with $a < z < M_C$. Hence M_C is not a supremum of a subset of $\mathcal{A}$. Summing-up, we do not change existing suprema or infima. □

Lemma 3. *Any countable, saturated and weakly archimedean BL-chain $\mathcal{A}$ embeds into a standard BL-algebra on $[0,1]$ by a complete embedding.*

Proof. Consider any enumeration $\mathcal{C}_0, ..., \mathcal{C}_n, ...$ of all Łukasiewicz, Gödel or product components of $\mathcal{A}$. In each component we replace 1 by its supremum. In other words, if d_i is the supremum of $\mathcal{C}_i \setminus \{1\}$ we replace $\mathcal{C}_i$ by $(\mathcal{C}_i \setminus \{1\}) \cup \{d_i\}$, thus getting a new set $\mathcal{C}_i'$, which, by abuse of language, we will still call a component. In this way, any two different components may either be disjoint or intersect in one of their endpoints. We write $C_i' < C_j'$ to mean that $C_i' \neq C_j'$ and that every element of C_i' precedes every element of C_j'. We write $C_i' <_0 C_j'$ to mean that $C_i' < C_j'$ and that C_i' and C_j' have a common endpoint (i.e., the minimum of C_j equals the supremum of $C_i \setminus \{1\}$). We write $C_i' <_1 C_j'$ to mean that $C_i' < C_i'$ and not $C_i' <_0 C_j'$. We proceed by induction; at each step i we embed C_i' into an algebra of the same kind on an interval $[a_i, b_i]$ (by a complete embedding) in such a way that: (a) $a_i = 0$ iff C_i is the first component, and $b_i = 1$ iff C_i is the last component; (b) if $C_i' <_0 C_j'$ then $b_i = a_j$; (c) if $C_i' <_1 C_j'$, then $b_i < a_j$.

Step n. Suppose that at step $n-1$ we have embedded all C_i' with $i < n$ into (algebras of the same kind on) intervals $[a_i, b_i]$ such that (a), (b) and (c) are satisfied. The construction proceeds as follows:

(1) If C_n' is the first component, then let $C_j' = \min \{C_i' : i = 1, ..., n-1\}$. Note that $a_j > 0$ by condition (a). If $C_n' <_0 C_j'$, then embed C_n' into $[0, a_j]$. Otherwise, embed C_n' into $[0, \frac{a_j}{2}]$.

(2) If C_n' is the last component, then let $C_j' = \max \{C_i' : i = 1, ..., n-1\}$. Note that $b_j < 1$ by condition (b). If $C_j' <_0 C_n'$, then embed C_n' into $[b_j, 1]$. Otherwise, embed C_n' into $[\frac{b_j+1}{2}, 1]$.

(3) If C_n' is the not the first component, but it is smaller than $C_0', ..., C_{n-1}'$, then let $C_j' = \min \{C_i' : i = 1, ..., n-1\}$. Note that $a_j > 0$ by condition (a). If $C_n' <_0 C_j'$, then embed C_n' into $[\frac{a_j}{2}, a_j]$. Otherwise, embed C_n' into $[\frac{a_j}{3}, \frac{2a_j}{3}]$.

(4) If C_n' is the not the last component, but it is greater than $C_0', ..., C_{n-1}'$, then let $C_j' = \max \{C_i' : i = 1, ..., n-1\}$. Note that $b_j < 1$ by condition (b). If $C_j' <_0 C_n'$, then embed C_n' into $[b_j, \frac{1+b_j}{2}]$. Otherwise, embed C_n' into $[\frac{1+2b_j}{3}, \frac{2+b_j}{3}]$.

(5) If there are $h, k < n$ such that $C_h' < C_n' < C_k'$, then let

$$C_i' = \max \{C_h' : C_h' < C_n' : h = 1, ..., n-1\},$$

$$C_j' = \min \{C_k' : C_n' < C_k' : k = 1, ..., n-1\}.$$

Embed C_n' into $[a_n, b_n]$, where: if $C_i' <_0 C_n' <_0 C_j'$, then $a_n = b_i$ and $b_n = a_j$; if $C_i' <_0 C_n' <_1 C_j'$, then $a_n = b_i$ and $b_n = \frac{a_j+b_i}{2}$; if $C_i' <_1 C_n' <_0 C_j'$, then $b_n = a_j$ and $a_n = \frac{b_i+a_j}{2}$; if $C_i' <_1 C_n' <_1 C_j'$, then $a_n = \frac{2b_i+a_j}{3}$ and $b_n = \frac{b_i+2a_j}{3}$.

Note that the idempotents ρ which are neither internal points of a Gödel component, nor common limit points of two consecutive components, are either the infimum of a family of left endpoints of components, or the supremum of a family of right endpoints of components, or both, and we only need to prove that such idempotents are mapped in such a way that the above suprema and infima are preserved. We only treat the case where ρ is both a proper supremum of right endpoints of components and a proper infimum of left endpoints of components, and we leave the other (similar, and a little bit simpler) cases to the reader. Thus we assume $\rho = \lim_n r_n = \lim_n l_n$ with $r_n < r_{n+1} < \rho < l_{n+1} < l_n$, where r_i and l_i are respectively right and left extremals of components of A, and we prove that if c_n, d_n and δ are the reals corresponding to r_n, to l_n and to ρ respectively, then $\delta = \lim_n d_n = \lim_n c_n$. Clearly, it suffices to prove that $\lim_n (d_n - c_n) = 0$. To this purpose, note that whenever we insert a new interval $[a_n, b_n]$ corresponding to a component C_n' inside an interval $[a, b]$ whose extremals have been previously introduced, the construction guarantees that $a_n - a \leq \frac{b-a}{2}$, $b - b_n \leq \frac{b-a}{2}$ and $b_n - a_n \leq \frac{b-a}{2}$. Now for every n we insert an interval of the form $[c'_m, c_m]$ and an interval of the form $[d_m, d'_m]$ inside $[c_n, d_n]$. This implies that $d_m - c_m \leq \frac{d_n - c_n}{2}$, and the claim follows. $\qquad\square$

5 Characterizing Standard Completeness: Propositional Case

We work in BL with an operator $*$ where A^* represents the greatest idempotent below A. In other words, we work in the logic whose equivalent algebraic semantics is the variety of representable BL-algebras with storage. The axioms for $*$ are (cf [21]:

(*1) $A^* \rightarrow (A \& A^* \& A^*)$
(*2) $(B \rightarrow (A \& B \& B))^* \rightarrow (B \rightarrow A^*)$
(*3) $(A \vee B)^* \leftrightarrow (A^* \vee B^*)$.

The rules of BL^* are:

$$\text{Modus Ponens: } \frac{A \qquad A \rightarrow B}{B}.$$

$$\text{Necessitation: } \frac{A}{A^*}.$$

Note that the axioms guarantee that $*$ has all the properties of an S4 modality. However, axiom (*3) is not valid in S4, and it is quite uncommon in modal logic: it has been introduced because it ensures representability of the corresponding algebras.

Let BL^* be the resulting logic. Note that BL^* is conservative over BL.

We consider the following infinitary rule:

$$\text{(R)} \qquad \frac{C \vee (A \rightarrow B^n) \qquad \text{all } n}{C \vee (A \rightarrow B^*)}.$$

In the sequel, $\vdash$ denotes derivability in BL^*, and $\vdash_R$ denotes derivability in BL^* plus the rule (R). Thus $\vdash_R$ is defined by adding to the definition of $\vdash$ the following clause:

If $d_1, ..., d_n, ...$ are derivations of $C \vee (A \rightarrow B), ..., C \vee (A \rightarrow B^n), ...$, from a set Γ of assumptions, then $\dfrac{d_1, ..., d_n, ...}{C \vee (A \rightarrow B^*)}$ is a derivation of $C \vee (A \rightarrow B^*)$ from Γ.

If Γ is any set of formulas, then $K(\Gamma)$ ($K_R(\Gamma)$ respectively) denote the smallest set of formulas which contains Γ and the axioms of BL^* and is closed under the rules of BL^* (under the rules of BL^* and under (R) respectively).

A set Γ is said to be a *theory* (an *R-theory* respectively) if $K(\Gamma) = \Gamma$ ($K_R(\Gamma) = \Gamma$ respectively). A theory is said to be *complete* iff for any pair A, B of formulas either $A \rightarrow B \in \Gamma$ or $B \rightarrow A \in \Gamma$.

Lemma 4. *Let Γ be any complete R-theory over BL^*, and let $\mathcal{L}_\Gamma$ denote the Lindenbaum sentence algebra of Γ. Then $\mathcal{L}_\Gamma$ can be embedded into a standard BL-algebra.*

Proof. The completeness of Γ makes sure that $\mathcal{L}_\Gamma$ is a chain. Hence by Lemma 3, it suffices to prove that $\mathcal{L}_\Gamma$ is weakly archimedean. Now $\mathcal{L}_\Gamma$ is a BL-chain with storage, and by the validity of (R), it satisfies condition (b) in Lemma 1. Thus by Lemma 1, $\mathcal{L}_\Gamma$ is weakly archimedean and weakly saturated. This ends the proof.   □

Lemma 5. $\Gamma \cup \{A\} \vdash_R B$ *iff* $\Gamma \vdash_R A^* \to B$.

Proof. The right-to-left direction is clear (using $\frac{A}{A^*}$ and then Modus Ponens). For the other direction, we work by induction on the derivation. If B is an axiom or A or belongs to Γ, the claim is clear. The induction steps corresponding to Modus Ponens or Necessitation are easy. We now consider the case where the last rule is (R). Thus assume that $B = E \vee (C \to D^*)$ is obtained from $E \vee (C \to D)$, $E \vee (C \to D^2),...,E \vee (C \to D^n),...$ by the rule (R). By the induction hypothesis we have derivations of $A^* \to (E \vee (C \to D)), ..., A^* \to (E \vee (C \to D^n)), ...$ From them we obtain derivations of $(A^* \to E) \vee ((C\&A^*) \to D)), ..., (A^* \to E) \vee ((C\&A^*) \to D^n)), ...$

Hence by the rule (R) we obtain a derivation of $(A^* \to E) \vee ((C\&A^*) \to D^*)$, which is provably equivalent to $A^* \to (E \vee (C \to D^*))$.   □

Lemma 6. *The rule* $\dfrac{(A^n \to B)^* \to C \quad \text{all } n}{(B \to A^*)^* \vee C}$ *is derivable in BL^* plus (R).*

Proof. From $(A^n \to B)^* \to C$ and from $(A^n \to B)^* \vee (B \to A^n)^*$, for every n we derive $(B \to A^n)^* \vee C$, and, using the valid schema $D^* \to D$, we also derive $(B \to A^n) \vee C$. By the rule (R) we get $(B \to A^*) \vee C$, and finally by Necessitation, by (*3) and $D^* \to D$, we conclude $(B \to A^*)^* \vee C$, as desired.   □

Lemma 7. *If for all n, $\Gamma \vdash_R (C^n \to B)^* \to A$ and $\Gamma \vdash_R (B \to C^*)^* \to A$, then $\Gamma \vdash_R A$.*

Proof. By Lemma 6, if for all n, $\Gamma \vdash_R (C^n \to B)^* \to A$, then $\Gamma \vdash_R (B \to C^*)^* \vee A$. If in addition $\Gamma \vdash_R (B \to C^*)^* \to A$, then $\Gamma \vdash_R A$.   □

We are ready to prove a syntactic characterization of the relation $\Gamma \models_{K_{TN}} A$ even for infinite Γ. Recall that in any standard BL-algebra there is a unique operator * making it a BL-algebra with storage. Thus we may consider a standard BL-algebra both as a BL-algebra or as a BL-algebra with storage.

Theorem 2. *For any set $\Gamma \cup \{A\}$ of BL or BL^* sentences, the following are equivalent:*

(a) $\Gamma \models_{K_{TN}} A$.
(b) $\Gamma \vdash_R A$.

Proof. $(b) \Rightarrow (a)$. It suffices to prove that (R) is valid in any standard BL-algebra $\mathcal{A}$. This reduces to prove that for all $x, y, z \in \mathcal{A}$, if $z \vee (x \to y^n) = 1$ for every n, then $z \vee (x \to y^*) = 1$. The claim is trivial if $z = 1$. Thus suppose $z < 1$, therefore $x \leq y^n$ for every n. If $y = 1$, then clearly $x \leq 1 = y^*$. Otherwise, let $\mathcal{C}$ be the unique Wajsberg component which y belongs to. Let $y_0 = \inf \{y^n : n \in \omega\}$. Then y_0 is an idempotent element, and $x \leq y_0 \leq y$. Thus $x \leq y^*$, and (R) is valid in $\mathcal{A}$.

$(a) \Rightarrow (b)$. Suppose $\Gamma \nvdash_R A$. We will construct a complete R-theory Γ^+ such that $\Gamma \subseteq \Gamma^+$ and $A \notin \Gamma^+$.

Before starting the construction, we warn the reader that by the presence of infinitary rules, many standard constructions do not work. For instance, one might be tempted to use Zorn's lemma to obtain a maximal R-theory Γ^+ extending Γ such that $A \notin \Gamma^+$. But in this case Zorn's lemma does not apply, as the union of a chain of R-theories may fail to be an R-theory: for instance, let $\Gamma_n = K_R(p \to q^n)$; then $\Gamma_1 \subseteq ... \subseteq \Gamma_n \subseteq ...$, and every Γ_n is an R-theory, but their union Γ^+ is not, as $p \to q^* \notin \Gamma^+$. Thus we will proceed in another way.

Let $(A_1, B_1), ..., (A_n, B_n), ...$ be an enumeration of all pairs of formulas of BL^*. We define inductively a sequence $\langle \Gamma_n : n \in \omega \rangle$ of R-theories with the following properties:

(a) $\Gamma_0 = K_R(\Gamma) \subseteq \Gamma_1 \subseteq ... \subseteq \Gamma_n \subseteq ....$

(b) For every n, $A \notin \Gamma_n$.

(c) For every n, either $A_n \to B_n \in \Gamma_{2n+1}$ or $B_n \to A_n \in \Gamma_{2n+1}$.

(d) For every n, if $A_n \to B_n \in \Gamma_{2n+1}$, then either for some k, $B_n^k \to A_n \in \Gamma_{2n+2}$, or $A_n \to B_n^* \in \Gamma_{2n+2}$.

(e) For every n, if $A_n \to B_n \notin \Gamma_{2n+1}$, then either for some k, $A_n^k \to B_n \in \Gamma_{2n+2}$, or $B_n \to A_n^* \in \Gamma_{2n+2}$.

Step 0: $\Gamma_0 = K_R(\Gamma)$.

Step $2n + 1$. If $A \notin K_R(\Gamma_{2n} \cup \{A_n \to B_n\})$, then let $\Gamma_{2n+1} = K_R(\Gamma_{2n} \cup \{A_n \to B_n\})$; otherwise, let $\Gamma_{2n+1} = K_R(\Gamma_{2n} \cup \{B_n \to A_n\})$. Note that in any case $A \notin \Gamma_{2n+1}$. Indeed, if $A \in \Gamma_{2n+1}$, then $\Gamma_{2n} \cup \{A_n \to B_n\} \vdash_R A$, $\Gamma_{2n} \cup \{B_n \to A_n\} \vdash_R A$, and by Lemma 5, $\Gamma_{2n} \vdash_R (A_n \to B_n)^* \to A$ and $\Gamma_{2n} \vdash_R (B_n \to A_n)^* \to A$. Since $\Gamma_{2n} \vdash_R (A_n \to B_n)^* \vee (B_n \to A_n)^*$, we would conclude $\Gamma_{2n} \vdash_R A$, against the induction hypothesis.

Step $2n + 2$. We distinguish two cases.

Case (a): $A_n \to B_n \in \Gamma_{2n+1}$. We have two subcases.

Subcase (a1): for some k, $A \notin K_R(\Gamma_{2n+1} \cup \{B_n^k \to A_n\})$. Then let k_0 be the minimum k with this property, and let $\Gamma_{2n+2} = K_R(\Gamma_{2n+1} \cup \{B_n^{k_0} \to A_n\})$. Note that $A \notin \Gamma_{2n+2}$.

Subcase (a2): for all k, $A \in K_R(\Gamma_{2n+1} \cup \{B_n^k \to A_n\})$. Then by Lemma 5, $\Gamma_{2n+1} \vdash_R (B_n^k \to A_n)^* \to A$ and since $A \notin \Gamma_{2n+1}$, by Lemma 7 we have that $(A_n \to B_n^*)^* \to A \notin \Gamma_{2n+1}$. Then let $\Gamma_{2n+2} = K_R(\Gamma_{2n+1} \cup \{A_n \to B_n^*\})$, and note that $A \notin \Gamma_{2n+2}$.

Case (b): $A_n \to B_n \notin \Gamma_{2n+1}$. Then $B_n \to A_n \in \Gamma_{2n+1}$, and the procedure is quite symmetric to Case (a) (just exchange A_n and B_n).

It is clear that the sequence $(\Gamma_n : n \in \omega)$ satisfies conditions (a), (b), (c), (d) and (e). Now let $\Gamma^+ = \bigcup \{\Gamma_n : n \in \omega\}$. Clearly Γ^+ is a complete theory extending Γ, and $A \notin \Gamma^+$, therefore by Lemma 4 to get the claim it is sufficient to show that Γ^+ is closed under (R) (warning: as noted before, the union of a chain of R-theories need not be an R-theory).

Thus assume that for some formulas D, E and F and for all k, $D \vee (E \to F^k) \in \Gamma^+$, and let us prove that $D \vee (E \to F^*) \in \Gamma^+$. Since Γ^+ is a complete theory, we have that either $D \in \Gamma^+$ or for all k, $E \to F^k \in \Gamma^+$. If $D \in \Gamma^+$, then $D \vee (E \to F^*) \in \Gamma^+$. If for all k, $E \to F^k \in \Gamma^+$, then by our construction we have that either for some h, $F^h \to E \in \Gamma^+$, or $E \to F^* \in \Gamma^+$. In the latter case, $D \vee (E \to F^*) \in \Gamma^+$. In the former case, since $E \to F^k \in \Gamma^+$ for all k and since $F^h \to E$ we derive $E \leftrightarrow F^h$ and $F^h \leftrightarrow F^{h+1}$. The last formula implies that in the Lindenbaum sentence algebra of Γ^+, (the equivalence class of) F^h is an idempotent element, therefore, E, F^h and F^* are provably equivalent. Then $E \to F^* \in \Gamma^+$, $D \vee (E \to F^*) \in \Gamma^+$, and Γ^+ is closed under (R). This concludes the proof.   □

6   Characterizing Standard Completeness: First-Order Case

We will work in the logic $BL^* \forall^+$ defined below.

Definition 12. $BL^* \forall^+$ *is the logic whose language is* $\mathbf{L}_1$ *plus the unary operator* **, and whose axioms and rules are:*

   The axioms and the rules of BL^* *(for formulas of the extended language).*
   The axioms and the rules of $BL\forall$ *(once again, for formulas of the extended language).*
   The axiom $\forall x B^*(x) \to (\forall x B^*(x))^*$ *(whose intended meaning is that the infimum of a set of idempotent elements is an idempotent).*

The logic $BL^* \forall R$ *is* $BL^* \forall^+$ *plus the rule (R).*

Note that the new axiom $\forall x B^*(x) \to (\forall x B^*(x))^*$ is true in any standard BL-algebra.

The derivability relation in $BL^* \forall^+$ will be denoted by $\vdash_1$, and the derivability relation in $BL^* \forall R$ will be denoted by $\vdash_{R1}$. We also recall from Section 2 that first-order semantic consequence relation in standard BL-algebras is denoted by $\models_{K_{TN}1}$.

Lemma 8. *Let* $\mathcal{A}$ *be a weakly saturated BL-chain, and let* $\mathcal{B}$ *be the saturated BL-chain constructed as in the proof of Lemma 2. Let* $\mathcal{M}$ *be a structure over* $\mathcal{A}$ *such that every axiom of* $BL^* \forall^+$ *is valid in* $(\mathcal{A}, \mathcal{M})$*. Then for any sentence* E *we have that* $\|E\|_{\mathcal{A}, \mathcal{M}} = \|E\|_{\mathcal{B}, \mathcal{M}}$*.*

Proof. The claim is clear if every Gödel component of $\mathcal{A}$ having an infimum has a minimum, because in this case the identity function on $\mathcal{A}$ is a complete embedding of $\mathcal{A}$ into $\mathcal{B}$. Now suppose that there are Gödel components of $\mathcal{A}$ with infimum but without minimum. Let $\mathcal{C}$ be any of them (thus the infimum γ of $\mathcal{C}$ is not an idempotent). Note that for every formula $D(x)$ we cannot have $\|\forall x D(x)\|_{\mathcal{A},\mathcal{M}} = \gamma$, otherwise we would have $\|\forall x D^*(x)\|_{\mathcal{A},\mathcal{M}} = \gamma = \|(\forall x D^*(x))^*\|_{\mathcal{A},\mathcal{M}} = \gamma^*$. Thus γ would be an idempotent, which is a contradiction.

We now proceed by induction on the complexity of E. The base step is clear, and the steps corresponding to connectives and to * are obvious, as $\mathcal{A}$ is a BL^* subalgebra of $\mathcal{B}$. For the $\forall$ step, the claim follows from the fact that $\|\forall x D(x)\|_{\mathcal{A},\mathcal{M}}$ cannot be the infimum of a Gödel component without minimum, and the remaining infima, i.e., those infima which are not infima of Gödel components without minimum, are preserved from $\mathcal{A}$ to $\mathcal{B}$. Finally, all suprema existing in $\mathcal{A}$ are preserved from $\mathcal{A}$ to $\mathcal{B}$, and this shows the $\exists$ step. $\qquad\square$

Definition 13. *A theory Γ over $BL^{*}\forall^{+}$ is said to be* Henkin *iff whenever $\forall x B \notin \Gamma$ (B any formula), then there is a constant c such that $B(x/c) \notin \Gamma$.*

Lemma 9. *Let Γ be a complete and Henkin R-theory over $BL^{*}\forall^{+}$, in a language with infinitely many constants, and let A be a formula such that $A \notin \Gamma$. Then $\Gamma \nvdash_{K_{TN}1} A$.*

Proof. Let D be the set of all constants in Γ, and define for every atomic formula B, $\mathcal{M}(B) = [B]$ (where $[B]$ denotes the equivalence class of B with respect to provable equivalence in Γ). Clearly, in this way we have defined a first-order structure $\mathcal{M}$ with domain D over $\mathcal{L}_\Gamma$. Now we prove that for every sentence F, we have $\|F\|_{\mathcal{L}_\Gamma,\mathcal{M}} = [F]$. The proof is by induction on F. The claim is trivial for F atomic, and the steps corresponding to connectives or to * are easy (for instance, using the induction hypothesis, we get $\|A \& B\|_{\mathcal{L}_\Gamma,\mathcal{M}} = \|A\|_{\mathcal{L}_\Gamma,\mathcal{M}} \& \|B\|_{\mathcal{L}_\Gamma,\mathcal{M}} = [A]\&[B] = [A\&B]$, and a similar argument works for the other connectives).

We now treat the $\forall$ step. Assume by induction hypothesis that for all $c \in D$, we have $\|B(x/c)\|_{\mathcal{L}_\Gamma,\mathcal{M}} = [B(x/c)]$. We need to prove that

(i) $\inf\{\|B(x/c)\|_{\mathcal{L}_\Gamma,\mathcal{M}} : c \in D\} = \inf\{[B(x/c)]; c \in D\}$ exists, and
(ii) $\inf\{[B(x/c)]; c \in D\} = [\forall x B]$.

Clearly, $[\forall x B]$ is a lower bound of all elements of the form $[B(x/c)]$. Now let C be any sentence such that $[C] \leq [B(x/c)]$ for every $c \in D$. Then for every c, $C \to B(x/c) \in \Gamma$. Since Γ is a Henkin theory, it follows that $\forall x(C \to B(x)) \in \Gamma$, therefore $C \to \forall x B(x) \in \Gamma$. Thus $[C] \leq [\forall x B(x)]$, and $[\forall x B(x)]$ is the greatest lower bound of the set $\{[B(x/c)] : c \in D\}$.

We now consider the $\exists$ step. Using the induction hypothesis, it is sufficient to prove that $[\exists x B] = \sup\{[B(x/c)] : c \in D\}$. That $[\exists x B]$ is an upper bound is clear. Now let C be any sentence such that $[B(x/c)] \leq [C]$ for every $c \in D$. Then for every $c \in D$, $B(x/c) \to C \in \Gamma$. Since Γ is a Henkin theory, it follows that $\forall x(B(x) \to C) \in \Gamma$, therefore $\exists x B \to C \in \Gamma$. Thus $[\exists x B] \leq [C]$, and $[\exists x B]$ is the least upper bound of the set $\{[B(x/c)] : c \in D\}$.

So far, we have shown that $\mathcal{L}_\Gamma$ is a BL^*-chain (as Γ is complete), and $\mathcal{M}$ is a first-order structure on it, such that for every sentence F, we have

$\|F\|_{\mathcal{L}_\Gamma, \mathcal{M}} = [F]$. It follows that $\|B\|_{\mathcal{L}_\Gamma, \mathcal{M}} = 1$ for all $B \in \Gamma$, and $\|A\|_{\mathcal{L}_\Gamma, \mathcal{M}} < 1$. Moreover, $\mathcal{L}_\Gamma$ is weakly saturated (being a BL* chain) and weakly archimedean, as Γ is an R-theory.

Now by Lemma 8, we can embed $\mathcal{L}_\Gamma$ into a weakly archimedean and saturated BL*-chain $\mathcal{B}$ such that for every sentence F we have $\|F\|_{\mathcal{L}_\Gamma, \mathcal{M}} = \|F\|_{\mathcal{B}, \mathcal{M}}$. Finally, by Lemma 3, $\mathcal{B}$ embeds into a standard BL-algebra $\mathcal{S}$ by a complete embedding Φ. Hence we obtain a first-order structure $\mathcal{N}$ on $\mathcal{S}$ letting, for every atomic sentence P, $\|P\|_{\mathcal{S}, \mathcal{N}} = \Phi(\|P\|_{\mathcal{B}, \mathcal{M}})$. Since Φ is a complete embedding, we have that for any sentence F,

$$\|F\|_{\mathcal{S}, \mathcal{N}} = \Phi(\|F\|_{\mathcal{B}, \mathcal{M}}) = \Phi(\|F\|_{\mathcal{L}_\Gamma, \mathcal{M}}).$$

Hence $\|B\|_{\mathcal{S}, \mathcal{N}} = 1$ for all $B \in \Gamma$ and $\|A\|_{\mathcal{S}, \mathcal{N}} < 1$. This completes the proof. □

Theorem 3. *Let $\Gamma \cup \{A\}$ be any set of sentences of $BL^*\forall$. Then $\Gamma \models_{K_{TN}1} A$ iff $\Gamma \vdash_{R1} A$.*

Proof. The proof of the right-to-left direction is similar to the proof of the analogous statement in Theorem 2. For the other direction, by Lemma 9, it is sufficient to show that if $\Gamma \nvdash_R A$, then there is a complete Henkin R-theory Γ^+ such that $\Gamma \subseteq \Gamma^+$ and $A \notin \Gamma^+$.

To this purpose, we first extend the language by countably many new constants. In the sequel, for any set Σ of sentences in the new language, $K_R(\Sigma)$ will denote the smallest R-theory over $BL^*\forall^+$ containing Σ, *in the language of $BL^*\forall^+$ added by the symbols of Σ.* Thus e.g. $K_R(\Gamma)$ does not contain any formula with constants not occurring in Γ.

Now consider: (a) an enumeration of all pairs (A_n, B_n) of sentences of the extended language; (b) a list $\langle C_n(x) : n \in \omega \rangle$ of all formulas of the extended language whose only free variable is x.

We define inductively a sequence $\langle \Gamma_n : n \in N \rangle$ of R-theories and a sequence $\langle E_n : n \in \omega \rangle$ of sentences with the following properties:

(a) $\Gamma_0 = K_R(\Gamma) \subseteq \Gamma_1 \subseteq ... \subseteq \Gamma_n \subseteq ....$

(b) For every n, $E_n \notin \Gamma_{3n}$, $BL^*\forall^+ \vdash A \rightarrow E_n$ and $BL^*\forall^+ \vdash E_n \rightarrow E_{n+1}$.

(c) For every n, either $A_n \rightarrow B_n \in \Gamma_{3n+1}$ or $B_n \rightarrow A_n \in \Gamma_{3n+1}$.

(d) For every n, if $A_n \rightarrow B_n \in \Gamma_{3n+1}$, then either for some k, $B_n^k \rightarrow A_n \in \Gamma_{3n+2}$, or $A_n \rightarrow B_n^* \in \Gamma_{3n+2}$.

(e) For every n, if $A_n \rightarrow B_n \notin \Gamma_{3n+1}$, then either for some k, $A_n^k \rightarrow B_n \in \Gamma_{3n+2}$, or $B_n \rightarrow A_n^* \in \Gamma_{3n+2}$.

(f) For every n, either $\forall x C_n(x) \in \Gamma_{3n+3}$ or there is a constant c such that $C_n(c) \rightarrow E_{3n+3} \in \Gamma_{3n+3}$.

Note that conditions (a),...,(f) guarantee that the union Γ^+ of all Γ_n is a complete and Henkin R-theory, and that $A \notin \Gamma^+$. That Γ^+ is a complete R-theory can be proved along the lines of Theorem 2. That $A \notin \Gamma^+$ follows from (a) and (b). We prove (assuming (a),...,(f)) that Γ^+ is Henkin. Suppose that $\forall x C_n(x) \notin \Gamma^+$. Then $\forall x C_n(x) \notin \Gamma_{3n+3}$, therefore by (f) there is a constant c such that $C_n(c) \rightarrow E_{3n+3} \in \Gamma_{3n+3}$. We claim that $C_n(c) \notin \Gamma^+$. Indeed, if $C_n(c) \in \Gamma^+$, there would be a $k \geq 3n + 3$ such that $C_n(c) \in \Gamma_k$, and since

$C_n(c) \to E_{3n+3} \in \Gamma_k$, we would obtain $E_{3n+3} \in \Gamma_k$, and finally, by (a) and (b), $E_k \in \Gamma_k$, which is excluded by (b).

The rest of the proof is devoted to the construction of sets Γ_n and sentences E_n satisfying conditions (a), (b), (c), (d), (e) and (f).

Step 0: set $\Gamma_0 = K_R(\Gamma)$ and $E_0 = A$.

Step $3n + 1$. If $E_{3n} \notin K_R(\Gamma_{3n} \cup \{A_n \to B_n\})$, then let $\Gamma_{3n+1} = K_R(\Gamma_{3n} \cup \{A_n \to B_n\})$; otherwise, let $\Gamma_{3n+1} = K_R(\Gamma_{3n} \cup \{B_n \to A_n\})$. Moreover, let $E_{3n+1} = E_{3n}$. Note that in any case $E_{3n+1} \notin \Gamma_{3n+1}$. This is shown as in the proof of Theorem 2.

Step $3n + 2$, (a). Suppose $A_n \to B_n \in \Gamma_{3n+1}$. If for some h, $E_{3n+1} \notin K_R(\Gamma_{3n+1} \cup \{B_n^h \to A_n\})$, then let $\Gamma_{3n+2} = K_R(\Gamma_{3n+1} \cup \{B_n^h \to A_n\})$; otherwise, let $\Gamma_{3n+2} = K_R(\Gamma_{3n+1} \cup \{A_n \to B_n^*\})$. Moreover, let $E_{3n+2} = E_{3n+1}$. Note that in any case $E_{3n+2} \notin \Gamma_{3n+2}$, see the proof of Theorem 2.

Step $3n + 2$, (b). Suppose now $A_n \to B_n \notin \Gamma_{3n+1}$ (and therefore $B_n \to A_n \in \Gamma_{3n+1}$). The construction is symmetric to that of Step $3n + 2$, (a) (just exchange A_n and B_n).

Step $3n + 3$, case (1). If $E_{3n+2} \notin K_R(\Gamma_{3n} \cup \{\forall x C_n(x)\})$, then let $\Gamma_{3n+3} = K_R(\Gamma_{3n+2} \cup \{\forall x C_n(x)\})$ and $E_{3n+3} = E_{3n+2}$.

Step $3n + 3$, case (2). If $E_{3n+2} \in K_R(\Gamma_{3n} \cup \{\forall x C_n(x)\})$, then take a new constant c not occurring in Γ_{3n+2} nor in E_{3n+2} (e.g., we may take the constant with minimum index having such property). Let Γ_{3n+3} be the smallest R-theory over $BL^*\forall^+$ containing Γ_{3n+2} *in the language of Γ_{3n+2} added with the new constant c*, and let $E_{3n+3} = E_{3n+2} \vee C_n(c)$.

Note that in any case $E_{3n+3} \notin \Gamma_{3n+3}$. This is evident if case (1) occurs. In case (2), if $E_{3n+3} \in \Gamma_{3n+3}$, then, by the definition of Γ_{3n+3}, we have that E_{3n+3} is also derivable from Γ_{3n+2}. Therefore, replacing c by a fresh variable in the derivation of E_{3n+3} (recall that c does not occur in Γ_{3n+2} nor in E_{3n+2}) and using the generalization rule, we would obtain that $\Gamma_{3n+2} \vdash_{R1} \forall x (E_{3n+2} \vee C_n(x))$. Therefore, using $(\forall 3)$, we would obtain $\Gamma_{3n+2} \vdash_{R1} E_{3n+2} \vee \forall x C_n(x)$. Since $\Gamma_{3n+2} \vdash_{R1} \forall x C_n(x) \to E_{3n+2}$, we would conclude $\Gamma_{3n+2} \vdash_{R1} E_{3n+2}$, which contradicts the induction hypothesis.

Now all conditions except from (f) are clearly satisfied by our construction. As regards to (f), if case (1) occurs, then $\forall x C_n(x) \in \Gamma_{3n+3}$ and there is nothing to prove; if case (2) occurs, then the constructions guarantees that for some constant c we have $C_n(c) \to E_{3n+3} \in \Gamma_{3n+3}$. This ends the proof.   □

7   Applications

In this section we investigate many applications of the results of the last two sections, namely, the case of Łukasiewicz and product logics, the Łukasiewicz logic with a probabilistic operator, and the complexity of first-order *BL* and product logics. But before we investigate these topics, we start from some general remarks.

Since BL, Ł and Π are finitely strongly standard complete, the rule (R) is admissible in any finite theory over any of the above mentioned logics. A non-trivial example of formulas A, B such that $A \to B^n$ is provable for every n is given by $A = p\&p$, and $B = \neg p \to p$. But also $A \to B^*$ is provable: the easy proof is left to the reader.

The situation is different for first-order extensions. Indeed, even finite semantic consequence relation in standard BL-algebras is not arithmetical, therefore there must be a finite set Γ of sentences, and formulas A and B such that $\Gamma \vdash_{BL*\forall+} A \to B^n$ for every n, but $\Gamma \nvdash_{BL*\forall+} A \to B^*$. Here is an example:

Example. Let U be a unary predicate, 0 be a constant, and let S be a unary function symbol (if we do not want functions symbols in our language, we may replace S by a binary predicate $S^+(x,y)$, but in this case we need two more axioms, i.e., $\forall x \forall y (S^+(x,y) \vee \neg S^+(x,y))$, and $\forall x \exists y S^+(x,y)$). Now let

$$\Gamma = \{\forall x (U(S(x)) \leftrightarrow U(x)^2)\}, \quad A = \forall x U(x) \text{ and } B = U(0).$$

(If we don't allow function symbols, then $\forall x (U(S(x)) \leftrightarrow U(x)^2)$ must be replaced by $\forall x \forall y ((S^+(x,y)\&U(y)) \leftrightarrow U(x)^2))$. Then it is easily seen that for every n, $\Gamma \vdash_{BL*\forall+} A \to B^n$. However, $\Gamma \nvdash_{BL*\forall+} A \to B^*$. To see this, let $\mathcal{C}$ be the cancellative hoop consisting of all powers of an element a, with $a^0 = 1$, $a^n \cdot a^m = a^{n+m}$, $a^n \leq a^m$ iff $m \leq n$, and with $a^m \to a^n = a^{\max\{n-m,0\}}$. Now let $\mathcal{W}_3$ be the three element MV-algebra, consisting of $0, 1$ and $\frac{1}{2}$, and let $\mathcal{A}$ be the ordinal sum of $\mathcal{W}_3$ and $\mathcal{C}$. Take D to be the set ω of natural numbers, and interpret 0 as the natural number 0 and S as the successor function on ω. Now evaluate $U(n)$ as a^{2^n}. Let $\mathcal{M}$ be the resulting structure on $\mathcal{A}$ with domain D. Then, it is easily seen that $\|\forall x (U(S(x)) \leftrightarrow U(x)^2)\|_{\mathcal{A},\mathcal{M}} = 1$. Moreover, $\|B^*\|_{\mathcal{A},\mathcal{M}} = 0$, and $\|A\|_{\mathcal{A},\mathcal{M}} = \frac{1}{2}$, therefore $\Gamma \nvdash_{BL*\forall+} A \to B^*$.

Remark 2. Since validity in standard BL-algebras is also non-arithmetical, the rule (R) is not admissible even when the set Γ of assumptions is empty. However, we have not been able to find a reasonably simple counterexample when $\Gamma = \emptyset$.

7.1   Strong Standard Completeness in Łukasiewicz and Product Logics

In the case of Łukasiewicz or product logics, the least idempotent below A is $\Delta(A)$. Therefore, the rule (R) becomes

(R)
$$\frac{C \vee (A \to B^n) \text{ all } n}{C \vee (A \to \Delta(B))}.$$

Now if L denotes any of Łukasiewicz or product logics and L_Δ denotes its extension by Δ, then we have:

$A \to \Delta(B) \vdash_{L_\Delta} \neg A \vee B$ and $\neg A \vee B \vdash_{L_\Delta} A \to \Delta(B)$.

Therefore the rule (R) may be rewritten as:

(R')
$$\frac{C \vee (A \to B^n) \text{ all } n}{C \vee \neg A \vee B}.$$

Now let L and L_Δ be as above, and let $L\forall$ and $L_\Delta\forall$ be their first-order extensions. Also, let $\models_{L1}$ stand either for $\models_{\text{Ł}1}$ or for $\models_{\pi 1}$, and let $\vdash_{LR1}$ have the same meaning as $\vdash_{R1}$, but with BL replaced by L. Then, it is possible to prove the analogues of theorems 2 and 3 for Łukasiewicz and for product logic. Here below we list the main differences in the proofs. First of all, every product or MV-chain is saturated, therefore we do not have to worry about saturation. Moreover, an MV-chain or a product chain is weakly archimedean iff it is archimedean. Finally, in the case of Łukasiewicz or product logic, the operator $*$ must be replaced by Δ. Thus Lemma 1 becomes:

Lemma 10. *An MV-chain or product chain is archimedean iff it satisfies the following condition:*
$(+')$ If for all n, $x \leq y^n$, then $x \leq \Delta(y)$, or equivalently, $x \vee \neg y = 1$.

Lemma 2 is not needed in the case of Łukasiewicz or product logic. Lemma 3 in the case of Łukasiewicz or product logic becomes just Proposition 4. Finally, lemmas 4, 5, 6 and 7 extend to Łukasiewicz and to product logic with obvious changes (e.g., write Δ for $*$, L for BL, etc.). Note that the analogue of the axiom $\forall x B^*(x) \to (\forall x B^*(x))^*$, that is, $\forall x \Delta(B(x)) \to \Delta(\forall x \Delta(B(x)))$ is provable in the expansion $L_\Delta\forall$ of $L\forall$ by means of Δ, therefore we do not need it. Thus we obtain:

Theorem 4. *Let $\Gamma \cup \{A\}$ be any set of sentences of $L_\Delta\forall$. Then $\Gamma \models_{L1} A$ iff $\Gamma \vdash_{LR1} A$.*

Problem 1. Is the operator Δ really needed in Theorem 4? The rule (R') does not involve Δ, and if L denotes either Ł or Π, then L_Δ is a conservative extension of L. The same holds for the first-order extension $L\forall$ of L. However, in order to prove that Δ is not needed, we should prove that conservativeness is preserved when the rule (R') is added, that is, that for every R'-theory T over L, T_Δ is an R'-theory which extends T conservatively.

7.2 Probability over Łukasiewicz Logic

In [11], Hájek introduces a logic of (classical) probability based on Łukasiewicz logic. Many authors also suggested an investigation of probability over many-valued events. This problem has been investigated in [23], and then it has been developed in many papers, cf e.g. [26], [25], [19], [9] and [24]. In particular, in [24], Mundici was able to extend the De Finetti no-Dutch-book criterion to Łukasiewicz logic. More precisely, recall that a *state* over an MV-algebra $\mathcal{A}$ is a map s from $\mathcal{A}$ into $[0,1]$ such that $s(1) = 1$, and whenever $x \cdot y = 0$, then $s(x \oplus y) = s(x) + s(y)$. A *probabilistic assessment* is a map σ from a subset of Lindenbaum sentence algebra $\mathcal{L}_{\text{Ł}}$ of Łukasiewicz logic into $[0,1]$. A probabilistic assessment is said to be *coherent* if there is a state over $\mathcal{L}_{\text{Ł}}$ which extends it. Now Mundici [24] gave a very interesting characterization of coherence of finite assessments by means of betting strategies. Consider a reversible book-maker **A** (i.e., one who accepts both positive and negative bets). Let σ be any finite assessment, i.e., a map from a finite subset of $\mathcal{L}_{\text{Ł}}$ into $[0, 1]$, and imagine the following situation: a bettor **B** is invited to bet any amount b_E of money (possibly negative, possibly 0) on every event $E \in Dom(\sigma)$. Then **B** pays $p_E = b_E \cdot \sigma(E)$ to **A** now, for each $E \in Dom(\sigma)$ (it is agreed that if $p_E < 0$, then **B** receives $-p_E$ from **A**). Then, a homomorphism v is chosen from $\mathcal{L}_{\text{Ł}}$ into the MV-algebra $[0, 1]_{\text{Ł}}$ on $[0, 1]$, and for each $E \in dom(\sigma)$, **B** receives $r_E = b_E \cdot v(E)$ from **A** for each $E \in Dom(\sigma)$ (again, if $r_E < 0$, then **B** pays $-r_E$ to **A**). A *Dutch book relative to* σ is a system of bets $\langle b_E : E \in Dom(\sigma) \rangle$ which ensures to **B** a win, independently of the choice of the homomorphism v. Then Mundici's result can be formulated as follows:

Proposition 5. *Let σ be a finite probability assessment. The following are equivalent:*

(i) σ is coherent.
(ii) There is no Dutch Book relative to σ.

Thus the concept of coherence has a very interesting counterpart in terms of bets. The following questions seem quite natural:

(1) Is there also a logical counterpart to the coherence problem for Łukasiewicz logic?
(2) Is there a logical approach allowing us to speak also of more general probabilistic judgements like: *A is at least as probable as B&C*, or: *the probability of A is equal to the sum of the probability of B and the probability of C?*

In order to answer these questions, following [11], we add a modality Pr to Łukasiewicz logic and we interpret the probability of a many-valued event E as the truth-value of the sentence $Pr(E)$. Then we introduce a logic ŁPr whose formulas are inductively defined as follows:

(i) Every formula of Ł is a formula of ŁPr.
(ii) The set of formulas of ŁPr is closed under connectives of Ł.
(iii) if A is a formula of Ł , then $Pr(A)$ is a formula of ŁPr.

Whilst in [11] and in [9] the semantics used is based on Kripke models, we would like to investigate semantics based on states. We will propose two different approaches.

In the first approach we consider:

An MV-algebra $\mathcal{A}$ having $[0, 1]_{\text{Ł}}$ as a subalgebra.
A state s on $\mathcal{A}$ (note that since $[0, 1]_{\text{Ł}}$ is a subalgebra of $\mathcal{A}$, s maps $\mathcal{A}$ into $\mathcal{A}$).
An evaluation v on $\mathcal{A}$.

Then we define for every formula A an element $\| A \|_{s,v}$ of $\mathcal{A}$ in the following inductive way:

$\| A \|_{s,v} = v(A)$ for A atomic.

For every binary connective $\circ$, $\| B \circ C \|_{s,v} = \| B \|_{s,v} \circ \| C \|_{s,v}$ (where the second occurrence of $\circ$ denotes its realization in $\mathcal{A}$).

$\| Pr(A) \|_{s,v} = s(\| A \|_{s,v})$.

The problem is then to characterize those formulas A such that $\| A \|_{s,v} = 1$ for every MV-algebra $\mathcal{A}$ containing $[0,1]_{\text{Ł}}$, for every state s and for every evaluation v on $\mathcal{A}$.

The second approach is as follows: let s be any state on the Lindenbaum sentence algebra $\mathcal{L}_{\text{Ł}}$ of Ł and v be any homomorphism of $\mathcal{L}_{\text{Ł}}$ into $[0,1]_{\text{Ł}}$. We define for every formula A a real number $\| A \|_{s,v}$ in the following inductive way:

$\| A \|_{s,v} = v([A])$ for A atomic, where $[A] \in \mathcal{L}_{\text{Ł}}$ denotes the equivalence class of A modulo provable equivalence in Ł .

For every binary connective $\circ$, $\| B \circ C \|_{s,v} = \| B \|_{s,v} \circ \| C \|_{s,v}$ (where the second occurrence of $\circ$ denotes its realization in $[0,1]_{\text{Ł}}$).

$\| Pr(A) \|_{s,v} = s([A])$.

In the present paper we will briefly discuss the second approach. We plan to develop the first one in a future paper.

Given a set $\Gamma \cup \{A\}$ of formulas, we write $\Gamma \models_P A$ to mean that for any state s and homomorphism v from $\mathcal{L}_{\text{Ł}}$ into $[0,1]_{\text{Ł}}$, if $\| B \|_{s,v} = 1$ for all $B \in \Gamma$, then $\| A \|_{s,v} = 1$. We say that a formula A of ŁPr is *valid* if $\emptyset \models_P A$ and that a set Γ of formulas of ŁPr is *satisfiable* if $\Gamma \not\models_P 0$.

Note that probabilistic judgements like A *is at least as probable as* $B\&C$ and *the probability of A is equal to the sum of the probability of B and the probability of C* are expressed by $Pr(B\&C) \rightarrow Pr(A)$ and by $\neg(Pr(B)\&Pr(C)) \wedge (Pr(A) \leftrightarrow (Pr(B) \oplus Pr(C)))$ respectively. One can also interpret assessments by means of sets of formulas of ŁPr. To this purpose, consider any condition of the form $Pr(E) = \alpha$. For each natural number $n > 1$, introduce a new variable p_n (which is supposed to represent $\frac{1}{n}$), and the axiom $(n-1)p_n \leftrightarrow \neg p_n$. Now for every rational $r = \frac{m}{n}$ with $0 \leq r \leq \alpha$, add the axiom $mp_n \rightarrow Pr(E)$, and for every rational $s = \frac{h}{k}$ with $\alpha \leq s \leq 1$, add the axiom $Pr(E) \rightarrow hp_k$. In this way, to each condition $Pr(E) = \alpha$ in an assessment σ, we associate a set $F_{E,\alpha}$ of formulas. Now let F_σ denote the union of all $F_{E,\alpha}$ such that $Pr(E) = \alpha$ is in σ. Then it is clear that F_σ is satisfiable iff σ is coherent.

We would like to find a formal system allowing us to derive all valid formulas of ŁPr. To this purpose, note that the following formulas are valid:

(a) All axioms of Ł (extended to all formulas of ŁPr).
(b) All formulas of the form $Pr(A)$: A an axiom of Ł.
(c) All formulas of the form $Pr(A \rightarrow B) \rightarrow (Pr(A) \rightarrow Pr(B))$.
(d) All formulas of the form $Pr(A \oplus B) \leftrightarrow (Pr(A) \oplus Pr(B \ominus (A\&B)))$.
(e) All formulas of the form $Pr(\neg A) \leftrightarrow \neg Pr(A)$, A a formula of Ł .

Moreover, the set of valid formulas is closed under Modus Ponens. Thus we introduce the following definition.

Definition 14. *ŁPr is the logic, in the language specified above, whose axioms schemata are (a), (b), (c), (d) and (e) and whose only rule is Modus Ponens.*

Remark 3. Even though the set of valid formulas is closed under Necessitation:
$\dfrac{A}{Pr(A)}$, *this rule is not valid for consequence relation with respect to the semantics under consideration: indeed, there may be a formula A, a state s and a homomorphism v such that* $v([A]) = 1$ *and* $s([A]) < 1$. *Thus we will not use this rule here. However, Necessitation is valid also for consequence relation with reference to the first semantics presented in this subsection. The philosophical counterpart of the use of Necessitation when dealing with consequence relation is the following: suppose that in some reasoning we* assume *that e.g. the sentence* tomorrow it will rain *will be absolutely true. Then, does this assumption imply that the above sentence has probability 1? We believe that both answers YES and NO to this question (and therefore, both choices, accepting or rejecting the Necessitation rule in deductions from assumptions) may be supported. In any case, we point out that, even though clearly inspired by [11] and by [9], our logic slightly differs from the logics presented there. This is why we used a different notation.*

In any case the axioms and the rules of LPr guarantee that whenever A is a theorem of L, then $LPr \vdash Pr(A)$. Thus the set of theorems is independent of the presence of Necessitation.

Lemma 11. *(i) If* $L \vdash A$, *then* $LPr \vdash Pr(A)$.
(ii) If $L \vdash A \to B$, *then* $LPr \vdash Pr(A) \to Pr(B)$.
(iii) If $L \vdash A$, *then* $LPr \vdash \neg Pr(\neg A)$.
(v) If $L \vdash \neg(A \& B)$, *then* $LPr \vdash \neg(Pr(A) \& Pr(B))$, *and* $LPr \vdash Pr(A \oplus B) \leftrightarrow (Pr(A) \oplus Pr(B))$.

Proof. (i) By induction on the length of the proof of A, using axiom (c) of LPr in the induction step.
(ii) Use (i) and axiom (c) of LPr. Note that (ii) implies that Pr is compatible with provable equivalence, that is, $L \vdash A \leftrightarrow A'$ implies $LPr \vdash Pr(A) \leftrightarrow Pr(A')$.
(iii) By (i) and axiom (e) of LPr.
(iv) If $L \vdash \neg(A \& B)$, then by (i), $LPr \vdash Pr(A \to \neg B)$, therefore by axiom (c), $LPr \vdash Pr(A) \to Pr(\neg B)$. By (e) we get $LPr \vdash Pr(A) \to \neg Pr(B)$ and $LPr \vdash \neg Pr(A) \& Pr(B)$. Moreover, by axiom (d) and recalling that Pr is compatible with provable equivalence, we get $LPr \vdash Pr(A \oplus B) \leftrightarrow (Pr(A) \oplus Pr(B))$.   □

We now consider the following problems:

Problem 2

(1) Is LPr *strongly complete*, i.e., is it true that if $\Gamma \models_P A$, then $\Gamma \vdash_{LPr} A$?
(2) Is LPr *finitely strongly complete*, i.e., is it true that if $\Gamma \models_P A$, for finite Γ, then $\Gamma \vdash_{L\,Pr} A$?
(3) Is LPr *complete*, i.e., is it true that if $\models_P A$, then $\vdash_{LPr} A$?

Clearly, question (1) has a negative answer, because even L is not strongly standard complete. We will see that strong standard completeness is obtained if we add an infinitary rule. We are not able to answer questions (2) and (3). Questions analogous to (2) and (3) have been solved positively (although in a slightly different context) in [9], under the additional assumption that modality free formulas only assume values of the form $\frac{m}{n}$ for some fixed natural number $n > 0$ and for $m = 0, 1, ..., n$.

In this paper, we will introduce a syntactic characterization of $\Gamma \models_P A$, even for Γ infinite. To this purpose, for every LPr-formula of the form $Pr(A)$, we introduce a new propositional variable p_A. Let for every formula C of LPr, C^- denote the result of substituting in C every subformula of the form $Pr(D)$ by p_D. Thus C^- is a Ł formula with possibly new propositional variables. For every set Γ of ŁPr formulas, Γ^- will denote the set $\{C^- : C \in \Gamma\}$. Moreover AX will denote the set of all axioms of LPr.

Lemma 12. *For every set $\Gamma \cup \{A\}$ of LPr formulas, we have: $\Gamma \models_P A$ iff $(\Gamma \cup AX)^- \models_Ł A^-$.*

Proof. For every evaluation e in $[0, 1]_Ł$ such that $e(B) = 1$ for every $B \in AX^-$, we define two functions v_e and s_e from $\mathcal{L}_Ł$ into $[0, 1]_Ł$ as follows: $v_e([A]) = e(A)$, and $s_e([A]) = e(p_A)$. It is easily seen that v_e and s_e are well-defined: for s_e, use the fact that Pr is compatible with provable equivalence, therefore if Ł $\vdash A \leftrightarrow A'$, then $e(p_A) = e(p_{A'})$. Moreover, v_e is clearly a homomorphism from $\mathcal{L}_Ł$ into $[0, 1]_Ł$. We now prove that s_e is a state. By Lemma 11 (i), $s_e([1]) = 1$. Further, if $[A\&B] = 0$, then by Lemma 11 (iv) and by our assumption on e, $e(p_A)\&e(p_B) = 0$, and $e(p_A \oplus p_B) = e(p_A) \oplus e(p_B)$. It follows that $s(A \oplus B) = e(p_A) \oplus e(p_B) = e(p_A) + e(p_B) = s(A) + s(B)$. Now by an easy induction we see that for every formula E of LPr one has $\| E \|_{s_e, v_e} = e(E^-)$. Thus if e is an evaluation which invalidates $(\Gamma \cup AX)^- \models_Ł A^-$, then the pair (s_e, v_e) invalidates $\Gamma \models_P A$.

Conversely, for every state s on $\mathcal{L}_Ł$ and homomorphism v from $\mathcal{L}_Ł$ into $[0, 1]_Ł$, we define an evaluation $e_{s,v}$ on $[0, 1]_Ł$ as follows. If p is not a new variable of the form p_A, then set $e_{s,v}(p) = v([p])$. Moreover for any new variable p_A, set $e_{s,v}(p_A) = s([A])$. These clauses uniquely determine the values of $e_{s,v}$ on all formulas of Ł. Clearly $e_{s,v}(B^-) = 1$ for every $B \in AX$, and by induction we can prove that for any formula F of LPr we have $e_{s,v}(F^-) = \| F \|_{s,v}$. Thus if the pair (s, v) invalidates $\Gamma \models_P A$, then $e_{s,v}$ invalidates $(\Gamma \cup AX)^- \models_Ł A^-$. $\quad\Box$

Theorem 5. *Let $\Gamma \cup \{A\}$ be a set of formulas of LPr. The following are equivalent:*

(a) $\Gamma \models_P A$.
(b) $(\Gamma \cup AX)^- \vdash_{LR} A^-$.

Proof. By Lemma 12 and Theorem 4. $\quad\Box$

Remark 4. A weakness of Theorem 5 consists in the use of the infinitary rule (R) (or (R')). As we said before, this rule is unavoidable when Γ is infinite. However, we conjecture that for finite Γ, (R) is redundant. If true, this conjecture would reduce the finite satisfiability problem for sentences of LPr to the satisfiability problem for Łukasiewicz logic. However, the conjecture seems not to be completely trivial, because, even if Γ is finite, the set $(AX \cup \Gamma)^-$ is infinite.

7.3   Complexity of First-Order Logics

In this subsection we use our characterization of semantic consequence in standard algebras in order to provide for a tight bound for the complexity of the sets of sentences of $BL\forall$ ($\Pi\forall$ respectively) which are valid in all standard BL (product respectively) algebras. We also prove a similar bound for $Ł_\Delta\forall$, $\Pi_\Delta\forall$ and $BL^*\forall$.

In the sequel, given a set X of natural numbers, X' denotes the halting set with oracle on X. Moreover we inductively define $X^{(0)} = X$, $X^{(n+1)} = (X^{(n)})'$. We also define $X^{(\omega)} = \{(n, m) : n \in X^{(m)}\}$, and $X^{(\omega+1)} = (X^{(\omega)})'$. The Turing degree of a set X is denoted by $d(X)$, and the Turing degree of any computable set is denoted by $\mathbf{0}$. Given a Turing degree $d = d(X)$, $d^{(n)}$, $d^{(\omega)}$ and $d^{(\omega+1)}$ denote the Turing degree of $X^{(n)}$, of $X^{(\omega)}$ and of $X^{(\omega+1)}$ respectively. A set is *arithmetical* if its Turing degree is bounded above by $\mathbf{0}^{(n)}$ for some n. It is well-known that a set is arithmetical iff it is definable in the standard model of natural numbers. In the sequel, V_{BL1} (V_{BL^*1} respectively) denotes the set of all sentences A of $BL\forall$ (of $BL^*\forall$ respectively) such that $\models_{K_{TN}1} A$. Moreover $V_{\pi 1}$ ($V_{\pi_\Delta 1}$ respectively) denotes the set of all sentences A of $\Pi\forall$ (of $\Pi_\Delta\forall$ respectively) such that $\models_{\pi 1} A$. Finally $V_{Ł1}$ ($V_{Ł_\Delta 1}$ respectively) denotes the set of all sentences A of $Ł\forall$ (of $Ł_\Delta\forall$ respectively) such that $\models_{Ł1} A$. Formulas are identified with their Gödel numbers, therefore the above defined sets can be considered as subsets of ω. In [20] and [15] it is shown that the theory of the standard model of natural numbers can be faithfully interpreted in any of V_{BL1} and $V_{\pi 1}$. Thus these logics (hence a fortiori V_{BL^*1} and $V_{\pi_\Delta 1}$) are not arithmetical. Moreover, whilst $V_{Ł1}$ is Π_2-complete (hence it is arithmetical), cf [27], $V_{Ł_\Delta 1}$ is not arithmetical [16]. The complexity of any of V_{BL1}, V_{BL^*1}, $V_{\pi 1}$, $V_{\pi_\Delta 1}$ and $V_{Ł_\Delta 1}$ is at least $\mathbf{0}^{(\omega)}$. In this subsection we show that such lower bound is rather tight.

Theorem 6. *Let Γ be any set of $BL^*\forall$ sentences, and let d be its Turing degree. Then the degree of the set $\{A : \Gamma \models_{K_{TN}1} A\}$ is bounded above by $d^{(\omega+1)}$. Similar results with BL^* replaced by $Ł_\Delta$ or by Π_Δ, and with $\models_{K_{TN}1}$ replaced by $\models_{Ł1}$, or, respectively, by $\models_{\pi 1}$.*

Proof. We prove the claim for $BL^*\forall$ sentences. The proof for the other cases is similar. We define inductively a sequence $\langle \Gamma_n : n \in \omega \rangle$ as follows: Γ_0 is the set of formulas derivable in $BL^*\forall^+$ from Γ. Given Γ_n, in order to define Γ_{n+1}, we first define Γ'_n to be the set of all formulas which are derivable from Γ_n by just one application of the rule (R), i.e., the set of all formulas $C = D \vee (A \rightarrow B^*)$ such that for every k, $D \vee (A \rightarrow B^k) \in \Gamma_n$. Then we define Γ_{n+1} to be the set of formulas which are derivable from formulas in $\Gamma_n \cup \Gamma'_n$ using the axioms and the rules of $BL^*\forall^+$. Then by theorem 3, V_{BL1} is the set of all sentences in $\bigcup_{n \in \omega} \Gamma_n$. Note that Γ_0 is computably enumerable in Γ; moreover, $C \in \Gamma'_n$ iff C has the form $D \vee (A \rightarrow B^*)$ and *for all* k, $D \vee (A \rightarrow B^k) \in \Gamma_n$. Thus Γ'_n is computably co-enumerable in Γ_n, and Γ_{n+1} is computably enumerable in Γ'_n. So Γ_{n+1} is Σ^0_2 in Γ_n. Thus, if we denote the Turing degree of Γ_n by d_n, we have that $d_1 \leq d^{(2)}$, $d_2 \leq d^{(4)}$, and in general, $d_n \leq d^{(2n)}$. Now consider the relation $R(A, n)$ defined for every formula A and for every natural number n, by $R(A, n)$ iff $A \in \Gamma_n$.

Then the Turing degree of R is bounded above by $d^{(\omega)}$. Finally, $\Gamma \models_{K_{TN}1} A$ iff $\exists n(R(A, n))$. It follows that $\{A : \Gamma \models_{K_{TN}1} A\}$ is computably enumerable in $d^{(\omega)}$, and its Turing degree is bounded above by $d^{\omega+1}$, as desired. $\Box$

Corollary 1. V_{BL1}, $V_{\pi 1}$ and their extension with $*$ (with Δ respectively), as well as $V_{L_\Delta 1}$ are recursively enumerable in $\mathbf{0}^\omega$. So their Turing degree is between $\mathbf{0}^{(\omega)}$ and $\mathbf{0}^{(\omega+1)}$. $\Box$

Corollary 2. For every natural number n, there is a sentence in V_{BL1}, $(V_{BL^*1}$, $V_{\pi 1}$, $V_{\pi_\Delta 1}$, $V_{L_\Delta 1}$ respectively) which cannot be derived with $\leq n$ nested occurrences of the rule (R).

Proof. A formula which is derivable with $\leq n$ nested occurrences of (R) is an element of Γ_n with $\Gamma = \emptyset$ (see the proof of Theorem 6). Now $\emptyset_n$ is arithmetical (its Turing degree is bounded above by $\mathbf{0}^{(2n)}$), and none of V_{BL1}, V_{BL^*1}, $V_{\pi 1}$, $V_{\pi_\Delta 1}$, $V_{L_\Delta 1}$ is arithmetical. The claim follows. $\Box$

The proof of Corollary 2 does not extend to V_{L1} because this set is arithmetical. Therefore it makes sense to ask the following problem.

Problem 3. Is there an upper bound for the number of nested applications of the rule (R) necessary to derive all sentences in V_{L1}?

Acknowledgement. We would like to thank Andrew Lewis for his contribution to Subsection 7.3. We also thank the anonymous referee, who contributed to improve the presentation of the paper.

References

1. Aglianó, P., Montagna, F.: Varieties of basic algebras I: general properties. Journal of Pure and Applied Algebra 181, 105–129 (2003)
2. Blok, W.J., Ferreirim, I.M.A.: On the structure of hoops. Algebra Universalis 43, 233–257 (2000)
3. Blok, W., Pigozzi, D.: Algebraizable Logics. Mem. Amer. Math. Soc. 396, vol.77, Amer. Math. Soc., Providence (1989)
4. Cignoli, R., Esteva, F., Godo, L., Torrens, A.: Basic fuzzy logic is the logic of continuous t-norms and their residua. Soft Computing 4, 106–112 (2000)
5. Cignoli, R., D'Ottaviano, I.M.L., Mundici, D.: Algebraic foundations of many-valued reasoning. Kluwer, Dordrecht (2000)
6. Cignoli, R., Torrens, A.: An algebraic analysis of product logic. Mult. Val. Logic 5, 45–65 (2000)
7. Esteva, F., Godo, L., Hájek, P., Montagna, F.: Hoops and fuzzy logic. Journal of Logic and Computation 13, 531–555 (2003)
8. Ferreirim, I.M.A.: On varieties and quasi varieties of hoops and their reducts, PhD thesis, University of Illinois at Chicago (1992)
9. Flaminio, T., Godo, L.: A logic for reasoning about the probability of fuzzy events. In: Fuzzy Sets and Systems (preprint 2006, to appear)

10. Glass, A.: Partially ordered groups. Series in Algebra, vol. 7. World Scientific, Singapore, New Jersey, London, Hong Kong (1999)
11. Hájek, P.: Metamathematics of Fuzzy Logic. Kluwer, Dordrecht (1998)
12. Hájek, P.: Fuzzy Logic and Arithmetical Hierarchy. Fuzzy sets and Systems 73, 359–363 (1995)
13. Hájek, P.: Fuzzy Logic and Arithmetical Hierarchy II. Studia Logica 58, 129–141 (1997)
14. Hájek, P.: Basic logic and BL-algebras. Soft Computing 2(3), 124–128 (1998)
15. Hájek, P.: Fuzzy Logic and Arithmetical Hierarchy III. Studia Logica 68, 129–142 (2001)
16. Hájek, P.: Arithmetical complexity and fuzzy predicate logics: a survey. Soft Computing 30, 1–7 (2005)
17. Hájek, P.: Some hedges for continuous t-norm logics. Neural Network World 12, 159–164 (2002)
18. Klement, E.P., Mesiar, R., Pap, E.: Triangular norms. Kluwer Academic Publishers, Dordrecht (2000)
19. Kroupa, T.: Representation and Extension of States on MV-algebras. Arch. Math. Log. 45, 381–392 (2006)
20. Montagna, F.: Three complexity problems in quantified fuzzy logic. Studia Logica 68, 143–152 (2001)
21. Montagna, F.: Storage Operators and Multiplicative Quantifiers in Many-valued Logics. Journal of Logic and Computation 14, 299–322 (2004)
22. Mundici, D.: Interpretations of AF C^* algebras in Łukasiewicz sentential calculus. Journal of Functional Analysis 65, 15–63 (1986)
23. Mundici, D.: Averaging the truth value in Łukasiewicz sentential logic. Studia Logica 55, 113–127 (special issue in honour of Helena Rasiowa) (1955)
24. Mundici, D.: Bookmaking over infinitely-valued events. International Journal of Approximate Reasoning (to appear)
25. Paris, J.: A note on the Dutch Book Method. In: De Cooman, G., Fine, T., Seidenfeleir, T. (eds.) Proceedings of the Second International Symposium on Imprecise Probabilities and their Applications, ISIPTA 2001, pp. 301–306. Shaker Publishing Company, Ithaca, NY, USA (2001)
26. Riečan, B., Mundici, D.: Probability on MV-algebras. In: Pap, E. (ed.) Handbook of Measure Theory, vol. II, pp. 869–900. North Holland, Amsterdam (2001)
27. Ragaz, M.E.: Arithmetische Klassification von Formelnmenge der unendlichwertigen Logik. ETH Zürich, Thesis (1981)
28. Ward, M., Dilworth, R.P.: Residuated lattices. Transactions of American Mathematical Society 45, 335–354 (1939)

The Automorphism Group
of Falsum-Free Product Logic

Giovanni Panti

Department of Mathematics
University of Udine
via delle Scienze 208
33100 Udine, Italy
panti@dimi.uniud.it

Abstract. A few things are known, and many are unknown, on the automorphism group of the free MV-algebra over $n-1$ generators. In this paper we show that this group appears as the stabilizer of $\mathbb{1}$ in the larger group of all automorphisms of the free cancellative hoop over n generators. Both groups have a dual action on the same space, namely the $(n-1)$-dimensional cube. The larger group has a richer dynamics, at the expense of loosing the two key features of the McNaughton homeomorphisms: preservation of denominators of rational points, and preservation of the Lebesgue measure. We present here some basic results, some examples, and some problems.

1 Preliminaries

Consider the usual product t-norm $\cdot$, but restrict its domain by discarding 0 from the real unit interval. The corresponding residuum is $a \to b = \min(1, b/a)$, and $\big((0,1], \cdot, \to, 1\big)$ is a residuated lattice. The usual machinery of many-valued logic applies, and we have a logical system akin to the product logic in [12, §4.1]. However, there is a key point of contrast: since 0 is not a truth-value, every n-variables term-definable function from $(0,1]^n$ to $(0,1]$ is continuous. As a matter of fact, this falsum-free product logic is the logic of cancellative hoops.

A *cancellative hoop* is an algebra $(A, +, \dotdiv, 0)$ such that $(A, +, 0)$ is a commutative monoid and the following identities are satisfied:

$$x \dotdiv x = 0,$$
$$x + (y \dotdiv x) = y + (x \dotdiv y),$$
$$(x \dotdiv y) \dotdiv z = x \dotdiv (y + z),$$
$$x \dotdiv (x \dotdiv y) = y \dotdiv (y \dotdiv x),$$
$$(x + y) \dotdiv y = x.$$

If one fixes $0 < c < 1$, then the exponential function to base c is an order-reversing isomorphism

$$\exp : \big(\mathbb{R}^+, +, \dotdiv, 0\big) \to \big((0,1], \cdot, \to, 1\big)$$

S. Aguzzoli et al.(Eds.): Algebraic and Proof-theoretic Aspects, LNAI 4460, pp. 275–289, 2007.

between $((0, 1], \cdot, \rightarrow, 1)$ and the positive cone $\mathbb{R}^+ = [0, \infty)$ of $\mathbb{R}$ endowed with the ordinary sum and the truncated difference $a \mathrel{\dot{-}} b = \max(0, a - b)$; note that $\exp(a \mathrel{\dot{-}} b) = \exp(b) \rightarrow \exp(a)$.

The following facts are known and can be found in [5], [7], and references therein.

1. $(\mathbb{R}^+, +, \mathrel{\dot{-}}, 0)$ generates the variety of cancellative hoops; this is a precise formulation of our previous statement that falsum-free product logic is the logic of cancellative hoops.

2. Every cancellative hoop is obtainable as the positive cone of a unique enveloping lattice-ordered abelian group (ℓ-group, for short), by setting $a \mathrel{\dot{-}} b = 0 \vee (a - b)$. This correspondence is 1-1 up to isomorphism, and is a categorical equivalence. Under restriction to the positive cones, ℓ-group homomorphisms correspond bijectively to hoop homomorphisms, and ℓ-group ideals (i.e., kernels of ℓ-group homomorphisms) correspond to hoop ideals. In the following we will identify cancellative hoops with positive cones of ℓ-groups without further ado.

3. The free n-generated cancellative hoop $\mathrm{Free}_n(\mathbf{CH})$ is the hoop of all continuous positively-homogeneous piecewise-linear functions with integer coefficients from $(\mathbb{R}^+)^n$ to $\mathbb{R}^+$, under pointwise operations.

In this paper we will study the automorphism group of $\mathrm{Free}_n(\mathbf{CH})$ and its dual action on the space of maximal ideals. It will turn out that this latter space is homeomorphic to the $(n-1)$-dimensional cube $[0, 1]^{n-1}$, and that the action is given by piecewise-fractional homeomorphisms with integer coefficients. The automorphism group of the $n - 1$-generated free MV-algebra sits naturally inside $\mathrm{Aut}\,\mathrm{Free}_n(\mathbf{CH})$ as the stabilizer of a specific element. Passing from this stabilizer to the full group one gains a much richer dynamics, at the expense of loosing the two key features of the McNaughton homeomorphisms: preservation of denominators of rational points, and preservation of the Lebesgue measure.

We assume familiarity with ℓ-groups, MV-algebras, Mundici's Γ functor, and the representation of the finitely generated free ℓ-groups and MV-algebras in terms of positively-homogeneous piecewise-linear functions and McNaughton functions, respectively [4], [3], [1], [11], [14], [6]. The present paper pursues the line of research in [16], [18], [17], [19]; some acquaintance with some of the above papers is a prerequisite as well.

2   Another Description of $\mathrm{Free}_n(\mathbf{CH})$

Let $n \geq 1$, and let G_n be the ℓ-group enveloping the free MV-algebra on $n - 1$ generators $\mathrm{Free}_{n-1}(\mathbf{MV})$, i.e., the unique ℓ-group such that $\mathrm{Free}_{n-1}(\mathbf{MV}) = \Gamma(G_n, \mathbb{1})$, where $\mathbb{1}$ is the function on $[0, 1]^{n-1}$ whose value is constantly 1. The elements of G_n are all McNaughton functions from $[0, 1]^{n-1}$ to $\mathbb{R}$. Let $x_1, \ldots, x_{n-1} \in G_n$ be the projection functions $[0, 1]^{n-1} \rightarrow [0, 1]$, and let $x_n = \mathbb{1} - (x_1 \vee \cdots \vee x_{n-1}) \in G_n$ (if $n = 1$, then $\{x_1, \ldots, x_{n-1}\}$ is empty, and $x_1 = \mathbb{1}$).

Theorem 1. *The free cancellative hoop over $n \geq 1$ generators $\mathrm{Free}_n(\mathbf{CH})$ is isomorphic to the positive cone G_n^+ of G_n, with $x_1, \ldots, x_n$ as free generators.*

Proof. The case $n = 1$ is clear, since $\mathrm{Free}_0(\mathbf{MV}) = \{0, 1\}$ and $G_0 = \mathbb{Z}$. Let $n > 1$, let $Q = (\mathbb{R}^+)^n$ be the positive octant of $\mathbb{R}^n$, and let $P \subset Q$ be the polyhedral cone spanned positively by $\{a_1 e_1 + a_2 e_2 + \cdots + a_{n-1} e_{n-1} + e_n : a_1, \ldots, a_{n-1} \in \{0, 1\}\}$, where $\{e_1, \ldots, e_n\}$ is the standard basis of $\mathbb{R}^n$. Denote by $\mathrm{F}\ell_n$ the free ℓ-group over n generators: its elements are all continuous positively-homogeneous piecewise-linear functions with integer coefficients from $\mathbb{R}^n$ to $\mathbb{R}$. In more detail, a function $F : \mathbb{R}^n \to \mathbb{R}$ is in $\mathrm{F}\ell_n$ iff it is continuous and there exists a finite complex Σ of rational polyhedral cones whose set-theoretic union is $\mathbb{R}^n$ and such that, for each cone $W \in \Sigma$, there exist $a_1, \ldots, a_n \in \mathbb{Z}$ satisfying $F(\alpha_1, \ldots, \alpha_n) = \sum a_i \alpha_i$ on W. Such a cone complex is usually called a *fan* [10], [9]. A fan is *unimodular* if all its cones are of the form $\mathbb{R}^+ u_1 + \cdots + \mathbb{R}^+ u_t$, where $u_1, \ldots, u_t$ belong to $\mathbb{Z}^n$ and are extendable to a $\mathbb{Z}$-basis of $\mathbb{Z}^n$. The *support* $|\Sigma|$ of the fan Σ is the set-theoretic union of all elements of Σ.

The projection functions $Y_i(\alpha_1, \ldots, \alpha_n) = \alpha_i$ are free generators for $\mathrm{F}\ell_n$. Let now I and J be the principal ideals of $\mathrm{F}\ell_n$ whose elements are all functions which are 0 in Q and in P, respectively. The description of $\mathrm{Free}_n(\mathbf{CH})$ given in §1(3) amounts to saying that $\mathrm{Free}_n(\mathbf{CH})$ is the positive cone $(\mathrm{F}\ell/I)^+$ of $\mathrm{F}\ell/I$, with free generators $Y_1/I, \ldots, Y_n/I$. Note that the element F/I of $\mathrm{F}\ell_n/I$ is identifiable with the restriction $F \upharpoonright Q$ of F to Q, and analogously for F/J and $F \upharpoonright P$; we shall tacitly use such identifications.

For every element ρ of the symmetric group over $n - 1$ letters, let N_ρ be the matrix obtained from the $n \times n$ matrix

$$\begin{pmatrix} 0 & 1 & 1 & \cdots & 1 & 1 \\ 0 & 0 & 1 & \cdots & 1 & 1 \\ 0 & 0 & 0 & \cdots & 1 & 1 \\ \vdots & \vdots & \vdots & \cdots & \vdots & \vdots \\ 0 & 0 & 0 & \cdots & 0 & 1 \\ 1 & 1 & 1 & \cdots & 1 & 1 \end{pmatrix}$$

by permuting its first $n - 1$ rows according to ρ, and let W_ρ be the unimodular cone spanned positively by the columns of N_ρ. Analogously, let M_ρ be the matrix obtained from

$$\begin{pmatrix} 0 & 1 & 1 & \cdots & 1 & 1 \\ 0 & 0 & 1 & \cdots & 1 & 1 \\ 0 & 0 & 0 & \cdots & 1 & 1 \\ \vdots & \vdots & \vdots & \cdots & \vdots & \vdots \\ 0 & 0 & 0 & \cdots & 0 & 1 \\ 1 & 0 & 0 & \cdots & 0 & 0 \end{pmatrix}$$

by permuting its first $n - 1$ rows according to ρ, and let R_ρ be the cone spanned by the columns of M_ρ. As proved in [16, Theorem 4.1], the set of all $(n-1)!$ W_ρ's and their faces is a unimodular fan Δ whose support is P, and the set of all R_ρ's and their faces is a unimodular fan Σ whose support is Q. The fans Δ and Σ are combinatorially isomorphic, and by mapping every W_ρ to the corresponding R_ρ in the obvious way we obtain a map

$$\Phi : P = |\Delta| \rightarrow Q = |\Sigma|,$$

which is an ℓ-equivalence [2, p. 120]. By [2, pp. 120-121], and taking into consideration the categorical equivalence of §1(2), Φ induces an isomorphism of cancellative hoops

$$\varphi : (F\ell/I)^+ \rightarrow (F\ell/J)^+,$$
$$F \upharpoonright Q \mapsto F \circ \Phi \upharpoonright P.$$

By direct inspection one easily sees that, for every $1 \leq i \leq n-1$ and every $W_\rho \in \Delta$, we have $Y_i \circ \Phi \upharpoonright W_\rho = Y_i \upharpoonright W_\rho$; hence $Y_i \circ \Phi \upharpoonright P = Y_i \upharpoonright P$ and $\varphi(Y_i/I) = Y_i \circ \Phi \upharpoonright P = Y_i \upharpoonright P = Y_i/J$ for every $1 \leq i \leq n-1$. We claim that the identity

$$\left[(Y_1 \vee \cdots \vee Y_{n-1}) + Y_n\right] \circ \Phi \upharpoonright P = Y_n \upharpoonright P$$

holds as well. Indeed, a typical point $u \in W_\rho$ is a column vector

$$u = N_\rho \begin{pmatrix} \alpha_1 \\ \vdots \\ \alpha_n \end{pmatrix}$$

for certain $\alpha_1, \ldots, \alpha_n \geq 0$, and $Y_n(u) = \alpha_1 + \cdots + \alpha_n$. On the other hand, we have

$$\Phi(u) = M_\rho \begin{pmatrix} \alpha_1 \\ \vdots \\ \alpha_n \end{pmatrix}$$

and $\left[(Y_1 \vee \cdots \vee Y_{n-1}) + Y_n\right](\Phi(u)) = (\alpha_2 + \cdots + \alpha_n) + \alpha_1$, which settles our claim. It follows that

$$\frac{Y_1 \vee \cdots \vee Y_{n-1}}{J} + \varphi\left(\frac{Y_n}{I}\right) = \varphi\left(\frac{Y_1 \vee \cdots \vee Y_{n-1}}{I}\right) + \varphi\left(\frac{Y_n}{I}\right)$$
$$= \varphi\left(\frac{(Y_1 \vee \cdots \vee Y_{n-1}) + Y_n}{I}\right)$$
$$= \frac{Y_n}{J},$$

whence $\varphi(Y_n/I) = \left[Y_n - (Y_1 \vee \cdots \vee Y_{n-1})\right]/J$. Let $X_1 = Y_1, \ldots, X_{n-1} = Y_{n-1}, X_n = Y_n - (Y_1 \vee \cdots \vee Y_{n-1})$; we have shown that $\mathrm{Free}_n(\mathbf{CH})$ is isomorphic to $(F\ell_n/J)^+$, with $X_1/J, \ldots, X_n/J$ as free generators.

Observe now that the affine plane $\pi = \{Y_n = 1\}$ cuts P along a cross-section $\pi \cap P$ which is an $(n-1)$-dimensional cube. Since the elements of $(F\ell_n/J)^+$ are positively homogeneous, and the group and lattice operations act pointwise, the restriction $F/J \mapsto F \restriction (\pi \cap P)$ is an immersion of $(F\ell_n/J)^+$ into G_n^+; we write f for $F \restriction (\pi \cap P)$. The range of the immersion is freely generated by the images of $X_1/J, \ldots, X_n/J$, namely $x_1, \ldots, x_n$, and coincides with G_n^+ since, as it is well known, the latter is generated by $x_1, \ldots, x_{n-1}, \mathbb{1} = x_n + (x_1 \vee \cdots \vee x_{n-1})$.

We have therefore three ways of looking at $\mathrm{Free}_n(\mathbf{CH})$: as $(F\ell_n/I)^+$ with free generators $Y_1/I, \ldots, Y_n/I$, as $(F\ell_n/J)^+$ with free generators $X_1/J, \ldots, X_n/J$, or as G_n^+ with free generators $x_1, \ldots, x_n$; the first of these is essentially the one discussed in [7]. In what follows, we always assume $n \geq 2$ and, if not otherwise specified, we identify $\mathrm{Free}_n(\mathbf{CH})$ with G_n^+ and $\mathrm{Free}_{n-1}(\mathbf{MV})$ with $\Gamma(G_n, \mathbb{1})$.

Let us remark that $x_1, \ldots, x_{n-1}, \mathbb{1}$ generate G_n^+, but they are not free generators (except in the case $n = 1$). Indeed, no strong unit g can belong to a free generating set for G_n^+, since the map sending g to 0 and all other generators to 1 cannot be extended to a homomorphism from G_n^+ to $\mathbb{R}^+$.

Theorem 1 makes clear the relationship between finitely generated free MV-algebras and free cancellative hoops. One obtains the free n-generated cancellative hoop by taking the positive cone of the ℓ-group enveloping the free $(n-1)$-generated MV-algebra and forgetting about any distinguished strong unit. It might be slightly annoying that the 0 function on $[0,1]^{n-1}$ means "false" in Lukasiewicz logic and "true" in falsum-free product logic, but things are promptly fixed by applying the $\neg$ involution to $\mathrm{Free}_{n-1}(\mathbf{MV})$, so that 0 means now "true" in both cases. It is reasonable to think of an element f of G_n^+ to be "sufficiently false" if it is never true, i.e., has never value 0 as a function from $[0,1]^{n-1}$ to $\mathbb{R}^+$. Equivalently, f is sufficiently false if it is a strong unit in G_n: for every $g \in G_n^+$ there exists an integer m such that the conjunction of f with itself m times $f + \cdots + f$ is falser (i.e., greater) that g. One then goes back from $\mathrm{Free}_n(\mathbf{CH})$ to $\mathrm{Free}_{n-1}(\mathbf{MV})$ by deciding that a certain sufficiently false f is actually the falsest proposition. The choice for f is large, but not arbitrary. Indeed, $\Gamma(G_n, f)$ and $\Gamma(G_n, g)$ are isomorphic as MV-algebras iff there exists an automorphism of G_n^+ that maps f to g. Therefore, $\Gamma(G_n, f)$ is isomorphic to $\mathrm{Free}_{n-1}(\mathbf{MV})$ iff f is in the orbit of $\mathbb{1}$ under the action of the automorphism group of $\mathrm{Free}_n(\mathbf{CH})$. We shall see in §1 that this orbit is countably infinite, even though $\mathrm{Aut}\, \mathrm{Free}_n(\mathbf{CH})$ does not act transitively on the set of strong units.

3 Dual Maps

The *spectral space*, or *dual space*, of an ℓ-group G is the set of all the *prime ideals* of G, i.e., the kernels of nontrivial homomorphisms from G to a totally-ordered group. This set is a topological space under the Zariski topology, in which a basic open set is the set of all kernels that avoid some fixed finite set of elements of G. The same description of the dual space applies both to MV-algebras and to commutative hoops: see [16] for a more general and detailed presentation. We are interested here in the *maximal spectrum* of the above structures, i.e., in the subspace of all kernels of nontrivial homomorphisms from G to $\mathbb{R}$ (to $[0,1]$ or to $\mathbb{R}^+$ in the case of MV-algebras or cancellative hoops, respectively). Fixing a strong unit in an ℓ-group does not affect the spectrum, which is also preserved by the categorical equivalences between ℓ-groups, MV-algebras, and cancellative hoops. In short, for every ℓ-group with strong unit (G, u), the spectra of G, of $\Gamma(G, u)$, and of G^+, are identifiable in the obvious way, and the same holds for the maximal spectra.

The key point in the use of spectral spaces is the functoriality of the construction: to every endomorphism σ of —say— the ℓ-group G it corresponds the *dual map* $\sigma^* : \operatorname{Spec} G \to \operatorname{Spec} G$ given by $\sigma^*(\mathfrak{p}) = \sigma^{-1}[\mathfrak{p}]$; the dual map is automatically continuous. A word of clarification is in order here: by definition, the trivial kernel G is excluded from the spectrum. Hence, we must discard those endomorphisms σ whose image $\sigma[G]$ is contained in some $\mathfrak{p} \in \operatorname{Spec} G$, for then $\sigma^*(\mathfrak{p})$ would be undefined. We leave to the reader the proof of the following simple fact.

Lemma 1. *Let σ be an endomorphism of the ℓ-group G. The following statements are equivalent:*

(a) for no $\mathfrak{p} \in \operatorname{Spec} G$ is $\sigma[G] \subseteq \mathfrak{p}$;
(b) for no $\mathfrak{m} \in \operatorname{MaxSpec} G$ is $\sigma[G] \subseteq \mathfrak{m}$;
(c) there exists a strong unit u of G such that $\sigma(u)$ is a strong unit;
(d) for every strong unit u of G, the image $\sigma(u)$ is a strong unit.

An analogous statement holds for cancellative hoops.

Endomorphisms satisfying the above conditions are called *nontrivial* in [16, p. 65]; note that endomorphisms of MV-algebras are automatically nontrivial. Nontrivial endomorphisms obviously form a monoid, and their dual maps are well defined, both on the spectrum and on the maximal spectrum. Of course, any automorphism is nontrivial.

Our goal in this paper is to start an analysis of the group of automorphisms of $\operatorname{Free}_n(\mathbf{CH})$ (or, rather, the dual group acting on the maximal spectrum). By way of comparison, let us sketch the situation for MV-algebras. The maximal spectrum of $\operatorname{Free}_{n-1}(\mathbf{MV})$ is homeomorphic to the $(n-1)$-cube $[0, 1]^{n-1}$ with the standard Euclidean topology, under the identification

$$[0, 1]^{n-1} \ni p \mapsto \{f \in \operatorname{Free}_{n-1}(\mathbf{MV}) : f(p) = 0\} \in \operatorname{MaxSpec} \operatorname{Free}_{n-1}(\mathbf{MV}). \quad (1)$$

Let σ be any endomorphism of $\operatorname{Free}_{n-1}(\mathbf{MV})$, and let $f_i = \sigma(x_i)$, for $1 \le i \le n - 1$. Then, under the identification (1), the map S dual to σ turns out to be $S(p) = (f_1(p), \ldots, f_{n-1}(p))$, and the mapping $\sigma \mapsto S$ is a contravariant monoid embedding: $\sigma \circ \tau \mapsto T \circ S$. A key point here is the existence of a distinguished measure on $[0, 1]^{n-1}$ —namely the Lebesgue measure— which is preserved under the duals of all automorphisms [15]. See [8], [19], [17] for various results on the automorphism group of $\operatorname{Free}_{n-1}(\mathbf{MV})$.

We now turn to cancellative hoops. As we noted before, the maximal spectrum of $\operatorname{Free}_n(\mathbf{CH})$ is identifiable with that of $\operatorname{Free}_{n-1}(\mathbf{MV})$, i.e., with the

$(n-1)$-cube. The correspondence (1) holds verbatim, by just substituting Free_{n-1} (**MV**) with $\text{Free}_n(\mathbf{CH})$.

Definition 1. *Let σ be a nontrivial endomorphism of $\text{Free}_n(\mathbf{CH})$, let $f_i = \sigma(x_i)$, for $1 \leq i \leq n$, and let $f_\sharp = f_n + (f_1 \vee \cdots \vee f_{n-1}) = \sigma(\mathbb{1})$. Since σ is nontrivial, $f_\sharp$ is a strong unit, and never takes the value 0. Moreover, $0 \leq f_i \leq f_\sharp$ for every $1 \leq i \leq n - 1$. Let $S_i(p) = f_i(p)/f_\sharp(p)$; the $n-1$ functions $S_i : [0,1]^{n-1} \to [0,1]$ are well defined. We denote by S the selfmap of $[0,1]^{n-1}$ given by $S(p) = \big(S_1(p), \ldots, S_{n-1}(p)\big)$.*

Theorem 2. *Assume the hypothesis and the notation of Definition 1. Then, under the above identification of $\text{MaxSpec}\,\text{Free}_n(\mathbf{CH})$ with $[0,1]^{n-1}$, the dual map of σ is S.*

Proof. Adopt all the definitions in the proof of Theorem 1. In that proof we showed that $\text{Free}_n(\mathbf{CH})$ is isomorphic to $(\text{F}\ell_n/J)^+$ with free generators $X_1/J, \ldots, X_n/J$. Let $u \in P$; then u can be given two sets of coordinates: the X-coordinates $\big(X_1(u), \ldots, X_n(u)\big)$, and the Y-coordinates $\big(Y_1(u), \ldots, Y_n(u)\big)$. The Y-coordinates are the "real world coordinates", i.e., the coordinates of u in terms of the standard basis of $\mathbb{R}^n$. The X-coordinates are the images of u under the free generators of $(\text{F}\ell_n/J)^+$. If we write $\alpha_i = Y_i(u)$ and $\beta_i = X_i(u)$, then the two sets of coordinates are related by

$$\alpha_i = \beta_i \text{ for } 1 \leq i \leq n - 1,$$
$$\alpha_n = \beta_n + (\beta_1 \vee \cdots \vee \beta_{n-1}),$$
$$\beta_n = \alpha_n - (\alpha_1 \vee \cdots \vee \alpha_{n-1}).$$

The functions in $\text{F}\ell_n$ are positively homogeneous, and the maximal spectrum of $(\text{F}\ell_n/J)^+$ is identifiable with the set of rays $\mathbb{R}^+ u = \{ru : r \geq 0\}$, for u a point of P. Let $F_1/J, \ldots, F_n/J \in (\text{F}\ell_n)^+$ be such that the restrictions of $F_1, \ldots, F_n$ to $\pi \cap P$ are $f_1, \ldots, f_n$. Lift σ to an endomorphism of $(\text{F}\ell_n/J)^+$, again denoted by σ, by setting $X_i/J \mapsto F_i/J$. We define a selfmap $\mathcal{S}$ of P as follows: if $u \in P$, then $\mathcal{S}(u)$ is the unique point of P whose X-coordinates are $\big(F_1(u), \ldots, F_n(u)\big)$. It is immediate that, for every $F/J \in (\text{F}\ell_n/J)^+$, we have $\big(\sigma(F)\big)(u) = F\big(\mathcal{S}(u)\big)$, and it follows that the map dual to σ acts on $\text{MaxSpec}(\text{F}\ell_n/J)^+$ by sending the ray through u to the ray through $\mathcal{S}(u)$. The rays are in 1-1 correspondence with the points of the cross-section $\pi \cap P = [0,1]^{n-1}$ in the obvious way. Summing up, S acts on $[0,1]^{n-1}$ as follows: given $p \in \pi \cap P$, construct the ray $\mathbb{R}^+\mathcal{S}(p)$ and intersect it with π. The intersection contains a single point, namely $\mathcal{S}(p)$. In terms of coordinates, the X-coordinates of $\mathcal{S}(p)$ are $\big(f_1(p), \ldots, f_{n-1}(p), f_n(p)\big)$, and its Y-coordinates are $\big(f_1(p), \ldots, f_{n-1}(p), f_\sharp(p)\big)$. Dividing by $f_\sharp(p)$, we project $\mathcal{S}(p)$ to $\pi \cap P$, and we obtain the point having Y-coordinates $(S_1(p), \ldots, S_{n-1}(p), 1)$, in accordance with the statement of the Theorem.

Corollary 1. *Assume the hypothesis and the notation of Definition 1. Then, for every $f \in \text{Free}_n(\mathbf{CH})$, we have $\sigma(f) = f_\sharp \cdot (f \circ S)$.*

Proof. Let F/J be the unique element of $(F\ell/J)^+$ such that $f = F \upharpoonright (\pi \cap P)$. Let S and p be as in the proof of Theorem 2. We have seen in that proof that $S(p) = f_\sharp(p) \cdot S(p)$. Since F is positively homogeneous, we obtain $(\sigma(f))(p) = (\sigma(F))(p) = F(S(p)) = F(f_\sharp(p) \cdot S(p)) = f_\sharp(p) \cdot F(S(p)) = f_\sharp(p) \cdot (f \circ S)(p)$.

A k-*cell* C in $\mathbb{R}^n$ is a compact convex polyhedron of affine dimension k. A *rational cellular complex* $\mathcal{C}$ is a finite set of cells such that: (1) all vertices of all cells in $\mathcal{C}$ have rational coordinates; (2) if $C \in \mathcal{C}$ and D is a face of C, then $D \in \mathcal{C}$; (3) every two cells intersect in a common face. The *support* of $\mathcal{C}$ is the set-theoretic union $|\mathcal{C}|$ of all cells in $\mathcal{C}$.

Let now $\sigma, f_1, \ldots, f_n, f_\sharp$ be as in Definition 1. We can always partition the $(n-1)$-cube in a rational cellular complex $\mathcal{C}$ in such a way that on each $(n-1)$-cell $C \in \mathcal{C}$ all functions $f_1, \ldots, f_{n-1}, f_\sharp$ are affine linear. Let us say that on C, and for $t \in \{1, \ldots, n-1, \sharp\}$, we have

$$f_t = a_1^t x_1 + \cdots + a_{n-1}^t x_{n-1} + a_n^t.$$

Then, in homogeneous coordinates, $S \upharpoonright C$ is given by

$$
\begin{pmatrix} \alpha_1 \\ \vdots \\ \alpha_{n-1} \\ 1 \end{pmatrix}
\mapsto
\begin{pmatrix} a_1^1 & \cdots & a_n^1 \\ \vdots & \cdots & \vdots \\ a_1^{n-1} & \cdots & a_n^{n-1} \\ a_1^\sharp & \cdots & a_n^\sharp \end{pmatrix}
\begin{pmatrix} \alpha_1 \\ \vdots \\ \alpha_{n-1} \\ 1 \end{pmatrix}. \tag{2}
$$

If σ fixes $\mathbb{1}$, then σ restricts to an endomorphism of the MV-algebra $\Gamma(G_n, \mathbb{1}) = \mathrm{Free}_{n-1}(\mathbf{MV})$. In this case the last row of the above matrix is $(0 \cdots 0\, 1)$, in accordance with [8, Theorem 2.6].

The possible dynamics of dual maps in falsum-free product logic is far richer that that in Łukasiewicz logic. The following example shows some of the possibilities.

Example 1. Let a, b be positive integers. Let $f_1 = b(x_1 \wedge x_2)$, $f_2 = a((x_1 \vee x_2) \dot{-} (x_1 \wedge x_2))$, and let σ be the endomorphism of $\mathrm{Free}_2(\mathbf{CH})$ determined by $x_i \mapsto f_i$. Since the 0-sets of f_1 and f_2 do not intersect, $f_\sharp = f_1 + f_2$ is a strong unit, and σ is nontrivial. By explicit computation, one easily sees that the map S dual to σ depends only on the ratio $q = a/b$, and has the explicit form

$$
S(x) = \begin{cases} x \cdot ((1 - 2q)x + q)^{-1}, & \text{if } 0 \le x \le 1/2; \\ (1 - x) \cdot ((1 - 2q)(1 - x) + q)^{-1}, & \text{if } 1/2 < x \le 1. \end{cases}
$$

We see here that, in contrast with the case of Łukasiewicz logic [16, p. 66], the map S does not determine σ: multiplying a and b for the same positive integer we get distinct σ's and the same S. We plot here the graphs of S for $q = 2/9$, $q = 1$, and $q = 9/2$, respectively.

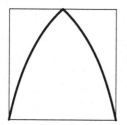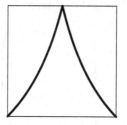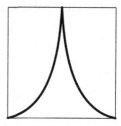

As shown in [16, Theorem 4.4], we get quite different dynamics:

1. If $q < 1$, then almost all (in the sense of Lebesgue measure) points have a dense S-orbit, and S is ergodic with respect to a uniquely determined probability measure absolutely continuous w.r.t. Lebesgue.
2. If $q = 1$, then almost all points have a dense orbit, but S does not preserve any probability measure absolutely continuous w.r.t. Lebesgue.
3. If $q > 1$, then almost all points are attracted to 0.

4   The Automorphism Group

We have seen in Example 1 that the map associating to a nontrivial endomorphism its dual map is not injective. Things go better in the case of automorphisms: we shall prove in Theorem 3 that if S is the dual of an automorphism σ, then S determines σ uniquely.

Definition 2. *Let S be an orientation-preserving homeomorphism of $[0,1]^{n-1}$. We call S a piecewise $\mathrm{SL}_n \mathbb{Z}$-homeomorphism if there exists a rational cellular complex $\mathcal{C}$ whose support is $[0,1]^{n-1}$ and whose $(n-1)$-cells are $C_1, \ldots, C_k$, and there exist matrices $A_1, \ldots, A_k \in \mathrm{SL}_n \mathbb{Z}$ such that, for every $1 \leq h \leq k$, A_h expresses $S \upharpoonright C_h$ in positively homogeneous coordinates (i.e., if $p = (\alpha_1, \ldots, \alpha_{n-1}) \in C_h$ and $S(p) = (\beta_1, \ldots, \beta_{n-1})$, then $A_h(\alpha_1 \cdots \alpha_{n-1} 1)^{tr}$ is positively proportional to $(\beta_1 \cdots \beta_{n-1} 1)^{tr}$).*

We call an automorphism of $\mathrm{Free}_n(\mathbf{CH})$ *orientation-preserving* or *orientation-reversing* according whether its dual homeomorphism is orientation-preserving or orientation-reversing. Of course the set of orientation-preserving automorphisms is a normal subgroup of $\mathrm{Aut}\,\mathrm{Free}_n(\mathbf{CH})$ of index 2, and every orientation-reversing automorphism is the composition of an orientation-preserving one with —say— the automorphism $x_1 \leftrightarrow x_2$.

Theorem 3. *Let σ be an orientation-preserving automorphism of $\mathrm{Free}_n(\mathbf{CH})$, with dual map S. Then S is a piecewise $\mathrm{SL}_n \mathbb{Z}$-homeomorphism of $[0,1]^{n-1}$. Conversely, every piecewise $\mathrm{SL}_n \mathbb{Z}$-homeomorphism is the dual map of a unique orientation-preserving automorphism.*

Proof. Taking into account the discussion after Corollary 1, we need only prove that, if C is an $(n-1)$-cell in $[0,1]^{n-1}$ in which $f_1 = \sigma(x_1), \ldots, f_{n-1} = \sigma(x_{n-1})$,

$f_\sharp = \sigma(\mathbb{1})$ are all affine linear, then the matrix

$$A = \begin{pmatrix} a_1^1 & \cdots & a_n^1 \\ \vdots & \cdots & \vdots \\ a_1^{n-1} & \cdots & a_n^{n-1} \\ a_1^\sharp & \cdots & a_n^\sharp \end{pmatrix}$$

in §3(2) has determinant 1. First of all, we extend uniquely σ to an automorphism of G_n, again denoted by σ. Let now $p = (\alpha_1, \ldots, \alpha_{n-1}) \in C$ be such that $\alpha_1, \ldots, \alpha_{n-1}, 1$ are linearly independent over $\mathbb{Q}$, and let $\mathfrak{m}_p$ be the maximal ideal of G_n whose elements are all McNaughton functions which are 0 in p. Evaluation at p provides a canonical isomorphism from $G_n/\mathfrak{m}_p$ to the totally-ordered subgroup H_p of $\mathbb{R}$ generated by $\alpha_1, \ldots, \alpha_{n-1}, \alpha_n = 1 - (\alpha_1 \vee \cdots \vee \alpha_{n-1})$ or, equivalently, by $\alpha_1, \ldots, \alpha_{n-1}, 1$. Let $q = S(p) = (\beta_1, \ldots, \beta_{n-1})$, and define analogously $H_q \simeq G_n/\mathfrak{m}_q$. Since $\sigma^{-1}[\mathfrak{m}_p] = \mathfrak{m}_q$, the map $f/\mathfrak{m}_q \mapsto \sigma(f)/\mathfrak{m}_p$ is an order isomorphism from $G/\mathfrak{m}_q$ to $G/\mathfrak{m}_p$. Denote by ψ the corresponding order isomorphism from H_q to H_p; by [13, Proposition II.2.2], ψ must necessarily be of the form $\psi(\alpha) = r\alpha$, for a uniquely determined positive real number r. Since $\mathbb{1}/\mathfrak{m}_p \mapsto f_\sharp/\mathfrak{m}_p$, we have explicitly $r = f_\sharp(p)$. It follows that H_p coincides with the group rH_q generated by the elements of the column vector

$$r \begin{pmatrix} \beta_1 \\ \vdots \\ \beta_{n-1} \\ 1 \end{pmatrix} = \begin{pmatrix} f_1(p) \\ \vdots \\ f_{n-1}(p) \\ f_\sharp(p) \end{pmatrix} = A \begin{pmatrix} \alpha_1 \\ \vdots \\ \alpha_{n-1} \\ 1 \end{pmatrix}.$$

Since $H_p = rH_q$ is isomorphic to $\mathbb{Z}^n$ as a group, A must have either determinant 1 or determinant -1, but the case -1 is excluded since S is orientation-preserving.

Conversely, let S be a piecewise SL_n $\mathbb{Z}$-homeomorphism over a rational cellular complex $\mathcal{C}$ as in Definition 2. For every $1 \le h \le k$, let $\Phi_h : \mathbb{R}^n \to \mathbb{R}^n$ be the non-singular linear transformation whose associated matrix w.r.t. the standard basis of $\mathbb{R}^n$ is A_h. Since A_h expresses $S \upharpoonright C_h$ in positively homogeneous coordinates, Φ_h maps bijectively the cone $\mathbb{R}^+ C_h$ onto $\mathbb{R}^+ S[C_h]$. Moreover, if p is a vertex common to C_h and C_t, then $\Phi_h(p) = \Phi_t(p)$; this follows because p has rational coordinates and $A_h, A_t \in \mathrm{SL}_n \mathbb{Z}$. Indeed, denoting by u the *primitive vector* along the ray $\mathbb{R}^+ p$ (i.e., the unique $u \in \mathbb{Z}^n \cap \mathbb{R}^+ p$ whose coordinates are relatively prime), then both Φ_h and Φ_t must map u to the primitive vector along $\mathbb{R}^+ S(p)$. We conclude that the map $\Phi : P \to P$ (P being the cone defined in the proof of Theorem 1) defined by $\Phi(v) = \Phi_h(v)$ for $v \in \mathbb{R}^+ C_h$, is piecewise homogeneous linear with integer coefficients and hence, by [3, Corollary 1 to Theorem 3.1], is induced by n elements $F_1, \ldots, F_n$ of $F\ell_n$ as $\Phi(v) = (F_1(v), \ldots, F_n(v))$. By [3, Corollary 2 to Theorem 3.1] and the categorical equivalence between cancellative hoops and positive cones of ℓ-groups, there exists a unique automorphism of $(F\ell_n /J)^+$ (namely, the one defined by $X_i/J \mapsto F_i/J$) whose dual map on rays is $\mathbb{R}^+ v \mapsto \mathbb{R}^+ \Phi(v)$. Taking into account the isomorphism between $(F\ell_n /J)^+$ and

G_n^+, and the correspondence between rays and $\mathrm{MaxSpec}(\mathrm{F}\ell_n/J)^+$ in the proof of Theorem 2, this concludes the proof of Theorem 3.

If $p = (\alpha_1, \ldots, \alpha_{n-1}) \in [0,1]^{n-1} \cap \mathbb{Q}^{n-1}$, the *primitive homogeneous coordinates* of p are the coordinates $(a_1, \ldots, a_{n-1}, a_n) \in \mathbb{Z}^n$ of the primitive vector along the ray $\mathbb{R}^+(\alpha_1, \ldots, \alpha_{n-1}, 1)$; the *denominator* of p is then $\mathrm{den}(p) = a_n$.

Theorem 4. *Let $\sigma, S, \mathcal{C}, A_1, \ldots, A_k$ be as in Theorem 3. If p is a point in the topological interior of some $(n-1)$-cell in $\mathcal{C}$, then the Jacobian matrix $J(p)$ of S at p is defined and its determinant has value $[f_\sharp(p)]^{-n}$. The following statements are equivalent:*

(a) $\sigma(\mathbb{1}) = \mathbb{1}$ (i.e., σ restricts to an automorphism of $\mathrm{Free}_{n-1}(\mathbf{MV})$);
(b) for every $p \in [0,1]^{n-1} \cap \mathbb{Q}^{n-1}$, $\mathrm{den}(S(p)) = \mathrm{den}(p)$;
(c) for every vertex $p \in \mathcal{C}$, $\mathrm{den}(S(p)) = \mathrm{den}(p)$;
(d) the last row of every A_h is $(0 \cdots 0\, 1)$;
(e) S preserves the Lebesgue measure λ on $[0,1]^{n-1}$ (i.e., $\lambda(T) = \lambda(S^{-1}T)$, for every measurable set T).

Proof. The statement about the Jacobian follows from [20, Proposition 2]. Note that the set of points in which S is not differentiable is contained in the union of the $(n-2)$-dimensional cells in $\mathcal{C}$. The latter is a Lebesgue nullset, so we can safely write $|J(p)| = [f_\sharp(p)]^{-n}$ throughout the $(n-1)$-cube (recall that $f_\sharp$ is a strong unit, so it never takes value 0). The equivalence of (a) and (d) is the content of [8, Theorem 2.6]. (d) $\Rightarrow$ (b) $\Rightarrow$ (c) is clear; we prove (c) $\Rightarrow$ (d). Fix $1 \leq h \leq k$, and choose n vertices $p_1, \ldots, p_n$ of C_h such that the matrix B whose columns are the primitive homogeneous coordinates of $p_1, \ldots, p_n$ is nonsingular. Since A_h has determinant 1, the columns of $A_h B$ give the primitive homogeneous coordinates of $S(p_1), \ldots, S(p_n)$. By (c), we have the identity $(a_1 \cdots a_{n-1}\, a_n)B = (0 \cdots 0\, 1)B$, where $(a_1 \cdots a_{n-1}\, a_n)$ is the last row of A_h. Since B is nonsingular, (d) follows. (a) $\Rightarrow$ (e) is proved in [15, Theorem 3.4]. If (e) holds, then $|J(p)|$ must be identically 1, so $f_\sharp^{-n} = [\sigma(\mathbb{1})]^{-n} = \mathbb{1}$, and (a) holds as well.

Let us say that a rational cellular complex $\mathcal{C}$ supported in $[0,1]^{n-1}$ is a *unimodular complex* if all $(n-1)$-cells in $\mathcal{C}$ are simplexes and, for each such $(n-1)$-simplex C, the primitive homogeneous coordinates of the vertices of C constitute an $n \times n$ integer matrix whose determinant has absolute value 1. It is well known that every rational cellular complex can be refined to a unimodular one (see, e.g., [9, Theorems III.2.6 and VI.8.5]). It easily follows from Theorem 3 that the most general automorphism of $\mathrm{Free}_n(\mathbf{CH})$ is obtained by choosing a combinatorial isomorphism between two unimodular complexes $\mathcal{C}$ and $\mathcal{D}$, both supported on $[0,1]^{n-1}$ (a *combinatorial isomorphism* is a bijection between the two sets of vertices that preserves all incidence relations between simplexes).

Example 2. Take $n = 3$, and let $\mathcal{C}, \mathcal{D}$ be the following unimodular complexes:

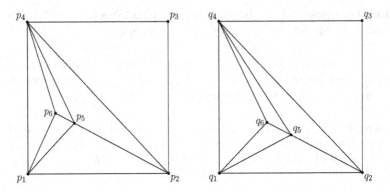

The primitive homogeneous coordinates of the inner vertices are

$$p_5 = \begin{pmatrix} 1 \\ 1 \\ 3 \end{pmatrix}, \qquad\qquad q_5 = \begin{pmatrix} 2 \\ 1 \\ 4 \end{pmatrix},$$

$$p_6 = \begin{pmatrix} 1 \\ 2 \\ 5 \end{pmatrix}, \qquad\qquad q_6 = \begin{pmatrix} 1 \\ 1 \\ 3 \end{pmatrix}.$$

We obtain a combinatorial isomorphism from $\mathcal{C}$ to $\mathcal{D}$ by mapping p_t to q_t, for $1 \leq t \leq 6$. If C_1 is —say— the simplex $\langle p_4, p_6, p_5 \rangle$, then A_1 is uniquely determined by

$$A_1 \begin{pmatrix} 0 & 1 & 1 \\ 1 & 2 & 1 \\ 1 & 5 & 3 \end{pmatrix} = \begin{pmatrix} 0 & 1 & 2 \\ 1 & 1 & 1 \\ 1 & 3 & 4 \end{pmatrix}.$$

Hence

$$A_1 = \begin{pmatrix} 4 & 1 & -1 \\ 2 & 2 & -1 \\ 7 & 3 & -2 \end{pmatrix},$$

and the restrictions of $f_1, f_2, f_3, f_\sharp$ to C_1 can be read from the rows of A_1:

$$f_1 \restriction C_1 = 4x_1 + x_2 - \mathbb{1};$$
$$f_2 \restriction C_1 = 2x_1 + 2x_2 - \mathbb{1};$$
$$f_\sharp \restriction C_1 = 7x_1 + 3x_2 - 2\mathbb{1};$$
$$f_3 \restriction C_1 = f_\sharp \restriction C_1 - (f_1 \restriction C_1 \vee f_2 \restriction C_1).$$

Note that the homeomorphism S of Example 2 is not differentiable along the 1-simplexes of $\mathcal{C}$. Things are smoother in dimension 1, i.e., for $n = 2$: first of all, a unimodular complex on $[0, 1]$ is determined by a finite set of rational vertices

$$\frac{0}{1} = \frac{a_0}{b_0} < \frac{a_1}{b_1} < \cdots < \frac{a_t}{b_t} = \frac{1}{1},$$

such that $a_j b_{j+1} - a_{j+1} b_j = 1$ for $0 \leq j \leq t - 1$. Two such complexes are combinatorially isomorphic iff they have the same number of vertices. If S is the dual of some automorphism of $\text{Free}_2(\mathbf{CH})$, then $|J(p)| = S'(p)$ for every p in which S is differentiable. By Theorem 4, S' equals either $f_\sharp^{-2}$ or $-f_\sharp^{-2}$, depending on whether S is orientation-preserving or orientation-reversing. It follows that, in dimension 1, all dual homeomorphisms are of class C^1 (i.e., are differentiable everywhere with continuous first derivative).

Example 3. The two sets of rational vertices

$$\frac{0}{1} < \frac{1}{2} < \frac{2}{3} < \frac{1}{1},$$

and

$$\frac{0}{1} < \frac{1}{3} < \frac{1}{2} < \frac{1}{1},$$

determine the map

$$S(x) = \begin{cases} x \cdot (x+1)^{-1}, & \text{if } 0 \leq x \leq 1/2; \\ (-x+1) \cdot (-5x+4)^{-1}, & \text{if } 1/2 < x \leq 2/3; \\ (2x-1) \cdot x^{-1}, & \text{if } 2/3 < x \leq 1; \end{cases}$$

whose graph is

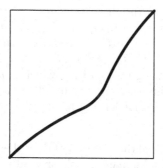

We see in this example that the duals of automorphisms of $\text{Free}_2(\mathbf{CH})$ may preserve no interesting probability measure. As a matter of fact, basic ergodic theory shows that the only probability measures on $[0,1]$ preserved by S are the affine combinations of the Dirac measures at 0 and 1.

5   Open Problems

Problem 1. We have seen that the automorphism group of the free MV-algebra over $n - 1$ generators $\text{Aut Free}_{n-1}(\mathbf{MV})$ is a (not normal) subgroup of $\text{Aut Free}_n(\mathbf{CH})$, namely the stabilizer of $\mathbb{1}$. Our first problem is to describe the space of laterals, i.e., the orbit of $\mathbb{1}$ under $\text{Aut Free}_n(\mathbf{CH})$. In equivalent terms, this means to characterize the set of strong units g of G_n such that $\Gamma(G_n, g)$ is isomorphic to $\mathrm{Free}_{n-1}(\mathbf{MV})$. The orbit of $\mathbb{1}$ is countably infinite (it is already infinite under the action, e.g., of the single automorphism of Example 3), but does not exhaust the set of strong units. As an example, the strong unit $g = (x_1 + \mathbb{1}) \wedge (-x_1 + 2\mathbb{1}) \in G_2^+$ is not in the orbit of $\mathbb{1}$, because $\Gamma(G_2, g)$ is not isomorphic to $\mathrm{Free}_1(\mathbf{MV})$ (e.g., it has not a quotient isomorphic, as an MV-algebra, to $\{0, 1/2, 1\}$). This should be compared with the case of real vector lattices, in which the automorphism group acts transitively on strong units; see [2, Lemma 4.2].

Problem 2. Given two rational points $p, q \in [0, 1]^{n-1} \cap \mathbb{Q}^{n-1}$, is it always true that there exists $\sigma \in \mathrm{Aut}\,\mathrm{Free}_n(\mathbf{CH})$ whose dual maps p to q? Much harder: provided that p and q have the same denominator, can σ be taken in $\mathrm{Aut}\,\mathrm{Free}_{n-1}$ $(\mathbf{MV})$?

Problem 3. $\mathrm{Aut}\,\mathrm{Free}_{n-1}(\mathbf{MV})$ is residually finite [8, p. 75]. What about Aut $\mathrm{Free}_n(\mathbf{CH})$? Is either group finitely generated?

Problem 4. Let $n \geq 3$, and let $g \in G_n^+$ be a strong unit in the orbit of $\mathbb{1}$, say $\sigma(g) = \mathbb{1}$. Then there exists a unique probability measure μ on $[0, 1]^{n-1}$ which is null on underdimensioned 0-sets (see [17, Definition 2.2]) and is invariant under the duals of all automorphisms of G_n^+ that fix g. Namely, μ is the push-forward $S_*\lambda$ of the Lebesgue measure λ via S: for every Borel set $A \subseteq [0, 1]^{n-1}$, we have by definition $\mu(A) = (S_*\lambda)(A) = \lambda(S^{-1}A)$. These facts follow from the main result of [17]; see also the discussion in [19, §2]. We only show here the invariance of $S_*\lambda$: choose $\tau \in \mathrm{Aut}\,G_n^+$ such that $\tau(g) = g$. Then $\sigma \circ \tau \circ \sigma^{-1}$ fixes $\mathbb{1}$, and hence its dual $S^{-1} \circ T \circ S$ fixes the Lebesgue measure. Therefore $\lambda = (S^{-1} \circ T \circ S)_*\lambda = (S_*^{-1} \circ T_* \circ S_*)\lambda$, and $S_*\lambda = T_*(S_*\lambda)$, as desired. Now the question is: given a strong unit g of G_n^+ which is *not* in the orbit of $\mathbb{1}$, does it always exist a probability measure on $[0, 1]^{n-1}$ which is invariant under the duals of all automorphisms that leave g fixed? If so, under which conditions is such a measure unique?

Problem 5. In [19] it is proved that for every odd n there exists an automorphism of $\mathrm{Free}_{n-1}(\mathbf{MV})$ whose dual is measure-theoretically isomorphic to a Bernoulli shift. What about even n?

References

1. Anderson, M., Feil, T.: Lattice-ordered groups. Reidel, Dordrecht (1988)
2. Beynon, W.M.: Duality theorems for finitely generated vector lattices. Proc. London Math. Soc. 31(3), 114–128 (1975)
3. Beynon, W.M.: Applications of duality in the theory of finitely generated lattice-ordered abelian groups. Can. J. Math. XXIX(2), 243–254 (1977)
4. Bigard, A., Keimel, K., Wolfenstein, S.: Groupes et anneaux réticulés. Lecture Notes in Math., vol. 608. Springer, Heidelberg (1977)
5. Blok, W.J., Ferreirim, I.M.A.: On the structure of hoops. Algebra Universalis 43(2-3), 233–257 (2000)

6. Cignoli, R., D'Ottaviano, I., Mundici, D.: Algebraic foundations of many-valued reasoning. Trends in logic, vol. 7. Kluwer, Dordrecht (2000)
7. Cignoli, R., Torrens, A.: Free cancellative hoops. Algebra Universalis 43, 213–216 (2000)
8. Di Nola, A., Grigolia, R., Panti, G.: Finitely generated free MV-algebras and their automorphism groups. Studia Logica 61(1), 65–78 (1998)
9. Ewald, G.: Combinatorial Convexity and Algebraic Geometry. Springer, Heidelberg (1996)
10. Fulton, W.: An introduction to Toric Varieties. Annals of Mathematics Studies, vol. 131. Princeton University Press, Princeton, NJ (1993)
11. Glass, A.M.W.: Partially ordered groups. Series in Algebra, vol. 7. World Scientific Publishing Co. Inc., River Edge, NJ (1999)
12. Hájek, P.: Metamathematics of Fuzzy Logic. Trends in logic, vol. 4. Kluwer, Dordrecht (1998)
13. Kokorin, A.I., Kopytov, V.M.: Fully ordered groups. Wiley, Chichester (1974)
14. Mundici, D.: Interpretation of AF C^*-algebras in Łukasiewicz sentential calculus. J. of Functional Analysis 65, 15–63 (1986)
15. Mundici, D.: Averaging the truth-value in Łukasiewicz logic. Studia Logica 55(1), 113–127 (1995)
16. Panti, G.: Generic substitutions. J. Symbolic Logic 70(1), 61–83 (2005)
17. Panti, G.: Invariant measures in free MV-algebras. In: Communications in Algebra (to appear), available at http://arxiv.org/abs/math.LO/0508445
18. Panti, G.: Dynamical properties of logical substitutions. Discrete Contin. Dyn. Syst. 15(1), 237–258 (2006)
19. Panti, G.: Bernoulli automorphisms of finitely generated free MV-algebras. J. Pure Appl. Algebra 208(3), 941–950 (2007)
20. Schweiger, F.: Multidimensional continued fractions, Oxford Science Publications. Oxford University Press, Oxford (2000)

Probability Theory on IF Events

Beloslav Riečan

Faculty of Natural Sciences, Matej Bel University
Department of Mathematics
Tajovského 40
974 01 Banská Bystrica, Slovakia
Mathematical Institute of Slovak Acad. of Sciences
Štefánikova 49
SK–81473 Bratislava
riecan@fpv.umb.sk

Abstract. Basic constructions of two different theories are presented. The first one is based on the Łukasiewicz connectives, the second on the max - min connectives. In both cases the joint observable is constructed. As an application the central limit theorem is proved.

1 Introduction

Although there are different opinions about IF-events, the following definitions are accepted generally. Let $(\Omega, \mathcal{S})$ be a measurable space. By an IF-event we mean any pair

$$A = (\mu_A, \nu_A)$$

of $\mathcal{S}$-measurable functions, such that $\mu_A \geq 0, \nu_A \geq 0$, and

$$\mu_A + \nu_A \leq 1.$$

The function μ_A is called the membership function and the function ν_A the non-membership function. The family $\mathcal{F}$ of all IF-events is ordered by the following way:

$$A \leq B \iff \mu_A \leq \mu_B, \nu_A \geq \nu_B.$$

Evidently the notion of an IF-event is a natural generalization of the notion of the fuzzy events (here $\nu_A = 1 - \mu_A$), hence also probability theory should have a similar property. And actually, two constructions were proposed independently ([4], [3]). It is interesting that both definitions can be regarded as a special case of a descriptive definition ([20], [26]). This descriptive definition has been based on the Łukasiewicz connectives

$$a \oplus b = \min(a + b, 1),$$

$$a \odot b = \max(a + b - 1, 0).$$

S. Aguzzoli et al.(Eds.): Algebraic and Proof-theoretic Aspects, LNAI 4460, pp. 290–308, 2007.

The operations can be naturally extended to IF-events by the following way. If $A = (\mu_A, \nu_A)$ and $B = (\mu_B, \nu_B)$ then

$$A \oplus B = (\mu_A \oplus \mu_B, \nu_A \odot \nu_B)$$

$$A \odot B = (\mu_A \odot \mu_B, \nu_A \oplus \nu_B)$$

It is easy to see that in the case of a fuzzy set $A = (\mu_A, 1 - \mu_A)$ the Łukasiewicz operations are obtained. Similarly as in the classical case and in the fuzzy case, probability is a mapping (in our case from $\mathcal{F}$ to the unit interval) which is continuous, additive and satisfies some boundary conditions. Here the main difference is in additivity. There are infinitely many possibilities how to define additivity

$$m(A) + m(B) = m(S(A, B)) + m(T(A, B))$$

where

$$S(A, B) = (S(\mu_A, \mu_B), T(\nu_A, \nu_B))$$
$$S, T : [0, 1]^2 \rightarrow [0, 1]$$

being such binary operations that

$$S(u, v) + T(1 - u, 1 - v) \leq 1.$$

In the present contribution we have choosen only two possibilities: the Łukasiewicz $S(a, b) = a \oplus b, T(a, b) = a \odot b$, and the Zadeh

$$S(a, b) = a \vee b = \max(a, b),$$
$$T(a, b) = a \wedge b = \min(a, b).$$

Namely, in these two choices we are able to formulate a meaningful theory including such fundamental assertions as the law of large numbers (a bridge between frequency and probablity) or central limit theorem (as a possible starting point to statistical inference).

Therefore we divide our results in to two parts. In the first part the Łukasiewicz connectives are used and the corresponding theory is based on the well known MV-algebra probability theory (Definition 2). Some possibilities for applications of the MV-algebra probability theory to the IF-events case is demonstrated on the IF-central limit theorem (Theorem 2). Although the MV-algebra considered in our IF-case is very simple, it would be not very economic to work only with the special case and do not use some known results contained in the general MV-algebra probability theory. On the other hand the simple formulations in the IF-events case could lead to a larger variety of possible applications.

Since we are not able to embed the max-min theory to some analogous MV-algebra we suggest another method based on the local representation of $\mathcal{F}$ by some Boolean algebras. And again this method is illustrated for to obtain a variant of the central limit theorem.

The Kolmogorov probability theory has 3 fundamental notions: probability, random variable, and expectation. In our fuzzy case an analogous situation occurs. The existence of the joint observable plays a crucial role in both theories.

It is interesting that the corresponding existence theorems (Theorem 1.2.5, Theorem 2.2.2) has been proved by some thoroughly different methods. Therefore it is hardly to expect that there exists a general method working for a larger set of pairs (S, T). In this moment this is an open problem.

Some ideas of the paper has been used separately in previous papers (e.g. the embedding theorem in the paper [24] about entropy of dynamical systems, the representation theorem in [26]) and here they are presented in a simple and clear way as a source for possible applications. All results of Chapter 2 are new and they have been inspired by the paper by M. Krachounov [6]. It was quite surprising for the author that also in the very general case a good probability theorems can be proved.

2 IF-Probability Theory

In this chapter we shall consider the family $\mathcal{F} = \{(\mu_A, \nu_A); \mu_A, \nu_A$ are $\mathcal{S}$-measurable non-negative real functions, such that $\mu_A + \nu_A \leq 1\}$. The crucial point in the first construction is the embedding the family of IF-events to an appropriate MV-algebra. We could consider a tribe instead of the family of all $\mathcal{S}$-measurable functions, of course it is very well known that any tribe containing constant functions coincides with the tribe of all $\mathcal{S}$-measurable functions with respect to a convenient σ-algebra $\mathcal{S}$.

In Section 1.1 basic facts about IF-probability theory are presented and the embedding of the theory to the MV-algebra probability theory is realized. Section 1.2 contains the proof of the existence of the joint observable. As an application the central limit theorem in Section 1.3 is presented.

2.1 Probability

Definition 1 (20). *Denote by $\mathcal{F}$ the set of all IF-events, by $\mathcal{J}$ the family of all compact intervals on $\mathbb{R}$. A probability is a mapping $\mathcal{P} : \mathcal{F} \to \mathcal{J}$ satisfying the following properties:*

  (i) $\mathcal{P}((1_\Omega, 0_\Omega)) = [1, 1], \mathcal{P}((0_\Omega, 1_\Omega)) = [0, 0]$;
  (ii) $\mathcal{P}(A) + \mathcal{P}(B) = \mathcal{P}(A \oplus B) + \mathcal{P}(A \odot B)$ for all $A, B \in \mathcal{F}$;
  (iii) $A_n \nearrow A \Longrightarrow \mathcal{P}(A_n) \nearrow \mathcal{P}(A)$.

Here $A_n \nearrow A$ means that $\mu_{A_n} \nearrow \mu_A, \nu_{A_n} \searrow \nu_A$. Of course, $\mathcal{P}(A_n) = [\mathcal{P}^\flat(A_n), \mathcal{P}^\sharp(A_n)] \nearrow \mathcal{P}(A) = [\mathcal{P}^\flat(A), \mathcal{P}^\sharp(A)]$ means that $\mathcal{P}^\flat(A_n) \nearrow \mathcal{P}^\flat(A), \mathcal{P}^\sharp(A_n) \nearrow \mathcal{P}^\sharp(A)$.

Theorem 1. *To any probability $\mathcal{P}$ there exist $\alpha, \beta \in [0, 1], \alpha \leq \beta$ and a Kolmogorovian probability $P : \Omega \to [0, 1]$ such that for any $A = (\mu_A, \nu_A)$,*

$$\mathcal{P}(A) = [(1 - \alpha) \int_\Omega \mu_A dP + \alpha(1 - \int_\Omega \nu_A dP), (1 - \beta) \int_\Omega \mu_A dP + \beta(1 - \int_\Omega \nu_A dP)].$$

Proof (26).
Recall that the probability by P. Grzegorzewski and E. Mrowka ([4]) can be obtained putting $\alpha = 0$ and $\beta = 1$, and the T. Gerstenkorn and J. Manko probability ([3]) putting $\alpha = \beta = \frac{1}{2}$.

Of course, from our point of view, more important is the possibility of embedding the family $\mathcal{F}$ to an MV-algebra $\mathcal{M}$. By the Mundici theorem, any MV-algebra $(M, \oplus, \odot)$ can be obtained as an interval $[0, u]$ in an l-group G where

$$a \oplus b = (a + b) \wedge u, a \odot b = (a + b - u) \vee 0.$$

In our case the appropriate group is the group $G = (R^2)^\Omega$ of all functions $(f, g) : \Omega \to R^2$. Here

$$(f_1, g_1) + (f_2, g_2) = (f_1 + f_2, g_1 + g_2 - 1),$$

$$(f_1, g_1) - (f_2, g_2) = (f_1 - f_2, g_1 - g_2 + 1)$$

$$(f_1, g_1) \leq (f_2, g_2) \Longleftrightarrow f_1 \leq f_2, g_1 \geq g_2$$

The neutral element is $(0_\Omega, 1_\Omega)$, our MV-algebra is

$$\mathcal{M} = \{(f, g); (0_\Omega, 1_\Omega) \leq (f, g) \leq (1_\Omega, 0_\Omega)\},$$

$$((f_1, g_1) + (f_2, g_2)) \wedge (1_\Omega, 0_\Omega) =$$
$$= (f_1 + f_2, g_1 + g_2 - 1) \wedge (1_\Omega, 0_\Omega) =$$
$$= ((f_1 + f_2) \wedge 1_\Omega, (g_1 + g_2 - 1) \vee 0_\Omega) = (f_1, g_1) \oplus (f_2, g_2).$$

$$((f_1, g_1) + (f_2, g_2) - (1_\Omega, 0_\Omega)) \vee (0_\Omega, 1_\Omega) =$$
$$= (f_1 + f_2 - 1_\Omega, g_1 + g_2) \vee (0_\Omega, 1_\Omega) =$$
$$= ((f_1 + f_2 - 1_\Omega) \vee 0_\Omega, (g_1, +g_2) \vee 1_\Omega) = (f_1, g_1) \odot (f_2, g_2).$$

Definition 2. *A mapping* $m : \mathcal{F} \to [0, 1]$ *is called a state, if the following properties are satisfied:*
(i) $m((1_\Omega, 0_\Omega)) = 1, m((0_\Omega, 1_\Omega)) = 0$;
(ii) $m(A) + m(B) = m(A \oplus B) + m(\odot B)$;
(iii) $A_n \nearrow A \Longrightarrow m(A_n) \nearrow m(A)$.

Proposition 1. *If* $\mathcal{P} = [\mathcal{P}^\flat, \mathcal{P}^\sharp] : \mathcal{F} \to \mathcal{J}$ *is a probability, then* $\mathcal{P}^\flat, \mathcal{P}^\sharp : \mathcal{F} \to [0, 1]$ *are states.*

Definition 3. *If* $(M, \leq, \oplus, \odot)$ *is an MV-algebra, then a state on M is a mapping* $m : M \to [0, 1]$ *satisfying the following conditions*
(i) $m(u) = 1, m(0) = 0$;
(ii) $m(a) + m(b) = m(a \oplus b) + m(a \odot b)$;
(iii)) $a_n \nearrow a \Longrightarrow m(a_n) \nearrow m(a)$.

Theorem 2. *To any state* $m : \mathcal{F} \to [0, 1]$ *there exists exactly one state* $\overline{m} : \mathcal{M} \to [0, 1]$ *such that* $\overline{m} \mid \mathcal{F} = m$.

Proof. Let $(f, g) \in \mathcal{M}$. Since $(f, g) + (0, 1 - g) = (f, 0)$, it is reasonable to define

$$\overline{m}(f, g) = m((f, 0)) - m((0, 1 - g)).$$

It is not difficult to prove that $\overline{m} : \mathcal{M} \to [0, 1]$ is a state, $\overline{m} \mid \mathcal{F} = m$. If $\nu : \mathcal{M} \to [0, 1]$ is any state such that $\nu \mid \mathcal{F} = m$, then

$$m(f, 0) = \nu(f, 0) = \nu(f, g) + \nu(0, 1 - g) = \nu(f, g) + m(0, 1 - g),$$

hence

$$\nu(f, g) = m(f, 0) - m(0, 1 - g) = \overline{m}(f, g).$$

Notation 1. *If* $\mathcal{P} : \mathcal{F} \to \mathcal{J}$ *is an IF-probability,* $\mathcal{P} = [\mathcal{P}^\flat, \mathcal{P}^\sharp]$, *then* $\overline{\mathcal{P}}^\flat, \overline{\mathcal{P}}^\sharp :$ $\mathcal{M} \to [0, 1]$ *are the extensions of* $\mathcal{P}^\flat, \mathcal{P}^\sharp$ *guaranteed by Theorem 2.*

2.2   Observables

Definition 4. *An IF-observable is a mapping* $x : \mathcal{B}(R) \to \mathcal{F}$ *satisfying the following conditions:*
  (i) $x(R) = (1_\Omega, 0_\Omega), x(\emptyset) = (0_\Omega, 1_\Omega)$
  (ii) $A \cap B = \emptyset \Longrightarrow x(A) \odot x(B) = (0_\Omega, 1_\Omega), x(A \cup B) = x(A) \oplus x(B)$;
  (iii) $A_n \nearrow A \Longrightarrow x(A_n) \nearrow x(A)$.

Since $\mathcal{F} \subset \mathcal{M}$, any observable $x : \mathcal{B}(R) \to \mathcal{F}$ is an observable in the sense of the MV-algebra probability theory ([33], [34]).

Proposition 2. *If* $\mathcal{P} = (\mathcal{P}^\flat, \mathcal{P}^\sharp) : \mathcal{F} \to \mathcal{J}$ *is an IF-probability, and x is an IF-observable, then the mappings* $\mathcal{P}^\flat \circ x, \mathcal{P}^\sharp \circ x : \mathcal{B}(R) \to [0, 1]$ *are probability measures.*

Proof. We prove only additivity. If $A \cap B = \emptyset$, then $x(A) \odot x(B) = (0_\Omega, 1_\Omega)$, hence

$$\mathcal{P}^\flat(x(A \cup B)) = \mathcal{P}^\flat(x(A) \oplus x(B)) + \mathcal{P}^\flat(x(A) \odot x(B)) =$$
$$= \mathcal{P}^\flat(x(A)) + \mathcal{P}^\flat(x(B)).$$

Definition 5. *The product $A.B$ of two IF-events A, B is defined by the equality*

$$A.B = (\mu_A \mu_B, 1 - (1 - \nu_A)(1 - \nu_B)).$$

Definition 6. *If x, y are IF-observables, then their joint IF-observable is a mapping* $h : \mathcal{B}(R^2) \to \mathcal{F}$ *satisfying the following conditions:*
  (i) $h(R^2) = (1_\Omega, 0_\Omega), h(\emptyset) = (0_\Omega, 1_\Omega)$;
  (ii) $A \cap B = \emptyset \Longrightarrow h(A) \wedge h(B) = (0_\Omega, 1_\Omega), h(A \cup B) = h(A) + h(B), A, B \in$ $\mathcal{B}(R^2)$;
  (iii) $A_n \nearrow A \Longrightarrow h(A_n) \nearrow h(A)$;
  (iv) $h(C \times D) = x(C).y(D), C, D \in \mathcal{B}(R)$.

Theorem 3. *To any IF-observables $x, y : \mathcal{B}(R) \to \mathcal{F}$ there exists their joint IF-observable.*

Proof. Put $x(A) = (x^\flat(A), 1 - x^\sharp(A)), y(B) = (y^\flat(B), 1 - y^\sharp(B))$. We want to construct $h(C) = (h^\flat(C), 1 - h^\sharp(C))$. Fix $\omega \in \Omega$ and put

$$\mu(A) = x^\flat(A)(\omega), \nu(B) = y^\flat(B)(\omega).$$

It is not difficult to prove that $\mu, \nu : \mathcal{B}(R) \to [0, 1]$ are probability measures. Let

$$\mu \times \nu : \mathcal{B}(R^2) \to [0, 1]$$

be the product of measures and define

$$h^\flat(A)(\omega) = \mu \times \nu(A).$$

Then $h^\flat : \mathcal{B}(R^2) \to \mathcal{T}$, where $\mathcal{T}$ is the family of all $\mathcal{S}$-measurable functions from Ω to [0,1]. If $C, D \in \mathcal{B}(R)$, then

$$h^\flat(C \times D)(\omega) = \mu \times \nu(C \times D) = \mu(C).\mu(D) =$$

$$= x^\flat(C)(\omega).y^\flat(D)(\omega),$$

hence

$$h^\flat(C \times D) = x^\flat(C).y^\flat(D).$$

Similarly $h^\sharp : \mathcal{B}(R^2) \to \mathcal{T}$ can be constructed such that

$$h^\sharp(C \times D) = x^\sharp(C).y^\sharp(D).$$

Put

$$h(A) = (h^\flat(A), 1 - h^\sharp(A)), A \in \mathcal{B}(R^2).$$

By Definition 5 we have for $C, D \in \mathcal{B}(R)$

$$x(C).y(D) = (x^\flat(C), 1 - x^\sharp(C)).(y^\flat(D), 1 - y^\sharp(D))$$

$$(x^\flat(C).y^\flat(D), 1 - (1 - (1 - x^\sharp(C))).(1 - (1 - y^\sharp(D))))$$

$$= (x^\flat(C).y^\flat(D), 1 - x^\sharp(C).y^\sharp(D))$$

$$= (h^\flat(C \times D), 1 - h^\sharp(C \times D))$$

$$= h(C \times D).$$

2.3   Central Limit Theorem

Proposition 3. *Let* $\mathcal{P} = [\mathcal{P}^\flat, \mathcal{P}^\sharp] : \mathcal{F} \to \mathcal{J}$ *be an IF-probability,* $x : \mathcal{B}(R) \to \mathcal{F}$ *an IF-observable. Then the mappings* $\mathcal{P}_x^\flat = \mathcal{P}^\flat \circ x, \mathcal{P}_x^\sharp = \mathcal{P}^\sharp \circ x : \mathcal{B}(R) \to [0,1]$ *are probability measures.*

Definition 7. *For any probability* $\mathcal{P} = [\mathcal{P}^\flat, \mathcal{P}^\sharp] : \mathcal{F} \to \mathcal{J}$ *and any IF-observable* $x : \mathcal{B}(R) \to \mathcal{F}$ *we define*

$$E_\flat(x) = \int_R t dP_x^\flat(t), E_\sharp(x) = \int_R t dP_x^\sharp(t),$$

$$\sigma_\flat^2 = \int_R (t - E_\flat(x))^2 dP_x^\flat(t),$$

$$\sigma_\sharp^2(x) = \int_R (t - E_\sharp(x))^2 dP_x^\sharp(t)$$

assuming that these integrals exist.

Definition 8. *Let* $g_n : R^n \to R$ *be a Borel function,* $x_1, ..., x_n : \mathcal{B}(R) \to \mathcal{F}$ *be IF-observables,* $h_n : \mathcal{B}(R^n) \to \mathcal{F}$ *their joint IF-observable. Then we define the IF-observable* $y_n = g_n(x_1, ..., x_n) : \mathcal{B}(R) \to \mathcal{F}$ *by the prescription*

$$y_n(A) = h_n(g_n^{-1}(A)).$$

Definition 9. *A sequence* (x_n) *of IF-observables is independent if for any* n

$$\mathcal{P}^\flat(h_n(A_1 \times ... \times A_n)) = \mathcal{P}_{x_1}^\flat(A_1).....\mathcal{P}_{x_n}^\flat(A_n),$$

$$\mathcal{P}^\sharp(h_n(A_1 \times ... \times A_n)) = \mathcal{P}_{x_1}^\sharp(A_1).....\mathcal{P}_{x_n}^\sharp(A_n),$$

where $h_n : \mathcal{B}(R^n)$ *is the joint observable of* $x_1, ..., x_n$.

Theorem 4. *Let* (x_n) *be a sequence of independent equally distributed, square integrable IF-observables,*

$$E_\flat(x_n) = E_\sharp(x_n) = a, \sigma_\flat^2(x_n) = \sigma_\sharp^2(x_n) = \sigma^2 (n = 1, 2, ...)$$

Then for any $t \in R$

$$\lim_{n \to \infty} \mathcal{P}^\flat(\frac{x_1 + ...x_n - na}{\sigma\sqrt{n}}((-\infty, t))) = \frac{1}{\sqrt{2\pi}} \int_\infty^t e^{-\frac{u^2}{2}} du$$

$$\lim_{n \to \infty} \mathcal{P}^\sharp(\frac{x_1 + ...x_n - na}{\sigma\sqrt{n}}((-\infty, t))) = \frac{1}{\sqrt{2\pi}} \int_\infty^t e^{-\frac{u^2}{2}} du$$

Proof. Proof. We have seen that $\mathcal{F} \subset \mathcal{M}$ where $\mathcal{M}$ is an MV-algebra and there exists states $\overline{\mathcal{P}}^\flat, \overline{\mathcal{P}}^\sharp : \mathcal{M} \to [0,1]$ such that $\overline{\mathcal{P}}^\flat|\mathcal{F} = \mathcal{P}^\flat, \overline{\mathcal{P}}^\sharp|\mathcal{F} = \mathcal{P}^\sharp$. Moreover, x_n are IF-observables, $x_n : \mathcal{B}(R) \to \mathcal{F} \subset \mathcal{M}$, hence also observables in the sense of MV-algebra probability theory. Therefore by theorem 2.12 of [33] (see also theorem 9.2.6. in [34]) and Theorem 3 we have

$$\lim_{n \to \infty} \overline{\mathcal{P}}^{\flat}(\frac{x_1 + \dots x_n - na}{\sigma\sqrt{n}}((-\infty, t))) = \frac{1}{\sqrt{2\pi}} \int_{\infty}^{t} e^{-\frac{u^2}{2}} du$$

and the analogous assertion holds for $\overline{\mathcal{P}}^{\sharp}$.

3   M-Probability Theory

Consider again a measurable space $(\Omega, \mathcal{S})$, where $\mathcal{S}$ is a σ-algebra of subsets of Ω,
    $\mathcal{F} = \{A = (\mu_A, \nu_A); \mu_A, \nu_A \text{ are non-negative, } \mathcal{S}\text{-measurable functions, } \mu_A + \nu_A \le 1 \}$.
    According to [6] we shall define the probability on $\mathcal{F}$ using max-min connectives instead of the Łukasiewicz connectives,

$$A \vee B = (\mu_A \vee \mu_B, \nu_A \wedge \nu_B),$$

$$A \wedge B = (\mu_A \wedge \mu_B, \nu_A \vee \nu_B).$$

For distinguishing the two theories we shall speak about M-probability.

In Section 3.1 the basic notions are discussed: M-probability and M-observable. Section 3.2 contains the proof of the existence of the joint M-observable. As an application Section 3.3 contains a version of the central limit theorem.

3.1 M-Probability and M-Observable

Definition 10. *Let $\mathcal{J}$ be the set of all compact intervals. A mapping $p : \mathcal{F} \to \mathcal{J}$ is called M-probability if the following properties are satisfied:*

(i) $p((1_\Omega, 0_\Omega)) = [1, 1], p((0_\Omega, 1_\Omega)) = [0, 0]$;
(ii) $p(A) + p(B) = p(A \vee B) + p(A \wedge B)$ for any $A, B \in \mathcal{F}$;
(iii)$A_n \nearrow A, B_n \searrow B \Longrightarrow p(A_n) \nearrow p(A), p(B_n) \searrow p(B)$.

Definition 11. 2.1.2. Definition. A mapping $\mu : \mathcal{F} \to [0, 1]$ is an M-state, if the following propertiers are satisfied:

(i) $\mu((1_\Omega, 0_\Omega)) = 1, \mu((0_\Omega, 1_\Omega)) = 0$;
(ii) $\mu(A) + \mu(B) = \mu(A \vee B) + \mu(A \wedge B))$ for any $A, B \in \mathcal{F}$;
(iii) $A_n \nearrow A, B_n \searrow B \Longrightarrow \mu(A_n) \nearrow \mu(A), \mu(B_n) \searrow \mu(B)$.

Proposition 4. *Let $p : \mathcal{F} \to \mathcal{J}$ be an M-probability. Put $p(A) = [p^{\flat}(A), p^{\sharp}(A)]$. Then the mappings $p^{\flat} : \mathcal{F} \to [0, 1], p^{\sharp} : \mathcal{F} \to [0, 1]$ are M-states.*

On the family $\mathcal{F}$ we have two notions: state and M-state. It is interesting what is a relation between these notions.

Theorem 5. *Any state $m : \mathcal{F} \to [0, 1]$ is an M-state on $\mathcal{F}$.*

Proof. By Theorem 1 there exist a probability $\mu : \mathcal{S} \to [0,1]$ and a constant $\alpha \in [0,1]$ such that for any $A \in \mathcal{F}$

$$m(A) = (1-\alpha)\int_\Omega \mu_A d\mu + \alpha(1 - \int_\Omega \mu_A d\mu).$$

Therefore

$$m(A) + m(B) = (1-\alpha)(\int_\Omega (\mu_A + \mu_B)d\mu) + \alpha(2 - \int_\Omega (\nu_A + \nu_B)d\mu).$$

Of course,

$$\mu_A + \mu_B = \mu_A \vee \mu_B + \mu_A \wedge \mu_B = \mu_{A\vee B} + \mu_{A\wedge B},$$

$$\nu_A + \nu_B = \nu_A \vee \nu_B + \nu_A \wedge \nu_B = \nu_{A\wedge B} + \nu_{A\vee B},$$

hence

$$m(A) + m(B) =$$

$$= (1-\alpha)\int_\Omega \mu_{A\cup B}d\mu + \alpha(1 - \int_\Omega \nu_{A\cup B}d\mu) + (1-\alpha)\int_\Omega \mu_{A\cap B}d\mu + \alpha(1 - \int_\Omega \nu_{A\cap B}d\mu) =$$

$$= m(A \vee B) + m(A \wedge B).$$

Corollary 1. *Any probability* $\mathcal{P} : \mathcal{F} \to \mathcal{J}$ *is an* M-*probability.*

Proposition 5. *For any* $(\Omega, \mathcal{S})$ *there exists an* M-*state* $m : \mathcal{F} \to [0,1]$ *that is not a state, hence there exists and* M-*probability that is not a probability.*

Proof. Fix $x_0 \in \Omega$ and put

$$m(A) = \frac{1}{2}(\mu_A^2(x_0) + 1 - \nu_A^2(x_0)).$$

Since $(\mu_A \vee \mu_B)^2 + (\mu_A \wedge \mu_B)^2 = \mu_A^2 + \mu_B^2$, it is not difficult to see that m is an M-state. Put

$$\mu_A(x) = \mu_B(x) = \frac{1}{4}, \nu_A(x) = \nu_B(x) = \frac{3}{4}$$

for any $x \in \Omega$. Then

$$m(A) = m(B) = \frac{1}{4}.$$

On the other hand

$$A \oplus B = (1_\Omega, 0_\Omega), A \odot B = (0_\Omega, 1_\Omega),$$

hence

$$m(A \oplus B) + m(A \odot B) = 1 + 0 \neq \frac{1}{4} + \frac{1}{4} = m(A) + m(B).$$

Although the probability theory on IF-events discussed in our Chapter 2 seems to be satisfactory, the previous facts lead us to an experience to create basic instruments for an alternative M-probability theory. Of course, the crucial notion is the notion of an M-observable.

Definition 12. *An M-observable is a mapping $x : \mathcal{B}(R) \rightarrow \mathcal{F}$ satisfying the following conditions:*

(i) $x(R) = (1_\Omega, 0_\Omega), x(\emptyset) = (0_\Omega, 1_\Omega)$;
(ii) $x(A \cup B) = x(A) \vee x(B), x(A \cap B) = x(A) \wedge x(B)$ for any $A, B \in \mathcal{B}(R)$;
(iii) $A_n \nearrow A, B_n \searrow B \Longrightarrow x(A_n) \nearrow x(A), x(B_n) \searrow x(B)$.

Proposition 6. *If $x : \mathcal{B}(R) \rightarrow \mathcal{F}$ is an M-observable, and $m : \mathcal{F} \rightarrow [0, 1]$ is an M-state, then $m \circ x : \mathcal{B}(R) \rightarrow [0, 1]$ is a probability measure.*

Proof. Evidently $m(x(R)) = m(1_\Omega) = 1$. Also continuity of $m \circ x$ is clear. Let $A \cap B = \emptyset$. Then $x(A) \wedge x(B) = x(\emptyset) = (0_\Omega, 1_\Omega)$. Therefore

$$m(x(A \cup B)) = m(x(A) \vee x(B)) + m(x(A) \wedge x(B)) =$$

$$= m(x(A)) + m(x(B)).$$

Definition 13. *Let $\mathcal{R}$ be an algebra of subsets of a set X. A mapping $\mu : \mathcal{R} \rightarrow [0, 1]$ is called an M-measure, if the following properties are satisfied:*

(i) $\mu(X) = 1, \mu(\emptyset) = 0$;
(ii) $\mu(A \cup B) = \mu(A) \vee \mu(B), \mu(A \cap B) = \mu(A) \wedge \mu(B)$ for any $A, B \in \mathcal{R}$;
(iii) $A_n \nearrow A, B_n \searrow B, A_n, B_n, A, B \in \mathcal{R} \Longrightarrow \mu(A_n) \nearrow \mu(A), \mu(B_n) \searrow \mu(B)$.

Proposition 7. *Let $x : \mathcal{B}(R) \rightarrow \mathcal{F}$ be an M-observable. Put $x(A) = (x^-(A), 1 - x^+(A))$, and for fixed $x_0 \in R$ define $\mu : \mathcal{B}(R) \rightarrow [0, 1], \nu : \mathcal{B}(R) \rightarrow [0, 1]$ by the formula*

$$\mu(A) = x^-(A)(x_0), \nu(A) = x^+(A)(x_0).$$

Then μ, ν are M-measures.

Proof. Consider the mapping μ, the proof for ν is analogous. First $\mu(X) = x^-(X)(x_0) = 1_\Omega(x_0) = 1, \mu(\emptyset) = x^-(\emptyset)(x_0) = 0_\Omega(x_0) = 0$. Further

$$\mu(A \cup B) = x^-(A \cup B)(x_0) = (x^-(A) \vee x^-(B))(x_0) = \mu(A) \vee \mu(B),$$

$$\mu(A \cap B) = x^-(A \cap B)(x_0) = (x^-(A) \wedge x^-(B))(x_0) = \mu(A) \wedge \mu(B).$$

The continuity of μ can be proved similarly.

The notion of an M-measure is an important tool in our theory. Because of the symmetry of μ the measure extenstion theorem can be proved.

Theorem 6. *For any M-measure μ defined on an algebra $\mathcal{R}$ there exists exactly one M-measure $\bar{\mu}$ on $\sigma(\mathcal{R})$ extending μ.*

Proof. See [17].

3.2 Joint Observable

Definition 14. *Let* $x, y : \mathcal{B}(R) \to \mathcal{F}$ *be M-observables. The joint M-observable of* x *and* y *is a mapping* $h : \mathcal{B}(R^2) \to \mathcal{F}$ *satisfying the following conditions:*

(i) $h(R^2) = (1_\Omega, 0_\Omega), h(\emptyset) = (0_\Omega, 1_\Omega);$
(ii) $h(A \cup B) = h(A) \vee h(B), h(A \cap B) = h(A) \wedge h(B)$ *for any* $A, B \in \mathcal{B}(R^2);$
(iii) $A_n \nearrow A, B_n \searrow B \Longrightarrow h(A_n \nearrow h(A), h(B_n) \searrow h(B);$
(iv) $h(C \times D) = \min(x(C), y(D))$ *for any* $C, D \in \mathcal{B}(R).$

Theorem 7. *For any M-observables there exists their joint M-observable.*

Proof. We must construct $h : \mathcal{B}(R^2) \to \mathcal{F}$. Here $h(A) = (h^-(A), 1 - h^+(A)) \in \mathcal{F}$, and $h^-(A), h^+(A)$ are functions from Ω to [0,1]. We shall construct the functions pointwisely: $h^-(A)(\omega), h^+(A)(\omega)$ as elements of [0,1]. Therefore fix ω. For any $A \in \mathcal{B}(R)$ put

$$\mu(A) = x^-(A)(\omega), \nu(B) = y^-(B)(\omega).$$

By this construction we obtain two mappings $\mu, \nu : \mathcal{B}(R) \to [0, 1]$ and we have seen (Prop. 7) that μ, ν are M-measures. Let $\mathcal{R}$ be the algebra of all sets of the form

$$\bigcup_{i=1}^{n} (A_i \times B_i),$$

where $n \in N, A_i = [a_i, b_i), B_i = [c_i, d_i) \in \mathcal{B}(R)$, and $(A_i \times B_i) \cap (A_j \times B_j) = \emptyset$ for $i \neq j$. Since the operations $a \vee b = \max(a, b)$ and $a \wedge b = \min(a, b)$ satisfy the distributive law, the expression

$$\bigvee_{i=1}^{n} (\mu(A_i) \wedge \nu(B_i))$$

does not depend on the choice of A_i and B_i. Therefore we can define

$$\kappa(\bigcup_{i=1}^{n} (A_i \times B_i)) = \bigvee_{i=1}^{n} (\mu(A_i) \wedge \nu(B_i)).$$

By this way we obtain a mapping $\kappa : \mathcal{R} \to [0, 1]$. We shall prove that κ is an M-measure. Evidently

$$\kappa(R^2) = \mu(R) \wedge \nu(R) = \min(1_\Omega(\omega), 1_\Omega(\omega)) = 1,$$

$$\kappa(\emptyset) = \mu(\emptyset) \wedge \nu(\emptyset) = 0.$$

Moreover
(I)
$$\kappa(A \times B) = \mu(A) \wedge \nu(B).$$

Further

$$\kappa(A \cup B) = \kappa(\bigcup_{i=1}^{n} (A_i \times B_i) \cup \bigcup_{j=1}^{m} (C_j \times D_j)) =$$

$$= \kappa(\bigcup_{i=1}^{n} \bigcup_{j=1}^{m} (A_i \times B_i) \cup (C_j \times D_j)) =$$

$$= \kappa(\bigcup_{i=1}^{n} \bigcup_{j=1}^{m} ((A_i \setminus C_j) \times B_i) \cup ((A_i \cap C_j) \times (B_i \cup D_j)) \cup ((C_j \setminus A_i) \times D_j)) =$$

$$= \bigvee_{i=1}^{n} \bigvee_{j=1}^{m} (\mu(A_i \setminus C_j) \wedge \nu(B_i)) \vee (\mu(A_i \cap C_j) \wedge \nu(B_i \cup D_j)) \vee (\mu(C_j \setminus A_i) \wedge \nu(D_j))$$

$$= \bigvee_{i=1}^{n} \bigvee_{j=1}^{m} (\mu(A_i) \wedge \nu(B_i)) \vee (\mu(C_j) \wedge \nu(D)j)) =$$

$$= \kappa(A) \vee \kappa(B).$$

Similarly

$$\kappa(A \cap B) = \kappa(A) \wedge \kappa(B).$$

Now we shall prove
(II)

$$A_n \in \mathcal{R}(n = 1, 2, ...), A_n \searrow \emptyset \Longrightarrow \kappa(A_n) \searrow 0.$$

Denote

$\mathcal{K} = \{C \in R^2; C \text{ is compact }\}.$
First we show that

(III) $\forall \varepsilon > 0 \forall A \in \mathcal{R} \exists B \in \mathcal{R}, C \in \mathcal{K}, B \subset C \subset A, \kappa(A \setminus B) < \varepsilon.$

Let $A = \bigcup_{i=1}^{n} (A_i \times B_i)$, $A_i, B_i \in \mathcal{B}(R)(i = 1, 2, ..., n)$. Since

$$A_i = [a_i, b_i) = \bigcup_{m=1}^{\infty} [a_i, b_i - \frac{1}{2m}] = \bigcup_{m=1}^{\infty} [a_i, b_i - \frac{1}{m})$$

and

$$A_i \setminus [a_i, b_i - \frac{1}{m}) \searrow \emptyset \quad (m \to \infty)$$

we have

$$\lim_{n \to \infty} \mu(A_i \setminus [a_i, b_i - \frac{1}{m})) = 0,$$

hence there exists m_i such that

$$\mu(A_i \setminus [a_i, b_i - \frac{1}{m})) < \varepsilon.$$

Put

$$E_i = [a_i, b_i - \frac{1}{m_i}), C_i = [a_i, b_i - \frac{1}{2m_i}].$$

Then

$$E_i \subset C_i \subset A_i$$

and
$$\mu(A_i \setminus E_i) < \varepsilon.$$

Similarly there exist
$$F_i \in \mathcal{R}, D_i \text{ compact}, F_i \subset D_i \subset B_i$$

such that
$$\nu(B_i \setminus F_i) < \varepsilon.$$

Put
$$C = \bigcup_{i=1}^{n}(C_i \times D_i), B = \bigcup_{i=1}^{n}(E_i \times F_i).$$

Then
$$\kappa(A \setminus B) = \kappa(\bigcup_{i=1}^{n}(A_i \times B_i) \setminus \bigcup_{i=1}^{n}(E_i \times F_i)) \leq$$

$$\leq \kappa(\bigcup_{i=1}^{n}((A_i \times B_i) \setminus (E_i \times F_i))) =$$

$$= \bigvee_{i=1}^{n} \kappa((A_i \times B_i) \setminus E_i \times F_i)) \leq$$

$$\leq \bigvee_{i=1}^{n} \kappa(((A_i \setminus E_i) \times R) \cup (R \times (B_i \setminus F_i))) =$$

$$= \bigvee_{i=1}^{n} (\mu(A_i \setminus E_i) \vee \nu(B_i \setminus F_i)) < \varepsilon.$$

Now return to a sequence $(A_n), A_n \in \mathcal{R}, A_n \searrow \emptyset$. Using (III) construct
$$B_n \in \mathcal{R}, C_n \in \mathcal{K}, B_n \subset C_n \subset A_n, \kappa(A_n \setminus B_n) < \varepsilon.$$

Put
$$D_n = \bigcap_{i=1}^{n} \in \mathcal{K}.$$

Then
$$\bigcap_{n=1}^{\infty} D_n \subset \bigcap_{n=1}^{\infty} A_n = \emptyset.$$

Since $\mathcal{K}$ is a compact family, there exists m such that
$$\bigcap_{i=1}^{m} B_i \subset D_m = \bigcap_{i=1}^{m} C_i = \emptyset.$$

We have
$$\kappa(A_m) = \kappa(A_m \setminus \bigcap_{i=1}^{m} B_i) =$$

$$= \kappa(\bigcup_{i=1}^{m}(A_m \setminus B_i)) \le$$

$$\le \kappa(\bigcup_{i=1}^{m}(A_i \setminus B_i)) = \bigvee_{i=1}^{m} \kappa(A_i \setminus B_i) < \varepsilon.$$

Also $\kappa(A_n) \le \kappa(A_m) < \varepsilon$ for any $n \ge m$. Therefore

$$\lim_{n \to \infty} \kappa(A_n) = 0.$$

Now if $B_n \in \mathcal{R}, B_n \nearrow B, B \in \mathcal{R}$, then $B \setminus B_n \searrow \emptyset$, hence

$$\kappa(B) = \kappa((B \setminus B_n) \cup B_n) = \kappa(B \setminus B_n) \vee \kappa(B_n)$$

$$\le \kappa(B \setminus B_n) \vee \bigvee_{i=1}^{\infty} \kappa(B_i).$$

Therefore

$$\kappa(B) \le \lim_{n \to \infty} \kappa(B \setminus B_n) \vee (\bigvee_{i=1}^{\infty} B_i) = \bigvee_{i=1}^{\infty} \kappa(B_i) \le \kappa(B),$$

hence

$$\kappa(B) = \lim_{i \to \infty} \kappa(B_i).$$

On the other hand $C_n \searrow C$ implies $C_n \setminus C \searrow \emptyset$,

$$\kappa(C_n) = \kappa((C_n \setminus C) \vee C) = \kappa(C_n \setminus C) \vee \kappa(C),$$

$$\bigwedge_{n=1}^{\infty} \kappa(C_n) = (\bigwedge_{n=1}^{\infty} \kappa(C_n \setminus C) \vee \kappa(C) = 0 \vee \kappa(C) = \kappa(C).$$

We have proved that $\kappa : \mathcal{R} \to [0,1]$ is an M-measure. By theorem 6 there exists exactly one M-measure $\overline{\kappa} : \sigma(\mathcal{R}) \to [0,1]$ such that $\overline{\kappa}|\mathcal{R} = \kappa$. By (I) we have

$$\overline{\kappa}([a,b) \times [c,d)) = \mu([a,b)) \wedge \nu([c,d)).$$

Fix $[c,d)$ and put

$$\mathcal{L} = \{A \in \mathcal{B}(R); \overline{\kappa}(A \times [c,d)) = \mu(A) \wedge \nu([c,d))\}.$$

Since $\mathcal{L}$ is monotone and $\mathcal{L} \supset \mathcal{R}_0 = \{[a,b); a < b\}$, hence $\mathcal{L} \supset \sigma(\mathcal{R}_0) = \mathcal{B}(R)$. Therefore

$$\overline{\kappa}(A \times [c,d)) = \mu(A) \wedge \nu([c,d))$$

for any $A \in \mathcal{B}(R)$. Further for fixed $A \in \mathcal{B}(R)$ consider the family

$$\mathcal{G} = \{B \in \mathcal{B}(R); \overline{\kappa}(A \times B) = \mu(A) \wedge \nu(B)\}.$$

By previous results, $\mathcal{G} \supset \mathcal{R}_0$. Since $\mathcal{G}$ is monotone, $\mathcal{G} \supset \sigma(\mathcal{R}_0) = \mathcal{B}(R)$, hence

$$\overline{\kappa}(A \times B) = \mu(A) \wedge \nu(B)$$

for any $A, B \in \mathcal{B}(R)$.

Now we can define for any $C \in \mathcal{B}(R^2)$

$$h^-(C)(\omega) = \overline{\kappa}(C).$$

We have $h^-(A \times B)(\omega) = \mu(A) \wedge \nu(B) = x^-(A)(\omega) \wedge y^-(B)(\omega)$, hence

$$h^-(A \times B) = x^-(A) \wedge y^-(B), A, B \in \mathcal{B}(R).$$

Similarly there exists to any $\omega \in \Omega$ an M-measure λ such that

$$\lambda(A \times B) = x^+(A)(\omega) \wedge y^+(B)(\omega),$$

hence putting

$$h^+(C)(\omega) = \lambda(C)$$

we obtain

$$h^+(A \times B) = x^+(A) \wedge y^+(B).$$

Now we define

$$h : \mathcal{B}(R^2) \to \mathcal{F}$$
$$h(C) = (h^-(C), 1 - h^+(C)).$$

It is easy to see that h satisfies the properties (i) - (iii) of definition 14. Moreover,

$$h(A \times B) = (h^-(A \times B), 1 - h^+(A \times B))$$

$$= (x^-(A) \wedge y^-(B), 1 - x^+(A) \wedge y^+(B))$$

On the other hand

$$x(A) \wedge y(B) = (x^-(A), 1 - x^+(A)) \wedge (y^-(B), 1 - y^+(B))$$

$$= (x^-(A) \wedge y^-(B), (1 - x^+(A)) \vee (1 - y^+(B)))$$

$$= (x^-(A) \wedge y^-(B), 1 - (x^+(A) \wedge y^+(B)))$$

$$= h(A \times B).$$

3.3   Central Limit Theorem

First recall the classical limit theorem.

Theorem 8. *Let $(\Omega, \mathcal{S}, P)$ be a probability space, (ξ_n) a sequence of independent, equally distributed, square integrable random variables, $E(\xi_n) = a, D(\xi_n) = \sigma^2, (n = 1, 2, ...)$. Then for any $t \in R$*

$$\lim_{n \to \infty} P(\{(\omega; \frac{\sum_{i=1}^n \xi_i(\omega) - na}{\sigma \sqrt{n}} < t\}) = \frac{1}{\sqrt{2\pi}} \int_\infty^t e^{-\frac{u^2}{2}} du$$

In our generalized case we have a sequence (x_n) of M-observables $x_n : \mathcal{B}(R) \to \mathcal{F}$ and the M-probability $\mathcal{P} : \mathcal{F} \to \mathcal{J}$,

$$\mathcal{P}(A) = [\mathcal{P}^-(A), \mathcal{P}^+(A)].$$

By Prop. 6 the mappings

$$\mathcal{P}^- \circ x_n, \mathcal{P}^+ \circ x_n : \mathcal{B}(R) \to [0,1]$$

are probability distributions. We can define the following quantities.

Definition 15. *Denote $\mathcal{P}^-_{x_n} = \mathcal{P}^- \circ x_n, \mathcal{P}^+_{x_n} = \mathcal{P}^+ \circ x_n$. Then we define*

$$E_-(x_n) = \int_R t d\mathcal{P}^-_{x_n}(t), E_+(x_n) = \int_R t d\mathcal{P}^+_{x_n}(t).$$

if the integrals exist, and

$$\sigma^2_-(x_n) = \int_R (t - E_-(x_n))^2 d\mathcal{P}^-_{x_n}(t), \sigma^2_+(x_n) = \int_R (t - E_+(x_n))^2 d\mathcal{P}^+_{x_n}(t),$$

if the integrals exist.

Definition 16. *Let $g_n : R^n \to R$ be a Borel measurable set (i.e. $A \in \mathcal{B}(R) \implies g_n^{-1}(A) \in \mathcal{B}(R_n)$). Let $h_n : \mathcal{B}(R^n) \to \mathcal{F}$ be the joint M-observable of $x_1, ..., x_n$. Then we define the observable*

$$y_n = g(x_1, ..., x_n) : \mathcal{B} \to \mathcal{F}$$

by the formula

$$y_n(A) = h_n(g_n^{-1}(A)), A \in \mathcal{B}(R).$$

Definition 17. *A sequence (x_n) of M-observables is independent if*

$$\mathcal{P}(h_n(A_1 \times ... \times A_n)) = \mathcal{P}_{x_1}(A_1) \cdot ... \cdot \mathcal{P}_{x_n}(A_n), A_1, ..., A_n \in \mathcal{B}(R),$$

i.e.

$$\mathcal{P}^-(h_n(A_1 \times ... \times A_n)) = \mathcal{P}^-_{x_1}(A_1) \cdot ... \cdot \mathcal{P}^-_{x_n}(A_n), A_1, ..., A_n \in \mathcal{B}(R),$$

$$\mathcal{P}^+(h_n(A_1 \times ... \times A_n)) = \mathcal{P}^+_{x_1}(A_1) \cdot ... \cdot \mathcal{P}^+_{x_n}(A_n), A_1, ..., A_n \in \mathcal{B}(R),$$

Theorem 9. *Let (x_n) be a sequence of independent, equally distributed, square integrable observables, $E_-(x_n) = E_+(x_n) = a, \sigma^2_-(x_n) = \sigma^2_+(x_n) = \sigma^2$. Then for any $t \in R$*

$$\lim_{n \to \infty} \mathcal{P}(\frac{x_1 + ... + x_n - na}{\sigma\sqrt{n}}((-\infty, t))) = \{\frac{1}{\sqrt{2\pi}} \int_\infty^t e^{-\frac{u^2}{2}} du\}$$

i.e.

$$\lim_{n \to \infty} \mathcal{P}^-(\frac{x_1 + ... + x_n - na}{\sigma\sqrt{n}}((-\infty, t))) = \frac{1}{\sqrt{2\pi}} \int_\infty^t e^{-\frac{u^2}{2}} du,$$

$$\lim_{n \to \infty} \mathcal{P}^+(\frac{x_1 + ... + x_n - na}{\sigma\sqrt{n}}((-\infty, t))) = \frac{1}{\sqrt{2\pi}} \int_\infty^t e^{-\frac{u^2}{2}} du.$$

Proof. Consider the probability space $(R^N, \sigma(\mathcal{C}), P^-)$, where $\mathcal{C}$ is the family of all cylinders and P^- is the product of the probability measures $\mathcal{P}_{x_1}^-, \mathcal{P}_{x_2}^-, \mathcal{P}_{x_3}^-, \ldots$. Define $\xi_n : R^N \to R$ by the formula

$$\xi_n((u_i)_{i=1}^\infty) = u_n$$

n=1,2,3,... Then

$$P_{\xi_n}(A) = P^-(\xi_n^{-1}(A)) = \mathcal{P}_{x_n}^-(A), A \in \mathcal{B}(R),$$

hence

$$E_-(x_n) = \int_R t dP_{x_n}^-(t) = \int_R t dP_{\xi_n}(t) = E(\xi_n),$$

and similarly

$$\sigma_-^2(x_n) = \sigma^2(\xi_n).$$

Moreover, if $T_n = (\xi_1, \ldots, \xi_n) : R^N \to R^n$, then

$$P^-(T_n^{-1}(A_1 \times \ldots \times A_n)) = P^-(\xi_1^{-1}(A_1) \cap \ldots \cap \xi_n^{-1}(A_n)) =$$

$$= P^-(\{(u_i); u_1 \in A_1, \ldots, u_n \in A_n\}) =$$

$$= \mathcal{P}_{x_1}^-(A_1) \cdot \ldots \cdot \mathcal{P}_{x_n}^-(A_n) = \mathcal{P}^-(h_n(A_1 \times \ldots \times A_n)),$$

hence

$$P_{T_n}^- = \mathcal{P}_{h_n}^- \ (n = 1, 2, \ldots)$$

Also we see that (ξ_n) are independent. If we put

$$\eta_n = \frac{\xi_1 + \ldots + \xi_n - na}{\sigma\sqrt{n}},$$

$$g_n : R_n \to R, g_n(u_1, \ldots, u_n) = \frac{u_1 + \ldots + u_n - na}{\sigma\sqrt{n}}$$

then

$$\eta_n = g_n \circ T_n,$$

$$P^-(\eta_n^{-1}((-\infty, t))) = P^-(T_n^{-1}(g_n^{-1}((-\infty, t)))) =$$

$$= P_{T_n}^-(g_n^{-1}((-\infty, t))) = \mathcal{P}_{h_n}^-(g_n^{-1}((-\infty, t)))+$$

$$= \mathcal{P}^-(y_n((-\infty, t))).$$

Therefore

$$\lim_{n\to\infty} \mathcal{P}^-(\frac{x_1 + \ldots + x_n - na}{\sigma\sqrt{n}}((-\infty, t))) =$$

$$= \lim_{n\to\infty} P^-(\eta_n^{-1}((-\infty, t))) = \frac{1}{\sqrt{2\pi}} \int_\infty^t e^{-\frac{u^2}{2}} du,$$

by Theorem 8. The relation

$$\lim_{n\to\infty} \mathcal{P}^+(\frac{x_1 + \ldots + x_n - na}{\sigma\sqrt{n}}((-\infty, t))) = \frac{1}{\sqrt{2\pi}} \int_\infty^t e^{-\frac{u^2}{2}} du,$$

can be proved similarly.

Ackowledgement. The paper was supported by Grant VEGA 1/2002/05.

References

1. Atanassov, K.: Intuitionistic Fuzzy Sets: Theory and Applications. Physica Verlag, New York (1999)
2. Cignoli, R.L.O., D'Ottaviano, I.M.L., Mundici, D.: Algebraic Foundations of Many-valued Reasoning. Kluwer, Dordrecht (2000)
3. Gerstenkorn, T., Manko, J.: Probabilities of intuitionistic fuzzy events. In: Hryniewicz, O., et al. (eds.) Issues in Inteligent Systems: Paradigms, EXIT, Warszawa, pp. 58–63 (2005)
4. Grzegorzewski, P., Mrowka, E.: Probability of intuitionistic fuzzy events. In: Grzegorzewski, P., et al. (eds.) Soft Methods in Probability, Statistics and Data Analysis, pp. 105–115. Physica Verlag, New York (2002)
5. Král, P., Renčová, M.: On the central limit theorem of general IF probabilities. In: Proc. Eleventh Int. Conf. IPMU, Paris, pp. 714–717 (2006)
6. Krachounov, M.: Intuitionostic probability and intuitionistic fuzzy sets. In: El-Darzi, E., Atanassov, K., Chountas, P. (eds.) First Intern. Workshop on IFS, Generalized Nets and Knowledge Engineering, pp. 18 - 24, pp. 714–717. Univ. of Westminster, London (2006)
7. Lendelová, K.: Measure theory on multivalued logics and its applications, PhD thesis. M.Bel University Banská Bystrica (2005)
8. Lendelová, K.: IF-probability on MV-algebras. Notes on IFS 11, 66–72 (2005)
9. Lendelová, K.: Strong law of large numbers for IF-events. In: Proc. Eleventh Int. Conf. IPMU, Paris, pp. 2363–2366 (2006)
10. Lendelová, K.: Conditional probability on L-poset with product. In: Proc. Eleventh Int. Conf. IPMU, Paris, pp. 946–951 (2006)
11. Lendelová, K., Michalíková, A., Riečan, B.: Representation of probability on triangle. In: Hryniewicz, O., Kaczprzyk, J., Kuchta, D. (eds.) Issues in Soft Computing - Decision and Operation research, Warszawa, EXIT, pp. 235–242 (2005)
12. Lendelová, K., Riečan, B.: Probability on triangle and square. In: Proc. Eleventh Int. Conf. IPMU, Paris, pp. 977–982 (2006)
13. Michalíková, A.: IFS-valued possibility and necessity measures. Notes on IFS 11(3), 73–77 (2005)
14. Michalíková, A.: Measurable elements on IF-sets. Notes on IFS 11(6), 26–28 (2005)
15. Michalíková, A.: Outer measure on IF-sets. In: El-Darzi, E., Atanassov, K., Chountas, P. (eds.) First Intern. Workshop on IFS, Generalized Nets and Knowledge Engineering, pp. 31–38. Univ. of Westminster, London (2006)
16. Michalíková, A.: Carathéodory outer measure on IF-sets. Math. Slovaca (accepted)
17. Mazureková, P., Riečan, B.: A measure extension theorem. Notes on IFS (accepted)
18. Petrovičová, J., Riečan, B.: On a characterization of IF probability. In: Torra, V., Narukawa, Y., Valls, A., Domingo-Ferrer, J. (eds.) MDAI 2006. LNCS (LNAI), vol. 3885, pp. 1–7. Springer, Heidelberg (2006)
19. Renčová, M., Riečan, B.: Probability on IF-sets: an elementary approach. In: El-Darzi, E., Atanassov, K., Chountas, P. (eds.) First Intern. Workshop on IFS, Generalized Nets and Knowledge Engineering, pp. 8–17. Univ. of Westminster, London (2006)
20. Riečan, B.: A descriptive definition of the probability on intuitionistic fuzzy sets. In: Wagenecht, M., Hampet, R. (eds.) Proc. EUSFLAT'2003, pp. 263–266. Zittau - Goerlitz Univ. Appl. Sci, Dordrecht (2003)

21. Riečan, B.: Representation of probabilities on IFS events. In: Lopez-Diaz, M., et al. (eds.) Advances in Soft Computing, Soft Methodology and Random Information Systems, pp. 243–246. Springer, Heidelberg (2004)
22. Riečan, B.: On the Law of Large Numbers on IFS Events. In: Advances in Soft Computing, vol. 2, pp. 677–680. Springer, Dortmundt, Germany (2004)
23. Riečan, B.: On the entropy on the Łukasiewicz square. In: Proc. Joint EUSFLAT - LFA 2005, Barcelona, pp. 330–333 (2005)
24. Riečan, B.: On the entropy of IF dynamical systems. In: Proceedings of the Fifth International workshop on IFS and Generalized Nets, Warsaw, Poland, pp. 328-336 (2005)
25. Riečan, B.: On the probability on IF-sets and MV-algebras. Notes on IFS 11(6), 21–25 (2005)
26. Riečan, B.: On a problem of Radko Mesiar: general from of IF probabilities. Fuzzy Sets and Systems 152, 1485–1490 (2006)
27. Riečan, B.: On IF - sets and MV - algebras. In: Proc. Eleventh Int. Conf. IPMU, Paris, pp. 2405–2407 (2006)
28. Riečan, B.: On the probability and random variables on IF sets. In: Applied artificial Intelligence. Proc. 7th FLINS Conf. World Scientific 2006, pp. 138–145 (2006)
29. Riečan, B.: On the probability theory on Atanassov sets. In: 3rd International IEEE Conference Intelligent Systems, pp. 730–732. Univ. of Westminster, London (2006)
30. Riečan, B.: On two ways for the probability theory on IF-sets. In: Soft Methods for Integrated Uncertainty Modelling, Advances in Soft Computing, pp. 285–290. Springer, Heidelberg (2006)
31. Riečan, B.: On two concepts of probability on IF-sets. Notes on IFS 12, 69–72 (2006)
32. Riečan, B.: On some contributions to quantum structures inspired by fuzzy sets (submitted to Kybernetika)
33. Riečan, B., Mundici, D.: Probability on MV-algebras. In: pap, E. (ed.) Handbook of measure Theory, pp. 869–909. Elsevier, Amsterdam (2002)
34. Riečan, B., Neubrunn, T.: Integral, Measure, and Ordering. Kluwer, Dordrecht (1997)
35. Valenčáková, V.: Conditional probability on IF-events (submitted to Math. Slovaca)

Author Index

Lecture Notes in Artificial Intelligence (LNAI)

Vol. 4585: M. Kryszkiewicz, J.F. Peters, H. Rybinski, A. Skowron (Eds.), Rough Sets and Intelligent Systems Paradigms. XIX, 836 pages. 2007.

Vol. 4578: F. Masulli, S. Mitra, G. Pasi (Eds.), Applications of Fuzzy Sets Theory. XVIII, 693 pages. 2007.

Vol. 4573: M. Kauers, M. Kerber, R. Miner, W. Windsteiger (Eds.), Towards Mechanized Mathematical Assistants. XIII, 407 pages. 2007.

Vol. 4571: P. Perner (Ed.), Machine Learning and Data Mining in Pattern Recognition. XIV, 913 pages. 2007.

Vol. 4570: H.G. Okuno, M. Ali (Eds.), New Trends in Applied Artificial Intelligence. XXI, 1194 pages. 2007.

Vol. 4565: D.D. Schmorrow, L.M. Reeves (Eds.), Foundations of Augmented Cognition. XIX, 450 pages. 2007.

Vol. 4562: D. Harris (Ed.), Engineering Psychology and Cognitive Ergonomics. XXIII, 879 pages. 2007.

Vol. 4548: N. Olivetti (Ed.), Automated Reasoning with Analytic Tableaux and Related Methods. X, 245 pages. 2007.

Vol. 4539: N.H. Bshouty, C. Gentile (Eds.), Learning Theory. XII, 634 pages. 2007.

Vol. 4529: P. Melin, O. Castillo, L.T. Aguilar, J. Kacprzyk, W. Pedrycz (Eds.), Foundations of Fuzzy Logic and Soft Computing. XIX, 830 pages. 2007.

Vol. 4520: M.V. Butz, O. Sigaud, G. Pezzulo, G. Baldassarre (Eds.), Anticipatory Behavior in Adaptive Learning Systems. X, 379 pages. 2007.

Vol. 4511: C. Conati, K. McCoy, G. Paliouras (Eds.), User Modeling 2007. XVI, 487 pages. 2007.

Vol. 4509: Z. Kobti, D. Wu (Eds.), Advances in Artificial Intelligence. XII, 552 pages. 2007.

Vol. 4496: N.T. Nguyen, A. Grzech, R.J. Howlett, L.C. Jain (Eds.), Agent and Multi-Agent Systems: Technologies and Applications. XXI, 1046 pages. 2007.

Vol. 4483: C. Baral, G. Brewka, J. Schlipf (Eds.), Logic Programming and Nonmonotonic Reasoning. IX, 327 pages. 2007.

Vol. 4482: A. An, J. Stefanowski, S. Ramanna, C.J. Butz, W. Pedrycz, G. Wang (Eds.), Rough Sets, Fuzzy Sets, Data Mining and Granular Computing. XIV, 585 pages. 2007.

Vol. 4481: J. Yao, P. Lingras, W.-Z. Wu, M. Szczuka, N.J. Cercone, D. Ślęzak (Eds.), Rough Sets and Knowledge Technology. XIV, 576 pages. 2007.

Vol. 4476: V. Gorodetsky, C. Zhang, V.A. Skormin, L. Cao (Eds.), Autonomous Intelligent Systems: Multi-Agents and Data Mining. XIII, 323 pages. 2007.

Vol. 4460: S. Aguzzoli, A. Ciabattoni, B. Gerla, C. Manara, V. Marra (Eds.), Algebraic and Proof-Theoretic Aspects of Non-classical Logics. VIII, 309 pages. 2007.

Vol. 4457: G.M.P. O'Hare, A. Ricci, M.J. O'Grady, O. Dikenelli (Eds.), Engineering Societies in the Agents World VII. XI, 401 pages. 2007.

Vol. 4456: Y. Wang, Y.-m. Cheung, H. Liu (Eds.), Computational Intelligence and Security. XXIII, 1118 pages. 2007.

Vol. 4455: S. Muggleton, R. Otero, A. Tamaddoni-Nezhad (Eds.), Inductive Logic Programming. XII, 456 pages. 2007.

Vol. 4452: M. Fasli, O. Shehory (Eds.), Agent-Mediated Electronic Commerce. VIII, 249 pages. 2007.

Vol. 4451: T.S. Huang, A. Nijholt, M. Pantic, A. Pentland (Eds.), Artifical Intelligence for Human Computing. XVI, 359 pages. 2007.

Vol. 4441: C. Müller (Ed.), Speaker Classification II. X, 309 pages. 2007.

Vol. 4438: L. Maicher, A. Sigel, L.M. Garshol (Eds.), Leveraging the Semantics of Topic Maps. X, 257 pages. 2007.

Vol. 4434: G. Lakemeyer, E. Sklar, D.G. Sorrenti, T. Takahashi (Eds.), RoboCup 2006: Robot Soccer World Cup X. XIII, 566 pages. 2007.

Vol. 4429: R. Lu, J.H. Siekmann, C. Ullrich (Eds.), Cognitive Systems. X, 161 pages. 2007.

Vol. 4428: S. Edelkamp, A. Lomuscio (Eds.), Model Checking and Artificial Intelligence. IX, 185 pages. 2007.

Vol. 4426: Z.-H. Zhou, H. Li, Q. Yang (Eds.), Advances in Knowledge Discovery and Data Mining. XXV, 1161 pages. 2007.

Vol. 4411: R.H. Bordini, M. Dastani, J. Dix, A.E.F. Seghrouchni (Eds.), Programming Multi-Agent Systems. XIV, 249 pages. 2007.

Vol. 4410: A. Branco (Ed.), Anaphora: Analysis, Algorithms and Applications. X, 191 pages. 2007.

Vol. 4399: T. Kovacs, X. Llorà, K. Takadama, P.L. Lanzi, W. Stolzmann, S.W. Wilson (Eds.), Learning Classifier Systems. XII, 345 pages. 2007.

Vol. 4390: S.O. Kuznetsov, S. Schmidt (Eds.), Formal Concept Analysis. X, 329 pages. 2007.

Vol. 4389: D. Weyns, H. Van Dyke Parunak, F. Michel (Eds.), Environments for Multi-Agent Systems III. X, 273 pages. 2007.

Vol. 4386: P. Noriega, J. Vázquez-Salceda, G. Boella, O. Boissier, V. Dignum, N. Fornara, E. Matson (Eds.), Coordination, Organizations, Institutions, and Norms in Agent Systems II. XI, 373 pages. 2007.

Vol. 4384: T. Washio, K. Satoh, H. Takeda, A. Inokuchi (Eds.), New Frontiers in Artificial Intelligence. IX, 401 pages. 2007.

Vol. 4371: K. Inoue, K. Satoh, F. Toni (Eds.), Computational Logic in Multi-Agent Systems. X, 315 pages. 2007.

Vol. 4369: M. Umeda, A. Wolf, O. Bartenstein, U. Geske, D. Seipel, O. Takata (Eds.), Declarative Programming for Knowledge Management. X, 229 pages. 2006.

Vol. 4363: B.D. ten Cate, H.W. Zeevat (Eds.), Logic, Language, and Computation. XII, 281 pages. 2007.

Vol. 4343: C. Müller (Ed.), Speaker Classification I. X, 355 pages. 2007.

Vol. 4342: H. de Swart, E. Orłowska, G. Schmidt, M. Roubens (Eds.), Theory and Applications of Relational Structures as Knowledge Instruments II. X, 373 pages. 2006.